C000141396

Neate:
Bank Confidentiality

Neate:
Bank Confidentiality

Third edition

General editor

Gwendoline Griffiths

the global voice of
the legal profession

Members of the LexisNexis Group worldwide

United Kingdom	LexisNexis UK, a Division of Reed Elsevier (UK) Ltd, Halsbury House, 35 Chancery Lane, LONDON, WC2A 1EL, and 4 Hill Street, EDINBURGH EH2 3JZ
Argentina	LexisNexis Argentina, BUENOS AIRES
Australia	LexisNexis Butterworths, CHATSWOOD, New South Wales
Austria	LexisNexis Verlag ARD Orac GmbH & Co KG, VIENNA
Canada	LexisNexis Butterworths, MARKHAM, Ontario
Chile	LexisNexis Chile Ltda, SANTIAGO DE CHILE
Czech Republic	Nakladatelství Orac sro, PRAGUE
France	Editions du Juris-Classeur SA, PARIS
Germany	LexisNexis Deutschland GmbH, FRANKFURT, MUNSTER
Hong Kong	LexisNexis Butterworths, HONG KONG
Hungary	HVG-Orac, BUDAPEST
India	LexisNexis Butterworths, NEW DELHI
Ireland	Butterworths (Ireland) Ltd, DUBLIN
Italy	Giuffrè Editore, MILAN
Malaysia	Malayan Law Journal Sdn Bhd, KUALA LUMPUR
New Zealand	LexisNexis Butterworths, WELLINGTON
Poland	Wydawnictwo Prawnicze LexisNexis, WARSAW
Singapore	LexisNexis Butterworths, SINGAPORE
South Africa	LexisNexis Butterworths, DURBAN
Switzerland	Stämpfli Verlag AG, BERNE
USA	LexisNexis, DAYTON, Ohio

© International Bar Association 2003

A CIP Catalogue record for this book is available from the British Library.

ISBN 0 406 95847 5

Typeset by Doyle & Co, Colchester
Printed by Cromwell Press, Trwobridge, Wilts

Visit LexisNexis UK at www.lexisnexis.co.uk

Preface

This publication represents one aspect of the activities of the Banking Committee (Committee E) of the Section on Business Law of the International Bar Association (IBA). Its past history is set out in the following introduction to the 1990 edition and the preface to the 1997 edition, which were both edited by Francis Neate. This new edition is the result of a session on Banking Secrecy and the Treatment of Information chaired by him at the IBA's Business Law International Conference in Cancun in November 2001. There was a good deal of lively debate and interest in what had become a topical matter.

It became apparent that there had been a number of developments in the field which merited the new edition to update the 24 existing chapters. The opportunity has been taken to add five new chapters by some of the participants at the conference whose jurisdictions had not been covered previously (Argentina, Brazil, Mexico, Panama and South Africa). Francis Neate asked me to edit this third edition. I am grateful to him for the opportunity to undertake such an interesting project and for his wise counsel on the process.

The revisions to the chapters which appeared in the 1997 edition illustrate the way in which the law is constantly and rapidly evolving in this area on a global basis. Both the existing chapters and the new chapters had to be amended further in the course of production. They are up to date as at 30 April 2003. Several contributors have mentioned forthcoming developments. In most jurisdictions, these continuing changes seem to be the result of a number of similar factors.

The erosion of banking secrecy detected by Francis Neate continues to gain momentum. Here the main factor seems to be the international effort to prevent the laundering of the proceeds of crime and the use of funds by terrorist organisations. Developments such as the provision of banking services on the Internet are thought to have made the banking system more vulnerable to abuse. The events of 11 September 2001 prompted further international initiatives, which are reflected in a plethora of new laws and regulations in many jurisdictions.

However, this is not always the overwhelming trend, since in some jurisdictions there is an attempt to preserve, or even promote, bank confidentiality by appropriate laws and regulations. There is a view that consumers should be protected against disclosure of their personal data to the maximum extent possible. The provision of banking services on the Internet is also relevant here, since there are concerns about the security of information passed between banks and their customers. The tendency for banks to outsource administrative functions, sometimes to service providers in different jurisdictions, also gives rise to concerns about the disclosure of information to third parties.

The result is that banks and financial institutions face a complex mixture of rights and obligations in dealing with information on their customers. They have to strike a proper balance between the rights of customers to privacy and their duties to law enforcement agencies and regulators. In most jurisdictions, this seems to be an area where sound and wide-ranging legal and regulatory knowledge needs to be coupled with practical and constructive advice.

Perhaps this is just one reflection of the increasingly 'global' business community in which bankers and their advisers work. In any event, this publication should prove to be a useful tool in understanding the issues involved in the relevant jurisdictions and working out appropriate solutions.

My thanks are due to all the contributors, who have spent a good deal of time on this project. They have responded courteously and efficiently to the various deadlines and comments and queries. Without their dedication this edition would not have been possible. I am sure that there are also a number of other members of their own law firms to whom thanks are due for their support.

For my own part, I have been most appreciative of the comments of Ashley Booker and the research of my colleague, Wendie Mensah, in relation to my chapter on England. Cliff Godfrey has provided invaluable advice and support, particularly in his review of the other contributions. My secretary, Yvonne Chandler, deserves a special word of thanks for her calm efficiency in co-ordinating the project. Finally, Ruth Eldon of the IBA has been unfailingly helpful and constructive throughout.

Gwendoline Griffiths
June 2003

Contents

International Bar Association
the global voice of the legal profession

THE IBA, THE SECTION ON BUSINESS LAW AND ITS COMMITTEE ON BANKING LAW

In its role as a dual membership organisation, comprising 16,000 individual lawyers and 191 Bar Associations and Law Societies, the International Bar Association (IBA) influences the development of international law reform and helps shape the future of the legal profession. Its Member Organisations cover all continents and include the American Bar Association, the German Federal Bar, the Japan Federation of Bar Associations, the Law Society of Zimbabwe and the Mexican Bar Association.

Grouped into three Sections – Business Law, Legal Practice, and Energy & Natural Resources Law – more than 60 specialist Committees provide members with access to leading experts and up to date information as well as top-level professional development and network-building opportunities through high quality publications and world-class Conferences. The IBA's Human Rights Institute works across the Association, helping to promote, protect and enforce human rights under a just rule of law, and to preserve the independence of the judiciary and the legal profession worldwide.

BANKING LAW COMMITTEE (E)

The Banking Law Committee (E) has over 2,400 members in 134 countries and membership is increasing steadily. Cross-border activities have become a dominant feature in the banking field, thus increasing the need for constant exchange of experience and for joint action among professionals. The Banking Law Committee supports this need through its regular specialised Conferences and working sessions at the major International Bar Association and Section on Business Law Conferences, as well as its regular Newsletter.

For further information about the International Bar Association and the Banking Law Committee, please contact:

International Bar Association
271 Regent Street
London W1B 2AQ
United Kingdom

tel: +44 (0) 20 7629 1206
fax: +44 (0) 20 7409 0456
email:member@int-bar.org
website: www.ibanet.org

Contributors

Jean-François Adelle – France

Jean-François Adelle, born in 1958, graduated from the law schools of Nancy and Paris Assas, the Paris Institute of Comparative Law (magna cum laude), and the University of Pennsylvania (LLM). He is also an Alumnus of the Paris Institute of Political Sciences. He was admitted to the bar in 1979. He worked as an associate with Shearman & Sterling and as a partner at Bignon Lebray Delsol & Associés, where he chaired the European Alliance of Commercial Law Affiliates from 2000–2001. He is now a partner at JeantetAssociés.

He practices mainly in the areas of financings and corporate finance. He has been regularly involved in acquisition, trade and project financings in a variety of sectors including telecommunications and energy. He also advises on private placements, M&A transactions, international cash pooling arrangements, financial products and public offerings of shares.

He is currently a member of the Financial Law Committee and the Chair of the Security Law Commission of Paris Europlace. He co-ordinated the CLA brochure on the change over to the Euro (1998) and the AFTE/CLA *Technical Guide to Centralized Management in Europe* (2000), of which he contributed the French sections.

André Andersson and Jesper Johansson – Sweden

Having graduated from University of Lund in 1986 (LLM and MBA), and having attended Christ Church College, Oxford (Diploma in Legal Studies) in 1987, André Andersson joined the Swedish law firm Mannheimer Swartling in 1987 and was made a partner in 1994. He is the chairman of the firm's Banking and Insurance Group. He specialises in lending and structured financing, including securitisation and leasing. His work also includes advice on clearing and settlement rules, supervisory issues relating to financial institutions and other regulatory matters.

Jesper Johansson joined Mannheimer Swartling in 2000, as a graduate from University of Uppsala (2000). He is a member of the firm's Banking and Insurance Group.

Marios Bahas – Greece

Born Athens, 1944. Having graduated from the University of Athens, Law School in 1967, Marios Bahas was admitted in the Supreme Court of Greece in 1979. He heads the Company/Commercial and Banking/Finance practice of Bahas, Gramatidis &

Partners. He advises on company and commercial issues in the context of mergers and acquisitions as well as litigation. In recent years, he has represented a number of boards of directors, banks and other companies. He is a member of the Athens Bar Association and the International Bar Association and he is a correspondent of *Tax Letter Europe* of the European Law Press. At present he serves as Senior Legal Advisor of the Egnatia Bank in Greece. He speaks Greek, English and French.

Manuel Barrocas and Margarida Caldeira – Portugal

Manuel Barrocas graduated from the University of Lisbon, Law School and was admitted to Bar in 1968. He is a founder partner and senior partner of Barrocas & Alves Pereira (formerly Barrocas & Sarmento). He has spoken at various international conferences on several legal themes, including corporate finance, and has written a number of law books published in Portugal and abroad. A member of the SBL Council of the IBA between 1994–1998, he has represented the IBA in Portugal, and is a member of several IBA Committees.

Margarida Caldeira graduated from the Catholic University of Portugal (Lisbon), Law School (1992) and is a postgraduate in EC law there (1992). Admitted to the Bar in 1991, she is a partner in the same firm practising in corporate and civil law, commercial contracts, EU law and competition law, pharmaceutical and consumer law. She is a member of the IBA and has been a speaker on several conferences on drafting international contracts.

Stefan Breitenstein – Switzerland

He graduated from the Law School of the University of Zurich and continued his legal education at the College of Europe in Brussels where he received the 'Diplôme des Hautes Etudes Européennes'. After his admission to the Zurich Bar, he completed his postgraduate studies at the University of Zurich with a Dr iur and received an LLM from Harvard Law School in 1988. He returned to Lenz & Staehelin in Zurich where he became a partner in 1994. He practises in corporate and financial law and he is head of the banking practice group of Lenz & Staehelin in Zurich.

Karl Delwaide and Isabelle Durand – Canada

Karl Delwaide is a senior partner at the Montreal office of Fasken Martineau Dumoulin LLP. He acts as legal counsel as well as a litigator, particularly in public and government regulation matters. He has expertise in issues relating to privacy, including the protection of information held or managed by a company as well as the protection of personal information and its use on the Internet. He has extensive experience of the courts and tribunals in this field. He is one of the founders of the National Protection of Information and Privacy Practice Group of Fasken Martineau. His diversified practice also includes advising companies in the natural resources industry and professional societies, as well as advising on various business regulation matters.

Isabelle Durand is an associate at the Montreal office of Fasken Martineau Dumoulin LLP. She practices in real estate and hypothecary and banking financing law.

Victor de Serière – The Netherlands

He graduated from Leyden University in 1972, and obtained an LLB at Cambridge University in 1974. He joined the law firm of Loeff Claeys Verbeke in 1976, and became a partner in 1980. He is now a partner in the banking and finance department of the Amsterdam office of Allen & Overy. He mainly works on structured finance transactions, securitisations, leveraged finance deals, restructurings and regulatory advice.

Herman Federspiel – Denmark

He graduated with a law degree from Copenhagen University Law School in 1966 followed by European law studies at the University of Paris. He was a lecturer in public international law at the University of Copenhagen from 1967–1968 and was a member of the Danish Ministry of Justice's Committee on Legislation for Commercial Agents. He was an associate with the law firm of Dragsted, Kromann, Nørregaard, Friis in Copenhagen from 1967–1972. He became a partner in the law firm of Per Federspiel (now Gorrissen Federspiel Kierkegaard) in 1974. His areas of practice include banking and finance, insolvency and general corporate work. He is a member of the IBA's Banking Committee and of the Danish Bar Association's Educational Committee.

Marcello Gioscia and Giuseppe de Falco – Italy

Marcello Gioscia is the partner of Ughi e Nunziante in charge of the banking and finance department, also specializing in corporate law and privatisation. He graduated in law at the University of Genoa and took the LLM at the Columbia University School of Law. He is the author of several publications in Italian, English and French. He was Co-Chairman of the Banking Committee of the IBA.

Giuseppe de Falco is a partner of Ughi e Nunziante involved in banking, finance, corporate and privatisation matters. He graduated in law and specialized in commercial law at the University of Naples and took the LLM in Banking and Financial Law at the London School of Economics. He was awarded a scholarship for a PhD concerning Regulation of the Securities Market and is the author of several publications in Italian and English.

Juan Miguel Goenechea – Spain

Juan Goenechea is a partner in the Madrid office of Uría & Menéndez. He joined the firm in 1982 and became a partner in 1990. From 1996 to 2000, he was head of the Latin America Practice Group. He specialises in mergers and acquisitions, corporate, banking and finance, securities and the Internet. He has been regularly involved in M&A in a wide variety of sectors, including financial and capital market businesses and internet companies. He also advises on tender offers in Spain and assists private equity funds and several leading Spanish listed companies. He is also experienced in appearing before domestic and international arbitration tribunals. He has been Professor of Commercial Law at the Universidad Pontificia de Comillas since 1985.

Ros Grady and Frances Russell-Matthews – Australia

Ros Grady is a partner in Mallesons Stephen Jaques, Melbourne, where she specialises in electronic banking, financial services and privacy law. A graduate of the University of Adelaide (1976), she was a solicitor in the Commonwealth Attorney General's Department and the Department of Consumer and Business Affairs before joining Mallesons (1988). Her practice covers Australia and various South East Asia countries. She has spoken at numerous conferences and published widely.

Frances Russell-Matthews was at the time that the Australian chapter was drafted a senior solicitor in the same office but has since left the firm. She advised financial service organisations, telecommunications and internet companies on privacy, financial services regulation and consumer credit legislation. A graduate of the University of Technology (Sydney) (1994), she was admitted in 1995. Prior to joining Mallesons (2001), she worked in the New South Wales Crime Commission, the Commonwealth Bank of Australia In-House Legal Team and with Gilbert and Tobin, Sydney.

Gwendoline Griffiths – England

Having graduated from St Anne's College, Oxford in 1977 she took her qualifying exams, trained and was admitted as an English solicitor in 1979. She is a finance partner at O'Melveny & Myers, based in their London office. Her specialisation is banking law, dealing mainly with transactional matters, although she also advises on regulatory issues. She has worked mainly in London but also in Singapore from 1984–1986. She spent a year on secondment at Citicorp Investment Bank from 1983–1984. Her previous published works include the English chapter of the AFTE/CLA *Technical Guide to Centralised Cash Management in Europe* (2000). Her memberships include the IBA where she is Vice Chair of the SBL Banking Law Committee, having previously been its Publications Officer.

Thomas Heather – Mexico

A partner in Ritch, Heather y Mueller, SC, Thomas Heather heads the workouts and restructurings and the mergers and acquisitions practice areas. He advised on the NAFTA negotiations and has been an arbitrator for the ICC's International Court of Arbitration. He chairs the Mexican Mediation Institute and the Financial Law Section of the Mexican Bar Association. After graduating from the Escuela Libre de Derecho and the University of Texas (LLM), he was a postgraduate at the National University of Mexico and the Universidad Panamericana. He worked at Thellen, Reid & Priest, New York, prior to his current firm. He has written extensively on legal and financial topics and is a director of a number of Mexican corporations.

Pavla Henzlová – Czech Republic

She received a doctorate in law from Charles University, Prague in 1980. Prior to being called to the Bar, she worked as an in-house lawyer and a legal consultant. She gained a wide range of experience from a three-year co-operation with a British law firm where she ran her own legal practice. After spending six years with Kocián Šolc Balaštík Law Office, she joined Klein Šubrt Došková in 2000. She has had a wealth of experience in many aspects of corporate and commercial law, advising Czech and international clients on investments in the Czech Republic in connection with mergers and acquisitions, securities transactions and banking.

Angela Itzikowitz – South Africa

Angela Itzikowitz is the Nedcor Professor of Banking Law at the University of the Witwatersrand, Johannesburg, where she teaches negotiable instruments, banking and financial markets law. She is also a professorial fellow at Queen Mary College, University of London, and a member of the Board of International Scholars, Banking and Finance Law Unit and the London Institute of Banking, Finance and Development Law (University of London). She is also a Founder Member of the Association of Banking Lawyers of Southern Africa (ABLASA). She is a partner at Edward Nathan and Friedland (Pty) Ltd, where she heads the Financial Markets Division. Her specialisation includes securitisation, title finance, swaps, derivatives and all regulatory aspects of banking and financial markets.

William Johnston – Ireland

He graduated in economics and administration (MA) from Trinity College, University of Dublin. He qualified as a solicitor in 1979 and since 1986 he has been a partner at Arthur Cox, currently heading the banking department. He is a member of the statutory Company Law Review Group where he chairs the committees considering ultra vires, creditor protection and registration of charges. As vice-chairman of the Business Law Committee of the Law Society he lectures on bank regulation. He is publications officer and newsletter editor for the SBL Banking Law Committee of the IBA. He is author of *Banking and Security Law in Ireland* (Butterworths, 1998), and co-author of *Structuring Company Lending after the Company Law Enforcement Act 2001* (Butterworths, 2001).

Péter Köves and Gábor Felsen – Hungary

The contributors are from Köves Clifford Chance, Budapest and both are registered members of the Hungarian Bar. Dr Köves is Managing Partner and head of the Finance Practice. He obtained a diploma in law with distinction (summa cum laude) in the Faculty of Law and Politics at the University Eötvös Loránd in 1983 and is a doctor of law. He has extensive experience in complex structured finance transactions in several sectors, and in litigation. He advises leading Hungarian and international companies, banks, advisory firms and government institutions. He was co-chairman of the IBA's East European Forum from 1994–1998.

Dr Felsen graduated from the Faculty of Law and Politics at the University Eötvös Loránd with distinction (summa cum laude) in 1997 and holds a diploma in banking law (1993-1994). He specialises in the area of finance law, with emphasis on structured finance transactions, derivatives and securitization.

Michael Kutschera, Thomas Schirmer and Alexander Kramer – Austria

The contributors are from the Vienna Office of Binder Grösswang Rechtsanwälte.

Dr Kutschera (New York University Law School MCJ 1983, Fulbright Fellow; University of Vienna Dr iur 1979) has been a partner since 1989. He specialises in M&A, banking and finance, capital markets, arbitration and international transactions. He is member of the Board of the Vienna Bar, Austrian Councillor of the IBA and Co-Chair of its Committee E (Banking Law).

Dr Schirmer (Tulane University Law School – New Orleans 1993, LLM, Fulbright Fellow; University of Innsbruck – Dr iur 1994, Mag iur 1989, Mag.rer.soc.oec. 1991) has been a partner since 1999, specialising in M&A, structured finance, cross-border leases and banking. He is a member of the IBA's Committee E (Banking Law).

Mag Kramer (University of Chicago Law School – LLM 1998; University of Vienna – Mag iur 1995) became an attorney-at-law at the firm in 2002, having previously been an associate. His specializations are M&A, banking and finance, and real estate.

Rafael La Porta Drago and Silvia G Poratelli – Argentina

The contributors are from Allende & Brea.

Rafel La Porta Drago is the co-managing partner, specialising in banking, capital markets, M&A and international transactions. He joined the firm after graduating from the University of Buenos Aires Law School (1960). He is active in the Buenos Aires Bar Association and is a visiting professor in Finance at the Universidad de San Andrés.

Silvia Poratelli is a Senior Associate. She joined the firm in 1996 as a graduate from the University of Buenos Aires (LLB, magna cum laude) where she was Editor-in-Chief of the *Law Review*. She also went to Harvard Law School, 1997 (MLL) and was an Associate with Sidley & Austin, New York from 1998–2000. She is a visiting professor of Corporate Law at the Universidad Torcuato Di Tella.

Jorge Nemr – Brazil

Born in São Paulo 1964, Dr Nemr graduated from the Law School of the University of São Paulo in 1987 and was a postgraduate at the Fundação Getúlio Vargas (FGV/SP) in Economical and Corporate Law. He has been a partner at Leite, Tosto e Barros Advogados since 2000, and he is the head of the International Area of the firm. Dr Nemr is a member of the International Bar Association (IBA), and of the International Criminal Law Association (ICLA).

Danforth Newcomb and Michael Gruson – United States

The contributors are from Shearman & Sterling.

Danforth Newcomb is a litigation partner in the New York office. His practice covers civil, administrative and criminal matters mostly acting for financial institutions. He is the author of articles on bank secrecy, fraud and money laundering. He received his JD degree from Columbia University in 1968.

Michael Gruson became a partner in 1973, practising in their New York and Frankfurt offices, and is presently Of Counsel. He received his legal education in Germany and in the US (1962, University of Mainz; MCL 1963, LLB 1965, Columbia University; Dr jur 1966, Freie Universität Berlin). Michael Gruson is the author of several books and many articles on issues of conflict of laws, on legal opinions and on US and European banking law. He also served as a visiting professor at various law schools.

Lauri Peltola and Helena Mäkinen – Finland

Lauri Peltola is a partner of Waselius & Wist. He graduated from the Helsinki University in 1974 and was admitted to the Finnish Bar in 1978. He worked for the Ministry of Trade and Industry, Competition Bureau, from 1975–1976, Procopé & Hornborg from 1976–1992 (partner 1980, head of London Branch 1984, secondment SG Archibald, Paris 1980), and Roschier Holmberg from 1993–2002 (head of London Branch 1993, partner 1995). He has extensive knowledge in the areas of banking and capital markets and cross-border M&A work.

Helena Mäkinen is a senior associate of Waselius & Wist. She received her LLM from the Helsinki University in 1996 and an LLMEur from the Europa-Institut at the University of Saarland in 2000. She was admitted to the Finnish Bar in 2002.

José Agustín Preciado Miró – Panamá

Born Panama, 1963, he obtained his law degree from Santa Maria La Antigua University in Panama City in 1987 and his LLM on International Trade and Banking from the Washington College of Law of the American University in 1989. He has acted as Chief Legal Counselor to the Minister of Government and Justice of Panama from 1992–1993, Chief General Counselor to the Minister of Housing and Urban Development from 1993–1994 and at present is Vice-Chairman of the Board of Directors of the Social Security Administration of the Republic of Panama. He is a partner at Sucre, Arias & Reyes, where, as part of the Finance and Banking team, he advises on bank contracts, banking operation and regulatory issues, insurance and securities.

Pit Reckinger – Luxembourg

He graduated from the University of Paris I (Panthéon-Sorbonne) with a maitrise en droit and received a postgraduate diploma in business law from the University of Paris I (Diplôme d'Etudes Approfondies en droit des affaires). He was called to the Luxembourg Bar in 1990. He joined Linklaters and Paines, solicitors in London, for a year before becoming a partner at Elvinger, Hoss & Prussen in 1994. His areas of practice include general corporate work, corporate finance, banking and insurance securities, public and private debt and stock issues, syndicated loans, stock exchange listings and investment fund registrations.

Jacques Richelle and Tom Thomas – Belgium

The contributors are from Linklaters De Bandt. Jacques Richelle graduated from Brussels University Law School (1988) and received an LLM from Southern Methodist

University School of Law (1989). After working for the Belgian Minister for Europe, he was called to the Brussels Bar in 1990 and joined De Bandt, van Hecke & Lagae (1992). A partner since 1998, he mainly practises banking law (transactional and regulatory aspects) and general financial law.

Tom Thomas graduated from the Universities of Namur and Leuven (1999), having spent an exchange year at the Humboldt University, Berlin. After an MSc in Theory and History of International Relations at the London School of Economics and Political Science, he was called to the Brussels Bar (2000). Then, he joined the Brussels firm of De Bandt, van Hecke, Lagae & Loesch (now Linklaters De Bandt) where he practises banking and financial law.

Thomas Schulz and Joachim Preussner – Germany

The contributors are from Nörr Stiefenhofer Lutz.

Dr Preussner is a partner in the Berlin office. He graduated from the Universities of Berlin and Freiburg/Brsg. He was admitted as a German attorney-at-law (1976). Prior to joining the firm, he worked in the banking sector, most recently as chief in-house counsel. He specialises in banking, corporate, public institutions and labour law and co-determination. He speaks German and English and is a member of the Banking Law Association and the Association of German Jurists.

Dr Schulz is a partner in the Munich office. A graduate of the University of Munich and Georgetown University Washington DC (LLM) (USA). He is a German attorney-at-law and a New York attorney and counselor-at-law. He was Counsel at the European Bank for Reconstruction and Development in London from 1996–1997. He specialises in corporate law, M&A, project and structured finance. He is on the Supervisory Board of Hettlage KGaA, Munich, and of Globalprint AG, Sassenberg.

Terje Sommer – Norway

Terje Sommer is a partner in Bugge, Arentz-Hansen & Rasmussen, a leading Norwegian law firm. He was born in Norway and obtained a law degree from Oslo University in 1969. He became an Advokat in 1973. From 1969 to 1989, he worked with Bergen Bank (now known as Den norske Bank) in Oslo holding various positions including General Counsel. From 1989 to 1991 he was General Manager of the bank's London branch. From 1991 to 2000, he was Resident Partner of Bugge, Arentz-Hansen & Rasmussen in London, returning to Oslo in 2000 to become a partner within the firm's Financial Markets Group.

Tomasz Wardyński – Poland

He is a founding partner of Wardyński & Partners specialising in international project finance, litigation, EU law and privatisation, and the restructuring of state enterprises. He graduated from the Faculty of Law in Warsaw University (1970), the College of Europe, Bruges (1973) and L'Institute des Hautes Etudes Europeannes, France (1974–1975). He was a visiting scholar at the American Bar Foundation (1985). He started legal practice in 1979. He was Chairman of the Foreign Commission of the Polish National Bar Association from 1988–1992 and member of the Ownership

Transformation Council of the Prime Minister of Poland from 1991–1996. He is an honorary advisor to the British Ambassador to Poland. He holds the British Order of Honorary Commander of the British Empire.

Alvin Yeo and Joy Tan – Singapore

The contributors are from Wong Partnership.

Alvin Yeo is Managing Partner and heads the Litigation, Arbitration and ADR Practice in which Joy Tan is a partner. He is also Joint Managing Director of Clifford Chance Wong. He practises in insolvency, restructuring, construction, civil engineering, intellectual property corporate and shareholder disputes. A graduate of King's College, London University, he was admitted to the English Bar (1987) and the Singapore Bar (1988). He was appointed Senior Counsel (2000) and is a member of the Law Reform Committee of the Singapore Academy of Law and the Inquiry Panel on complaints against lawyers.

Joy Tan graduated from Cambridge University (1991) with first class honours. She was admitted to the English Bar (1992) with an award from the UK Council of Legal Education, and the Singapore Bar (1993). Her main practice areas are banking, corporate and commercial disputes, and insolvency and restructuring.

Preface to the 1997 edition

Almost all the papers in this publication were first presented in May 1997 at the Annual International Financial and Banking Law Seminar of the Section on Business Law of the International Bar Association. Some of the papers were revised in the light of the discussion at the seminar. However, the reader should not assume that they take account of any changes in law occurring after May 1997.

This is the second edition of this publication, but it is the third occasion upon which members of the Banking Committee (Committee E) of the Section on Business Law of the International Bar Association have combined to publish a set of papers on this subject. The prior history was explained in my introduction to the previous edition in 1990, which is reproduced verbatim in this edition. It is reproduced not merely to explain the history, but more importantly because in that introduction I claimed to detect a number of trends in this area of the law, all of which I can now claim to be clear and unambiguous. In 1990, I detected the erosion of banking secrecy; in 1997 we can declare it dead and buried. In particular, the introduction throughout the European Union of money laundering legislation now means that no one can any longer feel confident that he can hide his money away in his bank safe from the prying eyes of government. Recent revelations about the alleged liberties which the Swiss banks have taken with Jewish money over the years have demoralised the Swiss and demolished the moral authority with which they once defended the principle of banking secrecy against all-comers. Whether or not we should welcome these trends is a different question. They are now clearly established and will not be easily reversed.

We have expanded the present edition to include papers not only from all countries of the European Union, but also from three countries on the eastern edge of the European Union, as well as papers from the other jurisdictions which were represented in the previous edition and a paper from Singapore which also covers Malaysia. Maybe, in the next edition, if time and energy permit, we will be able to expand still further to cover yet more jurisdictions.

The burden of editorial responsibility for the previous edition was shared by my friend, Roger McCormick, of Freshfields. He has recently become Chairman of the Banking Committee of the Section on Business Law and this has meant that he has not been able to take on an editorial role in connection with this edition, so this time the editorial responsibility has been entirely mine. I have greatly missed his constructive and efficient assistance.

My thanks are also due to all the contributors. Without their courteous and usually prompt and efficient co-operation, my task as editor would have been impossible. In fact, they made it very easy for me. Those with experience of organising a group of international business lawyers to contribute to a publication of this nature will not believe me when I say that almost all the contributors delivered their papers on time and responded to my requests promptly on almost every occasion. That is nevertheless true and I am very grateful to each and every one of them. I am also extremely grateful to my secretary, Eleanor Carter, and to Deborah Roberts of the IBA staff, who between them kept track of the papers and organised both the papers and me with their usual calm patience and efficiency.

Francis Neate
September 1997

Introduction to the 1990 edition

Francis Neate

In September 1979 at the Biennial Conference of the Section on Business Law of the International Bar Association, the Banking Committee (Committee E) conducted a comparative survey of the laws relating to banking confidentiality in a wide variety of jurisdictions. A large number of papers were read and subsequently published.[1] Switzerland, of course, led, followed by Austria, Germany and a number of other continental European jurisdictions. Then came the US, a stark contrast to Switzerland. The common law countries—England, Australia, New Zealand, Canada—brought up the rear. It was an interesting exercise. I delivered the English law paper at that conference. I emerged from the conference with a recollection of two striking contrasts.

The first contrast was the one between those countries, notably Switzerland, also Austria, in which breach of the banker's duty of confidence was enforced by the criminal law, and those where it was merely a civil obligation. In the former, enforcing the duty seemed to be straightforward. Everything was nicely cut and dried. One does not, after all, hesitate long when the choice is between performing one's duty and going to gaol. In the latter jurisdictions, by way of contrast, much doubt and uncertainty seemed to exist in some of the grey areas thrown up by the increasing internationalisation of banking business: to take one example, how should the branches or subsidiaries of a bank in one country respond to demands for information from the supervisory authorities in another country? There was an attractive simplicity to the certainty engendered by the harsh Swiss approach to these issues. On the other hand, it also seemed to encourage a rigidity which did not always make a lot of sense; whereas the greater flexibility permitted by those laws which provided merely for a civil duty appeared to me to permit a more pragmatic approach. After all, is serious harm likely to result to customers (unless they are criminals) from the disclosure of information to responsible supervisory authorities? Or, as an alternative way of looking at the problem, is there not greater risk overall to customers in general if the supervisory authorities are unable to do their job properly because of their failure to obtain information which is withheld in the interests of the few who might be damaged by its disclosure?

---

1   'Banking Secrecy' published by the International Bar Association in January 1980.

The second contrast lay in the extreme isolation of the US from most of the other countries. One of the principal causes of this was the very considerable resentment engendered in other countries by the recurring US tendency to extend its jurisdiction beyond its shores. The US representatives were themselves so sensitive to this resentment that one heard them apologising on more than one occasion for their authorities' behaviour; indeed, I cannot recall anyone during the 1979 conference trying to defend the US approach to the issue of jurisdiction.

However, another strong element contributing to the US isolation was the strong European feeling that the US banking and securities industries were overregulated. The US Securities and Exchange Commission was the body we all loved to hate. The European view seemed to be that our longer history had enabled us to develop systems of regulation and supervision which allowed for pragmatism and greater flexibility for sensible bankers and securities firms to conduct sensible business efficiently and quickly, without being trammelled by detailed regulations or the necessity of having a lawyer at their side every step of the way. In the English context, after the Financial Services Act and the 'Guinness' and 'Blue Arrow' scandals (among others) of the last decade, one might view this attitude with some amusement; alternatively, one might hark back to the 1970s, when this attitude was prevalent, with nostalgia for a golden age. But there is no doubt that such an attitude was widespread and was encouraged by many of the US bankers, lawyers and others then operating in Europe. It was natural enough for the US lawyer in private practice to look upon the SEC (or, in the case of banks, the Comptroller of the Currency) as the organisation primarily responsible for making his and his clients' lives so difficult; and to contrast this with the apparent freedom in Europe. In addition, he must have been worn down by the chore of endlessly explaining to his European counterparts the detailed ramifications of the activities of powerful regulatory organisations of which they had no experience and knew no equivalents. As to the US bankers and securities dealers, the experience of coming to Europe in the 1970s was a culture shock which many found liberating. I can remember many questions from US bankers in the early 1970s as to whether there was any fundamental legal impediment to the transaction being proposed; to which often the reply would be—why should there be? What do you have in mind? In consequence, there were few articulate defendants of the US approach to whom Europeans were exposed; rather, they were encouraged in their faith in their own systems by the majority of US practitioners in Europe. Scandals such as the IOS affair were conveniently forgotten.

One wonders also how far this divergence in attitude was reinforced by more deep-rooted historical and cultural attitudes. Certainly, it is a commonplace assertion that to declare an act a criminal offence is to reinforce the underlying belief that it constitutes a moral wrong. Everyone knows the historical reasons why Switzerland takes so seriously the banker's duty of confidence and treats breach of it as a criminal offence. In the paper on Swiss law delivered in 1979, these reasons were stated proudly and unequivocally. It may be a sign of the times that, in the equivalent paper in this publication, the statement is more muted. There can be no doubt that in 1979 the stringency of Swiss law on this subject was highly respected and the reasons for it well understood. In a sense, Switzerland was regarded as the acme of banking rectitude.

No doubt, there was (as there still is) a strong competitive element also. There always has been and always will be a huge quantity of international money, owing allegiance to no particular country, looking for a home where secrecy is guaranteed. Switzerland's assumed success in attracting a large proportion of this money has long been regarded with envy by bankers in other countries.

There may also have been an element of assertion of cultural superiority by the old world over the new, a recurring tendency in many parts of Europe after (if not also before) the Second World War.

Many of these factors were contributing to the apparent isolation, during the 1970s, of US attitudes to banking regulation and banking secrecy from the European attitude. Certainly, this isolation was apparent from the papers delivered and views expressed at the conference in 1979. Yet, even then, the discerning observer might have perceived the beginnings of a convergence in those attitudes. The most concrete indication was, perhaps, the Treaty of 25 May 1973 between Switzerland and the US concerning mutual assistance in criminal matters, which was mentioned in almost apologetic terms by the Swiss speaker at the 1979 conference as a minor tear in the enveloping fabric of Swiss banking secrecy, yet to some appeared to drive a coach and horses through the principle. In the United Kingdom, the Banking Act 1979 was strengthening the powers of the banking supervisors; legislation against insider trading was also mooted. This first came into effect in the Companies Act 1980.

Ten years later, one can see that a distinct shift in European attitudes has taken place. There appear to be several reasons for this. First, and perhaps foremost, the increasing globalisation of the banking and securities businesses presents a whole new range of problems to the domestic supervisors. It has become clear to them that the traditional concept of jurisdiction limited by territorial boundaries is wholly inadequate in the context of the developing global market. Simultaneously, there has been an increasing recognition of and determination to tackle the money laundering which is an inherent feature of international and organised crime. Finally, there has been a growing appreciation and acceptance, in the securities industry, of the principle of the 'integrity' of the market; in other words, that confidence in financial markets can only be preserved by the provision of simultaneous and, where possible, instantaneous access for all to all relevant information. The principal source of all these ideas has been the US. It is no longer isolated.

In the United Kingdom, the legal effect has been dramatic. As already mentioned, insider trading became a criminal offence in 1980. The attack on organised crime (particularly drug- or terrorist-related) has been stepped up to such an extent that, in one case today, a bank which merely suspects that it is handling the proceeds of crime itself commits a criminal offence if it fails to report its suspicion.[2] The investigatory powers of the authorities have been strengthened or, in the case of inquiries instituted by the Department of Trade under the Companies Acts, utilised to an extent never seen before. Market practices which, in the past, might have been considered dubious but would certainly have gone unpunished, if not undetected, have been ruthlessly stamped on. Finally, 'Big Bang'—presented as the 'deregulation'

---

2   Drug Trafficking Offences Act 1986.

of the securities industry—has been accompanied by the Financial Services Act, under which the securities industry is now regulated to an extent it has never known before.

Although the United Kingdom would, no doubt, claim that it has worked out (and is still working out) its own solutions, the similarities between the approach of the United Kingdom and that of the US are far more striking than the differences. No doubt many reasons can be offered for this convergence of attitudes, but I will limit myself to suggesting two. The first is obvious: the much-trumpeted 'victory' of the philosophy of the free market. There is no need to enter the debate over whether or not the philosophy is right, or whether it has been victorious over competing ideologies. It is sufficient to acknowledge that in the United Kingdom, in the last decade, this philosophy has been dominant and that the one field of activity to which its principles have been applied most vigorously has been the financial sector. This is not to say that the financial sector has been opened to unrestricted free enterprise. Rather, as already noted, it has been subjected to greater regulation than ever before. There have been substantial borrowings from the longer US experience of running an economy dedicated to the free enterprise principle. The paradox is that maintenance of the free market appears to require the strictest regulation of the market participants.

The second reason is more complex, but also represents a borrowing, albeit less conscious, from US experience. The increasing internationalisation of the banking and securities industries is rapidly eroding the cultural homogeneity of local financial markets. In the United Kingdom this process is already almost complete. Twenty years ago, the financial system in the United Kingdom was the preserve of the middle class 'establishment'. This is not to say that it was a closed shop. Many successful careers in the City of London started at the level of 'office boy' or the like. But the values of the City and its (unwritten) codes of conduct were those of the establishment and even those who did not 'belong' when they started aspired to join. The cynic would, of course, say that one reason why this way of doing things endured for so long was that, as with any system organised and run by and for the establishment, abuses of the system were ignored—at least until one section of the establishment began to disapprove of the activities of another, as happened in the insurance market at Lloyd's in the late 1970s. But that was not the whole story. The system enabled financial business to be conducted quickly and efficiently, with the minimum of regulation and relatively modest paper-work, because it was based to a considerable extent upon trust between the majority of participants engendered by shared standards and mutual understanding. However, much of this has been lost as a result of the internationalisation of the City of London which has been taking place over the last 20 years, considerably accelerated by 'Big Bang'.

Once again, one has to look to the US for the longest experience of organising a society comprising a mix of widely different cultures. Once again, one finds that the solution lies in the promulgation of regulations spelling out in great detail what behaviour is and is not permitted. When there are no shared assumptions, written rules are the only recourse; alternatively, if the only common understanding is that what is not forbidden is permitted, then a detailed list of what is forbidden must be provided.

All these factors have been at work in the United Kingdom over the last ten years and all have contributed to a very substantial shift in attitudes towards regulation of the banking and financial industries, which have been reflected in legislation. To return to the narrower scope of this book—the banker's duty of confidence—the same trend has occurred. In the paper on English law on this subject which I delivered to the conference in 1979, I said that the basic principle of English law was that the law will not permit you to keep your secrets by hiding them in a bank. At the time, this seemed to be a bold over-statement. Today, it is clearly right.

It was because I believed that there had been, over the last ten years, so clear a convergence of attitudes between the United Kingdom and the US, that I thought it would be interesting, in 1989, to revisit the subject of banking secrecy on a comparative basis, if only to discover to what extent a similar convergence might be found in other countries. Accordingly, at the Sixth Annual International Financial and Banking Law Seminar of the Section on Business Law of the International Bar Association, held in Copenhagen in May 1989, a session was devoted to this subject. A number of panellists, mainly but not exclusively from European jurisdictions, were invited to submit papers and a variety of case studies were discussed. The title of the topic was changed—from 'Banking Secrecy' to 'Use and Abuse of Confidential Information'. This change was deliberate, in order to ensure that two topics were dealt with which had scarcely featured in the 1979 papers. The first was insider trading. The second was the subject of conflict of interests. It is ironic that the principal reform associated with 'Big Bang'—the removal of enforced dual capacity in securities dealing—has introduced a whole league of new problems of this nature. Today, you may well find your trusted broker, whom you have instructed to buy shares for you, selling you his own at a considerable profit. In the banking context, the most interesting field in which these problems have started to arise is in the context of take-over bids. Target companies have been alarmed to find their own bank representing, or lending money to, the bidder. The Takeover Panel has addressed this kind of problem but, if the law also has a role to play, it seems likely that this will be found in the law relating to abuse of confidence. Similarly, the new fashion among banks and others of offering a 'one stop' service to customers, ranging from traditional banking to estate agency, stockbroking, merchant banking, equipment leasing, etc has introduced the temptation to weaken the duties of confidentiality traditionally owed by commercial banks in order to maximise 'cross-marketing' opportunities within the enlarged group of which the commercial bank forms part. It is relatively easy for banks to include standard terms in documentation with their customers in order to achieve this; if this practice is to be curbed, legislation will be required and the matter becomes one of public policy.

Insider trading, of course, has been given wide coverage in the media during the last decade. Some still see it as a 'victimless crime' or as merely 'an Anglo-Saxon obsession'. Many complain that, although laws have been enacted in various jurisdictions, they are not applied with much rigour. Indeed, insider trading is a classic example of the inherent weakness in 'harmonisation' measures in the international community. Legislative bodies do not actually catch international criminals by passing sophisticated new laws: it is how the laws are applied that matters.

The quality of the papers and of the discussion at the seminar in 1989 was uniformly excellent and it seemed worth while to repeat the 1979 experiment by producing a publication. A number of other contributors were, therefore, also approached and the original contributors revised their papers in the light of the discussion at the seminar. The results are contained in the following chapters. All European jurisdictions are covered except Sweden, together with the other leading common law jurisdictions: Australia and Canada, and, of course, the US.

It is for the reader to judge whether, and to what extent, the trends suggested above can be seen to be more widespread. I write merely from a United Kingdom perspective. Certainly, the jurisdictions covered in the following chapters vary considerably in their experience of the problems and the level of sophistication with which they have so far been addressed, and this is reflected to some extent in the papers in question. I would suggest, however, that the trends suggested above can be discerned in many of the countries in question; and further that, if the factors underlying and compelling those trends continue to exist, each country will eventually be forced to choose. One option will be to join the global market; in which case one would expect increasingly rigorous supervision of the financial industry, coupled with more exchanges of information and standardisation of supervisory criteria among the supervisors; an ever more vigorous attack on the money laundering activities of international crime; and ever more detailed rules designed to preserve the 'integrity' of the financial markets. Insider dealing will be made a criminal offence (if it is not already) and more strenuous efforts made to catch the offenders. The alternative is to join the 'off-shore haven' club, among whose members, no doubt, the concept of banking secrecy will be elevated to an ever higher moral plane. Members of the European Community will all have to make the same choice and it seems clear that this will be for the first option.

March 1990

1 Argentina

Rafael La Porta Drago
Silvia G Poratelli

GENERAL OVERVIEW

Argentine law has traditionally recognised a principle of bank secrecy consisting of both a bank's right to protect the privacy of its records and proprietary commercial information and a customer's right to privacy.

The first aspect of bank secrecy derives from the bank's constitutional right of privacy and, particularly, its right to engage in commercial activities (Argentine Constitution, ss 18 and 14 respectively). However, more emphasis has been placed on the bank's duty to protect its customers' right to privacy.

Until 1969, when it was for the first time specifically addressed by statute, the bank's duty of confidentiality was construed on the basis of the customers' constitutional right of privacy provided by the Argentine Constitution, s 18 and a combination of various other provisions of the Civil Code, the Criminal Code and the Civil and Commercial Procedural Code.

Some scholars construed such duty under the provisions of the Civil Code as an implied term of all contracts entered into between a bank and its customers, resulting from commercial usage and the parties' broader duty of good faith. An analogy was also drawn with the bailee's duty to maintain the confidentiality of the property delivered in bailment (Civil Code, s 2207). Based on this 'implied contract term' theory, if a bank disclosed information provided by a customer, such customer was said to be entitled to compensation for breach of contract, not only during the life of the contract but also before entering into it and following its termination. A violation by a bank of this duty of secrecy was also construed as a tort, ie an illicit act that gave rise to a customer's right to compensation for damages. In addition, when a violation of the duty of secrecy seriously affects a customer's private life, the Civil Code, s 1071bis, which prohibits the 'arbitrary disturbance' of another person's privacy – a language broad enough to cover a bank's indiscretion – may also apply.

In further support, the Criminal Code, s 156 prohibits those entrusted with a secret as a result of their job or profession from disclosing such secret, and the Civil and Commercial Procedural Code, s 444 allows a witness to refuse to disclose information considered as 'privileged communication'.

FINANCIAL INSTITUTIONS LAW

In 1969, Law no 18,061, which regulated the activities of banks and other financial institutions, for the first time specifically established a general duty of confidentiality applicable to banks, subject to certain exceptions. Although the spirit of the law was to protect the customers' privacy, it did not exclude the banks' right to protect their proprietary information. Law no 18,061 was later replaced by Law no 21,526 (the Financial Institutions Law), which addressed the duty of confidentiality in its s 39. Section 39 underwent a number of amendments over time that gradually limited the scope of this duty and broadened its exceptions.

The Financial Institutions Law governs all entities (either governmental or private) who regularly intermediate in the supply and demand of financial resources in Argentina, such as commercial banks, investment banks, mortgage banks, financial companies, savings and loan co-operatives etc. The Argentine Central Bank is the regulatory authority in charge of applying the provisions of the Financial Institutions Law, issuing regulations thereunder and supervising the activities of the banks and other financial entities.

The Financial Institutions Law, s 39, as currently in force, provides that banks and other financial institutions shall not disclose information about what is accounted for as deposits and other banks' liabilities.[1] This confidentiality duty does not apply when the disclosure is requested by:

1   a court, in a judicial proceeding;
2   the Argentine Central Bank;
3   the tax authorities; and
4   other banks and financial institutions (with the Argentine Central Bank's prior authorisation).

In addition, the bank's personnel are prohibited from disclosing any information about the bank's customers.

In 1981, the Supreme Court concluded that the Financial Institutions Law, s 39 is not only applicable to banks but also to individuals and companies who handle confidential information delegated to them by a bank.[2] The case involved a credit card processing company who refused to provide to the tax authorities certain information which had been furnished to it by the banks (and was at that time protected by the banks' duty of confidentiality). This ruling is particularly applicable to the outsourcing of services, and has become emphasised by the Habeas Data Law (Law no 25,326, discussed below), which makes the transferor of personal data jointly and severally liable with the transferee for any breach of confidentiality concerning that information. Additionally, the Habeas Data Law further prohibits the transfer of personal data to countries or international entities that do not provide an adequate level of confidentiality protection.

---

1   This limitation reflects a criterion previously suggested by the Argentine Supreme Court in the case *Banco de Londres y América del Sud* Fallos 302-1116 (1980).
2   *Argencard SA v Gobierno Nacional (Tribunal Fiscal de la Nación)* LL 1982-B 462 (1981).

Bank secrecy is limited to deposits and other banks' liabilities

As mentioned above, the Financial Institutions Law, s 39 applies only to what is accounted for as deposits and other banks' liabilities (the Confidential Transactions). This means that it does not apply to loans and other bank transactions accounted for as assets, nor to a broad range of transactions that are not reflected in the liabilities side of a bank's balance sheet. This limitation, which was not present in prior versions of s 39, is aimed at allowing banks to share information on creditworthiness of customers and prospective customers for purposes of protecting credit.

As part of this policy, all banks are required to supply information on their loans to the Central Bank on a monthly basis. These reports include:

1   information identifying the borrower (name, tax identification number, customer number, type of customer, place of residency, creditworthiness and whether or not customer is deemed to be an insider of the bank);
2   information relating to the debt (type, securities, refinancing, previsions made by the bank);
3   information on economic groups;
4   additional information on 'significant borrowers' (those who meet certain standards set by the Central Bank), such as principal activity etc; and
5   certain aggregate statistical information (Communication A3360, the Communication).

This data is processed by the Central Bank which in turn makes available certain parts of such information (list of borrowers, their credit rating and type and amount of their indebtedness, the Public Information) to the general public by means of publication on the Internet. Banks and financial institutions have also access to information relating to the average interest rates and remaining life of the loans. Pursuant to the Communication, banks and other financial institutions may not directly supply to third parties any information other than Public Information. Thus, all sharing of information on creditworthiness among banks and other credit risk institutions is centralised by the Central Bank.

The above limitation to the duty of confidentiality is aimed at allowing banks to share financial information for purposes of protecting credit, and it should not be interpreted as a general authorisation publicly to disclose any kind of information. Although there is no relevant case law on the subject, a reasonable argument under the National Constitution and the Civil Code could be made to prevent banks from arbitrarily disclosing private information outside the scope of the credit protection purpose implicit in the Financial Institutions Law, s 39. This argument is strengthened by the Communication, which prohibits banks from directly supplying information other than Public Information to third parties.

In addition, customers are further protected by the Financial Institutions Law, s 39's last sentence, which prohibits the bank's personnel from disclosing *any* information about the bank's customers, whether relating to Confidential Transactions or not. Disclosures made in violation of this provision may give rise to administrative penalties imposed by the Central Bank, and might subject the person or institution who disclosed the information to civil liability or, in certain cases, criminal prosecution (see Remedies below).

Exceptions

Court order

Pursuant to the Financial Institutions Law, s 39, para (a), a court may request a bank's report on otherwise confidential information in the context of a judicial procedure.

Other than in criminal procedures, a bank's duty to disclose confidential information in response to a court order is limited by general rules of civil procedure providing that:

1   the court's request must refer to concrete facts, clearly identified and at issue during the trial; and
2   the bank's report must result from its accounting records, documents and files (Civil and Commercial Procedural Code, ss 364 and 396, respectively).

Thus, during trial, a court will assess the admissibility of the request for confidential information and, if appropriate, will issue a subpoena ordering the bank to disclose the requested information in writing before the court. Note that the Financial Institutions Law, s 39's general rule prohibiting the bank's personnel from disclosing any information about the bank's customers together with the Civil and Commercial Procedural Code, s 444, which permits that a witness refuse to disclose information considered as 'privileged communication', may prevent a court from requiring a bank's employee to provide testimony about a bank's customer.

The foregoing principles do not apply to criminal procedures, which are of an inquisitive nature. Thus, at any stage of a criminal procedure, a bank may be required by a judge or a public prosecutor to disclose otherwise confidential information about one of its customers, without even giving notice to such customer.

Central Bank

The Financial Institutions Law, s 39, para (b) provides that information 'required by the Central Bank within its competence' is excluded from the banks' duty of confidentiality. All information received by the Central Bank is in turn protected by the Financial Institutions Law, s 40, which requires the Central Bank, its personnel and any external auditors to maintain the confidentiality of all information relating to Confidential Transactions.

The language in s 39, para (b) has recently become important within the context of a conflict between local banks (represented by the Argentine Association of Banks) and two Congress Committees created to investigate the flight of capital that followed recent exchange control measures taken by the Argentine government (the Committees). In July 2002, the Central Bank requested general information on certain operations from all Argentine banks, for the purpose of submitting such information to the Committees. Although banks spontaneously responded to such request providing non-confidential information, they refused to submit information on Confidential Transactions. Their main argument was that the Central Bank's request was made for purposes of providing a response to the Committees, which is not within the scope of its authority. In other words, the Central Bank's responsibility is to supervise the correct functioning of financial institutions and the financial market and not to serve as an 'access door' to other governmental organisations not included in the exceptions of s 39. Resolution of this conflict is still pending at the time of writing.

Tax authorities

Initially, the Financial Institutions Law, s 39, para (c) set forth a limited exception to the general principle of banks' secrecy, for the exclusive benefit of Argentina's national tax authorities (the National Tax Bureau). This exception was generally limited by the following requirements:

1   that the requested information refer to a particular taxpayer;
2   that such taxpayer is then under a tax audit; and
3   that a prior written notification be made.

The purpose of these limitations was to guarantee the protection of such taxpayer's right to due process.

The scope of this exception was gradually broadened in the following years. First, to benefit provincial and municipal tax authorities as well. Then, to exclude the application of points 1 and 2 above when the request is made by the National Tax Bureau.

As a result, today the National Tax Bureau has very broad powers to request otherwise confidential information from banks. However, as in the Central Bank's case, the National Tax Bureau *is* limited by (i) the scope of its own competence (ie it may not request information other than for purposes of investigating tax evasion and pursuing tax collections) and (ii) its own duty of confidentiality towards the tax payer.

As a corollary to the tax authorities' broad powers, in 1998, the National Tax Bureau issued a General Resolution pursuant to which banks and other financial institutions must monthly provide it with information on (i) companies or individuals who open one or more bank accounts and (ii) bank accounts that are credited during such month with an amount equivalent to Pesos 8,000 (approximately US$2,800 at the time of writing) or more in the aggregate.

Other banks

The Financial Institutions Law, s 39, para (d) refers to information requested by 'other financial institutions, with the prior express authorization of the Central Bank'. This exception was never implemented and has now become purposeless since its main objective – to facilitate the sharing of information on creditworthiness – has been accomplished directly by the Central Bank through the reception and redistribution of information on loans.

Furthermore, the exchange of information is nowadays usually made pursuant to the customer's consent, as further explained in the following paragraph.

OTHER EXCEPTIONS TO BANK SECRECY

Consent

Even within the limited scope of the Financial Institutions Law, s 39, it is generally agreed that disclosure made with the affected customer's consent does not constitute a breach of the bank's duty of secrecy.

As a particular application of this principle, the Argentine courts have decided that a bank cannot refuse to respond to a request made by the holder of a cheque returned unpaid to be provided with information that helps to identify and locate the issuer of such returned cheque. It is understood that a customer who issues a cheque has consented to such disclosure of information, which purpose is to allow the cheque's beneficiary to enforce its rights.[3]

A similar conclusion must be reached when a bank and its customer are opposite parties during a trial: the latter is assumed to have consented to the bank's disclosure of confidential information within the limited scope of the trial.

Another example is the previous consent given by borrowers of a loan secured by a mortgage, for purposes of securitisation of a loan portfolio by the bank acting as lender. Such consent is usually contained in the mortgage deed and relieves the bank from the obligation to notify the borrowers of the assignment of their loans, and it is also interpreted as a release of the confidentiality obligation regarding the credit record of the borrower.

In addition, as a general practice, Argentine subsidiaries and branches of foreign banks generally include in their printed forms a customer's consent to the sharing of information between said subsidiaries and branches, their parent institutions and other affiliates.

Illegal drugs

In 1989, the Argentine Congress passed Law no 23,737, which deals with illegal drug-related crimes. Section 26 of this law specifically provides that during the investigation of any of the crimes included therein, no bank secrecy may limit the task of the judge in charge of such investigation. The language of Law no 23,737, s 26, which is broader than that of the Financial Institutions Law, s 39, para (a), suggests that within the scope of this statute, a criminal judge may order any bank to submit generic information otherwise protected by such bank's duty of secrecy. However, a recent law on money laundering, referred to below, has in some ways superseded this statute in all matters related to bank's secrecy.

Money laundering

In May 2000, Law no 25,246 (the Money Laundering Law) was passed, aggravating penalties for money laundering and other forms of 'aiding and abetting'. The Money Laundering Law created a new government agency called the Financial Information Unit (FIU) with broad powers to investigate and prevent the laundering of assets connected with the traffic of drugs and arms, terrorist organisations, government corruption, minors prostitution and child pornography. The FIU, which is still in the process of becoming operative, has authority to require any kind of information from any public or private entity. However, when such information is confidential, the FIU must previously request a court authorisation.

---

3   *San Sebastián SA v Toro, Ximena* E LL 1984-C 485 (1984).

Pursuant to the Money Laundering Law, ss 20 and 21, banks and other financial institutions, as well as their officers and employees, are required to play an active role in monitoring their customers for purposes of preventing money laundering transactions. Thus, s 21 provides that banks will be required to:

1 Obtain and keep exhaustive information on its customers, particularly when any such customers act in representation of third parties, in which case banks should properly identify those third parties as well.

2 Inform the FIU of any 'suspicious act or transaction' performed by its customers; a 'suspicious act or transaction' is defined as any act or transaction which is:

   (a) unusual in light of the applicable activity's commercial usage and the experience and skill of the person(s) obliged to inform;

   (b) without economic or legal justification; or

   (c) of an uncommon or unwarranted complexity, in each case, either in an isolated or repeating fashion.

   It is worth noting that, pursuant to Decree no 169/2001, s 10, regulating the Money Laundering Law, banks and their officers are automatically exempted from their duty of confidentiality when complying with this obligation (ie they are not required to obtain a court's prior authorisation).

3 Not disclose to any customer or third party the existence of any investigations performed pursuant to the Money Laundering Law.

As a means to encourage compliance with the duty to inform about 'suspicious transactions', the Money Laundering Law exempts all good faith reports from any civil, commercial, labour, criminal and administrative responsibility.

Furthermore, the Money Laundering Law, s 24 provides that any violation of a bank's duty of information shall be penalised with a fine for an amount ranging from one to ten times the aggregate value of the transaction not informed to the FIU or, if such value cannot be determined, from Pesos 10,000 to 100,000 (approximately US$3,500 to 35,000 at the time of writing). This penalty may be imposed not only on the bank, but also on the officers or employees involved in the violation. In addition, banks are required to appoint an 'anti-money laundering compliance officer'.

As a counterbalance to the FIU's broad powers to obtain information, the FIU is subject to a strict duty of confidentiality. Thus, the Money Laundering Law, s 22 provides that the FIU's personnel (and all persons required to provide information to it, ie banks and their personnel) must maintain the confidentiality of all gathered information or risk penalties as serious as six-month to three-year periods of imprisonment (for individuals) or fines from Pesos 10,000 to 100,000.

Terrorism

A recent communication of the Argentine Central Bank,[4] issued upon a request made by the Federal Reserve Bank of New York in the context of a criminal investigation on terrorism, has required the Argentine financial institutions to report transactions performed by certain persons, listed in an Annex to that communication,

---

4   Communication B7701, 28 January 2003.

who are suspected of being involved in terrorist activities. However, the communication in question specifies that the information should be given in a generic manner and 'without identifying, for instance, persons or amounts involved, for purposes of maintaining bank confidentiality'.

REMEDIES

Damages

A customer is entitled to recover damages caused by any illegitimate disclosure of information made by its bank. The scope of compensation depends on whether the claim is based on tort or breach of contract. Most scholars predicate the first alternative, which results in the bank being liable for both direct and indirect damages. Alternatively, if a customer sues for breach of contract, indirect damages are imposed only if the bank has acted with malice.

In addition to compensation for economic damage, a customer is entitled to compensation for 'moral damage'. Exceptionally, if the circumstances of the case and the evidence produced by the claimant warrant it, a customer may obtain compensation exclusively for moral damage. However, note that in the imposition of moral damages, a court will mainly take into account the customer's 'affliction' caused by the arbitrary disclosure of financial information, and not the bank's inappropriate conduct: moral damage is not equivalent to 'punitive damages'.

Because Argentine law does not contemplate punitive damages and the Civil Code's system strongly relies on the strict demonstration of actual damages, there are almost no precedents of claims filed by customers harmed by their banks' breach of confidentiality (instead, most of the case law on bank secrecy deals with the banks' response to various kinds of information requests). In fact, the incentive to pursue a claim of this nature is very low, since a customer's ability to succeed in court will in most cases be hindered by the difficulty in proving the actual damage caused by the bank.

It is not usual to include a clause limiting the bank's responsibility for disclosure in the documentation signed between a bank and its clients (ie an application for opening a bank account) in Argentina. A probable explanation for this is that, given the low level of litigation in this area industry-wide, such a provision might reflect poorly on the bank's image without a noticeable benefit. In any event, any such provision should take into consideration that mandatory principles of Argentine law prohibit to waive in advance the wilful misconduct of the other party to a contract (that is, the limitation could only apply to negligent disclosures). Additionally, a court of law could disregard such limitation if it found the maximum liability amount so agreed unreasonably low; particularly taking into account that bank agreements are usually pre-printed forms (adhesion contracts) in which the client has little or no possibility to negotiate terms and conditions.

Habeas Data Law

The last amendment to the Argentine Constitution, which took place in 1994, granted to every person the right to access any public – or private, if it has the purpose of providing information to third parties – database or files that include personal data about such person, and the right to demand deletion, rectification, confidential treatment or updating of any false or discriminatory piece of data, as applicable (s 43).

In November 2000, the Argentine Constitution, s 43 was regulated by Law no 25,326 (the Habeas Data Law), aimed at protecting personal data contained in public or private databases. Pursuant to the Habeas Data Law, s 16, a person is entitled to file a habeas data claim requiring the holder of a database to maintain the confidentiality of his or her personal information, if such confidentiality is applicable. This section, combined with the Financial Institutions Law, allows a customer expeditiously to compel a bank to maintain the confidentiality of any personal information protected by the duty of secrecy. A preliminary injunction preventing a bank from disclosing information until the habeas data claim is solved adds efficiency to this proceeding.

Finally, the Habeas Data Law, s 10 provides that any person or company handling personal data must maintain its confidentiality even after termination of such person or company's relationship with the owner of such data; this section adds weight to the general prohibition of disclosure imposed on banks' personnel by the last sentence of the Financial Institutions Law, s 39.

Administrative penalties

A bank's breach of its duty of secrecy constitutes a violation of the Financial Institutions Law, regardless of whether or not it has caused any actual damage. Said violation is subject to administrative sanctions imposed by the Central Bank on the breaching bank and any of its responsible employees. These penalties include a formal warning, fines and temporary or permanent disqualification from holding a position or investing in a bank or other financial institution, as the Central Bank may deem appropriate, subject to appeal before court.

CONCLUSION

The principle of bank secrecy is protected by the Argentine Constitution and expressly regulated by the Financial Institutions Law. However, many exceptions to it have significantly limited its scope. First, as a general rule bank confidentiality does not apply to loans and other similar bank transactions. Second, subject to certain procedures, the courts, the Central Bank and the tax authorities are empowered to request disclosure of otherwise confidential information. In addition, banks must monthly report to the National Tax Bureau the opening of accounts and deposit of certain amounts with them.

Other exceptions to the principle of bank secrecy include: customer's consent, requests of information by a criminal judge persecuting drug-related crimes or by the FIU, a recently created money laundering government agency, and the obligation to report bank transactions performed by alleged terrorists to the Federal Reserve Bank of New York.

A bank's breach of its duty of secrecy is subject to administrative sanctions imposed by the Central Bank pursuant to the Financial Institutions Law. In addition, the

Habeas Data Law entitles a customer to obtain an injunction requiring a bank to maintain the confidentiality of his or her personal information.

Although a case could be made under various provisions of the Argentine Civil Code by a customer who has been harmed by its bank's breach of the confidentiality duty, the incentive to pursue a claim of this nature is very low, since the customer's ability to succeed in court will most probably be hindered by the difficulty in proving the actual damaged caused by its bank.

2 Australia

Ros Grady
*Frances Russell-Matthews**

INTRODUCTION

Australia is a federation of six states and two territories, together with a federal (Commonwealth) government. The Australian Constitution gives to the federal government the power to legislate throughout Australia with respect to banking.[1] Each of the states and territories can also legislate where there is a connection with its geographic area, subject to the supremacy of Commonwealth law where there is inconsistency.[2]

Whilst each of these nine governments has the power to legislate in respect of the banker's duty of confidence, there is no legislation in Australia which codifies the duty. There are many federal and state statutes which are relevant, but these mainly allow disclosure in certain circumstances and hence represent exceptions to the duty.

In the absence of legislation, the basis for the duty in Australia rests in common law and equity. The principles set out in the leading English case of *Tournier v National Provincial and Union Bank of England*,[3] discussed in depth in chapter 9, England, still succinctly summarise for Australian law purposes the principal scope of the duty and the category of exceptions to it.[4]

TOURNIER v NATIONAL PROVINCIAL AND UNION BANK OF ENGLAND[5]

The principles expressed in *Tournier* apply to banks. They are not usually regarded as having an application to building societies, credit unions or other financial institutions.[6]

---

*   The authors gratefully acknowledge the kind assistance of Gian Boeddu in preparation of this chapter. Since this chapter was first drafted, Frances Russell-Mathews has left the firm Mallesons Stephen Jaques.
1   Other than 'state banking', which covers the business of banking engaged in by a state itself as banker which is of little importance currently as all of the state banks have been privatised.
2   Commonwealth Constitution, s 109.
3   [1924] 1 KB 461. The principles in *Tournier* have been reaffirmed recently, amongst other cases, in *Christopher v Barclays Bank plc* [1998] All ER Rep 484.
4   See under Further duties of confidence in Australia below.
5   *Tournier v National Provincial and Union Bank of England* [1924] 1 KB 461.
6   *The Laws of Australia*, para 124.

However, the principles from *Tournier* have been reflected in the Code of Banking Practice. Both building societies and credit unions also have codes of practice. Section 12 of the Credit Union Code is very similar to the provisions in s 22 of the Code of Banking Practice. Section 11 of the Building Society Code is less similar to s 22 of the Code of Banking Practice, but still imposes duties of confidentiality. Alan Tyree concludes that *Tournier* would apply to building societies and credit unions on the basis that the judgment in *Tournier* was not limited strictly to the bank-customer relationship.[7]

REMEDIES FOR BREACH

As the common law duty lies in contract in Australia, normal contractual remedies exist for breach of contract.[8] Further, equitable remedies may exist on the basis of a breach of confidence or breach of fiduciary duty such as an injunction or damages.[9] There is also the possibility of bringing a claim under the tort of defamation, which depends entirely on the nature of the disclosure. Finally, there are statutory provisions in some cases. An example is the Privacy Act 1988. Section 36(1) provides (subject to s 36(1A)) that an individual may complain to the Privacy Commissioner about an act or practice that may be an interference with the privacy of the individual. Under s 36(1A), s 36(1) does not apply if the complaint is about an act or practice of an organisation that is bound by a privacy code approved by the Privacy Commissioner that contains a procedure for making and dealing with complaints to an adjudicator in relation to acts or practices that may be an interference with privacy and that is relevant to the act or practice complained of.

Section 52(1)(b)(iii) provides that, after investigating a complaint, the Commissioner may find the complaint substantiated and make a determination including a declaration that the complainant is entitled to a specified amount to compensate for any loss or damage suffered. Such loss or damage includes injury to the complainant's feelings or humiliation suffered by the complainant. The Privacy Commissioner, however, has in place a procedure of mediation and its success has resulted in only two determinations under s 52(1)(b)(iii) to date.

DISCLOSURE UNDER COMPULSION OF LAW

This is the first of the exceptions to the bank's duty of non-disclosure.

Confidentiality is not of itself sufficient to deny a request to produce information. Indeed, confidentiality may sometimes have to defer to a higher public interest which may be served by disclosure.[10] Gibbs ACJ in *Sankey v Whitlam*[11] said: 'Confidentiality is not a separate head of privilege, but may be a material

---

7   Tyree 'Does Tournier apply to building societies?' (1995) 6 J Banking and Finance Law and Practice 206.
8   *Federal Commissioner of Taxation v ANZ* (1979) 143 CLR 499 at 522.
9   See discussion under Further duties of confidence in Australia below.
10 *Campbell v Tameside Metropolitan Borough Council* [1982] 3 WLR 74. The principles in *Campbell* have been recently applied in *M v L* [1997] 3 NZLR at 424.
11 *Sankey v Whitlam* (1978) 142 CLR 1.

consideration to bear in mind when privilege is claimed on the ground of public interest.'[12] He then went on to comment:

> 'The court will of course examine the question with especial care, giving full weight to the reasons for preserving the secrecy of documents of this class, but it will not treat all such documents as entitled to the same measure of protection – the extent of protection required will depend to some extent on the general subject matter with which the documents are concerned.'[13]

The decision on whether there should be disclosure involves a balance between the public interest in protecting the confidence and the public interest in having all relevant material available for the determination of a dispute.[14] In *Trade Practices Commission v Queensland Aggregates Pty Ltd (No 2)*,[15] Shepherd J referred to the following statement of Lord Kilbrandon in *D v National Society for the Prevention of Cruelty to Children*:[16]

> '(I) In civil proceedings a judge has no discretion, simply because what is contemplated is the disclosure of information which has passed between persons in a confidential relationship (other than that of a lawyer and client), to direct a party to that relationship that he need not disclose that information even though its disclosure is: (a) relevant to and (b) necessary for the attainment of justice in the particular case. If (a) and (b) are established, the doctor or the priest must be directed to answer if, despite the strong dissuasion of the judge, the advocate persists in seeking disclosure. This is also true of all other confidential relationships in the absence of a special statutory provision ...
>
> (II) But where (i) a confidential relationship exists (other than that of lawyer and client) *and* (ii) disclosure would be in breach of some ethical or social value involving the public interest, the court has a discretion to uphold a refusal to disclose relevant evidence provided it considers that, on balance, the public interest would be better served by excluding such evidence ...
>
> (IV) The sole touchstone is the public interest, and not whether the party for whom disclosure is sought was acting under a "duty" – as opposed to merely exercising "powers". A party who acted under some duty may find it easier to establish that public interest was involved than one merely exercising powers, but that is another matter.
>
> (V) The mere fact that relevant information was communicated in confidence does not necessarily mean that it need not be disclosed. But where the subject matter is clearly of public interest, the *additional* fact (if such it be) that to break the seal of confidentiality would endanger that interest will in most (if not all) cases probably lead to the conclusion that disclosure should be withheld. And it is difficult to conceive of *any* judicial discretion to exclude relevant and necessary evidence save in respect of confidential information communicated in a confidential relationship.

12   (1978) 142 CLR 1 at 42–43.
13   (1978) 142 CLR 1 at 43.
14   *Campbell v Tameside Metropolitan Borough Council* [1982] 3 WLR 74. See also *National Tertiary Education Industry Union v Commonwealth of Australia* (2001) III FCR at 583.
15   (1981) 51 FLR 364.
16   [1978] AC 171.

(VI) The disclosure of all evidence relevant to the trial of an issue being at all times a matter of considerable public interest, the question to be determined is whether it is clearly demonstrated that in the particular case the public interest would nevertheless be better served by excluding evidence despite its relevance. If, on balance, the matter is left in doubt, disclosure should be ordered.'[17]

These principles were considered in the criminal context in the state of Victoria in *Falconer v Australian Broadcasting Commission*.[18] Vlado Rajicic had been a police informer and was given a new identity known only to a small group of police officers. The defendant proposed to broadcast photographs, identified as photographs of him. The plaintiff, a senior police officer, sought an interlocutory injunction to restrain publication. Ashley J undertook the balancing process and decided that the public policy considerations against disclosure of Rajicic's present identity were material to the exercise of his discretion and tended in favour of the interlocutory relief. He considered:

'There is the need to ensure "a flow of intelligence about planned crime and its perpetrators". Anonymity of informers, and their protection against those who would later wish them ill, are in my opinion matters of importance in the exercise of my discretion.'[19]

Therefore, in all cases where the court's indulgence is sought, the court will undertake this balancing approach when considering the competing public interests involved in the disclosure of confidential information. This approach was reiterated, again in a criminal context, in the state of South Australia as recently as in June 2000 in *R v Richard Edward Mason*.[20]

Subpoena

Requirements of the law

The courts do not give banking secrecy preferential protection over other types of confidential information. In court proceedings where evidence concerning a person's banking arrangement is relevant, that evidence can be obtained by subpoena. For example, in the state of Victoria, Order 42 of the Supreme Court (General Civil Procedure) Rules 1996 provides that a subpoena can be filed for production of a document or thing for evidence, or an order to attend for the purpose of giving evidence. The information requested in the subpoena is to be delivered to the court that issued the subpoena and not to the solicitors acting for the issuing party or the issuing party. In the absence of a reasonable excuse, failure to comply with a properly issued and served subpoena may constitute a contempt of court or a statutory offence.[21]

17   [1978] AC 171 at 245–246.
18   [1992] 1 VR 662.
19   [1992] 1 VR 662 at 671.
20   [2000] 74 SASR 105.
21   *Halsbury's Laws of Australia* para 105-315.

The principles in relation to setting aside subpoenas were discussed by Beach J in *Re ACI International Ltd*.[22] The fact that documents are confidential is usually not a ground for having the subpoena set aside, but is relevant to issues such as inspection and access.[23]

Effects on banker's duty of confidentiality

Robertson v Canadian Imperial Bank of Commerce[24] saw the Privy Council consider the issue of a bank complying with a subpoena. Lord Nolan said on disclosing the existence of the subpoena to a customer that it should be done 'if only as a matter of courtesy and good business practice'.[25] Lord Nolan declined to place an express duty on a bank to inform a customer. Respected Australian writer Weaver observes that the practice in Australia is not to tell the customer or to tell the customer at the last minute.[26] Lord Nolan, however, in the *Robertson* case suggested that it would be prudent to tell the customer of the existence of the subpoena to at least give the customer the opportunity of pursuing any available remedies.

The other issue of interest from the *Robertson* case was what information the bank should disclose. For example, a bank statement may show relevant deposits but may also show several other payments. One would expect the bank statements, if provided, should black out every other transaction aside from those which are relevant to the subpoena. The *Robertson* case held no firm view on the exact nature of the disclosure. A court and a customer would expect a bank to be extremely careful when answering a subpoena not to disclose information that is not required and is of a particularly sensitive nature. However, in this process it is for the bank to form its own opinion about each item of information and whether it comes within the terms of the subpoena.

In practice, the importance of the bank delivering the documents to the court, and not to the party that issued the subpoena, is critical for two reasons. First, to fall within the exception of compulsion of law the bank must comply with the law and the law only requires production to the court. Secondly, confidentiality will be a material factor in deciding issues of inspection and reproduction of the documents. If the documents are produced to a third party, then the party issuing the subpoena will not have to seek leave of the court to inspect, and the court will not have an opportunity to consider the issue of confidentiality.[27]

In relation to orders of foreign courts and foreign authorities, see the discussion at International requests for information, below.

---

22 (1986) 11 ACLR 240.
23 (1986) 11 ACLR 240 at 243.
24 [1995] 1 All ER 824.
25 [1995] 1 All ER 824 at 830.
26 This is on the basis that there is no legal duty to inform the customer and there is little a customer can do to intervene.
27 Particularly, where there are several parties to the litigation the court may limit inspection to the party that issued the subpoena.

Search warrants

Requirements of the law

The leading authority on search warrants is the decision of the Full Court of the High Court of Australia in *George v Rockett*.[28] The court acknowledged that a search warrant authorises an invasion of premises without the occupier's consent. State and Commonwealth statutes provide several mechanisms by which to obtain search warrants.[29]

> 'Nevertheless, in construing and applying such statutes, it needs to be kept in mind that they authorise the invasion of interests which the common law has always valued highly and which, through the writ of trespass, it went to great lengths to protect.'[30]

Effects on banker's duty of confidentiality

The statutes do not provide an exception for a bank's confidential information. However, the decision to issue a search warrant is a reviewable decision for the purposes of the Administrative Decisions (Judicial Review) Act 1977 (Cth). Further, in *R v Tillett*[31] the court held that the fact that a search warrant had been executed did not preclude relief by way of certiorari.[32]

Subject to any express requirements of law,[33] a bank in receipt of a search warrant in relation to one of its customers should be careful to exercise caution in assisting an officer's request. The possibility exists, although it is unlikely in relation to documents held by a bank, that the customer may make a claim for legal professional privilege in relation to documents the subject of a search warrant.[34] This may be relevant, for example, where a customer keeps highly confidential files (which would have to be within the ambit of the legal professional privilege test) in a safe deposit box at the bank. As the privilege is that of the customer, the bank must not do anything which inadvertently amounts to a waiver of the customer's privilege. Therefore, it is always sensible to involve the customer at the outset.

Prudence would also suggest that a bank, from a legal and commercial perspective, should inform a customer when it receives a search warrant in order to allow the

---

28   (1990) 170 CLR 104. The principles in *George v Rockett* have been recently applied in *Adler v Gardiner* (2002) 43 ACSR at 24.
29   As an example of a typical legislative prescription, see s 3E(1) of the Crimes Act 1914 (Cth) which provides:
     'An issuing officer may issue a warrant to search premises if the officer is satisfied by information on oath that there are reasonable grounds for suspecting that there is, or there will be within the next 72 hours, any evidential material at the premises.'
30   (1990) 170 CLR 104.
31   (1969) 14 FLR 101.
32   Certiorari is an administrative remedy issued by a superior court exercising its supervisory jurisdiction. It is only available after the inferior court has made a decision and it results (if awarded) in the quashing of the decision. See for an introductory discussion of Margaret Allars *Introduction to Australian Administrative Law* (1990) paras 6.103–6.113.
33   Eg National Crime Authority Act 1984, s 29B which makes it an offence to disclose the existence of a summons from the National Crime Authority.
34   *Baker v Campbell* (1981) 153 CLR 52.

customer to avail himself of all possible remedies, notwithstanding the bank's public duty to assist law enforcement officers in their investigations. This factor is important because search warrants generally precede criminal prosecution.

A bank officer should also request time to check the validity of the warrant and, in particular, ensure that the people named on the warrant are authorised to execute it and that they are the only people seeking to exercise it.

Corporations Act 2001 (Cth)

Requirements of the law

The principal function of corporate regulation is contained in the Corporations Act 2001 (Cth) (CA).[35] The provisions that are most relevant to the banker's duty of confidentiality, however, are contained in other statutory prescriptions which confer investigative powers upon certain corporate regulators.[36] Nonetheless, there are some sections in the CA which are relevant.

Section 983C of the CA provides that, where a court makes an order under s 983A to restrain dealing in respect of specified accounts with financial institutions that a person holds or maintains (whether in Australia or elsewhere), there is a duty on the financial institution where the order is directed to disclose to the Australian Securities and Investments Commission (ASIC) every account kept by the institution in the name of the person to whom the order relates, and any account that the institution reasonably suspects is held or kept for the benefit of that person. Further, the financial institution must permit ASIC to make a copy of, or to take an extract from, any account of the person or any of its books relating to that person.

Effects on banker's duty of confidentiality

These sections specifically apply to financial institutions. One difficulty is that the institution is required to form a judgment as to any account that it reasonably suspects is held for the benefit of that person. This is analogous to the difficulties with s 16 of the Financial Transaction Reports Act 1988 (Cth).[37] It raises the difficult issue of having to form a judgment on what is 'reasonable suspicion'.

Some indication as to the meaning of reasonable suspicion may be drawn from the High Court case of *George v Rockett*[38] where the Full Court quoted with approval the following statement of Kitto J in *Queensland Bacon Pty Ltd v Rees*:[39]

---

35 CA is an Act of the federal government enacted, in part, on the basis of a referral of legislative powers by the states to the Commonwealth.
36 See Australian Securities Commission and Australian Crime Commission investigations below.
37 We refer to the discussion under Disclosure of cash transactions under the Financial Transaction Reports Act 1988 below.
38 (1990) 170 CLR 104.
39 (1966) 115 CLR 266.

'A suspicion that something exists is more than a mere idle wondering whether it exists or not; it is a positive feeling of actual apprehension or mistrust, amounting to "a slight opinion, but without sufficient evidence", as *Chamber's Dictionary* expresses it. Consequently, a reason to suspect that a fact exists is more than a reason to consider or look into the possibility of its existence.'[40]

Income Tax Assessment Act 1936 (Cth)

Requirements of the law – s 263

Section 263 of the Income Tax Assessment Act 1936 (Cth) (ITAA) gives the Commissioner of Taxation (or any authorised officer),[41] at all times, full and free access to all buildings, places, books, documents and other papers for any of the purposes of the ITAA and the power to make extracts from, or copies of, any such books, documents or papers. Section 263(2) provides that an officer is not entitled to enter or remain on or in any building or place if, on being requested by the occupier for proof of authority, the officer does not produce an authority in writing signed by the Commissioner stating that the officer is authorised to exercise powers under s 263.[42] Section 263(3) places an obligation on the occupier of a building or place entered, or proposed to be entered, under sub-s (1) to provide the Commissioner or the officer with all reasonable facilities and assistance.

In *Simionato Holdings (No 2)*[43] it was assumed that s 263 powers could be used to obtain documents from a bank for use in proceedings to recover unpaid tax. It has also been held that communication of information, obtained in exercise of powers under s 263, to a liquidator did not breach the secrecy provision in s 16(2).[44] Section 16(2) provides:

'... an officer shall not either directly or indirectly, except in the performance of any duty as an officer, and either while he is, or after he ceases to be an officer, make a record of, or divulge or communicate to any person any information respecting the affairs of another person acquired by the officer ...'

The communication was found to be in the performance of a duty as an officer, as maximising the return to creditors in the liquidations, of which the Commonwealth was one for large amounts, and was a function and duty of the relevant tax officer's employment.[45]

The seriousness of the powers under s 263 is exemplified by the fact that it is an offence for a person to hinder or obstruct an Australian Taxation Office (ATO) officer exercising his right of access under s 263. Further, in the *Industrial Equity Case*,[46] the random selection of the taxpayer, which was being ordered under the Commissioner's policy to audit the top 100 companies, did not invalidate the s 263

40   (1966) 115 CLR 266 at 303.
41   Or any officer authorised by him.
42   In practice, the Australian Taxation Office officers carry identification cards with the ss 263 and 264 powers outlined on the back.
43   (1995) 60 FCR 375.
44   *Simionato Holdings Pty Ltd v FCT (No 2)* (1995) 60 FCR 375.
45   *Simionato Holdings Pty Ltd v FCT (No 2)* (1995) 60 FCR 375.
46   (1990) 21 ATR 934.

notices as the Commissioner was endeavouring to fulfil his statutory function of ascertaining the taxpayer's taxable income.

The requirements of s 263(3) mean that an officer should be able to make reasonable use of, for example, office space and facilities to extract information stored on computer.[47] The officer is also entitled to reasonable assistance in the form of advice and access to where relevant documents are located. An occupier who fails to provide the necessary facilities or assistance is liable for a fine of up to $3,300, if an individual, and up to $16,500 if a corporation.

Effects on banker's duty of confidentiality

A bank does not have any special protection from the provisions in s 263. Of particular relevance to a bank is that an authorised officer is entitled to take all reasonable and necessary steps to remove any physical obstruction to access but should not act in an excessive manner. This was illustrated in the case of *Kerrison v The Federal Commissioner of Taxation*[48] where the bank refused to open a safe deposit box or supply a key. The officer was entitled to attempt to open the box and, as that failed, to break open the box by the use of 'not excessive force'.

The ATO officers have been issued with guidelines on how they should exercise their powers of access.[49] The guidelines state, inter alia, that:

1 access requests should be avoided without prior notice unless there are exceptional circumstances;
2 officers should grant a request by the occupier to delay the search temporarily to enable professional advice to be obtained;
3 where it is expected that some of the records sought will be subject to legal professional privilege, the custodian should be given the opportunity to make a privilege claim;
4 where access is temporarily delayed to enable professional advice to be obtained, arrangements should be made to ensure there is no tampering with the records;
5 when acting under an access provision, answers can only be demanded to questions that are incidental to the exercise of the right of access (for example, the location of records); and
6 access to documents includes access to hard disc, CD-ROMs, magnetic tapes or other storage of electronic information.

It may be possible to request a delay to a s 263 search so that legal advice can be taken on the issues of the validity of the notice and legal professional privilege. This will not amount to an obstruction.[50] In *FCT v Citibank Ltd*, it was held that the

---

47 See *Australian Master Tax Guide* (1997) para 23-220.
48 (1995) ATC 4720.
49 *Australian Taxation Office Guidelines: Access and Information Gathering Powers* published by the Australian Taxation Office. The working title of the guidelines is 'Access and Information Gathering Manual' and it is one volume of approximately 1,000 pages. See in particular, para 2.11.1 in ch 2 on Notices.
50 Note that Division 149 of the Sch to the Criminal Code 1995 imposes a penalty for obstructing a tax officer of $2,000 or six months' imprisonment.

access powers in s 263 are restricted by the doctrine of legal professional privilege.[51] The validity of this proposition has been questioned in *Questions of Law Reserved (No 1 of 1998)*.[52] The doctrine of legal professional privilege protects communications made between a lawyer and his client for the predominant purpose of giving or receiving legal advice or for use in existing or anticipated litigation.[53]

It is also possible that the decision to utilise s 263 is reviewable under the Administrative Decisions (Judicial Review) Act 1977 (Cth). *Simionato Holdings Pty Ltd v FCT (No 2)*[54] is an example of a case where an application was made to seek orders of review under the 1977 Act of decisions and conduct of the Commissioner of Taxation in making a decision under s 263 of the ITAA. Importantly, under the 1977 Act a person who makes a decision to which the Act applies is required to furnish a person who is aggrieved by the decision with a statement in writing setting out the findings on material questions of fact, referring to the evidence or other material on which those findings were based and giving the reasons for the decision.[55]

Requirements of the law – s 264

Section 264 of the ITAA provides:

> 'The Commissioner may by notice in writing require any person, whether a taxpayer or not, ...—
> (a) to furnish him with such information as he may require; and
> (b) to attend and give evidence before him or before any officer authorized by him in that behalf concerning his or any other person's income or assessment, and may require him to produce all books, documents and other papers whatever in his custody or under his control relating thereto.'[56]

Section 264 cannot be used by the Commissioner to compel the production of documents subject to legal professional privilege.[57] The Commissioner can require a person to produce documents only where these documents are in the custody of or under the control of that person.[58] This includes persons who have the physical ability to produce the documents. This is relevant to a bank because of the High Court decision in *Comr of Taxation v ANZ Bank*.[59] That decision found that a bank

---

51   *FCT v Citibank Ltd* (1989) 20 FCR 403.
52   *Question of Law Reserved (No 1 of 1998)* (1998) 70 SASR 281.
53   A 'dominant purpose' test applies for evidentiary purposes in federal proceedings pursuant to ss 118 and 119 of the Evidence Act 1995 (Cth) and to a claim for legal professional privilege in relation to discovered documents on the basis of the High Court's decision in *Esso Australia Resources Ltd v The Commissioner of Taxation* (1999) 201 CLR 49.
54   (1995) 60 FCR 375.
55   Administrative Decisions (Judicial Review) Act 1977, s 13(1). Provided there is not an express exemption from complying with s 13(1) in the relevant Act.
56   S 264 also applies by operation of s 128Q to Division 11A, which deals with dividends, interest and royalties paid to non-residents and to certain other persons.
57   *Baker v Campbell* (1983) 153 CLR 52.
58   On this subject see *Simionato Holdings (No 2)* (1995) 60 FCR 375.
59   (1979) 143 CLR 499.

has custody or control of the contents of a safe deposit box kept on its premises and can therefore be compelled to produce its contents.[60]

A decision by the Commissioner to issue a notice under s 264 is reviewable under the Administrative Decisions (Judicial Review) Act 1977 (Cth).[61]

Again, the sanction for failure to comply with a s 264 notice is the risk that the person may be guilty of an offence. Both the ATO officer conducting the examination and the person being examined are entitled to have legal counsel[62] present at the examination to advise on legal issues such as legal professional privilege.[63]

The comments of Mason J in *Federal Commissioner of Taxation v Australia and New Zealand Banking Group Ltd*,[64] as quoted in *Industrial Equity Ltd v DCT*,[65] are the best illustration of the breadth of the powers in this regard. He said:

> 'The strong reasons which inhibit the use of curial processes for the purposes
> of a "fishing expedition" have no application to the administrative process of
> assessing a taxpayer to income tax. It is the function of the Commissioner to
> ascertain the taxpayer's taxable income. To ascertain this he may need to make
> wide-ranging inquiries, and to make them long before any issue of fact arises
> between him and the taxpayer. Such an issue will in general, if not always,
> only arise after the process of assessment has been completed. It is to the
> process of investigation before assessment that section 264 is principally, if
> not exclusively, directed.'[66]

Effects on banker's duty of confidentiality

Section 264 of the ITAA is a further example of where a bank can be compelled by law to override its common law duty of confidentiality to a client.[67]

---

60 The Commissioner's powers to require production of documents do not extend to authorising him to require persons to make copies of documents: *Perron Investments Pty Ltd v DCT* (1989) 25 FCR 187.
61 *Industrial Equity v FCT* (1990) 21 ATR 934. See, in particular, the majority judgment.
62 *Dunkel v DCT* (1990) 91 ATC 4142.
63 Note the comment by Weerasooria in his book *Banking Law and the Financial System in Australia* (5th edn, 2000) p 491 n 10 that, in view of the decision of the High Court in *Corporate Affairs Commission (NSW) v Yuill* (1991) 172 CLR 319, Australian decisions prior to 1991 on legal professional privilege may be affected by the 3:2 majority that held that the power conferred by s 295(1) of the Companies (NSW) Code in power and production of documents was not subject to legal professional privilege. See also *The Daniels Corpn International Pty Ltd v Australian Competition and Consumer Commissioner* [2002] HCA 49. Here the High Court held unanimously that ACCC powers in s 155 of the Trade Practices Act 1974 are subject to legal professional privilege.
64 (1979) 143 CLR 499.
65 (1990) 21 ATR 934 at 939.
66 (1990) 21 ATR 934 at 939.
67 S 218 of the ITAA is also relevant to a bank. It is where the Commissioner may collect tax from a person owing money to a taxpayer. Such a direction could be forwarded to a bank under s 218(1)(b). Importantly for a bank, s 218(4) provides that any person making any payment in pursuance of this section shall be deemed to have been acting under the authority of the taxpayer and of all other persons concerned and is indemnified in respect of such payment.

Tax file number legislation

A tax file number (TFN) is a unique number issued by the ATO for each taxpayer.[68] The object of the tax file number system is in part to detect non-disclosure of income and to enable the ATO to match the details of the income disclosed in a taxpayer's return with details which it receives from other sources.[69] Subject to certain exemptions, a failure by an investor to quote a TFN in connection with an investment means the investment body must withhold an amount on account of tax from any income which it becomes liable to pay in connection with that investment. Section 202D of the ITAA defines 'investment body' widely to include any financial institution. An investment body which refuses or fails to withhold the prescribed amount is required to pay a penalty of $1,000 or an amount equal to the amount which should have been withheld to the ATO.[70]

Bankers' books evidence provisions

Requirements of the law

Provisions exist in all Australian jurisdictions relating to the use of bankers' books in legal proceedings.[71] These provisions provide an expeditious method of receiving the contents of bankers' books into evidence. The provisions do not mean that the information does not have to be provided but rather allow it to be provided in a more convenient manner. The statutes include provisions relating to a banker's role in any legal proceeding to which their bank is not a party. As an illustration, s 58F of the Victorian Evidence Act 1958 provides:

> 'A person carrying on any business or an employee of that person shall not in any legal proceeding to which the person is not a party be compellable to produce any book of account, the contents of which can be proved under this Division or to appear as a witness to prove the matters, transactions and accounts therein recorded unless by order of a court made for special cause.'[72]

Effects on banker's duty of confidentiality

The sections provide uniformly (except for New South Wales) that a banker shall not be compellable to produce any bankers' book, the contents of which can be proved under the Act in question. Further, the banker shall not be compellable to appear as a witness to prove the matters, transactions and accounts recorded in the banker's

---

68   Ss 202A and s 202BA of the ITAA.
69   S 202 of the ITAA.
70   Guidelines covering the method of collection of TFN information in this and other situations are contained in the TFN guidelines 1992 (amended July 1997) issued by the Privacy Commissioner under s 17 of the Privacy Act 1988. S 221YHZC(1A) of the ITAA sets out the duties of an 'investment body'.
71   Queensland: Evidence Act 1977, ss 83–91 (books of account of any business); New South Wales: Evidence Act 1995, s 69; Victoria: Evidence Act 1958, ss 58A–58J (books of account of any business); Tasmania: Evidence Act 1910, ss 33–40; South Australia: Evidence Act 1929, ss 46–51; Western Australia: Evidence Act 1906, ss 89–96; Northern Territory: Evidence Act 1939, ss 43–47; Australian Capital Territory: Evidence Act 1971, ss 21–27.
72   Evidence Act 1958, s 58F (Vic).

books, unless by order of a judge. The object of the statutes is to save the time of bankers and protect them from the inconvenience of producing the originals of their books.[73]

The courts have adopted a wide interpretation of the concept of a banker's book. In *ANZ Banking Group Ltd v Griffiths*[74] the court held that:

> 'A print-out of banking information from a computer is capable of constituting a "banking record" within the meaning of section 46 of the Evidence Act 1929 (SA) whether it is produced by microfilming or by photocopying or by some other mechanical or electronic process.'[75]

The provisions apply to both civil and criminal matters. Clearly, if a bank is subject to a court order to produce its books this will be an exception to the bank's duty of confidentiality to its customer. The bank is, however, entitled to rely on the special rules outlined in the various bankers' books provisions in the different jurisdictions in order to avoid unnecessary inconvenience or cost.[76]

Disclosure of cash transactions under the Financial Transaction Reports Act 1988 (Cth)[77]

Requirements of the law

The Financial Transaction Reports Act 1988 (Cth) (FTRA) was enacted on the basis that cash transactions are used in the evasion of tax and for other illicit purposes. It applies to cash dealers, which is defined to include a financial institution, which in turn is defined to include a bank.[78] The FTRA is divided into three reporting divisions.

---

73 However, from the perspective of the duty of confidentiality, it is irrelevant whether the original or a copy of a document is produced.
74 (1990) ACLD 577.
75 (1990) ACLD 577 as quoted in Weerasooria, n 63 above.
76 See comments by Weerasooria, n 63 above, para 27.19 for further detail.
77 The Financial Transaction Reports Amendment Bill 1996 received Royal Assent on 17 April 1997. The principal object of this amendment was to give effect to several recommendations of 'Checking the cash: a report on the effectiveness of the Financial Transaction Reports Act 1988', a report of the Senate Standing Committee on Legal and Constitutional Affairs 1993. The recommendations that have been given legislative effect are access to financial transactions reports; information by state and territory revenue authorities; definition of transactions; inadmissibility of suspect transaction report information; increase in the reporting threshold for imported and exported currency and definition of the point at which currency transferred is considered to have been exported. The other features of the Bill were the introduction of significant cash transaction reporting by solicitors; consolidation of the powers and inspection of AUSTRAC to access and examine the records and record keeping systems of persons required to keep records under the Act; updating of the penalty provisions of the Act in accordance with current drafting practices and to align the quantum and expression of penalties with those in other Commonwealth statutes; updating other specific provisions that contain superseded terminology or are otherwise in need of modernising; and the making of minor technical amendments to correct minor drafting errors.
    The Financial Transactions Reports Act 1988 was amended in 2002 by the Suppression of the Financing of Terrorism Act 2002 (Cth) to provide for the reporting by cash dealers of transactions that they suspect are 'preparatory to the commission of a financing of terrorism offence'; or if information concerning the transaction 'may be relevant to investigation of, or prosecution of a person for, a financing of terrorism offence': see s 16(1A).
78 FTRA, s 3.

Division One requires a cash dealer to report any 'significant cash transaction' to the Australian Transaction Reports and Analysis Centre (AUSTRAC). A significant cash transaction is defined as a cash transaction involving the transfer of currency of not less than $10,000 in value.[79] The transaction must be reported regardless of whether it is suspicious.

Division Two, in particular s 16, requires that, where a cash dealer is a party to a transaction and the cash dealer has 'reasonable grounds to suspect' that information that the cash dealer has concerning the transaction may be relevant to an investigation into tax evasion, prosecution of a person for an offence against a law of the Commonwealth or of a Territory, or may be of assistance in enforcement of the Proceeds of Crimes Act 1987 (Cth), or may be relevant to investigation of, or prosecution of a person for, the financing of a terrorism offence (an offence under s 103.1 of the Criminal Code[80] or s 20 or s 21 of the Charter of the United Nations Act

---

79   FTRA, ss 3(1), 7(1).
80   S 103.1 of the Criminal Code provides that:
    '(1)   A person commits an offence if:
        (a)   the person provides or collects funds; and
        (b)   the person is reckless as to whether the funds will be used to facilitate or engage in a terrorist act.
    Penalty: Imprisonment for life.
    (2)   A person commits an offence under subsection (1) even if the terrorist act does not occur.
    (3)   Section 15.4 (extended geographical jurisdiction - category D) applies to an offence against subsection (1).'
    'Terrorist Act' is defined in s 100.1(1) to mean 'an action or threat of action where:
        (a)   the action falls within subsection (2) and does not fall within subsection (2A); and
        (b)   the action is done or the threat is made with the intention of advancing a political, religious or ideological cause; and
        (c)   the action is done or the threat is made with the intention of:
            (i)   coercing, or influencing by intimidation, the government of the Commonwealth or a State, Territory or foreign country, or of part of a State, Territory or foreign country; or
            (ii)   intimidating the public or a section of the public.'
    Section 100.1(2) provides that 'action falls within this subsection if it:
        (a)   causes serious harm that is physical harm to a person; or
        (b)   causes serious damage to property; or
        (ba)   causes a person's death; or
        (c)   endangers a person's life, other than a life of the person taking the action; or
        (d)   creates a serious risk to the health or safety of the public or a section of the public; or
        (e)   seriously interferes with, seriously disrupts, or destroys, an electronic system including, but not limited to:
            (i)   an information system; or
            (ii)   a telecommunications system; or
            (iii)   a financial system; or
            (iv)   a system used for the delivery of essential government services; or
            (v)   a system used for, or by, an essential public utility; or
            (vi)   a system used for, or by, a transport system.'
    S 100.1(2A) provides that 'action falls within this subsection if it:
    '(a)   is advocacy, protest, dissent or industrial action; and
    (b)   is not intended:
        (i)   to cause serious harm that is physical harm to a person; or
        (ii)   to cause a person's death; or
        (iii)   to endanger the life of a person, other than the person taking the action; or
        (iv)   to create a serious risk to the health or safety of the public or a section of the public.'

1945[81]) then the cash dealer must, as soon as practicable after forming that suspicion, prepare a report of the transaction and communicate the information contained in the report to AUSTRAC. Failure to report is an offence against s 28 and, if the offender is a body corporate, there is potential liability for a fine not exceeding $55,500. Some protection is afforded in s 16(5), which provides that a legal action does not lie against a cash dealer in relation to any action taken by the cash dealer under s 16 or in the mistaken belief that such action was required under the section.

Division Three requires a cash dealer to prepare a report to AUSTRAC if the cash dealer is the sender or recipient of an international funds transfer instruction.[82] One of the following conditions also must apply: the cash dealer is acting on behalf of or at the request of another person who is not a bank or the cash dealer is not a bank.[83] All international funds transfer instructions have to be reported regardless of the amount involved.

Effects on banker's duty of confidentiality

A cash dealer is prohibited from informing a client that the cash dealer has formed a suspicion, or that information has been communicated to AUSTRAC, or from giving the client any other information from which the client could reasonably be expected to infer that a suspicion had been formed, or that information had been so communicated.[84] A cash dealer who contravenes this section is guilty of an offence punishable on conviction by a fine not exceeding $11,100 or imprisonment for a term not exceeding two years or both. The fine for a corporation is up to $55,500.

---

81 Under s 20 of the Charter of the United Nations Act 1945:
　　'(1) A person commits an offence if:
　　　　(a) the person holds an asset; and
　　　　(b) the person:
　　　　　　(i) uses or deals with the asset; or
　　　　　　(ii) allows the asset to be used or dealt with; or
　　　　　　(iii) facilitates the use of the asset or dealing with the asset; and
　　　　(c) the asset is a freezable asset; and
　　　　(d) the use or dealing is not in accordance with a notice under section 22.
　　Penalty: Imprisonment for 5 years.
　　(2) Strict liability applies to the circumstances that the use or dealing with the asset is not in accordance with a notice under section 22 (authorised dealing).
　　(3) It is a defence if the person proves that the use or dealing was solely for the purpose of preserving the value of the asset.
　　(4) Section 15.1 of the Criminal Code (extended geographical jurisdiction - category A) applies to an offence against subsection (1).'
　　S 21 of the Charter of the United Nations Act 1945 provides that:
　　'(1) A person commits an offence if:
　　　　(a) the person, directly or indirectly, makes an asset available to a person or entity; and
　　　　(b) the person or entity to whom the asset is made available is a proscribed person or entity; and
　　　　(c) the making available of the asset is not in accordance with a notice under section 22.
　　Penalty: Imprisonment for 5 years.
　　(2) Strict liability applies to the circumstance that the making available of the asset is not in accordance with a notice under section 22 (authorised dealings).
　　(3) Section 15.1 of the Criminal Code (extended geographical jurisdiction - category A) applies to an offence against subsection (1).'
82 FTRA, s 17B(1)(a).
83 FTRA, s 17B(1)(b).
84 FTRA, s 16(5A).

AUSTRAC Guideline No 1 (Suspect Transaction Reporting) provides detailed information about reporting procedures. A suspect transaction report is filed on AUSTRAC Form 16 and all pertinent details are required. In relation to the principle of 'Know Your Customer', this guideline states:

> '. . . a significant part of international efforts (organised by the G7 group of nations) to curb money laundering focuses on financial institutions being aware of their customers' business activities. To a degree this coincides with an institution's own prudential requirements. Thus branches of financial institutions are encouraged to "know their customers" and where possible be able to judge whether the amount of cash or other monies going through accounts are consistent with the line of business or occupation being undertaken by the customer. The Act also requires the identification of new signatories to accounts and where customers try to avoid that requirement it might give rise to a suspicion of tax evasion or other illegal conduct.'[85]

The principle of 'Know Your Customer' is one foundation of the FTRA.

The FTRA is a clear exception to the banker's duty of confidentiality. Section 16(5) has been seen as a reinforcement of the exception of disclosure of information under compulsion of law.[86] An important provision in terms of gathering further information is s 16(4) of the FTRA. It provides that where a cash dealer communicates information to AUSTRAC under s 16(1) or (1A) the cash dealer shall, if requested to do so by either the director of AUSTRAC, the relevant authority[87] or an investigating officer who is carrying out an investigation arising from a report, give such further information as is specified in the request to the extent to which the cash dealer has that information.

Section 16(4) has the potential to have a large effect on the banker's duty of confidentiality in terms of the amount of information which is disclosed. It is not difficult to see how this section may be manipulated by an investigative agency. If an investigative agency was to indicate to the bank that a certain customer of the bank had been arrested on drug charges, the bank would then have reasonable grounds to suspect that information in relation to the customer's account may be relevant for an investigation or prosecution of the customer for an offence against a law of the Commonwealth, and would then be in the position of having to report under s 16(1) or 16(1A). On the basis of that report an investigative agency could use s 16(4) to obtain whatever further information they may require from the bank.

Section 17 provides that a dealer who fulfils his s 16 duty shall be taken, for the purposes of ss 81 and 82 of the Proceeds of Crime Act 1987, not to have been in possession of the information at any time.[88]

---

85   AUSTRAC *Guideline No 1: (Suspect Transaction Reporting)* p 15.
86   Tyree 'The Cash Transaction Reports Act 1988' (April 1990) J Banking and Finance Law and Practice 57.
87   A relevant authority is defined to include the Commissioner of the Australian Federal Police, the Chairperson of the NCA, the Commissioner of Taxation and the Comptroller-General of Customs.
88   FTRA, s 17.

The relevant sections of the Proceeds of Crime Act 1987 deal with the offence of money laundering. The major offence described in s 81 occurs when a person engages in certain transactions involving proceeds of crime and that person knows, or ought reasonably to know, certain facts.[89] The s 81 offence carries a maximum penalty of up to $200,000 and/or 20 years' imprisonment when the offender is a natural person, and $600,000 where the offender is a body corporate, and the lesser offence described in s 82 has a maximum penalty of up to $5,000 and/or two years' imprisonment for a natural person, and $15,000 for a body corporate. The intention of s 17 is to protect a bank from exposure under ss 81 and 82 of the Proceeds of Crime Act 1987. This may influence a bank to make a report. The comments however of Walter and Erlich are poignant:

> 'It must be pointed out that bankers are not trained to carry out the function of detecting crimes and that section 16 is drafted in wide and woolly terms; what do the expressions "reasonable grounds" and "suspect" mean?'[90]

Walter and Erlich highlight that the section is forcing the banker to make a judgment on what is suspicious behaviour. The difficulty for the bank is that a disclosure which is not sanctioned will leave the bank open to an action by its customer for a breach of confidentiality.[91]

The provisions, in particular s 17, have sustained further criticism from Weerasooria, who concludes that s 17 'says something alarming'.[92] It enacts that:

> 'Where a cash dealer, or a person who is an officer, employee or agent of a cash dealer commutes or gives information under section 16, the cash dealer or person shall be taken, for the purposes of sections 81 and 82 of the Proceeds of Crime Act 1987 not to have been in possession of that information at any time.'[93]

Therefore, the statute enacts that a bank is protected from committing an offence under the Proceeds of Crime Act 1987.[94]

The 2001–02 Annual Report of AUSTRAC reveals that the number of suspicious transactions reported has increased from 7,247 in 2000–01 to 7,809 in 2001–02. Reports lodged by the banking sector continued to provide most suspicious financial activity reported to AUSTRAC.[95]

Information gathering under the Proceeds of Crime Act 1987

Requirements of the law

The Proceeds of Crime Act 1987 gives various information gathering powers to Commonwealth and state enforcement agencies which may be used to search or obtain property in the possession of a financial institution. Further to this, Division 4 of Pt 3

89 Proceeds of Crime Act 1987, ss 81, 82.
90 Walter and Erlich 'Confidences – bankers and customers: powers of banks to maintain secrecy and confidentiality' (1989) 63 AU 413.
91 Walter and Erlich, n 90 above.
92 Weerasooria 'Tournier Turns 70' (December 1993) Australian Banker 314.
93 FTRA, s 17.
94 Weerasooria, n 92 above.
95 AUSTRAC *2001–2002 Annual Report*.

provides that a bank must retain each essential 'customer generated financial transaction document for the minimum retention period which is seven years after the day on which the account is closed'. This includes documents that relate to the opening or closing by a person of an account, the operation by a person of an account and the transmission of funds using the person's account in its original form.

Effects on banker's duty of confidentiality

The mere keeping of these records as required by the Proceeds of Crime Act 1987 does not override the banker's duty of confidentiality. But it does indicate that a bank may be required, in order to comply with the Proceeds of Crime Act 1987, to maintain the confidential material up to seven years after an account is closed. Therefore it cannot avoid disclosing documentation by putting in place a system of document destruction. These prescriptions merely ensure that the information in relation to customers' accounts is available to be examined in the event that an appropriate order is made by a court.

Disclosure under trade practices legislation

Requirements of the law

Section 155 of the Trade Practices Act 1974 (Cth) (TPA) provides that if the Australian Competition and Consumer Commission (ACCC)[96] has reason to believe that a person is capable of furnishing information, producing documents or giving evidence relating to a matter that constitutes, or may constitute, a contravention of the TPA or is relevant to the making of a decision in relation to exclusive dealing, a member of the ACCC may, by notice in writing served on that person, require that person to furnish to the ACCC any such information in writing or to produce to the ACCC any such documents or to appear before the ACCC to give evidence.[97]

Effects on banker's duty of confidentiality

There is no exemption for a bank from the operation of s 155. If a bank is in receipt of a notice under it, then a bank will be required to comply, unless some proper ground of challenge to the issue or the form of the notice can be established.

ASIC investigations

Requirements of the law

ASIC is a federal government agency with national operations which was established by the Australian Securities and Investments Commission Act 2001 (the ASIC Act).

---

96   Or the Chairperson of the ACCC, or the Deputy Chairperson of the ACCC.
97   Some exceptions do exist in s 155(2A), none of which are relevant to this discussion.

The function of ASIC is primarily to administer the CA. ASIC also provides administrative support to various boards such as the Australian Accounting Standards Board and has a role to play in advising on law reform.

Part 3 of the ASIC Act is entitled 'Investigations and Information Gathering'. Division 3 of Pt 3 relates to the inspection of books and provides, in s 30, that ASIC may give to a body corporate a notice to produce books about the affairs of a body corporate. These powers are mirrored in ss 31 and 33 in relation to securities and futures contracts and in s 32A in relation to the provision of financial services. Investigations conducted by ASIC may lead to the issue of a search warrant pursuant to the ASIC Act.[98] Failure to comply with the notice requiring production is a prerequisite for the issue of the search warrant. Therefore, the procedure is only available where ASIC's interest in particular documentation has already been revealed.[99]

Division Two (s 19) provides mechanisms for the examination of persons on oath. These powers can only be exercised if ASIC holds reasonable grounds for suspecting or believing that the person can provide information 'relevant to a matter' under investigation, and serves a written notice on the person in a prescribed form. ASIC may also require any person who is involved in the compilation or production of documents to explain any matter about them or to which any of them relate: s 37(a). In addition, ASIC may require a person to state where the documents may be found and the identity and whereabouts of the person who last had possession of them (to the best of their knowledge or belief): s 38.

A breach of any of the above sections without reasonable excuse is an offence under s 63 and the offender is liable to a penalty of $11,000 or imprisonment for two years or both.[100] A corporation can be fined up to $55,000 for breach.

Effects on banker's duty of confidentiality

In the *ASC v Zarro*[101] the Federal Court of Australia held that the bank's obligation of confidentiality was no reasonable excuse for non-compliance with a notice to produce documents in its possession. The decision in *ASC v Zarro* confirms that the requirements of the ASIC Act are an exception to the banker's duty of confidentiality. Spender J concluded that:

> 'However odious the conclusion may be, in my opinion, if objectively the documents sought do relate to the affairs of a body corporate the subject of an investigation by ASIC, the bank is obliged to produce them.'[102]

Spender J acknowledged that some comfort could be drawn by a bank from s 92 of the ASIC Act, which provides that a person complying with the ASIC Act 'is neither liable to a proceeding, nor subject to a liability, merely because the person has

98 Ss 35 and 36.
99 The Laws of Australia, n 6 above, paras 11.2 and 17.
100 There is also the power in s 70 of the Australian Securities and Investments Commission Act 2001 to apply for a court order forcing a person to comply with Pt 3.
101 (1991) 105 ALR 227. See also eg *Insurance & Superannuation Commission v Glaser* (1991) 79 FCR 505.
102 (1991) 105 ALR 227 at 235.

complied, or proposes to comply, with a requirement made, or purporting to have been made, under this Part'.[103]

Australian Crime Commission

Requirements of the law

The Australian Crime Commission (ACC) was established by the Australian Crime Commission Act 2002 (Cth) (ACCA).[104] Although created by federal legislation, it is also empowered by state and territory legislation.[105] (The Australian Crime Commission replaces the National Crime Authority established by the National Crime Authority Act 1984 (Cth).) The ACC can apply to a judge of the Federal Court or a court of a state or territory for the issue of a warrant where there are reasonable grounds for believing that there is in specified premises a thing connected with 'a special ACC operation/investigation' (referred to as 'things of the relevant kind') and that there could be a risk of concealment or destruction of that thing.[106] The issued warrant authorises entry for the purposes of search and seizure.

Section 28 of the ACCA gives a member of the ACC the power to summon witnesses and to take evidence. Section 29 gives a member of the ACC the power, by notice in writing served on a person, to require that person to produce a specified document or a thing specified in a notice which is relevant to an investigation that the ACC is conducting in performance of its special functions. Importantly, s 29A provides that a summons or a notice issued under s 28 or s 29 may provide that disclosure of information about the summons or notice, or any connected official matter, is prohibited, except in the circumstances, if any, specified in the notation. Section 29B provides that any person served with, or otherwise given, a summons or notice containing such a notation must not disclose the existence of the summons or notice or any information about it. If a disclosure is made, the maximum penalty is $2,200 or imprisonment for one year.[107] For a corporation, the fine is a maximum of $11,000.

Effects on banker's duty of confidentiality

There is no special treatment afforded to confidential information in the possession of a bank. A bank in receipt of an ACC warrant or notice properly issued and served will be required to comply with it regardless of the common law duty of

---

103 The Australian Securities and Investments Commission Act 2001 (Cth), s 92.

104 Australian Crime Commission Act 2002 (Cth), s 7.

105 See *The Laws of Australia*, n 6 above, para 11.2. The reference in this chapter to the National Crime Authority Act 1984 and the National Crime Authority should now be read as a reference to the Australian Crime Commission Act 2002, and the Australian Crime Commission, respectively. See also the Australian Crime Commission Establishment Act 2002 (Cth).

106 National Crime Authority Act 1984 (Cth), s 22.

107 S 29B(2) provides certain circumstances in which a person is entitled to make a disclosure including in para (b) disclosure to a legal practitioner for the purposes of obtaining legal advice or representation relating to the summons.

confidentiality. Further, s 29A would clearly prevent a bank advising an affected customer of the issue of a s 28 summons or a s 29 notice.

Commonwealth bankruptcy legislation

Requirements of the law

The Bankruptcy Act 1966 (Cth) (the Bankruptcy Act) provides a number of methods for a trustee in bankruptcy to obtain documents. Where information is sought in relation to a bankrupt's account, the trustee in effect is acting as the bankrupt. One example is if a bank is the subject of a written direction of the 'official receiver' under the Bankruptcy Act, the 'official receiver' will be entitled at all reasonable times to full and free access to all premises and books the subject of the written direction.[108] Considerations that are relevant when faced with court orders to disclose information are also relevant in this context.[109]

Section 77A of the Bankruptcy Act provides a 'bankruptcy investigator' who is conducting an investigation under s 19AA in relation to a person, the power to require a person to produce, at a specified time and at a specified place, specified books or classes of books. The purpose of this section is to extend the investigatory powers of the trustee as recommended by the Costigan Royal Commission.[110]

Another example is s 125 of the Bankruptcy Act, which is specifically directed at the situation where a prescribed organisation[111] (which includes a bank) has ascertained that an account holder is an undischarged bankrupt. In that case, unless the prescribed organisation is satisfied that the account is on behalf of some other person, it must inform the trustee in bankruptcy, in writing, of the existence of the account. Further payments out of the account are prohibited, except under an order of the court. If within one month from the date on which the prescribed organisation informed the trustee of the existence of the account, a copy of the court order has not been served on the prescribed organisation and it has not received written instructions from the trustee, the prescribed organisation is entitled to act without regard to any claim or right the trustee may have in respect of the account.

Effects on banker's duty of confidentiality

There is no specific exemption for banks from the operation and effect of these provisions and therefore they are another example of the compulsion of law exception.

The Privacy Commissioner has, however, publicly released advice as to the need for credit providers to make sure they are legally bound to release information requested in purported reliance on the Bankruptcy Act:

---

108 See Bankruptcy Act 1966, s 77AA in regard to official receiver's powers.
109 See discussion under Disclosure under compulsion of law above.
110 See McDonald *Bankruptcy Law and Practice* p 3607.
111 Prescribed organisation is defined to include a bank in s 125(3).

'To the extent that an Official Receiver requires a credit provider to disclose consumer credit information in accordance with the provisions of the Bankruptcy Act, the disclosure would be permitted by section 18N(1)(g) of the Privacy Act. It would be advisable for credit providers to obtain advice to ensure that they are legally bound to respond under a particular provision of the Bankruptcy Act in order to avoid breaches of section 18N of the Privacy Act.'[112]

Miscellaneous statutory provisions

Instances exist of the protection of the principles in *Tournier*,[113] for example, s 62(2) of the Banking Act 1959 which provides that information requested by the Reserve Bank shall not be furnished with respect to the affairs of an individual customer unless it relates to prudential matters. Another example is s 18N(1)(d) which limits (subject to some exceptions) disclosure by credit providers of personal information contained in reports relating to matters such as a customer's creditworthiness.[114]

Below is a list of examples of other statutes which impinge on the banker's duty of confidentiality at a Commonwealth and state level.[115]

Commonwealth statutes

1   *The Banking Act 1959*: s 61 provides for APRA to investigate and report on prudential matters in relation to banks about banks; s 62 provides that a bank must furnish to APRA such information in respect of its business as APRA directs, however it is limited by s 62(2); s 69 provides that a bank shall, within three months after 31 December in each year, deliver to the Treasury a statement of all sums of unclaimed moneys of not less than $100.

2   *The Life Insurance Act 1995*: s 140 empowers ASIC to enter a bank's premises without a search warrant where ASIC has reasonable grounds for believing that entry is necessary for the purpose of an investigation of the business of a company under this Act. ASIC must first issue a written notice to the bank stating that it proposes to investigate the business before launching an investigation (s 139(1)). This means that ASIC must give a bank prior notice before it exercises any right to enter the banks premises without a search warrant. ASIC may also obtain search warrants lawfully to enter a bank's premises under s 144. A search warrant authorises ASIC to enter the premises without prior notice or permission.

3   *The Privacy Act 1988*: under s 44 the Privacy Commissioner may give a written notice to a person requiring that person to give information or produce a document that is relevant to an investigation under the Privacy Act 1988. Under

---

112 See Credit Reporting Advice Summaries released by the Privacy Commissioner. See below for a brief discussion of the Credit Reporting Advice Summaries.

113 *Tournier v National Provincial and Union Bank of England* [1924] 1 KB 461.

114 Examples of situations where disclosure of a report or information is permitted include to a credit reporting agency for the purpose of being included in the relevant individual's credit information file (s 18N(1)(a)) or where the individual has consented (s 18N(1)(b)) or the disclosure is to a guarantor (s 18N(1)(ba)).

115 Statutes from Victoria and New South Wales are chosen as an illustration of legislation which exists at a state level.

s 18N(1), a credit provider in possession or control of a report must not disclose the report or any personal information derived from it to another person for any purpose unless specific exceptions listed in s 18N(1) apply such as in s 18N(1)(g). Section 18N(1)(g) provides for disclosure of the report or information if the particular purpose is required or authorised by or under law. See also cl 2.1 of the National Privacy Principles.

4   *The Trade Practices Act 1974 (TPA)*: under s 155 of the TPA, the Australian Competition and Consumer Commission (ACCC) has extensive powers to investigate possible contraventions of the TPA by requiring information and documents to be provided to it, or by entering premises to inspect and take copies of documents. A warrant or court order is not necessary in order for ACCC's officers to exercise the power to enter premises: s 155(2). However, the ACCC may also be able to obtain the issue of a search warrant under s 3E of the Crime Act 1914 (Cth). Section 155 of the TPA expressly overrides a bank's common law duties of confidentiality to the extent of any inconsistency with the TPA. However, the bank's common law duties of confidentiality are expressly preserved to the extent that the common law is capable if operating concurrently with the TPA: s 4M of the TPA.

Victorian Acts

1   *The Estate Agents Act 1980*: s 59(5A) provides that a financial institution has an obligation to advise the Estate Agents Licensing Authority of any overdrawing of an estate agent's trust account as soon as the financial institution knows of it. Section 60 provides a power to the Secretary to the Department of Justice to enter into arrangements with a financial institution in relation to the payment of interest and auditing of balances of trust accounts. Section 89 provides a power in the minister to freeze a trust account of a defaulting estate agent.

2   *The Legal Practice Act 1996*: s 191 provides that, despite any duty of confidence to the contrary, a bank must report a suspected offence in relation to a trust account established in that bank to the Legal Practice Board as soon as practicable after forming the suspicion.

New South Wales Acts

1   *New South Wales Crime Commission Act 1985*: s 17 provides for a member, by notice in writing served on a person, to require that person to attend at a specified time and place before a member of the Commission (or its staff) and to produce a specified document or thing specified in the notice, that is relevant to a Commission investigation. Section 18B(1) provides that a witness summoned to attend or appearing before the New South Wales Crimes Commission at a hearing is not (except as provided by s 18A) excused from answering any questions or producing any document or thing on the ground that the answer or production may incriminate or tend to incriminate the witness, or on any other ground of privilege, or on the ground of a duty of secrecy or other restriction on disclosure or on any other ground.

The High Court in *Johns v ASC*[116] considered the issue of regulators disclosing information obtained from a person or company to another regulator. Brennan J on this subject commented:

'A statute which confers a power to obtain information for a purpose defines, expressly or impliedly, the purpose for which the information when obtained can be used or disclosed. The statute imposes on the person who obtains information in exercise of the power a duty not to disclose the information obtained except for that purpose ... The person obtaining information in exercise of such a statutory power must therefore treat the information obtained as confidential whether or not the information is otherwise of a confidential nature.'

See, however, as an illustration, the ACA, in particular ss 19A and 20, which give the ACC powers to seek information from Commonwealth agencies, and s 59, which gives the ACC power to disclose information it has obtained to other regulators.

DISCLOSURE IN THE PUBLIC INTEREST

This is the second exception to the bankers' duty of confidentiality in *Tournier*.[117]

Weerasooria, in *Banking Law and the Financial System in Australia*,[118] concludes:

'While the right to disclose under this exception should not be lightly assumed, it would appear that it would apply in the following cases:
•   during time of war where the customer's dealings indicate that he is trading with the enemy;
•   during time of national emergency where a customer is reasonably suspected of treasonable activities against the state;
•   to prevent the perpetration or aid in the detection of serious frauds and crimes.'[119]

The decision of Staughton J in *Libyan Arab Foreign Bank v Banker's Trust Co*[120] is worthy of note in relation to this exception. In the context of the order of the US President on 8 January 1986 blocking all trade with Libya, Bankers Trust Co in New York were the subject of a claim (amongst others) of breach of confidence for disclosures to the US Federal Reserve Bank. The claim was defended on the basis that the bank was acting pursuant to a higher public duty. Staughton J stated:

'... it seems to me that the Federal Reserve Board, as the central banking system in the United States, may have a public duty to perform in obtaining information from banks ... I am prepared to reach a tentative conclusion that the exception applied in this case ... I need not reach a final conclusion on that point, because I am convinced that any breach of confidence there may have been caused the Libyan bank no loss.'[121]

---

116 (1993) 178 CLR 408.
117 *Tournier v National Provincial and Union Bank of England* [1924] 1 KB 461.
118 Weerasooria, n 63 above.
119 Weerasooria, n 63 above, p 492.
120 [1989] QB 728.
121 [1989] QB 728.

Australian courts have not resolved any of the uncertainty regarding this exception. Sheppard J in *Allied Mills v Trade Practices Commission (No 1)*,[122] when considering the balance between disclosure of private and confidential information and the public interest in the disclosure of iniquity, commented:

> 'The authorities establish that the public interest in the disclosure [sic] (to the appropriate authority or perhaps the press) of iniquity will always outweigh the public interest in the preservation of private and confidential information.'[123]

A bank, therefore, has to establish first whether the conduct amounts to 'iniquity'.

After reviewing the authorities, Sheppard J concluded that iniquity is wider than a crime or misdemeanour.[124] In *Allied Mills Industries Pty Ltd v Trade Practices Commission (No 1)*, a breach of the Trade Practices Act 1974, liability for which was only civil, amounted to iniquity because Sheppard J found Parliament had taken a serious view of the importance of the legislation from the standpoint of the public interest.[125]

Walter and Erlich suggest that, where bankers are involved, the judiciary may develop a test to weigh up whether the disclosure was justified. Walter and Erlich consider the following factors would be relevant to such an assessment:

1 whether the facts in front of the court display a situation a reasonable banker would understand to be one that would be in the public interest to disclose;
2 whether clear, real and extensive danger to the public exists;
3 whether the sole purpose for releasing the information was in the public interest and not a collateral purpose;
4 whether the bank has carefully considered whether its action would be constructive and in the public interest;
5 whether there is a lack of alternatives for the bank to pursue; and
6 whether the bank weighed up and balanced the harm that might flow from the disclosure, directly and indirectly.[126]

Weaver and Craigie suggest that, in the absence of any clear authority on this exception, the warning given by Sir John Paget in relation to the use of this exception remains as valid today as it was when he delivered it in 1924. 'It would be inadvisable for a banker to exercise his private judgment in such matters at the expense of the customer.'[127]

DISCLOSURE IN THE INTERESTS OF THE BANK

Traditionally, this exception has been considered relevant where the bank issues civil proceedings against a customer of the bank or in defence of civil proceedings.

---

122 (1981) 34 ALR 105. The issues enunciated by Sheppard J in *Allied Mills* were considered recently by Moore J in *King v AG Australia Holdings Ltd* (formerly GIO Australia Holdings Ltd) [2002] FCA 151.
123 (1981) 34 ALR 105 at 141.
124 (1981) 34 ALR 105 at 141.
125 (1981) 34 ALR 105 at 142.
126 Walter and Erlich, n 90 above, at 416.
127 Weaver and Craigie *Banker and Customer* p 2647.

It is also relevant where the bank wishes to make a disclosure to a potential guarantor of a customer.[128] There has not been a reported case directly under this exception in Australia.

The English case of *Sunderland v Barclays Bank Ltd*[129] is an example of a reported case under this exception, but it has not been judicially considered in Australia.[130] In *Sunderland v Barclays Bank Ltd* it was held to be in the bank's interest for the bank to disclose confidential information in reply to a demand for an explanation of what appeared to be discourteous behaviour. Further details of this case are given in the section of chapter 9, England, which deals with disclosure in the interests of the bank.

The only sensible basis for the decision in *Sunderland v Barclays Bank* is that Mrs Sunderland consented to the disclosure. Otherwise, we are left with the absurd position that a bank may disclose one customer's interests to another because the inquirer wants to know and will be offended if the bank does not disclose. The proper course for the bank to take would have been to show the inquirer that the dishonour was justified by reason of insufficient funds.

Bank of Tokyo Ltd v Karoon[131] is an example of where a bank sought to argue that it was in the interest of the bank to pass information between a parent company and a subsidiary in relation to a customer of the bank. The bank argued there had been no disclosure because the parent and subsidiary were part of the one corporate group, and if there was disclosure that it was in the interest of the bank. The court treated the parent and the subsidiary as separate entities and therefore held that there had been a disclosure. The purpose for the disclosure was to assist the parent in its interpleader to the court in England. The argument in relation to the disclosure being in the interests of the bank was found to be an issue that was more appropriate for the New York court to decide.

In Australia, the effect of *Bank of Tokyo Ltd v Karoon* is limited by the application of the Code of Banking Practice.[132] Section 12.2(a) changes to some extent the common law position in *Bank of Tokyo Ltd v Karoon* by providing that a bank may disclose to a related entity information necessary to enable an assessment to be made of the total liabilities (present and prospective) of the customer to the bank and the related entity.[133] Further, a bank may disclose to a related entity of the bank, which provides financial services which are related or ancillary to those provided by the bank, information concerning the customer unless the customer instructs the bank not to do so.[134]

---

128 See Guarantees below. In relation to responses in general to inquiries by guarantors see *Commonwealth Bank of Australia v Amadio* (1983) 151 CLR 447.
129 (1938) 5 LDAB 163.
130 For a discussion of *Sunderland v Barclays Bank Ltd* (1938) 5 LDAB 163 see Walter and Erlich, n 90 above, at 416.
131 [1987] 1 AC 45.
132 See discussion under Code of Banking Practice below.
133 Where the Code of Banking Practice seeks to alter the agreement between the bank and the customer (relying on s 1.3(b)) in a way that could disadvantage the customer (ie s 12.2(a)) then the bank will have to rely on a term in the original contract to the effect that it can change the terms of the contract at any time without consideration.
134 S 12.2(b) of the Code of Banking Practice.

Under Pt IIIA of the Privacy Act 1988 a credit provider such as a bank is also permitted to disclose to a related corporation certain consumer credit information relating to an individual.[135]

Such a disclosure would accordingly seem to be 'authorised by or under law' and hence within the s 18N(1)(g) exemption in the Privacy Act 1988 and be permissible notwithstanding that it is not clearly within one of the *Tournier*[136] exceptions (subject to any contractual limitations such as those arising by virtue of the Code of Banking Practice provisions discussed above). However since credit information is also personal information, it follows that a credit provider will be bound by both Pt IIIA *and* the National Privacy Principles (NPPs) when dealing with it. The two are independent in that an act or practice that does not breach the NPPs is not automatically acceptable under Pt IIIA and vice versa.

This independence of Pt IIIA from the NPPs is made explicit in s 164(4) of the Privacy Act 1988:

> 'To avoid doubt, an act done, or practice engaged in by an organisation without breaching an approved privacy code or the National Privacy Principles is not authorised by law (or by this Act) for the purposes of Part IIIA merely because it does not breach the code or the Principles.'

Accordingly, if the credit provider wants to disclose the credit information, it must, after first establishing that the disclosure is permitted under Pt IIIA, confirm that the disclosure is also allowed under the NPPs. In summary, the rule under the NPP is that personal information (including credit information) cannot be disclosed or used for a purpose (a secondary purpose) other than the primary purpose of collection unless one of the specified exceptions apply. The exceptions include (amongst others) a disclosure:

- where the secondary purpose is in relation to the primary purpose of collection and the individual concerned could reasonably have expected the disclosure (NPP 2.1(a));
- with consent (NPP 2.1(b));
- for certain direct marketing purpose (NPP 2.1(c)); and
- where the disclosure is required or authorised under law (NPP 2.1(g)).

DISCLOSURE BY EXPRESS OR IMPLIED CONSENT

It will usually be clear when a bank is entitled to disclose under the exception of express consent. A more difficult issue is where a bank seeks to rely on the exception of the implied consent of the customer.

It has been argued by some commentators[137] that the information a bank can disclose to a guarantor or intending guarantor is an example of an exception of express or

---

135 S 18N(1)(d).
136 *Tournier v National Provincial and Union Bank of England* [1924] 1 KB 461.
137 See Walter and Erlich, n 90 above, at 416.

implied consent.[138] The other area where this exception has traditionally been discussed is the giving of bankers' opinions.[139]

It is a well-established practice that banks give opinions concerning their customers' creditworthiness. Some debate has taken place on whether the practice of giving bankers' opinions has reached a level whereby it is a trade custom of which the customer is, or should be, aware and to which the customer gives implied consent. However, some commentators believe that the giving of bankers' opinions is not well known amongst customers, and, accordingly, an implied consent to the giving of bankers' opinions cannot be drawn from the custom of bankers.[140]

The position on bankers' opinions has been resolved by the provisions of ss 18A and 18B of the Privacy Act 1988. Section 18A provides for the Privacy Commissioner (after appropriate consultation) to issue a Code of Conduct concerning the activities of credit reporting agencies or credit providers that are connected with credit reporting. Section 18B provides that credit reporting agencies and credit providers must comply with the Code of Conduct.

The Credit Reporting Code of Conduct (which has statutory force under ss 18A and 18B) provides:

'A credit provider which is a bank may not disclose to another bank a "banker's opinion" relating to an individual's consumer credit worthiness, unless that individual's specific agreement to the disclosure of such information for a particular purpose has been obtained.'

Paragraph 71 of the Explanatory Notes to the Code further provides that:

'The provision by banks of opinions relating to an individual's commercial credit worthiness is unaffected by the provisions of the Code of Conduct or the Privacy Act.'

GUARANTEES

Disclosure to guarantors

There has been some confusion about what a bank can disclose to a guarantor or intending guarantor. Harvey CJ in *Ross v Bank of New South Wales*[141] found that a guarantor of a customer's loan account with a bank is not entitled to demand from the bank a copy of the loan account, but is entitled to information as to the balance then owing, the rate of interest charged and the amount, if any, realised by the bank in respect of collateral securities.[142] A guarantor is the guarantor of the loan obligations of the borrower, and this does not entitle a guarantor to information in relation to accounts held by the borrower in his capacity as a customer of the bank. Harvey CJ commented:

138 See discussion under Guarantees below.
139 See discussion of the Privacy Act 1988 below.
140 Walter and Erlich, n 90 above, at 419.
141 (1928) SR (NSW) 539.
142 (1928) SR (NSW) 539 at 542.

'So far as the plaintiff is concerned, I think her rights must be determined in exactly the same way as if the mortgagee creditor was not a bank at all, but was an ordinary mortgagee.'[143]

Arguably, when disclosing to a guarantor, the bank could fall under the exception of the disclosure either being in the interest of the bank or with express or implied consent.

The argument that disclosure to a guarantor is in the bank's interest could be justified on the basis that there has been considerable development in the law relating to guarantees and guarantors, particularly since the decision of the High Court in *Commercial Bank of Australia v Amadio*.[144] Therefore, a higher duty has been placed on banks to ensure that guarantors are aware of their obligations, and hence it is more likely to be accepted by a court that it was in the interest of the bank to provide information to a potential guarantor. This is particularly the case given the High Court's decision in *Garcia v National Australia Bank Ltd*[145] that a creditor may have a positive duty to take steps to explain a transaction to a guarantor.

The difficulty with this argument is that in the vast majority of cases there will be a simple alternative, namely to advise the customer that the customer must give consent for the disclosure of information to the guarantor if the loan facility is to be made available.

The effect of the Code of Banking Practice on guarantees

Requirements of the Code

Section 28 of the new Code of Banking Practice[146] applies to each guarantee and each indemnity obtained from a third party who is an individual, for the purpose of securing any financial accommodation or facility provided by a bank to another individual or a small business.[147]

Section 28.4(a) sets out a number of things which the bank must do before it takes a guarantee. These include giving the prospective guarantor a prominent notice advising (amongst other things) that the guarantor can request information about the transaction or facility to be guaranteed (including any facility with the bank to be refinanced by the facility to be guaranteed). Under s 28.4(b)(i), the bank must also tell the prospective guarantor about:

---

143 (1928) SR (NSW) 539 at 541.
144 (1983) 151 CLR 447.
145 (1998) 194 CLR 395.
146 On 12 August 2002, the Australian Banker's Association (ABA) launched a new Code of Banking Practice (New Code). The New Code sets standards of good banking practice for banks that adopt it when dealing with their individual and small business customers and their guarantors. The New Code will replace the existing Code of Banking Practice that the ABA adopted in November 1993. The ABA has said that the New Code should be operational by August 2003.
147 'Small business' is defined for these purposes in s 40 of the Code of Banking Practice to mean a business employing:
    (a) less than 100 full-time (or equivalent) employees if the business is or includes the manufacture of goods; or
    (b) in any other case, less than 20 full-time (or equivalent) employees.

- certain notices of demand made by the bank on the debtor and excesses, overdrawings or dishonours in relation to any facility the debtor has, or has had, with the bank within a specified time; and
- if any existing facility the bank has given the debtor will be cancelled, or if the facility to be guaranteed will not be provided if the guarantee is not provided.

Before accepting the guarantee under s 28.4, the bank has to provide a prospective guarantor with:

- a copy of any related credit contract or security contract;
- the final letter of offer provided to the borrower by the bank together with details of any conditions in an earlier version of that letter of offer that were satisfied before the final letter of offer was issued;
- any related credit report from a credit reporting agency;
- any current related credit insurance contract in the bank's possession;
- any financial accounts or statement of financial position given to the bank relevant to the facility to be guaranteed (and any other statement in the last two years relating to a facility the debtor has, or has had, with the bank where there has been a notice of demand issued and any excess, overdrawing or dishonour);
- certain statements of account relating to the facility; and
- any notice previously given to the borrower relevant to the facility to be guaranteed, with which the borrower has not complied.

The bank must also give the guarantor other relevant information (including any facility to be refinanced by the new facility) that the guarantor reasonably requests (but the bank does not have to give the guarantor its legal opinions). The guarantor must be given until at least the next day to consider the information, unless the person has received independent legal advice.[148]

Various exceptions and qualifications have been proposed to the abovementioned rules which have not been finalised at the time of writing.

These provisions represent a considerable change to the 'old' Code of Banking Practice. The old Code provisions on guarantees apply to only limited types of guarantees provided by individuals.[149] For example, they do not apply to an individual acting as a guarantor to secure financial accommodation provided to a corporation of which the guarantor is a director; or a trustee of a trust of which the guarantor is a beneficiary.

Effects on banker's duty of confidentiality

The provisions of the new Code of Banking Practice relating to guarantees would seem to have little direct effect on the banker's duty of confidentiality. If the bank cannot obtain the borrower's consent to provide the required information, then the banker will not be able to take the guarantee.

---

148 New Code of Banking Practice, cl 28.5.
149 See cl 17.1 of the current Code of Banking Practice.

The effect of the Consumer Credit Code on guarantees

Requirements of the law

Section 34(1) of the Consumer Credit Code provides that a credit provider must, at the request of a debtor or guarantor, provide a statement of the current balance of the debtor's account; any amounts credited or debited during the period specified in the request; any amounts overdue and when each such amount became due; and any amount payable on the date it became due. There are also provisions in s 34(2) in relation to the time within which the statement must be provided.

Section 51(1) further provides that, before the obligations under a credit contract are secured by guarantee, the credit provider must give to the prospective guarantor a copy of the contract document of the credit contract or proposed credit contract and a document in the form prescribed by the regulations explaining the rights and obligations of the guarantor. Failure to do so renders the guarantee unenforceable.[150]

Section 163(1) also provides that other contracts and documents must be provided to a guarantor on request. These include any credit related insurance contract in the credit provider's possession and any notice previously given to the debtor under this Code.

Effects on banker's duty of confidentiality

Unlike the provisions of the Code of Banking Practice, the provisions in the Consumer Credit Code require disclosure under compulsion of law with statutory force. It may be a defence to a claim for wrongful disclosure to a guarantor under the provisions of the Consumer Credit Code that disclosure was made under compulsion of law. However, to avoid any doubt on this issue, banks may wish to obtain an express consent to the relevant disclosures from the potential borrower as part of the loan application process.

AUSTRALIAN SECURITIES AND INVESTMENTS COMMISSION ACT 2001, S 12DA – EFFECT ON BANKER'S DUTY OF CONFIDENTIALITY[151]

Section 12DA of the ASIC Act imposes an obligation on a financial corporation to refrain from misleading or deceptive conduct in trade or commerce. One potential difficulty is that, under certain conditions, silence itself may be construed as misleading conduct. The general approach was formulated by French J in *Kimberley NZI Finance Ltd v Torero Pty Ltd*[152] in relation to s 52 of the TPA as being:

---

150 S 51(2).
151 For developments in relation to silence amounting to a breach of s 52 (which predated s 12DA of the ASIC Act) see Warren Pengilley 'Section 52: can the blind mislead the blind?' (March 1997) 5 Trade Practices LJ.
152 (1989) 11 ATPR 46-054.

'... unless the circumstances are such as to give rise to the reasonable expectation that if some relevant fact exists it would be disclosed, it is difficult to see how mere silence could support the inference that the fact does not exist ...'[153]

In *Kabwand Pty Ltd v National Australia Bank Ltd*[154] this issue arose in relation to a bank. A banker acted as banker for both the vendor and the purchaser of a business. The banker told the purchaser the business had 'an excellent cash flow situation'. The business, however, was unprofitable and the bank manager deliberately refrained from telling the purchasers. Did s 52 place an obligation on the manager to disclose that overrode the manager's duty of confidentiality? The court found there was no duty of disclosure since the bank was under a contractual duty of secrecy to its customer. The reasoning has been criticised by Alan Tyree on the basis that it is circular. 'There is no duty of secrecy if disclosure is under compulsion of law. There is compulsion if there is a reasonable expectation. But according to *Kabwand*, there is no reasonable expectation because there is a duty of secrecy.'[155]

It is important to note that in *Kabwand* the applicants did not plead a case that, once the banker had made the statement about the excellent cash flow of the business, s 52 imposed upon the banker an obligation to go on and give the true picture in relation to the business. Had that been done, the result might have been different.

CODES OF PRACTICE

There are a number of duties of confidentiality imposed by various Codes of Practice in Australia. For example:

1   The bank, building society and credit union and electronic funds transfer codes of conduct contain a duty of confidentiality.
2   The CUSCAL (Credit Union Corporation (Australia) Limited Privacy Code for their Quick Link Smart Card released in July 1996) addresses five key areas of privacy: the purposes for which information collected can be used, a prohibition on the smart card holder's personal information being amalgamated with transaction data, and storage and security, access and collection rights.
3   The Internet Industry Codes of Practice (first released in May 2002) deals with privacy issues only in very broad terms. For example, there is a requirement that the privacy of users' details obtained by Code subscribers in the course of business will be respected.
4   The Australian Direct Marketing Association (ADMA) Code of Practice (November 2001) sets out specific standards of conduct for ADMA members

---

153 (1989) 11 ATPR 46-054 at 53, 195. This approach has been applied recently in *Hadid v Lenfest Communications Inc* [1999] FCA 1798.
154 (1989) 11 ATPR 40-950. Hill J in *Winterton Construction Pty Ltd v Hambros Australia Ltd* (1992) 39 FCR 97 endorsed for a merchant bank the court's view in *Kabwand* of a bank's duty of confidence.
155 Tyree 'Section 52 and the Bankers Duty of Confidentiality' (June 1990) J Banking and Finance Law and Practice 144. In Daniel Clough's article 'Misleading and deceptive silence: Section 52, Confidentiality and the General Law' (1994) 2 Trade Practices LJ 76 at 93. See section entitled 'The Financier's Duty of Confidentiality: does it take precedence over section 52' therein.

who are participants in the direct marketing industry. Privacy principles similar to the NPPs are an integral part of this Code. They give consumers control over their personal information by limiting collection of customer information and requiring marketers (including banks) to identify themselves to consumers, tell them how to get in touch with them and what they intend to do with their personal information. Marketers must also give consumers the opportunity to block transfer of their contact details to any other marketer.

The most important code in the bank-customer relationship is the Code of Banking Practice.

CODE OF BANKING PRACTICE

As a result of the November 1991 House of Representatives Standing Committee on Finance and Public Administration[156] Report entitled *A Pocket Full of Change*,[157] the Code of Banking Practice was formulated. Since then, the Code has been revised to apply to all banking facilities provided in s 39.1 of the Code, and each bank publicly announces it has adopted the Code.[158] Since November 1996, as part of the movement towards the development and implementation of the Consumer Credit Code,[159] Australian banks have been advertising their adoption of the Code of Banking Practice and it is now growing in terms of its legal enforceability.

Once adopted, the terms of the Code become an express part of the contract between the bank and its customer. The new Code replaces the old definition of 'customer' (defined in s 1.1 of the amended Code to include an individual who 'acquires a Banking Service which is wholly and exclusively for his or her private or domestic use') with the definition of 'you' and 'your' (which is significantly different in that there is no personal or domestic use test and small businesses are covered). A breach of the Code is a breach of contract, and normal contractual remedies will be available.[160]

The intention of the new Code is that it should not impose obligations on banks relating to privacy and confidentiality in addition to their existing obligations under the Privacy Act 1988 and their general duty of confidentiality.[161]

Under s 22 of the new Code, a bank acknowledges that, in addition to the bank's duties under the Privacy Act 1988, the bank has a general duty of confidentiality towards its customer, except in the following circumstances:

---

156 The Martin Committee.

157 AGPS (1991).

158 There is also provision for a bank to adopt the Code by incorporating its terms into a contract with a customer: see cl 10.3 of the New Code.

159 The Consumer Credit Code provides for consumer protection regulation. It regulates the provision of credit for personal, domestic or household purposes.

160 See discussion under Remedies for breach above.

161 Cl 12.9 of the amended Code provides that a bank may not collect, use or disseminate information about a customer's political, social or religious beliefs, or affiliations, race, ethnic origins, national origins or sexual preferences, or practices except that it may collect or use such information for a 'proper commercial purpose'. This provision is not included in the New Code, but is covered by stricter provisions in s 6, NPP 10.1 and NPP 2.1 in the Privacy Act 1988.

- where disclosure is compelled by law;
- where there is a duty to the public to disclose,
- where it is in the bank's interests to require disclosure; or
- where disclosure is made with the customer's express or implied consent.

CONSUMER CREDIT CODE

The Consumer Credit Code provides for substantially uniform consumer credit regulation throughout Australia. It provides for the regulation of the provision of credit to individuals for domestic, personal or household use. Several provisions of the Consumer Credit Code impinge upon the banker's duty of confidentiality. See, in particular, the discussion in relation to guarantees above.

PRIVACY ACT 1988

The Privacy Act 1988 (Cth) (the Privacy Act) (incorporating the amendments made to it by the Privacy Amendment (Private Sector) Act 2000) applies basically to the private sector in relation to all dealings with the personal information of individuals. The NPPs in the Privacy Act set out how private sector organisations (including banks) should collect, use and disclose, keep secure and provide access to personal information.[162] The principles also give individuals the right to know what information an organisation holds about them and a right to correct that information if it is wrong.

The Federal Privacy Commission has written Guidelines to the National Privacy Principles to assist private sector organisations to meet their obligations in the handling of personal information. A series of Information Sheets has also been developed and provides more detailed explanations and good practice or compliance tips on various aspects of the NPPs and the private sector provisions.

The Privacy Commissioner has issued Tax File Number Guidelines concerning the collection, storage, use and security of tax file number information. These guidelines are interpreted under s 17(1) of the Privacy Act and have statutory force under s 18.

Part IIIA of the Privacy Act governs credit reporting and the use and disclosure of credit-sensitive information. It is these two areas which are of particular interest in the present context. Part IIIA would clearly apply to a 'bank', given that the definition of a 'credit provider' in s 11B(1)(a) specifically refers to a bank.

Part IIIA only regulates consumer credit information – that is, information relating to a 'loan'[163] to an individual to be used wholly or primarily for domestic, family or household purposes. These provisions, by definition, do not apply to data relating

---

162 Principle 1 – Collection; Principle 2 – Use and disclosure; Principle 3 – Data quality; Principle 4 – Data security; Principle 5 – Openness; Principle 6 – Access and correction; Principle 7 – Identifiers; Principle 8 – Anonymity; Principle 9 – Transborder data flows; Principle 10 – Sensitive information.

163 A 'loan' is broadly defined in s 6(1) of the Privacy Act to cover, in effect, any debt deferral arrangement.

to any person other than an individual (ie they would not apply to information concerning an incorporated company), aggregate bank data or data which does not identify an individual.

Broadly, Pt IIIA, as far as it relates to credit providers, regulates:

1   the accuracy and security of credit reports;[164]
2   access to, and alteration of, credit reports held by credit providers by customers;[165]
3   the purpose for which credit providers can use credit reports;[166]
4   the information which must be provided to an applicant where a credit application is refused wholly or partly on the grounds of a credit report in relation to the applicant;[167] and
5   disclosure by credit providers of a 'report' or personal information derived from a 'report'.[168]

The restrictions in the Privacy Act on disclosures of a 'report' or personal information derived from a 'report' are of particular relevance to the bankers' duty of confidentiality. In summary, s 18N prohibits the disclosure of such information for any purpose unless one of the various specified exceptions applies.

A 'report' is broadly defined to include:

1   any 'record' (which is in turn defined in s 6(1) to include a document, database or any pictorial representation of a person, subject to certain exceptions);
2   a 'credit report'; and
3   any other record or information, in any form, that has any bearing on an individual's creditworthiness, credit standing, credit history or credit capacity; other than publicly available information.[169]

A 'credit report' is essentially a report on creditworthiness obtained from a credit reporting agency, such as the Baycorp Advantage Business Information Services Ltd.[170]

The exceptions provided for in s 18N(1) relate to disclosures:

1   to a credit reporting agency for specified purposes;
2   with the specific agreement of the individual, to another credit provider for a particular purpose;
3   to a guarantor of a loan for enforcement purposes;
4   to a mortgage insurer for specified purposes;
4   to a dispute resolution authority;
6   to a minister, department or authority in a state or territory whose functions include the giving of mortgage credit, the management or supervision of schemes or arrangements involving mortgage credit;

164 S 18G.
165 Ss 18H and 18J.
166 S 18L.
167 S 18M.
168 S 18N.
169 S 18N(9).
170 S 6(1).

7   to a supplier for the purpose of allowing the supplier to determine whether to accept payment by means of a credit card or electronic transfer of funds;

8   to potential assignees;

9   to debt collectors;

10   to persons who manage loans for the credit provider;

11   to related corporations;

12   where disclosure for the particular purpose is required or authorised by or under law;

13   to the individual themselves or a person authorised in writing by the individual to seek access to the relevant report or information;

14   to a person authorised to operate an account maintained by the person; and

15   in a case where there has been a serious credit infringement and the disclosure is made to another credit provider or a law enforcement authority.

The exceptions to the rule in *Tournier*[171] differ somewhat from the circumstances where disclosure is authorised under Pt IIIA and the NPPs. In some respects, Pt IIIA expands the scope of disclosure by permitting disclosure on the basis that it is 'authorised' by law. The question is whether a disclosure 'authorised' by law for the purposes of Pt IIIA is permissible in derogation from the common law duty not to disclose. Where there is an express intention on the part of the legislature to override the common law, this issue is not problematic. For example, the Privacy Act itself expressly allows disclosures between related corporations.[172] Such a disclosure would accordingly seem to be 'authorised by or under law' and hence be within the s 18N(1)(g) exception and be permissible notwithstanding that it is not clearly within one of the exceptions to *Tournier*.[173] Many statutes 'authorise' (as opposed to 'require') disclosure, however in vague terms. In such instances, it is still arguable that Pt IIIA will still authorise disclosure on the basis of the s 18N(1)(g) exception.

The Pt IIIA provisions sit together with the NPPs in relation to banks' collection, use and disclosure of customer information. NPP 1 provides that an organisation (including a bank):

1   Must not collect personal information unless the information is necessary for one of its functions or activities.

2   Must collect personal information only by lawful and fair means and not in an unreasonable intrusive way.

3   Must, at or before the time (or as soon as practicable thereafter) it collects personal information about an individual from the individual, take reasonable steps to ensure that the individual is aware of the identity of the organisation and how to contact it; the fact that he can gain access to it; the purposes for which the information is collected; the organisations (or types of organisations) to which the organisations usually disclose information of that kind; any law which requires the particular information to be collected and the main consequences (if any) to the individual if any or part of the information is not provided.

---

171   *Tournier v National Provincial and Union Bank of England* [1924] 1 KB 461.

172   Privacy Act, s 18N(1)(d).

173   See discussion of *Bank of Tokyo Ltd v Karoon* [1987] 1 AC 45 under Disclosure in the interests of the bank above.

In addition, NPP 1.4 provides that where it is reasonable and practicable to do so, an organisation must collect personal information about an individual only from that individual.

Under NPP 1.5, if the information is collected from someone else, the organisation must take reasonable steps to make sure that the individual whose information it is aware of the matters set out in NPP 1.3 except to the extent this would pose a serious threat to their life or health.

Under NPP 2.1, a bank must not use or disclose personal information (including credit information) about an individual for a purpose (the secondary purpose) other than the primary purpose of collection unless:

- the secondary purpose is related to the primary purpose of collection, and, if the personal information is sensitive information, directly related to the primary purpose of collection, and the individual would reasonably expect the organisation to use or disclose the information for the secondary purpose;
- the individual has consented to the use or disclosure; or
- if the information is not sensitive information and the use of the information is for the secondary purpose of direct marketing:
    '(i)   it is impracticable for the organisation to seek the individual's consent before that particular use; and
    (ii)   the organisation will not charge the individual for giving effect to a request by the individual to the organisation not to receive direct marketing communications; and
    (iii) the individual has not made a request to the organisation not to receive direct marketing communications; and
    (iv) in each direct marketing communication with the individual, the organisation draws to the individuals attention; or prominently displays a notice, that he or she may express a wish not to receive any further direct marketing communications; and
    (v)   each written direct marketing communication by the organisation with the individual (up to and including the communication that involves the use) sets out the organisations business address and telephone number and, if the communication with the individual is make by fax, telex or other electronic means, a number or address at which the organisation can be directly contacted electronically;' or
- one of the other provisions in NPP 2.1(d)–(h) apply, including the use or disclosure of the personal information as required or authorised by or under law (NPP 2.1(g)).

Under the NPPs, an organisation must also:

- take reasonable steps to make sure that the personal information it collects, uses or discloses is accurate, complete and up-to-date (NPP 3);
- take reasonable steps to protect the personal information it holds from misuse and loss and from unauthorised access, modification or disclosure (NPP 4.1);
- take reasonable steps to destroy or permanently de-identify personal information if it is no longer needed for any purpose for which the information may be used or disclosed under NPP 2 (NPP 4);

- set out in a document clearly expressed policies on its management of personal information on request (NPP 5.1); and
- on request by a person, take reasonable steps to let the person know, generally, what sort of personal information it holds, for what purposes, and how it collects, holds, uses and discloses that information (NPP 5.2).

If an organisation holds personal information about an individual, it must provide the individual with access to it on request subject to certain exceptions (including if the denial of access is authorised or required by law (NPP 6.1(h), NPP 6.1)). However, where providing access would reveal evaluative information generated within the organisation in connection with a commercially sensitive decision – making process, the organisation may under NPP 6.2 give the individual an explanation for the commercially sensitive decision rather than direct access to the information.

NPP 6.3–6.7 provide for:

3   access to be given to personal information by mutually agreed intermediaries;
4   the charges for access to personal information (these must not be excessive and a charge must not be made for a request for access);
5   the organisation to take reasonable steps to correct information so that it is accurate, complete and up-to-date;
6   to take reasonable steps if an individual requests it to associate with information a statement that it is not accurate, complete or up-to-date, where the organisation disagrees that this is the case; and
7   provide reasons for denial of access or a refusal to correct personal information.

NPP 8 provides that wherever it is lawful and practicable, individuals must have the option of not identifying themselves when entering transactions with an organisation.

NPP 9 sets out the conditions under which an organisation in Australia or an external territory may transfer personal information about an individual to someone (other than the organisation or the individual) who is in a foreign country. Such transfers are authorised only if:

- the organisation reasonably believes that the recipient is subject to a law, binding scheme or contract which effectively upholds principles for fair handling of the information that are substantially similar to the WPPs;
- the individual consents to the transfer;
- the transfer is necessary for the performance of a contract between the individual and the organisation, or for the implementation of pre-contractual measures taken in response to the individual's request;
- the transfer is necessary for the conclusion or performance of a contract concluded in the interest of the individual between the organisation and the third party;
- all of the following apply:
  - the transfer is for the benefit of the individual;
  - it is impracticable to obtain the consent of the individual to that transfer; and
  - if it were practicable to obtain such consent, the individual would be likely to give it; or

- the organisation has taken reasonable steps to ensure that the information which is transferred will not be held, used or disclosed by the recipient of the information inconsistently with the NPPs.

NPP 10 restricts an organisation from collecting sensitive information about an individual unless certain specified conditions are satisfied. 'Sensitive information' is defined in s 6 of the Privacy Act as an information or an opinion about an individual's:

- social or ethnic origin;
- membership of a political association;
- religious beliefs or affiliations;
- philosophical beliefs;
- membership of a professional or trade association;
- membership of a trade union;
- sexual preference or practices;
- criminal record that is also personal information (as defined); or
- 'health information' (which is separately defined).

Credit Reporting Code of Conduct

The Privacy Act's rules applicable to credit providers must be read in conjunction with the Credit Reporting Code of Conduct (the Credit Reporting Code) which has been issued by the Privacy Commissioner under s 18A of the Privacy Act. The Credit Reporting Code has statutory force by virtue of s 18B of the Act.

The Credit Reporting Code, like Pt III of the Act, applies only to consumer credit information and supplements Pt IIIA.

Among other things, the Credit Reporting Code requires credit providers (including banks) and credit reporting agencies:

1 to deal promptly with individual requests for access and amendment of personal credit information;
2 to ensure that only permitted and accurate information is included in an individual's credit information file;
3 to keep adequate records in regard to any disclosure of personal credit information;
4 to adopt specific procedures in settling credit reporting disputes; and
5 to provide staff training on the requirements of the Privacy Act.

Credit Reporting Advice Summaries

Part IIIA of the Privacy Act (and the NPPs as relevant) must also be read in conjunction with the Credit Reporting Advice Summaries issued by the Privacy Commissioner. These advice summaries do not have force of law, but nevertheless clarify the Privacy Commissioner's view of many of the ambiguities inherent in s 18N(1). By way of example, the Privacy Commissioner is apparently of the view that a disclosure by a credit provider to certain service providers (such as lawyers, accountants, authors, consultants and mailing houses) in connection with the management of loans provided by the credit provider may be regarded as a permitted 'use' of information rather than as a prohibited 'disclosure', provided the credit provider maintains control of the information and there are appropriate confidentiality provisions.[174] Such explanations of s 18N(1) are useful, but they do not have the force of law and consequently there must be some uncertainty in relying on them.

Interaction between the Privacy Act 1988 and *the Tournier* case

Part IIIA of the Privacy Act bears on the banker's common law duty of confidentiality as established by the *Tournier* case.

For example, the *Tournier* duty of confidentiality attaches at the commencement of the bank-customer relationship, commensurate with its contractual nature, and terminates when the relationship comes to an end.

The Privacy Act, in contrast, operates with statutory force in relation to personal information, including certain consumer credit personal information. It is not affected by the commencement or cessation of the bank-customer relationship. Hence, the Privacy Act imposes obligations on credit providers (including banks) in a wider set of circumstances than *Tournier* does.

Furthermore, the rule in *Tournier* applies in respect of information, such as account information, concerning the conduct by the bank of the customer's business, irrespective of its source and purpose of collection. Part IIIA and the NPPs regulate, however, credit providers in respect of all information that comes within the broad definition of a 'report'. This latter class of information is clearly broader than the class of information in respect of which the *Tournier* duty of confidentiality attaches.

Many other aspects of Pt IIIA and the NPPs exceed the *Tournier* duty of bank confidentiality. For example, the obligations concerning the collection of personal information, accuracy and security safeguards, restrictions on internal use of credit reports and permitted customer access are not represented at common law. In contrast, the *Tournier* duty is confined to disclosure (and, to some degree, use).

The common law duty of non-disclosure also differs, however, from its counterpart provisions in Pt IIIA and NPP 2. The best way to specify the differences is to examine the impact of Pt IIIA and NPP 2 upon the four exceptions to the common law rule.

Disclosure under compulsion of law

An example at common law is where a bank is required to give evidence concerning a customer's account in civil or criminal proceedings.

Under Pt IIIA of the Privacy Act[175] and NPP 2.1(g), the disclosure of a credit report by a credit provider is permitted if it is 'required or authorised by or under law'.

---

174 Para 10.24 of the Credit Reporting Advice Summaries issued by the Privacy Commissioner.
175 Privacy Act, s 18N(1)(g).

'Required' connotes compulsion such as mandatory legislation[176] or court order. An example is the Financial Transaction Reports Act 1988 (Cth) which requires 'cash dealers', inter alia, to supply reports of any transactions that they suspect on reasonable grounds may be relevant to the investigation of tax evasion or a federal offence.

'Authorised' indicates a right or entitlement, such as the right to disclose information under the Proceeds of Crime Act 1987 (Cth) (for example, the right under s 46 of the Act to adduce evidence in relation to a proposed restraining order on property where the person appearing has an interest in the property), or the right to disclose confidential legal information under the common law exceptions to legal professional privilege. The 'compulsion of law' exception to *Tournier* would not appear to allow disclosure on this basis.

The Credit Reporting Code contains the following explanation by the Privacy Commissioner of this exception which indicates it should be broadly interpreted and, in particular, that it should cover any disclosure allowed by *Tournier* (except to the extent that one of the other specific exceptions in s 18N indicates to the contrary):

> '... where the disclosure is required or authorised by or under law. This applies to both statute law and common law. It is not limited to Commonwealth law but applies also to state law, and laws of other Australian jurisdictions to which credit providers may be subject. It also includes statutory provisions authorising warrants and other instruments for searching premises, obtaining information etc.'[177]

Disclosure in the public interest

Part IIIA of the Privacy Act contains no general public interest exception to its disclosure rules, but it does permit disclosure in circumstances where, on reasonable grounds, a credit provider believes than an individual has committed a serious credit infringement. A 'serious credit infringement' is defined in s 6(1) of the Privacy Act to mean:

> 'an act done by a person:
> (a) that involves fraudulently obtaining credit, or attempting fraudulently to obtain credit; or
> (b) that involves fraudulently evading the person's obligations in relation to credit, or attempting fraudulently to evade those obligations; or
> (c) that a reasonable person would consider indicates an intention, on the part of the first-mentioned person, no longer to comply with the first-mentioned person's obligations in relation to credit.'

In such a case, information may be passed on to another credit provider or to a law enforcement agency.[178]

---

176 Eg the Income Tax Assessment Act 1936 (Cth), ss 263, 264 (power to inspect and seize documents and to require disclosure of income and assets for use as evidence).
177 Para 74 of Explanatory Notes to Credit Reporting Code.
178 Privacy Act, s 18N.

NPP 2.1(e), 2.1(f) and 2.1(h) provide clear general public interest exceptions to the disclosure rules otherwise set out in NPP 2.1. Under NPP 2.1(e) an organisation may use and disclose personal information about an individual other than for the primary purpose of collection where it reasonably believes that the use or disclosure is necessary to lessen or prevent:

1   a serious and imminent threat to an individual's life, health or safety; or
2   a serious threat to public health or public safety.

NPP 2.1(f) provides for use and disclosure of personal information by an organisation where there is reason to suspect that unlawful activity has been, is being or may be engaged in, and the organisation uses or discloses the personal information as a necessary part of its investigation of the matter or in reporting its concerns to relevant persons or authorities.

NPP 2.1(h) provides for use and disclosure of personal information by an organisation where it reasonably believes that the use or disclosure is reasonably necessary for one or more of the following by or on behalf of an enforcement body:

1   the prevention, detection, investigation, prosecution or punishment of a criminal offence, breaches of a law imposing a penalty or sanction or breaches of a prescribed law;
2   the enforcement of laws relating to the confiscation of the proceeds of crime;
3   the protection of the public revenue;
4   the prevention, detection, investigation or remedying of seriously improper conduct or prescribed conduct; and
5   the preparation for, or conduct of, proceedings before any court or tribunal, or implementation of the orders of a court or tribunal.

Disclosure in the interest of the bank

The counterpart of this exception in Pt IIIA of the Privacy Act is narrower. It permits disclosure to a person recognised and accepted in the community as being appointed for the purpose of settling disputes between credit providers and customers, for the purpose of settling such a dispute.[179]

Disclosure by consent

At common law, there is scope for implying consent in certain circumstances. As far as individual consent goes, Pt IIIA of the Privacy Act should probably be regarded as recognising only express consent to disclosure.[180]

In particular, Pt IIIA affects the giving of 'bankers' opinions'. It requires the specific consent of the individual to be given before a credit report or information may be disclosed by one credit provider to another.[181] This clearly covers the giving of

179 Privacy Act, s 18N(1)(bc).
180 Privacy Act, s 18N(1)(b).
181 Privacy Act, s 18N(1)(b).

bankers' opinions. It could be argued that, if at common law banks do have the implied consent of their customers to give opinions (which in itself may be debated),[182] then the practice of giving opinions is 'authorised' by law.[183] On this view, it should not be necessary to rely on the s 18N(1)(b) exception. Instead, there could be reliance on the s 18N(1)(g) exception for disclosures which are 'authorised' by law.

However, it would be anomalous to regard Pt IIIA otherwise than as being intended to prevent the giving of bankers' opinions without consent. This is so notwithstanding the wide view expressed by the Privacy Commissioner as to what 'authorised' by law means.

The position is made clear by the Credit Reporting Code, which provides that 'a credit provider which is a bank may not disclose to another bank a "banker's opinion" relating to an individual's consumer credit-worthiness unless that individual's specific agreement to the disclosure of such information for the particular purpose has been obtained'.[184]

This conclusion is supported by the provision in NPP 2.1(b) for the use or disclosure of personal information by consent of the individual concerned. Any implied consent for these purposes ideally should be asked within the Privacy Commissioner's Guidelines. The safest position to adopt is to act on a customer's proactive response to a consent question. However, the value of a 'Yes' answer to a consent question which relates to personal information which may be gathered over a long period may diminish over time if no steps are taken to 'refresh' the consent.

State privacy legislation

The following state privacy legislation may also be relevant to the bankers' duty of confidentiality.

Fair Trading Act 1987 (South Australia)

Part V of the Fair Trading Act 1987 (South Australia), which deals with fair reporting, is broad in scope and is not confined to credit. It applies to any communication made to a trader by a reporting agent or another trader of any information relating to a person, except where the person concerned is aware of the communication and the information. Such a communication is a 'prescribed report'.

---

182 See on bankers' opinions above.
183 Privacy Act, s 18N(1)(g).
184 Credit Reporting Code, cl 2.16. See discussion on bankers' opinions above. The same would apply in respect of information relating to a prospective guarantor's creditworthiness where the purpose for which the borrowing was made is not relevant to the question of whether the opinion may be sought. What is relevant is the kind of information sought in respect of the guarantor. His prior consent may only be required if the information relates to the guarantor's consumer creditworthiness. Para 71 of the Explanatory Notes to the Code of Conduct confirms this view and states that '[t]he provision by banks of opinions relating to an individual's commercial creditworthiness is unaffected by the provisions of the Code of Conduct or the Privacy Act'.

A reporting agency is generally defined to mean a person that carries on the business of providing prescribed reports. A trader is a person who, in the course of a business, supplies, or offers to supply, goods or services. It is arguable that the provision of credit constitutes the supply of services.

A trader is required to notify an individual of certain information, including the name and address of a relevant credit reporting agency, where the trader:

1   denies a prescribed benefit sought by the individual, or grants a prescribed benefit sought by the individual on less favourable terms compared with other persons to whom the trader has granted prescribed benefits; and
2   has obtained a prescribed report on the individual in the last six months.

A prescribed benefit includes a benefit of a commercial nature.

The legislation also deals with a person's right to gain access to information held by a reporting agency, and a person's right to dispute the accuracy of that information.

It may apply where a credit provider uses a prescribed report in respect of commercial credit. However, where a bank issues a banker's opinion (in respect of consumer or commercial credit), then it arguably could be caught by the legislation as a reporting agency.

Credit Reporting Act 1978 (Victoria)

The Credit Reporting Act 1978 (Victoria) only deals with credit reporting. However, it is not limited to consumer credit. It also applies to commercial credit, and may apply to companies as well as individuals, despite its apparent restriction to 'consumers'. That is because a 'consumer' is defined as 'any person with respect to whom a *credit report* is made or with respect to whom any information is held by a *credit reporting agent*' [185] A 'credit report' is in turn broadly defined in s 2. There is no 'consumer purposes' test. A '"*credit report*" means any written, oral, or other communication with respect to the credit worthiness, credit standing, or credit capacity of a person but does not include a report containing information solely as to transactions or experiences between the person making the report and the person who is the subject of the report'.

The Act primarily deals with the notification by a user of a credit report, to an individual, of the refusal of credit, and the individual's subsequent rights to obtain access to information held by the relevant 'credit reporting agent' (a person who engages in the practice of providing credit reports),[186] and to dispute the accuracy of that information.

A 'credit reporting agent' has the following further obligations (amongst others):

1   to give an affected consumer access to information compiled by the agent and the right to request corrections;[187]

---

185 S 2.
186 See s 2 definitions.
187 S 6(1) and (2).

2   to advise an affected consumer where amendments are made to relevant credit information, and to advise the consumer and any or all persons who have been supplied with information concerning the consumer in the previous six months and any other person requested by the consumer.[188]

Interrelationship between the Privacy Act 1988 and state legislation

Section 3 of the Privacy Act provides that the Privacy Act is not to affect the operation of a state or territory law that 'makes provision with respect to the collection, holding, use, correction, disclosure or transfer of personal information (including such a law relating to credit reporting or the use of information held in connection with credit reporting) and is capable of operating concurrently with this Act'.

The Commonwealth therefore does not purport to cover the field in relation to credit reporting. Accordingly, if there is no inconsistency with the Commonwealth Act, the relevant provision of the state law should be complied with, otherwise the Privacy Act prevails.

INTERNATIONAL REQUESTS FOR INFORMATION

Hypothetical[189]

The branch[190] of your client bank in the UK is approached by the Financial Services Authority (FSA) in relation to various transactions which are thought to have been improper but do not give rise to criminal liability, but are suspected to have been undertaken by various customers of the bank in London possibly with the connivance of officers of the bank. The FSA wishes the bank to make available all its records to its investigators. All these records are held in Australia by the head office of the bank.

Application of legal principles to the hypothetical[191]

The bank's duty not to disclose information about a customer to a third party applies, even when the third party is a wholly owned subsidiary of the bank and operates, in practice, as a part of the bank.[192] Each foreign branch of the bank is regarded as independent of its parent body.[193] Therefore, care must be taken in the transfer of information between branches.[194] Consent to the transfer of information to another

---

188 S 6(3).
189 In relation to cross-border issues, one should bear in mind the power of the Australian Taxation Office to issue offshore information notices pursuant to s 264A.
190 If the branch is in fact a subsidiary, it will be treated as a separate legal entity and the issue of which documents are in its control or possession will be assessed on that basis.
191 Australian law would not prevent the disclosure of information to the SIB if the information did not identify particular customers. However, it is assumed for the purposes of the hypothetical that customer specific information may be disclosed, and that the SIB is operating under legislative powers (not court powers).
192 *Bank of Tokyo Ltd v Karoon* [1987] 1 AC 45.
193 *Power Curber International Ltd v National Bank of Kuwait SAK* [1981] 3 All ER 607.
194 See discussion under Privacy Act 1998 above.

office of the same bank, in the ordinary course of the banking business may readily be implied in the contract between the bank and its customer. However, consent to the forwarding of customer details to another branch in another country in response to an order of a foreign court, or to bring information within the jurisdiction of a foreign authority, would rarely be implied.[195]

First exception: disclosure under compulsion of law

One qualification to the *Tournier* case[196] is disclosure under compulsion of law. Where there is a statutory duty to disclose information, any contractual duty owed by a bank to the depositor is overridden by the statutory duty.[197]

The first issue in the above hypothetical is the appropriate law governing the contract. Normally, the law in force in the place where the account is held by the customer will govern the obligations under it.[198] Therefore in the above hypothetical the account would be governed by the principles in *Tournier* as well as any applicable legislation in England.

The consequences of this may be seen in *XAG v A Bank*,[199] in which an injunction was sought by a customer in London to prevent the London branch of the bank from answering a subpoena served upon its New York headquarters by the US Justice Department. It was held that English law governed the banking contract, that insufficient reason had been demonstrated for failing to uphold the confidentiality of the documents, and that the binding legal obligation in England would probably be an adequate excuse to any contempt proceedings prosecuted in the US for the failure to produce the documents.[200] In the hypothetical the accounts are held in London, and therefore it is likely that English law will be the law governing the obligation to disclose.

COMPULSION OF LAW – RELEVANT AUTHORITIES

There is no Australian decision on what amounts to compulsion of law in an international context. However, English and Hong Kong cases provide that the compulsion of law exception does not include an order directed by a foreign court requiring the production of documents of a branch overseas.[201] In *FDC Co Ltd v Chase Manhattan NA*, Huggins VP said:

> 'In Tournier's case the English Court of Appeal indicated four qualifications to an otherwise absolute obligation of secrecy. Although Mr Saville contends that the plaintiffs are seeking to widen the ambit of the resulting obligation, it

---

195 *FDC Co Ltd v Chase Manhattan Bank NA* [1990] 1 HKLR 277 at 283–284. This case has been considered in *Bank of Valetta plc v National Crime Authority* (1999) 164 ALR 45.
196 *Tournier v National Provincial and Union Bank of England* [1924] 1 KB 461.
197 *Federal Commissioner of Taxation v The Australian and New Zealand Banking Group Ltd* (1979) 143 CLR 499 at 521.
198 *Libyan Arab Foreign Bank v Bankers Trust Co* [1989] QB 728 at 746, per Staughton J.
199 [1983] 2 All ER 464.
200 Lee Aitken 'The bank's duty of confidence in transnational proceedings' (June 1994) J Banking and Finance Law and Practice 109 at 111.
201 *FDC Co Ltd v Chase Manhattan Bank NA* [1990] 1 HKLR 277.

seems to me his argument seeks to narrow it. It does so by construing the first qualification (disclosure under compulsion of law) as including an order of a foreign court to produce documents which are in Hong Kong. Such a construction was never within the contemplation of the judges in Tournier's case and in my view a term so construed would not be reasonable.'[202]

In *Power Curber International Ltd v National Bank of Kuwait SAK,*[203] Lord Denning MR stated:

'Each branch has to be licensed by the country in which it operates. Each branch is treated in that country as independent of its parent body. The branch is subject to the orders of the courts of the country in which it operates; but not to the orders of the courts where its head office is situate.'[204]

In *MacKinnon v Donaldson,*[205] Hoffman J considered the situation where a plaintiff under the banker's books provisions in England had obtained an ex parte order against a US bank, which required the US bank to produce books and other papers held at its head office in New York in the English court. The plaintiff then issued a subpoena duces tecum against an officer of the bank at its London office. Hoffman J held in discharging the order and the subpoena:

'In principle and on authority, it seems to me that the court should not, save in exceptional circumstances, impose such a requirement upon a foreigner, and, in particular, upon a foreign bank. The principle is that a state should refrain from demanding obedience to its sovereign authority by foreigners *in respect of their conduct outside the jurisdiction*' (emphasis added).[206]

Hoffman J considered it relevant that in the case there were two other methods by which the documents could have been obtained without infringing US sovereignty and without Citibank losing the protection of a New York court order. First, the plaintiff could have applied directly to a court in New York under provisions of US or New York legislation. Secondly, the plaintiff could have applied to a master under the English Rules of the Supreme Court for the issue of letters of request to the courts of New York specifying the documents required to be produced.[207]

XAG v A Bank is also relevant (as mentioned above and in the consideration of subpoenas from other jurisdictions in the section on extra-territorial aspects of compulsion of law in chapter 9).

---

202 [1990] 1 HKLR 277 at 283.
203 [1981] 3 All ER 607.
204 [1981] 3 All ER 607 at 1241.
205 [1986] Ch 482.
206 *MacKinnon v Donaldson* [1986] Ch 482 at 493. The principle in *MacKinnon* was applied by Habersberger J in *Gao v Zhu* [2002] VSC 64.
207 This is on the basis that the US and the UK are both parties to the Hague Convention on the taking of evidence abroad in civil or commercial matters and, subject to any questions of privilege or public policy under New York law, the English court is entitled under the Convention to the assistance of the New York courts in obtaining evidence for the purposes of any pending action.

APPLICATION OF THE RELEVANT AUTHORITIES TO THE HYPOTHETICAL

In considering the application of these cases to the hypothetical example, and assuming that English law applies because the account is held in London, the following facts will be important:

1   whether the documents sought by the FSA relate to conduct of the Australian bank in England or outside England; and
2   whether there are existing alternative methods available to obtain the documents.

If the relevant activities took place in England, then on the authority of *MacKinnon v Donaldson*, the court is likely to take the view that it is a legitimate exercise of the subject matter jurisdiction of the English court and therefore appropriate. In such a case it should not matter where the documents are physically held at the time of the request for production. If the bank is trading in England and the activities to which the request for production relates occurred in England, it would appear not to infringe any principle of sovereignty for the English authorities to require the branch trading in its jurisdiction to produce documents relating to that trading, provided that those documents remain within its control. It would be an all too easy device for foreign branches trading in a foreign jurisdiction to escape regulatory scrutiny merely by moving the documents offshore.

However, the position would appear to be different if the relevant activity took place outside the jurisdiction. In these circumstances it is likely the court would take the view that it is an illegitimate exercise of English subject matter jurisdiction in effect to use a compulsory process such as a subpoena to obtain documents situated abroad relating to transactions conducted abroad.[208] Significantly, a Memorandum of Understanding exists between the ASIC and the FSA for mutual assistance in relation to the provision of documents to each other. Legislative provision to enable the ASC to honour its obligations under the Memorandum of Understanding is provided in the Mutual Assistance in Business Regulation Act 1992 (Cth). Section 5(1) provides:

'The object of this Act is to enable Commonwealth regulators to render assistance to foreign regulators in their administration or enforcement of foreign business laws by obtaining from persons relevant information, documents and evidence and transmitting such information and evidence and copies of such documents to foreign regulators.'

The existence of this alternative would be a relevant factor for the court to take into account in considering the position.

The position may also be different depending on the source of the power to compel the production of the documents. If the source of the power is legislative, then the position may well turn on the proper interpretation of the legislative provisions.

A bank finding itself in these circumstances should consider notifying its customer of the existence of the court order and of its intention to comply (bearing in mind that a refusal to comply may cause adverse consequences on the client's branch in

---

208 *MacKinnon v Donaldson* [1986] Ch 482.

London). The bank should request that the customer consent to the disclosure of the information.[209] If the customer objected to the disclosure, then the customer could seek an injunction and in those injunctive proceedings, the bank could bring to the attention of the court all relevant factors.[210]

Second exception: disclosure in the public interest

It is unlikely that a bank could claim an exception to its duty of confidentiality on the basis that there is a duty to the public to disclose the information to the foreign authority. It is difficult to see what the duty to the public is in this context.[211]

Third exception: disclosure in the interests of the bank

The possibility of relying on the third exception to the banker's duty of confidentiality, where the interest of the bank requires disclosure has been limited by the decision in *Libyan Arab Foreign Bank v Bankers Trust Co*,[212] where Staughton J rejected out of hand the argument that disclosure to the US authorities was required in Bankers Trust's own interest on the basis of this exception.[213]

Fourth exception: disclosure with the customer's consent

The possibility of relying on the customer's express or implied consent will naturally be limited in situations where the customer itself is the subject of the investigation. However, a customer may be willing to give its express consent to the disclosure of information to a foreign authority where the customer is particularly concerned with its role as a corporate citizen or acutely aware of its public duty.[214]

Effect of the Privacy Act 1988 (Cth)

The Privacy Act restricts the manner in which banks may deal with information about a natural person. The Privacy Act does not restrict the bank from disclosing:

1   data in respect of companies and other incorporated bodies;
2   aggregate bank data; or
3   data with respect to specific transactions or credits which do not identify the customer.

Further, the Privacy Act does not prevent disclosure if the disclosure and use of personal information is required or authorised by or under law,[215] or the use of the

---

209 On occasions, the terms of the production order may prohibit such disclosure.
210 *XAG v A Bank* [1983] 2 All ER 464.
211 See discussion under Disclosure in the public interest above.
212 [1989] QB 728.
213 [1989] QB 728.
214 See Staughton J's comments on this exception in *Libyan Arab Foreign Bank v Bankers Trust Co* [1989] QB 728 at 770–771.
215 Privacy Act, s 18N(1)(g). See also NPP 2.1, in particular NPP 2.1(g) and 9.

report or information for that purpose is required or authorised by or under law.[216] Other exceptions are discussed above.

The key issue is whether 'authorised by or under law' is a reference to only Australian law or whether it is wide enough to be interpreted to mean laws of a foreign jurisdiction as well. However, given the decisions in the *Federal Commissioner of Taxation v The Australian and New Zealand Banking Group Ltd*,[217] *FDC Co Ltd v Chase Manhattan Bank NA*[218] and *Power Curber International Ltd v National Bank of Kuwait SAK*,[219] the most likely conclusion is that it would be interpreted as meaning Australian law only.

Note clause 10.40 of the Credit Reporting Advice Summaries released by the Privacy Commissioner, where in relation to this subject he commented:

> 'It is important to note that the disclosure by the credit provider must itself be authorised or required. That is, section 18N(1)(g) and NPP 2.1(g) may not necessarily be satisfied if the request is made by a person or body who is performing functions which are authorised by law. Credit providers who have been requested to disclose information under law should therefore request some evidence of the particular authority under which disclosure by the credit provider is required or authorised.'[220]

It is also important to note that any transborder data flow of personal information must be in accordance with NPP 9 requirements. NPP 9 authorises the transfer of personal information about an individual to someone who is in a foreign country subject to prescribed conditions, including the recipient of the information being subject to a law, binding scheme or contract which effectively upholds principles for fair handling of the information in a way substantially similar to the NPPs (NPP 9(a)), or the disclosing organisation taking reasonable steps to ensure that the transferred information will not be held, used or disclosed by the recipient inconsistently with the NPPs (NPP 9(f)).

Effect of the Proceeds of Crime Act 1987 and Financial Transaction Reports Act 1988

The disclosure obligation under the Proceeds of Crime Act 1987 and Financial Transaction Reports Act 1988 requires disclosure only to Australian authorities. Neither Act authorises disclosure by the bank to authorities of non-Australian governments. However, s 27(1)(d) of the Financial Transaction Reports Act 1988 provides that the Director of AUSTRAC may, in writing, authorise the Commissioner of the Australian Federal Police (the AFP Commissioner) to have access to information obtained by the Director under Pt II of the 1988 Act for the purposes of communicating the information to a foreign law enforcement agency. The AFP Commissioner may communicate that information to a foreign law enforcement agency if the

---

216 Privacy Act, s 18L(1)(e). See also NPP 2.1
217 (1979) 143 CLR 499, in particular, the comments of Gibbs ACJ at 521.
218 [1990] 1 HKLR 277, in particular, the comments of Huggins VP at 281.
219 [1981] 1 WLR 1233, in particular, the comments of Lord Denning at 1241.
220 The Credit Reporting Advice Summaries do not cover the issue of foreign courts or foreign authorities.

Commissioner is satisfied that the agency has given appropriate undertakings as to the protection of the confidentiality of the information and its use.

Effect of the Foreign Proceedings (Excess of Jurisdiction) Act 1984

Even if disclosure fell within one of the exceptions discussed above, disclosure may still be prohibited by the Attorney-General. Under s 7 of the Foreign Proceedings (Excess of Jurisdiction) Act 1984 the Commonwealth Attorney-General may, by order in writing, prohibit, inter alia, the production of a document which is in Australia, in a foreign court. This is based on the assumption that the FSA obtained a court order.

He may only make an order under s 7 if he is satisfied that:

1   the making of an order is desirable for the protection of the national interest;
2   the assumption of jurisdiction by the foreign court, or the manner of exercise by the foreign court, is contrary to international law or is inconsistent with international comity or international practice; or
3   the taking of that action, for an authority, or the manner of taking that action, is contrary to international law or is inconsistent with international comity or international practice.[221]

THE EFFECT OF OUTSOURCING ON THE BANKER'S DUTY OF CONFIDENTIALITY

Hypothetical

Consider the situation where an Australian bank wishes to engage a contractor to analyse certain data concerning customers of the bank.

Is it possible for the bank to avoid contravening its duty of confidentiality towards its customer by engaging as employees of the bank the relevant personnel of the contractor to analyse data on customers for the bank and by contracting with the contractor for those employees to have exclusive use of the contractor's computer to avoid any disclosure to staff of the contractor?

Application of legal principles to the hypothetical

Effect of the Privacy Act 1988

The difficulty with the first proposition is that s 18N(1) of the Privacy Act prohibits a 'credit provider' from disclosing a 'report' concerning the customer or 'personal information derived from a report'.[222] However, s 8(1)(a) of the Privacy Act avoids a breach of s 18N(1) where the disclosure is to an employee of the credit provider. Section 8(1)(a) provides:

---

221 Foreign Proceedings (Excess of Jurisdiction) Act 1984, s 6.
222 See discussion of the relevant provisions above.

'For the purposes of this Act:

(a) an act done or practice engaged in by, or information disclosed to, a person employed by, or in the service of, an agency, file number recipient, credit reporting agency or credit provider in the performance of the duties of the person's employment shall be treated as having been done or engaged in by, or disclosed to, the agency, recipient, credit reporting agency or credit provider.'

Therefore, by engaging the relevant staff of the contractor as genuine employees of the bank, the bank could avoid making a disclosure that is prohibited by s 18N(1).

However, the employment of the contractor by the bank must not be a sham to avoid the prescriptions in the Privacy Act. The bank would be obliged to comply with all laws in relation to those new employees including taxation laws and labour laws. All arrangements would need to be fully and properly documented.

There is also the possibility that the disclosure might be made directly to the contractor on the basis of the Privacy Commissioner's views relating to disclosures to service providers.

Section 8(1) of the Privacy Act would appear effectively to permit a flow of information between a credit provider and a person 'employed by, or in the service of, ... a credit provider in the performance of the duties of the person's employment ...' There is an argument that this provision extends to service providers of the relevant credit provider.

The difficulties with this view are:

1   the reference to 'the person's employment' in s 8(1)(a) is inconsistent with the concept that an independent contractor might be covered by the provisions; and
2   certain specific exemptions to the prohibition on disclosure of credit sensitive information in s 18N(1) would not seem to be necessary if this view were correct (see, for example, s 18N(1)(c), (ca) and (f) which permit disclosures to certain service providers in order to perform particular functions).

Nevertheless, the Privacy Commissioner has expressed the view that the provision of personal information to an external contractor in connection with the management of loans could be regarded as a 'use' of information rather than a prohibited 'disclosure' if the credit provider retains control over any use by the contractor of that information. In this situation the Privacy Commissioner has said that the credit provider should ensure that the third party agrees to abide by strict standards (according to the standards laid out in the Privacy Act) to safeguard the information and to ensure that no other uses of personal information are permitted. In particular, there should be a prohibition on disclosure to third parties.

The Privacy Act does not contain the distinction between a 'use' and a 'disclosure' of information contemplated by the Privacy Commissioner. Nevertheless, it is unlikely that a bank would be considered to be in breach of the Privacy Act simply because it relied on the Privacy Commissioner's views.

A further dimension is given to this question by the application of NPP 2.1(a) to the Privacy Act. NPP 2.1(a) provides for an organisation to use or disclose personal information about an individual for a purpose (the secondary purpose) other than the primary purpose of collection provided that:

- the secondary purpose is related to the primary purpose of collection, and if the personal information is sensitive information directly related to the primary purpose for collection; and
- the individual would reasonably expect the organisation to use or disclose the information for the secondary purpose.

It would seem reasonable, on this basis, that a bank's disclosure to its contractors would be reasonably expected by the bank's customers. Alternatively, the bank could rely, in accordance with NPP 2.1(b), on the consent of its customers to the use and disclosure of their personal information in this way. However, there are other relevant obligations under the NPPs for both the bank and its contractors. These are:

- The obligations under either NPP 1.3 or NPP 1.5 to take reasonable steps to make an individual aware of certain information. For the bank this means that it must take reasonable steps to ensure its customers are made aware of the disclosure (NPP 1.3(d)). It could make a general statement to this effect in the NPP 1.3 notice and give more detail in a readily available privacy policy. There are a number of ways that the contractor could meet its obligations under NPP 1.5 to take reasonable steps to make individuals aware of NPP 1.3 matters. The contractor would not have to notify the customers itself if the bank discloses all the details of the contractual arrangements to its customers. Alternatively, if the relevant service contract included very strong and comprehensive privacy provisions placing stringent obligations on the contractor and the bank monitored the contractor's compliance with these, and the NPPs, and took ultimate responsibility for any breaches, the contractor may not need to take any steps under NPP 1.5.
- The obligations under NPP 2.1(b) relating to data quality (any information used must be accurate, complete and up-to-date).
- The obligations under NPP 4 to ensure that the information is held securely.
- The obligations under NPP 5.2 for openness (especially in the requirement to let people know how the information is used).
- The obligations under NPP 6 to provide individuals with access (with some exceptions) to any information it holds about them. The contractor and the bank would need to work out between themselves which organisations in the first instance would take responsibility for giving the customers access.

Effect of the Code of Banking Practice

The Code of Banking Practice does not have a provision corresponding with s 8(1)(a) of the Privacy Act. However, it is considered that it is implicit that a use by an employee of confidential information in the course of their duties would not be regarded as a breach of the Code.

EFFECT OF THE BANKER'S DUTY OF CONFIDENTIALITY ON A BANK'S DESIRE TO PARTICIPATE IN DIRECT MARKETING OR MARKET RESEARCH

Hypothetical

The bank wants to provide a market researcher with a customer's name, telephone number and customer type, possibly also information concerning the customer's accounts from which the market researcher can contact the customer and conduct an interview.[223]

Application of legal principles to the hypothetical

The four relevant heads of law for this issue are the banker's common law duty of confidentiality, the Privacy Act, the Code of Banking Practice and the Australian Direct Marketing Association Code of Practice (ADMA Code). A disclosure by the bank to such third-party agencies separate from the bank is likely to constitute a breach of the bank's obligations under each of the four heads, unless appropriate consents from relevant customers are obtained beforehand.

In the case of the bank's common law duty, such consent might be obtained in an implied form by the bank notifying the customers of its intentions, indicating that the bank proposes to proceed with the disclosure unless the customer indicates their objection. In relation to the Privacy Act, the bank's obligations under the Code of Banking Practice (which are to comply with the Privacy Act and the bank's general duty of confidentiality towards its customers) and the bank's obligations under the ADMA Code, (which substantially replicates those in the NPPs), the bank would need to ensure the disclosure came within one of the exceptions to the prohibition. The exception most likely to apply would be the 'consent' exception in s 18N(1)(ga)(ii).[224] (If the information disclosed did not contain credit information (ie if Pt IIIA did not apply), the 'consent' exception which would apply would be s 13A and 13B NPP 2.1(b)).

However, to overcome the prohibition contained in s 18N(1) of the Privacy Act, the consent of the customer would need to comply with s 18N(1)(ga)(ii). This would involve the bank obtaining from each relevant customer an authorisation in writing in favour of the marketing agency. Logistically, this is a difficult and impractical course unless the consent is obtained at the time the account is opened.

It is not considered that a bank could, under the Privacy Act, make a disclosure to an external marketing agency in reliance on the Privacy Commissioner's view that

---

223 The Direct Marketing Code of Practice of the Australian Direct Marketing Association sets out specific standards of conduct for participants in the direct marketing industry in relation to consumers. Many banks have adopted this Code, which then has the force of a contract between the bank and its 'consumers'.

224 See above.

disclosure to certain service providers is not in fact prohibited 'disclosure', but is instead a permitted 'use' of information.[225] That is because those views by the Privacy Commissioner appear only to apply where the disclosure is for the loan management purposes of the credit provider.

A bank may be restricted by the Privacy Act in its own use of some credit restrictive information for marketing purposes (ie even if it does not disclose the relevant information to an external marketing agency). We refer here to the use of a 'credit report' for such purposes.[226]

The Privacy Commissioner, in the Credit Reporting Advice Summaries on the subject of marketing, acknowledges that a credit provider sometimes seeks to use credit reports relating to individuals for the purposes of soliciting further business from the individual concerned.

He also acknowledges that s 18L of the Privacy Act, listing the circumstances under which the credit provider may use the information derived from a credit report obtained from a credit reporting agency, does not include any provision enabling use of such information for the purposes of soliciting further business. For this reason, the Privacy Commissioner recommends that credit providers have procedures in place to ensure the separation of consumer credit report information from other information held on the credit provider's files in order to prevent unlawful uses of the consumer credit report information. In the event of a complaint, the Commissioner would expect the credit provider to be able to identify whether information which it held about an individual was derived from a consumer credit report or from other sources.

If, however, the credit provider does not use the information contained in or derived from a credit report issued by a credit reporting agency in the course of soliciting business from individuals, then s 18L limitations on use would arguably not apply.

Sections 13A and NPPs 2.1(a) and 2.1(b) would apply to the disclosure of the customers' personal information. The disclosure would amount to an interference with the privacy of an individual unless the marketing purpose of the information is directly related to the primary purpose for which it was collected, and the individual would reasonably expect the organisation to use or disclose the information for that 'secondary purpose' (NPP 2.1(a)) or the individual has consented to its disclosure for that purpose (NPP 2.1(b)). Parallel provisions and restrictions are found in Pt E, clauses 1 and 2 of the ADMA Code. NPP 2.1(c) exceptions would not apply to the facts, because they apply only to the use of personal information, not to its disclosure.

The use of a subsidiary to conduct market research

This variation raises for consideration an exception contained in s 18N(1)(d) of the Privacy Act, which applies where the report or information is disclosed by an

---

225 See above.
226 As mentioned above, a 'credit report' is defined in s 6(1) of the Privacy Act to mean, in effect, a report on consumer creditworthiness from a credit reporting agency.

incorporated credit provider to another corporation that is related to the credit provider.

However, the application of that exception is qualified by s 18Q which, by reference to s 18L, places limits on the use of personal information obtained by a related corporation from a credit provider. Section 18L requires a credit provider to use a credit report (as mentioned above, a report issued by a credit reporting agency) only for assessing credit applications, unless one of the specified exceptions applies. None of the exceptions appears to be relevant to direct marketing. If, accordingly, any of the information given to the subsidiary includes a credit report, then the subsidiary could not use that information for the purposes proposed. If the s 18N(1)(d) exception is to be relied on, it would be very important that the information provided to the subsidiary did not include a credit report, or any information derived from such a report.

There is also an argument that the effect of s 18Q(1)(a) is that a corporation in the position of the subsidiary may use a credit report disclosed to it under s 18N(1)(d) in the circumstances permitted by s 18L, but may not make any use whatsoever of any other information disclosed to it under s 18N(1)(d).

However, in the present writers' view, all s 18Q(1)(a) does is restrict the use of the sensitive information contained in a credit report (subject to s 18L). It does not restrict the use of any other information which might be received from a related corporation.

We conclude that s 18Q(1)(a) would not restrict the use of information disclosed under the 18N(1)(d) exemption for disclosures between related corporations, except to the extent that it contains information which is a credit report for the purposes of the Privacy Act.

Provided the information did not contain a credit report, we could also get there another way, under the provisions of NPP 2.1(a) (if the customer would reasonably expect the use and disclosure of their information in relation to the primary purpose for which it was collected), or NPP 2.1(b) (with the customer's consent). Once it has the information, the subsidiary can then rely on NPP 2.1(c) to permit its use of the information (which is clearly not sensitive information) for the secondary purpose of direct marketing) if:

- it is impracticable for the credit provider to seek the customer's consent before the disclosure;
- the credit provider will not charge the customer for giving effect to their request not to receive marketing communications;
- the customer has not made a request to the credit provider not to receive direct marketing communications;
- in each direct marketing communication with the customer, the credit provider draws to the customer's attention; or prominently displays a notice, that he may express a wish not to receive a direct marketing communication; and
- each *written* direct marketing communication by the credit provider with the customer (up to and including the communications that involves the use) sets out the credit provider's business address and telephone number and, if the communication with the individual is made by fax, telex or other electronic means, a number or address at which the credit provider can be contacted electronically.

Secondment of market research employees to the bank

Is it possible to second employees of a market research agency to a bank to overcome the legal obstacles in relation to the banker's duty of confidentiality?

Provided the employees are truly employees of the bank, there would be no disclosure of information beyond the bank and the contact would be between a representative of the bank and the customers. Hence, the bank's obligations under common law and the Code of Banking Practice to maintain confidentiality would not appear to be breached.

As far as the Privacy Act is concerned, s 8(1)(a) avoids the breach of s 18N(1) where the disclosure is to an employee of the credit provider. This provision makes clear that disclosures to employees of a credit provider are to be treated as disclosures to the credit provider. However, considerations in relation to any employee should be borne in mind.[227]

Consequences of a breach

As to the consequences of a breach of any obligations, a breach of common law duty will give rise to a right in a relevant customer to seek damages for breach of duty or an injunction to prevent any further breach, or both. The fallout upon the bank in terms of damaging customer relations would be a more serious consideration. Breaches of the Code of Banking Practice are a breach of contract and therefore remedies which are usually attracted by a breach of contract are available. The penalties for a breach of the Privacy Act are serious and include under s 18N(2) that a credit provider that knowingly or recklessly contravenes sub-s (1) is guilty of an offence punishable by a fine not exceeding $150,000.

FURTHER DUTIES OF CONFIDENCE IN AUSTRALIA

It is well established that the banker's duty of confidence principally arises out of the contractual relationship with the customer. There is also a duty of confidentiality that arises in equity and the possibility of a fiduciary relationship. Further, there may also be an express term in the contract between a banker and a corporate customer in relation to confidentiality.

Equitable duty of confidence

The equitable duty of confidence was considered and recognised by the High Court in *Commonwealth v John Fairfax & Sons Ltd*.[228] The duty consists of two elements:[229] the information is of its nature confidential, and it is imparted in circumstances

---

227 Factors such as payroll tax and worker's compensation are two of the more important considerations to bear in mind.
228 (1980) 147 CLR 39. The equitable duty of confidence has been discussed by the High Court in *Australian Broadcasting Corpn v Lenah Game Meats Pty Ltd* (2001) 185 ALR 1.
229 There is some doubt over whether there is a third element which is an unauthorised use which causes detriment to the claimant. See discussion in Meagher, Gummow and Lehane *Equity Doctrines and Remedies* (3rd edn) para 4109.

where the recipient could reasonably expect to have realised that it was under an obligation to keep the information confidential.[230] The test to apply was discussed in *Castrol Australia Pty Ltd v Emtech Associates Pty Ltd*.[231] In the context of the bank-customer relationship the test may apply as follows: if a bank received information from a customer in the course of the bank-customer relationship and the bank knew or ought to have known that it was receiving the information in confidence, and a reasonable banker would consider that that information should only be used for the purpose for which it was supplied, the bank would be unable to use the information for an unrelated purpose. Therefore, the equitable duty of confidence applies to use of confidential information as well as disclosure. An equitable duty of confidence can exist concurrently with a contractual obligation.[232]

Concurrency of contractual rights and equitable principles

The concurrency of contractual rights and the underlying equitable principles based on breach of confidence give more substance to the duty.[233] This allows it to withstand legislative attempts to narrow the duty. It is also relevant where a court has resisted a foreign court's attempts to require disclosure on the basis that the protection under local law of the duty of confidence has been seen in the public interest, and not merely as the protection of a private right.

The further importance of the concurrency of the equitable duty is that it fills the position prior to a contract forming between a bank and a prospective customer, and, as expressed by Walter and Erlich, continues 'hovering' over the contractual obligation throughout the life of the contract and continues to exist after the life of the contract.[234]

Fiduciary relationship

Further substance is added to the bank-customer relationship by the possibility of a fiduciary duty being owed where the bank gives financial advice, for example, when the bank takes on the role of investment adviser or provides a service where the customer is relying upon the bank's advice.[235]

Nature of fiduciary relationship[236]

In *Hospital Products Ltd v United States Surgical Corpn*,[237] Mason J said:

230 See Meagher, Gummow and Lehane, n 229 above, para 4109 and ch 41 in general on confidential information.
231 (1980) 33 ALR 31.
232 *Stephens Travel Service International Pty Ltd, Receivers and Managers Appointed v Qantas Airways Ltd* (1988) 13 NSWLR 331; and *A-G v Guardian Newspapers Ltd (No 2)* [1988] WLR 776.
233 See Francis Neate and Roger McCormick Bank Confidentiality (1st edn, 1990).
234 Walter and Erlich, n 90 above.
235 *Commonwealth Bank of Australia v Smith* (1991) 42 FCR 390; *Hospital Products Ltd v United States Surgical Corpn* (1984) 156 CLR 41.
236 On fiduciary relationship in a commercial matrix see Lehane 'Fiduciaries in a commercial context' in Finn (ed) *Essays in Equity* (1985).
237 (1984) 156 CLR 41.

'The accepted fiduciary relationships are sometimes referred to as relationships of trust and confidence or confidential relations ... The critical feature of these relationships is that the fiduciary undertakes or agrees to act for or on behalf of or in the interests of another person in the exercise of a power or discretion which will affect the interests of that other person in a legal or practical sense. The relationship between the parties is therefore one which gives the fiduciary a special opportunity to exercise the power or discretion to the detriment of that other person who is accordingly vulnerable to abuse by the fiduciary of his position.'[238]

The nature of a fiduciary duty must be viewed in the context of the terms of any contract:

'That contractual and fiduciary relationships may co-exist between the same parties has never been doubted. Indeed, the existence of a basic contractual relationship has in many situations provided a foundation for the erection of a fiduciary relationship. In these situations, it is the contractual foundation which is all-important because it is the contract that regulates the basic rights and liabilities of the parties. The fiduciary relationship, if it is to exist at all, must accommodate itself to the terms of the contract so that it is consistent with, and conforms to, them. The fiduciary relationship cannot be superimposed upon the contract in such a way as to alter the operation which the contract was intended to have according to its true construction.'[239]

The possibility of a fiduciary relationship existing between a banker and a customer will depend to a large extent on the character of the customer. As Gibbs CJ, as he then was, said in *Hospital Products Ltd v United States Surgical Corpn*:

'... the fact that the arrangement between the parties was of a purely commercial kind and that they had dealt at arm's length and on an equal footing has consistently been regarded by this court as important, if not decisive, in indicating that no fiduciary duty arose ...'[240]

Mason J, as he then was, said in his judgment:

'True it is that a promise or a contractual term may be so precise in its regulation of what a party can do that there is no relevant area of discretion remaining and therefore no scope for the creation of fiduciary duty ...'[241]

In the joint judgment of Woodward, Northrop and Sheppard JJ in the Federal Court in *Paul Dainty Corpn Pty Ltd v National Tennis Centre Trust*,[242] in reliance on the High Court's decision in *Hospital Products Ltd v United States Surgical Corpn*, their Honours in *Paul Dainty* considered that the authorities made it clear that equity

---

238 (1984) 156 CLR 41 at 96–97. See also the wider discussion of fiduciary relationships applying *Hospital Products Ltd* (and other decisions) in *Distronics Ltd v Edmunds* [2002] VSC 454.
239 (1984) 156 CLR 41 at 95. See the unreported decision of Sundberg J in *Drambo Pty Ltd v Westpac Banking Corpn Ltd* (1 August 1996, matter number OG92/91), in particular, his comments at 132 on the judicial consideration of the above statement.
240 (1984) 156 CLR 41 at 70.
241 *Hospital Products Ltd v United States Surgical Corpn* (1984) 156 CLR 41 at 98.
242 (1990) 22 FCR 495.

will not impose fiduciary obligations on parties who have entered into ordinary and arm's length commercial relationships, which fully prescribe the respective powers and duties of the parties. This is particularly so when the parties involved are substantial corporations having equal bargaining power, and they agree to limit the scope of the contract.[243]

Remedies for breach of fiduciary obligations

The scope for different fiduciary relationships calls for a wide variety of remedies. A fiduciary may of course be restrained by injunction from breaching his fiduciary duty. A fiduciary who profits from a breach of duty is liable to account for that profit. Where the profit can be traced into identifiable property in the hands of the defaulting fiduciary, proprietary remedies may be appropriate. Where the breach of duty by a fiduciary causes loss to his principal, it is well established that compensation is available in the exclusive jurisdiction of equity to make good the loss. Finally, a fiduciary relationship may co-exist with contract, and a fiduciary may owe his principal duties, breach of which sounds in damages in tort, or gives rise to other common law remedies.[244]

CONTRACTING OUT OF DUTIES OF CONFIDENCE

If a financial institution were to seek to contract out of its duties of confidence, or to exercise a broad contractual discretion to avoid them, its conduct may, depending on the character of the relevant transaction, be held to be unconscionable conduct under ss 12CA, 12CB and 12CC of the ASIC Act or s 51AC of the TPA.

Section 12AC of the ASIC Act prohibits a person in trade or commerce from engaging in conduct in relation to financial services if the conduct is unconscionable within the meaning of the unwritten law. (The conduct prohibited by s 12CB of the ASIC Act is excluded from the application of s 12AC.) Section 12CB(1) of the Act prohibits conduct that is, in all the circumstances, unconscionable, in connection with the supply or possible supply of financial services to a person. 'Financial services' is defined by s 12CB(5) for these purposes as 'a reference to financial services of a kind ordinarily acquired for personal, domestic or household use'.

Section 12CC of the ASIC Act prohibits any person (in trade or commerce) from engaging in conduct that is, in all the circumstances, unconscionable:

'. . . in connection with
(a) the supply or possible supply of financial services to another person (other than a listed public company);or
(b) the acquisition or possible acquisition of financial services from a person (other than a listed public company).'

---

243 (1990) 22 FCR 495 at 515–516.
244 See Meagher, Gummow and Lehane, n 229 above, paras 547–554.

Under s 12AC(1) of the ASIC Act, the above provisions extend to:

'. . . the engaging in conduct outside Australia by:

(a) bodies corporate incorporated or carrying on business outside Australia;

(b) Australian citizens; or

(c) persons ordinarily resident in Australia.'

Section 51AC(3) of the TPA mirrors for a corporation's supply or possible supply of goods or services to a person in trade or commerce the same prohibition of unconscionable conduct as s 12CC of the ASIC Act provides for the supply of financial services.

PRIVACY ACT 1988 PROVISIONS FOR SECURITISATION ARRANGEMENTS

Section 11B(4A)–(7) of the Privacy Act make special provision for those persons carrying on a business involved in securitisation arrangements and/or managing loans that are the subject of such arrangements. Section 11B(4B) provides that while that person is performing a task that is reasonably necessary for purchasing or funding a loan (including credit enhancement of a loan) or managing a loan, or processing an application for a loan by means of the arrangement (being a loan that has been provided by, or in respect of which, application has been made to a credit provider) (each a 'securitisation transaction'), for the purposes of the Privacy Act:

'(a) the person is taken to be another credit provider; and is subject to the same obligations under the Privacy Act as any other credit provider; and

(b) the loan is taken to have been provided by, or the application for the loan is taken to have been made to, both the person and the first-mentioned credit provider.'

Section 11B(4C) of the Privacy Act provides that nothing in the Act prevents a s 18N(9) report from being disclosed if the disclosure is reasonably necessary for the Securitisation Transaction; and the disclosure takes place between a person to whom s 11B(4B) applies in relation to the relevant loan and the credit provider or another person to whom that subsection applies in relation to that loan.

For the above purposes, s 11B(4E) provides that the reference to 'managing a loan' does not include a reference to any act relating to the collection of payments that are overdue in respect of any relevant loan.

3 Austria

Michael Kutschera
Thomas Schirmer
Alexander Kramer

BANK'S DUTY OF CONFIDENTIALITY

Introduction

Austrian law expressly recognises and protects a bank's duty of confidentiality (sometimes referred to as 'bank secrecy') with respect to information received by or relating to its customers. This duty is primarily governed by s 38(1) to (4) (scope and exceptions) and s 101 (criminal liability) of the Banking Act (BWG) and supplemented by several provisions of a procedural nature such as the Revenues Penal Code and the Criminal Procedure Code.

Section 38(5) of the BWG, a provision of constitutional law, affords special protection to the provisions of s 38(1) to (4) of the BWG by stipulating that an amendment of these provisions requires – similar to an amendment of a provision of constitutional law – a quorum of at least 50% and a majority of two-thirds of the deputies to the National Counsel (Nationalrat, the more powerful of Austria's two Houses of Parliament).[1]

Since 1 January 1994, the provisions on bank secrecy were partly amended, in particular with regard to money laundering, as Austrian law and banking practice initially permitted the opening of anonymous accounts in certain cases. In order to avoid the abuse of the Austrian banking system for the purpose of money laundering, Austrian banks in 1989 agreed on the wording of a uniform declaration, according to which each bank voluntarily undertook a number of duties to prevent such abuse.[2] These duties were expanded by another declaration on additional duties of diligence in 1992, the compliance with which still was voluntary.

Due to increasing national and international political pressure, as well as the fact that Austria became a full member of the EEA in 1994 and of the EU in 1995, most of the duties contained in the above-mentioned two declarations were implemented

---

1 With regard to the predecessor provision of s 38(5) BWG, s 23a KWG, see the critics by Jabornegg 'Neues zum Bankgeheimnis' (1990) WBl at 30 and 61.
2 For the wording, see the first edition of this book, p 33ff and Economy (1989) at 34 and 36.

into s 39ff of the BWG.[3] Furthermore, money laundering was rendered a criminal offence. By amendment of s 40 of the BWG, with effect from 1 November 2000, the potential to open anonymous accounts was finally abolished: BWG, s 40(1), no 1. This was supplemented by a new s 40(6), according to which no payments may be made on existing savings accounts unless the identity of the holder was registered by the bank. As of 30 June 2002, savings accounts of still unidentified holders need to be particularly labelled by the bank and no payments into and no withdrawals from such accounts are permissible unless the holder has been identified.

As of 1 January 2002, the amount as of which banks are under a duty to register the identity of their customer in connection with cash transactions not within an ongoing business relationship between bank and client was changed from ATS 200,000 to €15,000. As of 31 October 2000, this duty to register also applies to payments into and, as of 30 June 2002, to withdrawals from saving accounts in cases where the amount paid in or withdrawn exceeds €15,000.[4] Since 1 October 1998, the duty to register the identity of a customer has also existed if there is reasonable suspicion that the client is engaged in transactions which serve the purpose of money laundering: BWG, s 40(1), no 3.

THE BANK'S DUTY OF CONFIDENTIALITY

Section 38(1) of the BWG reads:

> 'The credit institutions, their shareholders, organ members, employees, as well as persons otherwise becoming active for the credit institutions, are prohibited from disclosing or exploiting secrets which were entrusted to, or to which access was made available for, them on the basis of the business relationship with clients or on the basis of s 75 (3)[5] hereof exclusively (Bank Secrecy). If, in the conduct of their official activities, organs of public authorities or of the Austrian National Bank, receive information which is subject to the Bank Secrecy, they shall maintain the Bank Secrecy as an official secret from which they may be released only in one of the cases set forth in s 38 (2). The duty of confidentiality applies without limit as to time.'

---

3   See Klippl *Geldwäscherei* (1994) p 56.
4   Following these amendments, the European Commission has abandoned its complaint of 28 July 1998 against the Republic of Austria as to the compatibility of Austrian law with the provisions of Council Directive 91/308/EEC on the prevention of the use of the financial system for the purpose of money laundering.
5   Section 75 of the BWG (like its predecessor provision in the KWG, s 16) provides that credit institutions and finance institutions, as well as contract insurance businesses, have to provide certain data (name and address of the borrower and the amount borrowed) on large borrowings (more than €350,000) to the Austrian National Bank, which collects them and has to pass them on to other credit and finance institutions, to contract insurance businesses and deposit protection facilities (et al) upon request. BWG, s 38(1) to (3) apply also to finance institutions and to contract insurance businesses in respect of BWG, s 75(3): see BWG, s 38(4). BWG, s 38(4) was last amended as per 1 May 1999, extending the application of the provisions on bank secrecy and the exceptions thereto also to guarantee schemes except for the co-operation required by BWG, ss 93 to 93b with other guarantee schemes, to deposit guarantee schemes and to investor compensation schemes.

The provisions contained in BWG, s 38 contain elements of private as well as public administrative law.[6] The expressly stipulated confidentiality obligation on the part of public authorities which gain access to information which is subject to bank secrecy or the supervision of the banks' compliance with the provisions on bank secrecy within the framework of the general supervision of banks certainly constitute elements of public administrative law. On the other hand, BWG, s 38 also defines the scope of a duty of private law which forms part of every contractual relationship between a bank and its customers. Views are split on whether or not the duties imposed by the statutory bank secrecy can be contracted away in whole or in part.[7]

The elements contained in the above s 38(1) of the BWG can be described as follows:

1   BWG, s 1(1) defines as a credit institution (hereafter bank) whoever is authorised to conduct banking transactions (explicitly enumerated and defined in s 1(1) of the BWG) on the basis of the BWG or any other provision of federal law. Views are split on whether the bank secrecy also applies to institutions which conduct banking transactions without authorisation, ie which have not received the necessary banking licence.[8] The Austrian National Bank is not subject to the bank secrecy provisions of the BWG, but to its own provisions. Finance institutions, ie institutions authorised to conduct specific finance transactions as defined in BWG, s 1(2) without qualifying as credit institutions, as well as contract insurance businesses, are principally also not subject to the bank secrecy.[9]

2   It is the prevailing view that the term 'shareholders' as used in s 38 of the BWG means all shareholders of a bank, including shareholders of banks which are publicly traded.[10] 'Organ members' are the holders of offices which are provided for in the applicable corporate law. A trustee in bankruptcy is deemed an organ member of the bank.

'Persons otherwise becoming active for the banks' are physical and other persons which are not integrated into the banks' internal organisation, including their outside counsel, other experts as well as other banks employed for the accomplishment of banking transactions.[11]

6   See Arnold 'Das Bankgeheimnis' ZGV Service 1/1981, p 20; Avancini, Iro and Koziol *Österreichisches Bankvertragsrecht* (1987) vol I, p 103ff; Frotz 'Die Bankauskunft nach österreichischem Recht' in Hadding and Schneider (ed) *Bankgeheimnis und Bankauskunft in der Bundesrepublik Deutschland und in ausländischen Rechtsordnungen* (1986) p 257; Jabornegg, Strasser and Floretta *Das Bankgeheimnis* (1985) p 31ff; Laurer 'Das Bankgeheimnis in der Entwicklung von Lehre und Rechtsprechung' (1986) ÖJZ at 385.

7   See Arnold, n 6 above, p 20; Arnold 'Zum Bankgeheimnis, Anmerkungen zu einer kontroversiell diskutierten Rechtsthematik – zugleich eine Buchbesprechung' (1986) ÖBA 359 at 360; Avancini, Iro and Koziol, n 6 above, vol I, p 104; for a mandatory nature, Jabornegg, Strasser and Floretta, n 6 above, p 34ff.

8   Avancini, Iro and Koziol, n 6 above, vol I, p 106; Jabornegg, Strasser and Floretta, n 6 above, p 55; for banks with concession only, Arnold, n 6 above, p 4; Frotz, n 6 above, p 257.

9   An exception contained in BWG, s 38(4) with regard to the information passed on according to BWG, s 75(3); see n 5 above. In respect of finance institutions, however, the statutory language is not very clear as to the question bank secrecy applies even beyond BWG, s 75(3); for a broader application, see Laurer in Fremuth, Laurer, Linc, Pötzelberger and Strobl *Kommentar zum Bankwesengesetz* (1999) p 476; compare with Klippl, n 3 above, p 31.

10   Arnold, n 6 above, p 5; Avancini, Iro and Koziol, n 6 above, vol I, p 108; Jabornegg, Strasser and Floretta, n 6 above, p 56ff; Kastner 'Kreditwesengesetz und Gesellschaftsrecht' (1980) JBl 62 at 70.

11   Avancini, Iro and Koziol, n 6 above, vol I, p 110ff; Jabornegg, Strasser and Floretta, n 6 above, p 65ff.

Physical persons may be simultaneously shareholders, organ members, employees of, or persons otherwise becoming active for, the same bank.

3 'Secrets' are facts, proceedings and conditions of factual or legal nature which are known to a limited group of persons only and to which other interested persons cannot gain access at all or can gain access with difficulty only. Further, an objective interest to keep the facts in question secret is required, but regularly presumed on the part of the clients.[12]

4 'Clients' are persons that deal with the banks in the context of banking transactions. It is not necessary that such transactions actually close.[13] Since bank secrecy is unlimited in time, it continues to exist after termination of the contractual relationship, and even after the death (or liquidation) of the client. If a bank gains access to a secret relating to a client in a manner other than through the business relationship, there is no duty of confidentiality upon the bank pursuant to bank secrecy.[14] Non-clients, and therefore not directly entitled to bank secrecy, are third parties with respect to which the banks receive confidential information from clients. The banks are nevertheless obliged towards their clients not to disclose secrets relating to third parties which they learn from clients.[15]

5 'Disclosing' a bank secret generally means making it known (or allowing it to become known by refraining from taking reasonable action to prevent disclosure) to somebody who did not know it before. There is quite a dispute about the scope of those persons to whom bank secrets may be disclosed on the ground that such persons would also be subject to bank secrecy with respect to the relevant information (for example, other bank employees etc). One view holds that a bank secret may only be disclosed to those others within the same organisation (bank) with reasonable grounds for learning about the secret in question, such grounds depending on the relevant internal organisation.[16] The opposite view advocates that bank secrets may be freely passed on within the same organisation (bank) provided only that the recipients of the information themselves are strictly bound by bank secrecy as well.[17] Another controversial question is whether bank secrecy shall prevail over the (bank's) supervisory board's or the shareholders' right to information.[18]

---

12 Arnold, n 6 above, p 8; Burgstaller 'Der strafrechtliche Schutz wirtschaltlicher Geheimnisse' in Ruppe (Hrsg) *Geheimnisschutz im Wirtschaftsleben* (1980) p 13; Frotz, n 6 above, p 237; Jabornegg, Strasser and Floretta, n 6 above, p 37; the required interest might become very weak after decades of time – see Laurer, n 9 above, p 458.

13 Laurer, n 9 above, p 458.

14 Exception: BWG, s 75(3), see n 5 above.

15 Arnold, n 6 above, p 8; Avancini, Iro and Koziol, n 6 above, vol I, p 114ff; Haushofer, Schinnerer and Ulrich *Die österreichischen Kreditwesengesetze* (1980) s 23/16; Jabornegg, Strasser and Floretta, n 6 above, p 40ff; Laurer, n 9 above, p 457.

16 Avancini, Iro and Koziol, n 6 above, vol I, p 125; Jabornegg, Strasser and Floretta, n 6 above, p 137ff; Bzoch and Bittner *Bankwesengesetz 1993* (1995) s 38-5, by referring to a decision of the Austrian Supreme Court (OGH) in 1991 (OGH 4 Ob 114/91) according to which bank secrecy was violated since secrets were disclosed to other bank employees within the same bank who themselves were obliged by the bank's duty of confidentiality, even though they had no dealings with the client's affairs. Note, however, that the decisive ground for the holding of this decision was the abuse of information for reasons of unfair competition.

17 Laurer, n 6 above, at 389 and n 9 above, p 456.

18 See Greiter 'Das Auskunftsrecht des Aktionärs und des Partizipanten gemäß § 112 AktG' (1989) ÖJZ 524 at 526 and 528.

6   'Exploiting' a bank secret is generally interpreted as an economic exploitation of a bank secret to the detriment of the bank's client in question.[19] One of the leading commentaries holds that a bank is entitled to use clients' secrets for its own business dispositions, provided such use does not adversely affect the clients in question, further for its own dispositions towards the clients even if that affected them adversely and, finally, for its usual counselling of other clients, provided that the secret is thereby not indirectly disclosed or that the clients in question are not otherwise adversely affected.[20]

7   Bank secrets disclosed to courts or other public authorities become official secrets[21] and generally must not be disclosed to other courts or public authorities or exploited by the latter as a basis for the initiation of proceedings of any kind. To this extent the (transformed) bank secrecy prevails over the general duty of public authorities to mutual assistance.[22] Furthermore, official secrecy is lifted once a trial has commenced.[23]

CUSTOMER'S REMEDIES FOR BREACH OF CONFIDENCE

Injunction

If a breach of bank secrecy is threatened, whether for the first time or continuing, the client will be entitled to injunctive relief and, in rare cases, also to removal (Beseitigung) of the breach, for example, by causing a bank to reclaim passed on information which still enjoys the character of a secret. For a client's claim to an injunction or to removal no fault is required on the part of the person against whom such remedy is sought.[24]

Damages

A client who suffers damages through a violation of bank secrecy is entitled to reimbursement in accordance with the general principles of tort law. The client will generally be entitled to reimbursement of pecuniary damages which have been caused by such violation through the fault of a tortfeasor. If the party in breach is a bank (or one of those for whom a bank is liable), pecuniary damages will include lost

---

19   Avancini, Iro and Koziol, n 6 above, vol I, p 125ff; Haushofer, Schinnerer and Ulrich, n 15 above, s 23/7; Jabornegg, Strasser and Floretta, n 6 above, p 86; Schinnerer 'Zur Problematik einer gesetzlichen Regelung des börslichen Insider-Geschäftes in Österreich' (1985) ÖBA at 271.

20   Avancini, Iro and Koziol, n 6 above, vol I, p 126.

21   A release from the duty of non-disclosure of official secrets shall be limited to the grounds of BWG, s 1(2); according to Laurer, n 9 above, p 458 this shall also be applied to the information duties under the Act on Information Duties (against, however, the Austrian Administrative Court (VwGH) 89/17/0028 (1992) ÖBA at 89).

22   Avancini, Iro and Koziol, n 6 above, vol I, p 127; Jabornegg, Strasser and Floretta, n 6 above, pp 69ff, 124ff.

23   Avancini, Iro and Koziol, n 6 above, vol I, p 127; Liebscher 'Das Bankgeheimnis im In- und Ausland' (1984) ÖJZ 253 at 255.

24   Avancini, Iro and Koziol, n 6 above, vol I, p 163ff; Jabornegg, Strasser and Floretta, n 6 above, p 160ff.

profit; if the tortfeasor is one of the other persons subject to bank secrecy, this will often but not always be the case.[25]

It is the prevailing view that the right to damages may be contracted away in respect of a tortfeasor's lower levels of fault (at least for slight negligence) and that provisions to that effect contained in the bank's general conditions are valid if such conditions have become a part of the contractual relationship between the bank and the client.[26] A bank will be liable for all its agents and other personnel, whether employed or not, which inflict damage upon clients through a (faulty) breach of bank secrecy. On the other hand, such agents and other personnel will also be protected by the above disclaimer as to lower degrees of negligence.[27]

If breaches of bank secrecy cause damage to third parties (other clients or non-clients), the Austrian Supreme Court (OGH) held in a recent decision that third parties (in this case another client) are not entitled to damages towards the bank in cases where it breaches bank secrecy towards another client.[28]

Termination of business relationship

A client who is the victim of a violation of bank secrecy by a bank or a tortfeasor whose actions are attributed to such bank will be entitled to terminate the contractual relationship with the bank with immediate effect.[29]

Criminal punishment

A physical person who discloses or exploits facts which are subject to bank secrecy with the malicious intent to enrich himself or a third party or to affect another adversely is subject to criminal punishment (imprisonment for up to one year or fines), but shall only be prosecuted upon application of the person whose interest in confidentiality was impaired: BWG, s 101. Public officials in breach of bank secrecy may be subject to (even more serious) criminal punishment for the offence constituted by a breach of the official secret.

Action by bank regulatory authorities

The bank regulatory authority, the Financial Market Authority (Finanzmarktaufsichtsbehhörde, FMA)[30] has to intervene in cases of breaches of the

---

25   Arnold, n 6 above, p 20; Avancini, Iro and Koziol, n 6 above, vol I, p 164ff; Jabornegg, Strasser and Floretta, n 6 above, p 162ff.
26   Avancini, Iro and Koziol, n 6 above, vol I, p 165ff; Frotz, n 6 above, p 267ff; compare with Jabornegg, Strasser and Floretta, n 6 above, p 163.
27   Avancini, Iro and Koziol, n 6 above, vol I, p 165ff.
28   OGH 27.2.2002 (2002) ecolex at 194.
29   Avancini, Iro and Koziol, n 6 above, vol I, p 168; Jabornegg, Strasser and Floretta, n 6 above, p 164.
30   With effect as of 1 April 2002, the FMA was established as new supervisory authority for banks, securities and capital markets, insurance companies and pension funds.

bank secrecy attributable to a bank: BWG, s 70(4). The most severe consequence is the withdrawal of the bank's banking licence.[31]

EXCEPTIONS TO THE GENERAL DUTY OF NON-DISCLOSURE

Section 38(2) of the BWG provides for nine exceptions to bank secrecy. It is the general consensus that this list is not exhaustive.[32] The following text describes those exceptions set forth in BWG, s 38(2) as well as those which are based on other provisions or principles of law.

Customer's consent

There is no bank secrecy if the client 'expressly consents in writing' to the disclosure or exploitation of a secret: BWG, s 38(2), no 5. A valid consent must be clearly formulated in writing and signed by the client. If a secret relates to non-clients, the waiver has nevertheless to be issued by the client who passed the secret on to the bank. It is not clear how precisely the waived secrets have to be defined in the declaration of consent. The OGH has held that a reasonably defined waiver, by signing the application form for the opening of a bank account which contains a corresponding clause, was valid.[33] A general waiver of bank secrecy without limit as to time (in particular, the future) or scope could be qualified as invalid.[34] The general conditions currently used by banks do not provide for such a sweeping waiver of bank secrecy. It is not clear whether a waiver of bank secrecy can be revoked at any time.[35]

Litigation between bank and client

There is no bank secrecy if the disclosure is 'necessary for the resolution of legal issues arising out of the relationship between banks and clients' (BWG, s 38(2), no 7). This exception relates to litigation between the bank and its client only.

---

31 Avancini, Iro and Koziol, n 6 above, vol I, p 170ff; Jabornegg, Strasser and Floretta, n 6 above, p 165ff.
32 Arnold, n 6 above, pp 12, 18ff; Avancini, Iro and Koziol, n 6 above, vol I, p 129; Jabornegg, Strasser and Floretta, n 6 above, p 93; restrictively, Laurer, n 9 above, p 454, according to whom additional exceptions (ie information duties, eg under the General Civil Code (ABGB) or the Act on Foreign Exchange Control (DevG)) could prevail over bank secrecy only if enacted as a provision of constitutional law or as an exception based upon a provision of judicial criminal law.
33 OGH 29.1.1997 (1997) ecolex at 498; this decision was criticised by Wilhelm 'Formularmäßige Entbindung vom Bankgeheimnis' (1997) ecolex at 490.
34 Laurer, n 9 above, p 464; Arnold, n 6 above, p 17; Avancini, Iro and Koziol, n 6 above, vol I, p 131ff; Frotz, n 6 above, p 244ff; Jabornegg, Strasser and Floretta, n 6 above, p 99ff.
35 Against a revocation at any time: Laurer 'Bankgeheimnis' 386 FN 19; and Laurer, n 9 above, p 465. For a revocation at any time: Arnold, n 6 above, p 17; Avancini, Iro and Koziol, n 6 above, vol I, p 139; Frotz, n 6 above, p 245; Jabornegg, Strasser and Floretta, n 6 above, p 103.

General information on customer's economic situation

There is no bank secrecy for 'generally phrased information on the economic situation of a business', as usually given by banks, unless the former expressly objects thereto (BWG, s 38(2), no 6); this exception only applies to business clients as opposed to private customers. The bank will have to balance the interests of the clients and those of the recipients of the bank's information. It may only give a general picture of their clients' state of affairs without directly or indirectly disclosing exact data.

Balancing of interest

This exception is not set out in statutory law. It has been argued in the literature that probably no bank secrecy exists if, upon a balancing of the client's interest in confidentiality with conflicting interests of the bank or third parties, the bank's or such third parties' interests appear to be significantly overriding.[36] After all, the expressly codified exceptions to bank secrecy are provisions on special conflict of interest situations in which the law stipulates that other interests prevail over bank secrecy. Therefore, the balancing of interests in cases not statutorily provided for must result in a clear preponderance of those interests which conflict with bank secrecy. Accordingly, the OGH, in confirming this view, held in one decision that in principle a bank is not bound to bank secrecy if an overriding interest in the disclosure exists.[37]

Typical cases are those where the bank or its employees would incur (criminal) punishment by non-disclosure of bank secrets, or civil litigation in cases with third parties who themselves are under the bank's duty of confidentiality.

Payment of another's debt, surety

There is probably no bank secrecy if the bank is asked by a surety or a person who actually has posted or is contemplating posting security for an obligation by a bank's client towards such bank for information on such debtor's financial state.[38]

The OGH held in various decisions that bank secrecy had to be lifted for third parties who have paid a client's debt to the bank, for which debt such third parties were personally liable or have posted other security. Such third parties are assignees of the (bank) creditor's rights by operation of law. Such third parties are further entitled, inter alia, to delivery of all other security posted for the debt in question and of such other documents or information (namely the underlying credit agreements, other suretyship agreements, drafts and the correspondence executed by the other sureties

---

36 See Arnold, n 6 above, p 19; Avancini 'Der Auskunftsanspruch des Bürgen gegenüber dem Gläubiger – Zugleich ein Beitrag zum Bankgeheimnis' (1985) JBl 193 at 204ff; Avancini, Iro and Koziol, n 6 above, vol I, p 161ff; Frotz, n 6 above, p 254ff; Jabornegg, Strasser and Floretta, n 6 above, p 142ff; Steiner 'Zur Aufklärungspflicht der Kreditunternehmung bei Wechseldiskontgeschäften' (1983) JBl 189.
37 OGH 29.1.1997 (1997) ecolex at 491.
38 See Avancini, n 36 above, at 193ff; Steiner, n 36 above, at 189ff; against: Laurer, n 9 above, p 454.

or the debtor and relating to the debtor's credit account, but not the internal memoranda and correspondence signed by the bank) as are necessary for the payers to pursue their right of recourse against the debtor and against others who have posted security for such debt.[39] The OGH also expanded this exception to the pledgee's right of information about the pledgor's financial state in order to evaluate whether or not to claim for an additional pledge by the pledgor.[40]

Criminal proceedings

There is no bank secrecy in Austrian penal courts in connection with initiated judicial criminal proceedings nor to Austrian fiscal penal authorities (Finanzstrafbehörden) in connection with initiated penal proceedings because of intentional fiscal offences (vorsätzliche Finanzvergehen) except for fiscal irregularities (ie fiscal offences of a lesser degree, Finanzordnungswidrigkeiten). The above provision, which is contained in BWG, s 38(2), no 1, forms the core of the exceptions to bank secrecy by virtue of compulsion of law.

Criminal proceedings are proceedings with respect to such crimes or offences (including certain crimes and offences of a fiscal nature) as shall be conducted by the regular court system. Fiscal offences are certain offences provided for in the Revenues Penal Act (for example, tax fraud and smuggling) and other fiscal offences defined as such in other statutes. Fiscal offences are only offences against the federal tax system; they may be subject to judicial criminal punishment or to administrative (fiscal) penal punishment. Fiscal penal authorities are administrative agencies.

Whether or not courts or fiscal penal authorities may request the disclosure of bank secrets depends mainly on whether or not a relevant proceeding is deemed 'initiated' and whether or not there is (sufficient) 'connection' between the proceeding and the requested disclosure. A resolution of these issues must take the generally advocated principle into consideration that the exception to bank secrecy in connection with criminal and certain administrative penal proceedings shall not enable the prosecution to gather information for potential crimes or offences ('fishing expeditions'), but only to corroborate (or dispel) well-founded and reasonably defined suspicions of such crimes or offences.[41]

'Initiated' criminal proceedings

Under Austrian law, a criminal proceeding is normally conducted in three stages. The initial stage is the preliminary inquiry (Vorerhebung) conducted under the guidance of the public prosecution, which in turn employs police or courts for the actual inquiry. The next phase is the preliminary investigation (Voruntersuchung) in which a judge is in charge. This is followed by the trial as the last stage. A preliminary

---

39   OGH 2.2.1984 (1984) SZ 57/29; OGH 29.4.1986 (1986) JBl at 511; Avancini, Iro and Koziol, n 6 above, vol I, p 157; Frotz, n 6 above, p 252ff; Jabornegg, Strasser and Floretta, n 6 above, p 151ff.
40   OGH 7.11.1991 (1992) ÖBA at 654, which is, however, disputed by two major commentators (Jabornegg (1997) ÖBA at 655ff; Laurer, n 9 above, p 454).
41   Arnold 'Entscheidungsanmerkung' (1986) AnwBl at 417; Avancini, Iro and Koziol, n 6 above, vol I, p 141; see also Jabornegg, Strasser and Floretta, n 6 above, p 110ff.

investigation can be directed against one or more identified persons only, whereas a preliminary inquiry may also be directed against unknown perpetrators.

Whether a criminal proceeding should be deemed initiated upon the commencement of preliminary inquiries or only upon the opening of a formal preliminary investigation was resolved by a decision of the OGH,[42] which held that the taking of any measures against known or unknown perpetrators in the course of criminal proceedings, including the stage of preliminary inquiries, constituted the initiation of criminal proceedings.

'Initiated' fiscal penal proceedings

Fiscal penal proceedings are formally initiated by a decree pursuant to the Revenues Penal Code (FinStrG), ss 82, 83, subject to appeal. The suspect must receive notice of such initiation. A fiscal penal proceeding is to be initiated if there is suspicion of a fiscal offence unless the offence can probably not be proven, suspected facts do not constitute a fiscal offence or the suspect has not committed the offence or cannot be prosecuted or punished for it.

Sufficient 'connection'

There is a sufficient connection between proceedings and bank secrets if there is an objectively ascertainable relevance for the requested information to the proceedings in question. This is a question of degree and there are only a few court decisions on the point.[43] It is, however, the prevailing view that such relevance may also exist for the bank secrets of one party in relation to a crime or fiscal offence of a third party in which the former did not participate.[44]

Search and seizure

In the context of fiscal penal proceedings, s 89(4) of the FinStrG provides that such evidence which is in the custody of banks and which concerns secrets within the meaning of the BWG, s 38(1) may only be seized if it is 'directly connected' with the intentional fiscal offence(s) (not just fiscal irregularities) for which bank secrecy is (already) lifted pursuant to the BWG, s 38(2), no 1.

This limitation applies not only for the benefit of the party whose suspected fiscal offence formed the basis of the initial search order, but also for the benefit of third parties. The direct connection between the originally suspected fiscal offence and one on the part of such third party which comes into the open in the course of a search and seizure is probably only present if it turns out that the third party is a direct accessory to the original suspect's fiscal offence. A closely related but formally separate fiscal offence, a crime or other contravention of law certainly, will probably not suffice.[45]

---

42   OGH 18.1.1989 (1989) JBl at 454; see also Weber 'Das Bankgeheimnis bei eingeleiteten gerichtlichen Strafverfahren' (1990) RdW 435.
43   See eg OGH 11 Os 171/86; VWGH 15.4.1997, 93/14/0080.
44   Avancini, Iro and Koziol, n 6 above, vol I, pp 141, 144; Jabornegg, Strasser and Floretta, n 6 above, p 108ff; Liebscher, n 23 above, at 254. Against a lifting of bank secrecy: Arnold, n 6 above, p 13.
45   Arnold 'Die Finanzstrafgesetznovelle 1985' (1986) ZGV at 7; Avancini, Iro and Koziol, n 6 above, vol I, p 146.

If the bank formally alleges that information was seized in violation of bank secrecy, such information must be sealed and a formal decision on the legality of the seizure must be issued, which is subject to appeal.

Finally, s 98(4) of the FinStrG provides that evidence seized in violation of the above must not be used for the rendering of the decision (punishment order) to the detriment of the accused or of an accessory. This provision is interpreted to mean (in addition) that the fiscal authorities must not use such evidence in an initiated proceeding and no court or other public authority may use it to commence proceedings whatsoever against those involved.[46]

There is probably one exception to the above: the fiscal authorities which receive such privileged information may use it for an assessment (or reassessment) of the original suspect's taxes.[47]

The corollary to s 89(4) of the FinStrG is s 145a of the Criminal Procedure Code (StPO). Under this provision banks (and persons acting for banks) are under a duty to hand over all documents concerning the type and scope of the business relationship with the client as well as business transactions and other business operations related thereto to the authorities if, based upon specific facts, it must be assumed that the business relationship of a client with a bank is connected to the rendering of a criminal act (crimes or offences). Such context must also be assumed if the business relationship is used for the transfer of an economic benefit which was derived from or received for a criminal act or which is under the disposition of a criminal organisation. Under the same prerequisites, persons acting for banks are under a duty to testify as witnesses on such business operations. The existence of this duty of a bank (or persons acting for a bank) must be ascertained by way of a decision of the judge presiding over the preliminary investigation, which needs to contain the facts giving rise to the connection between the business relationship and the subject matter of the preliminary investigation as well as a description of the documents to be handed over by the bank. Section 145(2) of the StPO affords the bank the right to request a sealing of the seized documents. In such a case, a panel of three judges resolves on whether the documents may be searched or whether they must be returned to the bank. Their ruling cannot be appealed. In case of a seizure of objects beyond the limitations set by s 145a of the StPO, a criminal judgment rendered on the basis of such evidence could be appealed as void.

Bank secrecy and foreign legal proceedings

Letters rogatory

In the absence of applicable treaties, legal assistance to foreign authorities is governed by the Act on Extradition and Legal Assistance in Matters of Criminal Law (ARHG). Pursuant to the ARHG, s 50, legal assistance may be granted by or through Austrian

---

46   Arnold, n 45 above, at 9; Avancini 'Neueste gesetzliche Regelungen zum Bankgeheimnis'(1986) RdW at 299; Avancini, Iro and Koziol, n 6 above, vol I, p 146.
47   Avancini, n 46 above, at 299; Avancini, Iro and Koziol, n 6 above, vol I, p 147.

courts to foreign courts, foreign public prosecutors and foreign prison authorities, provided there is reciprocity. Legal assistance shall not be granted if, inter alia:

1 the offence on which the request for legal assistance is based is:
  (a) not subject to judicial criminal punishment under Austrian law,
  (b) of a political nature,
  (c) of a military nature, or
  (d) a violation of revenues, monopolies, or customs laws, or a breach of exchange control, rationing, import or export control laws;
2 the request is made by a country the criminal procedure and enforcement system of which does not meet certain human rights standards;
3 the special requirements under Austrian law for certain measures (in particular, seizure and opening of mail or wire-tapping) are not met;
4 the legal assistance would lead to a breach of Austrian law providing for duties of confidentiality which shall be maintained in regard to penal courts as well; or
5 the compliance with the request for legal assistance would be contrary to the public policy or other essential interests of the Republic of Austria.

It is the prevailing view[48] that legal assistance shall be granted on the basis of the ARHG if its conditions are met *and* the special requirements and limits under which bank secrecy may be lifted in purely domestic proceedings are fulfilled.

Austria is also a party to the European Convention on Mutual Assistance in Criminal Matters of 20 April 1959 (the European Mutual Assistance Convention). The main requirements for and exceptions to Austria's duty to render legal assistance under it are:

1 Legal assistance will only be granted for offences which are subject to judicial criminal punishment in the requesting country *and* in Austria (art 1(1) and Austrian Reservation thereto).
2 Legal assistance will not be granted in respect of political or *fiscal* offences (Austrian Reservation to art 2a).
3 Legal assistance will not be granted if it impairs Austria's sovereignty, security, ordre public or other essential interests (art 2b; Austria has made a Reservation to art 2b declaring that it understood as 'other essential interests', in particular, respecting the duties of confidentiality provided for by Austrian law).
4 'Austria will only comply with requests for search or seizure if such search or seizure is in accordance with Austrian law' (Austrian Reservation to art 5(1)).

In 1983, Austria, by ratifying the Additional Protocol to the European Mutual Assistance Convention (the Additional Protocol), waived the exception as to fiscal offences for violations of revenues, tax and customs laws. Upon ratification of the Additional Protocol, Austria made a declaration in which it stated that it would grant legal assistance in criminal proceedings relating to revenues, tax and customs laws subject to the condition that, in accordance with the duties of confidentiality provided for by Austrian law, information and evidence received by way of legal

---

48 OGH 16.12.1993 (1994) ÖBA at 728; OGH 9.3.1995 (1996) JBl at 532; Avancini, Iro and Koziol, n 6 above, vol I, p 149; Jabornegg, Strasser and Floretta, n 6 above, p 156; Laurer, n 6 above, at 393.

assistance will only be used in the criminal proceeding for which legal assistance was requested and in revenues, tax, or customs proceedings directly connected to such proceeding.

In an additional unilateral Declaration, Austria withdrew the Reservation it made to art 2a with respect to those parties to the European Mutual Assistance Convention which had not become parties to the Additional Protocol, and announced that it would henceforth apply art 2a of the European Mutual Assistance Convention in accordance with domestic law, ie the ARHG.[49]

Consequently, there now seems to be two groups of parties to the European Mutual Assistance Convention: those who are parties to the Additional Protocol and to whom legal assistance will be granted in criminal proceedings of a fiscal nature; and those who are not parties to the Additional Protocol and to who such assistance will, in the absence of further bilateral treaties, not be granted. We believe that the above-mentioned special requirements and limits under which bank secrecy may be lifted in a domestic proceeding will apply likewise to the grant of legal assistance under the Convention (to either group), this in view of the above Reservation to art 2b and the declaration on duties of confidentiality made in connection with the ratification of the Additional Protocol.[50, 51]

On 29 May 2000, the Council of the European Union established the Convention on Mutual Assistance in Criminal Matters between the member states of the EU (2000/C 197/01) which aims at supplementing the provisions and facilitating the application between the EU member states of, inter alia, the European Mutual Assistance Convention and the Additional Protocol.

Under its art 3, mutual assistance shall also be afforded in proceedings brought by the administrative authorities in respect of acts, which are punishable under the national law of the requesting or requested member state, or both, by virtue of being infringements of the rules of law, and where the decision (by administrative authorities) may give rise to proceedings before a court having jurisdiction in particular criminal matters. In addition, mutual assistance shall also be afforded in connection with proceedings which relate to offences or infringements for which a legal person may be held liable in the requesting member state. Further, on 16 October 2001 the Council of the European Union established the Protocol to the Convention on Mutual Assistance in Criminal Matters between the member states of the EU (2001/C 326/01), which shall form an integral part of said convention. It details member states' duties with regard to requests for information by other member

---

49   For a detailed description of the above, see Laurer, n 6 above, at 391ff; Schütz 'Die Anfechtung des Bankgeheimnisses aufgrund eines ausländischen Amtshilfeersuchens in Strafsachen' (1996) JBl at 502ff and OGH 9.3.1995 (1996) JBl at 532.
50   Avancini, Iro and Koziol, n 6 above, vol I, p 149.
51   On 8 November 2001, the Council of Europe passed a Second Additional Protocol to the European Convention on Mutual Assistance in Criminal Matters. Under the new art 1(3) of the European Convention on Mutual Assistance in Criminal Matters, 'mutual assistance may also be afforded in proceedings brought by the administrative authorities in respect of acts which are punishable under the national law of the requesting or the requested Party by virtue of being infringements of the rules of law, where the decision may give rise to proceedings before a court having jurisdiction in particular criminal matters'. The Second Additional Protocol has not yet entered into force.

states on bank accounts, banking transactions and for the monitoring of banking transactions. According to its art 7, a member state shall not invoke banking secrecy as a reason for refusing any co-operation regarding a request for mutual assistance from another member state. To date (September 2002), both this Convention and this Protocol have not been adopted by Austria.

In addition to the above, Austria has entered into a number of bilateral treaties, some of which supplement the European Mutual Assistance Convention. A good example is the Treaty between Austria and the Federal Republic of Germany Supplementing the European Convention for Mutual Assistance in Criminal Matters and Facilitating its Application, dated 31 January 1972, which expands the scope of the European Mutual Assistance Convention. In particular, the covered offences include proceedings for violations of revenues, tax, customs and monopolies laws. Further, the police authorities of either country shall render, and may request, mutual assistance as well.

Indeed, the Administrative Court has held with regard to the predecessor provision of s 38 of the BWG, s 23 of the Credit System Act (KWG, the predecessor code of the BWG, which was replaced by the BWG as of 1 January 1994), and the OGH has held that s 38 of the BWG, did not prevent an Austrian administrative agency from granting legal assistance to a German authority in fiscal matters.[52] Upon compliance with such requests, the Austrian authorities had to act in accordance with Austrian law and thus had the same rights as if they were themselves the investigating authorities in a purely domestic proceeding. This older decision was severely criticised by one author,[53] who believed that the lifting of bank secrecy in fiscal matters violated an essential interest of Austria contained in art 2b of the Convention, in particular, in view of the Reservation made to art 2b and to the Declaration referred to above. Therefore, Austria should deny legal assistance in all fiscal matters if such assistance led to a revelation of bank secrets. However, most other[54] commentators agreed with the court's ruling on the legality of such legal assistance and emphasised that care should be taken that the requirements for the limits to the disclosure and use of bank secrets were indeed fulfilled and respected upon the rendering of legal assistance involving bank secrets. The latter decision confirmed this view.

Summary

Austrian authorities will not render legal assistance to foreign authorities in civil matters if such assistance is contrary to bank secrecy. Austria will render legal assistance in criminal matters in accordance with applicable treaties or the ARHG even if that requires a lifting of bank secrecy, provided the requirements for and the limits to a lifting of bank secrecy in a purely domestic situation are fulfilled and

---

52 VwGH 21.10.1983 (1984) ÖStZB at 189; OGH 16.12.1993 (1994) ÖBA at 728.
53 Beiser 'Entscheidungsanmerkung' (1984) RdW at 192; Beiser 'Das österreichische Bankgeheimnis (§ 23 KWG) im Verhältnis zum Ausland, insbesondere zur Bundesrepublik Deutschland' (1985) ÖJZ at 178; see also Arnold 'Entscheidungsanmerkung' (1984) AnwBl at 172.
54 Avancini, Iro and Koziol, n 6 above, vol I, p 150; Jabornegg, Strasser and Floretta, n 6 above, p 156; Laurer, n 6 above, at 393.

respected. If provided for in applicable treaties, such (foreign) criminal matters may include fiscal offences and both requesting authorities and authorities rendering legal assistance may be administrative agencies as well.

Money laundering

There is no bank secrecy in cases in which there is a duty to disclosure under s 41(1) and (2) of the BWG (BWG, s 38(2), no 2), ie in connection with a founded suspicion of money laundering. Basically, s 41 provides as follows:

1   If there is reasonable suspicion (i) that a transaction which has already occurred, is in progress or is about to occur serves the purpose of money laundering, or (ii) that a client has violated its duty to disclose fiduciary relationships pursuant to BWG, s 40(2), banks (including financial institutions) shall without delay inform the relevant authority (to be determined according to the Austrian Security Police Act) thereof and shall, until the case has been solved, stop any further execution of the transaction unless there is danger that a delay in the transaction would complicate or obstruct the investigation of the case.

2   Banks shall without undue delay inform the authority of all requests by customers to pay out saving deposits if such requests were made after 30 June 2002 and the identity of the account holder has not yet been established according to s 40(1) of the BWG (see Introduction above) and the payment shall be made from a saving deposit with a balance of at least €15,000. Such payouts may only be effected seven days after the customer's request.

3   Banks (including financial institutions) shall, upon request, provide the authority with all information which the latter deems necessary to prevent or prosecute money laundering.

4   The authority is entitled to request that a transaction already in progress or about to occur with respect to which there is reasonable suspicion that it may serve the purpose of money laundering shall not be carried out or shall be provisionally delayed and that requests by customers to pay out funds may only be carried out by the bank with the authority's approval.

5   The banks (including financial institutions) shall keep secret towards their clients and third parties all proceedings designed to implement these provisions.

In order to fulfil these duties, banks are under an obligation to request disclosure of the identity of their clients (i) when entering into a continuous business relationship, (ii) in all other transactions involving a total amount of at least €15,000 (irrespective of whether the transaction is carried out in a single operation or in several operations which are obviously closely linked to each other), (iii) if there is founded suspicion that the client (even unknowingly) participates in transactions that serve the purpose of money laundering or (iv) if, after 31 October 2000, payments to saving accounts and, as of 30 June 2002, withdrawals from saving accounts are carried out and the amount paid in or withdrawn exceeds €15,000: BWG, s 40(1). Further, banks shall request the customer to declare whether it intends to execute the continuous business relationship or the other transaction for its own or for someone else's account and the customer shall comply with that request. If the customer declares to act for someone else's account it must disclose the trustor's identity to the bank: BWG, s 40(2).

Enforcement proceedings

There is no bank secrecy with respect to requests for information on a person's claims against banks (as guarnishees) which were attached in enforcement proceedings.[55]

Guardianship court

There is no bank secrecy in a guardianship court where the client is a minor or a ward: BWG, s 38(2), no 4. This provision complements the guardianship court's right and duty regularly to examine whether a minor's or a ward's property and funds held in trust for the minor or the ward are invested as statutorily prescribed. A request for information made by the guardianship court requires concrete evidence with respect to the relevance of the information as to the funds of the minor or the ward.

Inventories of estates by the probate court

There is no bank secrecy towards the probate court and its aides, ie notaries public fulfilling court functions during probate proceedings, in the case of a client's death, namely in connection with compiling of inventories or other determination of the assets and obligations which belong to the estate of a deceased person: BWG, s 38(2), no 3. Again, a request for information made by the probate court requires concrete evidence of the assets or liabilities forming part of the estate. Even though the exception pursuant to s 38(2), no 3 principally applies to requests for information by Austrian probate courts in Austrian probate proceedings only, requests by (competent) foreign probate courts in foreign probate proceedings must be deemed to be Austrian probate proceedings and must therefore be complied with by the Austrian probate court in accordance with the laws of Austria, if the foreign court has its jurisdiction within a member state of the Hague Convention on Civil Procedure or any other (bilateral) international convention.[56]

Tax liabilities of deceased persons

There is no bank secrecy in respect of the banks' duty according to s 25(1) of the Inheritance and Gift Tax Act to 'give notice to the fiscal authorities of assets belonging to or deposited with them for the disposition of a deceased person' (ie assets which were held in deposit or administered for the deceased in the course of the banks' business) within one month from the death becoming known to the banks: BWG, s 38(2), no 8.

---

55   Laurer, n 9 above, p 454; Arnold, n 6 above, p 22; Avancini, Iro and Koziol, n 6 above, vol I, p 158; Jabornegg, Strasser and Floretta, n 6 above, p 153ff.
56   Laurer, n 9 above, p 475ff ; OGH 1.12.1998 (1999) EvBl at 100.

Assessment of the banks' taxes

There is no bank secrecy to the extent that a disclosure of bank secrets is necessary for the assessment of taxes to be paid by the banks themselves: BWG, s 38(3). Certainly, bank secrets obtained by the (fiscal) authorities in such manner are subject to official secrecy and must not be passed on to other public authorities or used in whatever manner in regard to third parties to which such bank secrets relate.

Exchange control, income tax, FMA, deposit protection facilities, bank auditors, Ombudsman, Audit Office, trustee in bankruptcy

There is further no bank secrecy with respect to the Austrian National Bank's right to certain information in matters of exchange control,[57] with respect to certain notice requirements under the Income Tax Act or other revenue laws, further, in regard to the right to information of, and the duty of disclosure to, the FMA in its function as bank regulatory authority (BWG, s 69ff) and as securities supervisory authority (BWG, s 38(2), no 9),[58] the deposit protection facilities (BWG, s 38(2), no 2 in connection with ss 93 and 93a), the bank auditors (BWG, s 38(2), no 2 in connection with s 61(1)), the Audit Office (Rechnungshof) and the Ombudsman (Volksanwalt), and towards the trustee in bankruptcy in bankruptcy or reorganisation proceedings.

Foreign bank regulatory authorities

Pursuant to s 77 of the BWG, the FMA may give official information to foreign bank regulatory authorities provided:

1   the ordre public, other essential interests of the Republic of Austria, bank secrecy and the revenues law duty of confidentiality are not violated thereby;
2   there is reciprocity; and
3   a similar request for information made by the FMA would be in accordance with the purposes of the BWG.

The FMA may provide official information only if s 77(5) to (7) of the BWG (specifying the countries to whose authorities official information may be transferred and the tasks under which such transfer is permissible) or applicable treaties do not provide to the contrary. At present there is no such treaty; in particular, Austria has not ratified the Convention on International Assistance in Administrative Matters. Section 77 of the BWG does not grant to foreign bank regulatory authorities a specific right to request information, but specifies definitely the limits of the FMA upon granting international legal assistance.

---

57   VwGH 28.10.1994 (1995) WBl at 256.
58   It should be noted that upon the establishment of the FMA, BWG, s 38(2)9 has not been amended accordingly. Therefore, it still mentions its predecessor, the Federal Securities Supervisory Authority (Bundes-Wertpapieraufsicht, BWA) as the authority towards which bank secrecy shall be lifted. It is disputed whether this non-amendment has the consequence that no exception to the duty of bank confidentiality shall exist towards the new FMA in its function as securities supervisory authority. See Brandl and Wolfbauer (2002) ecolex at 294ff, according to whom bank secrecy shall not be lifted towards the FMA as securities supervisory authority. Against: Painz and Tauböck (2002) ecolex at 132ff.

Furthermore, the FMA may give information on large borrowings in the sense of s 75(3) of the BWG to the relevant authorities of any member state of the EU upon its request (BWG, s 75(5)) provided:

1 the requesting member state maintains a similar register on large borrowings;
2 there is reciprocity;
3 the data will be used for bank regulatory purposes only; and
4 the given information is subject to the professional secrecy pursuant to art 30 of Council Directive 2000/12/EC.

CONFLICTS OF INTEREST AND FIDUCIARY DUTIES

Conflicts of interest might occur both between the interests of the bank and its client and between the interests of two or more clients of the same bank. As a matter of general contract law, the contractual relationship between the bank and its client entails certain mutual fiduciary duties and duties of care (Schutz- und Sorgfaltspflichten).[59] Particularly with respect to securities transactions, the bank's contractual duties also entail the duty to inform and advise the client (Aufklärungs- und Beratungspflichten) properly.[60]

From this follows, first, that the client's interests shall always prevail over the interests of the bank. For example, a bank clearly must not recommend a transaction in which it may gain financial benefit by giving incomplete, biased or one-sided information or objectively detrimental advice to the client. In addition, the bank is prohibited from obtaining advantage from any kind of 'frontrunning', ie the advantageous conclusion of (adverse or similar) nostro transactions by the bank itself, for example, on the occasion of large client orders. On the other hand, there seems to be the prevailing view that a bank shall not be obliged to take into account its client's interests in the course of conducting nostro transactions. If, for example, the bank intends to buy a large stake in a certain company which makes a price increase foreseeable, it shall not be obligated to inform a selling client; however, the bank must refrain from any recommendation as to the selling of these shares by its clients.[61]

Secondly, from the contractual (in particular, the fiduciary) duties set out above it follows that the banks are under an obligation towards their clients to avoid, as far as possible, any situations which would expose them to a conflict of interests between clients. Often, for example, a bank represents a client whom it assists with the borrowing of money and at the same time it tries to place the shares among other clients, for example, private investors who are interested in buying shares in such company. The borrowing client may expect that its financial and economic situation will not be disclosed by the bank; the private investor, on the other hand, may expect to be informed about the risks of this investment. With respect to situations where the bank's role is limited to the financing of a risky undertaking (as opposed to the role as an investment adviser), the OGH held that the duty to inform an investor should not be interpreted too broadly, since a reasonable investor may be

59 Avancini, Iro and Koziol, n 6 above, vol I, p 42ff.
60 Avancini, Iro and Koziol, n 6 above, vol II, p 588ff.
61 Avancini, Iro and Koziol, n 6 above, vol II, p 605ff.

expected to know of the principle that the higher the profit opportunities, the higher is the risk. A duty to inform would only exist in exceptional instances, if the bank actually was aware of, for example, atypical risks of the participation.[62] No general duty of the bank exists to inform the client of all circumstances that may influence the client's investment decision.[63]

The duty of confidence pursuant to bank secrecy might also conflict with the bank's duty to inform and advise its clients. There is the prevailing view that the interest of another client of the bank in being informed and advised properly does not constitute an exception to bank secrecy. Consequently, the bank may – without the client's express and written consent – only provide general information on the economic situation of such a client, even if the other client seems to need further information with regard to a proper investment decision.[64] This view was confirmed by the OGH, which held that a financing bank, if under a duty to inform the private investor about the undertaking to be financed, must either refrain from the contemplated transaction or, prior to the information of the client about its concerns, obtain the undertaking's consent (provided that general information on the undertaking's economic situation would not have been sufficient) in order to comply with bank secrecy.[65]

The conflict of interest problems may gain particular relevance in situations where a bank gains access to insider information, for example, because it assists an issuer of securities or because an executive board member of the bank or a bank employee serves as a member of the supervisory board of another company at the same time.[66] Such conflict might arise both in nostro transactions of the bank itself and in transactions of other clients to whom the bank gives advice (for example, with regard to the sale or purchase of securities or the granting of credits or loans to other bank clients). According to the rules on insider trading (which are dealt with in detail below), both the trading in and the recommendation of securities by a bank having insider information as to these securities as well as the disclosure of insider information constitutes a criminal offence. Thus, a bank is not only prohibited from exploiting information obtained from one of its clients in its own transactions, but also is neither entitled nor obliged to pass on insider information to any other of its clients.[67]

INSIDER TRADING AND CHINESE WALLS

Until 1989, Austrian law did not contain any statutory provisions on insider trading at all.[68] In order to address the problem of insider trading, the Vienna Stock Exchange

---

62   OGH (1995) ÖBA at 146ff and 627ff.
63   OGH (2002) RdW at 341.
64   Avancini, Iro and Koziol, n 6 above, vol II, p 614ff.
65   OGH (1995) ÖBA at 627ff; OGH (1998) ÖBA at 733.
66   For details see Koziol 'Pflichtenkollisionen im Wertpapiergeschäft bei Übernahme von Aufsichtsratsmandaten durch Mitarbeiter der Bank' in Enzinger, Hügel and Dillenz *Aktuelle Probleme des Unternehmensrechts* (1993) p 351ff.
67   See eg OGH (2002) RdW at 341.
68   Only a minority view held that ss 23 and 34 of the KWG covered insider trading: cf Roth 'Der Wall Street-Skandal und das österreichische Kapitalmarktrecht' (1987) RdW pp 221, 222). In addition, ss 121 and 122 of the Austrian Penal Code which sanction certain offences involving the disclosure of professional, trade and business secrets were considered to cover insider trading.

issued Guidelines for the Prevention of Insider Trading in 1987.[69] As of 1 December 1989, a new Stock Exchange Act (BörseG) came into effect, ss 26 and 82 of which dealt with the problems of insider trading for the first time in Austrian law.[70] In accordance with these provisions, 'Insider Rules of the Chamber of the Vienna Stock Exchange' were issued as of 6 July 1990.

With effect from 1 October 1993, the law on insider trading has been changed fundamentally by the introduction of two new provisions of the BörseG – ss 48a and 48b – and by an amendment of s 82. In particular, the provisions on liquidated damages as a compulsory sanction for insider violations were abolished and replaced by criminal punishment and administrative penal punishment, complemented by supporting measures for the prevention of insider trading. Thus, the Austrian law on insider trading does not contain an explicit provision that creates a statutory basis for claims under civil law in situations involving insider trading.[71] Since 1993, these have been consolidated by further amendments and, concomitantly, the FMA has been made the responsible supervising authority with respect to insider trading situations.

Criminal offence

The core[72] of the provisions on insider trading is s 48a of the BörseG, a provision of criminal law which covers both primary insiders (insiders) and secondary insiders (tippees).[73]

According to s 82(1) of the BörseG, it shall constitute a criminal offence (imprisonment for up to two years or fines) if a person who qualifies to be an insider exploits insider information in the course of trading with securities with the malicious intent to obtain an economic advantage for himself or a third person, provided such person (the insider) (i) either buys or sells, or recommends to a third party the sale or purchase of such securities or (ii) or discloses such information to a third party without being obliged thereto.

In addition, a person who does *not* qualify to be an insider (a tippee) is subject to criminal punishment (imprisonment for up to one year or fines) if he knowingly exploits insider information that was communicated to it or which it learned otherwise with the same malicious intent as set out above, provided such person (the tippee) buys or sells such securities: BörseG, s 48a(2).

---

69 For the wording and details of these Guidelines, see the first edition of this book, p 48ff; see further Schinnerer 'Zur Problematik einer gesetzlichen Regelung des börslichen Insider-Geschäftes in Österreich' (1985) ÖBA 271 at 273.

70 The sanctions of a violation of insider trading contained in these provisions were limited to contractual consequences, ie liquidated damages, which, however, turned out to be inefficient and were thus applied in a single instance only (Decision of the Chamber of the Vienna Stock Exchange of 7 February 1992). In a number of other instances, there was suspicion about insider trading only, which could not be proven: see Hausmanninger *Insider Trading* (1997) p 354ff. For the wording of these provisions, see the first edition of this book, p 51.

71 Of course, it might be possible to have recourse to statutory provisions of a more general nature to find a legal basis for such claims: see Hausmanninger, n 70 above, p 408ff.

72 Sceptical, however, Hausmanninger "Organisatorische Maßnahmen zur Verhinderung mißbräuchlicher Verwendung oder Weitergabe von Insiderinformation nach der BörseGNov 1993' (1993) ÖBA at 848, because of its inefficiency in practice.

73 See Hausmanninger, n 70 above, p 371ff.

The elements contained in these two provisions, are partly defined in s 48a of the BörseG itself. They can be described as follows:

1   'Insider' is deemed to be any person having access to insider information due to his profession, occupation, task or participation in the share capital of the issuer. This definition does not only cover the issuer of securities (including its organ members, employees and shareholders who hold any direct or indirect participation in the issuer that enables them to have access to insider information of the issuer, and the organ members of such shareholders), but also persons receiving insider information due to a temporary contractual relationship with the issuer (for example, the issuer's attorneys, accountants, public relations advisers and other consultants), further institutional investors, market makers, brokers, journalists and, in particular, banks.[74]

2   The qualification as a 'secondary insider' does not necessarily require that the secondary insider was aware of whether or not the received information was – directly or indirectly – communicated to it by a (primary) insider. Thus, a secondary insider is any person who learns or knows of any insider information, irrespective of the source of the information and the means of how it learned of the insider information, provided only it does not qualify as a primary insider.

3   'Insider information' is any information about a certain confidential (ie not known to the broad public) fact (as opposed to rumours, opinions) which is connected either to securities or to the issuer of securities and which could have a material impact on the price development of the securities if the fact became known to the public.[75]

4   'Securities' are defined as certain specified instruments (particularly shares, debt obligations, bonds, bills and other negotiable securities, subscription rights, options, futures and other financial and derivative instruments) provided they are admitted for trading on a market (i) which is regimented and supervised by officially approved authorities, (ii) directly or indirectly accessible by the public and (iii) on which trade occurs on a regular basis.

Ancillary measures, Standard Compliance Code and disclosure of insider information

In addition to the criminal sanctions set out above, Austrian law requires the establishment of organisational measures in order to prevent the abuse and the passing-on of insider information. Section 82(5) of the BörseG imposes on any issuer for the purpose of preventing insider transactions the duty:

1   to notify its employees and any other persons becoming otherwise active for the issuer of the prohibition of abuse of insider information;

2   to establish, and supervise the compliance with, internal guidelines for the passing-on of information within the enterprise; and

3   to adopt appropriate organisational measures to prevent any abuse or passing-on of insider information.

---

74   See Hausmanninger, n 70 above, p 372ff.
75   See Hausmanninger, n 70 above, p 376ff.

In addition to the issuer, these duties are also imposed on banks and institutional investors (contractual insurance companies and pension funds) (BörseG, s 48b), on all members of the stock exchange (BörseG, s 18, no 5) and stock exchange dealers (BörseG, s 36(6)). Violation of these duties is subject to administrative penalties (fines of up to €20,000) and disciplinary sanctions (elimination or suspension from participation in the stock exchange). In addition, ss 13 no 2, 14 and 16 to 18 of the Act on the Supervision of Investment Services in the Securities-Field (Wertpapieraufsichtsgesetz) contain further compliance provisions for banks engaged in investment services relating to securities which also aim at the prevention and tracking of insider transactions.[76]

Section 82(5a) of the BörseG authorises the FMA to issue a regulation setting out principles for the passing-on of information within the enterprise pursuant to 1 above, as well as for the establishment of organisational measures pursuant to 3 above. These principles shall, in particular, preclude the possible creation, and assist in tracing, of situations involving insider trading. Based thereon, the FMA has issued, with effect as of 1 April 2002, a Compliance Code (Emmittenten-Compliance-Verordnung) for issuers of securities admitted on an Austrian stock exchange for official listing or regulated over-the-counter trading. However, the Compliance Code does not apply to banks, pension funds, insurance companies and as certain investment firms: s 2(2) of the Compliance Code.

Consequently, with regard to banks, pension funds and insurance companies, the rules of compliance which have been formulated by these businesses themselves since 1993 on the basis of s 82(5) of the BörseG in the form of guidelines setting forth certain minimum standards remain in existence and applicable.[77]

The Standard Compliance Code of Austrian Banks of 1999 (SCC), sets forth certain minimum standards to which all of the Austrian banks agreed to adhere. According to the SCC, every bank has to appoint at least one person responsible for the compliance with the SCC (the compliance officer).The SCC further recommends the creation of separate 'areas of confidentiality' within the bank's internal structure by adopting appropriate internal organisational measures order to prevent an exchange of confidential information. Any compliance-relevant information held in one area may in general not leave that area. Every employee of an area of confidentiality needs to agree in writing to refrain from transmitting confidential information – both inside the bank and to third parties – by way of the ordinary bank information channels. The creation of such Chinese Walls is not regarded as a mandatory minimum standard, but shall depend on the size of the bank. Disclosure of information to another area of confidentiality is permitted only if it is limited to cases of absolute necessity and if the confidentiality of the compliance relevant information is preserved. A communication may thus occur only with the knowledge of the area

---

76 For a summary see eg Hausmaninger 'Anpassungs- oder Ergänzungsbedarf des Standard Copliance Code der österreichischen Kreditinstitute ('SCC')? Eine Analyse im Lichte der neuen Compliance-Bestimmungen des BörseG und WAG' (1998) ÖBA at 678ff.
77 Standard Compliance Code of Austrian Banks (1999); Directive According to Sec 48a in Connection with Sec 82 subs 5 BörseG for Pension Funds (1995); and Compliance Guidelines for the Avoidance of Insider Trading for Insurance Companies (1994).

manager and the compliance officer. The contents, source and the dates of disclosure and receipt of information shall be documented. Employees that permanently or temporarily switch from one area of confidentiality to another shall not disclose or exploit in the new area confidential knowledge they have acquired in the old area of confidentiality.

The compliance officer shall further keep a (strictly confidential, internal) 'watch list' of securities and derivatives with respect to which the bank holds material investment and price-relevant information which is not yet publicly available. The placing on this list itself has no immediate legal consequences. It will, however, facilitate the monitoring of nostro trading or employee transactions that could raise the suspicion that confidential information has been exploited in an unfair manner. In this context, reporting duties of the bank's departments and employees to the compliance officer in cases of large orders (combined with the prohibition against 'frontrunning') and any other compliance relevant information are established. In addition to the watch list, the compliance officer must keep and distribute throughout the bank[78] a 'restricted list' (Sperrliste), which includes securities and derivatives with respect to which information is received that might have an immediate material impact on the price development. These titles shall be removed from the official list of recommendations. Employee and nostro transactions in these titles, as well as active advice and recommendations by the bank, are substantially restricted.

Finally, s 82(6) of the BörseG[79] principally requires any issuer of securities which are admitted for official listing or regulated over-the-counter trade to disclose without undue delay any new fact that occurred in the issuer's field of activity, provided it qualifies as materially affecting the price development of the security because of its impact on the course of the issuer's business, its economic position or earnings. Prior to such notification to the public, the issuer must file a notification of these facts to the FMA and to the Stock Exchange.

---

78   This list is otherwise, however, subject to bank secrecy pursuant to BWG, s 38.
79   Besides this general duty, special disclosure provisions applicable exist, eg in connection with share buy-backs or a change in the issuer's ownership structure.

4   Belgium

Jacques Richelle
Tom Thomas

INTRODUCTION

Banks' duty of confidentiality (or 'duty of discretion' as referred to by the Belgian Supreme Court (Cour de Cassation/Hof van Cassatie)) is a long-established concept under Belgian law, even though its principle has never been embodied in a statutory provision. Case law is scarce in this matter and has not been of much help in determining the scope of banks' obligations and the remedies available to clients in case of breach. The main decision in this area was rendered on 25 October 1978 by the Supreme Court,[1] which held that a breach of a bank's duty of confidentiality is not a criminal offence.

Exceptions to the confidentiality rule can be found in general statutory provisions applicable not only to banks, such as the Judicial Code or the Code of Criminal Procedure.

Other exceptions are specific to banks, and can be found in specific statutes, such as the various Tax Codes, the laws on consumer credit and the law on money laundering.

Since the 1990s, the scope of these specific exceptions has been extended in several areas. The most important examples are to be found in the Income Tax Code, in the legislation on consumer credit (including the specific law on mortgage credit) and in the law on money laundering.

NATURE OF THE DUTY OF CONFIDENTIALITY

The duty of confidentiality as a civil law concept

Contractual and other grounds

A bank may be liable for damages incurred by its clients due to the breach of its duty of confidentiality. The nature of this duty and its resulting liability depend on the circumstances.

---

1   Cass, 25 octobre 1978, *Pas* 1979, I, 237 and *JT* 1979, 371-378, note A Bruyneel.

When a bank and its client reach an agreement, the duty of confidentiality arises out of the contract itself. Whether expressly provided for in the agreement or, as in most cases, merely implied, this duty is undoubtedly contractual.

The nature of the duty of confidentiality is not so clear, however, in the absence of a contract, for example, during the negotiation process or when a person cashes a bank cheque as a one-time operation. Legal authors have put forward many legal grounds on which to enforce a bank's duty of confidentiality in such circumstances:

1   in tort, under art 1382 of the Civil Code;
2   on the basis of an implied pre-contractual agreement;
3   on the basis of a sui generis contract; and
4   on the basis of the culpa in contrahendo doctrine.

It seems that, in most cases, liability could be based on an implied agreement of confidentiality, independent from any subsequent formal contract.

If evidence of such an agreement cannot be provided, however, art 1382 of the Civil Code is always applicable.

Client's remedies

If the duty of confidentiality is contractual, the client may claim damages for breach of contract (arts 1142 and 1145 of the Civil Code).

As far as tortious liability is concerned, pursuant to art 1382 of the Civil Code, the client may be awarded damages if he can establish (i) that there has been a breach of the duty of confidentiality, (ii) damage and (iii) a causal link between the two.

A judgment of 25 February 2000 by the Court of First Instance of Brussels[2] (Tribunal de Première Instance/Rechtbank van Eerste Aanleg) awarded moral damages to a client whose bank had mistakenly communicated information regarding the client's financial situation beyond what had been asked by the auditor to whom the information was communicated. The court was of the opinion that both material and moral damage can be suffered when a bank breaches its duty of confidentiality. The moral damage consists not only of the broken relationship of confidence between the bank and its client, but also of the fact that private information has been communicated to a third party, which has offended the client.

Scope of the duty of confidentiality

The scope of banks' duty of confidentiality is very broad. It may be approached from three different angles.

TYPE OF OPERATIONS

The duty of confidentiality applies to banking operations in the broad sense: deposit taking, credit, transfer of funds, foreign exchange, financial advice, the rental of a

2   Civ Bruxelles, 25 février 2000, *RDC* 2001, 860, note J Buyle et M Deliernieux.

safety deposit box, letter of credit etc. Such duty would not apply to activities unrelated to banking, such as the operating of a travel agency.

ORIGIN OF THE INFORMATION

The duty of confidentiality extends to all facts a banker comes across in the course of his business relationship with his client. This includes information released directly by the client himself as well as that known by the banker from any other source (for example, banker's own investigation, client blacklists). Mere hints or facts suspected by the banker are also included.

Some legal authors have suggested that (i) facts known by the banker in another capacity (for example, as a friend) and (ii) facts discovered by the banker by a mere coincidence are not included in the scope of the duty of confidentiality because they do not come to the banker's attention 'in the course of his business relationship with the client'. Such drawing of a fine line must be handled very cautiously.

TYPE OF INFORMATION

The duty of confidentiality applies to various types of information, including:

1 facts about the client himself, for example, financial situation, commercial practices or strategy etc;
2 types of banking operations, for example, the opening of an account or line of credit, the transfer of funds, the receipt of funds etc; and
3 the amounts involved, account balances etc.

It must be added that the mere disclosure of the existence of a business relationship does not seem to constitute a breach of a bank's duty of confidentiality under Belgian law.

The breach of the duty of confidentiality does not constitute a criminal offence

In its decision of 25 October 1978, the Belgian Supreme Court[3] (Cour de Cassation/ Hof van Cassatie) clearly held that the breach of bankers' duty of confidentiality does not constitute a criminal offence. The issue before the court was whether bankers should come under the scope of application of art 458 of the Criminal Code, which provides that physicians, surgeons, health officers, pharmacists and all other persons who, because of their status or profession, are confided secrets will be, subject to certain exceptions, fined and/or imprisoned if they reveal these secrets.

The court held that this article does not apply to bankers because they are merely held to a duty of 'discretion'. The court added that neither the nature of their duties nor any statutory provision makes them subject to art 458 of the Criminal Code.

3 See n 1 above.

The judgment of 25 October 1978 is very short. Hints as to the court's reasoning can be found in previous decisions and in the comments of legal authors:[4]

1   Bankers do not have any legal monopoly as is the case with the professions mentioned in art 458.
2   Entering into a relationship with a banker does not necessarily involve confiding secrets in him; at least, it is not the banker's primary function.
3   It is not deemed as socially important for a banker to keep the secrets he is told as it is for a lawyer or a physician; the latter have a much more intimate relationship with their clients, whose trust is essential to their function; patrimonial interests, such as property and goods, are seen as less worthy of legal protection than personal interests, such as life and physical integrity.

These arguments have been the subject of controversy among legal authors. Whatever the underlying reasoning, however, the rule of law is clear: bankers are not criminally liable for revealing secrets confided to them by their clients.

EXCEPTIONS TO THE DUTY OF CONFIDENTIALITY

Introduction

Exceptions to the rule of confidentiality are based on either general law concepts applied by legal scholars, general procedural rules applicable to any party in civil or criminal proceedings or specific statutory provisions.

Client's consent

The client can relieve the bank of its duty of confidentiality, either expressly or implicitly. The underlying reasoning for this rule is that the bank's duty only protects its client's private material interests, not any larger public interest.

Interest of the bank

A bank is allowed to release information about its client when its own material interest is at stake. Whether or not such disclosure is limited to judicial proceedings to which the bank is a party is the subject of controversy among legal authors.

Information to persons within the sphere of confidentiality

Certain persons may require information from the bank because of their special relationship with the client. Such persons may be those associated with, or those that have taken over, the management of the client's assets and are, therefore, included within the sphere of confidentiality. These situations should not be considered as real exceptions, but rather as flexible applications of the rule of confidentiality.

---

4   See eg A Bruyneel 'Le secret bancaire en Belgique après l'arrêt du 25 octobre 1978', *JT* 1979, 371-378.

The following categories can be drawn up:

1 Persons representing the client, including representatives of persons lacking legal capacity, the client's agents (for example, the directors of a corporation), the trustee of a bankrupt company or person, the company's liquidator etc.

2 Persons continuing the client's legal status after his death, for example, the legal heir or the heir by will having accepted the estate as a whole (légataire universel/algemene legataris).

3 Persons having the same right as the client to assets in the bank's possession, for example, the spouse under certain circumstances. The bank must advise the client's spouse of the opening of any account or renting of a safety deposit box (art 218 of the Civil Code). The spouse may request information from the banker as to the client's assets, provided he or she can show evidence that such money or property is jointly owned by the couple.

Criminal proceedings

Introduction

A bank can be compelled to disclose information about its client's operations at various stages of criminal proceedings, ie during the investigation process and by the court at the trial hearings. In these cases, its duty of confidentiality is irrelevant: the bank must testify through its representatives or accept a search, just like any other person.

The same rules apply if the bank is itself under investigation or on trial. In that case, however, its fundamental right to remain silent supersedes any duty of disclosure. Therefore, the bank cannot be forced to testify.

Investigation stage

The judge leading the investigation (juge d'instruction/onderzoeksrechter) has the power:

1 To compel the bank to disclose confidential information about its client (art 71ff of the Code of Criminal Procedure – Code d'Instruction Criminelle/Wetboek van Strafvordering – hereinafter referred to as CCP).

    The judge may request the public prosecutor (procureur du roi/procureur des konings and his substituts/substituten) or the federal police (police fédérale/federale politie) to interrogate the banker. If the banker refuses to testify before the judge leading the investigation, he can be fined and forced to appear (CCP, art 80).

    At this stage, false testimony is not a criminal offence. The witness can modify his testimony up until the close of the trial. However, this traditional rule has been called into question by some legal authors and courts.[5]

2 To order a search (perquisition/opzoeking) at the bank (CCP, art 87).

    This is the judge's most effective alternative, since the bank may not oppose the search. The banker may, however, include his own written comments in the official minutes of the search. He will do so when:

5   See eg A Bruyneel 'Le secret bancaire en Belgique après l'arrêt du 25 octobre 1978', *JT* 1979, 375.

> (a) a procedural rule has been violated, for example, if the judge lacks territorial jurisdiction; or
> (b) the search is unrelated to the charges brought against the person under investigation.
>
> This may lead the trial court to eventually reject as evidence any material found during the search.

It is important for the banker to distinguish the official, formal investigation described above from an unofficial investigation led by the public prosecutor. In the latter case, as there is no legal obligation for the banker to answer any questions, his duty of confidentiality should keep him from disclosing any confidential information.

Trial stage

At the trial hearings, the trial court may order a banker, in the same manner as for any other person, to testify (CCP, arts 153, 190 and 315). A refusal to testify then leads to the same consequences as at the investigation stage (CCP, arts 157, 189 and 355).

Spontaneous disclosure

CCP, art 30 provides that anybody who witnesses an attempt to commit a crime against the 'public safety' or the life or property of an individual must advise the public prosecutor. Faced with such situation, the banker would not be liable to the client for disclosing information evidencing the attempted crime.

Subpoenas from foreign jurisdictions

Belgium is a party to the European Convention on Mutual Assistance in Criminal Matters, signed in Strasbourg on 20 April 1959, supplemented by the Council Act of 29 May 2000, and to various other bilateral and multilateral treaties. Under the European Convention, a subpoena from a signatory state must be executed by the judicial authorities of the receiving state in accordance with the latter's own procedural rules. Therefore, once the subpoena is accepted by the Belgian authorities, the banker finds himself in the same situation as when faced with a subpoena from a Belgian judge.

In the absence of an international treaty, the foreign subpoena must be authorised by the Belgian Minister of Justice (art 873 of the Judicial Code).

A specific procedure for foreign subpoenas ordering searches or the production of documents is set out in art 11 of the Law of 15 March 1874 on extradition.

Conclusion

A banker faced with criminal proceedings has very little room within which to manoeuvre. In most cases, in order to avoid criminal sanctions, he will have no other options than to disclose information about his client or undergo a search.

In these circumstances, the bank will not be liable to its client for breach of the duty of confidentiality, provided that it stays within the general limits of disclosure. This would require the bank, for instance, to limit its answers to the specific questions asked during the testimony and to mention any procedural irregularities related to the search that it is aware of. The bank will never be liable to its client if the latter is eventually convicted of the charges pending at the time of the investigation or trial.

Civil proceedings

Banks' testimonies and production of documents

The rules relating to evidence in Belgian civil proceedings are based on two principles:

1 litigants and third parties must co-operate in the search for the truth; and
2 the court has the power to force them to do so.

The court has the power to compel litigants (arts 871 and 877 of the Judicial Code – Code Judiciaire/Gerechtelijk Wetboek, hereafter referred to as JC) and third parties (JC, arts 877 and 878) to produce documents. If they fail to comply with the court's order, they may have to pay damages to the party to whom their conduct has caused a damage (JC, art 882). Similar rules apply to testimonies (JC, arts 915 and 916). In addition to possible damages, a refusal to testify may also lead to criminal penalties, including imprisonment (art 495bis of the Criminal Code; see also art 495).

In a judgment of 29 June 1995,[6] the Commercial Court of Namur held that this duty of disclosure does not entail an obligation of the bank to *comment* on the disclosed documents.

As in criminal proceedings, the banker, despite his duty of confidentiality, is subject to the same rules of disclosure as any other person.

This broad duty of disclosure is, however, qualified by two sets of rules.

THE COURT'S SUBPOENA MUST BE VALID

This rule is laid down in JC, art 929 which, by its terms, only applies to testimony. It is widely accepted, however, that the same rules apply to the production of documents (see JC, arts 878 and 882 and the Van Reepinghen Report,[7] on which the 1967 enactment of the Judicial Code was based).

JC, art 929 provides that:

1 witnesses may request the court to be relieved of their duty to testify because of a legitimate reason (motif légitime/wettige reden);
2 professional secrecy, among other things, is to be deemed a legitimate reason; and

6   Comm Namur, 29 juin 1995, *JT* 1996, 328.
7   Charles Van Reepinghen, Ministerie van justitie, *Verslag over de gerechtelijke hervorming,* Belgisch staatsblad, 1964 (2 vols: 842+543 pp).

3   the court must hear the witness and the (other) parties before reaching a decision as to this request.

Bankers' duty of confidentiality is not generally deemed a duty of professional secrecy within the meaning of JC, art 929. In specific circumstances, however, such duty of confidentiality can constitute a legitimate reason for not testifying or producing documents. Therefore, the judge would have to take the bank's request into consideration and balance the bank's duty of confidentiality with the requirements of the search for the truth. Legal authors agree that such request by the bank is not likely to succeed, as courts would construe the 'legitimate reason' concept narrowly.

THE SUBPOENA MAY BE OPPOSED FOR A 'LEGITIMATE REASON'

The tests of such legitimacy are laid down in JC, arts 877 (production of documents), 915 (testimony at the request of the litigant) and 916 (testimony at the request of the court). They can be summarised as follows, the first test applying to both testimony and presentation of documents, the following two only to the latter:

1   the subpoena must present the evidence of a relevant and specific fact: requests which are too broad (for example, 'all documents in your possession') or too vague (for example, 'any relevant document available') do not meet this test;
2   there must be specific and serious presumptions that the document is in the hands of the person requested to produce it – a mere suspicion of the possession of the document is therefore not enough; and
3   the document must exist at the time of the request – a demand to draft a new document will be rejected.

With regard to subpoenas from foreign jurisdictions, Belgium is party to many bilateral or multilateral treaties, including the International Convention on Civil Proceedings, signed in The Hague on 1 March 1954. As in criminal proceedings, the general principle of execution of the subpoena in accordance with the procedural rules of the party requested to produce a document is applied.

In the absence of an international treaty, the foreign subpoena must be authorised by the Belgian Minister of Justice (JC, art 873).

In conclusion, as in criminal proceedings, the bank does not have many options when requested to testify or produce documents regarding its clients. It will not be liable to its client for breach of its duty of confidentiality, provided it has verified the validity of the subpoena, has raised any available legitimate reason to oppose disclosure and has stayed within the general limits of its duty of disclosure.

Garnishee orders

INTRODUCTION

A creditor of a bank's client may have the bank garnished as a third party owing money or property to the client-debtor. The garnishment order may be either a mere sequestration pending the outcome of litigation (saisie-arrêt conservatoire/bewarend beslag onder derden), or a step in the execution of a judgment (saisie-arrêt exécution/ uitvoerend beslag onder derden). The procedures are strictly regulated by JC, art 1386ff.

Garnishment obviously entails disclosure of information by the garnishee, ie by the bank.

THE BANK MUST BE THE CLIENT'S DEBTOR — SPECIFIC PROBLEMS

In order for the garnishment procedure to be valid, the bank must be the client's debtor for a particular amount of money or property, which corresponds to the garnishee order. Questions which arise concern what is to be considered as a debt in a bank-client relationship:

The bank's safe. If the client leaves property to be kept by the bank in the bank's safe, the bank has the duty to deliver it back to the client, at his request. The bank is thus the client's debtor. If the client rents a private safety deposit box at the bank, however, the bank is a mere lessor and is not a debtor with regard to any of the property contained therein.

Line of credit. This issue is not yet settled in Belgian law. A decision by the attachment judge (juge des saisies/beslagrechter) of Brussels has declared valid the application of the garnishment procedure to a line of credit,[8] but case law to the contrary also exists and some legal authors disagree.[9] The practical significance of such garnishee order in this case, however, is limited as the bank can, in principle, revoke the line of credit as a result of loss of confidence vis-à-vis its client at the time it receives the notice of the order.

Pending operations. The amount of the debt is equal to the credit balance of an account at the time notice of the order is given to the bank. Some operations prior to that date, but affecting the balance at a later stage, must also be taken into account. Such is the case for cheques signed by the account holder but not yet presented for payment at the bank. Such is not the case, however, for transfers of funds ordered prior to the garnishee order but not yet executed by the bank.

Operations taking place after the notice is given do not affect the amount of the debt subject to the order.

BANKS' DUTY TO DISCLOSE

Upon receipt of notice of a garnishee order relating to one of its clients, a bank must disclose to the creditor (with a copy for the client), within a 15-day period, the following information (JC, arts 1452–1456):

1   In the case whereby the bank is currently the client's debtor:
    (a) the origin of the debt, ie type of account or other banking operation from which the debt derives;

---

8   Tribunal de première instance Bruxelles, chambre des saisies, 10 avril 1986, Saisie - Saisie-arrêt conservatoire (unpublished).
9   See eg Bruxelles, 16 juin 1989, *JLMB* 1989, 802, note G De Leval.

(b)   the amount of the debt;

(c)   the terms of payment, if any; and

(d)   the specific conditions of the debt, if any.

2   In the case whereby it has never been the client's debtor, the bank may simply so declare.

3   In the case whereby it is no longer a debtor, the bank must state when and how the debt was paid off and produce any relevant document evidencing such fact.

The bank must also disclose prior orders of which it received notice. It is not clear whether the bank must inform the creditor of accounts with a debit balance. The bank may always turn to the attachment judge for information regarding the extent of the required disclosure.

Failure to issue such statement within the 15-day period or any misrepresentation of facts may result in the bank being held liable for part or all of its client's debts. Fraud, bad faith or negligence can constitute possible grounds for a such measure, but it is left entirely up to the attachment judge whether and to what extent such a penalty will be imposed. For instance, a short delay for technical reasons or which causes the client's creditor no harm will normally not be penalised by the attachment judge.

CONCLUSION

In view of the penalty at stake, the bank must be careful to adhere strictly to the requirements of the garnishee order. Its role is not to protect its client, who has at his disposal various means of opposing wrongful or abusive garnishments by his creditors. The bank is not expected, for instance, to oppose an order relating to amounts much greater than the client's debt. Many banks seem, however, to have the habit of disclosing and blocking any increase in the credit balance after notice of the garnishee order is given, until the credit equals the client's debt to his creditor. Such a practice is overly cautious and lacking in any legal grounds.

Information to the tax authorities

Introduction

A distinction must be drawn between:

1   income tax; and

2   registration, inheritance and value-added taxes.

Specific statutory provisions as to bank confidentiality, ie limits to a Tax Administration's powers of investigation into bank records with respect to their clients, only apply to income tax. It is important to note that these provisions were amended by Royal Decree of 20 December 1996 (published in the Belgian State Gazette of 31 December 1996), limiting banks' rights to invoke their duty of confidentiality in order to oppose the Income Tax Administration's investigations.

Income tax

The Income Tax Administration may request from any individual or corporation information and relevant material necessary to determine the tax liability of that party or of any third party (art 315ff of the Income Tax Code 1992 – Code des Impôts sur les Revenus 1992/Wetboek van de Inkomstenbelastingen 1992, hereafter referred to as ITC).

As far as banks are concerned, this broad duty of disclosure is qualified by ITC, art 318(1), which provides that the Income Tax Administration may not check banks' books or records in order to determine their clients' tax liability. Some case law has complemented this rule by rendering it illegal for the Income Tax Administration to request banks to disclose information about clients that the Administration itself is not allowed to seek out in the bank's records.

However, if in the course of an inquiry related to a bank's own tax situation, the Administration discovers relevant information leading to the suspicion that a mechanism exists or is being prepared by which the client is trying to avoid the taxation of his income illegally (mécanisme de fraude fiscale/mechanisme van belastingontduiking), then the Administration is allowed to investigate into the bank's records in order to determine the client's tax liability (ITC, art 318(2)). This article does not require the bank's involvement in the fraudulent mechanism, as was the case before.

Furthermore, if a tax investigation leads to a criminal investigation, the specific duty of confidentiality provided for in ITC, art 318(1) is no longer relevant, as the general rules on criminal proceedings will apply (see above). In addition, if the Banking and Finance Commission, whose mission includes the supervision of banks and investment firms, discovers special mechanisms (mécanismes particuliers/ bijzondere mechanismen) having as their purpose or as a consequence the promotion of fiscal fraud by third parties and put in place by banks (or investment firms) and where the Banking and Finance Commission has knowledge about the fact that these special mechanisms constitute a tax offence punishable by criminal sanctions for the banks (or investment firms) concerned themselves, it must advise the judicial authorities and no longer the Income Tax Administration, as was the case until 1999 (art 46 of the Law of 2 August 2002).

In a judgment of 23 October 2001,[10] the Antwerp Court of Appeal (Cour d'Appel/Hof van Beroep) has clarified the scope of the fiscal banking secrecy rules laid out in ITC, art 318 with regard to Banksys, the operator of the electronic payment system in Belgium and provider of ATM's and bank card payment terminals (for example, in shops). The Tax Administration had asked Banksys to provide it with information regarding the electronic payments made through a terminal placed by Banksys in the taxpayer's shop and obtained such information. The taxpayer claimed that the Tax Administration had violated the fiscal banking secrecy rule as laid out in ITC, art 318 by obtaining the information in such a way. The Tax Administration claimed that Banksys is not a bank. The court held that Banksys is indeed not a bank, but only a system-operating intermediary, which rents or sells payment terminals, linked to a central computer. The prohibition on seeking out bank records laid out in ITC, art 318(1) is as such not directly applicable to Banksys, but the court held that the Tax Administration had nonetheless violated the banking secrecy rule by attempting

10   Antwerpen, 23 oktober 2001, *RW* 2002-2003, afl 1, 27.

to bypass the prohibition laid out in ITC, art 318 by trying to obtain the same information from Banksys, which is, moreover, not the owner of the electronic data which are processed through its installations.

ITC, arts 335 and 336 provide that information discovered by one Tax Administration may be used by another to determine another category of tax. It seems, however, that the Income Tax Administration may not use this provision as a basis for requesting other Tax Administrations to obtain from a bank the information the Income Tax Administration needs regarding one of the bank's clients. Such a construction of the ITC would render meaningless the limits to the Income Tax Administration's power of investigation. ITC, art 318 was enacted in 1980, over 40 years after ITC, arts 335 and 336, and it should be understood as limiting the rule of co-operation among the various Tax Administrations. Some legal authors have however identified this co-operation between Tax Administrations as presenting a potential risk to banking confidentiality.[11]

When a taxpayer contests the taxation of his income, the Income Tax Administration may require information from his bank in order to investigate the validity of the complaint (ITC, art 374). It is accepted, however, that the taxpayer may forbid his bank from disclosing any information, even though such attitude will obviously greatly undermine his chances of a successful complaint. Banks often spontaneously refuse to release information that could reveal the identity of other clients.

Registration tax

Various types of operations, such as the sale of real estate, are subject to registration and payment of a tax to the Registration Administration (Administration de l'Enregistrement et des Domaines/Administratie der Registratie en Domeinen). Banks may be compelled by this administration's controllers (acting by virtue of an authorisation of a highly ranked official) to disclose any information and document deemed relevant to the determination of the exact amount of tax to be paid, when the bank or one of its clients is subject to such taxation (art 183 of the Registration Tax Code – Code des Droits d'Enregistrement/Wetboek Registratierechten).

Inheritance tax

The following rules of disclosure only apply when the deceased is a Belgian resident. Non-residents are not subject to Belgian inheritance taxes, except with regard to real estate, which is irrelevant in a bank-client relationship.

Banks have a passive duty of disclosure similar to the one related to registration taxes: the Registration Administration (which is also in charge of the collection of inheritance taxes) may request information from banks related to any operation of the deceased, his or her spouse or heir, or any third party that took place before or

---

11   See eg E De Baenst 'La protection de la confidentialité en matière fiscale', *JDF* 1991, 193 (quoted in D Mareels et M Bihain 'Le secret bancaire en droit fiscal belge', *JDF* 1996, 193-240) and I Quinet et L Herve 'Préparation à un contrôle fiscal: droits et devoirs de l'administration fiscale', *Pacioli* n° 50, 15.03.1999.

after the death and that may affect the taxation of the inheritance (art 100 of the Inheritance Tax Code – Code des Droits de Succession/Wetboek Successierechten).

In addition, banks must maintain a record of all clients depositing sealed envelopes or parcels or renting safety deposit boxes, along with the identity of their spouses. They must also maintain a list of signatures of all of a client's mandatees or co-lessees who request to have access to the envelope, parcel or safety deposit box. These records are transmitted to the Registration Administration (art 102-1 of the Inheritance Tax Code). The following disclosures occur in the event of death of a client or his or her spouse:

1   The banker must transmit to the Registration Administration a list of all of the client's funds, securities or other properties in the bank's possession, before paying or delivering them back to the estate (art 97 of the Inheritance Tax Code).
2   If the banker is in possession of sealed envelopes or parcels or if the client has rented a safety deposit box, the banker must:
     (a)   notify the Registration Administration of the intended opening of the envelope, parcel or safety deposit box, at least five days in advance; and
     (b)   transmit a list of the contents of the envelope, parcel or safety deposit box at the time it is opened. The Registration Administration may send one of its agents to witness such opening (arts 98 and 101 of the Inheritance Tax Code).

Value added tax

Banks, like any other party subject to VAT, must list, in regular VAT returns, all operations with clients who are themselves subject to VAT.

Banks also have a positive duty of disclosure. If the bank is itself subject to an investigation from the VAT Administration, it must supply the VAT controllers, at their request, with all the registers and documents the bank, like any other party subject to VAT, is required to maintain pursuant to the VAT Code, as well as any other information (arts 61, §1 and 62, §2 of the VAT Code). If the investigation targets third parties (whether or not clients), the bank is under the same duty to disclose such other information, provided the request is authorised by a highly ranked official (art 62bis of the VAT Code).

Disclosure of bank accounts abroad

It must be noted that Royal Decree of 20 December 1996 amended ITC, art 307, §1 and introduced the obligation for Belgian individuals to list in their income tax return all their bank accounts with banks abroad. This obligation is being contested on various grounds by legal authors, but has nevertheless been applicable to tax returns filed since 1997.

This provision is complemented by the new art 315(2) of the ITC, according to which the Income Tax Administration may request from individuals all documents relating to their foreign bank accounts.

Supervision by the Banking and Finance Commission

The Banking and Finance Commission ('BFC') supervises banks directly and through accredited statutory auditors (Law of 22 March 1993 on the Legal Status and Supervision of Credit Institutions and Law of 2 August 2002 on the Supervision of the Financial Sector and Financial Services). Neither auditors nor members of the Banking and Finance Commission may reveal any information they come across in the course of their supervisory activities, subject to certain exceptions, such as:

1   criminal proceedings;
2   the filing of a complaint by the BFC with the public prosecutor's office with respect to discovered offences; and
3   the communication of information to foreign supervisory authorities, to the extent such authorities are bound by similar secrecy rules.

A breach of this rule leads to the criminal sanctions provided for in art 458 of the Criminal Code (arts 7 and 8 of Royal Decree no 185 of 9 July 1935, as amended by the Law of 22 March 1993, and art 74ff of the Law of 2 August 2002).

The BFC may enter into reciprocal agreements with foreign supervisory authorities in order to organise exchanges of information and supervision abroad (art 77 of the Law of 2 August 2002). Such agreements (Memoranda of Understanding) have already been entered into with most other EU member states' supervisory authorities.

Outsourcing

Banks wishing to outsource a certain number of services (for example, IT services) will have to make sure that the appropriate technical and organisational measures are taken to ensure that confidential information is not used by the outsourcer nor disclosed to third parties. Data protection rules will have to be complied with as well. If a disclosure of confidential information occurs as a consequence of the outsourcing, the bank may be held liable for damages. The BFC, which should be informed of any proposed outsourcing by banks, will examine the scope of any proposed outsourcing project and evaluate whether the limits of the outsourcing are clearly defined and whether the outsourcing meets the prudential requirements regarding the proper organisation and functioning of the bank.

Communication of information among banks

Information to the Belgian National Bank (Consumer Credits Centre)

Two types of credit information must be notified by banks to the Belgian National Bank, which operates the Consumer Credits Centre, established by the Law of 10 August 2001 on the Consumer Credits Centre (as implemented by the Royal Decree of 7 July 2002). This Centre replaces the formerly separate positive and negative databases. The National Bank has the task of registering in the Consumer Credits Centre:

1   consumer credit agreements;
2   mortgage loan credit agreements (covered by the Law of 4 August 1992); and
3   default payments under consumer credit and mortgage loan credits.

The Consumer Credits Centre is composed of a positive and a negative section.

POSITIVE SECTION

Banks are compelled to notify the National Bank of any grant (or acquisition) of a credit or a loan, irrespective of the amount. The information registered includes personal data regarding the credit recipient, the name and address of the creditor (or the assignee), the type of credit, the amount of the credit, the amount actually drawn down, the periodicity of the credit and specific additional information depending on the type of credit. The positive section of the Consumer Credits Centre basically contains all credit information, whether or not the client has defaulted. Notification must be made within two business days after the conclusion of the agreement (or repayment of the credit).

NEGATIVE SECTION

All defaults under consumer credits and mortgage loan credits must be reported to the negative section of the Consumer Credits Centre, provided that certain criteria are met, depending on the type of credit (for example, when an amount due under a mortgage credit loan has not been paid within three months after the maturity date). Defaults have to be notified to the Consumer Credits Centre within eight business days of their being ascertained. Regularisations also have to be reported to the Centre.

CONSULTATION

Consultation of the Consumer Credits Centre (both positive and negative sections) is mandatory for banks prior to any offer of credit to a consumer (20 or 15 calendar days prior to a consumer credit or a mortgage credit loan respectively). The information disclosed is basically the same as the information which has to be registered in the Consumer Credits Centre, excluding, however, the name of the creditor or assignee and the number and language of the credit agreement(s).

Credit recipients have the right to access their file in the Consumer Credits Centre and can request rectification or removal of incorrect information.

Private databases

The Law of 12 June 1991 on Consumer Credit allows, under specific conditions, the setting up of private databases on consumers and their credit situation. The said law determines the type of information that may be included in the databases, as well as the categories of persons to whom and the purpose for which the information may be disclosed. Such private databases may be positive only.

A consumer must be informed of his initial inclusion in such a database. Consumers involved are entitled to have access to the information at all times and have the right to request that false or irrelevant data be amended or omitted.

Prior to the Law of 12 June 1991, private organisations had already set up databases to gather information for their members regarding their clients, especially in case of defaults or frauds. Such private blacklists are not necessarily limited to information on consumers. An example of such private blacklist is the one organised by the Union Professionnelle du Crédit/Beroepsvereniging van het Krediet.

Some legal authors seem to agree that such private blacklists are legal, whether they are 'positive' or only 'negative'. This exception to banks' duty of confidentiality is accepted on the following grounds:

1   disclosure is made to other banks – their duty of discretion prevents information from being leaked to the general public;
2   such disclosure is justified by a higher social and economic interest – safer and healthier credit for the public as a whole; and
3   the system only affects 'bad' clients, ie those who do not accurately disclose the existence of other credits to their bankers and those who have defaulted on previous credits.

On 5 June 1991, the Court of Appeal of Liège held a Belgian bank and the Union Professionnelle du Crédit liable for damages to a client for keeping outdated information on a blacklist.[12] The client's default was partly due to technical problems and had been cleared soon after. The default was still mentioned on the blacklist, however. Notwithstanding the absence of evidence that the client had been refused other credits because of the incorrect data, the court nevertheless held that the burden of the investigation undertaken by the client to discover the existence of the blacklist constituted recoverable damages. The court held that the plaintiff's right to privacy had been violated because the blacklist was secret and did not allow amendments to the data in case of a subsequent change in the debtor's situation, for example, the reimbursement of his debt or a judicial decision declaring the debt to be null and void.

The court seems to agree that blacklists are lawful provided they meet certain tests regarding disclosure and updating. These tests are similar to those established in the Law of 12 June 1991 on Consumer Credit.

In addition to the specific provisions of the Law of 12 June 1991, and for information on individuals not related to consumer credits, such databases must be operated in accordance with the Law of 8 December 1992 on the Protection of Privacy, which imposes obligations on the manager of a database with respect to the inputting of information, the information to be provided to the individuals, its internal treatment and its disclosure to third parties.

By a decision of 15 September 1994,[13] the President of the Commercial Court of Brussels held that a bank which had used data found on transfer forms (used by its clients to transfer funds to another bank) to approach these clients for a specific marketing campaign had breached the Law of 14 July 1991 on Trade Practices. Part of the unlawful practice spotted by the President of the court was the use of data handled in breach of the provisions of the Law of 8 December 1992 on the Protection of Privacy.

12   Liège, 5 juin 1991, *JT* 1992, 36.
13   Prés Comm Bruxelles, 15 septembre 1994, *DAOR* 1995, liv 34, 85.

Money laundering

Applicable laws and BFC circulars

The Law of 11 January 1993 (the Money Laundering Law) implemented the EEC Council Directive of 10 June 1991 on the prevention of the use of the financial system for money-laundering purposes in Belgium.[14]

The Money Laundering Law has been amended on several occasions to extend its scope of application and the notion of 'illegal origin' of the funds which is included in the definition of money laundering. The events of 11 September 2001 have led to a number of legislative initiatives in order to further widen the scope of the existing legislation.

The Banking and Finance Commission issued circulars for the credit institutions under its supervision to specify the practical measures to be taken in order to comply with the Money Laundering Law. A circular was also sent to banks' auditors requesting them to comment in their reports on the implementation of the Money Laundering Law by the banks.

Definition of money laundering

According to art 3 of the Money Laundering Law, the concept of money laundering includes certain types of transactions (listed in the Money Laundering Law) aimed at acquiring, holding, using, converting, transferring etc goods or funds having an illegal origin. These goods or funds are considered as having an illegal origin if they derive from certain offences (listed in the Money Laundering Law) including terrorism, organised crime, drug dealing, illegal arms trade, trade in human beings, exploitation of prostitution, illegal trade in human organs or tissues, 'severe and organised tax fraud' involving complex mechanisms or international schemes etc. A draft law of 15 January 2003 aims, inter alia, at explicitly including the financing of terrorism in this list of offences.

Measures to be taken by banks

In addition to a general duty to take all necessary measures to implement its provisions, the Money Laundering Law imposes the following obligations upon banks in order to prevent the use of such institutions by persons trying to launder money:

1   properly identifying the clients and other persons involved in any financial operation;
2   the maintaining of records related to the identification of the clients (and of these other persons) for a period of five years after the end of the relationship;
3   the issuing of reports on any operation that could be linked to money laundering;
4   the heightening of employees' awareness of the Money Laundering Law;

14   Council Directive 91/308/EEC.

5   the designating of one or more employees responsible for the implementation of the Money Laundering Law within the financial institution; and

6   the declaring of money laundering operations, or suspicion thereof, to the Committee for the Handling of Financial Information.

Specifically, banks must prepare certain documents and check the identity of both regular and occasional clients. As soon as a client enters into a relationship pursuant to which he will become a regular client, the identification should be made by means of documentary evidence, a copy of which needs to be retained. It is not necessary for a client to have an account with the bank to be considered 'regular'. Occasional clients must be identified:

1   where they wish to carry out a transaction involving an amount of €10,000 or more, even if this amount is spread over different operations between which there seems to be a link; and

2   each time a client wants to carry out a transaction which is suspected of being a money-laundering operation, even if the amount involved is below €10,000.

Client identification is not required if the client is (i) a credit institution, (ii) a financial institution, (iii) itself subject to the identification and other obligations imposed by the Money Laundering Law or (iv) a life insurance company and the amount of premiums is limited.

Reporting certain transactions could lead to a breach of the bank's duty of confidentiality (for example, when a 'clean' transaction is mistakenly reported). Therefore, the Money Laundering Law provides immunity against criminal or civil proceedings to banks which have reported a transaction in good faith even if, in retrospect, there was no reason for suspicion (art 20 of the Money Laundering Law).

The Money Laundering Law applies in principle to all banks (and other actors) having their head or branch office in Belgium. The international context has, however, shown that money laundering criminals are increasingly looking for countries and regions with absolute banking secrecy. The Money Laundering Law was amended by a recent Law (3 May 2002), which has added the possibility of extending by Royal Decree the duty to report all transactions and facts (irrespective of the amount) involving natural or legal persons domiciled, registered or having their residence in a state or region, the legislation of which is regarded as inadequate by a competent international institution (ie the Financial Action Task Force on Money Laundering, FATF) or which does not co-operate in the fight against money laundering (art 14ter of the Money Laundering Law). A direct link between the transaction or facts and the state or region concerned is required. Extensions to a number of states and regions by Royal Decree are to be expected.

Committee for the Handling of Financial Information

The Money Laundering Law set up a Committee for the Handling of Financial Information. Its tasks include the follow-up of the declarations made by banks on money laundering operations. When faced with serious indications of money laundering, the Committee must forward the information to the Public Prosecutor's Office. It should be noted that the Committee for the Handling of Financial Information is itself bound by a strict duty of secrecy, subject to certain exceptions comparable to those for the BFC mentioned above (for example, testimonies before court, in the framework of the international fight against fraud and money laundering etc).

Brokerage in transferable securities

For the time being, the Law of 6 April 1995 on Secondary Markets and on the Status and Supervision of Investment Companies, Brokers and Investments Advisers provides for specific supervisory powers entrusted to the Management Committee of the Stock Exchange regarding the operations carried out by brokers, including banks, on transferable securities (art 20).

The Management Committee of the Stock Exchange may request any information from brokers in order to ensure that relevant laws and regulations are being complied with. It has far-reaching investigative powers, including the right to conduct on-site inspections.

Specific rules apply in case the Management Committee suspects that insider trading is occurring or that the price of listed securities is being manipulated by fraudulent means.

The Law of 2 August 2002, the relevant provisions of which will soon enter into force, has reformed the supervision of the financial markets and has centralised supervision into the BFC, which will soon take over the supervisory tasks and powers from the Management Committee as described above. It should be noted that the powers of the BFC are more extensive than those of the Management Committee and include, inter alia, the possibility of imposing penalties.

CONCLUSION

This description of banks' duty of confidentiality has placed much more emphasis on the exceptions to the rule, which are more specific to Belgian law, than on the duty itself.

In many circumstances, the banker will not be allowed to use his duty of discretion to oppose requests for disclosure.

It must be recalled, however, that the rule of confidentiality, in its principle and scope, and the potential liability in case of breach of such rule are clearly established in Belgium. Therefore, a bank, if required to disclose information to public authorities or private persons regarding its client's operations, must not depart from its traditional cautious conduct: it must ensure that procedural rules have not been violated and limit the release of information or documents to the minimum required.

5   Brazil

Jorge Nemr

INTRODUCTION

The legal duty of bank secrecy in Brazil was formerly ruled by art 38 of Law no 4,595, of 31 December 1964, for almost 40 years. Bank secrecy is currently ruled by Complementary Law no 105, of 10 January 2001, regulated, on the same date, by Decree no 3,724, one of the several measures recently adopted by the Union with the purpose of intensifying the fight against tax evasion.

When it was created, the legal duty of bank secrecy caused great controversy, mainly in questions involving the Public Power. It is worth noting that developments over the last few years have not been sufficient to clarify the matter, considering that the legislative evolution, the new Constitution of 1988 and several other new situations have contributed to the continual arising of doubts in connection with this matter.

Bank secrecy is currently a worldwide practice. It emerged in view of the ethical and moral requirements of certain professional categories. With social evolution, values were established, among them trust and discretion. Such ethical requirements changed into moral rules, then into technical rules and finally into legal rules.

It is worth noting that bank secrecy appeared as a variant of professional secrecy. It developed as a means of protection for private interests, but with society's approval, as bankers were acquainted with businesses, assets and even family secrets.

BANK SECRECY UNDER BRAZILIAN LAW

After the arrival of the Portuguese Royal Family in Brazil in the nineteenth century, Banco do Brasil, the first Brazilian bank, was created. This bank was liquidated in 1829 as a result of the excessive expenses of the Crown, the return of the Royal Family to Lisbon, Brazil's gaining of independence and the struggle for political consolidation in the new empire.

With the creation of new banks, several laws were enacted to regulate banking operations, clearly evidencing the concern of the government with the appropriate functioning of the system.

The enactment of the Brazilian Commercial Code of 1850 provided bank secrecy with a certain legal protection, as mercantile secrecy could also be applied to banks and transactions thereof. Based on this rule, the banks refused to supply information on their transactions and their clients, even in response to judicial requests.

In 1940, with the enactment of the current Criminal Code, the violation of professional secrecy was typified among crimes against the inviolability of secrets. The purpose thereof was to protect the privacy of the citizen against a possible indiscretion of necessary confidences. Despite the fact that no express reference was made to bankers and professionals of the area, the legal writing and the case law placed them among the persons covered by the norm. At that time, bank secrecy was criminally established, providing for a penalty of detention or fines for violators.

Little by little, the Public Power, particularly in judicial or tax-related matters, started to reduce the strictness of compliance with bank secrecy rules. Some decisions of the courts supported the unconditional character of bank secrecy, while others defied such character. The conservative legal writing of that time insisted on the inviolability of secrecy. However, this view did not prevail and bank secrecy, absolute in origin, became relative, with limits expressly set forth in law.

REGULATION OF THE MATTER

Law no 4,595, of 31 December 1964, was enacted to reorganise the banking system. Article 38 of this Law, which provided for bank secrecy, was revoked by Complementary Law no 105, of 10 January 2001, regulated, on the same date, by Decree no 3,724.

In contrast to the preceding provision, it is now provided that the violation of secrecy may be decreed *when it is necessary for the investigation of occurrence of any illicit act, in any phase of the inquiry or the judicial proceeding*, especially in cases of crimes of terrorism; illicit traffic of narcotics or similar drugs, contraband or traffic of weapons, ammunitions or material destined to the production thereof; extortion upon kidnapping; crimes against the national financial system, against the Public Administration, the tax order and the social security; laundering of money or occultation of goods; rights and amounts or crimes practiced by a criminal organisation: art 1, para 4, of Complementary Law no 105/2001.

Among the measures adopted by the Union to intensify the fight against tax evasion, an important measure is the potential for tax authorities and agents of the Union, states, federal district and municipalities to violate the bank secrecy of taxpayers, without previous authorisation from the Judiciary Power.

Such power, as mentioned above, was granted to the tax authority by means of Complementary Law no 105/2001, regulated, on the same occasion, by Decree no 3,724/2001. According to art 6 of this Law, provided an administrative procedure has been commenced or a tax proceeding is in progress, the administrative authority and the tax agents may request information shown on documents, books and registers of the financial institutions, including deposit accounts and financial investments relative to the taxpayers.

Note that there is permission for the violation of bank secrecy even before the commencement of the administrative procedure, as the law mentions 'inspection proceeding in progress', ie during the inspection.

Leaving aside the arguments relative to the material constitutionality of the law in question, it is worth mentioning that the violation of bank secrecy is an extremely controversial issue in Brazil, as this may involve the violation of privacy and of intimacy, assured as a fundamental right by item X of art 5 of the Federal Constitution. The individual rights and guarantees are included in the so-called immutable clauses, the abolition of which may not be the object of resolution: art 60, para 4 of the Federal Constitution.

DEFINITION OF BANK SECRECY

Several scholars have defined 'bank secrecy'. We may cite a few, such as, for example, Malagarriga, who defines bank secrecy as 'the obligation imposed to the Banks of not revealing to third parties, without a justified cause, information relative to their clients to which they may have knowledge as a consequence of the legal relations which bind them'.[1]

According to Sichtermann, bank secrecy is the 'right corresponding to the obligation of the bank of not providing any information whatsoever, whether on the accounts of its clients, whether on subsequent facts to which they may have knowledge in view of its relations with clients'.[2]

Finally, in accordance with the concept of Sérgio Carlos Covello, a Brazilian scholar, bank secrecy may be defined as 'the obligation which the Banks have of not revealing, except for just cause, the information they may obtain by virtue of their professional activity'.[3]

LEGAL NATURE

Over time, the ethical duty which bankers had to maintain the secrecy of the banking transactions of their clients was changed into an obligation of a mandatory nature. Therefore, the single moral duty, the violation of which could simply produce a social disapproval, became a legal duty, with criminal sanctions for those who had the duty of maintaining secrecy.

It may be noted that it concerned a negative covenant, not liable to extinction even upon the release of the financial institution before the client. Besides persisting in time, it was an erga omnes obligation, as the duty of non-disclosure of the information by the bank applied to any person, except as provided by law.

1   Malagarriga, Juan Carlos 'El Segreto Bancário' Buenos Aires, Abeledo-Perot, 1970
2   Covello, Sérgio Carlos 'O Sigilo Bancário' Leud, 2001
3   Covello, Sérgio Carlos 'O Sigilo Bancário' Leud, 2001

THE RELATIVITY OF BANK SECRECY

The right to bank secrecy, just like other rights, is not absolute. According to the teachings of Ariel Dotti:

> '. . . all rights, since the most fundamental one which is life, are subject to privations and limitations: death and imprisonment penalties, patrimonial sanctions, confinement, banishment, searches and seizures, expropriations, seizures under legal process and so many other measures in progress with the purpose of satisfying collective or individual interests, are examples thereof. Such limitations result from the imposition of life in society in its most diversified expressions.'[4]

In order to avoid contraventions of other general rights, society must restrict certain rights in some circumstances. In certain circumstances there is a conflict of interests between intimacy, which is a private interest of the individual, and the information which may be relevant to the state or to other citizens.

As already mentioned, on 11 January 2001, Complementary Law no 105 was enacted, which regulates the secrecy of transactions of financial institutions and makes up part of the governmental package in its fight against tax evasion and avoidance in Brazil.

A great debate was created in connection with art 6 of this legal rule, which provides for the possibility of violation of bank secrecy by tax authorities and agents of the Union, states, federal district and municipalities, without the necessity of previous judicial authorisation.

In order to regulate this legal provision, the federal government enacted Decree no 3,724/2001, providing for the violation of bank secrecy by tax agents, and defining that such measure shall only be possible when there is an inspection proceeding in progress and provided that it occurs, in the concrete case, in one of 11 situations where bank verification is deemed indispensable by the competent authority.[5]

Under this scenario, it is extremely important to analyse the question of the violation of bank secrecy without judicial authorisation in view of the fundamental rights relative to private life and data secrecy, set forth in items X and XII of art 5 of the Federal Constitution, respectively.

As stated by Professor Pedro Luís Piedade Novaes,[6] the Universal Declaration of Human Rights, signed by Brazil on 10 December 1948, provides, in art XII, that:

> '. . . no one shall be subjected to arbitrary interference with his privacy, family, home or correspondence, nor to attacks upon his honor and reputation. Everyone has the right to the protection of the law against such interference or attacks.'

This is also the wording of art 11, item '2', of the American Convention of Human Rights, ratified by Brazil on 25 September 1992.

---

4   Dotti, René Ariel, 'Proteção da Vida Privada e Liberdade de informação' São Paulo Editora RT, 1980
5   See Appendix, Decree No. 3.724, of 10 January 2001, Art. 3, items I-XI
6   Professor Pedro Luis Piedade Novaes 'O Sigilo Bancário e a Lei Complementar No. 105/ 2001 Brazilian Institute of Tax Planning Studies of the IBPT, 2001.

Bank secrecy, therefore, is a fundamental right, protected by the Constitution of 1988 as an immutable clause, which may not be abolished or limited even by a Constitutional Amendment, as provided by art 60, para 4, item IV of the Federal Constitution.

However, the legal writing and case law in Brazil has understood that no public liberty is absolute, and that therefore there will be situations where two or more fundamental rights are in conflict with each other.

In order to resolve this tension between constitutional principles, one may resort to the principle of proportionality, imported from German law, which provides that, there being two constitutional principles in conflict, one must place on them an imaginary balance in order to sacrifice that of lesser social relevance.

In the instant case, we find precisely such a conflict of rules: on the one hand, the individual right to bank secrecy and, on the other, the public interest, which is represented by the intent of the tax authorities of verifying a possible tax evasion or crime. One must, therefore, assess both rights in order to decide which of them shall prevail in the concrete case.

Initially, it is worth mentioning that the present matter is not new, there being decisions rendered by the High Court of Justice and by the Federal Supreme Court, which define the rules to be followed for the violation of tax secrecy under the Federal Constitution of 1988.[7] The Federal Supreme Court, in this regard, has already stated that the violation of bank secrecy is legal when there is a relevant public interest, such as that of an investigation based on a reasonable suspicion of criminal infraction, provided that duly ordered by the Judiciary Power.[8]

Following this rationale, Celso Bastos clarifies that:

> '. . . the breakage of bank secrecy is only admissible when based on reasons with fundaments, when there is a relevant public interest, such as that of a criminal investigation or criminal procedural finding of facts or by virtue of the exceptionality of the motive, provided that a judicial authorization is rendered.'

Likewise, the High Court of Justice has decided that:

> '. . . the legal order authorizes the breakage of bank secrecy, under exceptional situations. Should it imply, however, a restraint to the citizen's privacy right, assured by the constitutional principle, it is indispensable to evidence the necessity of the information requested, with the strict compliance with the authorizing legal conditions.'

---

7   HCJ (Special Appeal 1997/0075348-4, D.J.U. 15.12.1997 / Appeal in Writ of Mandamus (1998/0098502-6) Justice Fernando Gonçalves FSC (Decision rendered by Justice Sepúlveda Pertence in IC No. 901.6-DF, D.J.U. 23.02.1995 / Writ of Mandamus 23964-DF, reporting Justice Celso de Mello, D.J.U. 21.06.2002

8   FSC, Writ of Mandamus No. 21.729-4 DF, D.J.U 19.10.2001.

According to the unanimous understanding of the Federal Supreme Court, even before the enactment of Complementary Law no 105/2001, the violation of bank secrecy may take place in two cases: (i) under a Parliamentary Inquiry Committee (CPI); and (ii) upon a judicial order, provided that both exceptional situations are duly justified.

In this regard, art 6 of Complementary Law no 105/2001, by establishing the violation of bank secrecy without a judicial authorisation, diverges from the present understanding of the Federal Supreme Court, for which reason it may not be admitted in Brazil's legal system, under penalty of violation of art 5, items X and XII of the Federal Constitution.

For discussion purposes only, even if Complementary Law no 105/2001 provided for the violation of bank secrecy upon judicial authorisation, such rule would only be valid in the event of investigation of tax crimes and not in the case of administrative proceedings aiming at ascertaining tax credits in favour of the Public Treasury. This is so because, applying the principle of proportionality and placing such rights under observation, it means to assert that bank secrecy must only be extinguished for the investigation of crimes, as the latter concerns a relevant public interest which is more important than the privacy right of the individual or of the legal entity.

It is worth pointing out that the governmental assurances that the violation of bank secrecy shall be carried out with full prudence and responsibility and under the rules set forth by Decree no 3,724/2001 are not convincing, and do not have the power to transform art 6 of Complementary Law no 105/2001 into a provision sheltered by the Constitution.

It is worth clarifying that in Brazil's legal system it is widely accepted that the violation of bank secrecy may only be decreed by a judicial order or in cases (within limits) where other bodies are, by express mention of the Federal Constitution, held equivalent to the Judiciary Power, as is the case of the CPIs: art 58, para 3 of the Federal Constitution.

It should be noted that the Federal Constitution does not grant to the Federal Revenue Office, in any of its articles, the status of body held equivalent to the Judiciary Power, for which reason the violation of bank secrecy as provided by art 6 of Complementary Law no 105/2001, without the intervention of a judge or court, is completely unreasonable. Otherwise, the preparation of a law regulating the violation of bank secrecy would not be necessary, as the Federal Revenue already has the means to catch supposed evaders, by means of a joint action with the Public Prosecution, which, in the capacity of holder of the public criminal action, would require in court, with justifications, the disclosure of bank secrecy. This would not be the case of unconstitutionality, being in agreement with the current understanding of the Federal Supreme Court regarding bank secrecy.

In short, if the Brazilian government intends to impose morals on the country by adopting measures which aim at fighting tax evasion crimes, it must first respect the Federal Constitution, at the risk of placing itself on a level even lower than that of the persons whose investigation is intended. This would be so because while the evaders are violating the law, the government (including the Legislative and Executive Powers) would be violating the Federal Constitution and the international treaties ratified by Brazil.

Unless the Federal Supreme Court drastically changes its understanding, which was confirmed by nine out of the eleven justices which constitute part of its present plenary composition, the violation of bank secrecy without judicial authorisation must be declared unconstitutional, as it violates items X and XII of art 5 of the Federal Constitution.

LEGAL LIMITS

In Brazil, there are several limitations of public order for bank secrecy. When there was not any express law on the matter, information on the personal and patrimonial life of the citizens was not provided. The compulsory disclosure was only admitted in special cases, and with due cautions.

The limits of bank secrecy in Brazil may only be established by a complementary law of the Union and, therefore, only another complementary law of the Union may provide for the exceptions thereof, in addition to those already in existence. Municipal or state laws may not regulate this matter. A law which admits exceptions to general rules, or restricts rights, covers only the cases which it specifies. Hence, banks may only provide public authorities with the information permitted by law, in the manner provided by such law, under penalty of violation of the obligation which is imposed thereto and the consequent imposition of sanctions.

The legal restrictions on bank secrecy may not be used for the purpose of carrying out a deep investigation of a citizen's life. The violation of secrecy, when so ordered, must be restricted to the period of occurrence of the facts which are being investigated. This is so because the public interest which is being protected by the decree of violation of secrecy may not violate human dignity, which is fundamental to the maintenance of the state and to society.

The state, in the exercise of the jurisdictional function, very often needs to investigate facts in order to render a just solution to the case under analysis. However, such facts may, time and again, be covered by bank secrecy, thus preventing the solution of the case by the Justice. For such reason, the legislation in force requires banks to provide information to the Justice, removing the banking barrier before the Judiciary Power. Bank secrecy may only cover the just and legitimate interests of the client. Any illicit interest would represent an injury to third parties and, therefore, the legal conscience may not protect it under the veil of secrecy.

With the enactment of Complementary Law no 105/2001, the authorities and the tax agents of the Union, state, federal district and municipalities may only examine documents, books and registrations of financial institutions, including those relative to deposit accounts and financial investments, when there is an administrative procedure commenced or a tax proceeding in progress and when such examinations are considered indispensable by the competent administrative authority.

The result of the examinations, the information and the documents referred to by this article shall be maintained in secrecy, with due regard to the tax legislation: art 6 and sole paragraph of Complementary Law no 105/2001. According to Decree no 3,724/2001, which regulates art 6 of Complementary Law no 105/2001, the examination of the information which characterises the violation of secrecy may only take place when there is an inspection proceeding in progress and when such examinations are deemed indispensable.

On the other hand, the inspection proceeding would only commence by virtue of an express order contained in a Writ of Tax Proceeding (MPF) by a tax auditor of the Federal Revenue. However, in cases of evident verification of an instance of violation of tax legislation which may jeopardise the interests of the National Treasury, the inspection proceeding must be commenced immediately and, within five days of the date of commencement, a special MPF shall be issued, by means of which the investigated party shall be officially informed thereof.

According to Professor Gilberto Marques Bruno,[9] such provisions evidently render the taxpayers quite vulnerable before the condition assured by law, which grants to the public agents, under the form of an inspection proceeding, the possibility of examining the registrations of financial transactions.

Therefore, even if we take into account that the violation of secrecy in transactions of financial institutions keeps, in its essence, the purpose of the federal government of fighting tax evasion, we may question the admissibility of a complementary law granting competence to the tax authorities which compose the structure of offices and functions of the Federal Revenue Office, and granting them powers of verification of secret data and information which, up to then, could only be disclosed upon the intervention and approval of the Judiciary Power, with the appearance of total violation of the Principle of Inviolability of Data Secrecy, consecrated by item X of art 5 of the Federal Constitution, as mentioned above.

More than a governmental instrument designed to fight tax evasion, the text contained in Complementary Law no 105/2001 and regulated by Decree no 3,724/2001 may become a mechanism of indiscretion to satisfy the collecting requirements of the tax authorities, resulting in real invasion of taxpayers' privacy.

NATURAL LIMITS

The natural limits of bank secrecy arise either from the wishes of the secrecy's holder or from the nature of the banking transactions, or, in addition, from the rules of civil law. They indicate to what extent a bank is authorised to disclose the secrets without violating its duty.

The natural limits must be sought mainly in the rules of civil law. If there is any doubt, the obligation of secrecy must prevail. For financial institutions, it is preferable to deny the information and let the interested party resort to the courts to obtain the information, rather than to inform and risk violating the secrecy and becoming subject to criminal, administrative and civil penalties.

Without violating bank secrecy, the bank may and must supply to the client information regarding his current account, such as balance, credits and debts, copies

---

9   Professor Bruno 'Quebra do Sigilo Bancário', Estudos do IBPT, Instituto Brasileiro de Planejamento Tributário, 2001

of cheques drawn, name of the person who paid an instrument of credit to his benefit placed in collection with the establishment. However, the bank must not disclose more than what is necessary for compliance with its power. This means that it must not disclose facts which do not concern its obligation, under penalty of violating the intimacy of a third party, being thus liable therefor.

In the event of representatives or attorneys of the client, it is necessary that the bank analyse, on a case-by-case basis, the powers granted in the power-of-attorney to the attorney-in-fact. For example, if the attorney-in-fact was given powers to open a current account only, there would be no reason for giving him access to subsequent business information concerning the client. In relation to legal entities, only those vested with representation powers may share the secrecy. In Brazilian law, the partners which do not have access to the secrecy and wish to exercise their right to information must proceed in accordance with the provision of art 18 of the Commercial Code.

In the event of heirs and successors, they may have access to information protected by bank secrecy, as they may need such information in order to carry on the business and safeguard their own interests. However, the access to secrecy must be limited to strictly patrimonial information. Information that is not necessary to safeguard the patrimonial interests of the heirs must remain undisclosed.

The client of the bank may authorise it to supply information to third parties and the bank may not decline to do so. This is due to the fact that the obligation of secrecy exists in order to preserve the intimacy of the client, and it would not be reasonable that its strictness reached the point of imposing itself even against the will of the protected interested party. Only the interested party may select the information which must remain secret. There are circumstances where a client may have reason to disclose certain information about his banking transactions (such as the number of transactions, punctuality, balance in current account etc) in order to evidence his financial credibility.

With respect to marital relationships, bank secrecy applies to spouses, even if the information is necessary to proceed with a conjugal separation. In such cases, the interested party must resort to the Judiciary Power.

The bank accounts in Brazil's system may also be 'joint' (where several persons hold an account). In such cases, each holder has the right to be informed on the patrimonial character relative to the operation of the bank account. This is so because each act practised by a holder affects the juridical sphere of the others. The bank must inform each holder of the balance of the current account, cheques drawn, withdrawals and deposits made etc. However, personal information of a holder which does not relate to the operation of the current account must not be supplied to the other holder without due authorisation.

Finally, in litigation between a bank and its client, the financial institution may disclose any and all information regarding the client with the purpose of avoiding damage. However, the bank may disclose only facts strictly necessary to the defence of its rights and must not disclose those facts of which it has knowledge and which do not benefit the bank and cause damage to the client.

BANKING INFORMATION

Banks hold important information which discloses the moral and patrimonial profile of a person, and which may contribute to the regularisation of the financial system. However, they have the right to be silent by virtue of the secrecy which they are committed to respect. The supply of information may conflict with the obligation of secrecy. Information requested by third parties and by other banking establishments may only be supplied upon authorisation of the client; without authorisation, the bank must deny information to whoever is requesting it. If the financial institution has filed a lawsuit against the client or protested an instrument of credit representing a debt, this becomes public and, therefore, the bank may inform that a client is in default. With the exception of this case, the bank has the duty to be silent, given that one of its main virtues is discretion.

With regard to the issue of secrecy, there is an interesting question: with respect to the Central Bank, would such prohibition be valid, taking into account that the banks' obligation of keeping secrecy is extendable to all, and may only be disregarded upon a judicial order? The answer is Yes.

According to art 2 of Complementary Law no 105/2001, the duty of secrecy applies to the Central Bank in relation to the transactions it may carry out and to the information it may obtain in the exercise of its functions.

The secrecy, including information regarding deposit accounts and investments held with financial institutions, may not be detrimental to the Central Bank of Brazil in the performance of its functions of inspection, encompassing the investigation, at any time, of illegal acts practiced by controlling parties, administrators, members of chart boards, managers, attorneys and representatives of financial institutions, not even while proceeding to an inquiry in a financial investigation submitted to special regime: art 2, para 1 of Complementary Law no 105/2001.

The commissions charged with the inquiries may examine any documents relative to assets, rights and obligations of financial institutions, of its controlling parties, administrators, members of chart boards, attorneys, managers and representatives, including current accounts and transactions with other financial institutions.

The bank has the obligation to inform the Central Bank of the amount of its transactions, its assets, its liabilities etc. However, this is related to the inspection power held by the Central Bank. It does not have the power to violate bank secrecy, which is a rule of public order. Allowing that the Central Bank obtains any and all information from the financial institutions would mean to grant to the state, by means of a supervision body, the permission to investigate in full the intimacy of the clients of banks. Therefore, there is the bank secrecy before the Central Bank, which, being a financial institution itself, must comply with such legal provision.

Law no 9,613, of 3 March 1998, (the Money Laundering Law) defined the crime of 'money laundering' and created the Council of Financial Activities (COAF), with the function of gathering information on illegal transactions. In art 11, the Law establishes that banks must inform the competent authorities or COAF of any transactions or proposals of transactions which present serious indications of occultation or laundering of money; this provision is confirmed by art 2, para 6 of Complementary Law no 105/2001. Such information, besides violating bank secrecy, disregards the general right to intimacy set forth by art 5, item X of Brazil's Federal Constitution, and submits banks to civil liability, in addition to other penalties. In the present writer's view, the administrative regime of information (that is, without being submitted to the approval of the Judiciary Power) which the Money Laundering Law intended to create, is unconstitutional.

LEGAL GUARANTEE

A legal rule usually provides, in principle, for a penalty previously established for cases of non-compliance. Such penalty is imposed on the person or on their assets, and has the purpose of remedying the injury caused by the non-compliance with the duty. The penalty brings the external force and the coercion necessary for the effectiveness of the right. It is the extreme method to which the state has to resort in order to obtain the due regard to the rules of behaviour in order in a certain time and place. The penalty also works psychologically on the public as, generally, people comply with the obligation in order to avoid the penalty.

Penalties can be criminal or civil. Criminal penalties have a repressive or punitive character and civil penalties are for the purpose of reparation, but both have a preventive nature, since ordinary persons do not wish the imposition of penalties of restrictive nature on their personal or patrimonial freedom.

With respect to bank secrecy, the law provides for a criminal and administrative penalty in the event of non-compliance. The violation thereof is punished with the a penalty of imprisonment from one to four years, and a fine of up to 200 times the highest minimum wage in force in Brazil.

PREVENTIVE RELIEF

Avoiding the violation is the best protection that can be given to bank secrecy. The trouble caused by the violation of an interest is a wrong which the legal system can hardly reinstate satisfactorily. The preventive relief is the most efficient protection of the personal rights, and especially the intimacy right, which, as any right, exists to be exercised. In Brazilian law, there is no specific measure for the preventive protection of intimacy, nor of bank secrecy.

However, in Brazil's legal system there are writs of prevention, with the purpose of ensuring the efficacy of executive measures, supporting provisionally a right which, in principle, seems unquestionable, until the merits are finally decided. The writ of prevention has the purpose of assuring the proper progress of the main lawsuit which was filed or shall be filed, assuring its function of settlement of the litigation or of satisfaction of the credit. One may notice, therefore, that the writ of prevention is a legal instrument used in order to avoid an injury.

The Brazilian Code of Civil Procedure allows the judge to determine the writs of prevention or provisional measures which he deems proper in order to maintain entire and unattainable the juridical good aimed at by the parties, when there is a fair and justified fear that one of the parties causes, prior to the final decision, a severe injury, which is difficult to be repaired, to the other party's right.

There are two indispensable requisites of the writs of prevention: the *periculum in mora* and the *fumus boni iuris*; the first is the possibility of damage resulting from the delay in the final judgment of the issue and the second is the probability of the existence of the right claimed by the claimant. As a rule, both requisites are present in the case of a violation of bank secrecy. The violation of bank secrecy represents a severe injury, as it offends one of the most valuable personal rights. Such injury is difficult to remedy, mainly in relation to the moral damage, and for this reason it is preferable to prevent than to compensate. We may see, therefore, that the writ of prevention seeks the preventive defence of the good protected by bank secrecy, both in its patrimonial aspect and in its exclusively moral aspect.

However, in order to prevent injury by means of a writ of prevention, the party wishing to preserve the secrecy should also file a main lawsuit, which may be an indemnification lawsuit or a merely declaratory lawsuit.

REPARATION OF DAMAGE

Article 186 of the New Civil Code protects any and all subjective right and imposes the obligation of indemnification by a party which caused damages to third parties. By imposing the civil liability on the violator, the legislator protects bank secrecy, not only for the right of reparation assured to the injured party, but also for the unfavourable situation imposed on the violator, as this is required to remedy the damage. Such an obligation holds the violator back from committing the violation again, and discourages others from committing the same violation. The civil liability repairs the damages or, at least, attempts to mitigate the consequences thereof.

In order to define the illicit behaviour justifying a penalty, one must verify what the violation consists of. Violating is the action of disclosing the information under secrecy, thus causing an undue invasion of a third party's privacy. With the violation of bank secrecy, privacy, which is a protected juridical good, is damaged due to the acknowledgement or disclosure of protected information and facts. The disclosure may be made directly or indirectly, in writing, orally or even by gestures.

However, not all disclosure made by a bank is a violation of bank secrecy, as there may be reasons that justify it. In order to render the bank liable, the disclosure must be against the law; that is, must be in absolute non-compliance with the legal system. Otherwise, its behaviour is legal and does not imply the burden of indemnification. Its liability shall only be excepted upon evidence that the damage occurred by virtue of force majeure, legitimate self-defence, or by virtue of strict compliance with the legal duty.

Upon the occurrence of a damage, the relevant indemnification, for which the re-establishment of a state or situation under the law are intended, must be provided for, with the purpose of erasing the effects of the illegal behaviour. It must be sufficiently wide to cover the whole damage arising from the non-compliance with the obligation.

We may define 'damage' as any injury to a juridical good, which may reach things, provisions, features of the person and products of the mind. With respect to the violation of bank secrecy, the indemnification must cover the material damages as well as the extra-patrimonial damages.

Material damages are relatively easy to ascertain, whether upon comparison with other goods of the same type or upon evaluation made by experts on the matter. On the other hand, in the event of non-material damages, the indemnification is at the judge's discretion, which may be significant to the extent of being symbolic, and therefore inefficient, or excessive, causing an unlawful enrichment.

Alternatively, extra-patrimonial damages, especially those arising from a violation of the right to privacy, honour and image, are assured by art 5 of Brazil's Constitution. Due to the difficulty in evaluating the extent of such types of damage in order to establish an indemnification, such compensation, under Brazilian law, is fixed by arbitration according to the judge's sensible criteria.

Under Brazilian law, it is not necessary to evidence moral damages in the instant case. The judge is likely to presume them; that is, to consider the occurrence thereof until evidence to the contrary. The burden of proof, in the event of a violation of bank secrecy, rests with the offender, who must show the non-existence of damage, thus suppressing the presumption.

The indemnification lawsuit for the occurrence of violation of bank secrecy may only be filed by the client of the bank or by an authorised third party. Being a private interest, the compensation of the damage caused may not be claimed, on its own initiative, by members of the Public Prosecution or determined by the own initiative of the judge. In cases where the violation of bank secrecy applies to more than one person (an absolutely plausible situation), each holder has the right to claim the reparation of the damage individually suffered. Therefore, the compensations are distinct and may be claimed in independent lawsuits.

Finally, it is worth mentioning that, being an extremely invasive action, the violation of bank secrecy may not take place without the approval of the Judiciary Power. The unjustified investigation into someone's life is absolutely incompatible with the fundamental rights assured by the Federal Constitution.

It remains clear, therefore, that the measure under discussion may only be justified on the grounds of strong evidence or indications, clearly defined, of the practice of irregularities capable of giving good reason for the adoption of such extreme measures.

CONCLUSION

Finally, it is worth mentioning that the breakage of bank secrecy, being a measure of extreme violence, may not take place without the consent of the Judiciary Power. The groundless invasion of someone's life is a conduct absolutely incompatible with the fundamental rights assured by the Federal Constitution.

It remains clear, therefore, that the measure under discussion may only be justified upon strong evidences or indications, clearly defined, of the practice of irregularities capable of giving good reason for the adoption of such an extreme measure.

It is worth mentioning that the Brazilian legal system has established that the breakage of bank secrecy may only be decreed by a judicial decision (within the limits already mentioned) where other bodies, by express reference of the Federal Constitution, are held equivalent to the Judiciary Power, such as the Parliamentary Inquiry Committees (art 58, para 3, of the Federal Constitution.)

An example which corroborates the foregoing is the amendment to Decree No 4,489, of 28 November 2002, after a lot of pressure made by lawyers and by society, as provided by Decree No 4,545, of 26 December 2002.

The first Decree (No. 4,498/02), which complemented the regulation of the utilisation of information covered by bank secrecy for purposes of inspection by the Federal Revenue, allowed the indiscriminate access, by the Federal Revenue Office, to information regarding financial operations of all clients involving, within the period of one month, amounts in excess of R\$5,000.00 (for individuals) and R\$10,000.00 (for legal entities), and the financial institutions had the obligation of sending such information on a monthly basis to the tax authorities as from 1 January 2003.

Displeased with the content of this Decree, the Brazilian Bar Association issued an opinion pointing out defaults of legality and unconstitutionality of the first Decree, which contributed for the enactment, by the President of the Republic, Fernando Henrique Cardoso, of a new Decree (4,545/02), which, in practice, revokes the first one, excluding the financial institutions' obligation to send information on their clients to the tax authorities.

Notwithstanding the enactment of the new Decree, it is worth informing that the Federal Revenue may yet have access to the clients of the financial institutions, however without the facility granted by Decree No 4,489/02, as it must request such information to the financial institutions by means of the filing of the relevant administrative proceeding or tax procedure.

The appendix below contains relevant extracts from Brazlian legislation.

APPENDIX

Complementary Law no 105, of 10 January 2001

Provides on the secrecy of transactions of financial institutions, and addresses other matters.

THE PRESIDENT OF THE REPUBLIC

I hereby state that the National Congress has decreed and I sign the following Complementary Law:

Art. 1. The financial institutions shall keep secrecy of their active and passive transactions and services rendered.

Paragraph 1 – For the purposes of this Complementary Law, the following are considered financial institutions:

I – banks of any kind;

II – distributors of securities;

III – exchange and securities brokers;

IV – companies of credit, financing and investments;

V – companies of real estate credit;

VI – administrators of credit cards;

VII –leasing companies;

VIII – administrators of over-the-counter organized market;

IX – credit unions;

X – associations of savings and loans;

XI – stock exchanges and futures and commodities exchanges;

XII – entities of liquidation and clearance;

XIII – other companies which, by virtue of the nature of their transactions, may be so considered by the National Monetary Council.

Paragraph 2 – Companies of commercial stimulation or factoring, for the purposes of this Complementary Law, shall comply with the rules applicable to the financial institutions set forth in paragraph 1.

Paragraph 3 – The following do not represent violation of the secrecy duty:

I – the exchange of information between and among financial institutions, for records purposes, including by means of risk centrals, in compliance with the rules enacted by the National Monetary Council and by the Central Bank of Brazil;

II – the supply of information mentioned in registrations of drawers of bad checks and of debtors in default, to entities of credit protection, in compliance with the rules enacted by the National Monetary Council and by the Central Bank of Brazil;

III – the supply of the information referred to in paragraph 2 of article 11 of Law no 9,311, of October 24, 1996;

IV – the information, to the competent authorities, of the practice of criminal or administrative violations, encompassing the supply of information on transactions which involve funds arising from any criminal practice;

V – the disclosure of secret information with the express consent of the interested parties;

VI – the provision of information in the terms and conditions set forth in articles 2, 3, 4, 5, 6, 7 and 9 of this Complementary Law.

Paragraph 4 – The breakage of secrecy may be decreed when so necessary for the investigation on the occurrence of any illicit act, in any phase of the inquiry or judicial procedure, and especially in the following crimes:

I – terrorism;

II – illicit traffic of narcotics or similar drugs;

III – contraband or traffic of weapons, ammunitions or material destined to the production thereof;

IV – extortion upon kidnapping;

V – against the national financial system;

VI – against the Public Administration;

VII – against the tax order and the social security;

VIII – laundering of money or occultation of goods, rights and amounts;

IX – practiced by a criminal organization.

Art. 2. The duty of secrecy is extendable to the Central Bank of Brazil, in relation to the transactions it carries out and to the information it obtains in the exercise of its functions.

Paragraph 1 – The secrecy, including as to deposit accounts and investments held with financial institutions, may not be opposed to the Central Bank of Brazil;

I – in the performance of its functions of inspection, encompassing the investigation, at any time, of illegal acts practiced by controlling parties, administrators, members of chart boards, managers, attorneys and representatives of financial institutions;

II – while proceeding to an inquiry in a financial investigation submitted to special regime.

Paragraph 2 – The commissions charged with the inquiries mentioned by item II of paragraph 1 may examine any documents relative to assets, rights and obligations of financial institutions, of its controlling parties, administrators, members of chart boards, managers, attorneys and representatives, including current accounts and transactions with other financial institutions.

Paragraph 3 – The provision of this article applies to the Securities and Exchange Commission (CVM) in cases of inspection of transactions and services in the securities market, including in financial institutions which are listed companies.

Paragraph 4 – The Central Bank of Brazil and the Securities and Exchange Commission, in their areas of competence, may execute conventions:

I – with other public bodies monitoring financial institutions, with the purpose of carrying out joint inspections, in compliance with the respective competences;

II – with central banks or inspection entities of other countries, seeking:

a) the inspection of branches and subsidiaries of foreign financial institutions operating in Brazil and of branches and subsidiaries abroad of Brazilian financial institutions;

b) the mutual cooperation and the exchange of information for the investigation of activities or transactions which imply the investment, negotiation, occultation or transfer of financial assets and of securities in connection with the practice of illicit acts.

Paragraph 5 – The duty of secrecy provided by this Complementary law shall be extendable to the inspection bodies mentioned in paragraph 4 and to the agents thereof.

Paragraph 6 – The Central Bank of Brazil, the Securities and Exchange Commission and the other inspection bodies, in their areas of competence, shall provide to the Council of Financial Activities – COAF, mentioned in article 14 of Law no 9,613, of March 3, 1998, the information of registration and of operation of amounts relative to the transactions set forth in item I of article 11 of the mentioned Law.

Art. 3. The Central Bank of Brazil, the Securities and Exchange Commission and the financial institutions shall provide the information required by the Judiciary Power, preserving their secret character by means of the restrict access by the parties, which may not use them for purposes foreign to the proceeding.

Paragraph 1 – The providing of information and the supply of secret documents requested by a commission of administrative inquiry destined to ascertain the liability of a public servant for violations committed in the exercise of his/her functions, or which is connected to the functions of the office in which he/she is vested, shall depend on the previous authorization of the Judiciary Power.

Paragraph 2 – In the cases of paragraph 1, the requirement of breakage of secrecy does not depend on the existence of a judicial procedure in progress.

Paragraph 3 – In addition to the cases set forth in this article, the Central Bank of Brazil and the Securities and Exchange Commission shall provide to the Attorney General of the Union the information and documents necessary to the defense of the Union in lawsuits where it is involved.

Art. 4. The Central Bank of Brazil and the Securities and Exchange Commission, in their areas of competence, and the financial institution shall provide to the Federal Legislative Power the secret information which, fundamentally, are necessary to the exercise of their respective constitutional and legal competences.

Paragraph 1 – The parliamentary inquiry committees, in the exercise of their constitutional and legal competence of wide investigation, shall obtain the secret information and documents which they need, directly from the financial institutions, or through the intermediation of the Central Bank of Brazil or of the Securities and Exchange Commission.

Paragraph 2 – The requests mentioned in this article must be previously approved by the Plenary Session of the Deputies Chamber, of the Federal Senate, or of the plenary of their respective parliamentary inquiry committees.

Art. 5. The Executive Power shall regulate, including as to the periodicity and to the limits of amount, the criteria according to which the financial institutions shall inform to the tax administration of the Union the financial transactions carried out by the users of their services.

Paragraph 1 – For the purposes of this article, the following are considered financial transactions:

I – deposits in cash and on credit, including in savings accounts;

II – payments made in currency or in checks;

III – issuance of orders of credit or similar documents;

IV – redemptions in accounts of deposits in cash or on credit, including of savings;

V – loan agreements;

VI – cashing of trade acceptance bills, promissory notes and other credit instruments;

VII – acquisitions and sales of fixed-income variable-income securities;

VIII – investment funds;

IX – acquisitions of foreign currency;

X – conversions of foreign currency into national currency;

XI – transfers abroad of currency and other amounts;

XII – transactions with gold as financial asset;

XIII – transactions with credit cards;

XIV – transactions of leasing; and

XV – any other transactions of similar nature which may be authorized by the Central Bank of Brazil, Securities and Exchange Commission or other competent body.

Paragraph 2 – The information transferred as provided in the *caput* of this article shall be restricted to data related to the identification of the holders of the transactions and the aggregate amounts monthly operated, it being forbidden the insertion of any element which allows the identification of their origin or the nature of the expenses made therewith.

Paragraph 3 – Financial transactions carried out by the direct and indirect administrations of the Union, of the States, of the Federal District and of the Municipalities are not included in the information referred to in this article.

Paragraph 4 – Upon the receipt of the information referred to in this article, should indications of failures, incorrectness or omissions, or of tax violation, be detected, the interested authority may require the information and the documents it may need, as well as carry out an inspection or an audit for the proper investigation of the facts.

Paragraph 5 – The information referred to in this article shall be maintained under tax secrecy, as provided by the legislation in force.

Art. 6. The authorities and the tax agents of the Union, State, Federal District and Municipalities may only examine documents, books and registrations of financial institutions, including those relative to deposit accounts and financial investments, when there is an administrative procedure commenced or a tax proceeding in progress and when such examinations are considered indispensable by the competent administrative authority.

Sole Paragraph – The result of the examinations, the information and the documents referred to by this article shall be maintained in secrecy, with due regard to the tax legislation.

Art. 7. Without prejudice to the provision of paragraph 3 of article 2, the Securities and Exchange Commission, upon the commencement of an administrative inquiry, may request to the competent judiciary authority the disclosure, before financial institutions, of information and documents relative to assets, rights and obligations of an individual or a legal entity submitted to its regulating power.

Sole Paragraph – The Central Bank of Brazil and the Securities and Exchange Commission shall keep a permanent exchange of information on the results of the inspections they carry out, of the inquiries they commence and of the penalties they impose, whenever the information are necessary to the performance of their activities.

Art. 8. The compliance with the requirements and formalities set forth in articles 4, 6 and 7 shall be expressly declared by the competent authorities in the requests addressed to the Central Bank of Brazil, to the Securities and Exchange Commission or to the financial institutions.

Art. 9. Whenever the Central Bank of Brazil and the Securities and Exchange Commission, in the exercise of their functions, verify the occurrence of a crime defined by law as of public action, or indications of the practice of such crimes, they shall inform it to the Public Prosecution, adding to the communication the documents necessary to the investigation or evidencing of the facts.

Paragraph 1 – The communication mentioned in this article shall be made by the Presidents of the Central Bank of Brazil and of the Securities and Exchange Commission, delegation of competence being admitted, within the maximum term of fifteen days as of the receipt of the procedure, with the opinion of the respective legal departments.

Paragraph 2 – Regardless of the provision of the *caput* of this article, the Central Bank of Brazil and the Securities and Exchange Commission shall inform to the competent public bodies the irregularities and the administrative illicit acts of which they have knowledge, or indications of the practice thereof, enclosing the relevant documents.

Art. 10. The breakage of secrecy, with the exception of the cases authorized in this Complementary Law, constitutes a crime and submits the responsible persons to a penalty of reclusion, from one to four years, and fine, with the application of the Criminal Code, as the case may be, without prejudice of other applicable penalties.

Sole Paragraph – All that omit, unreasonably delay or untruly render the information required in the terms of this Complementary Law are subject to the same penalties.

Art. 11. The public servant which utilizes or causes the utilization of any information obtained as a consequence of the breakage of secrecy provided by this Complementary Law is personally and directly liable for the consequent damages, without prejudice of the objective liability of the public entity, should it be evidenced that the servant acted in accordance with an official orientation.

Art. 12. This Complementary Law shall become effective as of the date of its publication.

Art. 13. Article 38 of Law No 4,595, of December 31, 1964, is hereby revoked.

Brasilia, January 10, 2001; 180th of the Independence and 113th of the Republic.

FERNANDO HENRIQUE CARDOSO

José Gregori; Pedro Malan; Martus Tavares

Decree no 3,724, of 10 January 2001

> *Regulates article 6 of Complementary Law No 105, of January 10, 2001, relatively to the request, access and utilization, by the Federal Revenue Office, of information regarding transactions and services of financial institutions and entities held equivalent thereto.*

THE PRESIDENT OF THE REPUBLIC, empowered with the attribution granted by item IV of the Constitution, and in view of the provision of Complementary Law No 105, of January 10, 2001,

DECREES:

Art. 1. This Decree provides, in the terms of article 6 of Complementary Law No 105, of January 10, 2001, on the request, access and utilization, by the Federal Revenue Office, of information regarding transactions and services of financial institutions and entities held equivalent thereto, in compliance with article 1, paragraphs 1 and 2 of the mentioned Law, as well as establishes procedures to preserve the secrecy of the information obtained.

Art. 2. The Federal Revenue Office, through a servant holding the function of Tax Auditor of the Federal Revenue, may only examine information relative to third parties, mentioned in documents, books and registrations of financial institutions and of entities held equivalent thereto, including those relative to accounts of deposits and of financial investments, when there is an inspection proceeding in progress and when such examinations are considered indispensable.

Paragraph 1 – Inspection proceeding shall be deemed as the modality of tax proceeding referred to by article 7 and followings of Decree No 70,235, of March 6, 1972, which provides on the tax administrative procedure.

Paragraph 2 – The inspection proceeding shall solely commence by virtue of a specific order called Writ of Tax Proceeding (MPF), instituted by an act of the Federal Revenue Office, with the exception of the provisions of paragraphs 3 and 4 of this article.

Paragraph 3 – In cases of evident verification of contraband, improper clearance or any other violation to the tax legislation, where the delay of the beginning of the tax proceeding may jeopardize the interests of the National Treasury, due to the possibility of subtraction of the evidence, the Tax Auditor of the Federal Revenue shall immediately commence the inspection proceeding and, within five days as of the date of commencement, a special MPF shall be issued, by means of which the investigated party shall be officially informed thereof.

Paragraph 4 – The MPF shall not be required in cases of inspections proceedings which are:

I – carried out during customs clearance;

II – internal, of customs review;

III – of vigilance of and repression to contraband and improper clearance, carried out in an ostensive operation;

IV – relative to the automatic treatment of tax returns (tax inspections).

Paragraph 5 – For the purposes of this article, the MPF must comply with the following:

I – the competent tax authority to issue the MPF shall be the holder of the office of General Coordinator, Superintendent, Delegate or Inspector, member of the structure of offices and functions of the Federal Revenue Office;

II – it shall contain, at least, the following information:

a) the denomination of the tax or of the contribution object of the inspection proceeding to be accomplished, as well as the corresponding assessment period;

b) the term for the accomplishment of the inspection proceeding, extendable at the discretion of the authority which issued the MPF;

c) name and enrollment number of the Tax Auditors of the Federal Revenue responsible for the performance of the MPF;

d) name, telephone number and office address of the immediate chief of the Tax Auditors of the Federal Revenue mentioned in the previous indent;

e) name, enrollment number and signature of the authority which issued the MPF;

f) internet access code which shall allow the investigated subject, target of the inspection proceeding, to identify the MPF.

Paragraph 6 – The examination referred to in the *caput* shall not apply to the inspection proceeding mentioned in item IV of paragraph 4 of this article.

Art. 3. The examinations referred to in the caput of the previous article shall only be considered indispensable in the following cases:

I – undervaluation of amounts of transactions, including of foreign trade, of purchase or sale of goods or rights, based on the corresponding market prices;

II – obtaining of loans of non-financial legal entities or of individuals, when the investigated subject fails to evidence the effective receipt of the resources;

III – practice of any transactions with individuals or legal entities resident or domiciled in a country which meets the conditions set forth in article 24 of Law No 9,430, of December 27, 1996;

IV – omission of net revenues or gains arising from financial investments of fixed or variable income;

V – expenses or investments in amounts in excess of the available revenue;

VI – remittance abroad, for any reason, by means of a non-resident account, of amounts incompatible with the availabilities declared;

VII – cases set forth in article 33 of Law No 9,430, of 1996;

VIII – legal entity classified, under the National Corporate Taxpayers' Register, in the following register situations:

a) cancelled;

b) unqualified, in the cases set forth in article 81 of Law No 9,430, of 1996;

IX – individual not enrolled with the Individual Taxpayers' Register (CPF) or whose registration was cancelled;

X – denial, by the lawful holder of the account, of the actual holding or of liability for the financial operation;

XI – indication that the lawful holder is a representative of the actual holder.

Paragraph 1 – The provisions of items I to IV shall not apply when the differences assessed do not exceed ten percent of the market or declared prices, as the case may be.

Paragraph 2 – It shall be deemed an indication of representation, for the purposes of item XI of this article, when:

I – the available information relative to the investigated subject indicate a financial operation ten times in excess of the declared available revenue, or in the absence of Income Tax Return, the annual amount of the operation exceeds the limit established in item II of paragraph 3 of article 42 of Law No 9,430, of 1996;

II – the record of the investigated subject with the financial institution, or entity held equivalent thereto, contains:

a) false information as to address, revenues or net worth; or

b) revenue lower than ten percent of the annual amount of the operation.

Art. 4. The information mentioned in the *caput* of article 2 may be requested by the competent authorities to issue the MPF.

Paragraph 1 – The request mentioned in this article shall be formalized upon a document denominated Request of Information on Financial Operation (RMF) and shall be addressed, as the case may be, to:

I – the President of the Central Bank of Brazil or the representative thereof;

II – the President of the Securities and Exchange commission or the representative thereof;

III – the president of the financial institution, or entity held equivalent thereto, or the representative thereof;

IV – the manager of the bank branch.

Paragraph 2 – The RMF shall be preceded by a service of process to the investigated subject for the rendering of information on financial operation, necessary to the accomplishment of the MPF.

Paragraph 3 – The investigated subject is liable for the veracity and integrity of the information rendered, with due regard to the applicable criminal legislation.

Paragraph 4 – The information rendered by the investigated subject may be the object of corroboration with the institutions mentioned by article 1, including through the Central Bank of Brazil or the Securities and Exchange Commission, as well as comparison with other information available at the Federal Revenue Office.

Paragraph 5 – The RMF shall be issued based on a circumstantiated report, prepared by the Tax Auditor of the Federal Revenue in charge of the execution of the MPF or by his/her immediate chief.

Paragraph 6 – In the report cited in the previous paragraph, it must be mentioned the motivation of the proposal of issuance of the RMF, which evidences, precisely and clearly, that this is a situation covered by the indispensability requirement set forth in the previous article, with due regard to the principle of reasonability.

Paragraph 7 – In the RMF, at least the following must be mentioned:

I – name or corporate name of the investigated subject, address and number of enrollment with the CPF or CNPJ;

II – number of identification of the MPF to which it is related;

III – the information requested and the period which the request concerns;

IV – name, enrollment number and signature of the authority which issued the request;

V – name, enrollment number and office address of the Tax Auditors of the Federal Revenue in charge of the execution of the MPF;

VI – manner of presentation of the information (in paper or magnetic means);

VII – deadline for delivery of the information, as provided by the applicable legislation;

IX – internet access code which shall allow the requested institution to identify the RMF.

Paragraph 8 – The issuance of the RMF presumes the indispensability of the information requested, as provided by this Decree.

Art. 5. The information requested as provided by the previous article:

I – encompass:

a) data mentioned on the records of the investigated subject;

b) individualized amounts of the debts and credits made within the period;

II – shall:

a) be presented, until the deadline established in the RMF, to the authority which issued it or to the Tax Auditors of the Federal Revenue responsible for the execution of the corresponding MPF;

b) subsidize the investigation proceeding in progress, with due regard to the provision of article 42 of Law No 9,430, of 1996;

c) make part of the tax administrative procedure underway, when they pertain to the evidence of the voluntary assessment.

Paragraph 1 – The documents regarding the debts and the credits, in the cases set forth in items VII to XI of article 3, may only be requested by means of certified copies.

Paragraph 2 – Information not utilized in the tax administrative procedure, in the terms of an act of the Federal Revenue Office, must be delivered to the investigated subject, destroyed or obliterated.

Paragraph 3 – All that omit, unreasonably delay or falsely provide to the Federal Revenue Office the information referred to by this article shall be subject to the penalties established by article 10, *caput*, of Complementary Law No 105, of 2001, without prejudice to the penalties applicable according to the tax or regulatory legislation, as the case may be.

Art. 6. In compliance with the provision of article 9 of Complementary Law No 105, of 2001, the Central Bank of Brazil and the Securities and Exchange Commission, through their respective Presidents or servants who were delegated competence for the specific purpose, shall voluntarily inform to the Federal Revenue Office, within the maximum term of fifteen days, the irregularities and the administrative illicit acts of which they have knowledge, or indications of the practice thereof, enclosing the relevant documents, whenever such facts may imply any violation to the federal tax legislation.

Sole Paragraph – The non-compliance with the provision of this article constitutes an administrative and disciplinary violation of the manager or servant who causes it, without prejudice to the application of the provision of article 10, *caput*, of Complementary Law No 105, of 2001, and other applicable civil and criminal penalties.

Art. 7. The information, the results of the tax examinations and the documents obtained by virtue of the provision of this Decree shall be maintained under tax secrecy, as provided by the pertinent legislation.

Paragraph 1 – The Federal Revenue Office shall maintain the control of the access to the tax administrative procedure, and the responsible for the receipt thereof shall in all times be recorded, in the event of circulation.

Paragraph 2 – In the issuance and handling of the information, the following must be complied with:

I – the information shall be sent in two sealed envelopes:

a) one external, which shall contain only the name or the function of the addressee and its address, without any annotation which indicates the degree of secrecy of the content;

b) one internal, on which the name and the function of the addressee, its address, the number of the MPF or of the tax administrative procedure must be inscribed, and on which a note that it deals with secret matter must be clearly indicated;

II – the internal envelope shall be sealed and its forwarding shall be enclosed by a receipt;

III – the receipt destined to the control of the custody of the information shall contain, necessarily, indications on the sender, the addressee and the number of the MPF or of the tax administrative procedure.

Paragraph 3 – It is incumbent upon the persons responsible for the receipt of secret documents:

I – to verify and to register, as the case may be, indications of any violation or irregularity in the correspondence received, informing the fact to the addressee, which shall inform it to the sender;

II – to sign and date the respective receipt, as the case may be;

III – to provide for the registration of the document and for the control of the handling thereof.

Paragraph 4 – The internal envelope may only be opened by the addressee or its authorized representative.

Paragraph 5 – The addressee of the secret document shall inform to the sender any indication of violation, such as erasures, irregularities of printing or of paging.

Paragraph 6 – Secret documents shall be stored under special conditions of safety.

Paragraph 7 – Information sent by electronic means shall necessarily be cryptographic.

Art. 8. The servant which utilizes or allows the utilization of any information obtained under this Decree, for a purpose or in a case different from that set forth by law, regulation or administrative act, shall be administratively liable for the non-compliance with the official duty of complying with legal or regulatory rules, referred to by article 116, item III, of Law No 8,112, of December 11, 1990, if the fact does not imply a more serious violation, without prejudice of his/her liability in the appropriate action to recover and of the applicable criminal liability.

Art. 9. The servant which divulges, discloses or facilitates the divulgation or disclosure of any information dealt with by this Decree, stored by information technology systems, records of documents or files of procedures protected by tax secrecy, with violation to the provision of article 198 of Law No 5,172, of October 25, 1966 (National Tax Code), or in article 116, item VIII, of Law No 8,112, of 1990, shall be subject to the penalty of dismissal, set forth by article 132, item IX, of the mentioned Law No 8,112, without prejudice of the applicable civil and criminal penalties.

Art. 10. The servant which allows or facilitates, upon the attribution, supply or loan of password or otherwise, the access of unauthorized person to information systems, data banks, records or files of procedures which contain the information mentioned in this Decree, shall be administratively liable, as provided by the specific legislation, without prejudice of the applicable civil and criminal penalties.

Sole Paragraph – The provision of this article also applies should the servant unduly use the restricted access.

Art. 11. It is a violation by the servant of the official duties of exercising with zeal and dedication the functions of the office and of compliance with legal and regulatory rules, as provided by article 116, items I and III, of Law No 8,112, of 1990, without prejudice of the applicable criminal and civil liability, as provided by articles 121 to 125 of such Law, if the fact does not imply a more serious violation:

I – the failure to proceed with the due caution in the storage and utilization of his/her password, or lend it to another servant, however qualified he/she may be;

II – to access unjustifiably information systems of the Federal Revenue Office, records of documents or files of procedures, which contain information protected by tax secrecy.

Art. 12. The investigated subject who deems to have suffered damages for the undue utilization of the information requested, in the terms of this decree, or for the abuse of the requiring authority, may address a petition to the General Magistrate (*Corregedor-Geral*) of the Federal Revenue Office, with a view to investigating the fact and, as the case may be, to imposing the penalties applicable to the servant responsible for the violation.

Art. 13. The Federal Revenue Office shall issue instructions necessary to the execution of the provisions of this Decree.

Art. 14. This Decree shall become effective as of the date of its publication.

Brasilia, January 10, 2001; 180th of the Independence and 113[th]of the Republic.

FERNANDO HENRIQUE CARDOSO

Pedro Malan

Federal Constitution of 1988

Art. 5. All persons are equal before the law, without any distinction whatsoever, Brazilians and foreigners residing in the country being ensured of inviolability of the right to life, to liberty, to equality, to security and to property, under the following terms:

(...)

X – the privacy, private life, honor and image of persons are inviolable, and the right to compensation for property or moral damages resulting from their violation is ensured;

(...)

XII – the secrecy of correspondence and of telegraphic, data and telephone communications is inviolable, except, in the latter case, by court order, in the cases and in the manner prescribed by law for the purposes of criminal investigation or criminal procedural finding of facts;

Art. 60. The Constitution may be amended on the proposal of:

(...)

§ 4. No proposal of amendment shall be considered which is aimed at abolishing:

(...)

IV – individual rights and guarantees.

Law 9,613, of 3 March 1998 (the Law on Money Laundering)

CHAPTER VI

CUSTOMER IDENTIFICATION AND RECORD-KEEPING

Art. 10. The legal entities referred to in Section 9 hereof shall:

I – identify their customers and maintain an updated record in compliance with the provisions set forth by the competent authorities;

II – keep an up-to-date record of all transactions, in national and foreign currency, involving securities, bonds, credit instruments, metals, or any asset that may be converted into cash, and that exceeds an amount set forth by the competent authorities and in accordance with the requirements they may issue;

III – comply with notices sent by the Council established under Section 14 hereof, within the time period stipulated by the competent judicial authority. The judicial proceedings pertaining to such matters shall be conducted in a confidential manner.

Paragraph 1 – In the event that the customer is a legal entity, the identification mentioned in item I of this Section shall include the individuals who are legally authorized to represent it, as well as its owners.

Paragraph 2 – The reference files and records mentioned in items I and II of this Section shall be kept during a minimum period of five years, counted from the date the account is closed or the date the transaction is concluded. The competent authorities may decide, at their own discretion, to extend this period of time.

Paragraph 3 – The registration under item II of this Section shall also be made whenever an individual or legal entity, or their associates execute, during the same calendar month, transactions with the same individual, legal entity, conglomerate or group that exceed, in the aggregate, the limit set forth by the competent authorities.

(...)

Section 14. The Council for Financial Activities Control (COAF) is hereby instituted, under the jurisdiction of the Ministry of Finance, for the purpose of regulating, applying administrative sanctions, receiving pertinent information, examining and identifying any suspicious occurrence of illicit activities set forth in this Law. The actions of COAF shall not conflict with the jurisdiction of other agencies.

Paragraph 1 – COAF shall be the agency responsible for issuing the instructions set forth in Section 10 to the legal entities specified in section 9 that are not subject to any specific regulatory or surveillance agency. In these cases, COAF shall also be responsible for defining the entities and applying the sanctions set forth in Section 12.

Paragraph 2 – COAF shall also be responsible for coordinating and advancing suggestions for the adoption of systems of cooperation and exchange of information designed to enable rapid and efficient responses in the struggle against the practice of concealment or disguise of assets, rights and valuables.

Section 15. COAF shall notify the competent authorities whenever it finds evidence of the existence of crimes defined in this Law, of clear indications of the occurrence of such crimes, or of any other illicit activity, so as to enable such authorities to take the appropriate measures.

Section 16. The members of COAF shall be civil servants of outstanding reputation and capability, named by act of the Minister of Finance and chosen among the career personnel of the Central Bank of Brazil, the Securities and Exchange Commission, the Superintendence of Private Insurance, the General Attorney Office for the National Treasury, the Secretariat of Federal Revenue, the Brazilian Agency of Intelligence, the Federal Police Department, and the Ministry of Foreign Affairs. In the last three cases, the Ministers having jurisdiction over each such entity shall nominate the members.

Paragraph 1 The Chairperson of the Council shall be appointed by the President of the Republic, acting on a recommendation of the Minister of Finance.

Paragraph 2 The decisions of COAF regarding the application of administrative sanctions may be appealed to the Minister of Finance.

Section 17. COAF's internal organization and mode of operation shall be set forth in bylaws to be approved by a decree of the Executive Branch.

(...)

Law 10,467, of 11 June 2002

Adds Chapter II-A to Title XI of Decree-Law No 2,848, of December 7, 1940 – Criminal Code, and a provision to Law No 9,613, of March 3, 1998, which 'provides on crimes of 'laundering' or occultation of assets, rights and amounts, the prevention of the utilization of the Financial System for the illicit acts set forth in this Law, creates the Council of Control of Financial Activities ('COAF'), and addresses other matters'.

THE PRESIDENT OF THE REPUBLIC

I HEREBY STATE THAT THE NATIONAL CONGRESS HAS DECREED AND I SIGN THE FOLLOWING LAW:

Art. 1. The purpose of this Law is to give effectiveness to Decree No 3,678, of November 30, 2000, which enacts the Convention on the Fight Against the Corruption of Foreign Public Servants in Commercial Transactions, concluded in Paris, on December 17, 1997.

Art. 2. Title XI of Decree-Law No 2,848, of December 7, 1940 – Criminal Code, shall be in force with the inclusion of the following Chapter II-A:

'TITLE XI

....

CHAPTER II-A

CRIMES PRACTICED BY AN INDIVIDUAL AGAINST A FOREIGN PUBLIC ADMINISTRATION

Active corruption in international commercial transactions

Art. 337-B. To promise, offer or give, directly or indirectly, an undue advantage to a foreign public servant, or to a third party, in order to cause him/her to practice, omit or delay an official act in connection with an international commercial transaction.

Penalty – incarceration from one (1) to eight (8) years and fine.

Sole Paragraph – The penalty shall be increased of one third (1/3) if, by virtue of the advantage or promise, the foreign public servant delays or omits an official act, or practices it in violation of an official duty.

Traffic of influences in international commercial transactions

Art. 337-C. To request, demand, collect or obtain, for oneself or for a third party, directly or indirectly, an advantage or a promise of advantage with the purpose of affecting an act practiced by a foreign public servant in the exercise of his/her functions, in connection with an international commercial transaction.

Penalty – incarceration from two (2) to five (5) years and fine.

Sole Paragraph. The penalty is increased of a half if the agent alleges or suggests that the advantage is also destined to a foreign servant.

Foreign public servant

Art. 337-D. For criminal purposes, a foreign public servant is deemed as any person who, even if on a temporary basis or without compensation, exercises a public office, employment or function in State entities or in diplomatic representations of a foreign country.

Sole Paragraph – A person who exercises an office, employment or function in companies controlled directly or indirectly by the public power of a foreign country or in international public organizations shall be held equivalent to a foreign public servant.'

Art. 3. Article 1 of Law No 9,613, of March 3, 1998, shall be in force with the inclusion of the following item VIII:

'Art.1 ....

VIII – practiced by an individual against the foreign public administration (articles 337-B, 337-C and 337-D of Decree-Law No 2,848, of December 7, 1940 – Criminal Code).

....' (NR)

Art. 4. This Law shall become effective as of the date of its publication.

Brasilia, June 11, 2002, 181st of the Independence and 114th of the Republic.

FERNANDO HENRIQUE CARDOSO

Miguel Reale Júnior

NEW CIVIL CODE (LAW 10,406, OF JANUARY 10, 2002))

TITLE III

Illicit acts

'Art. 186. The person who, due to a voluntary action or omission, negligence or imprudence, violates a right and causes a damage to a third party, even of an exclusively moral nature, commits an illicit act.'

6 Canada

Karl Delwaide
Isabelle Durand[1]

INTRODUCTION

This chapter examines Canadian legal aspects of the relationship between a bank and its customers. The analysis has become more complicated and the implications potentially more significant as a result of increasingly aggressive and innovative efforts by Canadian banks to diversify into new areas of financial services, assisted by a sweeping reform of the financial sector legislation in 1992 which blurred some of the distinctions between the so-called 'four pillars' of the Canadian financial system: banking, insurance, trust companies and the securities industry. These factors have also been influenced by the apparent willingness of Canadian courts to impose responsibilities and obligations upon banks which reflect their new powers and activities and which go beyond those which banks have traditionally assumed.

The relationship between a bank and its customers has always been multifaceted but, in the past, relatively straightforward in regard to each facet. It is one of debtor and creditor as regards the money in the customer's account, but is better characterised as one of agent and principal with respect to the bank's obligations to pay the customer's cheques. Canadian courts have held, however, that under the appropriate circumstances, a bank may be held to be a fiduciary in relation to its customer.[2] In addition to judicial development, there are increasing statutory responsibilities, some expanded by recent legislative initiatives, that apply in new areas of activities for Canadian banks, such as securities dealing and investment banking.

Moreover, concerns about the 'dirty' money of crime have recently led to the adoption, at the federal level, of a new money laundering legislation under which banks have a mandatory reporting obligation for prescribed and suspicious transactions, as well as for cross-border movements of large amounts of currency. In parallel, customer concerns regarding the potential abuse of personal information have resulted, in 2000, in the introduction of a new privacy protection statute at the

---

1 The text of this chapter was originally written by James E Fordyce and Elizabeth Shriver of Osler, Hoskin & Harcourt.
2 D Waters 'Banks, Fiduciary Obligations and Unconscionable Transactions' [1986] 65 Can BR 37.

federal level, an initiative that had already been implemented in 1994 in the province of Quebec. The new federal Protection of Information in the Private sector and Electronic Documents Act[3] (PIPEDA) also imposes new duties on banks, not only with their customers but also with their own employees, as they now have to state the purpose for which they collect or gather any personal information and the use they will make of it. Consequently, Canadian banks now have to take into consideration accrued confidentiality requirements for the personal information of their customers and the newly enacted obligatory disclosure of transactions that meet given standards of either importance or dubiousness.

These developments and the ongoing administration and regulation of these activities are complicated by the Canadian constitutional structure, which is a federal system that places banks under the overlapping jurisdictions of the federal and provincial governments. While banking per se is a federal matter governed by the federal Bank Act,[4] other financial transactions in which banks or their subsidiaries are involved, such as securities matters, are primarily under provincial jurisdiction. Moreover, to the extent not specifically dealt with by federal banking legislation, matters such as contract law and agency are governed by the laws (common law and statutory) of each province.[5] A good example of this somewhat complicated pattern can be illustrated by the statutes regulating privacy in the private sector which have been enacted both at the federal and at the provincial levels. It is likely that both provincial and federal privacy statutes will generally be found applicable to banks doing business in the provinces where such a legislation has been implemented, which is currently only the case in Quebec.

THE BANK'S DUTY OF CONFIDENTIALITY

Confidentiality is fundamental to the relationship between a bank and its customers. In Canada, as in the other Commonwealth jurisdictions, the bank's legal duty of confidentiality is founded in the common law and consists of an implied contractual

---

3   RSC 2000, c 5.
4   RSC 1991, c 46. Although banks in Canada are governed by federal law and may (and normally do) carry on business through branches in one or more provinces, ss 461 and 462 of the Bank Act provide, in essence, for a 'branch of account' for each deposit account of a customer, which is the situs of the debt owing by the bank to the customer in respect of that account and also provide that notices of process or assignment and the like relating to an account only bind the bank if served on the branch of account. Apart from providing relief to banks with many branches in different provinces (up to 1,000 or more), these provisions codify and refine the common law as to situs of the contract of confidentiality between a bank and its customer and hence the governing law of such contract.
       It should also be noted that the Bank Act applies to foreign banks carrying on the business of banking in Canada. Currently, these banks may only do so by way of subsidiaries and not by way of branches (the federal government announced in February 1997 plans to introduce a foreign bank branch regime into Canada).
5   While there may be some variation between the laws of the Canadian common law provinces, mainly as a result of statutory provisions, it may in general be said that laws applicable to commercial operations are similar in each of those provinces. In addition, the laws in the Province of Quebec are based on the French civil law system, which, although often similar in result to that found in the common law provinces, nevertheless further complicates the regulatory system.

duty (subject to certain exceptions) not to divulge information about its customer's accounts to third parties without the consent of the customer, as laid down in the leading English case of *Tournier v National Provincial and Union Bank of England*.[6] Although the principle is easy to state, its ultimate scope continues to evolve such that the potential breadth always remains somewhat unclear. The exceptions to the confidentiality principle, as discussed below, have been further refined in the courts, but the main spur to development of the law in this area has come from statutory enactments that delimit the bank's obligations of secrecy and clarify the circumstances under which a bank is entitled or even bound to disclose what would otherwise be confidential information.

Exceptions to the duty of confidentiality

While the *Tournier* case is more fully discussed in the chapter relating to English law, in brief, the case outlines four exceptions to the bank's duty of confidentiality:

1   the bank may disclose information when the customer consents to the disclosure expressly or by necessary implication;
2   disclosure may be made when it is necessary to the bank's interests;
3   the bank must disclose confidential customer information when it is so compelled by law; and
4   disclosure is permitted where there is a public duty to do so.

These exceptions are discussed in light of relevant developments in Canadian law.

Disclosure with express/implied consent of the customer

As a general principle, no disclosure is authorised beyond what is necessary by implication in order to carry out the customer's instructions. Thus, as indicated in *Tournier*, it is clearly permissible to disclose customer account information when the bank has been asked to give a credit reference. However, consent is not to be implied simply because the banker believes disclosure to be in the customer's best interest, particularly if it is possible to contact the customer to ascertain directly whether permission would be given. In addition, the information which may be disclosed in a credit reference without express consent is limited.[7]

Disclosure in the bank's own interest

In *Tournier* this exception was discussed as referring to cases where a bank brings an action against its customer for payment of a debt owed. Obviously, it is necessary under such circumstances to disclose the amount owed even though this would

---

6   [1924] 1 KB 461.
7   In the Ontario case of *Hull v Childs & Huron and Erie Mortgage Corpn* [1951] OWN 116, HCJ, where the customer had signed a series of blank cheques, the financial institution was held liable for breach of its duty of secrecy because it disclosed to the bearer of the cheques the total amount of money in the account so as to enable him to withdraw it all. The court held that it was unwarranted for the bank to infer that the customer intended all of his funds to be withdrawn by virtue of his having given someone blank cheques.

otherwise be in breach of the bank's duty of confidentiality.[8] This exception does not apply, however, to cases where the bank is a third party to a proceeding. In addition, when courts do interpret this exception, by necessity they will construe it narrowly, as Taylor JA noted in *Canadian Imperial Bank of Commerce v Sayani* (discussed below):

> 'The scope of [the bank's own interest] exception must, of course, be a limited one, for if the bank could make disclosure of its customer's confidential information whenever this served its interests, the duty of confidentiality would have little meaning ...'[9]

In some cases, an exchange of information in the bank's own interest is supported by a statutory provision. For example, the federal Competition Act[10] contains express provisions setting out conditions under which banks are permitted to have agreements or arrangements with one another which might otherwise be considered as anti-competitive. Among the permitted arrangements are those for the exchange of credit information. As noted above, the exchange of customer information or 'networking' among banking and certain non-banking members of a bank group has been restricted but, in Canada, the debate over whether such a restriction is appropriate has turned more on whether the ability to 'network' would provide an unfair advantage to bank-owned insurance companies over independent insurance companies than on issues of confidentiality.

Compulsion of law

In keeping with increased legislation relating to the bank's duty to keep customer information confidential, the bank's duty to disclose confidential information under compulsion of law is defined primarily by an ever-increasing web of statutory provisions.

LEGISLATION RELATING TO EVIDENCE

There are federal and provincial statutes which generally provide that a bank must disclose records in its possession where they could serve as evidence in the course of civil, criminal or arbitral proceedings not involving the bank. However, a court order is usually required before the bank can be compelled either to appear as a witness or to produce a customer's records.[11]

---

8   Cases invoking this exception are relatively rare; however, the exception was recently reaffirmed by the British Columbia Supreme Court in *Royal Bank of Canada v Vincenzi* [1994] BCJ no 772, DRS 94-09701.
9   [1993] 83 BCLR (2d) 167 at 176, BCCA.
10 RSC 1985, c C-34, as amended, s 49.
11 Eg see the Canada Evidence Act RSC 1985, c C-5. The provisions in the Evidence Act ensure that bank records are not seized every time one of its customers is in litigation, and they take precedence over the Criminal Code provision RSC 1985, c C-46, which permits seizure of records where there are reasonable grounds to believe the records will afford evidence of the commission of an offence: *R v Mount, ex p Toronto Dominion* (1967) 1 OR 179, HCJ. In general terms, these provisions are not dissimilar to those of the Bankers' Books Evidence Act 1879 which has been widely adopted in British Commonwealth jurisdictions.

TAX LEGISLATION

Under the Income Tax Act,[12] Revenue Canada may examine a third party's records if they relate to a taxpayer and the third party must answer any relevant questions. Therefore, a bank may be required to provide for inspection to Revenue Canada a customer's bank records and respond to inquiries on the customer's transactions. These provisions have been interpreted to mean that a bank can be required to disclose records of transactions even if the result would mean disclosing private information of the bank's customers who are not themselves under investigation.[13]

SECURITIES AND CORPORATE LAW

The provincial securities Acts provide broad powers of investigation, search and seizure which Securities Commission staff utilise in investigating securities law matters. These are frequently used to investigate a wide range of securities-related activities such as allegations or suspicions of insider trading or other misuse of confidential information.[14]

MONEY LAUNDERING AND TERRORISM LEGISLATION

Proceeds of Crime (Money Laundering) and Terrorist Financing Act

By virtue of the Proceeds of Crime (Money Laundering) and Terrorist Financing Act[15] (the Act) and its recent amendments and regulations, banks conducting business in Canada now find themselves faced with a series of new reporting obligations.

In essence, the Act and its subsequent regulations establish a mandatory reporting system for prescribed and suspicious transactions, as defined by the Act and regulations (see below). This system applies to a broad range of individuals and entities operating in Canada, including domestic and foreign banks, trust and loan companies and other intermediaries, as well as lawyers, accountants, real estate brokers and certain Crown-owned entities. Where circumstances warrant, these entities are now required to identify their clients, create and maintain records and report financial transactions and/or the cross-border movement of funds. In addition, these entities are required to develop and implement policies aimed at ensuring compliance

---

12   RSC 1985, 5th Supp, s 231.2. Revenue Canada must obtain authorisation for such third party disclosure through ex parte application to a judge. Effective 20 June 1996, the Income Tax Act was amended to repeal requirements that a judge must be satisfied that: (i) there was a reasonable expectation that the third party has failed or would fail to comply with the Act; and (ii) that the information was not otherwise readily available. This amendment dramatically increases the power of Revenue Canada to embark upon judicially authorised 'fishing expeditions'.

13   *Canadian Bank of Commerce v A-G of Canada* (1962) 35 DLR (2nd) 49, SCC.

14   Eg see the Ontario Securities Act, RSO 1990, c S-5, as amended. There are also powers that can be granted to inspectors under the corporate law statutes. See eg the Ontario Business Corporations Act, RSO 1990, c B-16, Pt XIII. In the Canadian context these latter powers are used less frequently than in some other jurisdictions given the broad powers and responsibilities of securities regulators. Investigations under the powers of the corporate statutes tend to focus on internal matters involving the corporation and its directors or holders of its securities.

15   SC 2000, c 17.

with the Act and its regulations. The objective of the Act is to implement specific measures to detect and deter money laundering and the financing of terrorist activities and to facilitate the investigation and prosecution of money laundering offences.

The Financial Transactions and Reports Analysis Centre of Canada

To help meet its objective, the Act establishes the Financial Transactions and Reports Analysis Centre of Canada (FINTRAC).[16] FINTRAC's principal role is to collect, analyse, assess and disclose information in order to assist in the detection, prevention and deterrence of money laundering and of the financing of terrorist activities, as well as acting at arms length with law enforcement agencies and other entities to which it is authorised to disclose information.[17] It is therefore to FINTRAC which the banks must report the financial transaction information requiring disclosure pursuant to the Act.

Transactions which a bank must report

SUSPICIOUS TRANSACTIONS

Banks must report to FINTRAC, in the prescribed form and manner, every suspicious transaction. That is, banks must report every financial transaction that has occurred in the course of their activities and in respect of which there are reasonable grounds to suspect that the transaction is related to the laundering of money or the financing of a terrorist activity.[18] More precisely, the bank activities which may trigger this obligation to report include the remitting or transmitting of funds and the issuing or redeeming of money orders, traveller's cheques or other similar negotiable instruments, except cheques payable to a *named person or entity*.[19]

PRESCRIBED TRANSACTIONS

Banks must also report certain 'prescribed' transactions. A prescribed transaction is a cash transaction or electronic fund transfer of CDN$10,000 or more.[20] Also considered to be prescribed transactions are two or more transfers or transactions made within 24 hours that together total an amount of CDN$10,000 or more.[21]

INFORMATION TO BE PROVIDED IN REPORT TO FINTRAC

The information which must be included in a report to FINTRAC is lengthy and includes elements such as the identity of the parties involved, the accounts involved and the sum of the transaction. In the event that the bank does not possess certain

---

16   SC 2000, c 17, s 40.
17   SC 2000, c 17, s 40.
18   SC 2000, c 17, s 7.
19   Proceeds of Crime (Money Laundering) and Terrorist Financing Suspicious Transaction Reporting Regulations, SOR/2001-317, s 4.
20   SOR/2002-184, s 12.
21   SOR/2002-184, s 3.

elements of such information, it must make all 'reasonable efforts' to obtain it and provide it to FINTRAC.[22]

PENALTIES

Violation of any of the provisions of the Act or its regulations is punishable by fines ranging from CDN$50,000 to 2,000,000 and/or imprisonment up to a maximum of five years.[23]

OTHER LEGISLATION

In addition to the foregoing, there are many other statutes in Canada, ranging from bankruptcy to public inquiries, which can also apply as exceptions to the duty of confidentiality.[24]

Public duty to disclose

This rarely-used exception was referred to in *Tournier* in the context of preventing acts that might present a danger to the state and the decision seemed to imply that there would be a wide range of circumstances in which this exception might apply.

In a sense, the primary 'public duty' obligations come under specific legislation such as the traditional evidence legislation or the new 'money laundering' provisions. The legislated duty in these situations relieves the bank of having to decide whether a sufficiently high public good would be served by disclosure so as to supersede the private duty to maintain confidentiality. This difficult judgment, combined with the ever broadening legislative requirements, may explain why this has been a little used exception.[25]

Common law developments limiting disclosure

The Privy Council appears to have expanded the scope of a bank's obligation to its customer when the bank is presented with a legally enforceable demand by a third

22   SOR/2002-184, s 53.
23   SC 2000, c 17, s 75.
24   Bankruptcy and Insolvency Act RSC 1985, c B-3: the Act imposes on the bank an affirmative duty to inform the Trustee in Bankruptcy if the bank discovers that its customer is an undischarged bankrupt. In addition, banks may be ordered by the court to produce the records or accounts of a company winding-up under the provisions of the Winding-Up and Restructuring Act RSC 1985, c W10.
       Inquiries Act RSC 1985, c I-13: banks can also be subject to the Inquiries Act which provides that in the course of an inquiry any person can be subpoenaed to appear, testify and produce any documents in his possession which relate to the subject matter of the inquiry. This provision is particularly far-reaching since there are at least 47 federal statutes which confer powers of inquiry by reference to the Inquiries Act and hence any of these statutes could be used to impose a duty of disclosure. See R Regan 'You don't say' (1982) 89 Canadian Banker 32 at 34.
25   In *Canadian Imperial Bank of Commerce v Sayani* [1993] 83 BCLR (2d) 167, BCCA, the court held that a bank's disclosure of a customer's indebtedness to the bank to prevent a trust company's reliance on the customer's misrepresentation of its indebtedness was a valid exercise of the public duty exception.

party for information about the customer. In *Robertson v Canadian Imperial Bank of Commerce*,[26] a case in which the original action was heard by the High Court of Justice of Saint Vincent and the Grenadines, the Privy Council held that a bank has the following additional obligations in such a situation:

1   when a bank receives a demand for information about a customer from a third party, the bank must use best efforts to inform the customer of the demand, unless the legal authorities have requested that the bank refrain from such notification; and

2   a bank must exercise care to give only that information that is specifically required by and relevant to the inquiry.

The factual background of the case involved a previous collection action, in which a subpoena duces tecum was issued to the Canadian Imperial Bank of Commerce (CIBC) with respect to the accounts of a customer in order to show that a cheque had been deposited to the customer's account. The manager of the CIBC branch attended in court with a monthly statement of the customer's account, which showed numerous other transactions, including an overdraft, that were not relevant to the action. Following the collection action, the customer sued CIBC for breach of contract and for negligence in disclosing the information about his account without his consent.

At the trial court level,[27] the judge held that a subpoena is not a court order to disclose in breach of a contractual duty of confidentiality, and that CIBC therefore had a duty either to secure its customer's consent, or ask the court to order it to testify and to produce the documents in question. As CIBC had done neither, it had breached its duty to its client. The Eastern Caribbean Court of Appeal[28] agreed that the subpoena was not a court order, but rejected the finding that CIBC had a duty to seek to avoid the disclosure, citing *Barclays Bank*[29] as authority for the proposition that the duty to maintain confidentiality does not exist within the four *Tournier* exceptions.

The Privy Council, however, ruled that the 'compulsion of law' exception in *Tournier* did not take away CIBC's obligation to advise its customer of the receipt of the subpoena. The obligation, however, was not an 'absolute duty', because the bank may either be unable to contact the customer or because the bank may, in certain situations, be entitled or compelled by public duty not to so inform the customer. The major example cited by the Privy Council in this regard was an instance where the legal authorities requesting the information also requested that the disclosure remain confidential from the customer. *Robertson* indicates that banks must not view the legal compulsion exception as absolving them of the duty to the customer. To the contrary, the ruling places additional responsibility on banks to ensure that

26   [1995] 1 All ER 824, [1994] 1 WLR 1493, PC.
27   *Robertson v Canadian Imperial Bank of Commerce* (unreported, 1988), St Vincent and The Grenadines HCJ, no 340.
28   *Robertson v Canadian Imperial Bank of Commerce* (unreported, 1990), Eastern Caribbean CA, St Vincent and The Grenadines, Civil Appeal no 4.
29   *Barclays Bank plc (trading as Barclaycard) v Taylor* [1989] 3 All ER 563, [1989] 1 WLR 1066, CA.

the fiduciary duty of confidentiality remains paramount, and instils in the bank the responsibility, where appropriate, to narrow the intrusion by the legal authorities as much as possible.[30]

An interesting interpretation was placed on the public duty exception in *Canada Deposit Insurance Corpn v Canadian Commercial Bank*.[31] There, the plaintiff deposit insurance corporation (an agency of the federal government) brought an action against a bank which had gone into receivership in order to obtain access to the bank's records directly, rather than by way of discovery. Such access would enable it more effectively to seek recovery of funds it had paid out to the bank's depositors. The court held that this case fell under *Tournier*'s public duty exception, and that the public interest required that disclosure be made in this more efficient way.

Statutory limitations on disclosure

For many years, Canadian legislators had not seen fit to disturb the common law traditions as the foundation of the confidential relationship. Currently, however, the parameters of permissible disclosure of customer information by a bank are statutorily defined at the federal level, and provincial governments have also implemented similar legislation.

The Act regarding Personal Information Protection and Electronic Documents

In April 2000, the federal government adopted the Act regarding Personal Information Protection and Electronic Documents (PIPEDA). This new Act literally incorporates under its Sch I the principles of the Canadian Standards Association (CSA) *Model Code for the Protection of Personal Information*,[32] which was itself based on the 1980 *Guidelines on the Protection of Privacy and Transborder Flows of Personal Data* of the Organization for Economic Co-operation and Development (OECD).

Application of the PIPEDA

The PIPEDA came into force on 1 January 2001, and applies to:

'every organization in respect of personal information that the organization collects, uses or discloses in the course of commercial activities; or is about an employee of the organization and that the organization collects, uses or discloses in connection with the operation of a federal work, undertaking or business.'[33]

This provision clearly includes banks as organisations who collect personal information. However, for a period of three years, until 1 January 2004, s 30 of the Act provides that the requirements of the Act do not apply to:

30   For a more complete discussion of *Robertson*, please see the Commentary by E K Rowan-Legg 'New Developments in Bank's Duty of Confidentiality' 26 Canadian Business Law Journal 455.
31   [1989] AJ no 44, no 8503-23319, Alta QB.
32   CAN/CSA-Q 830-96.
33   PIPEDA, s 4(1).

'any organization in respect of personal information that it collects, uses or discloses within a province whose legislature has the power to regulate the collection, use or disclosure of the information, unless the organization does it in connection with the operation of a federal work, undertaking or business or the organization discloses the information outside the province for consideration.'[34]

The interest of this three-year interim period is limited for banks, as they are considered, under the Act, as 'federal undertakings',[35] and therefore escape the provisions of s 30 as far as their activities are concerned.

The 'consideration' criteria, on the other hand, relates more specifically to the acquisition of personal information for a sum of money or for another advantage. 'Consideration' is not a defined term, but is generally defined as the cause, motive, price or impelling influence which induces a contracting party to enter into a contract. A typical enterprise dealing with personal information for consideration would be a credit reporting agency operating in Quebec and selling personal information to persons or entities located outside the province. The Act would therefore apply to the activities of such a company even during the three year period.

Application of the PIPEDA in each province

The Governor in Council has the power to exempt an organisation, a class of organisations, an activity or a class of activities from the application of Pt 1 of the PIPEDA with respect to the collection, use or disclosure of personal information that occurs in a province, if the Governor in Council is satisfied that the Legislature of that province has implemented legislation that is 'substantially similar' to Pt 1. Importantly, the former Industry Minister, John Manley, publicly stated that Quebec's Act Respecting the Protection of Personal Information in the Private Sector[36] (PPIA) meets the 'substantially similar' standard and, consequently, organisations subject to the PPIA will be exempt from the future imposition of the PIPEDA for intra-provincial collection, use or disclosure of personal information. The transfer of personal information from a province to a location outside the province, however, still is subject to the PIPEDA. Both Acts will therefore have to be observed by entities carrying an enterprise in the province of Quebec.

Principles

The principle underlying the PIPEDA is that personal information should not be collected, used or disclosed without the prior knowledge and consent of the

---

34 PIPEDA, s 30(1), which remains in force for three years starting January 2001, under s 30(2).
35 See PIPEDA, s 2(1), which includes banks in the definition of 'federal undertakings', under sub-s (g). This is consistent with the provisions of the Constitutional Act of 1867 which divides federal and provincial fields of jurisdiction.
36 RSQ, c P-39.1.

individual concerned, subject to limited exceptions in the Act,[37] a principle that is also part of the CSA Model Code.[38] Other principles include the accountability of the organisation gathering the information,[39] the necessity of identifying the purposes of the collection,[40] the limitation of the collection, use and disclosure of the information to the identified purposes[41] and the necessity for the information to be maintained accurate.[42]

The consent of the concerned individual can be either express or implied under the PIPEDA, and the express character of the consent relates directly to the sensitivity of the information implied. It should be noted, however, that health and financial information is almost always considered sensitive.[43] Banks should therefore seek the express consent of the individuals whose personal information they gather. Moreover, the Act provides that the consent must be given for specific purposes, which implies that the individual must be aware, at the time of his consent, of the use that will be made of the personal information he provides. This gives rise to a delicate situation, where the object of the collection of personal information must be clearly stated for the organisation validly to use the collected information, but must not be too broadly worded or a court may hold that the person who agreed could not know all the implications of the consent. A detailed and complete description of the motives for which the information is gathered, the use that will be made of it and the people to whom it may be communicated, is therefore advised. Moreover, the Act provides individuals with a right to access their personal information file detained by an organisation, and to make corrections to incorrect or false information.[44]

The Privacy Commissioner, who is in charge of the application of the Act, has already proceeded to numerous inquiries relating to complaints from individuals. Banks are prime targets for such inquiries, and the cases are numerous were they were ordered to provide individuals with specific information. For instance, a bank was ordered to provide an individual with the personal information on which it had based its refusal to issue him a credit card, and banks were also ordered to provide individuals with personal information regarding their credit rating when required to do so by the individuals.[45]

---

37   Eg see PIPEDA, s 7(3)b) and c) for situations where the communication of personal information without a consent is allowed (for the purpose of collecting a debt owed by the individual to the organisation, or for disclosure made to a governmental entity that made a request for the information).
38   PIPEDA, Sch I, s 4.3; principle 3 of the CSA Model Code.
39   PIPEDA, Sch I, s 4.1; principle 1 of the CSA Model Code.
40   PIPEDA, Sch I, s 4.2; principle 2 of the CSA Model Code.
41   PIPEDA, Sch I, ss 4.4 and 4.5; principles 4 and 5 of the CSA Model Code.
42   PIPEDA, Sch I, s 4.6; principle 6 of the CSA Model Code.
43   The form of consent will vary depending on the sensitivity of the information involved: see PIPEDA, Sch I, s 4.3.4.
44   PIPEDA, Sch I, s 4.8; principle 8 of the CSA Model Code.
45   Decisions rendered on 29 and 30 April 2002, for instance, available on the site of the Privacy Commissioner at www.privcom.gc.ca, the names of the parties implied are kept confidential.

Provincial legislation

It is relevant to consider provincial legislation since, as noted above, under the Canadian constitutional system, it is likely that the provincial statutes will be found applicable concurrently to the PIPEDA, and that organisations located in provinces where privacy protecting statutes have been adopted will have to comply to both. So far, the decisions rendered generally recognised the applicability of the PPIA to federal undertakings. Where both the PIPEDA and the PPIA stem from the same Model Code and principles, they do, however, suffer some differences, especially in the exceptions they allow to the necessity of consent for the collection, use and disclosure of personal information, as well as for the cases where communication of personal information can be refused to an individual.

Among the provinces, Quebec has taken the lead in legislating privacy protection. In 1994 (partly in January and partly in July), the PPIA came into effect, making Quebec the only Canadian province that currently has privacy legislation concerning the private sector.[46] The Act applies to any personal information, whatever the nature of its medium and whatever the form in which it is accessible, whether written, graphic, taped, filmed, computerised or other.[47] 'Personal Information' is defined to be 'any information which relates to a natural person and allows that person to be identified',[48] and therefore cannot relate to a moral person or a corporation as only the personal information relating to individuals is covered by the Act. The Act is based on the same principle as the federal Act, and the consent of an individual must be obtained in order to collect, use or disclose his personal information. This consent must always be express. Indeed, the Act states that 'consent to the communication or use of personal information must be manifest, free, and enlightened, and must be given for specific purposes'.[49] A consent that does not meet these three conditions is therefore deemed to be null. As for the 'specific purposes', it involves the same necessity for cautious drafting as the federal Act requires, as the description of the purposes for which the individual consents must be broad enough to allow for proper use of information, but must not be too general in order to qualify as 'specific'.

Interestingly, the Act provides, under s 17, that a:

> 'person carrying on an enterprise in Quebec who communicates, outside Quebec, information relating to persons residing in Quebec ... must take all reasonable steps to ensure that the information will not be used for purposes not relevant to the object of the file or communicated to third persons without the consent of the persons concerned and, in the case of nominative lists, that the persons concerned have a valid opportunity to refuse that personal information concerning them be used for purposes of commercial or philanthropic prospection and, if need be, to have such information deleted from the list.'

---

46 As stated by the Privacy Commissioner of Canada in his review of the provincial acts that have been adopted, so far, to deal with the protection of personal information in the private sector. Available at www.privcom.gc.ca/legislation/leg-rp_f.asp.
47 PPIA, s 1.
48 PPIA, s 2.
49 PPIA, s 14.

Companies operating in Quebec, such as banks, that communicate personal information outside the province should take steps to ensure that this provision is respected. If the receiving country or location does not have a legislative system ensuring the same protection of personal information, contractual provisions should be drafted to that effect.

It should be noted, moreover, that the fact for a company to communicate personal information pertaining to Quebec residents outside the province was covered by the Act, even if this company did not have an office in Quebec.[50] The notion of 'carrying on an enterprise' does not relate to a specific location, but to the question of whether or not juridical acts involving personal information took place with regards to personal information. Personal information stored electronically on a server that is not located in Quebec would therefore be covered as well.

As for the other Canadian provinces, they all, with the exception of Newfoundland and Labrador, have a privacy legislation dealing with the public (governmental) sector, but have not, so far, adopted any Act similar to the Quebec Act with regards to the private sector. Four provinces are currently considering legislative options pertaining to the regulation of the private sector,[51] and the Ontario government has published, in February 2002, a new legislative document entitled the 2002 Act for the Protection of Personal Information, which is to serve two purposes: it will at the same time constitute a bill for the Parliament to adopt eventually, and a consultation paper for Ontario citizens and organisations to comment on its contents. This initiative, which is similar to the ones that occurred in New-Brunswick in May 1998, in Manitoba in March 1999 and in British-Columbia in October 1999, allow for a conclusion that legislation regulating the collection and use of personal information in the private sector should be adopted in the near future in these provinces.

Provincial consumer reporting legislation, such as the Consumer Reporting Act in Ontario,[52] govern the operations of credit bureaux. The legislation does not require explicit consent before a credit reference can be given by a bank or other credit granting agency. It does, however, differentiate between 'credit' information and 'personal' information. If personal information is to be supplied or if a report is to be requested from a credit bureau regarding a customer, the customer must be notified in a prescribed manner prior to making a request for a credit report or providing such personal information. As a matter of routine, however, this notification is incorporated into standard forms, such as applications for loans, used by banks, and credit reports are routinely given and obtained by Canadian banks on their customers through independent credit reporting agencies, as well as by way of direct reports to other banks. Normally, a bank will not knowingly give a credit report other than to another financial institution or a bona fide credit reporting agency.

---

50   *Institut de l'Assurance Canadien v Guay* [1998] CAI 431, Cour du Quebec.
51   These four provinces are New-Brunswick, British-Columbia, Manitoba and Ontario.
52   RSO 1990, c C-33.

Electronic documents legislation

The growing use of electronic-form documents and the increasing importance of ecommerce have led, in several Canadian provinces, to the adoption of statutes regulating the form and validity of electronic documents and signatures.[53] The federal Parliament has also adopted a similar legislation,[54] but its reach extends only to federal governmental institutions, which renders the obligations of the Act of little interest for private entities such as banks. As for the provincial Acts, which apply to private entities, their purpose is generally to ensure that electronic documents have a legal status equivalent to the one of paper-based documents, thus permitting the use of electronic-based documents as evidence, and enabling enterprises and companies to convert their paper documents into more convenient electronic files.

The Quebec example

The Quebec Act entitled the Act to Establish a Framework for Information Technology[55] is one of these statutes. It details the parameters under which organisations may validly transfer paper-based documents to an electronic support. The act also provides for protection measures with regards to confidential information (which is broader than personal information, since it covers any information that has been declared by law to be confidential), and therefore imposes an additional obligation on entities that employ electronic means to communicate or process their information and data. Just like all the other provincial statutes dealing with electronic documents, it also requires that the technology used to create, access or communicate electronic-based documents allow for the integrity of such documents to be maintained.

The Act applies to both governmental and private entities, and therefore to banks (with the exception of constitutional incompatibilities). The Act states that when the information contained in a document is declared by law to be confidential, its confidentiality must be protected by means appropriate to the mode of transmission, including on a communication network.[56] The person who is responsible of the access to such a document must therefore ensure that its confidentiality is protected by controlling access to this document, through a restricted view technique or any other technique that prevents unauthorised persons from accessing the confidential information or from otherwise accessing the document or the components providing access to the document.[57] The Act is silent as to which specific technologies would

---

53 In Alberta, the Electronic Transactions Act (Bill 21); in British-Columbia, the Electronic Transactions Act; in Manitoba, the Electronic Commerce and Information, Consumer Protection Amendment; in New-Brunswick, the Electronic Transactions Act; in New-Foundland and Labrador, the Act to Facilitate Electronic Barriers to the Use of Electronic Communication; in Nova-Scotia, the Electronic Commerce Act 2000; in Ontario, the Electronic Commerce Act 2000; in Prince-Edward Island, the Electronic Commerce Act; in Saskatchewan, the Act respecting Electronic Information and Documents; and in Yukon, the Electronic Commerce Act.

54 The Act regarding Personal Information Protection and Electronic Documents (SC 2002, c 5) is the applicable federal statute.

55 RSQ, c C-1.1.

56 S 34 of the Act.

57 S 25 of the Act.

be considered appropriate, and banks must therefore ensure that the above-listed criteria are fulfilled by electronic services such as online banking or email communications that contain confidential information. Moreover, the Act requires that a link be established between an electronic document and a person to give a full legal effect to the document.[58] To do so, any technology may be used, to the extent that it allows the identity and location of the communicating person to be confirmed, as well as its link to the document, and that it allows for the document to be identified, and its destination and origin to be determined at any given time. The Act also requires that documents containing confidential information remain unmodified, and sets, in its s 6, the standard as follows:

> 'the integrity of a document is ensured if it is possible to verify that the information it contains has not been altered and has been maintained in its entirety, and that the medium used provides stability and the required perennity to the information.'

Once again, no specified technology is required, and banks who store information that is confidential on electronic documents must therefore ensure that their technological means meet those standards.

Limitations on networking

As mentioned above, one of the critical concerns posed by the efforts of financial institutions to bridge the gaps between the 'four pillars' of the Canadian financial services industry for marketing purposes – sometimes referred to as 'networking' – is the protection of confidential customer information. In the Canadian context, insurance companies and financial intermediaries are among the largest private sector collectors and users of personal information. The customer information which insurance companies possess is ideal for the target marketing of non-insurance products, while the very large branch networks of Canadian banks, with financial data relating to enormous numbers of bank customers, is very fertile ground for targeting sales of insurance products.

The federal government has attempted to deal with the threat to customer confidentiality by imposing a regulatory regime[59] designed to restrict the networking of insurance products by deposit-taking institutions, including banks, factoring corporations, financial leasing corporations, information services corporations, investment counselling and portfolio corporations and mutual fund corporations, amongst others. Generally speaking, the regime prohibits banks and their subsidiaries from providing, directly or indirectly, customer or employee information to an insurance entity. Banks and trust and loan companies are also prohibited from providing a telecommunications device that links their customers to an insurance entity if it is primarily for the use of customers in Canada. The regulations also require that such deposit-taking institutions must ensure that their customers are

---

58   S 38 of the Act.
59   See the Insurance Business (Bank) Regulations SOR/92–330, ss 8–10 and the Insurance Business (Trust and Loan Companies) Regulations SOR/92-331, ss 8–10. The two regulations are substantially identical.

aware that the premises of any insurance entity adjacent to a bank or trust and loan branch are clearly separate and distinct.

As noted above, in the development of these restrictions, more attention appears to have been paid to the concerns of the independent insurance companies about competition from the banks than to issues of confidentiality of bank customer information.

International aspects

Canadian banks have always operated in the international arena and the nature and scope of these activities have developed and expanded along with the general trend of globalisation of the financial services sector. The interaction of rules of different jurisdictions in connection with these activities can result in conflict of legislative goals and, therefore, courts and legislators have attempted to deal with banks or others caught between conflicting rules. While Canada, like many other countries, has enacted legislation which may contribute to such dilemmas faced by banks, the actual use of power under such rules has been very sparing since governments no doubt wish to avoid disturbance of international comity.

Provisions to restrict demands for information

As an example of such a rule, when Canadian banks are subpoenaed by foreign courts to provide information regarding customer accounts, they may be protected from having to breach their customers' confidence by virtue of the blocking legislation in the Foreign Extraterritorial Measures Act (FEMA).[60] This statute provides that the Attorney-General of Canada can block the production, disclosure or identification of any records in the possession or control of a Canadian citizen or a person resident in Canada if he believes that significant Canadian interests in international trade will be adversely affected. Such an order can be made in response to an order by a foreign tribunal, a foreign court judgment or measures taken by a foreign state. The term 'records' is defined very broadly so as to include virtually any stored or recorded information. If the Attorney-General makes such an order and believes that it may not be complied with, he may apply to a superior court to seize the records in question for safekeeping. Contravention of a blocking order by the Attorney-General is an indictable offence, even if it is committed outside Canada, and is punishable by a fine of up to CDN\$10,000 or a prison term of up to five years. There are, however, no reported cases where this legislation has been used to prevent disclosure of confidential customer records by a Canadian bank. In practice, as noted above, because Canadian courts and governments generally follow principles of international comity, the FEMA's blocking powers have been invoked very rarely and only when there is a political or foreign policy rationale behind the making of a blocking order.

The Competition Act may also be used to block the implementation of foreign judgments, decrees, orders or other processes in Canada if the Competition Tribunal

60 RSC 1985, c F-29.

finds that their effect would be detrimental to competition, trade or industry in Canada without providing compensating advantages. These blocking provisions generally parallel those of the FEMA and do not appear ever to have been invoked.

Procedures for agreed exchange of information

Although Canadian legislators have attempted to ensure there would not be inappropriate compulsion of information tribunals, they have also co-operated to facilitate exchange in appropriate circumstances. Perhaps the best recent example is the Memorandum of Understanding (MOU) executed in January 1988 between several Canadian provincial securities regulators and the US Securities and Exchange Commission. These MOUs provide for broad exchange of information in the interest of regulating securities markets which are increasingly international in scope. When combined with the broad powers of search and seizure provided to provincial securities regulators, the MOUs increase the potential for confidential information being distributed to an even wider group.

Domestic proceedings to obtain information from foreign banks or branches

Although there is Canadian legislation to block information going abroad in circumstances where it would be contrary to Canadian policy, the same can occur in reverse where a Canadian court attempts to overcome restrictions on disclosure in a foreign jurisdiction. The conditions under which Canadian courts will insist on disclosure of records from a foreign bank have been explored in *Frischke v Royal Bank of Canada*[61] and *Re Spencer and the Queen*.[62]

Frischke involved an appeal from a court order requiring Royal Bank employees in Panama to give evidence about certain customers' accounts in breach of Panamanian law. The court, in allowing the appeal, refused to use its jurisdiction over the Royal Bank to order it to compel its Panamanian employees to break their own country's laws.

Frischke was distinguished in *Re Spencer*, however. There, the Crown sought to call an employee of the Royal Bank as a witness on charges against a customer of the bank under the Income Tax Act. While a subpoena of this kind would present no problems in the normal case, the employee was at the material time manager of the Royal Bank's Bahamian branch, and was being asked to give evidence regarding transactions which had been made in the Bahamas, contrary to bank confidentiality provisions of Bahamian law. The Ontario Court of Appeal held that compellability of a witness was a matter for the lex fori and that in Canada, this witness was compellable. He was not being forced to give any evidence in contravention of Canadian laws even though he might be exposed to liability in another jurisdiction.

On appeal to the Supreme Court of Canada, the Court of Appeal decision was upheld on the grounds that even if the giving of evidence in Canada constituted a crime in

---

61   (1977) 80 DLR (3d) 393.
62   (1983) 145 DLR (3d) 344, Ont CA, *affd* (1985) 21 DLR (4th) 756, SCC.

the Bahamas, the courts and the public have a right to the evidence. To permit a witness to refuse to testify would be to permit a foreign country to frustrate the administration of justice in Canada with regard to a Canadian citizen. It was suggested by Estey J, however, that comity would require that the witness be allowed to make an application to that foreign jurisdiction to permit disclosure before the court compels him to do so.

To date, there has been no decision by a Canadian court that resolves the conflicting jurisprudence found in *Frischke* and *Spencer*. The recent trend, however, appears to indicate that bank secrecy laws of a foreign jurisdiction will generally not be a sufficient bar to the production of evidence if the action falls properly under the jurisdiction of the Canadian court and the bank is a party to the action. Most recently, in *Arab Bank v Coopers & Lybrand*,[63] Halperin J of the Quebec Superior Court held that representatives of four plaintiff banks should be compelled to testify regardless of bank secrecy laws in their home jurisdictions of Germany and Switzerland. The judge took the position that, the plaintiff banks having chosen to litigate in a forum where the law did not adhere to the same rigid rules of banking secrecy as found in their own jurisdictions, they should be required to comply with the rule of Canadian law as regards compellability of testimony.

Similarly, in the Ontario case of *Comaplex Resources International v Schaffhauser Kantonalbank*,[64] the issue considered was whether the Swiss banking secrecy laws, which apparently prohibited disclosure by the defendant bank of such documents and information, could form a valid basis for the defendant bank's refusal to answer the questions and produce the documents in Canada. Master Sandler of the Ontario High Court of Justice decided that neither *Frischke* nor *Spencer* applied to the *Comaplex* case, and instead based his decision on US cases which have held that, procedurally, a person should not be permitted to invoke foreign law prohibitions against the disclosure of information in an application to compel the disclosure. Rather, the objection should only be raised at the time that the court is considering sanctions for breach of an order to disclose.

CONFIDENTIALITY IN THE CONTEXT OF A FIDUCIARY RELATIONSHIP

As noted above, although the traditional bank-customer relationship is normally one of debtor and creditor or principal and agent, under the appropriate circumstances it can become a fiduciary relationship. Such a relationship goes beyond confidentiality and may impose additional duties upon a bank. In Canada, a fiduciary relationship has been found to arise when a bank steps outside its conventional relationship and gives advice to a customer, upon which the customer relies (to the bank's knowledge) and from which the bank stands to receive a benefit or, alternatively, when the bank misuses information obtained from a customer. Although it is possible that such a relationship can arise in circumstances where a bank is confining itself to more traditional banking activities, the circumstances in which it

---

63   Indexed as [1996] QJ no 1436, no 500-05-002564-936.
64   [1989] 42 CPC (2d) 230.

may be created are being expanded as banks move into the securities dealing and investment banking fields and take a broader and more active role in areas such as trading, investment management, take-overs and mergers and acquisitions.

Establishment of fiduciary relationship

The leading Canadian case dealing specifically with a bank's fiduciary duties towards its customers continues to be *Standard Investments Ltd v Canadian Imperial Bank of Commerce.*[65] In this case, the plaintiffs attempted to acquire control of a publicly quoted trust company. They sought the advice and assistance of the bank's president, who agreed to help them. Unbeknownst to the president, however, the bank's chairman had already decided to have the bank purchase for its own account just under 10% of the share of the trust company in order to thwart an anticipated take-over attempt, which some speculated was to be made by the plaintiffs. An outside director of the bank was also a director of the trust company and controlled or influenced significant shareholdings in the trust company. Both this director and the trust company were important customers of the bank. In addition, when it became clear there was a fight for control, the bank subsequently assisted another of its customers in the purchase of a 44% interest in the trust company which, together with the bank's 10% interest (which it subsequently sold to that other customer), effectively prevented the plaintiffs' take-over from being successful.

It was held at the Court of Appeal that a fiduciary relationship had been created. The plaintiffs had 'bared their souls' to the bank by providing it with confidential information regarding their take-over plans. In addition, the plaintiffs relied on the advice and assistance of the bank in their endeavour and the bank was aware of that reliance. Finally, the bank itself had obtained a benefit through the increased business that resulted from the plaintiffs' relationship with the bank as a result of their previously transferring accounts to the bank. Thus, all the criteria for the establishment of a fiduciary relationship were satisfied. As a result, the court held that the bank had a duty to disclose its conflict of interest.

It might be noted that there were actually two conflicts at play in this case. First, there was a conflict between the bank's interests and those of its customers, the plaintiffs. Secondly, there was the conflict between the interests of plaintiffs and those of the bank's other customers who, to the knowledge of the bank, wanted to prevent the take-over from occurring. The Court of Appeal acknowledged that the bank probably had a legal obligation not to disclose the second conflict. However, the court said that if the bank was either unwilling or unable to disclose the nature of the conflicts, it should have said that it was unable to advise the plaintiffs due to existing conflicts of interest. Alternatively, if the bank was unwilling or felt unable to disclose to a customer that a conflict existed, the bank should simply have refused to advise the plaintiffs on the matter. In fact, the court found the bank did neither of these things but rather allowed the plaintiffs to believe, over the course of seven years, that their take-over bid had a chance of success. The bank was, therefore, held

65   (1985) 52 OR (2d) 473, CA.

to be in breach of its duties to them. Damages were assessed at the amount of the plaintiffs' purchase price of the trust company shares, plus the interest lost from what would have been safe investments, minus the amount received in dividends and ultimate proceeds from the plaintiffs' sale of the shares (which fell substantially in value when the third party was able to acquire control).

Although the courts have been careful to point out that the question of whether a fiduciary relationship will be found to exist depends on all of the circumstances of a given case, there appear to be some common threads. For example, where the bank goes further than simply to explain the nature and effect of a transaction, and advises on its merit, it may be held to have 'crossed the line' from a normal debtor-creditor relationship into one involving fiduciary duties.[66]

Reliance by customer

It would appear, however, that in order for a fiduciary relationship to be established, there must also be an element of special reliance or confidence placed in the bank by the customer, either by virtue of communication of particular knowledge or by reason of ignorance or infirmity of the customer. In either case, the bank must either know, or be in circumstances where it ought to know, of the reliance being placed upon it. Once that reliance is found, then a fiduciary relationship may be said to exist and the breach thereof, by misuse of information provided or by permitting the bank's own interests to conflict with those of the customer, is actionable.

Standard Investments provides an illustration of a finding of reliance by reason of the customer having provided particular information, notwithstanding that the customer's principals were experienced businessmen. An example of reliance found by reason of the circumstances of the customer (a more common situation) is *Hayward v Bank of Nova Scotia*,[67] where the trial judge found a fiduciary relationship to exist where a highly respected small-town bank manager undertook to advise a farm widow in modest circumstances on investments in exotic cattle, for which she was proposing to borrow from the bank against the security of the family farm. Through dealings with the promoter of the investment (who was also heavily indebted to the bank and behind in his obligations in respect of that debt) the bank manager had gained considerable knowledge of the exotic cow business. His enthusiasm for the business was not shared to the same extent by his superiors, although their doubts were not fully communicated to the bank manager.

At trial, the case turned on the naivety of the customer and the faulty advice provided by the bank manager coupled with the inequality of bargaining position. Little, if anything, was said about where the proceeds of the investment were to go. Presumably, they went to pay down the promoter's loans, which would, of course, be of advantage to the bank since he was behind in his payments. The Court of Appeal reluctantly affirmed the trial decision disapproving, however, the trial judge's reliance on the inequality of bargaining position as being relevant to the breach of fiduciary duty

---

66   Waters, n 2 above, at 58.
67   (1984) 45 OR (2d) 542, HC, *affd* 510 OR (2d) 193, CA.

as opposed to the creation of the fiduciary relationship. However, the court again made no clear reference to what appeared to be a direct conflict between the bank's interest in having support for the cow business and its obligation to provide appropriate advice to the widow. In both judgments, the courts appeared to rely upon the decision of the English Court of Appeal in *Lloyds Bank Ltd v Bundy*.[68] The reasons of the Court of Appeal in *Hayward*, however, also referred to the later decision of the House of Lords in *National Westminster Bank plc v Morgan*,[69] quoting from Lord Scarman's speech,[70] to the effect that the presumption of undue influence cannot arise from the evidence of the relationship of the parties without there also being evidence that the transaction itself is wrongful, in that it constitutes an advantage taken of the party subjected to the influence. Thus, the notion that a fiduciary relationship can be established by reason of inequality of bargaining power alone was rejected.

Provision of special skills

More recently, the Supreme Court of Canada has articulated more precisely the required components of a fiduciary relationship in *Hodgkinson v Simms*.[71] The case, while dealing with an accounting firm, not a bank, has clear implications for the potential liabilities of which banks must be cognisant as they enter into non-traditional financial services areas, such as dealing in securities. The case is notable as well for its finding of a fiduciary duty even though the plaintiff investor was a relatively sophisticated individual familiar with the investment markets.

In *Hodgkinson*, the plaintiff, a 30-year-old stockbroker, sought the defendant accountant's advice to shelter some of his income in conservative investments. The accountant advised the plaintiff to invest his money in some real estate ventures in which, unbeknownst to the plaintiff, the accountant also had an interest. When the real estate market collapsed, the plaintiff lost most of his investment and sued the defendant for breach of fiduciary duty and breach of contract.

While the trial court found for the plaintiff in both claims, the British Columbia Court of Appeal found a breach of contract, but held there was no fiduciary duty to the investor because the choice to invest was entirely his. On appeal, a majority of the Supreme Court of Canada overturned the Court of Appeal's ruling and found that a fiduciary duty did exist, despite the apparent lack of 'vulnerability' of the plaintiff.

Two elements were crucial to the court's decision. The first was the finding that a 'power-dependency relationship' existed between the parties. The court noted that for this type of relationship to exist, there must be more than a simple undertaking by one party to provide information and execute orders for the other, as in most everyday transactions between a bank customer and a banker. However, it may exist when the complexity and/or importance of the subject matter make it reasonable for the customer or adviser to expect that the adviser or banker is exercising his special

68   [1974] 3 All ER 757.
69   [1985] All ER 821.
70   [1985] All ER 821 at 827.
71   [1994] 9 WWR 609, SCC.

skills in the customer's best interest.[72] The second element was the court's ruling that the existence of the fiduciary relationship flows not from the plaintiff's ability to protect himself from harm, but from the nature of the parties' reasonable expectations of the relationship. The case, although not dealing specifically with a bank's fiduciary duty to a customer, thus suggests the need for banks to use caution when providing advice or special services beyond routine banking transactions, regardless of the level of sophistication of the customer.

Standard Investments and cases such as *Hayward*, which were decided in the early and mid-1980s, indicated that the courts were becoming more willing to find the existence of a fiduciary relationship. A strand of case law from the late 1980s gave some indication that the courts were again becoming less inclined to superimpose a fiduciary relationship on the dealings between a bank and its customers, particularly if the plaintiffs are themselves knowledgeable business people.[73] It remains to be seen, however, whether these more recent cases will really assist the bank in circumstances such as contested take-overs where the parties do have a significant degree of investment experience and sophistication. *Hodgkinson* and the cases which have subsequently followed it, however, reinforce the concept that a bank may not assume that a fiduciary duty is unlikely to be found simply because the bank is dealing with a 'sophisticated' customer.

CONFLICTS OF INTEREST AND CONFIDENTIALITY

As mentioned in the preceding discussion, banks have duties of confidentiality in the normal course of a banking relationship. *Where* the relationship can be characterised as fiduciary, a bank may have an affirmative duty to disclose a conflict of interest or at least not to act in a transaction if to do so would result in a conflict of interest. As the range of activities in which banks and their affiliates are engaged has increased, so has the potential for such conflicts.

Internal conflicts

Perhaps the most straightforward conflict is the situation where a director or officer of the bank is considered to have an interest in a transaction to which the bank is a party. Prior to the 1992 reform of Canadian financial institutions legislation, the Bank Act took a conventional corporate law approach and provided that, except under specified circumstances, a director could not attend or vote at a board or committee meeting at which the bank is considering whether to advance funds to him, to a firm of which he was a member or a corporation of which he was a director. In addition, the old Bank Act set out certain restrictions on loans to officers, employees and directors of a bank and to entities in which officers or directors of a bank have interests.[74]

---

72 [1994] 9 WWR 609 at 629–630, SCC.
73 Eg see *Continental Bank of Canada v Hunter* (Alta CA) 6 November 1986; and *Sugar v Peat Marwick Ltd* (1989) 66 OR (2d) 766.
74 Bank Act, ss 418 and 491.

The 1992 revisions of the Bank Act, as amended by the new financial institutions legislation noted above, instituted a much more comprehensive regime to restrict such transactions. The rationale for this change stemmed partly from the concern over self-dealing in the context of the failures of financial institutions in Canada and abroad, and partly from the widening scope of operations, investments and affiliations that banks have acquired under the revised legislation. This restrictive code regulates transactions between a bank and related parties that might be in a position to exert influence over the bank's decision-making. Such related parties include senior officers, shareholders and directors of the bank, their spouses and minor children, and entities controlled by those individuals. The Bank Act also empowers the Superintendent of Financial Institutions to designate related parties at its discretion. Any person whose interest in the bank, or relationship with either the bank or a related party, might reasonably be expected to influence the exercise of the best judgment of the bank in respect of a transaction – for example, a major creditor or debtor of the bank – may be designated a related party.

In addition, the Bank Act stipulates that every bank must institute an independent Conduct Review Committee consisting of a majority of directors not affiliated with the bank. The Committee is charged with monitoring the bank's procedures for complying with the self-dealing regime.

These provisions are potentially more significant than may first appear because there is in Canada a relatively small number of major banks, all of which tend to have large boards of directors, coupled with a significant, and increasing, concentration of ownership in Canadian business.

External conflicts

A more frequent and increasing occurrence is that of conflicts of interest resulting from transactions involving customers of the same bank. In the field of hostile take-overs, the interaction of the concentration of ownership of Canadian business and the relatively small number of large Canadian banks can make such conflicts particularly problematic. As in the US, most Canadian bids are financed with a significant amount of debt. It is not uncommon in a major take-over bid in Canada to find that most of the major Canadian banks hold significant amounts of debt of the target. As a result, in order to preclude any claim of conflict, the acquirer may seek to finance the acquisition debt completely from non-Canadian bank sources, although this can raise other problems, such as withholding tax. At the very least, the target's 'relationship' banks would be expected to preclude themselves from financing a hostile take-over bid.

Conflicts can also arise between the interests of the bank and those of its customers as exemplified in *Standard Investments Ltd v Canadian Imperial Bank of Commerce*,[75] where the bank purchased shares in the target trust company for its own account while simultaneously 'assisting' the plaintiff customers in their take-over bid and also keeping the plaintiffs' important banking business. As noted above, the court

75   (1985) 52 OR (2d) 473, CA.

held that the bank could have resolved the conflict by either disclosing to the customers the nature of the conflict or by simply refusing to advise them on their take-over plans.

Securities dealings

The potential of conflict may now also arise between the banks' lending activities and the underwriting and selling activities of their new securities affiliates. When banks were permitted to enter the securities business, the securities regulators expressed concern about the potential for conflict if a securities firm was underwriting and distributing debt or equity securities of a third-party issuer in circumstances where that issuer was significantly indebted to, or otherwise connected in a material way with, the securities dealer's bank affiliate. Accordingly, a complex set of regulations is now in place to attempt to meet these concerns.[76]

Under these regulations, the bank's securities affiliate must prepare a statement of policies outlining how it will deal with the securities of connected issuers and must send the policy to the regulators and to customers. If a third party issuer is considered 'connected' to the bank, then any prospectus of the issuer in which the securities affiliate is an underwriter must disclose the existence and nature of the relationship in bold print on the cover of the prospectus, with a more detailed description in the body of the prospectus. The interpretation and application of these provisions is made difficult by the subjective nature of their application.

An issuer is considered 'connected' to a bank when:

1   the level of indebtedness or other relationship of the issuer with the bank is such as to lead a potential purchaser of securities to question the independence of the issuer from the bank; or
2   there is a reasonable likelihood such investor would consider such indebtedness or other relationship important in his investment decision.

In addition to the disclosure requirements, there are certain prohibited activities in respect of connected issuers. As an example, the securities affiliate is not permitted to underwrite securities of any connected issuer, or those of its bank affiliate, unless an independent dealer underwrites at least the same proportion as the bank's securities affiliate.

The concern about conflicts between banks and their securities affiliates has also been noted by the federal banking regulators. At the time that Canadian banks were first authorised by the federal authorities to acquire securities dealers, guidelines were set up outlining procedures for federally regulated financial institutions, such as banks, to obtain approval for the acquisition of more than a 10% interest in a Canadian corporation, such as a securities firm.[77] Among other things, the guidelines require the applicant to outline specifically their policies and procedures 'for effective handling of any conflicts of interest that may arise between the bank and the securities firm'.

---

76   See Pt XIII of the regulations to the Ontario Securities Act.
77   Office of the Superintendent of Financial Institutions of Canada, Guideline 18 *Re Shareholdings by Federally Regulated Financial Institutions in Securities Dealers*, 27 July 1989.

COMBATING MISUSE OF CONFIDENTIAL INFORMATION

The entry by Canadian banks into the field of securities activities has also increased the potential for misuse of confidential information. In the context of the new multi-service approach of contemporary Canadian banking, this problem can arise more often as a result of the bank's obligations to different clients in its various areas of business. For example, problems could arise if confidential information moved between a bank's commercial lending operations and its securities sales or trading functions or related activities. Information held by one department or affiliate could materially affect the decisions made in the other if that information were available to it.

Segregation of information

To date, the methods which have been utilised to deal with these potential concerns have evolved, or been derived, primarily from the North American securities experience and practice. The principal approach is to rely on concepts such as Chinese Walls, or other systems which are intended to provide for segregation of information within separate areas and departments so as to allow financial institutions to conduct activities in all areas of the financial services sector without improper use of information.

As discussed further below, most banks and other financial institutions active in a range of financial services have instituted procedures to avoid potential conflicts of interest by preventing the transmission of information among departments or to subsidiaries. In addition to Chinese Walls, restricted securities lists such as so-called 'grey' or 'watch' lists which prevent or restrict trading by employees or departments in specified securities are now commonly employed.[78]

The additional responsibilities, and the steps taken to deal with them, have not arisen solely by virtue of expanding the banks' areas of permitted activity. At the same time as the restrictions on the activities of banks and other financial institutions have been reduced, securities legislators have also been introducing expanded rules relating to insider trading or other misuse of confidential information.

Regulation of insider trading

Regulation of insider trading is considered within the legislative competence of both levels of government. The federal government (through the Bank Act and the Canada Business Corporations Act[79]) and the provinces (through securities statutes)

---

78   A 'grey' list refers to a list of companies for which a dealer has been retained on a matter which represents, or makes the dealer otherwise aware of, material undisclosed information in respect of a public company. As the information is not public, only certain senior officers of the dealer would be aware of the companies on the grey list and would be responsible to ensure the dealer undertook no trading or other improper activity. A 'restricted' list is broadly circulated within the dealer and used for companies for which the dealer will not trade due to the activities of the dealer or the issuer. At this stage, the nature of the dealer's activities have been disclosed publicly but the restriction on trading continues.

79   See the Bank Act, Pt IV, Div H and regulations; the Canada Business Corporations Act RSC 1985 c C-44, Pt XI; and the Ontario Securities Act RSC 1990 c S-5, s 74.

have enacted legislation dealing with insider trading. The legislation typically precludes trading on the knowledge of a material fact or a material change concerning a public company which has not been generally disclosed.[80] It also precludes informing or 'tipping' anyone about such information, except in the necessary course of business. In either case, in order for the trading or tipping to be an offence the party in question must be in a 'special relationship' with the public company. The term special relationship is broadly defined, however, and includes any party that engages or proposes to engage in a business or professional activity on behalf of a party such as a prospective bidder. As a result, a bank which proposes to fund or advise a bidder is in a special relationship and subject to the legislation and can only disclose material information to the extent it can conclude it is in the necessary course of business to do so.

Tightened standards

In certain provinces, insider trading legislation has become increasingly stringent both in scope of application and potential fines. For example, previously it was possible to defend a charge of insider trading by showing that, although the vendor or purchaser of securities was *aware* of material undisclosed information, it *did not make use* of it in making the trade. Therefore, if material undisclosed information was known by persons in different departments in a financial group it did not preclude trading, so long as the party did not make use of the information in trading. The regulators became increasingly concerned that it would be difficult to prove whether or not a party made use of the information and accordingly the regulators have removed the exception. The vendor or purchaser must show that persons who participated in the decision to implement the trade *did not have access* to the information.

This change has had an impact on the methods by which certain financial institutions conduct their activities. For instance, in the past, it would not have been unusual for one or more members of senior management of a bank to have knowledge of the major activities of, or developments in, more than one department. They could have had knowledge of undisclosed negative information about an issuer emanating from the corporate lending department, and at the same time been aware of principal trading, research or underwriting in securities of the issuer in other departments. Under the previous test, mere knowledge alone was not a sufficient base for a case of improper trading, the issue was whether the bank made use of such information in any securities dealings. Under the new and more restricted exception, the information must now be kept separate from all persons who may be considered to participate in trading decisions.

Mandatory policies for confidential information

At the same time as they narrowed the exception, securities regulators have introduced provisions which provide that the existence and maintenance of policies relating to

80   Ontario Securities Act, s 74.

confidential information will be a factor in discharging the burden of proof in any action for breach of the rules.[81] Some other jurisdictions have questioned whether segregating or compartmentalising information, through Chinese Walls or otherwise, can ever solve these concerns. In the new provisions, however, the Canadian securities regulators have specifically endorsed the concept of Chinese Walls. In fact, they have gone further and implemented a policy to serve as a guideline for establishing a Chinese Wall.[82]

The provisions acknowledge that the particular procedures that are appropriate for a given company or industry will vary and require that parties dealing with confidential market-sensitive information must set out their policies in writing. The policy outlines suggested procedures in the areas of employee education, containment of information, restriction of transactions and compliance. The policy is drafted primarily for dealers in securities, but also states that financial institutions in general should consider how they might implement procedures to protect themselves from allegations of insider trading. In fact, the policy has found the support of the Canadian Bankers Association.[83]

It is reasonable to conclude that in determining an appropriate standard, whether in litigation or in order to prevent it, the guidelines prescribed by the securities regulators, and the steps taken by others to attempt to follow them, are likely to be a standard against which activity will be tested.

Effectiveness of Chinese Walls – the courts' view

Although the regulators have endorsed the concept of Chinese Walls, there may be some question as to how the Canadian courts will react. In addition to the issue of fiduciary duties, the *Standard Investments* case,[84] discussed above, also considered the problem of the bank's responsibility for the conflicting acts and intentions of two or more responsible officers, in that case the president and chairman. The court's solution was to extend a doctrine of 'identification' for corporate responsibility which had previously been enunciated by the Supreme Court of Canada[85] in the context of criminal actions and apply it to civil actions regarding corporate breaches of fiduciary duties.[86]

Under this extension of the 'identification' doctrine, the court in *Standard Investments* held that it is possible for a corporation to have more than one directing mind in the same field of operations and that one person's lack of knowledge about the actions of the other will not serve to protect the corporation from liability for the actions of either or the combined effect of both. It commented that:

---

81   Ontario Securities Act, regulations, s 175d.
82   OSC Policy 10.2 *Guidelines for the Establishment of Procedures in Relation to Confidential Information* (1989) 12 OSCB 2387.
83   Regulations to the Ontario Securities Act, s 175.
84   *Standard Investments Ltd v Canadian Imperial Bank of Commerce* (1985) 52 OR (2d) 473, CA.
85   *Canadian Dredge and Dock Company Ltd v The Queen* (1985) 19 DLR (4th) 314, SCC.
86   The test for establishing that an employee's actions can be attributed to the corporation involves showing that the action: (i) was within the field of operation assigned to him; (ii) was not totally in fraud of the company; and (iii) was by design or result partly for the benefit of the company.

'In civil cases, where the element of *mens rea is* not applicable, when there are two or more directing minds *operating within the same field assigned to both* of them, the knowledge, intention and acts of each becomes together the total knowledge, intention and acts of the corporation which they represent.'[87]

It could be argued that the court was, in effect, implying that a company could not in some way keep separate the knowledge it has within separate departments. Although this case can be distinguished on its unusual facts, and although there has been legislative action by the securities regulators supporting Chinese Walls, these judicial comments may be used to question the appropriateness and effectiveness of Chinese Walls from a judicial perspective. It is likely, however, that where a Chinese Wall is sufficiently effective so as to preclude a finding that the directing minds of the corporation are operating in the same field, the court may well accept the effectiveness of the Chinese Wall.

CONCLUSION

In the last few years, the Canadian financial industry has undergone unprecedented change in both the domestic regulatory environment and the international market for financial services. The broader powers Canadian banks now possess, many as a result of their own requests, have unquestionably opened up new opportunities for them. It is clear, however, that banks must be mindful that Canadian courts and regulators are prepared to impress these new powers with new duties and responsibilities. While there has been some legislative encroachment on the general rule of bank confidentiality, particularly in the tax and money laundering areas, these initiatives have been accepted in Canada as representing intrusions for justifiable public policy reasons. Moreover, these incursions to some extent are counterbalanced as legislators begin to take a pro-active role in protecting the privacy of personal information, and in dealing with potential conflicts of interest that arise inevitably as the scope of activities undertaken by banks increases.

87   (1985) 52 OR (2d) 473 at 494, CA.

7   Czech Republic

Pavla Henzlová

INTRODUCTION

The confidentiality principle has always existed, in general terms, in all spheres of law in the legal system of the Czech Republic, and the bank confidentiality principle is, in fact, only a modification of this, although perhaps one of the most sensitive. It is therefore necessary to stress that bank confidentiality does not represent a brand new concept in the law of the Czech Republic, although the current legal regulation of banking was only adopted after 1989. Regardless of continuous discussions concerning the definition, content and practical application of bank confidentiality, the relevant legal regulation of banking has created a new foundation for the further development of the whole banking system, including, inter alia, bank confidentiality aspects. In addition, the legislation of the Czech Republic has been through significant changes and development since the publication of the second edition of this book in 1998, which changes and development have been required particularly in respect of a harmonisation of the Czech legal system with the EU legal system. Important amendments have also been adopted in the sphere of banking, which quite obviously affected also the basic principles of the bank confidentiality regulation. It should be noted that a bank under the law of the Czech Republic does not mean only a 'bank' in its limited sense, but any legal entity established in the form of a joint stock company which obtained a licence from the Czech National Bank to accept deposits from the general public and to provide credits.

The purpose of this chapter is not to provide an extensive jurisprudential essay, but to outline the basic principles of bank confidentiality under the law of the Czech Republic and to stress potential problems which might occur in connection with the application, protection and breach of bank confidentiality in the Czech Republic.

THE BASIC RULE OF CONFIDENTIALITY

The source of confidentiality

The general provisions on bank confidentiality under Czech law have been incorporated, quite logically, into the Act on Banks (no 21/1992 Coll, as amended), the Act on the Czech National Bank (no 6/1993 Coll, as amended) and the Decree of the Czech National Bank on Requirements for a Licence to operate as a Bank (no 166/2002 Coll – the Decree on Requirements for a Licence to operate as a Bank).

In addition to these Acts being the main sources of bank confidentiality, which in general terms apply to both the banks established and registered in the Czech Republic as joint stock companies and branches of foreign banks, there exists a number of other Acts and legal rules which regulate, deal with or affect bank confidentiality, for example, the Foreign Exchange Act (no 219/1995 Coll, as amended), the Act on Provisions against the Legalization of Profits from Criminal Activity (no 61/1996 Coll, as amended – the Money Laundering Act), the Act on Protection of Personal Data (no 101/2000 Coll, as amended – the Personal Data Protection Act), as well as the provisions in the double taxation treaties between the Czech Republic and foreign countries (since there might also be an international aspect under certain circumstances).

Bank confidentiality rules, which are common to all banks registered and operating in the Czech Republic and apply also to all branches of foreign banks operating as banks in the Czech Republic, are clear: all banking transactions and banking financial services, including the state of bank accounts and deposits, are subject to bank confidentiality. There is, however, one unclear 'detail': none of the provisions on bank confidentiality defines the contents of bank confidentiality, which fact, unfortunately, brings some uncertainty into the whole issue.

Since the banks, as legal entities, are bound by bank confidentiality, employees of the bank (including members of the board of directors, who must always be employees of the bank), members of its supervisory board and persons providing bank supervision are also obligated to keep all matters relating to interests of the bank and its clients confidential. This obligation to maintain professional confidentiality remains in existence even after the termination of an employment or similar relationship.

It is also important to stress that, although the relevant provision of the Act on Banks only imposes this obligation on employees and other representatives of Czech banks, it follows logically from the other provisions of the Act, in particular, from the provisions on bank supervision by the Czech National Bank (the central bank), that the same rules also apply to employees and representatives of the branches of foreign banks.

A foreign bank which applies for a banking licence for its branch in the Czech Republic must in addition provide the Czech National Bank, which is a licensing authority, with a written covenant by the banking supervisory authority in its own country to inform the Czech National Bank of any changes to the concept and application of the principles of bank confidentiality in that country, in particular, as they affect the branches of banks established abroad.

The confidentiality rules appear not only in the abstract sphere of rights and obligations to be observed from a legal point of view, but the accent is also placed on the technical, administrative and organisational provision and protection of data and information to be secured by the bank or by the branch of a foreign bank. Specification and details of the data protection system constitute mandatory requirements of an application for a banking licence.

The same confidentiality requirements, as applied to the bank, are also imposed on supervisory, regulatory and other bodies of state administration or courts if they dispose of bank information by virtue of law. The same principle applies to the employees and representatives of such bodies and authorities as regards professional confidentiality.

The nature and extent of bank confidentiality

Bank confidentiality can be viewed from different aspects according to the different legal relations in which it applies and according to the different positions of the entities or natural persons involved. The three basic legal aspects of bank confidentiality will be dealt with in more detail below. This section summarises the general concepts of the different views on this issue.

The activities of banks and branches of foreign banks are subject to bank supervision by the Czech National Bank. The Czech National Bank acts vis-à-vis banks as a general licensing, supervisory and regulatory authority (together with the Ministry of Finance, under certain circumstances). The Czech National Bank performs supervision as regards observance of the law and of the regulations which it issues, and imposes remedies and measures, which will be specified below, if it discovers any breach or shortcoming in the activities of a bank or a branch of a foreign bank as set out in the Act on Banks. All persons involved in the provision of bank supervision by the Czech National Bank vis-à-vis banks are subject to the obligation to keep all information obtained during the supervision confidential. By virtue of law, such persons are entitled to disclose such information to the authorities supervising the financial market and financial institutions in the Czech Republic and also to similar authorities abroad, as well as to the relevant EU bodies in connection with fulfilment of international treaties.

All measures and actions taken under the Act on Banks against a bank or a branch of a foreign bank which has breached any of its mandatory obligations or the law (in general) are of an administrative law nature. The consequences of such a breach are regulated and specified in the Act on the Czech National Bank and the Act on Banks. Measures and remedies ordered and taken by the Czech National Bank are of an administrative law character, which means that the procedure against the bank or the branch of a foreign bank which breached bank confidentiality would be governed by the Administrative Procedure Act (no 71/1967 Coll, as amended). The Czech National Bank would act in the procedure as the administrative body. With the exception of the Act on Banks, Czech law in general does not define a breach of bank confidentiality as a particular title for a remedy or recourse, either under civil law or under criminal law. This does not mean, however, that the person or entity affected by the breach might not seek a civil law remedy or that the relevant employee or representative of the bank or the branch of the foreign bank who disclosed the confidential bank information would not, under certain circumstances, be accused of a criminal offence.

Any bank customer (a legal entity or a natural person) may apply to a civil court for damages or satisfaction or for another remedy in the event that he or it has sustained damage in connection with a breach of bank confidentiality. Under the law of the Czech Republic, a liability for damage cannot be limited or even excluded by an agreement between a bank and its customer.

In some cases, a breach of bank confidentiality might be classified under criminal law, although the Criminal Code (Act no 140/1961 Coll, as amended) does not specify a breach of bank confidentiality as a separate criminal offence. In the event that an employee, representative or other person involved in banking operations discloses or misuses confidential bank information and fulfils thereby the factual substance of a specific criminal offence, he will be responsible under criminal law.

Recourse against breach of bank confidentiality

It has been mentioned above that responsibility for a breach of bank confidentiality is reflected in three spheres of law: administrative, civil and criminal, although the level of protection provided by each of these is not always equal and adequate.

Administrative law concept

As discussed above, the Czech National Bank carries out and executes the supervision of banks, including branches of foreign banks, as regards their observance of the law and regulations issued by the Czech National Bank. In the event that the Czech National Bank discovers a shortcoming, a breach of the law or any other activity on the part of the bank violating the interests of its customers, it will be authorised to take the measures and actions specified in the Act on Banks and set out below. A bank activity which violates the interests of its customers is determined by the Act to be, in particular:

1   violation of the terms of a banking licence;
2   violation of the Act, special laws, legal regulations and measures issued by the Czech National Bank; or
3   conduct of transactions in a manner which is detrimental to the depositor's interests, or which jeopardises the reliability and stability of the banking system.

In accordance with the Act, the Czech National Bank is authorised to take the following measures and actions:

1   to request that adequate redress be made by the bank or the branch of a foreign bank or that the bank or the branch of a foreign bank restrains the relevant unauthorised activities or provides for personnel changes;
2   to change the bank licence by elimination or restriction of some of the licensed activities;
3   to impose a receivership on the bank (this may not apply to a branch of a foreign bank);
4   to impose a penalty of up to 50 million Czech Crowns; and
5   to reduce the registered capital of the bank under certain conditions.

Despite quite a wide range of administrative remedies under the Act on Banks, apparently only the remedies specified under 1 above would apply in the event of a breach of bank confidentiality and remedies under 2 and 4 if the remedy under 1 is not complied with or in cases of some urgency.

In addition to the remedies listed above which might be imposed by the Czech National Bank, the Act on Banks also provides that the bank licence may be withdrawn from a bank or a branch of a foreign bank by the Czech National Bank in agreement with the Ministry of Finance. Such a remedy would apply in the event that serious shortcomings or breaches persist in the conduct of a bank or a branch.

In any case, the remedy or recourse in the event of the disclosure of confidential information may only apply on the basis of an administrative procedure in which proper and sufficient evidence of a breach of confidentiality has been presented, which might in many cases be the most difficult issue.

In addition, the administrative remedy is directed against the bank only and therefore does not provide a direct recourse to the customer affected by the breach of confidentiality.

Civil law concept

Under general civil law principles, a customer may take a civil law action against the bank or a foreign bank through its branch either for damages, for satisfaction, for a restraint of disclosure of information or for removal of the consequences of a breach of bank confidentiality. The civil law procedure would be based on and would follow the Civil Proceedings Code (Act no 99/1963 Coll, as amended), which stipulates the conditions and rules governing the conduct of civil law proceedings, including the court's decisions and remedies.

The legal action for damages or for satisfaction would probably be very problematic, since the customer would have to determine the damage he or it sustained in connection with a breach of bank confidentiality or to estimate the satisfaction he or it considers appropriate.

A claim for removal of the consequences of a breach of bank confidentiality would also be more likely to raise questions as to its practicability than to provide some positive compensation to the customer, and a potential recourse against the bank in the form of an injunction to restrain the disclosure of confidential information may not be regarded as an adequate remedy.

The length of the civil law process unfortunately adds a further argument in support of this sceptical viewpoint. Czech law does not prescribe any period in which the court would be obliged to issue its injunction. And, although Czech law provides for the institution of preliminary measures which may be imposed by the court in order to achieve a rapid and effective preliminary solution of a current situation before the proceedings are completed and the injunction is issued, it would not be advisable to rely on this since it is always at the discretion of the court and, according to general practice, the courts are rather reluctant to award preliminary measures. Should, however, a preliminary measure be awarded, then the court is obliged to do so within seven days following the submission of the relevant petition by the claimant (customer).

Although the customer affected by a breach of bank confidentiality may claim a remedy through civil law proceedings, under present conditions a civil law action (an event where the injunction satisfies the customer's claim) probably cannot be regarded in most cases as a sufficient and adequate recourse and protection for bank customers.

Criminal law concept

A breach of confidential bank information by employees or representatives of a bank or a branch of a foreign bank might also be classified as a criminal offence under the Criminal Code, in which case such a breach might fall into one of the following categories of criminal offences:

1   *The unauthorised disposal of personal data.* In accordance with the definition of this criminal offence, any person who discloses or makes available confidential data and information which he obtained in connection with his employment or other position where he was obliged to maintain professional confidentiality will be sentenced to imprisonment for up to three years (or five years if he has caused substantial damage by this criminal offence or if he has officially published such confidential information), or he will be subject to a financial penalty or a ban on his professional activity.

2   *The misuse or damage to records of a data system.* In accordance with the definition of this criminal offence, any person who, in pursuit of unauthorised financial profit, gains access to a data system and misuses or damages the data it contains will be sentenced to imprisonment for up to one year (or up to five years if he has caused extensive damage), or he will be subject to a financial penalty or a ban on his professional activity.

3   *The misuse of information in the conduct of business (insider dealing).* In accordance with the definition of this criminal offence, any person who, in pursuit of unauthorised profit, misuses confidential information which he gained through his employment or other position in a business operation or in the course of the trading of goods or securities will be sentenced to imprisonment for up to three years (or up to 12 years if he gained extensive profit), or he will be subject to a financial penalty or a ban on his professional activity.

The above three are examples of the most typical criminal offences which occur in the event of the unauthorised disposal and disclosure of confidential information directed against employees and other representatives of banks and branches of foreign banks. Although the Criminal Code sets out quite severe punishments and penal sentences, the question arises as to whether such measures represent any real prevention of a breach of professional confidentiality since the success of criminal proceedings will always be dependent upon the production of sufficient evidence. Given the sophisticated methods used by potential offenders, this could be hard to achieve and could prove to be a weak point in the whole concept of criminal responsibility in this area.

The provisions and rules summarised above would also reasonably apply to branches of foreign banks.

EXCEPTIONS TO THE BASIC RULE OF CONFIDENTIALITY

The obligation on the part of the banks and their employees and representatives to keep bank information confidential is not absolute. The Act on Banks sets forth circumstances under which a bank is either authorised or even obliged to disclose confidential information.

The disclosure of confidential information with a customer's consent

Except for the cases specified in the Act on Banks, the bank may disclose confidential information only with the customer's consent. Although the Act does not specify the form of such consent, for the sake of the protection of both the bank and the customer it should always be in written form and duly signed by the customer or a statutory representative of the customer, provided that the customer is a legal entity. The consent should also specify the extent and purpose of the disclosure of confidential information.

Basic rules on disclosure of confidential information in the interests of the bank and in the public interest

In all cases, release from the obligation to keep information confidential on grounds of public interest or in the interests of the bank must be based upon the general provisions of the Act on Banks, under which a bank will be entitled or obliged to disclose confidential information by virtue of the law. In addition to the cases mentioned below, the amended Act on Banks now implements rules under which the bank is authorised to disclose confidential information either in its own interests or in the public interest.

Under these new rules, the bank is entitled to exchange information on customers' bank accounts and solvency and credibility with another bank. Such information may, however, be exchanged between the banks only through an entity which is not a bank. Nevertheless, the ownership interests in such an entity may be held only by banks. Further, the bank is permitted to inform other banks, any third party or even the general public of the name of any client who is in a default with fulfilment of his or its obligations vis-à-vis the bank for the period exceeding 60 days. This permission, however, does not apply to branch offices of foreign banks.

The disclosure of information on the customer and his or its business in connection with criminal information made by the bank, which is a general obligation in the case that a suspicion of a criminal offence exists, will not be regarded as a breach of bank confidentiality, ie in the event that the information gives rise to criminal proceedings.

The same rule applies in the event that the bank fulfils its obligations under the Money Laundering Act. Under this Act, the bank is obliged to inform the Ministry of Finance of any 'unusual business' carried out by its customers. The Act defines 'unusual business' as behaviour, the nature, extent or specification of which apparently exceeds the nature or extent of certain kinds of business of the customer. In the event that the bank discovers such 'unusual business', it shall inform the

Ministry of Finance forthwith, within five days at the latest, of the discovery of such 'unusual business'.

In the event of disclosure of confidential information under the law, the statutory body of the bank will release the relevant employees, members of the supervisory board and other persons providing banking supervision from their obligations to keep professional information confidential in order to provide the necessary information and to allow co-operation with the relevant authorities. Such a release will always be in writing, and will also be delivered to the relevant authority that has requested the information.

Disclosure of information

While the above dealt with the general principles of the authorised disclosure of confidential information and, in particular, with the instances when confidential information is disclosed in an action to be taken at the bank's discretion, the following specifies cases when the bank, and also a branch of a foreign bank, is requested by the relevant authorities to disclose confidential information.

Authorities which may request information

Under the Act on Banks the bank (and therefore, obviously, also a foreign bank through its branch) shall disclose confidential information without the consent of the customer on the written request of and to:

1   the body of bank supervision, ie the Czech National Bank (and the Ministry of Finance under certain circumstances);
2   the courts for the purposes of civil law proceedings;
3   the authorities involved in criminal proceedings;
4   the tax authorities for the purpose of tax proceedings;
5   the Ministry of Finance and the Securities Commission for the purposes of its supervisory activities;
6   the Ministry of Finance under conditions stipulated in the Money Laundering Act;
7   the social security and health insurance authorities;
8   the court executives authorised to carry out executions in respect of the customer; and
9   the labour office in connection with a return of funds obtained from the state budget.

The basic characteristics of the obligations to disclose bank information

The characteristic features set out below show the basic and typical situations in which the bank may be approached by the relevant authorities (see above), in order to disclose confidential information:

THE CZECH NATIONAL BANK IN ITS SUPERVISORY CAPACITY

Under the Act on the Czech National Bank, the bank is obliged to inform the Czech National Bank, at its request, of any matter which is subject to bank confidentiality, such as, for example, bank transactions, banking services, the state of bank accounts and deposits, in order that the Czech National Bank may supervise and review the bank's compliance with generally binding legal regulations when performing its activities and operations. In the course of this supervision, the Czech National Bank may impose on the bank the administrative law remedies and measures, specified above at 'Administrative law concept' under 1 to 5.

THE COURTS FOR THE PURPOSES OF CIVIL LAW PROCEEDINGS

A civil court's request for confidential information would be based on the Civil Proceedings Code. The purposes behind a request for the disclosure of bank information can vary. A bankruptcy proceeding may serve as a typical example. However, the power of the court is not unlimited. For instance, some problems might occur if, for example, the civil court ordered the enforcement of a judgment through an assignment of money from the bank account of the debtor on the request of the creditor. The creditor should specify in his request the number of the relevant account. In the event that he does not know the number of the account, he may request the court to obtain this information, but the only possibility given to the court is to ask the debtor. If the debtor ignores the request of the court, the only remedy available is to impose on the debtor a fine of up to 50,000 Czech Crowns. This means that the principle of statutory exemptions from the obligation to maintain bank confidentiality is not unconditional and, especially in the event of civil proceedings, will probably always depend on the particular issue.

AUTHORITIES INVOLVED IN CRIMINAL PROCEEDINGS

Under the Criminal Procedure Code (Act no 158/1992 Coll, as amended), the courts, state attorneys, investigators and police (the relevant branch) are authorised to request confidential information from the bank under the following conditions:

1   the request is made in relation to criminal proceedings in progress; and
2   the requested information is necessary for the clarification of a criminal offence or for the estimation of the personal financial standing of the accused or for the purpose of enforcing a judgment.

On being approached by the authorities involved in the criminal proceeding, the bank is not entitled to consider whether the above conditions have been met.

The amendment to the Criminal Code brought a new provision to Czech criminal proceedings, that is the 'freezing' of bank deposits in an account. Under the relevant provision of the Criminal Code, the chairman of the criminal court senate, the state attorney, the investigator or the relevant police authority may issue an order to the bank requesting that it secure (block) its customer's deposits in the event of a suspicion that:

1   the deposits have been designated for the commitment of a criminal offence;
2   the deposits have been used for the commitment of a criminal offence; or
3   the deposits have resulted from a criminal offence.

In comparison with the position of the civil court, which is rather unclear vis-à-vis the bank, the position of the criminal court and the other authorities involved in criminal proceedings is undisputable, in that it has been strengthened even further by the adoption of the new provision (mentioned above) on the 'freezing' of deposits.

TAX AUTHORITIES

The tax authorities, ie in most cases the relevant finance offices, may request the disclosure of bank information for the purpose of a tax assessment during tax proceedings, in accordance with the Act on Administration of Taxes and Fees (no 337/1992 Coll, as amended). The tax authorities may approach the bank in the event that a suspicion exists of the concealment of the customer's income or if the customer does not co-operate with the tax authority or if any other suspicion exists of a breach of tax law by the customer.

THE MINISTRY OF FNANCE AND THE SECURITIES COMMISSION AS SUPERVISORY BODIES

A typical example of involvement on the part of the Ministry of Finance and the Securities Commission with bank confidentiality is the statutory supervision exercised by the Ministry and the Securities Commission in relation to a bond (in particular to a mortgage bond) issued under the Act on Bonds (no 530/1990 Coll, as amended). From their positions as licensing and regulatory bodies in relation to bond issues, the Ministry of Finance and the Securities Commission may request confidential bank information in the event that the issuer of the bonds (a bank in the case of mortgage bonds) is suspected of a breach of the Act on Bonds or any other obligation related to the relevant bond issue.

THE MINISTRY OF FINANCE IN RELATION TO THE MONEY LAUNDERING ACT

Some aspects of this issue have already been dealt with in connection with the bank's obligation to inform the Ministry of Finance under the Money Laundering Act (see above). In addition to the bank's obligation, the Ministry of Finance is authorised to perform its own investigation regarding an 'unusual business transaction' and to request the bank to present the ministry with all information and documents on 'unusual businesses', or to allow the employees of the ministry access to relevant information and documents and to request information on all persons involved in such 'unusual businesses'. Furthermore, the ministry may order that the bank postpone the performance of the customer's instruction, which is subject to review by the ministry, for a period from 24 to 72 hours from the time that the ministry obtained information on the 'unusual business' from the bank.

In the event that the bank does not fulfil its obligation to advise the ministry or to provide the ministry with the requested evidence and documents under this Act, the ministry may impose a penalty of up to 2 million Czech Crowns (or up to 10 million Czech Crowns if the bank repeatedly fails to comply with its obligation or fails to fulfil its obligation for a 12-month period). The statutory barred period for a penalty to be imposed by the ministry for the non-fulfilment of the obligations under this Act is two years from the end of the year in which the 'unusual business' occurred.

All of the above authorities are obliged to observe the confidentiality of bank information obtained from the bank. They may only disclose such information under the same conditions and for the same reasons as those applying to the bank. The consequences of a breach of bank confidentiality by the relevant authorities would probably be the same as above. The same applies to their employees and representatives as regards their observance of professional confidentiality.

THE SOCIAL SECURITY AND HEALTH INSURANCE AUTHORITIES

The social security and health insurance authorities may request the disclosure of bank information for the purpose of proceedings related to mandatory social security and health insurance contributions, in accordance with the Act on Social Security (no 100/1988 Coll, as amended) and Health Insurance (no 48/1997 Coll, as amended). The relevant authorities may approach the bank in the event that the customer does not pay the contributions or for the purpose of in the execution of the due contributions.

THE COURT EXECUTIVES

The court executive may request the disclosure of bank information for the purpose of execution of an effective court judgment against the customer to be carried out under the Executory Rules (no 120/2001 Coll, as amended) in the event that the execution is to be provided by payment from the customer's bank accounts.

DISCLOSURE OF CONFIDENTIAL INFORMATION IN RELATION TO FOREIGN AUTHORITIES

Rules similar to those which apply to the observance or compulsory disclosure of confidential information in the Czech Republic will probably apply in other countries. However, the 'exchange' of banking information might be rather problematic. Although Czech law makes a distinction between rendering information in the course of providing legal assistance or, in general, on the request of a judicial authority (ie courts), and rendering information on the request of another authority (ie banking or administrative authority), the procedure in both situations will be very similar.

Disclosure of confidential information on a court's request

Under principles of Czech law, legal assistance in relation to foreign countries may be provided either in accordance with an international treaty or upon a reciprocity principle if an international treaty with the relevant country does not exist. Basically, legal relations between countries with different jurisdictions are regulated by the Act on International Private and Proceedings Law (no 97/1963 Coll, as amended), which, inter alia, sets out basic principles of international legal assistance. In addition to this Act, a number of treaties on legal assistance exist between the Czech Republic and other countries. The Czech Republic is also a signatory of some multilateral international treaties, for instance, the European Treaty on Legal Assistance in Criminal Matters. As a random selection, countries with which the Czech Republic has entered into treaties on legal assistance include Switzerland, France, Spain, Belgium, Italy, Austria, Greece and Cyprus.

In principle, a foreign court may approach a bank in the Czech Republic, when seeking confidential information, only after complying with certain requirements stipulated either by the Act on International Private and Proceedings Law or by the relevant international treaty.

The treaties on legal assistance also usually designate the authorities of the relevant countries involved, which will be authorised to mediate between contacts in the provision of legal assistance. If a treaty does not exist or if the treaty does not designate the relevant authority, the mediation of contacts between the parties of two different countries will be governed by the Governmental Decree on Contacts of State and other Authorities with Offices and Authorities of Other Countries (no 31/1951 Coll).

Examples of procedure in connection with the disclosure of confidential information on a court's request

In order to clarify this, some typical examples are as follows:

1   If, for instance, a court in a country with which the Czech Republic has not entered into any treaty on legal assistance requests confidential information (whether in civil or criminal proceedings), the request of the court or other judicial authority must be submitted to the relevant country's Ministry of Justice (or a similar authority). The ministry will pass this request to the Ministry of Foreign Affairs (or a similar authority). The Ministry of Foreign Affairs will then forward the request to the Ministry of Foreign Affairs of the Czech Republic and this ministry will pass the request to the Ministry of Justice of the Czech Republic, which will eventually serve the request on the relevant court for a settlement, ie depending on other circumstances mentioned below, the court may request the bank to provide it with confidential information.

2   In the event that a treaty on legal assistance exists, the procedure would depend on the regulation of the mutual contacts between the relevant authorities of the two countries. Provided that the contacts are at ministerial level (for instance, treaties with Belgium, Italy, Portugal, Greece, Spain and Switzerland), the requests of the courts or other judicial authorities are delivered by the Ministry of Justice (or by an authority with a similar capacity) of the relevant country to the Ministry of Justice of the Czech Republic. The Ministry of Justice will then serve the request on the relevant court.

3   In the event that the mutual contacts between the two countries are at consular level, the Ministry of Justice or a similar authority of the relevant foreign country will forward the request to the Ministry of Foreign Affairs (or a similar authority) and this ministry will pass the request to the consulate of the relevant country in the Czech Republic. The consulate will then serve the request directly on the court in the Czech Republic. Depending upon the other circumstances, the court may request that the bank provide confidential information.

The same procedure will apply in reverse when a court in the Czech Republic requests confidential information from a bank abroad.

Therefore, the whole procedure regarding the means of delivering the request to the relevant court in the Czech Republic depends on:

(a) whether a treaty on mutual legal assistance exists and also whether the treaty covers the spheres of both civil and criminal law, or only one of these; and

(b) how the contacts between the two countries have been regulated, ie which state authorities have to be involved in the delivery process.

The delivery of the request, however, forms only a part of the total of all legal steps to be taken and considered in connection with the provision of confidential bank information to a foreign court.

Provided that all of the procedure for delivery of the request as described above has been duly completed, a Czech court will provide legal assistance on the request of a foreign judicial authority only on condition that reciprocity exists between the Czech Republic and the relevant country. Reciprocity may be based either on a treaty on mutual legal assistance or, in the event that such a treaty does not exist or that the existing treaty does not regulate reciprocity, on mutual practice between the two countries.

Disclosure of confidential information on the request of another foreign authority

A similar situation will then occur if another foreign authority, other than the courts, requests confidential bank information.

In the event that the request falls within the capacity of the state administrative body of the Czech Republic and not the Ministry of Justice, the request will be forwarded to the relevant state administrative body, which in this case might be the Czech National Bank or the Ministry of Finance. The Czech National Bank or the Ministry of Finance (as the case may be) would then follow a similar procedure to that of a court, ie they might at their discretion and depending on other circumstances request the confidential information from the bank.

The requested legal assistance will always be based on the laws of the Czech Republic, which means that the Czech court, or the Czech National Bank or the Ministry of Finance (as the case may be) will approach the bank with a request to provide confidential information only in the case that the disclosure of such information is in compliance with the law. Otherwise, the requested authority will refuse to provide the assistance sought. Obviously, the bank would be obliged to provide the confidential information only under the conditions and circumstances set out in the Act on Banks, as explained above.

It has been mentioned above that the procedure similar to that when a court requests confidential information would apply in the event that an administrative body requests such information. For instance, if the banking supervisory authority in the foreign country requires information from a Czech bank (which might also be a wholly owned subsidiary of a foreign bank), such a request would have to go through the Czech Ministry of Foreign Affairs, which means that the requesting authority would have to forward its request to the relevant state administrative authority of its country first, and the request would then be passed by this authority to the Ministry of Foreign Affairs of the Czech Republic. The ministry would then serve the request on the relevant state administrative body, ie the Czech National Bank or the Ministry of Finance, which would then approach the bank.

The provision of confidential information would therefore be based on the same principles as in the case of the provision of information on the request of a court, ie information would be provided in accordance with an international treaty, if it exists, otherwise under the general principles of Czech law as described above.

The situation does not seem to be any less complicated where an international treaty exists between the Czech Republic and a relevant foreign country. For instance, the double taxation treaties presume an exchange of information between the relevant tax authorities of the two countries. However, at the same time, some of the treaties stipulate that such a provision shall not apply to any confidential information, including bank confidential information (the treaty with Switzerland, for example), or stipulate that the requested party is not obliged to disclose any confidential information.

This means that if the relevant authority from a foreign country insists that the Czech bank make confidential information available, regardless of whether an international treaty exists, the authority would have to pass the whole procedure through the state administrative bodies.

It is doubtless unnecessary to stress that the relevant Czech administrative authority could approach the bank with a request to disclose confidential information and that the bank could do so only in the event that reciprocity in exchange of information between the Czech Republic and the relevant foreign country has been established and that such a disclosure was not contrary to Czech law. This means that the information might only be made available if its disclosure fell within the cases, specified by the Act on Banks, in which a bank may provide confidential information.

Disclosure of confidential information maintained by a branch of a foreign bank

It is necessary to emphasise that the above provisions and procedure would apply in the event that the confidential information was requested from a bank being a Czech legal entity, ie a bank incorporated under Czech laws as a joint stock company or a state monetary institution and registered in the commercial register in the Czech Republic. As far as branches of foreign banks are concerned, although they must comply with general requirements imposed on any bank in order to obtain a banking licence and must be registered in the commercial register, they are not regarded as Czech legal entities. Therefore, in the event of a Czech court or a state administrative body requesting information from a foreign bank with its branch office in the Czech Republic, it should approach the foreign bank through its branch, since the Act on Banks does not enable the Czech courts or state administrative bodies to request confidential information directly from the branch.

The whole concept of bank confidentiality as applied to the branch of a foreign bank would then be based on the Act on Banks, as explained above. That is to say, when the head office of a foreign bank in a foreign country is affected by a civil, criminal or administrative investigation in the Czech Republic through its branch office, it would be obliged, in respect of the activities of the branch, to keep confidential all banking information obtained and collected by the branch and to disclose it only on the legal basis stipulated by the Act on Banks. If the head office of a foreign bank refused to provide the information requested, although all statutory requirements had been met, it would be exposed to the risk that relevant measures might be imposed on it by the Czech National Bank.

The same rules then apply in the case of a branch of a Czech bank abroad, subject to potential differences in the concept of a branch of a foreign bank in some countries.

For example, if a court in England requests that all account records of the customer of a Czech bank be made available, it will have to follow the procedure described above since no treaty on mutual legal assistance between the Czech Republic and the UK exists.

The same rules apply in the event that the information is required by a state administrative body or by a banking supervisory authority.

PROCESS OF TRACING OF FUNDS

In the process of tracing funds which have been the subject of a criminal offence or of any illegal disposal, all the procedures and measures which have been dealt with above might apply, in general. This means that the elements of banking supervision by the Czech National Bank, of interference executed by the Ministry of Finance, as well as the elements of criminal law and also of the civil law would appear at various stages of such a process. There would, however, be differences, depending upon whether the funds could be traced in the Czech Republic or whether they disappeared abroad.

Tracing of funds in local banks

The process of tracing funds will always face the barrier of bank confidentiality and the rather strict rules on the possibility of compelling banks to disclose confidential information. Although the process of tracing funds has two basic legal aspects, the administrative law aspect and the criminal law aspect, in the whole concept of the law of the Czech Republic, only certain authorities involved in criminal proceedings are authorised to carry out effective interference with such a process.

Moreover, even if it were suspected that funds resulting from an illegal business or criminal activity were deposited in banks, only the courts would have the power to compel the bank to make available the confidential information about such funds.

The reasons for and examples of the court's interference have been set out above.

An example of tracing funds might be as follows: if the customer of a bank was defrauded by its employee, who illegally transferred the money to other bank accounts in other banks in the Czech Republic, the customer may lay a criminal information against its employee with the relevant body involved in criminal proceedings and the investigator would commence a criminal investigation.

In accordance with the Criminal Proceedings Code, only the chairman of the criminal senate, the state attorney, the investigator or a relevant police body within criminal proceedings may issue an order to block the deposits in a bank account, provided a justified suspicion exists that the money is connected with a criminal offence. The authority ordering a block on the deposits must also state in its order all the details related to the relevant account.

In the event that details of such a bank account are not available or that the customer and the authorities referred to above do not have sufficient information as to where the funds have been transferred, after the criminal proceedings have been commenced against the employee, the state attorney or the chairman of a criminal senate will approach the customer's bank with the request that the bank provide all information about the movements and disposal of funds in the customer's accounts. Under such circumstances, the bank shall be obliged to disclose the confidential information, as explained above.

The Money Laundering Act also signifies a substantial contribution towards greater transparency of banking transactions. The basic provisions and obligations imposed on banks in the Czech Republic in the event of the appearance of 'unusual business' are dealt with above. Under this Act the Ministry of Finance would be obliged to inform the competent bodies involved in criminal proceedings, in the case of any suspicion of a criminal offence.

The Ministry of Finance may also interfere with the banking operations to a certain extent, provided that it has been informed by the bank that a suspicion exists that the relevant deposits were the result of criminal activity. In such a case the Ministry may order a suspension of the banking operation for a period from 24 to 72 hours from the time it has been notified by the bank.

The Czech National Bank in its supervisory capacity also plays a role in the process of tracing funds. It is, however, necessary to stress that the Czech National Bank, in its position as a supervisory authority, would probably be involved only in the investigation and measurement of frauds or similar fraudulent actions having an effect on a large number of people or of very wide scope (for instance, frauds in investment funds, which are quite frequent). In such situations the bank would also be obliged to disclose all confidential information in relation to the fraud and the offenders.

It follows from the examples given that, despite all the above-mentioned instruments which might help to trace and identify funds which resulted from or were the subject of a criminal offence, the practical application does not seem to be very efficient. Under current legal regulations none of the authorities, ie neither the Ministry of Finance and the Czech National Bank nor the authorities involved in criminal proceedings, can execute its powers to stop any movements of money quickly and with immediate effect, as the obligatory procedural steps to be taken are in practice so complicated and lengthy that the authorities are unable to compete with all the possible fraudulent actions which may be taken by offenders.

Tracing of funds abroad

As indicated above, tracing funds which have disappeared on being transferred to Czech bank accounts is likely to be very difficult, lengthy and of uncertain outcome. The chances of succeeding in tracing funds which have disappeared abroad are minimal, despite the fact that transfers of money abroad are regulated by law and, moreover, that the bank must always be involved in such transfers. (The obligations of the banks in cases where criminal activity is suspected have been described above.)

The rules of foreign exchange control, including those dealing with transfers of money abroad, are set out in the Foreign Exchange Act. Some of the basic principles of the Foreign Exchange Act are as follows.

Under this Act:
1   any no-cash transfers abroad or any trading in foreign currency may only be made through a bank or a branch of a foreign bank which is authorised by a foreign exchange licence issued by the Czech National Bank to carry out foreign exchange transactions;
2   a Czech legal entity or a natural person may open an account abroad without a foreign exchange permission, he or it is only obliged to inform the Czech National Bank of such an account – the same applies to any deposit of money into a bank account abroad;
3   a Czech legal entity or a natural person may also fulfil its or his financial obligations towards a foreign entity or a foreign natural person without a foreign exchange licence;
4   a foreign legal entity or a foreign natural person may transfer foreign currency abroad without any restrictions or without the need to obtain foreign exchange permission; and
5   the bank shall be obliged to inform the Ministry of Finance and the Czech National Bank of any violation of foreign exchange rules it discovers.

These provisions of the Foreign Exchange Act have been included here in order to demonstrate that, although foreign exchange control may interfere to a limited extent with the free disposal of money by Czech legal entities and physical persons, there is, on the other hand, quite a large range of possibilities for legally transferring money abroad. Moreover, despite the fact that the Foreign Exchange Act imposes the obligation to obtain foreign exchange permission for certain operations, the avoidance of which might result in a fine under the Act (the maximum fine may be up to 50 million Czech Crowns) or even in a punishment under the Criminal Code in serious cases, which states that any person who, in contradiction of foreign exchange regulations, disposes of Czech Crowns or foreign currencies will be sentenced to imprisonment for up to three years (or up to six years if he committed the offence as a member of an organised group or if he committed the criminal offence in breach of his professional obligations) or will be subject to a ban on his professional activity or to a financial penalty, a potential criminal is probably not very likely to observe foreign exchange rules.

In addition, as already noted, neither the Ministry of Finance nor the Czech National Bank can execute its authority to stop or restrict a transfer of funds. The Ministry of Finance may only order the suspension of a bank transaction for up to 72 hours in the event of the suspicion of money laundering (under the Money Laundering Act).

The only means of tracing funds exists at the moment when the funds are actually transferred abroad, through criminal proceedings initiated in the Czech Republic.

But even if the criminal court obtains confidential information from a Czech bank as to where the funds have been transferred abroad, further steps towards banks abroad would have to be taken through the complicated procedure described above. In addition, such a procedure would be successful, where the money was actually deposited in a bank account abroad, only if the concept of bank confidentiality in the country in question permitted disclosure of confidential information on the request of the relevant court in such country and if reciprocity existed in provision of legal assistance with the Czech Republic.

MISCELLANEOUS

Insider dealing

Insider dealing, even if it is not specifically defined, is to a certain extent regulated by the Act on Banks. It is possible to say that, in general terms, the prevention of insider dealing has been incorporated into the principle of the maintenance of professional confidentiality by all employees and representatives of banks, who are obliged to keep confidential all information obtained in the course of their employment or functions at the bank and related to the interests of the bank and its customers. This rule also applies to the employees and representatives of a foreign bank who work or perform their activities in a branch of the relevant bank in the Czech Republic.

The Act on Banks also stipulates that the bank may not do business with persons with whom the bank has a special relationship if such a transaction would not be made with other clients because of the nature, purpose or risk of such business. For the purposes of the Act on Banks, the following persons shall be regarded as having a special relationship with a bank:

1   members of the bank's statutory body and directors of the bank;
2   members of the bank supervisory board;
3   legal entities holding a controlling interest in the bank;
4   persons close to the persons and entities mentioned under 1, 2 and 3 above;
5   legal entities in which any of the persons listed under 1, 2 and 3 above hold an ownership interest in the registered capital which exceeds 10% of the total amount of that capital;
6   major shareholders of the bank and any legal entity under their control; and
7   members of the Banking Board of the Czech National Bank.

Any bank breaching the relevant provision of the Act on Banks, under which it may not do business with the persons listed above, would be exposed to an administrative penalty by the Czech National Bank.

Certain preventive measures against insider dealing might also be found in the regulation of employment matters in the Czech Republic. Most banks insist on a provision in a contract of employment in respect of the members of its management and other employees above a certain level in the bank's hierarchy, under which the employees in question are forbidden to deal in information learnt in the course of their functions within the bank.

Taking into account the aforementioned consequences of a breach of bank confidentiality and the fact that, under Czech law, insider dealing would only be a modified version of a misuse of confidential information, insider dealing might be subject to:

1   a civil law action – in respect of the potential damage sustained by the customer;
2   a criminal action – in respect of unauthorised dealing with personal data and misuse of information in doing business (both criminal offences have been dealt with above); or
3   a labour law penalty – dismissal, demotion, damages.

However, the basic condition of any penalty which might be applied to an unauthorised 'dealer' in confidential information will always be sufficient evidence of such dealing and a credible valuation of the potential damage or profit the 'dealer' gained, which will always be a crucial issue in any relevant proceeding.

Therefore, the question of insider dealing will always depend to a large extent upon the moral principles of those who have access to confidential information.

Personal Data Protection Act

The Personal Data Protection Act provides, in general, for the protection of data concerning natural persons. At the moment no similar Act exists which would provide data protection for legal entities.

Although the current legal banking regulations do not define or determine the contents of the term 'bank confidentiality' or 'professional confidentiality', based on the definition of 'personal data', 'collection of personal data' and 'processing of personal data', the provisions of the Personal Data Protection Act would apply to a bank information system which collects and processes bank information about the bank's customers being natural persons. The reason for this assumption is the general and broad application of the Data Protection Act and, at the same time, the requirement set out in the Act on the Czech National Bank and in the Act on Banks that the Czech national Bank co-ordinates and develops a banking information system based on data systems of all entries regarding the customers, their bank operations and disposal of bank accounts operated and maintained by a bank (including data of natural persons).

In accordance with the definition set out in the Personal Data Protection Act, 'collection of personal data' means a systematic collection of data for the purposes of their processing and 'processing of personal data' means any operation regarding any storing, disposals, records, use, classification and maintenance of personal data.

The personal data in banking systems may be operated and used only in accordance with the Act on Banks or with the consent of the relevant natural person. The Act on Banks and the Act on the Czech National Bank specify not only the obligation of the bank to meet the requirements of a data system, but also set out the conditions under which the data may be disclosed.

The principle of 'Know your Customer'

The principle of 'Know Your Customer', which might eliminate potential problems between the bank and its customers and vice versa is, quite obviously, not specifically regulated in any of the banking-related Acts. However, it is possible to trace certain indications of this rule in some of the Acts which have already been dealt with above. An attempt to control the nature of customers appears in the Decree on Requirements for a Licence to operate as a Bank. For instance, when the founders of the bank apply to the Czech National Bank for a banking licence, they must present the main intentions of the bank regarding the granting of loans and obtaining deposits, in particular as regards the nature of the future customers – ie whether the bank will concentrate on natural persons or commercial companies, from which of the main sectors of the economy the customers will be drawn etc. This is not a typical example of the Know Your Customer principle. Nevertheless, the requirement may eliminate in advance the situation whereby the bank faces problems with customers, which would otherwise be unacceptable from the point of view of the banking sector as a whole. In the event that the Czech National Bank traces any potential problems, it will either refuse to issue a banking licence or it may persuade the applicant to change its concept. This rule applies to local applicants for a banking licence as well as to foreign banks intending to set up branches in the Czech Republic.

Rules which might relate to the Know Your Customer principle are mainly contained in the Money Laundering Act. Under the provisions of this Act, the bank must carry out a so-called 'customer's identification' in the event that the customer makes a banking transaction the value of which exceeds 500,000 Czech Crowns. The identification means the verification of the full name, personal number or date of birth and permanent address as regards natural persons and the verification of the business name, registered offices, identification number and identification of the representative as regards legal entities.

The banking transaction connected with the identification duty under the above provisions means:

1   any banking operation exceeding the amount of 500,000 Czech Crowns;
2   purchase, sale or exchange of any securities or derivatives of different issuers between the same contracting parties with the transaction price exceeding the amount of 500,000 Czech Crowns;
3   the payment of an amount exceeding 500,000 Czech Crowns by a betting shop, gambling shop or casino; or
4   the payment of the insurance premium exceeding the amount of 500,000 Czech Crowns.

In addition to the above-mentioned identification in the event that the customer makes a banking transaction the value of which exceeds 500,000 Czech Crowns, the following banking transactions are subject to the identification duty:

1   any suspicious transaction;
2   opening a bank account or concluding a contract on a deposit; and
3   the rental of a safety-deposit box.

The bank is obliged to keep all customer identification data for a period of ten years following the completion of the relevant banking transaction.

Other than by the special provisions of the Money Laundering Act, the most natural way of getting information about a customer is through the formalities connected with any opening of a bank account or, to a greater extent, any granting of a bank loan, as stipulated by the Act on Banks.

On opening a bank account, the customer must disclose to the bank all data as mentioned above in connection with the identification duty. Such data must be supported by relevant documentation. The Act on Banks also states that the bank is obliged to request proof of identity (ie personal data supported by relevant documents in the case of natural persons, or an extract from the Commercial Register in the case of a legal entity) in the event of any transaction exceeding 100,000 Czech Crowns or when renting a safety deposit box.

The arrangements between the bank and the customer regarding a bank loan are in addition based on the requirement that the customer be entitled to use the loan only for the purposes precisely specified in the loan agreement. The bank usually requests that a security be provided by the customer. As a result of all these formalities, the bank might be in a position to estimate the nature and legal status of the customer, at least to some extent.

Regardless of attempts to rate and estimate the standing and probity of the customers, as implemented by the rules mentioned above, the main responsibility for the estimation of customers and the prevention of potential risks will always lie with the bank and, in particular, with its employees and representatives.

Conflicts of interests

Under the present legal regulation of the banking system in the Czech Republic, no provision exists which would prevent the bank from providing both the usual commercial services for its customers and, at the same time, offering advisory services and assistance in investments. However, the relevant provisions of the Act on Banks stipulates that the bank, as well as a branch of a foreign bank, is obliged not to (i) use the information obtained in connection with investment transactions for the purposes of credit transactions and vice versa and (ii) use the information obtained in connection with investment transactions of the customers for the purposes of its own investment transactions.

In order to comply with the above obligations, the bank is required to implement relevant measures in its organisational, operation and control system to secure the separation of investment transactions and credit transactions. The compliance of the bank with the above-mentioned obligations must be already proved when the bank applies for the banking licence under the Decree on Requirements for a Licence to Operate as a Bank, where the bank must precisely specify its technical, organisational and operation prerequisites for the separation of investment transactions and credit transactions.

In addition, a principle of 'statutory collision' exists and is applicable under laws of the Czech Republic. This is the situation where a bank is obliged to refuse to act for a customer in the same matter in which it acts for another customer if the interests of the two customers are in a mutual conflict. This is a basic principle of professional ethics which appears in general in the Czech legal system. In other cases, for instance, if the bank acts for clients whose interests might be in conflict under other circumstances, though not in the matter in question, some sort of Chinese Wall would probably be created, depending on the internal arrangements and rules of each bank.

SUMMARY

Although the information contained in this chapter seems to indicate that the bank confidentiality concept in the Czech Republic faces many problems, various factors should be taken into account. As with the whole system of economy, the Czech Republic's legal system is still quite new and is subject to continuous development. The concept of bank confidentiality has not yet been worked out thoroughly, so that some gaps continue to appear, in particular, as regards the tracing of funds and the prompt and effective intervention in connection with money laundering or other criminal actions in the banking sphere.

Nevertheless, although some legal institutions still do not operate as intended, nor with the desired result, certain positive progress has already been achieved in this sphere. We can only hope that the further development of banking, supported by a continuous integration of the Czech Republic's legislation into the EU legislation, will bring more transparency and certainty to this entire issue.

8 Denmark

Herman D Federspiel

INTRODUCTION

Danish law recognises a duty of confidentiality owed by a bank with regard to the affairs of its customers both to private third parties and to public authorities. The original motive for banks to observe confidentiality was that it served the bank's business interests; a client was only likely to entrust its business to a bank which treated their affairs as confidential. While it originally was a right for the banks, it subsequently became an obligation which clients could invoke as part of the contractual relationship between the bank and its customers. Bank secrecy is statutorily regulated and since 1990 violations have been subject to criminal liability.

THE BANK'S DUTY OF CONFIDENCE

Source of the obligation

The individual's right to privacy is an important principle of Danish law, deriving some authority both from international treaties like The UN Convention on Civil and Political Rights (art 17), the European Convention on Human Rights (art 8)[1] as well as from the Danish Constitution (art 72). On a more commercial level, s 10 of the Act on Marketing[2] prohibits a person who is an employee or has a contractual relationship with a particular business enterprise from obtaining or trying to obtain 'by improper means' knowledge of its business secrets. If the person has lawfully acquired knowledge or possession of business secrets, the person may not disclose or make use of such secrets if such disclosure or use has not been authorised. Similarly, a recipient of such information is unauthorised to use the information if it has been obtained in contravention of s 10. Section 10 of the Act on Marketing is sanctionable both by civil and criminal remedies. Chapter 27 of the Danish Criminal Code[3] makes it a criminal offence to obtain unauthorised access to another person's data or business secrets. Other legislation expresses this principle as well. In consequence, bank confidentiality has developed in parallel with these legal developments.

---

1   Incorporated into Danish law by Act no 285 of 29 April 1992, now Consolidated Act no 750 of 19 October 1998.
2   Consolidated Act no 699 of 17 July 2000 as amended.
3   Consolidated Act no 779 of 16 September 2002 as amended.

In Denmark there has not been much discussion about the legal qualification of bank confidentiality. For a long time bank confidentiality (or secrecy) was based only on custom and usage, which gradually obtained the force of 'customary' law. Under Danish law, customary law means a practice generally followed during a considerable period and considered by those concerned to have become legally binding. The obligation of confidentiality can now also be said to be an implied term in the contractual relationship between the bank and its customer which can be waived by the customer. By Act no 306 of 16 May 1990 the Danish Bank Act was amended, now 'codifying' the banks' duty of confidentiality. The codification of the duty of confidentiality can now be found in the Act on Financial Business,[4,5] which applies to all financial undertakings.[6,7] The first sentence of s 4(1) of the Act on Financial Business states in the unofficial translation provided by the Danish Financial Supervisory Authority:

> 'Members of boards of directors, members of local boards of directors or similar organs, members of the committee of shareholders in a financial undertaking other than a savings bank, auditors and inspectors and their deputies, founders, valuation officers, liquidators, managing directors, responsible actuaries, general agents and administrators in an insurance company and other employees shall not without due cause disclose or use confidential information obtained during the performance of their duties.'

Section 4(2) of the Act on Financial Business provides for the following:

> 'Any person receiving information pursuant to subsection (1) hereof shall fall within the scope of the duty of silence [duty of confidentiality] specified in said subsection (1).'

Section 77(1) of the Act on Financial Business provides that a violation of s 4(1) shall be punishable by fine or imprisonment for up to four months, unless a more severe penalty is incurred under other legislation.

Thus, these sections of the Act on Financial Business make it a criminal offence for the bank and its employees to transmit or utilise, without due cause, confidential information with which they have become acquainted during the performance of their functions. The statute has two purposes:

1   protection against disclosure of confidential information about the bank itself, for instance, accounts, engagements in particular credits, exposures, strategies, general and particular dispositions and what in general is considered business secrets; and

---

4   Consolidated Act no 660 of 7 August 2002.
5   12 March 2003 the Minister of Economic and Business Affairs introduced a new bill on the Act on Financial Business. If the bill is passed in its proposed form, the provisions on confidentiality will be found in another part of the Act.
6   Financial undertakings are defined as (i) investment companies; (ii) insurance companies (including lateral pension funds); (iii) banks; and (iv) mortgage credit institutions.
7   The Financial Supervisory Authority has issued a guidance letter on the rules of confidentiality of financial undertakings, published 25 October 2002 on the official website of the Danish Financial Supervisory Authority at www.ftnet.dk.

2   protection of the bank's customers against transmission of or disclosure of confidential information which the customer has entrusted to the bank. The Act on Financial Business, thus, complements the general rules contained in the Data Protection Act.[8]

Pursuant to s 6 of the Act on Financial Business, information on purely private affairs may not be passed on without obtaining prior written consent from the customer, unless such disclosure is justified under s 4(1) or s 5(2). What constitutes 'purely private affairs' is not defined in the Act; however, the term is likely to apply to information on the customer's religious beliefs, race and ethnic origin. Further, s 9 of the Act on Financial Business provides that all banks must establish and publish guidelines for the transfer of customer data and the bank must once a year inform its customers of which type of information may be disclosed with the customer's consent, the purpose or purposes for which such disclosure may take place and the recipients of the information: s 10(3). Secrets relating to the bank's own affairs are also protected by the general rules in s 10 of the Act on Marketing and s 160 of the Companies Act,[9] which make it a criminal offence for directors, registered managers, auditors and certain others to disclose confidential information of a company. The Act on Financial Business goes further as it also includes employees and information on customers.

It is irrelevant to the application of the provisions on confidentiality in the Act on Financial Business whether the disclosure of information is conducted by electronic or non-electronic means.

Definition and extent of bank confidentiality

Danish banking law does not have a definition of 'confidential information'. The term is interpreted widely as including everything which the customer has told the bank about his affairs and which is not public knowledge. Even information that a particular person is a client of the bank is confidential. Information supplied by a third party or information which the bank has collected elsewhere or in connection with its dealings with the client is protected as well; in the following, no distinction will be made between information supplied by the customer or by a third party.

The duty of confidentiality has two aspects. One is that the information may only be passed on or disclosed with due cause. The other is that it may not be utilised for purposes other than those for which it was acquired. For instance, confidential information may only be disclosed to such other persons or departments within the bank which have a business reason to obtain the information. The Financial Supervisory Authority has held that the auditor's minute book, which could contain confidential customer information, could not be passed on to a bank's shareholders' committee as there was no business reason to disclose the matter to the committee.[10]

The obligation of confidentiality or secrecy is not absolute. The statute only extends to disclosure 'without due cause'. If the information is publicly available, there is no duty of confidentiality. This is, for instance, the case where the bank has obtained

8   Act no 429 of 31 May 2000 as amended.
9   Consolidated Act no 9 of 9 January 2002 as amended.
10   Decision of the Financial Supervisory Authority of 22 February 1995, mentioned in the annotated edition of the Bank Act by C Boye Jacobsen et al (1996) p 391.

judgments over its customer or where expedited proceedings have been initiated in the Bailiff's Court, in which case the bank may report such information to credit rating agencies. Information which may be obtained publicly with the Commerce and Companies Agency, in a land registration book or similar public registers may also be disclosed by a bank without consent.

The duty of confidentiality continues after the termination of the client relationship. The Danish Financial Supervisory Authority held in a ruling in 1995 that in principle a bank could not deliver its historical records from the middle of the nineteenth century to a local museum, but would have to examine in each case whether the records transmitted could be considered confidential, in which connection, of course, the length of time and other circumstances could be taken into consideration.[11]

REMEDIES FOR BREACH OF CONFIDENCE

The customer has several remedies in case of breach of confidence, not only under criminal and civil law, but also under what could be called 'administrative law'.

Administrative law

In Denmark, it is most likely that a customer fearing disclosure without due cause of information subject to bank confidentiality or having been exposed thereto will file a complaint with the Financial Supervisory Authority. The Financial Supervisory Authority will then be obliged to take action in its capacity as the administrative authority supervising compliance with banking laws. In most cases, a letter from the Supervisory Authority will determine the matter. The decision can be brought before the Danish Commerce and Companies Appeal Board and the ordinary courts.

Criminal sanctions

As the Act on Financial Business makes it a criminal offence for the bank or its employees to breach bank confidentiality, the customer – or the Financial Supervisory Authority – may ask the prosecution to institute criminal proceedings against the bank and/or the disclosing employee for any breach of confidence. The sanctions are fines and, in the case of physical persons and in very serious cases of violation, could be imprisonment.

Civil remedies

An effective remedy under civil law for a customer appears to be the right to obtain an injunction against the bank under Ch 57 of the Administration of Justice Act.[12] An injunction is an order by the Bailiff's Court prohibiting the bank from making disclosure and will require a subsequent affirmation by an ordinary court under ss 634–639 of the Administration of Justice Act. It is a preliminary legal measure

11   Decision of the Financial Supervisory Authority of 5 April 1995.
12   Consolidated Act no 777 of 16 September 2002 as amended.

granted by the court at short notice and after summary proceedings. Failure to comply with the order will constitute a criminal offence. An injunction would only make sense if it can be obtained before disclosure or to stop continuing disclosures.

If the bank violates bank secrecy, the client will always be entitled to initiate civil proceedings before the ordinary courts requesting a so-called declaratory judgment that the bank was not justified in the disclosure and/or claiming damages for any losses suffered. In most cases this may not be an adequate remedy as Danish courts will only award damages to the extent that the claimant can show an actual loss suffered as a result of the violation of the bank secrecy. Normally, it would be difficult, if not impossible, to prove a loss in this situation. Danish law does not recognise punitive damages. Should a customer be able to show an actual loss, it is unlikely that the bank would be able to limit the amount of claims for damages a customer may try to seek from the bank in the event of breach of confidentiality in their standard terms and conditions. It is not customary for Danish banks to include such a limitation in their standard terms and conditions. It follows from general principles of Danish law that disclaimers limiting the liability of a bank would not be upheld in a Danish court of law if the loss were caused by the bank's wilful misconduct or gross negligence.

Another sanction is the disciplinary sanction which the bank may invoke against employees who have acted in breach of bank confidentiality. A case of clear breach of bank confidentiality may entitle the bank to dismiss the employee by termination of the employment contract without notice and the bank would be entitled to claim damages from the employee for losses suffered: s 4 of the Act on the Legal Relationship between Employers and Employees.[13]

EXCEPTIONS TO THE DUTY OF CONFIDENCE

Express and implied consent

The customer is the master of the information that has been submitted to the bank. The customer's consent, therefore, releases the bank of its duty of confidentiality. The consent must be obtained voluntarily and be specific and be informed. Under s 10 of the Act on Financial Business, the consent must be given in writing. The consent must state which information may be disclosed, who may receive the information and for what purpose the information may be disclosed.[14] Consent cannot be given in advance in the general terms and conditions. The consent requirements in the Act on Financial Business should be construed in accordance with the similar provisions in the Data Protection Act. Examples of express consents are where, for instance, the customer asks the bank to confirm the customer's creditworthiness to the customer's trade creditors, providers of credit facilities or credit card companies.

One of the oldest examples of exceptions to bank confidentiality has been the custom of banks giving information on a confidential basis about customers' creditworthiness without specific consent. It was unclear whether the giving of this

---

13   Consolidated Act no 691 of 20 August 2002.
14   Cf guidance letter, Financial Supervisory Authority, n 7 above.

information was an exemption from bank confidentiality based on customary law or whether it was based on an implied consent from customers on the grounds that generally it was in their interest.

This area has now been regulated by the Ministry of Justice's Executive Order no 531 of 15 June 2000. The Association of Danish Banks, the Financial Council, has issued supplementary guidelines. The information may only be given to the bank's own business customers, non-Danish businesses,[15] Dankort A/S, businesses within the PBS Group, Danish and non-Danish banks, public institutions, Danish or non-Danish credit rating agencies, foreign embassies and, subject to the customer's express consent, to others. The bank passing on the information must be convinced that the inquiring bank has an acceptable commercial reason for obtaining information and that the inquiring bank will treat the information confidentially. Furthermore, no specific information may be passed on, for instance, the amount of any bank balances, credits, cheques returned unpaid, arrears etc, but only information in general terms, for example, whether the customer is considered good for a certain credit, ownership, management, its line of business, capital, turnover and earnings in descriptive language, account relation, liquidity and any special risk issues. However, specific financial information which cannot be obtained from the Danish Commerce and Companies Agency may not be passed on without the consent of the customer. Disclosure in respect of private customers may only be given in the case of guarantees, and then only to the bank benefiting from the guarantee. If the customer's consent has been obtained, information may, furthermore, be given in connection with the application for a charge card or in connection with the purchase of real estate. Finally, information may be given if the customer has explicitly requested it in writing. Information that is especially sensitive, such as that on race, colour, criminal records, health etc, or of a purely private nature, such as that on family affairs and significant social problems, may not be passed on.

The bank is obliged to inform its customer within four weeks the first time that it has disclosed information and the customer is entitled to see the disclosure upon request, although not the name of the addressee. In any event, the customer may specifically request the bank not to pass on information in which case any subsequent disclosure is unauthorised.

An implied consent from the customer is also supposed to apply in cases of a bank disclosing certain information to its customer's guarantor, such as, for example, the balance on the credit or loan. If the guarantor has had to repay the loan, he is entitled to be informed of any securities given by the customer in respect of which the guarantor has a right to subrogate. The bank may also disclose to a guarantor if certain property or assets which the customer has given as security is put up for sale.[16]

Danish courts have in published decisions not had the opportunity to take any position as to the validity or non-validity of the so-called Consent Directives issued

---

15 Information about a customer's creditworthiness may only be passed on to businesses outside the EU/EEA if the member state in question has a sufficient level of protection. A list of secure countries may be found at the official website of the Data Protection Agency at www.datatilsynet.dk.

16 R Jørgensen *Fagskrift for Bankvæsen, marts* (1981) p 73.

under US practices. Consent Directives are understood to be documents whereby a customer or former customer of the bank authorises or directs the bank to disclose certain information concerning his dealings with the bank to the US authorities. A person can, by a court order, be compelled to sign the consent under the threat of fines or imprisonment for failure to sign.

The extent of the duty of confidentiality owed by a Danish bank is governed by Danish law and any consents to disclosure must be in accordance with Danish law. It is doubtful whether a Danish court would consider a Consent Directive as fulfilling the requirement to consent which must be freely given as a dispositive act. There is no published court decision of any guidance.

Disclosure in the interests of the bank

Legal proceedings involving the bank as a party

It is generally held that a bank, for the purpose of protecting its own interest as a party in legal proceedings which take place in public, may submit in court confidential information about its affairs with the counter party, whether the bank is the claimant or defendant. The right of disclosure must be limited to what is relevant and necessary for the particular case.

Legal proceedings involving third parties

The bank may also be involved in cases where a third party is in legal proceedings with a client of the bank regarding a particular asset in respect of which the bank has an interest. The bank is entitled in court to disclose to the third party any security interests, rights of set-off and other preferential rights. For instance, in the case of a forced sale requested by a third party of a piece of real estate owned by the client of a bank, the bank may disclose its claims and any such further information necessary for the courts and other lien holders to determine the amount of the bank's claim. The Financial Supervisory Authority has further ruled that a bank is entitled to disclose to a third party who has levied execution or has taken a second priority interest in an asset in which the bank has a first security interest the amount of the bank's claim on the pledgor (the bank's customer).[17]

A special situation has arisen in connection with the so-called Financial Services Complaints Board, which is an institution to resolve disputes among banks and consumers and in certain matters business people. The Board consists of members appointed by the Consumer Council and the Finance Council, hereunder a chairman and two deputy chairman, who must all meet the requirements for the appointment as a High Court judge. The Financial Supervisory Authority has held that it is not in violation of the confidentiality obligation if the bank in its defence of a complaint reveals confidential information about a third party if this is necessary for the bank's

---

17   Decision of the Financial Supervisory Authority of 6 May 1996, referred to in the *Annual Report 1996* of the Financial Supervisory Authority, p 134; O Simonsen UFR 1980 B 246; Jørgensen, n 16 above, p 73; and G Wenning UFR 1996 B p 49ff.

defence.[18] The Financial Supervisory Authority noted in its decision that the members of the Complaints Board were bound by a duty of confidentiality as laid down in the constitutive documents of the Board.

DISCLOSURE FOR THE PERFORMANCE OF ADMINISTRATIVE TASKS

A bank may disclose 'usual' customer information for the performance of administrative tasks, hereunder as part of outsourcing: s 5(1) of the Act on Financial Business. The information may be passed on to group companies as well as non-group companies. What constitutes 'administrative tasks' is not defined in the Act, but according to the preparatory works the term should be interpreted broadly. Examples of administrative tasks are the joint preparation and distribution of account statements and insurance summaries, as well as reporting of other companies' information to the tax authorities etc. The Financial Supervisory Authority has in a decision stated that the disclosure of usual customer information to an opinion research institute was in accordance with s 5(1) as the conduct of a customer satisfaction study could be characterised as an administrative task.[19] However, the information may not be passed on for marketing or advisory purposes, and only information necessary for the performance of the administrative task may be passed on.

Further, according to s 5(2) information may be disclosed to a limited company owned wholly by the Labour Market Supplementary Pension Scheme and to the Labour Market Supplementary Pension Scheme and to the administrative company of a joint administrative organisation under the Danish Insurance Business Act for the performance of administrative tasks. Again, information may only be passed on for the performance of administrative tasks. However, under s 5(2) information of a purely private nature may also be passed on if necessary for the performance of administrative tasks. According to s 5(3), any person or company to whom information is transmitted pursuant to sub-ss (1) and (2) shall be bound by the duty of confidentiality laid down in s 4(1). The bank passing on the information is obliged to ensure that the recipient is aware of this duty of confidentiality.

'Usual' customer information is defined in Executive Order no 1075 of 17 December 2001 issued pursuant to the Act on Financial Business and includes general information such as name, sex, address, occupation, trade category, organisation of business and certain financial information such as customer category, number of accounts etc, but not specific information on customer affairs, such as arrears, income figures etc. Further, specifically for bank customers and customers of investment companies, usual information is also information on the buyer and seller in securities trades, the quota code, information in respect of the security and/or the underlying asset, instrument name, spot/term/repo-pricing etc. The Executive Order is exhaustive and information not listed in the Executive Order cannot be considered as usual customer information.

---

18 *Annual Report 1987* of the Financial Supervisory Authority, p 60.
19 Decision of 17 April 2002, published on the official website of the Danish Financial Supervisory Authority at www.ftnet.dk.

Disclosure within the banking group

Section 7(1) of the Act on Financial Business provides that information may be disclosed to a bank's parent company for the purpose of risk management of undertakings within the group if the parent company is a financial undertaking or a financial holding company.[20] This does not apply to information on purely private affairs. Further, information on private customers may not be disclosed for the purpose of risk management, unless information on a private customer concerns commitments which are or may become significant in size: s 7(2). The information may only be passed on to a foreign company if such company is subject to a duty of confidentiality comparable to the duty of confidentiality stipulated in s 4(1) of the Act on Financial Business.

Disclosure for marketing and advisory purposes

Pursuant to s 8(1) of the Act on Financial Business, information regarding private customers may not be disclosed for marketing or advisory purposes unless such private customer has consented thereto in writing. However, general customer information on private customers may be disclosed to group undertakings[21] without the consent of the customer, under three conditions:

1   the information is general customer information forming the basis for separation of customer categories;
2   such disclosure is necessary to enable the undertaking receiving such information to pursue justifiable interests and regard for the customer does not override such interests; and
3   the group undertaking to which the information is disclosed must be subject to a duty of confidentiality as set out in s 4(1) (s 8(2)).

Examples of usual customer information are, according to the preparatory works: name, address, sex and age. Further, information on whether the customer owns real estate, owns a car or similar information is usual customer information. However, more detailed information of a personal or financial nature and information which reveals purely private matters may not be disclosed. Usual customer information on business customers may be disclosed for marketing or advisory purposes to a financial undertaking under a duty of confidentiality as specified in s 4(1). The provisions complement the general rules of the Data Protection Act which apply to financial undertakings as well as to other undertakings. The Data Protection Act as a rule only applies to the processing of data on individuals. Consequently, information may

---

20   For the purpose of the Act on Financial Business, a financial holding company is a parent company whose exclusive or principal activity is ownership of capital interests in subsidiaries which are financial undertakings or finance institutions, and where at least one subsidiary is a financial undertaking. Branches of Danish financial undertakings in other EU/EEA member states are subject to the provisions of the Act on Financial Business in accordance the principle of 'home-state-supervision'. Further, as a rule, the provisions of the Act apply to branches of financial undertakings in countries outside the EU and countries with which the EU has entered into an agreement.

21   For the purpose of the Act on Financial Business, a 'group' is defined as a parent company and its subsidiaries. A 'parent company' is defined as an undertaking which (i) holds the majority of the voting rights of an undertaking, (ii) is a shareholder and entitled to appoint or remove the board of directors, management board or similar, (iii) exercises a controlling influence on an undertaking, or (iv) commands the majority of the voting rights within the undertaking.

only be passed on without the consent of the customer pursuant to s 8(2) if the customer has not objected thereto under s 36 of the Data Protection Act.

Facilitation of securitisations

In Denmark, no legislation has been passed to ensure that questions of bank confidentiality do not impede the use of a bank's assets in securitisations, nor is such legislation contemplated.[22]

Where disclosure is by compulsion of law

Compulsion by order of court

DUTY TO TESTIFY

Employees of banks are in general subject to the same duty to testify in court as other persons: s 168 of the Administration of Justice Act. The rules do not exempt bank employees as is the case in respect of certain professions such as lawyers, clergymen, doctors and certain others. However, the court may rule under s 170(3) that evidence should not be given with respect to matters where according to statutory law the witness is subject to a duty of confidentiality and such duty has a substantial importance. When deciding whether this exemption should apply, the court will have to weigh, on the one hand, the general interest in the protection of confidentiality between a bank and its client and, on the other, the interests of the court in having the appropriate relevant information and evidence to ensure that justice is done; the court will attach importance as to whether the party requesting the bank officer to give evidence could obtain the requested information by other means. A court ruled in 1979 that a bank employee was compelled to give evidence in the Bailiff's Court about a customer's bank balances in a case concerning a creditor levying execution on the assets of the customer on the grounds that the customer himself would have been compelled to disclose this.[23] The rules of testifying apply in civil as well as in criminal cases.

DUTY TO SUBMIT DOCUMENTS

Although Danish law does not recognise the concept of pre-trial discovery rights, a party may during legal proceedings require the court to impose on the other party to the litigation the duty to submit certain documents in accordance with rules of disclosure: s 298 of the Administration of Justice Act. No 'fishing expeditions' are allowed as the party requesting a particular document to be disclosed must indicate the circumstances which should be proved by the document. The court may dismiss such a request on the same grounds as testifying may be exempted, namely accepting

---

22 Further, see decision by the Financial Supervisory Authority of 25 May 2000 concerning a credit swap agreement entered into by a bank and a third party. The Financial Supervisory Authority assumed that the customer was not informed of the credit swap agreement. The third party would under the agreement acquire engagements from a defined loan portfolio when certain credit 'events' occurred. When such events occurred, the third party would be informed of the bank customer's name and as a minimum be informed that the bank customer's engagement was failing. The Financial Supervisory Authority found such credit swap agreement to be a violation of the bank secrecy obligation.

23 UFR 1979 p 216 VLK.

that such documents should be covered by the duty of confidentiality under the Act on Financial Business. In 2002 the Supreme Court ruled that a bank must make anonymous and submit transcripts of its board minutes and its recommendations to the board in respect of negotiations concerning a share issue.[24] During legal proceedings the court may also upon request by a party impose on a third party the obligation to show or submit documents which may be of importance to the case: s 299 of the Administration of Justice Act. Again, the court may dismiss such a request on the same grounds as testifying may be exempted: s 170(3) of the Administration of Justice Act.

ARBITRATION PROCEEDINGS

In arbitration proceedings a court of arbitration does not have the power to force persons to testify. However, under the Act on Arbitration, s 5,[25] the court of arbitration may seek assistance from the ordinary courts and thereby compel persons to testify. Through these means confidential information could be disclosed in an arbitration court in the same manner as in proceedings before the ordinary courts.

BANKRUPTCY

The Bankruptcy Court is entitled, according to s 240 of the Bankruptcy Act,[26] to summon before it any person whom the court thinks capable of giving information on the business or affairs of the bankrupt; the general obligation of testifying will apply as set out in the Administration of Justice Act, ss 169–172. The court may on the same grounds as mentioned earlier exempt a bank officer from testifying.

Bank confidentiality continues while a bank is under insolvency proceedings or bankruptcy, although the bankruptcy proceedings may justify some wider entitlement to disclosure.[27] The liquidator is entitled to all information necessary to administer and realise the assets and wind up the estate, and the bank must release such information. Creditors of a bank under bankruptcy do not have any access to confidential information.

Compulsion by statute

THE TAX CONTROL ACT

It is reasonable to conclude from the Danish Tax Control Act,[28] which regulates the obligations of banks (and others) to provide information, that there is hardly any bank secrecy vis-à-vis the tax authorities. The situation is, however, no different in relation to other types of business or profession. The Act distinguishes between three types of disclosure requirements: reporting obligation upon request; reporting obligation upon inspection in the bank; and automatic reporting. The obligation to report automatically without request has, in particular, increased significantly in

---

24   UFR 2002 p 1734 H.
25   Act no 181 of 24 May 1972 as amended.
26   Consolidated Act no 118 of 4 February 1997 as amended.
27   Ruling by the Financial Supervisory Authority, as upheld in a decision by the Ministry of Business' Appeal Board of 10 August 1995.
28   Consolidated Act no 726 of 13 August 2001 as amended.

recent years. It is worth mentioning that the statutory powers of the tax authorities are continuously being vested on lower levels within the tax authorities to require disclosure and are aimed at an increasingly wider range of persons.

It follows from s 8D of the Tax Control Act that banks must upon request provide the tax authorities with such information as is deemed by the authorities to be of substantial importance for the tax assessment. The statute does not contain any details as to the extent of this obligation on the bank or, in other words, what documentation can be required to be submitted, or how far back information can be requested. It must be assumed that the authorities as far as possible must first request the information from the taxpayer himself.

Section 8G(2), of the Tax Control Act gives the tax authorities the right to undertake inspections in the banks in order to carry out on the spot examination of accounting records, agreements and other documents.

The Tax Control Act further provides a substantial number of instances where banks are now required annually and without request to give certain information on their customers. The requirements comprise, inter alia, pension arrangements (s 8F), deposits and accrued interest (s 8H), loans and accrued interest (s 8P), information on balance and accrued interest on mortgage deeds in real estate in custody (s 8Q), redeemed interest coupons, interest on bonds and value at year end (s 10A), dividend from unit trusts etc (s 10A), information on transfer of bonds and interest coupons (s 10B), agreements on transfer of forward contracts and certain other assets (s 10B).

The reporting requirements only extend to banks subject to Danish jurisdiction. However, private individual taxpayers who have deposits or securities held in custody by non-resident banks (or other non-resident institutions) are required to agree with the relevant foreign bank or institution that it annually without request advises the Danish tax authorities of the size of deposits, securities deposited, interest accrued and the relevant balances at year end. In addition, the Danish resident taxpayer must provide the tax authorities with a power of attorney authorising Danish tax authorities to obtain information directly from the account: Tax Control Act, ss 11A and 11B. Presumably, this is an attempt by the tax authorities to obtain the taxpayer's consent thus releasing the foreign bank of its duty of confidentiality. If the foreign bank or institution by law is prohibited from such disclosure or does not wish to undertake it, dispensation can be obtained in certain cases.

VALUE ADDED TAX AND SOCIAL LEGISLATION

According to s 75(3) of the Value Added Tax Act,[29] banks must upon request give the VAT authorities any information about their financial relationship with named registered enterprises. Various legislation on social pensions and unemployment insurance provide the authorities with similar rights to obtain certain information upon request.

FOREIGN TAX AUTHORITIES

Denmark has ratified and acceded to a number of international treaties and conventions concerning mutual assistance in tax matters, both regarding administrative assistance

29   Consolidated Act no 804 of 16 August 2000 as amended.

and as assistance in the recovery of tax claims. These treaties etc affect disclosure obligations of banks. Among the most wide-reaching is the EEC Council Directive of 19 December 1977,[30] as amended, implemented by Act no 635 of 13 December 1978. Also applicable is the Council of Europe and OECD Convention on Mutual Administrative Assistance in Tax Matters, implemented by Act no 132 of 26 February 1992, and the Nordic Treaty (Denmark, Sweden, Norway, Finland, Iceland, Greenland and the Faroe Islands) of 7 December 1989, as supplemented, on Assistance in Tax Matters.

The treaties impose on Danish tax authorities the obligation to assist foreign tax authorities with information on residents subject to Danish jurisdiction. This may involve passing on such information which the tax authorities already have on their own files, either upon request or, sometimes, spontaneously. They also require Danish tax authorities upon request to 'take all relevant measures to provide the applicant state with the information requested': art 5 of the Council of Europe/OECD Convention. This authorises the Danish tax authorities to pass on information otherwise subject to bank confidentiality – although member states are permitted not to provide assistance if this would involve disclosing information subject to 'professional secrecy': art 21. Danish tax authorities may assist if (i) permitted to do so under the provisions of the Danish Tax Control Act in similar circumstances involving Danish resident taxpayers, and (ii) if the applicant tax authority under its domestic laws would be entitled to demand the requested information.

The Nordic Tax Treaty provides for automatic exchange of certain relevant bank information, for example, on annual accrued interest on deposits and balances at year end, value of securities at year end including coupons redeemed during the year.

Many bilateral double taxation treaties which Denmark has concluded also include provisions on mutual assistance, although often not as specific as provided under the above-mentioned treaties. It must be assumed that in cases where the Danish tax authorities are required to disclose information otherwise subject to bank secrecy, the customer cannot raise any objections thereto based on the bank's duty of confidentiality. See also the Commentaries to art 26 of the OECD Model Tax Convention. It should be noted that if criminal proceedings have been initiated, whether in Denmark or abroad, the tax authorities are not entitled to pass on information administratively, but only by compulsion of court.

COMPETITION COUNCIL AND CONSUMER OMBUDSMAN

The Competition Council is, according to s 17 of the Act on Competition,[31] entitled to demand all information which is deemed necessary for the affairs of the Competition Council or to decide whether a certain matter is comprised within the law. This entitlement to information also relates to customer information with a bank if the Competition Council deems it appropriate. It is possible to demand that confidential customer information is not released for circulation among the members of the Competition Council. There are certain other restrictions as to this information.

30   Council Directive 77/799/EEC.
31   Consolidated Act no 539 of 28 June 2002.

The Consumer Ombudsman is also entitled to demand all information which is deemed necessary for the performance of his duties, unless it is the Consumer Ombudsman's intention to institute criminal proceedings against the bank.

POLICE AND CRIMINAL INVESTIGATIONS

The police have no right as part of their investigations to require bank officers to disclose or pass on confidential customer information, nor to demand submission of particular records or invoke other legal measures, unless sanctioned by the court. In criminal matters, employees of banks are subject to the same duty to testify in court as in civil matters, which means that testimony must be given unless the court rules under s 170(3) of the Administration of Justice Act that evidence should not be given due to the duty of confidentiality. Sections 801 and 803 of the Administration of Justice Act provide for the court to authorise documents to be disclosed or assets (bank accounts) to be confiscated. In addition, the court may sanction in special cases searches of records, bank balances or documents to be undertaken by the police under s 793 of the Administration of Justice Act. It is held that under very extraordinary circumstances banks are permitted to disclose confidential customer information prior to a court order, especially if otherwise the prevention or investigation of a crime would seriously suffer, against an undertaking from the police to obtain a court order subsequently.

If the police know which bank is in possession of the information requested, the court order of disclosure will, of course, be directed to that bank. If the police do not know which bank is holding the account, the courts have authorised a procedure whereby all banks through the Financial Council (the Association of Danish Banks) are ordered by the court to notify the police if they have an account in the accused person's name. Thereafter a specific order of disclosure will be requested from the court in respect of the particular bank, but subject to prior opportunity for the bank to question the basis on which the order is sought.[32]

In cases of disclosure, the police must show that the documents or records may be of importance as proof in connection with an identified crime. The bank may invoke, as in case of oral testimony, s 170(3) of the Administration of Justice Act that the records should not be disclosed due to the duty of confidentiality. Unless the bank can show that the police by other means and without prejudicing the purpose of the request may obtain the same information, the court will normally give effect to the request by the police.

MONEY LAUNDERING AND FINANCING OF TERRORISM – LEGISLATION

There is one exception where confidential customer information may be passed on and even spontaneously must be offered without either customer consent or a court order, and this is in connection with the Money Laundering Directive,[33] as implemented by the Danish Act no 348 of 9 June 1993, now Consolidated Act no

---

32   UFR 1995, p 333 Ø
33   Council Directive 91/308/EEC.

734 of 30 August 2002. The statute provides rules for the banking and financial services business to put in place various systems and control functions to identify customers and report suspicious transactions to the police. The Act also applies to lawyers, accountants and tax advisors, real estate brokers, insurance brokers and certain others.

Money laundering is defined as including conversion, transfer, acquisition, possession or application of money assets or concealment, or attempted concealment, of their form, origin, localisation, movements or ownership with knowledge or suspicion that the money is derived from violation of the Criminal Code. Terrorism is defined in s 114 of the Criminal Code as the commitment of manslaughter, gross violence, false imprisonment, obstruction of road safety and unlawful disturbances of the operation of ordinary means of communication or gross vandalism where the said violations are committed in such a way as to endanger human life or cause significant financial loss, hijacking of means of transportation, serious violation of the Danish Arms Act (Våbenoven)[34] and arson for the purpose of scaring people or unlawfully forcing public authorities or international organisations to act or not to act or destabilising or ruining basic political, constitutional, financial or social structures of a country or international organisation when the act, due to its character or the connection in which it appears, may seriously damage a country or international organisation.

It is a requirement that banks (and others covered by this legislation) must draw up written internal rules on warrantable controls – and communication procedures. Banks must ensure that their employees are aware of the procedures and relevant money laundering legislation, and must ensure that effective training procedures are in place.

The statute stipulates that customers must be required to produce satisfactory evidence of identity when a business relationship is opened, for example, the establishment of an account or custody. The customer must identify himself as to name, address, personal registration number or business registration number or similar documentation.

If it is not a question of a business relationship, opening of an account or a custody, identification must be required in case of a transaction, or linked transactions, the value of which is more than €15,000.

If the value of the transaction is not known at the time when it is initiated, identification must be required at the earliest stage at which there are reasonable grounds to believe that the value of the transaction is €15,000 or more.

Irrespective of the amount of the transaction, identification must be required when there are reasonable grounds for suspicion that the transaction concerns money laundering or financing of terrorism.

If the bank has suspicion that the transaction takes place on behalf of another party, third-party identification must be requested.

It follows from ss 10 and 10a of the Money Laundering Act that if there is a suspicion that a transaction is associated with money laundering or financing of terrorism, there is an obligation for the bank to examine the transaction further. This can be done by, for instance, an examination of the background for the transaction, by

---

34   Consolidated Act no 67 of 26 January 2000 as amended.

control telephone calls to other institutions involved, checks of the civil register and surveillance of the transaction over a period. If the suspicion cannot be dispelled, the transaction must be put on hold, until the Public Prosecutor (white-collar crime) has been notified. If, in the case of suspicion of money laundering, it is not possible to avoid carrying through the transaction or the purpose would be revealed, the transaction can be continued and the police notified immediately thereafter. The police are then entitled to demand such further information of the bank, production of documents etc, which can be demanded under a 'normal' criminal investigation, ie a court order. In the case of suspicion of financing of terrorism, transactions with respect to the specific account or person may only be carried pursuant to agreement with the Public Prosecutor (white-collar crime). The Money Laundering Act specifically states that information disclosed to the police in good faith cannot be considered a violation of the duty of confidentiality. The bank and its employees are bound by a duty of confidentiality not to disclose that the police have been informed about suspicions of money laundering.

Extra-territorial aspects of compulsion of law

OBTAINING INFORMATION FROM DANISH BANKS FOR USE IN FOREIGN CIVIL PROCEEDINGS

Foreign court orders requesting Danish banks or their employees to give information or to testify abroad are not enforceable in Denmark. However, Danish courts may in accordance with the provisions of s 347 of the Administration of Justice Act and applicable treaties render judicial assistance following requests from foreign courts on the taking of evidence or the undertaking of other judicial acts.

Denmark has ratified the Hague Convention on Civil Procedure of 1 March 1954, and the Convention on the Taking of Evidence Abroad in Civil or Commercial Matters of 18 March 1970. In addition, Denmark has concluded with the UK a Civil Procedures Convention[35] and with the Nordic Countries an Inter Nordic Convention on Evidence.[36] Accordingly thereto, persons subject to Danish jurisdiction may be compelled to give evidence before a Danish judge in accordance with the request from the foreign judicial authority and the courts shall apply the appropriate measures of compulsion to the same extent as provided by Danish law. According to art 11 of the Convention on the Taking of Evidence Abroad, the person concerned may refuse to give evidence in so far as he has a privilege or duty to refuse to give evidence under Danish law or under the law of the state which has requested the evidence. This means that Danish procedural rules are applicable and may in the circumstances be invoked so that the Danish court may deny a testimony, if necessary to protect bank confidentiality: s 170(3) of the Administration of Justice Act or where this is provided under foreign law. Denmark has exercised its rights under art 23 of the Convention to declare that it will not execute requests issued for the purpose of obtaining pre-trial discovery of documents.

---

35 Convention of 29 November 1932, cf Executive Order no 206 of 24 May 1933.
36 Convention of 28 April 1974, cf Executive Order no 100 of 15 September 1975.

In cases where the request originates from countries that are not members of the various treaties, the assistance of Danish courts may be rendered nonetheless upon request by a foreign judicial authority and the Danish courts will, based on the principle of comity, normally comply with the request as provided under s 7 of Act no 161 of 18 December 1897.

OBTAINING EVIDENCE ABROAD FOR USE IN DANISH PROCEEDINGS

Where a claimant before a Danish court wishes to obtain evidence from a foreign bank, application must be made to the Danish court for permission to obtain such evidence in accordance with s 342 of the Administration of Justice Act. A Danish court is not likely to issue any subpoenas or orders for disclosure, but will request the information in accordance with the aforementioned Hague Convention on Civil Procedure and the Convention on the Taking of Evidence Abroad in Civil or Commercial Matters and certain bilateral conventions.

Whether the foreign court will assist is a matter of local law.

ENFORCEMENT OF PRELIMINARY LEGAL MEASURES

It may be relevant to seek to enforce in Denmark foreign preliminary measures such as, for example, the freezing of assets in the form of an arrest or an injunction against moving assets, for instance money from an identified person's account with a certain bank. Article 25 of the Brussels Convention also applies to preliminary legal measures. In many cases, the wish could be to have a simultaneous 'surprise effect' in different states in order to increase the possibility of collecting losses as a result of a fraud. In the case *Denilauer v SNC Couchet Frères* (125/1979),[37] the European Court of Justice held that ex parte interim measures are not covered by art 25. The other party must have been notified about the court hearing where the preliminary measure was adopted. No surprise effect is therefore possible, but Danish courts will otherwise give effect to preliminary measures if the other party has been duly notified.

INTERNATIONAL JUDICIAL ASSISTANCE IN CRIMINAL MATTERS

The general principle is that the executive authorities of foreign states cannot operate in Denmark nor are foreign court orders enforceable. Denmark has, however, ratified the European Convention of 20 April 1959 on Mutual Assistance in Criminal Matters and, accordingly, Denmark shall execute, in the manner provided for under Danish law, any letters rogatory relating to a criminal matter and must grant the necessary assistance for the purpose of procuring evidence and transmitting records or documents. Search and seizure of property or documents can also be effected, but assistance may be refused if Denmark considers that the request relates to a political or fiscal offence or if it is likely to prejudice ordre public or other essential national interests.

In connection with its signature thereto, Denmark has reserved its rights to make the execution of judicial assistance concerning search or seizure of property dependent

37   [1980] ECR 1553, [1981] 1 CMLR 62.

on the offence being related to acts punishable under both the law of the requesting country and Danish law and that the offence motivating the request is an extraditable offence and, furthermore, that the execution of the request for assistance is consistent with Danish law.

There are no provisions under Danish law that provide coercive measures to force a witness to appear in proceedings held abroad. If a Danish bank official were to appear voluntarily before a foreign court which has ordered him to testify in respect of confidential customer information protected under Danish law, he would be in violation of s 4(1) of the Act on Financial Business and thus subject to criminal liability. It is possible that any punishment by a Danish court will be reduced or fall away as provided by s 84 of the Criminal Code. In the reverse situation where a foreign bank officer is testifying in a Danish court on matters in respect of which he is bound by bank confidentiality rules in his home state, Danish law does not offer any relief. In determining whether the officer in question were to give evidence, the court may be guided by s 170(3) of the Administration of Justice Act, under which the officer could be exempted from testifying if the duty of confidentiality imposed by his home country is deemed to outweigh the interest of clarifying the factual issues of the Danish case.

Danish courts have also agreed to provide assistance to the authorities of non-treaty countries based on a principle of comity, although they are not bound to do so.

THE MEDIA

It has been discussed[38] whether a bank may in certain cases be entitled to disclose confidential information about its customers to the media in order to correct false information detrimental to the bank's interests. In general, the answer is no. In the circumstances, it may be permissible for a bank to disclose information of an expected loss on a certain client, for instance, if it is deemed necessary to refute exaggerated rumours about the size of the loss and its importance for the bank's solidity. If the bank in the media has been accused of certain actions or inactions, for instance, in the termination of credit with resultant insolvency or bankruptcy for large enterprises, the bank is probably prevented from presenting its views or correcting information to the extent that this would affect its duty of confidentiality. This situation could be different if the customer itself has submitted incorrect information to the public in order to place the bank in an unfavourable light. There are no published judgments or rulings from the Financial Supervisory Authority defining this area, but one has to assume that the bank's duty of confidentiality is rather strict.

---

38 Jørgensen, n 16 above, p 74.

REGULATION OF FINANCIAL MARKETS

Powers of regulatory bodies to require the disclosure of information

Financial Supervisory Authority

Under the Act on Financial Business, s 67, banks are obliged to provide information on a regular basis to the Supervisory Authorities which are also entitled to request such information both about the general affairs of the bank as well as particular information on identified customers. The Supervisory Authorities are entitled to carry out inspections in the bank and to demand access to all papers, contracts etc.

Other EU Supervisory Authorities are also entitled to carry out inspections in Danish branches of EU banks: s 66(4) of the Act on Financial Business. The staff are presumably entitled to give such information to the foreign Supervisory Authority which the Danish Financial Supervisory Authority may demand from banks subject to the supervision of Danish authorities on the grounds that the Foreign Supervisory Authority can request the host authorities to undertake the inspections: arts 29(2) and 56(7) of the Directive of 20 March 2000 on the taking up and pursuit of business of credit institutions.[39] Branches established in Denmark by virtue of the European Passport are presumably not bound by the statutory confidentiality provisions of the Danish Act on Financial Business, but are subject to similar provisions of their home country legislation in addition, of course, to any contractually agreed terms.

According to s 73 of the Act on Financial Business, employees of the Supervisory Authorities are obliged under criminal law to keep secret all knowledge obtained during the course of their activities. According to s 152 of the Criminal Code, the penalty for any violation could be up to two years' imprisonment.

The Second Banking Directive[40] and the so-called BCCI Directive[41] resulted in substantial amendments to the then Bank Act concerning the right of the Supervisory Authority to pass on confidential information it has obtained during the performance of its duties. Of particular interest is the right under the now s 67(5), cf s 73(5), nos 14–15 of the Act on Financial Business to pass on confidential information to other Supervisory Authorities within the EU and also to similar institutions outside the EU on the basis of an international co-operation agreement, provided such information in the relevant country outside the EU is subject to, at a minimum, the same statutory duty of confidentiality as the Danish Financial Supervisory Authority and such passing on is required for the recipients to perform their duties. Further, confidential information originating from within the EU may only be passed on to such country outside the EU if the authority disclosing the information has expressly given its permission thereto and the information may only be used for the purposes specified in the permission. In certain limited circumstances, the Financial Supervisory Authority is also entitled to pass on confidential information to standing committees of the Danish Parliament and the relevant government minister.

---

39   Council Directive 2000/12/EC.
40   Council Directive 1989/646/EC.
41   Council Directive 1977/780/EC.

Central Bank requirements

Pursuant to the Danish Ministry of Industry's Executive Order on Foreign Exchange Regulations no 658 of 11 July 1994, Danmarks Nationalbank (the Central Bank) may also request information relating to foreign exchange transactions by physical or legal entities in Denmark for statistical reasons. Furthermore, currency dealers must advise Danmarks Nationalbank of all payments above the counter value of DKK 100,000 made to physical or legal entities outside of Denmark or similar incoming payments and in respect of payments above DKK 250,000 also about the legal nature of the payments. In this connection, Danmarks Nationalbank may request any further information relating to details of such payments from Danish resident individuals or companies.

Danmarks Nationalbank is an independent institution governed by a statute dating from 1936 and employees of the bank are bound there under by special duties of confidentiality, violations of which are subject to penalties under the Criminal Code.

Insider trading and insiders' disclosure requirements

Source of regulation

The prohibition on insider trading is provided in ss 34–37 of the Act on Securities Trading[42] which make insider trading a criminal offence. The prohibition applies not only to any person buying, selling or otherwise dealing in listed securities while in possession of insider information, but also to the passing on of such information. Further, defined insiders are under an obligation to notify the issuing company of their shareholdings and the issuing company must on a daily basis through the stock exchange publish the net change in the total insiders' shareholdings.

Which securities

The prohibition relates to all securities listed on or dealt with on a stock exchange, authorised market place or similar regulated market for securities. The securities may be issued by companies organised within or outside Denmark. Also included are non-quoted instruments which are linked to one or more securities listed on a stock exchange or dealt with on an authorised marketplace as well as units in investment associations, special purpose associations and similar foreign investment institutes.

Inside information

Section 34(2) of Act on the Securities Trading Act defines inside information as non-published information on issuers of securities, on securities or on market conditions concerning these, which are capable of impacting the 'formation of the price' of one or more securities if the information was made public. What seems to be decisive is whether investors, advisers or other participants of the stock market may be expected to attach such importance to the non-published piece of information that it is likely to affect the decision of whether at all to trade the security or at what price.

---

42   Consolidated Act no 587 of 9 July 2002.

Applicable persons

The prohibition applies to any physical or legal person who has inside information. It is therefore irrelevant whether the insider has a corporate or contractual association to the issuer or whether he is just a 'tippee' or the taxi driver who unintentionally overhears a discussion on a price-sensitive issue. The factual possession of inside information deprives the person of the entitlement to deal. The prohibition will also exclude two persons with the same inside information from dealing with each other. In order to constitute a criminal offence it must be proved that the insider knew or ought to have known that it concerned inside information.

Security traders, for example, banks, are not prohibited from executing customary orders from customers or performing functions as market makers (s 35(3)) even though they are in possession of inside information, but if the bank has knowledge or a suspicion that the buyer or seller has inside information, the bank is prohibited from executing any trade (s 35(2)).

Passing on of inside information

The Act on Securities Trading also includes a prohibition against passing on inside information unless the passing on or disclosure takes place in connection with the insider's occupation, trade or function: s 36(1). It is irrelevant how the person acquired the inside information whether as part of his occupation or by accident. It is difficult to interpret the exemption in s 36(1). Clear cases are statutory disclosure obligations to public authorities and obligations to testify in court as provided under the rules of the Administration of Justice Act.

Disclosure requirements

Pursuant to s 37(2) of the Act on Securities Trading defined insiders in listed companies are under an obligation to notify the issuing company of their shareholdings. For the purpose of the rules, insiders are, inter alia: (i) members of the Board of Directors and the Board of Management in the listed company and its parent company; (ii) staff that, due to their position within the issuing company or its parent company, may be expected to have access to inside knowledge, for instance, managerial staff referring directly to the supervisory board or the board of management and internal auditors; (iii) the auditors of the issuing company and its parent company; and (iv) certain other categories having access to inside information.

The issuing company must make a list of all insiders and notify the individual insider when he is added to the list. Insiders must notify the issuing company of their shareholdings and, further, notify the company of any change in their shareholdings. Such notification must take place immediately, ie on the same trading day. In addition to shares owned personally by the insider, shares in the issuing company held by certain other connected persons and companies must also be reported.

It should be noted that the insiders' disclosure requirements under these rules are towards the issuing company only, and not directly to the stock exchange. The general shareholder disclosure requirements, however, continue to apply.

Further, the issuing company must on a daily basis through the stock exchange publish the net change in the total insider's shareholdings during the previous trading day, unless the net change is less than DKK 50,000 in market value and, on a quarterly basis, the issuing company is further required to publish the total shareholdings of the insiders.

The Financial Supervisory Authority has issued Executive Order no 774 of 13 September 2002 pursuant to s 37.

Chinese Walls etc

The prohibition against insider trading applies to companies and other legal persons. In accordance with the theory of the unity of a legal person when members of the management have inside information, the company as such must be considered in possession thereof. This principle also applies in respect of other employees who take part in the decision-making process concerning securities or who as a result of their position in the company may bind the company. The consequence is that not only the persons who in actual fact are in possession of inside information are prevented from trading on behalf of the company, but also other persons without knowledge are prevented from trading on behalf of the company in affected securities.

This strict theoretical point of view creates difficulties for banks and financial institutions. The internal segregation of information between departments of a bank (Chinese Wall) is seen as a practical possibility for a bank to prevent misuse of information which is the basis for the offence of insider trading.

Whether a bank in the establishment of Chinese Walls can immunise itself against the offence of insider trading must be decided on a concrete basis, and the courts have not had the opportunity to express any views thereon.

Each case will have to be decided on its own merits and with particular reference to the concrete facts. Accordingly, even though a bank may be able to demonstrate that there has been no misuse of confidential information, the Financial Supervisory Authority and/or the courts may find the circumstances to be such that the bank should be precluded from acting in a particular capacity.

DATA PROTECTION LEGISLATION

From 1978 to 2000 Denmark had a legal framework regarding electronic data processing, storage and passing on of private data based on two separate Acts, the Private Registers Act and the Public Authorities Registers Act. In 2000 the Data Protection Act, which implements the EC Data Protection Directive,[43] entered into

43   Council Directive 95/46/EC.

force. The Data Protection Act applies to financial undertakings and, thus, complements the rules set out in the Act on Financial Business. This Act affects banks both as regards storage of confidential customer (and other) information as well as their rights to disclose such information. The Data Protection Act applies to all personal data, regardless of whether the data is kept in manual or electronic form. The Act generally regulates the systematic processing of personal data about individuals and not legal persons, but does under certain circumstances also apply to data concerning organisations, ie when processing is carried out for credit information agencies, or to warn third parties against business or employment relations is involved. The collection of data may only be undertaken for specified, explicit and legitimate purposes and all data must be processed in accordance with good data processing practice as determined by the Danish Data Protection Agency. Further, the personal data must be relevant, sufficient and not excessive, in relation to the purposes for which they are collected and processed. The data must be kept up to date, the bank must implement controls to ensure that it does not process inaccurate or misleading data and the bank may not store personal information so that identification of the data subject is permitted for a longer period of time than necessary for the purpose of the processing of the data.

The processing of personal data (other than sensitive data or data of a purely private nature) is permitted if either:

1   the data subject has consented to the data processing;
2   the data processing is necessary for the data subject's performance of a contract or in order to take steps as requested by the data subject prior to entering into a contract;
3   the processing is necessary to protect the vital interests of the data subject;
4   the processing is necessary to carry out a task which is in the public interest;
5   the processing is necessary to perform a task carried out in the exercise of official authority vested in the controller or a third party to whom the data are disclosed;
6   processing is necessary for the purpose of legitimate interests pursued by the controller or by a third party to whom the data are disclosed, and such interests are not outweighed by the data subject's interests; or
7   the processing is necessary for the data controller to comply with a legal obligation (s 6).

Sensitive data, defined as data on racial or ethnic origin, political opinions, religious or philosophical beliefs, trade union membership, and data concerning health or sex life, may only be processed if either: (i) the data subject has given its explicit consent to such processing; (ii) the processing is necessary in order to protect the vital interests of the data subject or a third party and the data subject is physically or legally unable to give his consent; (iii) the processing is in respect of information which has been made public by the data subject; or (iv) the processing is necessary for the establishment, exercise or defence of legal claims(s 7). Data of a purely private nature is defined as data regarding criminal matters, serious social problems and other matters which are considered as purely private in nature. Such purely private data may only be disclosed if: (i) the data subject has given its explicit consent to such disclosure; (ii) the disclosure of the data is necessary in order to protect a legitimate interest and said interest clearly outweighs the consideration to the data subject; (iii) the disclosure is necessary for the performance of an authority's activities or the disclosure is needed in order for an authority to make a decision; and (iv) the disclosure is required so that a person or a company may perform tasks for an official authority. When undertaking data processing the bank is under no obligation to notify the Danish Data Protection Agency unless the processing will involve the processing of sensitive data and data of a purely private nature. If, however, the bank undertakes data processing of sensitive or purely private data, the permission of the Danish Data Protection Agency must be obtained beforehand.

The Data Protection Act does not specifically regulate the transfer of personal data to countries within the EU, or to countries which have entered into an agreement with the EU which contains provisions equivalent to those of the Data Protection Directive. Thus, transfer to said countries must only comply with the general rules regarding processing and the specific rules on disclosure of personal data set out in the Data Protection Act. Data may in general only be transferred to a third country if such country ensures an adequate level of protection.

Special rules apply to, among others, cash cards and payment cards associated to specific holders pursuant to the Act on Certain Payment Instruments[44] which compliments the Data Protection Act in respect of such cards. Pursuant to s 13 of the Act on Certain Payment Instruments, information showing where and how cardholders have used their cards may only be processed where (i) it is necessary for the completion or correction of payment transactions or other functions, (ii) it is necessary for law enforcement, (iii) where it is necessary to prevent abuse, or (iv) where it is authorised by law. Further, information showing where cardholders have used their cards may be processed where (i) it is necessary for the issuer in order to counsel the cardholder to ensure appropriate use of the payment instrument and the information only concerns the type of payment transactions carried out by the cardholder or (ii) the issuer needs to process the information in order to adapt payment systems to ensure that such systems are safe, efficient and up-to-date and no information is generated at cardholder level.

SUMMARY

Under Danish law bank confidentiality (secrecy) is statutorily regulated and violations are subject to criminal sanctions. There do not appear to be published judgments where sanctions have been imposed. Most issues are determined administratively by the Financial Supervisory Authority. Bank confidentiality in its more traditional form is under attack to the extent that it is felt to conflict with public interests. This is evidenced most significantly in tax and anti-money laundering legislation. The size of banks and their customers and their respective importance to the national economy has led to a demand and pressure on banks to disclose information on customers to an ever-increasing number of regulatory and public authorities. It must, however, be assumed that principles of privacy which are important in Denmark will maintain a core of confidence between a bank and its customer. However, as shown above, complicated rules have been introduced by the legislator to restrict banks and other institutions from passing on customer information other than that justified by administrative and regulatory purposes.

44 Act no 414 of 31 May 2000.

9 England

Gwendoline Griffiths

INTRODUCTION

Under English law, a bank owes a duty of confidence to its customer. The right to confidence is that of the customer, not of the bank (so that where a customer can be compelled to disclose his secrets, his bank can be compelled to do so as well). There is no precise definition of the scope of this basic duty. There are also numerous exceptions to the duty, both statutory and at common law, which are often as imprecise as the duty itself.

Banking confidence was considered by the Jack Committee Report on Banking Services Law in February 1989. It recommended that the statutory exceptions should be codified in a single statute. It found that they constituted a 'massive erosion' of the duty of confidence.

However, the UK government rejected the concept of a single statute. It preferred a voluntary Code of Banking Practice to deal with this and other issues raised by the Committee. A Banking Code was drawn up by the British Bankers' Association (BBA), the Building Societies Association and the Association for Payment Clearing Services (APACS). Its sixth edition came into effect on 1 March 2003. Most, though not all, banks have adopted the Code, which applies to personal customers only. The BBA and APACS have also developed a Business Banking Code for banks to follow when dealing with business customers (generally with turnovers of up to £1,000,000). Its second edition came into force on 1 March 2003 and it deals with confidentiality in a similar way to the Banking Code.

The government also denied that there had been a 'massive erosion' of the duty. They considered that the statutory exceptions only operated where public policy overrode the need to preserve confidence (such as the international attempt to prevent the laundering of proceeds of crime).

The number of statutory exceptions has increased since then, particularly in view of the events of 11 September 2001. The burden on banks has also increased because of the nature of their statutory obligations, some of which require banks to disclose information voluntarily on suspicion of the commission of certain offences, failure to disclose itself being a criminal offence.

Conversely, banks, and most other UK businesses, are subject to legislation designed to protect individuals with regard to the processing and transfer of personal data. The first EU-wide Directive was passed in 1995.[1] The increasing use of electronic communications as well as developments such as the outsourcing by banks of some of their functions and the transfer of data for processing to other jurisdictions has resulted in a number of other EC Directives in this area. The Data Protection Act 1998 came fully into force on 31 October 2001.

Accordingly, banks have to try to reconcile a number of different rights and obligations in their day-to-day dealings with their customers. This chapter considers the implications for banks operating in the 2000s of the various ways in which the duty arises and the exceptions to it. It also looks at related issues which arise in relation to the regulation of the financial and securities markets.

THE BASIC DUTY OF CONFIDENCE

Under English law the contract between a bank and its customer is governed by the laws of the place where the account is kept, in the absence of agreement to the contrary. The duty of a bank to keep its customer's affairs confidential is often merely an implied term of the contract between bank and customer. The duty is subject to certain exceptions but otherwise extends to all information which the bank has about its customer.

The starting point is *Tournier v National Provincial and Union Bank of England*.[2] Tournier was a customer of the defendant bank. A cheque was drawn by another customer of the defendant in favour of Tournier who endorsed it to a third person with an account at another bank. On the return of the cheque to the defendant, its manager inquired of the other bank to whom it had been endorsed and was told it was a bookmaker. The defendant disclosed that information to third persons.

Tournier brought an action for breach of an implied contract that the defendant would not disclose to third persons the state of his account or any related transactions. Atkin LJ described the duty of confidence in his judgment:

'It clearly goes beyond the state of the account, that is, whether there is a debit or a credit balance, and the amount of the balance. It must extend at least to all the transactions that go through the account, and to the securities, if any, given in respect of the account; and in respect of such matters it must, I think, extend beyond the period when the account is closed, or ceases to be an active account ... I further think that the obligation extends to information obtained from other sources than the customer's actual account, if the occasion upon which the information was obtained arose out of the banking relations of the bank and its customers—for example, with a view to assisting the bank in coming to decisions as to its treatment of its customers ... In this case, however, I should not extend the obligation to information as to the customer obtained after he had ceased to be a customer.'

1   Directive 95/46/EC of the European Parliament and of the Council of 24 October 1995.
2   [1924] 1 KB 461.

This was confirmed as the correct position by May LJ in *Lipkin Gorman v Karpnale Ltd*,[3] who stated that 'the correctness of the principles of law stated by the majority in *Tournier*'s case has not been doubted since the case was decided'.

Where a customer fears that his bank is about to breach, or has already breached, its obligation of confidence, he has two remedies available to him. He may sue for damages after disclosure or for an injunction to restrain disclosure or a repetition of a previous disclosure. Before granting an injunction the court will require to be satisfied that an award of damages will not be an adequate remedy. In practice damages will rarely be an adequate remedy. Once disclosure has taken place, the damage is done and, in many cases, it is difficult to measure the customer's loss in monetary terms. Exemplary or punitive damages are not normally awarded by English courts.

Accordingly, the main protection for the customer is his ability to obtain an injunction restraining the bank from making disclosure. Failure to comply with such an order would, in most circumstances, constitute a contempt of court. However, the court will not grant an injunction without some evidence that a disclosure is threatened and damages will not be adequate. The customer has a dilemma, because disclosure can very easily take place before he knows about it.

SCOPE OF THE DUTY AND OTHER CONFIDENTIALITY REQUIREMENTS

Tournier's case[4] applies to all types of customers. However, it gives only limited guidance about the scope of the basic duty or the information subject to it.

Bankes LJ summarised the position:

> 'The duty is a legal one arising out of contract ... it is not absolute but qualified. It is not possible to frame any exhaustive definition of the duty. The most that can be done is to classify the qualifications and to indicate its limits.'

Where a bank or other financial institution adopts the Banking Code and/or the Business Banking Code the duty of confidence owed to the relevant types of customer is reinforced by express statements about treating information as private and confidential. The Codes provide customers with a complaints procedure for breaches which is ultimately covered by the Financial Ombudsman Service.

In any event, where a customer is an individual, the processing of personal data will also be covered by the Data Protection Act 1998. This basically requires data to be processed fairly and lawfully (which will include compliance with English common law and statutes, as well as art 8 of the European Convention on Human Rights, the requirement for the respect of privacy). Data processing has to be undertaken in a secure environment and personal data cannot be sent to destinations which are not within the EEA unless:

---

3   [1989] 1 WLR 1340 (rvsd on different grounds [1991] 2 AC 548).
4   *Tournier v National Provincial and Union Bank of England* [1924] 1 KB 461.

1   the relevant country has adequate data protection legislation (such as Hungary
     or Switzerland) and the individual has consented; or
2   the 'safe harbour' created by the US and the EU applies.

Finally, banks may enter into confidentiality agreements or undertakings with
customers under which contractual obligations arise. Such a contractual duty of
confidentiality was considered by the Court of Appeal in *United Pan-Europe
Communications NV v Deutsche Bank AG (2000)*.[5] There the bank had given the
claimant company confidentiality undertakings in relation to the preparation of
Information Memoranda for syndicated loan facilities. The bank had subsequently
competed with the claimant and acquired a target company. The court held that the
bank had breached its duty of confidence (amongst other things) and as a result
granted an injunction to prevent it selling on the shares which it had acquired
pending a subsequent trial.

EXCEPTIONS, LIMITS AND QUALIFICATIONS

There are various exceptions, limits and qualifications to the above-mentioned duties
of confidence and there are usually express exceptions in contractual confidentiality
undertakings.

The case of *Christofi v Barclays Bank plc*[6] illustrates the fact that the limits of the
Tournier duty are to be ascertained in accordance with common sense. There it was
held that it was neither sensible nor necessary to impose a duty on a bank to withhold
information from a person who the bank would expect to already be in possession of
it under a statutory scheme.

Tournier's case[7] also set out the following qualifications:

1   where the disclosure is made with the express or implied consent of the customer;
2   where the interests of the bank require disclosure;
3   where disclosure is under compulsion of law; and
4   where there is a duty to the public to disclose.

Some of these also apply to the other confidentiality requirements mentioned above.
The qualifications are considered in more detail below.

THE QUALIFICATIONS TO THE DUTY

Express or implied consent of the customer

Express consent

If a bank notifies a customer that it proposes to disclose specified information and
the reason, and actually receives consent (preferably in writing) from the customer,
there will be no breach of duty. However, if notice is given to a customer by the bank

---

5   Case No: 2000/0420/A3.
6   [1999] 4 All ER 437, CA.
7   *Tournier v National Provincial and Union Bank of England* [1924] 1 KB 461.

and the customer does not reply, the bank will not be entitled to assume implied consent. Under the Data Protection Act 1998, consent from individuals should be 'explicit' if the data is 'sensitive' (which includes details of racial or ethnic origin, medical history and criminal convictions), although under the Act, implied consent is sufficient for other data.

Whilst the Banking Codes generally reflect *Tournier*'s case[8] and its qualifications, they only provide for express (and not implied) consent. They refer to the customer asking the bank to reveal information or giving it permission (which in the case of a banker's reference must be in writing). The customer's permission is also required before disclosure of information to a third party giving a guarantee or security in respect of the customer.

Express provisions consenting to disclosure of information can be important in documentation for larger transactions such as syndicated loans where lenders may wish to transfer their interests in the future, in documentation for transactions which may later be the subject of securitisation and in inter-creditor deeds where banks with separate relationships may want to share information on a customer.

IMPLIED CONSENT

There is little decided case law on what constitutes implied consent. There had been a well-established practice of banks giving references to other banks on customers on the basis of implied consent. However *Turner v Royal Bank of Scotland plc*[9] held that the practice was not sufficiently notorious to constitute an implied term of the bank-customer contract.

The question of implied consent arises in relation to the US' practice of consent directives. Under these, a customer or former customer authorises or directs its bank to disclose information to the US authorities. A person can be compelled to sign the consent under the threat of fines or imprisonment. It is not clear that a consent directive amounts to a consent sufficient to justify disclosure of information in England and there is no English authority on this. The preferred view is that a consent obtained by compulsion of law in another jurisdiction cannot operate in effect retrospectively to support a claim that consent be implied as a term of the contract between banker and customer under English law.

Some guidance may be obtained from the attitude of the English court towards other orders from foreign jurisdictions purporting to have extra-territorial effect. These are dealt with below in the section on the extra-territorial aspects of compulsion of law. However, the conflict between the attempt by a court in one jurisdiction to assert extra-territorial jurisdiction, on the one hand, and the duty of confidence owed by a bank in another jurisdiction to its customers, on the other, is something which has yet to be resolved satisfactorily.

---

8   *Tournier v National Provincial and Union Bank of England* [1924] 1 KB 461.
9   [2001] All ER (D) 139, CA.

The Cayman Islands courts have considered the question of 'consents' given under the order of a foreign court and their effect on a bank's duty of confidence. In *Re ABC Ltd*,[10] the applicant bank applied to the Grand Court, Cayman Islands, for a direction as to whether it would be entitled under the relevant Cayman Islands law to disclose confidential information pursuant to a 'consent' signed by its client under a US court order. The court held that the applicant bank would not be entitled to disclose in such circumstances. Summerfield CJ stated:

'In the absence of other direct authority in England, this decision, which applies the principles in *Tournier*, may assist in considering the position in English law. Arguably "consent" under this *Tournier* exception is consent "voluntarily and freely given in the exercise of an independent and uncoerced judgment". This exception is dependent on the customer's consent being maintained at the time the bank makes disclosure. A practical solution may be to require a letter from the customer giving his express consent to the disclosure of the relevant information. Conversely, if the customer withdraws his consent prior to the bank making disclosure, the bank would probably be breaching its duty of confidence if it complied with the consent directive.'

Disclosure in the interests of the bank

This exception was illustrated in *Tournier*'s case by an example of a bank issuing a writ claiming payment of an overdraft, stating on the face of it the amount of the overdraft.

Another example arose in *Sunderland v Barclays Bank Ltd*.[11] The bank dishonoured the plaintiff's cheque because she was betting. The plaintiff telephoned the bank to complain. The husband interrupted the conversation to take up his wife's case, and was informed that most cheques passing through the wife's account were in favour of bookmakers. Du Parcq LJ thought that, in the circumstances, the interests of the bank required disclosure since it was being forced to give a reason for the policy it adopted. However, it was also noted that since the husband joined the conversation, the bank had the customer's implied consent to disclose the information to him.

More recently, the interpretation of this exception has been considered in the cases of *XAG v A Bank*[12] in the High Court in London and *FDC & Co Ltd v The Chase Manhattan Bank NA*[13] in the Hong Kong Court of Appeal. In both cases, customers obtained interlocutory injunctions to restrain their banks from disclosing information in order to comply with subpoenas of US courts. The banks argued that it was in their interest to disclose, because otherwise they would be in contempt of court in the US. These arguments were rejected on the ground that the banks' 'interest' in disclosure was of a different character to that contemplated in *Tournier*.

---

10   (1985) FLR 159.
11   (1938) Times, 25 November.
12   [1983] 2 All ER 464.
13   Civil Appeal no 65 1984.

Where disclosure is made under this exception, it must be limited strictly to information necessary to protect the bank's interest. Disclosure will be necessary and permissible under this exception if there is litigation between the bank and its customer or if the bank brings an action against a guarantor. The Banking Codes also give the prevention of fraud as a relevant example.

Since *Tournier*'s case, two major areas of concern have arisen in relation this exception.

Other group companies

Whilst a bank may think it appropriate to release confidential information about its customers without their consent to other companies within its group, some of which may be non-banking subsidiaries, the English courts have taken a different view. In *Bank of Tokyo Ltd v Karoon*[14] it was held that, for confidence purposes, each corporate entity within the banking group must be viewed as separate.

The Jack Committee recommended that to enable a banking group to be run in a cost effective way, the law should allow confidential information to be passed between the holding company, being a bank, and its banking subsidiaries without the need for customer consent. The government took the view that disclosure should only be allowed where the purpose of the disclosure is to protect against loss. However the Banking Codes just provide that this exception will not be used to give information to anyone else, including companies in the same group, for marketing purposes.

Credit reference agencies

Credit reference agencies collect information on the creditworthiness of individuals (from various public sources and banks and other providers of credit) and then sell it to subscribers, normally potential lenders. There is some doubt as to which exception is applicable (if any) – 'consent of the customer', or 'duty to the public' or 'interests of the bank'.

The government's response to the Jack Committee proposals on the disclosure of 'black' information (about customers in default) was that banks must be able to continue to make such disclosures since shared information provides the best means of ensuring that borrowers are creditworthy and prevents the average consumer from having to bear the costs of bad debts through higher charges. However, if a bank wishes to pass on any 'white' information (about customers not in default), it must seek the customer's consent.

The Banking Codes provide that if a bank intends to disclose information about undisputed personal debts which are in default and in respect of which no satisfactory proposals for repayment have been received following a formal demand, it must give at least 28 days' notice of that intention to the customer. This notice period is designed to allow the customer to remedy the position before the agencies are notified.

14   [1987] 1 AC 45.

It is unclear whether those in favour of disclosing 'white' information to agencies without the customer's express consent would seek to justify it under one of the exceptions to *Tournier*. It is also as yet unclear what view the courts would take. However, the Banking Codes do provide that, as part of the account-opening process, a customer should be told whether account details will be passed to credit reference agencies or checks made with them.

Disclosure by compulsion of law

It is under this exception that the most inroads have been made into the duty of confidence and the other confidentiality requirements. The Jack Committee identified at least 19 statutory exceptions in 1987. Its list was not exhaustive and there have been a number of new statutes and regulations since then. This exception arises as a result of court orders as well as statutes. Its extra-territorial aspects are also dealt with below.

Compulsion by order of court

SUBPOENAS

Where a court seeks to compel a bank not a party to pending proceedings to disclose information it will normally do so by subpoena duces tecum, which requires an authorised officer of the bank to produce documents at trial. The subpoena must specify with reasonable particularity the documents or identifiable categories of documents which are to be produced. The Court of Appeal in *Omar v Omar*[15] confirmed that the documents to be produced should be identified either individually or compendiously, and that each document should be shown to be likely to exist, to be relevant to some issue in the proceedings and to be admissible evidence in respect of that issue, as well as to be necessary for fairly disposing of the action. 'Documents' include films, tape recordings and computer records. The subpoena may be refused or set aside if the request is irrelevant, fishing, speculative or oppressive.

BANKERS' BOOKS EVIDENCE ACT 1879

Alternatively, an order may be sought under s 7 of the Bankers' Books Evidence Act 1879 which states: 'on the application of any party to a legal proceeding a court or judge may order that such party be at liberty to inspect and take copies of any entries in a banker's book for any of the purposes of such proceedings.'

The Act defines 'legal proceedings' to mean 'any civil or criminal proceedings or enquiry in which evidence is or may be given, and includes an arbitration'. 'Banker's books' are defined to include 'ledgers, day books, cash books, account books, and all other books used in the ordinary business of the bank', whether these records are in written form or on microfilm, magnetic tape or any other form of mechanical or

---

15   (11 October 1996, unreported), CA.

electronic data retrieval mechanism. However, letters in a correspondence file and records of conversations or meetings between bank employees and the customer are not included.[16]

Section 3 provides that 'a copy of any entry in a banker's book shall in all legal proceedings be received as prima facie evidence of such entry, and of the matters transactions and accounts therein recorded'. The Act follows the principle that if a customer is involved in civil or criminal proceedings, he subjects himself to the necessity of disclosure and this will apply equally to his bank.

There are distinctions between civil and criminal proceedings in the application of s 7. In criminal proceedings, the position is as stated in *Williams v Summerfield*:[17]

'... in criminal proceedings, justices should warn themselves of the importance of the step which they are taking in making an order under section 7; should always recognise the care with which the jurisdiction should be exercised; should take into account among other things whether there is other evidence in the possession of the prosecution to support the charge ...'

He warned against 'fishing expeditions' such as when 'a police officer seeking to make investigations of a suspect bank account started legal proceedings for that purpose and no other'.

In civil proceedings, the statutory power to order inspection should not be inconsistent with, and not overreach, the general law of discovery.[18] Bankers' books relating to an account of the party to litigation will be ordered to be disclosed if they are relevant to the litigation and not privileged.

In very specific circumstances the court can authorise the inspection of a bank account of a person who is not a party to the proceedings. In *DB Deniz Nakliyati TAS v Yugopetrol*[19] it was said that the party seeking inspection must show:

'that the bank account of the third party is in substance the account of a party to the litigation, or is one in which that person is so much concerned that items in it would be admissible evidence material to the question of his liability; and that there are very strong grounds, almost amounting to certainty, that there are material items in the account relevant to the matters in issue.'

DISCLOSURE ORDERS

The Court of Appeal in *Bankers Trust Co v Shapira*[20] extended the circumstances in which an order for discovery (now disclosure) could be used to coerce banks to reveal details of its customers' accounts. It was held that the court's power to order discovery of information at the earliest stages of an action to give effect to a defrauded

---

16   *Re Harglen Ltd* [2001] 1 All ER 376.
17   [1972] 3 WLR 131.
18   See *Parnell v Wood* [1892] P 137; *South Staffordshire Tramways Co v Ebbsmith* [1895] 2 QB 669; *Pollock v Garle* [1898] 1 Ch 1; *Waterhouse v Barker* [1924] 2 KB 759.
19   [1992] 1 All ER 205.
20   [1980] 1 WLR 1274.

plaintiff's equitable right to trace and recover property may be used to order a bank to disclose documents and correspondence relating to the account of a customer who is prima facie guilty of fraud, even though such material would normally be subject to the banker-customer obligation of confidence. In *Arab Monetary Fund v Hashim (No 5)*[21] limits were placed on this. It was held that the plaintiff must demonstrate that the information sought may lead to the location or preservation of assets to which the plaintiff is, or may be, entitled. General disclosure will not be ordered.

In two other cases the courts have also permitted the use of confidential information disclosed pursuant to a court order, for purposes which fell outside the strict terms of the order.

In *Bank of Crete SA v Koskotas (No 2)*[22] it was alleged that the former chief executive of the plaintiff bank had misappropriated bank funds. The London branches of certain banks were ordered to disclose information relating to certain customers in proceedings for the recovery of funds. The order stipulated that the information could be used only for the purposes of the plaintiff's action. However, the Governor of the Bank of Greece established an investigation team to look into the whereabouts of the missing funds. The investigation team wanted to use the material disclosed pursuant to the English court's order for the purposes of the report (which would then have to be disclosed to the Bank of Greece under Greek law).

The bank faced a dilemma between complying with an English court order and complying with Greek law. The judge said that these were exceptional circumstances and disclosure to the Greek investigatory team was ordered.

In *Omar v Omar*[23] the plaintiffs were seeking to recover funds allegedly misappropriated from their father's estate. They obtained an order for the disclosure of information from the London bank of one of the defendants. After the bank had supplied the information, the plaintiffs sought leave to amend their statement of claim to include claims based on the disclosed information and to add two personal claims against certain of the defendants. They also sought disclosure of further information. It was held that the proposed 'other' purposes were entirely legitimate within the framework of the main tracing claim and their application was allowed.

Compulsion by statute

Most of the statutory provisions entitle the relevant statutory body to compel a bank to produce information relevant to any matter which it is authorised to investigate. However, other provisions require a bank to disclose information to the appropriate authority of its own volition on suspicion of the commission of certain criminal offences. Banks are also required to carry out inquiries as to the identity and suitability of a potential customer (usually in order to determine whether the funds in question are derived from illegal activities). The penalties for failure to comply

---

21 [1992] 2 All ER 911.
22 [1993] 1 All ER 748.
23 [1995] 3 All ER 571.

vary with each piece of legislation. The following list is not exhaustive but deals with the more important provisions.

Section 745 of the Income and Corporation Taxes Act 1988 (ICTA) gives the Inland Revenue wide investigatory powers if it suspects non-compliance with the provisions of ICTA which prevent the transfer of assets abroad to evade English tax. In *Clinch v Inland Revenue Comrs*,[24] the court considered a notice served by the Commissioners under s 481 of ICTA 1970 (the predecessor to s 745 of ICTA). Mr Clinch maintained that the notice was void because it was merely a 'fishing expedition' and did not sufficiently identify the customers or transactions in which the Revenue was interested. Alternatively, it was invalid because it was unduly oppressive or burdensome. The court held that in the circumstances the notice was valid, although the court could intervene if such a notice went substantially beyond that required to decide whether tax had been unlawfully evaded. The burden of proving oppression is a heavy one. Such a notice can only be served on someone in England in relation to documents and files in England.

The Inland Revenue also has other powers under the Taxes Management Act 1970 (TMA) to oblige banks to disclose information. Notices served on a bank under s 20(3) TMA were considered in *R v Inland Revenue Comrs, ex p Banque Internationale a Luxembourg SA*.[25] The Revenue were investigating large-scale tax avoidance schemes, which had been financed by the bank. At the instigation of its customers, the bank challenged the validity of the notices on various grounds, including their impingement on the privacy and right to confidentiality of the bank and its customers in violation of art 8 of the European Convention on Human Rights. The court held the notices were valid. As far as art 8 was concerned, there was ample justification for the impingement as required by art 8(2) of the Convention.

Section 236 of the Insolvency Act 1986 applies where an administration order is made in relation to a company, an administrative receiver is appointed, a company goes into voluntary liquidation, a provisional liquidator is appointed or a winding-up order has been made by the court. The court has the power to summon before it any person whom the court thinks capable of giving information concerning the promotion, formation, business, dealings, affairs or property of the company.

Under s 236(3) the court, on the application of the office holder, can require any such person to submit an affidavit to the court containing an account of his dealings with the company and produce any books, papers or other records in his possession or under his control relating to the company. Failure to comply with the order could result in a warrant being issued for that person's arrest and the seizure of any books,

---

24   [1973] 3 WLR 862.
25   [2000] STC 708.

papers etc. This section has been used against banks and is wide-ranging and potentially penal in effect. It has even been used in relation to documents held abroad.[26]

The effect of s 236 was also considered in relation to a letter of request for assistance and documents from the Supreme Court of South Australia under s 426 of the Insolvency Act 1986 in *Re JN Taylor Pty Ltd*.[27] Section 426 provides for co-operation on insolvency matters between the English courts and other courts in the UK and other relevant countries and territories (mainly in the Commonwealth). The request for production of documents was granted since there was no serious risk that it would result in claims against the bank by third parties for breach of confidentiality. However, the request for examination of certain bank officers was not granted since, had s 236 of the Act applied, it would almost certainly have been refused.

POLICE AND OTHER CRIMINAL INVESTIGATORS

Recent years have seen a spate of new legislation in this area. Notably, anti-money laundering and anti-terrorism legislation requires banks to disclose confidential information simply if there are reasonable grounds to believe that a customer is engaged in any one of a number of specified offences. This directly conflicts with the view in *Tournier*'s case that the giving of information to the police in regard to a customer suspected of a crime would be unwarranted.

Problems can be caused for banks (and others) by their related statutory obligations not to 'tip off' individuals whom they suspect of such offences. In *Bank of Scotland v A Ltd, B & C*,[28] the bank faced a dilemma as it had reported a suspected fraud to the authorities, but then was instructed by its customer to pay out the relevant monies. The bank could not then defend any action against it by the customer for non-payment without 'tipping off' the customer. The Court of Appeal gave helpful guidance on ways in which the bank could have minimised its problems by seeking directions from the Serious Fraud Office as to what could be disclosed and then applying to the court. The court took the view that in most cases seeking directions from the court in this way should lead to a practical solution being found to protect the interests of the public as well as those of the bank.

There is a further complication in the interaction between the Data Protection Act 1998 and legislation dealing particularly with anti-money laundering and anti-terrorism. Here, the concern arises from an individual's right of access to his personal data as opposed to the bank's or other financial institution's obligations not to 'tip-off' an individual about whom suspicions have arisen. This led HM Treasury to issue 'The UK's Anti-Money Laundering Legislation and the Data Protection Act 1998: Guidance Notes for the Financial Sector' in April 2002. This offers advice on how to deal with a 'Subject Access Request' under the Act in such circumstances. Although it is not legally binding, the Information Commissioner has been consulted

---

26 *Re Mid East Trading Ltd* [1998] 1 All ER 577.
27 [1998] BPIR 347.
28 [2001] 3 All ER 58.

and supports the approach taken. The Guidance Notes, and other useful information, are available on HM Treasury's website.[29]

The following is a summary of some of the legislation relating to criminal investigations.

POLICE AND CRIMINAL EVIDENCE ACT 1984

Section 9 of the Police and Criminal Evidence Act 1984 provides that a constable may obtain access to 'special procedure material' for the purposes of a criminal investigation by making an application under Sch 1 to the Act. 'Special procedure material' is defined as 'material other than items subject to legal privilege and excluded material, in the possession of a person who acquired or created it in the course of any trade, business, profession or other occupation and holds it subject to an express or implied undertaking to hold it in confidence'. This would include a bank. Excluded material means personal records, human tissue and tissue fluid and journalistic material held in confidence. The police can apply for such an order at any stage if they believe that the special procedure material will assist their investigation of a serious arrestable offence.

Barclays Bank plc v Taylor; Trustee Savings Bank of Wales and Border Counties[30] made clear that where the police have obtained an order under s 9(1) a bank is obliged to comply with it, is not in breach of the duty of confidence by so doing and is under no obligation to oppose the application, probe the evidence given in respect of it or give notice to its customer that the application being made.

CRIMINAL JUSTICE ACT 1987

The Criminal Justice Act 1987 empowers the Director of the Serious Fraud Office (SFO) to investigate any suspected offence which appears to involve serious or complex fraud (s 1(3)). Under s 2 any person can be required to answer questions, furnish information or produce documents. Section 2(10) provides that a person cannot be required to do so if:

> 'he owes an obligation of confidence by virtue of carrying on any banking business unless—
> (a) the person to whom the obligation of confidence is owed consents to the disclosure or production; or
> (b) the Director has authorised the making of the requirement or ..., a member of the Serious Fraud Office ... has done so.'

By s 2(1) the Director can make such a requirement for the purpose of an investigation under s 1, if it appears to him that there is good reason to do so. There are no specific provisions in the Act which allow the Director's authority to be questioned. Section 2(13) provides that any person who without reasonable excuse fails to comply with a requirement shall, on summary conviction, be guilty of an offence punishable by imprisonment or a fine. Judicial review of the Director's power of investigation was

29   www.hm-treasury.gov.uk/mediastore/otherfiles/money_laundering.pdf.
30   [1989] 1 WLR 1066.

unsuccessfully sought in *R v Director of Serious Fraud Office, ex p Saunders*.[31] The court rejected the argument that the power under s 2 lapsed once a suspect had been charged. It was said, strictly obiter, that the SFO was entitled to obtain self-incriminating material in the possession of a third party including material arising out of civil proceedings (although the court expressed a reservation as to the extent to which this could be required in view of the subject's rights against self-incrimination). Subsequently, in *Saunders v United Kingdom*,[32] the European Court of Human Rights (ECHR) held that Mr Saunders' right to a fair trial had been violated because statements he had made under legal compulsion to that statutory inspector had been disclosed in criminal proceedings against him. However in *R v Morrissey*; *R v Staines*,[33] on the use of similar compulsory powers under another Act, it was held that the ECHR could not repeal, even partially, an English statute on the basis of its ruling in *Saunders* so that the court should not exclude evidence obtained in that way.

There is little helpful authority on what would constitute a 'reasonable excuse' under s 2(13) for failure to comply with a requirement for information. In *Ex p Saunders* the court said that an undertaking given by the third party to the Vice-Chancellor not to disclose the documents concerned to any person without leave of the court was a reasonable excuse. However, it is unlikely that a bank receiving such a requirement would be able to question the decision of the Director to authorise it.

COMPETITION ACT 1998

By s 26 of the Competition Act 1998, the Competition Director is empowered to require any person to produce documents or information to him for the purposes of an investigation of an infringement under Ch I or II under s 25 of the Act. The Director can apply to the court for a warrant to enter premises and search for documents under s 26 or 27 of the Act. The measures under the 1998 Act apply to companies. However, the Enterprise Act 2002 also contains provisions aimed at tackling corporate fraud, which apply to individuals. It is expected that the competition law provisions of the 2002 Act will come into force during 2003.

FINANCIAL SERVICES AND MARKETS ACT 2000

Part XI of this Act gives the Financial Services Authority information gathering and investigatory powers. These are dealt with below in the section on the regulation of the financial markets.

ANTI-MONEY LAUNDERING AND ANTI-TERRORISM

Background

The 1988 Basle Committee statement of principles on suppressing money laundering through national and international banking systems is one of various international

---

31 [1988] Crim LR 837.
32 (1996) Times, 18 December.
33 (1997) Times, 1 May.

and European initiatives which have resulted in UK legislation in this field. In the EU, the first Money Laundering Directive[34] was implemented from 1 April 1994. It has now been amended by a second Directive.[35] This has extended the requirement to combat money laundering to cover the proceeds of all crimes and applies not only to the financial sector, but also to other non-financial activities and professions (including lawyers) which are vulnerable to misuse by money launderers.

Post-11 September 2001, there have been further legislative changes in the UK to focus amongst other things on the financial arrangements of terrorist organisations. Before then the UK anti-money laundering regime was contained in three statutes, the Criminal Justice Act 1993 (CJA), the Drug Trafficking Act 1994 (DTA) and the Terrorism Act 2000 and one statutory instrument, the Money Laundering Regulations 1993.[36] Now the regime has been consolidated and expanded, so that banks (and others in the regulated sector) face a complex set of obligations with corresponding offences and penalties which can apply to individual officers and employees as well as the institutions themselves. The current position is reflected below.

Proceeds of Crime Act 2002

Part 7 of the Proceeds of Crime Act 2002 (POCA) deals with money laundering and came into force on 24 February 2003. It replaces and expands the earlier anti-money laundering legislation (CJA and DTA), with the exception of the terrorism legislation which had already been strengthened (as mentioned below).

The new money laundering offences under POCA are:

1   to conceal disguise convert transfer or remove from the UK criminal property (s 327);
2   to become concerned in an arrangement which a person knows or suspects facilitates the use or control of criminal property (s 328); and
3   to acquire use or have possession of criminal property (s 329). There is no distinction between the original criminal and a later recipient of the proceeds of crime.

Criminal property is property which:

1   is or represents a person's benefit from criminal conduct; and
2   the alleged offender knows or suspects constitutes or represents such a benefit (s 340(3)).

Criminal conduct is conduct which is an offence in any part of the UK, or would be an offence in the UK if it occurred there (s 340(2)). This is a key change to the previous legislation as the offences apply to the proceeds of all crimes, not just drug trafficking, terrorism or serious crime. In addition, there are no de minimis limits and no need for the conduct to have any connection with the UK.

POCA also creates three new offences of failure to disclose (which again broaden the previous position):

---

34   Council Directive 91/308/EEC.
35   Council Directive 2001/97/EC.
36   SI 1993/1933.

1   persons in the regulated sector (which include bank employees) who obtain information in the course of business which gives reasonable grounds for suspecting money laundering, commit an offence if they fail to make a report (s 330);
2   a money laundering reporting officer (MLRO) in the regulated sector commits an offence if an employee makes a report to the MLRO that gives reasonable grounds for suspicion, but the MLRO does not make an onward suspicious transaction report (STR) to the National Crime Intelligence Service (NCIS) (s 331); and
3   MLROs not in the regulated sector can also commit an offence if they do not make an STR when they know or suspect as a result of a disclosure to them that a person is engaged in money laundering (s 332).

However, an individual will have a defence if there is a reasonable excuse for his non-disclosure or he has not been provided with appropriate anti-money laundering training by his employer. The court will also consider whether any appropriate guidance was followed.

Section 333 deals with tipping off, and a person commits an offence if:

1   he knows or suspects that a disclosure has been made under POCA; and
2   he makes a disclosure which is likely to prejudice any resulting investigation.

The above offences carry penalties of a fine and/or imprisonment (up to a maximum of 14 years' under ss 327, 328 and 329, and of five years' under ss 330, 331, 332 and 333).

As with the previous regime, NCIS may give permission to transact a prohibited act under ss 327, 328 or 329. Under s 335 a person must be treated as having the appropriate consent if a disclosure is made to NCIS and he does not receive a notice of refusal within seven working days after the date of disclosure. Even if a notice of refusal is received in that period, a person will be treated as having the appropriate consent if a further 31 days elapse after the notice of refusal. Whilst these provisions are helpful, the speed of banking transactions may still mean that banks face difficulties in dealing with their customers after a disclosure has been made.

There are also helpful provisions on disclosures in ss 337 and 339. A disclosure which satisfies the conditions of s 337(1) or which includes additional information required by a form specified under s 339 is not to be taken to breach any restriction on the disclosure of information (howsoever imposed). As a result there will be no breach of any duty of confidence or other similar requirement.

The Money Laundering Regulations 1993, 2001 and 2003

The original Money Laundering Regulations[37] came into force on 1 April 1994 and complement the provisions of the relevant statutes. The Regulations provide guidelines for those involved, inter alia, in the banking or financial services business and there are criminal penalties for non-compliance. They relate to various matters,

---

37   SI 1993/1933.

including the setting up of systems and training to prevent money laundering, such as identification procedures ('Know Your Customer'), internal reporting procedures and external reporting requirements.

As far as disclosure of information is concerned, internal reporting procedures have to satisfy certain requirements under reg 14. They must identify an 'appropriate person' (the MLRO) to whom a report can be made of to a knowledge or suspicion of money laundering. Any such report must be considered in the light of all other relevant information to determine whether there is such knowledge or suspicion. The MLRO must have reasonable access to other information which may assist. Finally, there must be a mechanism for the MLRO to disclose the information to the police (NCIS) if he knows or suspects that the person the subject of the report is engaged in money laundering.

Regulations 15 and 16 impose a duty on any 'supervisory authority' and any 'secondary recipient' of information from a supervisor, to disclose evidence of money laundering to NCIS. Inspectors appointed under certain statutes must disclose also such information to NCIS or to their appointing supervisory authority. Again, the disclosure of information in any of the circumstances set out above will not be a breach of any restriction imposed by statute or otherwise.

The 1993 Regulations were supplemented by the Money Laundering Regulations 2001[38] which came into force in full on 15 July 2002. Amongst other things the 2001 Regulations added certain types of money service businesses to the financial business covered by the 1993 Regulations.

However it is now proposed to consolidate the Money Laundering Regulations by means of the Money Laundering Regulations 2003. These will reflect the second EU Money Laundering Directive[39] (principally by widening their application to all those in the regulated sector) as well as ensuring that more recent legislation (such as POCA) is taken into account. They were due to come into force by 15 June 2003 to meet the requirement to implement the Directive. The UK now intends to lay the Regulations by that date, but to allow a period of three months before they come into force.

The Financial Services Authority Anti-Money Laundering Rules 2001

The Financial Services Authority (FSA) published its Anti-Money Laundering Rules 2001 as part of its efforts to reduce financial crime. The Rules run parallel to, but are separate from, the Regulations. They apply to banks (and other firms) regulated by the FSA. The Rules mirror the Regulations and provide the FSA with the power to prosecute for breaches of the Regulations as well as the Rules.

Banks (and their employees) have to comply with both the Regulations and the Rules, and can be subject to criminal liability for breach of the Regulations as well as regulatory sanctions for breach of the Rules. The FSA can impose fines and, in extreme cases, remove authorisation (and thus the ability to carry on business). Like

---

38   SI 2001/3641.
39   Council Directive 2001/97/EC.

the Regulations, the Rules require regulated businesses to set up and operate anti-money laundering arrangements. In December 2002 the FSA imposed its first fine on a bank for breach of the Rules.

Joint Money Laundering Steering Group Guidance Notes

The Joint Money Laundering Steering Group (JMLSG) is made up of the leading UK trade associations in the financial services industry (including the British Bankers Association). Its aim is to promulgate good practice in countering money laundering and to give practical assistance in interpreting the legislative regime. Its Guidance Notes are not mandatory, but they provide an indication of what is expected and, when tailored to a bank or other firm's own risk base, they can provide a safe harbour. They were originally drafted in relation to the 1993 Regulations and they take account of the FSA Rules. They are being updated to take account of POCA and the proposed 2003 Regulations. A more radical revision of the Guidance Notes is also planned in 2004.

Anti-terrorism

The Terrorism Act 2000 (which replaced the previous Prevention of Terrorism Acts) remains in force. It defines terrorism as 'the use or threat of action ... designed to influence the government or to intimidate the public ...made for the purposes of advancing a political religious or ideological cause'. This is wider than the previous definition, and covers acts both within and outside the UK. The 2000 Act contains a comprehensive set of provisions to address terrorist money laundering. It deals with money or property likely to be used for terrorism (including lawful money donated to terrorists) as well as the proceeds of terrorist acts (such as kidnapping). It includes a money laundering offence (s 18) as well as a reporting requirement, with an offence of failure to report (s 19) and a tipping-off offence (s 39).

On 13 December 2001 the Anti-Terrorism Crime and Security Act 2001 came into force with a wide range of provisions, some of which deal with terrorist money laundering in a similar way to POCA (which at the time was a bill in Parliament). They include the addition of a new s 21A to the 2000 Act, which creates a new offence of 'failure to disclose' for banks and others in the regulated sector, which sits alongside the s 19 offence of failure to report, which continues to apply to everyone in the UK. The key difference is that s 21A applies not just to a failure to report any actual knowledge or suspicion, but also a failure by an institution or person to identify and report 'reasonable grounds for knowing or suspecting money laundering'. This introduced an objective test for liability. The penalty for failing to report is a fine and/or up to five years' imprisonment.

The 2001 Act also strengthened the powers of the police in investigations into terrorist money laundering. The 2000 Act allows the police to obtain disclosure orders; however, under the 2001 Act they may obtain account monitoring orders requiring financial institutions to provide information about named account holders. These new orders will make the obligations of banks and other financial institutions much clearer and make it easier to pass on information without any fear of breaching confidentiality obligations. The police also have powers of seizure and restraint (to freeze funds during investigations) as well as eventual forfeiture.

Finally, the government has introduced a series of sanctions to give effect to decisions of the UN Security Council and the EU Council of Ministers. For example, The Terrorism (United Nations Measures) Order 2001[40] makes it an offence to make funds or finances or related services available to terrorists without a licence from the Treasury or to contravene a decision to freeze funds, and creates related tipping-off offences. The Bank of England publishes lists of terrorist suspects and banks and financial institutions are obliged to check if they hold any accounts for them. If so, they must freeze the account and report it to the Bank of England as well as NCIS. The Bank of England's notices are available on its website.[41] Again, a bank can face a dilemma, since little assistance is given on identifying a terrorist suspect. As a result it can be potentially faced with notifying and freezing the assets of an individual who may be innocent or breaching sanctions by allowing a terrorist suspect to slip through the net.

Extra-territorial aspects of compulsion of law

Two particular aspects will be considered. An attempt by an overseas claimant to obtain confidential information from a bank in England and the reverse situation. The position varies depending on whether the proceedings are civil or criminal.

OBTAINING EVIDENCE IN ENGLAND FOR USE IN FOREIGN CIVIL PROCEEDINGS

Two methods are used to obtain information from banks in England for use in foreign proceedings – letters rogatory and subpoenas.

Letters rogatory from other jurisdictions

'Letters rogatory' or 'letters of request' involve a request for evidence made by the foreign court to the court in the country where records are maintained, in order to obtain the information without directly or indirectly infringing that country's sovereignty. The use of such letters is regulated by the Hague Convention on the Taking of Evidence Abroad in Civil or Commercial Matters 1970 which led to the Evidence (Proceedings in Other Jurisdictions) Act 1975. It enables an English court to make an order for the obtaining of evidence for civil proceedings in other courts or tribunals upon a request from that court or tribunal, if the evidence requested relates to proceedings 'which either have been instituted ... or whose institution ... is contemplated' (s 1(b)).

Such an order only requires the person to whom it is addressed to produce specified documents which are in his possession, custody or power. A person cannot be compelled to give any evidence which he could not be compelled to give in civil proceedings instituted under the jurisdiction of the court making the order. Therefore, the extent of disclosure to a foreign court cannot exceed that which would be available in England.

The Act was considered by the House of Lords in *Re Westinghouse Uranium Contract*,[42] where Westinghouse was the defendant in proceedings for a breach of

---

40   SI 2001/3365.
41   www.bankofengland.co.uk/sanctions.
42   [1978] 2 WLR 81.

contract in the US. Part of its defence was an allegation of a cartel which included RTZ, an English company. The US Court for the District of Virginia issued letters rogatory to the English High Court seeking orders for representatives of RTZ to attend for oral examination in London. RTZ claimed privilege which was upheld by the English Court of Appeal. The US federal judge upheld a claim by witnesses to privilege under the Fifth Amendment. The US Department of Justice then intervened and applied for an order in the US court compelling testimony in return for the provision of immunity on the grounds that it was required for a grand jury investigation into violations of the US anti-trust laws and with a view to issuing criminal proceedings.

The House of Lords upheld RTZ's claim of privilege and also held that the provisions of the Act did not enable an English court to make an order to provide evidence to be used for investigatory purposes such as Grand Jury proceedings. The Act does extend to the obtaining of evidence for the purposes of criminal proceedings, but specifically limits this to proceedings which have been instituted. Grand jury proceedings were held not to be criminal proceedings which had been instituted, rather they were merely investigatory. Consequently, the English courts will not recognise or assist proceedings of this nature.

The issues at stake in the *Westinghouse* case were considered so important that the Attorney-General intervened to bring to the notice of the House of Lords the government's opposition to extra-territorial recognition of the US investigatory jurisdiction (at least in relation to English companies or persons).

More recently, letters of request were considered in *First American Corpn v Sheik Al-Nahyan*,[43] where it was held that, where appropriate, the court should accede to a letter of request, particularly where the litigation arose out of fraud practiced on an international scale. However, in that case the court had to bear in mind the need to protect intended witnesses from an oppressive request.

Subpoenas from other jurisdictions

Foreign courts can ignore issues of comity by serving subpoenas on local offices of international banks in order to obtain information relating to their overseas branches. Often, the bank is placed in the position of refusing to comply and being held in contempt of court, or obeying and then infringing the secrecy laws of the country in which the information is maintained.

The effect of a foreign subpoena was considered in the case of *XAG v A Bank*.[44] There the London branch of an American bank was injuncted from producing documents relating to accounts held in London which were required by a New York District Court. As the accounts were opened and maintained in London, it was held that the banker-customer relationship was centred in London and governed by English law. The court had to determine the balance of convenience with regard to:

---

43   [1998] 4 All ER 439, CA.
44   [1983] 2 All ER 464.

1   the fact that the order of the New York Court would take effect in London in breach of both a private interest (the banker-customer contract) and the public interest (the obligation of confidence);

2   the effect of the subpoena and the fact that, under the US doctrine of foreign government compulsion, the New York court would not hold the bank liable in contempt for complying with the injunction of the English court which had jurisdiction over the branch where the documents were located; and

3   the fact that although the court would not be 'enforcing' a foreign revenue or penal law, by permitting the subpoena to be enforced in London, the mere fact of not impeding it would involve a measure of assistance and approbation of a breach of the obligation of confidence which the court would normally, in the public interest, maintain.

Leggatt J summarised the balance of convenience thus:

> 'On the one hand, there is involved in a continuation of the injunction impeding the exercise by the US court in London of powers which, by English statutes, would be regarded as excessive, without in so doing causing detriment to the bank: on the other hand, the refusal of the injunctions, or the non-continuation of them, would cause potentially very considerable harm to the [group], which cannot be disputed, by suffering the bank to act for its own purposes in breach of the duty of confidence admittedly owed to its customers.'

A similar view was taken by the Hong Kong Court of Appeal in *FDC Co Ltd v Vanguard International Manufacturing Ltd Inc and Garpeg and The Chase Manhattan Bank NA*.[45] The Hong Kong court refused to treat the fact that the bank had been exposed to considerable financial penalties and possible loss of banking licence in the US as a ground for allowing a breach of banking confidence. The majority of the Court of Appeal were of the opinion that for the purpose of this case, the Hong Kong branch of Chase should be considered as an entirely different entity, separate from the New York branch. This view has since been confirmed in the English decision of *Bank of Tokyo Ltd v Karoon*.[46]

Finally, the balancing test has also been applied in relation to letters rogatory. In *Re State of Norway's Application*,[47] Kerr LJ regarded as significant factors to weigh in the balance the nature, scope, quality and effect of a foreign court order or request.

OBTAINING EVIDENCE ABROAD FOR USE IN ENGLISH CIVIL PROCEEDINGS

A party that has brought proceedings in England may wish to obtain evidence from foreign banks which are not a party to the proceedings. Most commonly, this situation arises where funds have been misappropriated and transferred through various (unwitting) banks. In such circumstances there are four principal avenues available: letters rogatory; subpoenas; court orders for disclosure; and applications to the court in the country in which the relevant bank is situated.

45   Civil Appeal no 65 1984.
46   [1987] AC 45.
47   [1986] 3 WLR 453.

Letters rogatory to foreign courts

An English court can make a letter of request to obtain information from parties abroad. The reception that such a request receives from the foreign court is largely dependent on whether the country concerned is a party to a convention or treaty with the UK. Such a convention may be bilateral (such as the UK's conventions with Turkey, Poland or Greece) or multilateral (such as the Hague Convention on the Taking of Evidence Abroad in Civil and Commercial Matters 1970 which includes countries such as Belgium, Germany and the US). Some countries are not party to any such convention.

The procedure for obtaining information is obviously more straightforward in the case of convention countries. The principal difference between bilateral conventions and the Hague Convention is that the former usually only apply to willing witnesses. So, if a bank based in such a country refused to provide information, it could not be compelled to do so. Where a witness is willing to provide information or where, as in some circumstances under the Hague Convention, he can be compelled to do so, the information is not confined to purely oral evidence. The letter of request can seek the production of documents as well. In *Panayiotou v Sony Music*[48] the court rejected a contention that a party could not issue a letter of request that sought the production of documents alone.

If a witness is based in a non-convention country, a letter of request can be issued by the English court. However, the receiving court is not under any obligation to compel the witness to attend to give evidence or to produce documents. Whether the foreign court will assist is a matter of local law.

Subpoenas and disclosure orders

The English courts have adopted a very restrictive approach when faced with the question of whether a foreign bank can be compelled to disclose information by subpoena, an order under s 7 of the Bankers' Books Evidence Act 1879 or an order pursuant to the principles set out in *Bankers Trust Co v Shapira*[49] (which have been considered above in relation to banks operating in England).

For example, in the criminal case of *R v Grossman*,[50] the Court of Appeal refused an order under s 7 which would have required disclosure in England of a bank's books held in the Isle of Man relating to an account there. One of the grounds for refusal was that the account concerned was outside the jurisdiction, and conflict of jurisdictions should be avoided.

The case of *Mackinnon v Donaldson, Lufkin and Jenrette Securities Corpn*[51] concerned an ex parte order under s 7 obtained by the plaintiff against a US bank (which was not a party to the litigation); the plaintiff was alleging fraud against a certain company and individual defendants. The order required the bank to produce

48   [1994] Ch 142.
49   [1980] 1 WLR 1274.
50   (1981) 73 Cr App Rep 302.
51   [1986] Ch 482.

books and other papers, held at its head office in New York, which related to an account of one of the defendants. In addition, the plaintiff issued a subpoena against an officer of the London branch of the bank. Hoffman J, in discharging the order and the subpoena, said that on principle, the court should not, save in exceptional circumstances, impose on the foreigner and in particular a foreign bank which would owe a duty of confidence to its customer regulated by the law of the country where the customer's account was kept, a requirement to produce documents outside the jurisdiction concerning business transacted outside the jurisdiction. He said that the need to exercise the court's jurisdiction with due regard to the sovereignty of others is particularly important in the case of banks, who are in a special position because their documents are concerned not only with their own business, but with that of their customers.

The English court's approach to jurisdictional conflicts of this nature appears to be somewhat different from that of the US courts (as discussed above). Apart from exceptional circumstances, the English courts will voluntarily restrict their own jurisdiction within their own territorial limits and, in the interests, inter alia, of comity, leave matters outside those territorial limits to the courts of the relevant jurisdiction. It is also interesting to note that in a decision of the New York Federal District Court in *Laker Airways v Pan American World Airways*,[52] Brieant J quashed a subpoena served on two English banks at their New York offices requiring them to produce documents held in England which related to transactions which took place in England. Brieant J was apparently of the view that the subpoena was 'inappropriate' and constituted 'an end run around the Hague Convention'.

Applications to the foreign court

There is nothing to prevent a claimant who has brought proceedings in England from bringing proceedings for disclosure of documents in the courts of the country in which the bank in question is based. Whether the foreign court will grant such an order will depend on local law. However, the English courts have indicated that there is nothing improper in obtaining evidence in this manner and using it in England. In *South Carolina Insurance Co v Assurantie Maatschappij 'De Zeven Provincieir'*,[53] the plaintiff, having commenced proceedings in England, applied to the US court for an order for pre-trial discovery (which is not, as a general rule, permitted in England) against a non-party. The court refused to grant an injunction in favour of the defendants restraining the plaintiff from taking any further steps in the US proceedings.

Injunctions or disclosure orders in aid of foreign proceedings: Brussels and Lugano Conventions

In *Republic of Haiti v Duvalier*[54] the plaintiffs had commenced proceedings in France for the recovery of funds allegedly embezzled by the defendants. They also

52   1985 ECC 15, 38, 336.
53   [1987] AC 24.
54   [1990] 1 QB 202.

made an application in the English courts to restrain the defendants from dealing with their assets wherever situated, and compelling them to disclose information relating to their assets. Staughton LJ said, at 216–217:

'It is beyond question that the injunction ... was a most unusual measure, such as should very rarely be granted. But this case is most unusual.

It is not the nature or the strength of the republic's cause of action which puts it in that category. What, to my mind, is determinative is the plain and admitted intention of the defendants to move their assets out of the reach of the courts of law, coupled with the resources they have obtained and the skill they have hitherto shown in doing that, and the vast amount of money involved [\$120 million]. This case demands international co-operation between all nations. As the judge said, if ever there was a case for the exercise of the court's powers, this must be it. Or to quote Kerr LJ in the *Babanaft* case,[55] at p 33D–E: "some situations ... cry out – as a matter of justice to the plaintiffs – for disclosure orders and Mareva type injunctions covering foreign assets of defendants even before judgment". And I think that this is such a case.'

Whilst the disclosure order was granted against the defendant and not a third party bank, at least one commentator cites the *Duvalier* case to support the proposition that such disclosure can be ordered against a third-party bank.

Originally, the Civil Jurisdiction and Judgments Act 1982 only allowed the English court to grant interim or protective relief in aid of substantive proceedings in a state which had ratified the Brussels Convention (a 'Brussels state') or in a state which had ratified the Lugano Convention (a 'Lugano state'). However, the Civil Jurisdiction and Judgments Act 1982 (Interim Relief) Order 1997[56] extended the English court's power so that it may now grant interim relief (including disclosure orders) in support of proceedings in foreign countries other than Brussels or Lugano states.

OBTAINING EVIDENCE IN ENGLAND FOR USE IN FOREIGN CRIMINAL PROCEEDINGS

The Criminal Justice (International Co-operation) Act 1990 makes provisions for the obtaining of evidence in England by foreign authorities for use in criminal proceedings. The 1990 Act was passed in part to enable the UK to ratify the European Convention on Mutual Assistance in Criminal Matters 1959.

Section 4 of the 1990 Act enables the Secretary of State, when requested to do so by a foreign criminal court, to nominate an English court to receive such of the evidence requested as appears to him to be appropriate. He must be satisfied that:

1   an offence under the relevant law has been committed, or there are reasonable grounds for suspecting that one has been committed; and

---

55   *Babanaft Intl Co SA v Bassatne* [1989] 1 All ER 433.
56   SI 1997/302.

2   proceedings in respect of that offence have been instituted there, or the offence is being investigated.

For the purpose of satisfying himself, the Secretary of State shall regard a certificate issued by the foreign court or appropriate authority to that effect as conclusive.

Additionally, where the offence concerned is a 'fiscal offence', the Secretary of State shall not make provision for the taking of evidence unless:

1   the request emanates from a Commonwealth country or is made under a treaty to which the UK is party; or
2   he is satisfied that the conduct constituting the offence would constitute a similar offence if it had been committed in the UK.

Section 4(5) provides that evidence includes documents and other articles as well as oral evidence of a witness. Assistance is potentially available to any foreign country, though in some circumstances it is more readily available to countries party to the Convention, and to Commonwealth countries.

The Convention provides that a state which receives a request can refuse to provide assistance in certain circumstances. Where an offence is, or is connected with, a political offence or where the request is likely to prejudice the sovereignty, security, public order or other essential interests of the country, then the request may be refused.

Additionally, the UK has reserved the right to refuse to assist, inter alia, in circumstances in which UK law recognises privilege, non-comparability or another exemption from giving evidence.

It is clear from the Convention that the Secretary of State retains an overriding discretion to refuse to provide assistance. It is likely that banking confidence would be taken into account, and any interference with it would only be permitted in exceptional circumstances unless, for example, one of the *Tournier* exceptions apply.

OBTAINING EVIDENCE ABROAD FOR USE IN ENGLISH CRIMINAL PROCEEDINGS

Section 3 of the 1990 Act provides that a judge or magistrate can issue a letter requesting assistance from another state to obtain evidence outside the UK where it appears that:

1   an offence has been committed or there are reasonable grounds to suspect that one has been committed; and
2   proceedings in respect of that offence have been instituted or the offence is being investigated.

The application can be made by a prosecuting authority (for example, the Attorney-General, the Director of Public Prosecutions, any Crown Prosecutor or the Director of the Serious Fraud Office) or by any defendant charged in the proceedings.

Additionally, a designated prosecuting authority can issue a letter of request without making an application to the court. In all such cases, bar those of urgency, the request must be screened by the Secretary of State.

Duty to the public to disclose

With regard to this final exception in *Tournier*, Bankes LJ said that many instances might be given where a bank is justified in disclosing its customers' affairs on the grounds that there is a duty to the public to do so. However he did not give any. Scrutton LJ said that a bank 'may disclose the customer's account and affairs ... to prevent frauds or crimes' and Atkin LJ considered that the right to disclose exists 'to the extent to which it is reasonably necessary ... to protect the bank, or persons interested, or the public, against fraud or crime'.

As mentioned above, since *Tournier* the passing of various statutes have imposed duties of disclosure. Thus the 'disclosure under compulsion of law' exception in *Tournier* now includes cases where a duty to the public to disclose has been recognised and imposed by statute. One has to assume that these statutory intrusions into the bank's obligation of confidence have taken place because banks have construed their duty to the public more narrowly.

However, this public duty exception is not yet completely moribund. The case of *Libyan Arab Foreign Bank v Bankers Trust Co*[57] concerned the US Presidential Order of 8 January 1986 freezing Libyan assets under the control, inter alia, of overseas branches of US banks. One of the claims made by the plaintiffs involved the scope of this exception. Staughton J said:

'But presuming (as I must) that New York law on this point is the same as English law, it seems to me that the Federal Reserve Board, as the central banking system in the United States, may have a public duty to perform in obtaining information from banks. I accept the argument that higher public duty is one of the exceptions to a banker's duty of confidence, and I am prepared to reach a tentative conclusion that the exception applied in this case.'

More recently, in *Price Waterhouse v BCCI Holdings (Luxembourg) SA*,[58] Millet J accepted in principle that the public interest exception could be relied on to justify the disclosure of confidential information to an inquiry set up to review the Bank of England's performance of its statutory functions.

However, in *Pharaon v BCCI*,[59] Rattee J held that whilst a greater public interest in making documents available in relation to proceedings relating to fraud overrode the public interest in upholding the duty of confidence, the disclosure should be limited to what was reasonably necessary to achieve the purpose of the public interest in disclosure.

REGULATION OF FINANCIAL MARKETS

Dealings in the financial and securities markets in the UK and their regulation also raise issues for banks (and others) in relation to confidentiality.

---

57   [1989] QB 728.
58   [1992] BCLC 583.
59   [1998] 4 All ER 455.

For many years, the City of London conducted a system of self-regulation which relied on an unwritten code of fair play between those operating in the financial markets. Under governmental pressure, the system expanded with the establishment of the City Panel on Takeovers and Mergers as the main supervisory body. However, in the 1980s there was a radical overhaul of the system, which is now supported by a considerable degree of statutory regulation. Some regulatory measures were contained in the Company Securities (Insider Dealing) Act 1985 (now to be found in the Criminal Justice Act 1993) and the Companies Act 1985. However, the principal statute, the Financial Services Act 1986, has now been effectively replaced by the Financial Services and Markets Act 2000 (FSMA) which set up the Financial Services Authority (FSA).

The functions of Self-Regulatory Organisations (such as IMRO, the PIA and the SFA) as well as the supervisory functions of other bodies, such as the Bank of England and the Building Societies Commission, have been transferred to the FSA. As a result the regulation of banking, securities, insurance and other financial services has been brought under one roof.

Information gathering by the FSA

FSMA requires the FSA to monitor firms (that is banks and the other types of financial services organisations which it regulates) to ensure that they comply with the requirements of FSMA. The FSA is also required to take certain steps to co-operate with other regulators (such as the Takeover Panel and Foreign Regulators) under which it can supply information to them. For these purposes the FSA needs to have access to a broad range of information.

It receives notifications and reports from firms themselves but it also has statutory powers to gather information itself, including the power to require the provision of information to it (FSMA, s 165). It also has certain investigatory powers (FSMA, ss 168 and 169). There are certain limitations on its powers, but it may require the disclosure of information subject to banking confidentiality to its investigators in certain circumstances (FSMA, s 175(5)). Failure to comply without reasonable excuse can lead to the defaulter being treated as if he were in contempt of court (FSMA, s 177).

The FSA will not itself disclose confidential information without lawful authority – for example, under an applicable exception in the Financial Services and Markets Act 2000 (Disclosure of Confidential Information) Regulations 2001[60] or with the consent of the person from whom that information was received and (if different) to whom the information relates (FSMA, s 348(1)).

However under FSMA, s 348(4), information is not confidential information if it has already been made available to the public in a way not precluded by that section or it is summarised so that information relating to a particular person cannot be ascertained.

60   SI 2001/2188.

In *Barings plc (in liquidation) v Coopers & Lybrand*,[61] the Court of Appeal took the view that transcripts of evidence given during an inquiry into the collapse of Barings were subject to similar restrictions on disclosure in s 82 of the Banking Act 1987 (the predecessor to FSMA, s 348(4)). This disapproved dicta in a previous case relating to the BCCI inquiry and reinforced the view that maintaining confidentiality encourages voluntary disclosure from banks which facilitates effective supervision. However, as the transcripts had been exhibited to affidavits sworn in the course of other proceedings, it was also held that they had been made available to the public and so could be disclosed.

If a firm enters into a material outsourcing arrangement it must ensure that its suppliers deal in a co-operative way with the FSA as far as access and the provision of information are concerned.

Insider dealing and market abuse

Insider dealing in corporate securities involves the utilisation of unpublished price sensitive information obtained through a privileged relationship to make a profit or avoid a loss by dealing in securities the price of which could be materially affected by public disclosure of that information.

Section 52 of the Criminal Justice Act 1993 (CJA) makes it a criminal offence for an individual who has information as an 'insider' to deal in securities to which the information relates. It is also an offence to encourage another person to deal in such securities, or to disclose the information other than in the course of the individual's profession or employment.

Information acquired by virtue of the insider's connection with his own company or by virtue of his employment gives rise to primary insider dealing.

Of more importance to banks is the prohibition on secondary insider dealing or 'tippee' trading. Sections 52 and 57(2)(b) deal with the situation where a person *obtains* inside information from an individual who is a director, shareholder etc of a company. If the 'tippee' then uses that information and deals on the Stock Exchange or investment exchange, he may be guilty of an offence (subject to certain defences). The information must be obtained directly from the person connected with the company or indirectly through any number of people forming a chain between the 'tippee' and the insider.

There has been a paucity of case law dealing with secondary insiders. The first case in which a prosecution was brought against a 'tippee' (under the earlier provisions of the 1985 Act) was *A-G's Reference (No 1 of 1988)*.[62] The Attorney-General referred the issue of the passive receipt of information to the Court of Appeal. In its view (subsequently upheld by the House of Lords) a recipient of price-sensitive information, who dealt in the relevant securities, had 'obtained' the information, whether he had procured it or came to it without any positive action on his part. This

---

61   [2000] 3 All ER 910.
62   [1989] 1 All ER 321.

would clearly catch a bank employee overhearing a conversation in the lift at work and, realising that what he was hearing was price sensitive, dealing in securities on the strength of it.

FSMA introduced a new market abuse regime which is set out in the FSA's Code of Market Conduct. Amongst other things it supplements the existing criminal offence of insider dealing, providing wider civil offences which will require a lower standard of proof and which are likely to result in more enforcement actions. Market abuse (as defined in FSMA, s 118) is behaviour which:

1   occurs in relation to a qualifying investment traded on a prescribed market;
2   involves the misuse of information and/or is likely to give a false or misleading impression and/or is likely to distort the market;
3   falls below the standard reasonably expected by the regular user of the market; and
4   does not fall within a safe harbour.

As well as this primary offence, there is a secondary offence of requiring or encouraging under FSMA, s 123. The FSA has power to impose penalties under FSMA as well as to enforce the CJA.

Chinese Walls

FSMA provides for two types of safe harbour from the offence of market abuse. The FSA can recognise in its Code of Market Conduct compliance with specific provisions of the City Code on Takeovers and Mergers (FSMA, s 122). It can also grant safe harbour status to certain of its own rules (FSMA, s 118(8)). That status has been given to its Conduct of Business (COB),r 2.4 on Chinese Walls, which applies to all firms (including banks) conducting designated investment business.

Establishing a Chinese Wall is one of the methods which can be used by a firm to manage a conflict of interest fairly. COB, r 2.4 sets out the circumstances when the FSA would consider it appropriate for a firm to withhold or not use information which it would otherwise have to disclose to or use for the benefit of a client. It is also the only information rule made so far under FSMA, s 147. COB, r 2.4.4 provides:

> '(1) when a firm establishes and maintains a Chinese Wall (that is an arrangement that requires information held by a person ... carrying on one part of its business, to be withheld from ... persons ... for whom it acts ... in another part of its business), it may:
> (a) withhold or not use the information held; and
> (b) ... permit persons employed in the first part of its business to withhold information ... from those employed in that other part ...'

but only to the extent that the business of one of them involves designated investment business or related activities.

Information may also be withheld or not used when required by an established arrangement maintained between different parts of the business in the same group. A Chinese Wall arrangement has to be monitored to ensure it is effective.

Whilst effective Chinese Walls are recognised by the FSA, there is no direct authority from an English court as to whether Chinese Walls within banks are effective to prevent conflicts of interest. However, there is a line of reported cases relating to conflicts of interest arising in firms of solicitors and accountants.

The courts are now applying the principles in *His Royal Highness Prince Jefri Bolkiah v KPMG*.[63] There the issue was whether accountants which had provided litigation support services to a former client, and possessed information confidential to him, could undertake work for another client with an adverse interest. The House of Lords held that the duty was not to disclose or misuse confidential information. For the court to intervene there must be a real risk of disclosure and not merely a theoretical or fanciful risk. If there was, it was up to the firm to show that even so there was no risk that the information would come into the possession of those acting for the second client. The court should restrain the firm from acting, unless it was satisfied that effective measures had been taken to ensure that no disclosure would occur. The court considered that an effective Chinese Wall needed to be an established part of the organisational structure of a firm and not created ad hoc.

These principles were considered in *Young v Robson Rhodes*[64] in the context of a proposed merger of two accountancy firms. Whilst a risk of disclosure was considered to be real, the court held that, in that case, ad hoc Chinese Wall arrangements would be sufficient. More recently, in *Koch Shipping Inc v Richards Butler*,[65] which involved a solicitors firm, the court again held that the proper test was whether there was a real risk of disclosure, and that in that case there was no such risk given that undertakings had been given by the relevant solicitor not to discuss the information with anyone. It was held that the court should take a 'robust view' in such cases and not be persuaded that there was a real risk, when it was no more than fanciful or theoretical.

Accordingly, whilst for many years the courts appeared reluctant to accept that Chinese Walls are effective, this appears now to be changing. Additionally, banks may be able to distinguish the management of conflicts within solicitors' firms (where client information is usually privileged as well as confidential) from arrangements within banks. Finally, a Chinese Wall which complies with the FSA COB Rules is arguably more effective than the ad hoc segregation of information within a firm of solicitors or accountants.

However, even so, there will be customers who will not be persuaded that Chinese Walls are completely effective in ensuring confidentiality. A substantial customer has the option of moving its business away from its bank. The consequences of a substantial customer removing its business may be a factor in a bank's decision whether it or a member of its group acts for that customer's competitor. However, that sanction would not be available to a past customer, nor perhaps to a less substantial customer, who would be left with having to seek redress in the courts to restrain an alleged misuse of confidential information by an injunction.

---

63 (1999) 2 WLR 215.
64 [1999] 3 All ER 524.
65 [2002] EWCA Civ 1280, [2002] All ER (D) 316 (Jul).

As an injunction is a discretionary equitable relief, the court, when considering an application for an interlocutory injunction founded upon an arguable claim, would apply a test as to where the balance of convenience lies: namely, which party would suffer more if an injunction were to be granted or refused. In addition, the court would have to be satisfied that monetary damages would not be an adequate remedy. A fundamental point would be whether the Chinese Walls erected by the bank were sufficiently effective to justify the refusal of an interlocutory injunction.

It is now open for a bank to argue that the regulatory framework that exists for banks in relation to Chinese Walls can be relied upon to prevent the informal flow of information within an organisation; accordingly, that it sets the standard of behaviour which customers are entitled to expect from their banks and which the courts should enforce as one of the accepted terms of the banker-customer relationship.

CONCLUSION

In England, banks face an increasingly difficult task in balancing and reconciling their various duties and obligations with regard to information on their customers and its confidentiality. Whilst customers may have greater expectations about the preservation of banking confidentiality (given the Banking Codes and such measures as the Data Protection Act 1998), banks find themselves facing a number of dilemmas, particularly given the statutory erosions to the duty of confidence. Ultimately, the public interest may well result in bank confidentiality being no longer the rule but the exception in England.

10   Finland

Lauri Peltola
Helena Mäkinen

INTRODUCTION

Bank confidentiality is one of the fundamental elements of the banking business in Finland; persons depositing funds as well as other customers of the banks operating in Finland must be able to rely thereon that information regarding their dealings with the bank or, indeed, themselves or their businesses will not be disclosed to third parties (except in circumstances as permitted by law and as explained below). Lack of trust in the maintenance of a high degree of confidentiality in the Finnish banking industry would certainly lead to, among other things, funds being directed into countries where confidentiality regulation would be more adequate. On the other hand, bank confidentiality cannot be absolute, and there are circumstances where the disclosure by a bank of confidential information is allowed and an unwilling bank may even be compelled by law to disclose such information. Somewhat paradoxically, in certain special circumstances the failure by the bank to disclose information may even constitute a criminal offence in itself.

Bank confidentiality, ie the bank's duty of non-disclosure of information, applies to all information that the bank has received in a customer relationship or otherwise in connection with carrying on the banking business and which information is not public knowledge. There are no set time limits for the extinction of the duty of non-disclosure and, thus, such duty does not end at the termination of a customer relationship, for example.

The scope of bank confidentiality was in certain respects considered in connection with the civil and criminal litigations, which were prompted by the very severe crisis of the Finnish banking industry in the first half of the 1990s. In the interests of maintaining bank confidentiality some of the proceedings were conducted either entirely or partly without admittance of the public to the courtroom, and certain evidence involving information subject to bank confidentiality was declared partly or wholly secret for a fixed period of time (under law, however, a maximum of 40 years). Such consequence of the bank confidentiality provisions is, naturally, as such, very much in conflict with the leading principle under the Finnish Procedural Code of court proceedings being open to the public, and it certainly has been sometimes difficult for the courts to find a fair balance to resolve the collision between these two principles in a satisfactory manner.

In court proceedings involving a bank, the bank may – and in many cases it should for the purposes of maintaining confidentiality – request that any material containing information subject to bank confidentiality presented to the court be declared secret. However, the Finnish courts have wide powers to consider and decide upon the matter independently.

The above shows the difficulties, which the banks are facing in dealing with bank confidentiality matters in a way which appropriately satisfies the sometimes very much conflicting interests of the various parties involved in the matter, including the society in general.

LEGAL FRAMEWORK

The principal statute governing matters regarding Finnish banking business is the Act on Credit Institutions of 1993 (the Credit Institutions Act). The Credit Institutions Act has been amended since 1993, latest as of 1 April 2003, whereby the EC E-money Directive[1] was implemented in Finland. The Credit Institutions Act includes specific provisions on the duty of non-disclosure which apply to credit institutions and financial holding companies, financial institutions and ancillary banking services undertakings belonging to the same consolidation group with the credit institution, agents of the credit institution and other companies representing the credit institution, as well as to collectives of credit institutions (including, for example, guarantee and investor protection funds and the Finnish Bankers' Association). All the above entities will be (on most occasions) referred to here, for the sake of simplicity, as the 'bank'. Furthermore, the term 'bank' used herein may also include, inter alia, Finnish investment firms and branch offices in Finland of foreign credit institutions or investment firms.

Prior to the Credit Institutions Act, the confidentiality obligations of the banks were regulated by various banking statutes dating from 1970. Prior to those statutes, bank confidentiality was considered as an essential principle of banking business established by custom. The scope of the confidentiality obligation in the Credit Institutions Act to a large extent corresponds to that of the former specific legislation and that established by practice.

Pursuant to the Act on Operations in Finland of a Foreign Credit and Financial Institution of 1993, the provisions on bank confidentiality included in the Credit Institutions Act also apply to branches and representative offices in Finland of foreign credit and financial institutions.

In addition to s 94 of the Credit Institutions Act, the focal provision concerning bank confidentiality, similar provisions on confidentiality obligation are included in, inter alia, the Securities Market Act of 1989, the Act on Book-Entry System of 1991, the Act on Collective Investment Schemes of 1999 as well as in the Act on Investment Firms of 1996, which implements in Finland the EC Investment Services Directive[2] and applies to the provision in or into Finland of investment services. In

---

1   Council Directive 2000/46/EC.
2   Council Directive 93/22/EEC.

addition, the Act on Supervision of Finance and Insurance Conglomerates of 2002, which sets forth requirements for the operations and supervision of finance and insurance conglomerates and the entities belonging to such conglomerates, such as credit institutions, investment firms and insurance companies, includes a similar rule of confidentiality.

Pursuant to the Act on Unfair Business Practices of 1978, which applies also to the banks, no person may unlawfully acquire or try to acquire information on a trade secret, nor may such trade secret be used or disclosed. Anyone employed by or carrying out a task for the entity must not use information on such trade secret for his own benefit or disclose such trade secret to gain benefit for himself or to the detriment of another person.

Further statutes that can be relevant when assessing the bank's confidentiality obligation include, inter alia, the Personal Data Act of 1999 and the Act on Preventing and Clearing Money Laundering of 1998 (the Money Laundering Act) which provides the banks with an obligation to identify their customers and report suspicious transactions. The Act on Publicity of the Operations of Public Authorities of 1999 contains exemptions from the authorities' general obligation to keep confidential documents that have been ordered as confidential or include information which is confidential under law. Moreover, several statutes include specific provisions providing authorities with a right to disclose confidential information to other authorities.

In addition to the above, the Finnish Bankers' Association has in 2001 issued the Instructions on Bank Confidentiality, which include the rules of interpretation of the bank confidentiality provisions, as understood by the Finnish banks.

DEFINITION AND EXTENT OF BANK CONFIDENTIALITY

According to s 94 of the Credit Institutions Act, an employee or an officer, including any member or a deputy member of any statutory body of a bank, such as a member of the supervisory board of the bank (ie a credit institution or a financial holding company, financial institution or ancillary banking services undertaking belonging to the same consolidation group with the credit institution, an agent of the credit institution or other company representing the credit institution or a collective of credit institutions) must not disclose information concerning the financial standing or private circumstances or the business or trade secret of a customer of the bank or of some other (non-customer) person related to the bank's activities. Such other (non-customer) person can be, for instance, a person who has been in negotiations with a bank and has delivered confidential information to the bank but no customer relationship was established. Bank confidentiality covers all information that the customer wishes to keep secret and that is not public knowledge or has not become publicly known. As a main rule, even information that a particular person is a customer of the bank is confidential. The duty of non-disclosure applies not only to an employee or officer of the bank, but also to any other person who is carrying out a service or an assignment for the bank, for instance, a person carrying out ADP, mailing or cleaning services for the bank. The duty of non-disclosure continues even after the employment/assignment has ended.

The Credit Institutions Act expressly provides that confidential information may not be disclosed at the general meeting of shareholders of the bank.

By law, a bank is under an obligation to disclose to the public information on its activities and financial standing. However, the information to be so disclosed by the bank must be compiled in the way that the disclosure of an individual person's confidential matters is excluded.

SANCTIONS AND REMEDIES

A breach by a person of the confidentiality obligation contained in the Credit Institutions Act (or, inter alia, that of the Act on Investment Firms or the Securities Market Act) is a criminal act. Sanctions include a fine and/or imprisonment for a maximum period of one year, unless the breach is of minor importance or unless more severe sanctions apply under other legislation. In addition, under the general principles of criminal law, profit made out of criminal activity may be confiscated.

Pursuant to the provisions of the Act on Compensation for Damage or Loss of 1974, a breach of the confidentiality provisions may lead to the obligation to compensate any damage or loss caused by the breach. The Securities Market Act, the Credit Institutions Act, the Act on Investment Firms and the Act on Supervision of Finance and Insurances Conglomerates include specific provisions on the liability to compensate for loss or damage in the case of a breach of the provisions in these acts, including the confidentiality provisions.

Under Finnish law, monetary damages are the general remedy available for a person who has suffered financial loss or damage as a consequence of another person's negligent action. In case of a breach of the confidentiality provisions, damages are often not a very adequate remedy, as the very disclosure of the confidential information in breach of the confidentiality obligations may in itself be the most damaging injury caused. The injured party may also find it difficult to quantify such damage in monetary terms. Exemplary or punitive damages are, however, not available under Finnish law. On the other hand, disclosure of confidential information may often take place without the advance knowledge of the person concerned so that no remedy other than damages can be applied.

However, should the person become aware of a danger of an unauthorised disclosure by a bank, he may file an application for an injunction by the District Court having jurisdiction in the matter. Such an injunction can be given initially as an interim measure without hearing the party against which the injunction is to be addressed, ie the bank. According to the Procedural Code, injunction proceedings are to be dealt with expeditiously by the court.

Furthermore, the Credit Institutions Act provides that if a credit institution does not in its activities comply with the provisions of the said act or the regulations given by virtue of it, including the confidentiality provisions, the Finnish Financial Supervision Authority (the FSA), the supervisory authority for the Finnish financial and banking markets, may order the credit institution to fulfil its obligations, non-compliance with such an order leading to a sanction in the form of a fine. The Act on Supervision of Finance and Insurance Conglomerates includes a similar provision.

If a bank in its operations fundamentally breaches any banking acts, decrees or regulations given by the authorities by virtue of such acts or decrees, including the non-disclosure obligations, the licence of the bank may be revoked by the Ministry of Finance upon the proposal of the FSA or the operations of the bank may be restricted for a certain period of time.

As regards the operations of foreign banks in Finland, the FSA (or in the case of a non-EEA bank, the Ministry of Finance) may order a branch or representative office of a foreign bank in Finland to discontinue its operations in Finland, if such branch or representative office is fundamentally or repeatedly in breach of Finnish banking legislation or regulations. Alternatively, the operations of the branch may be restricted for a certain period of time. Furthermore, if the branch has not complied with the relevant laws, regulations and byelaws, the branch may be dismissed from the membership of the Finnish Investor Protection Fund.

EXCEPTIONS TO THE CONFIDENTIALITY OBLIGATION

The interests of society require that there are circumstances where an absolute bank confidentiality must be overruled. Such circumstances are covered by various specific statutes by virtue of which confidential information can or must be released by the bank to various authorities and also to certain private entities, such as, for instance, credit reference agencies. The interpretation of such exemptions allowing the disclosure is, owing to the nature of such provisions, however, generally, restrictive.

This chapter deals with some of the most important exceptions to the confidentiality obligation.

Customer consent

The consent given by the customer (in this context and later in this chapter 'customer' also means any person other than a customer of the bank on whom confidential information is held by the bank) to the bank to make a disclosure, naturally, allows the bank to do so. Section 94 of the Credit Institutions Act contains an express reference to customer consent as a ground for legitimate disclosure of information by the bank.

The Credit Institutions Act does not specify the form of the customer consent required, ie whether the consent has to be express or whether an implied consent would be sufficient. Nevertheless, it would seem logical, as the non-disclosure of information is always presumed, that (except for, possibly, in certain rather special circumstances) only on the basis of an express consent by the customer, whether written or oral, the bank is allowed to disclose information regarding the customer. For the purposes of avoiding problems of proof, it is also certainly prudent for the bank to obtain the consent from the customer in writing. The agreement between the bank and the customer may contain provisions allowing the disclosure by the bank of otherwise confidential information without specific consent being obtained each time.

Obviously, the term 'consent by the customer' opens a variety of – often very difficult – further issues, such as whether, in the case of a joint account, consent by one account holder or both is required; whether a consent given not by the holder of the account but by someone authorised by the account holder to operate the account is acceptable; or, indeed, whether the bank may accept a 'consent' given by the customer in circumstances where the customer faces a prison sentence, or may have been exposed to some other type of mental duress of which the bank possibly was or should have been aware.

Some of these difficult situations may be covered by the contractual terms between the customer and the bank. In some cases the general principles of law or an established banking practice or the Instructions on Bank Confidentiality issued by the Finnish Bankers' Association may provide guidance. The bank may, however, find itself in a very uncomfortable position in certain cases where claims for the disclosure are made on the basis of customer consent, whereas some other party is insisting on the confidentiality being maintained basing his view on 'defects' in such a consent or the bank itself is aware of the existence of such 'defects'. Maintaining confidentiality in circumstances where disclosure should have been made can lead to claims for damages against the bank, whereas an unjustified disclosure can lead, in addition to damages, also to criminal sanctions.

An implied 'consent' for disclosure may be construed in circumstances where the customer himself has made an inquiry or complaint to the authorities on the bank's dealings with him. Such a request by the customer should allow the bank concerned to disclose to the authorities all information, which is relevant to address the issues raised by the customer.

Interests of the bank

For the purposes of customer services, marketing and risk management, a bank may disclose confidential information to a Finnish or foreign entity belonging to the same group, consolidation group or finance and insurance conglomerate, provided that such entity is subject to the above or similar confidentiality obligation. The disclosed information may, however, not include data which the Personal Data Act defines as sensitive or data based on registered information on payments between a customer and an entity not belonging to the same group, consolidation group or finance and insurance conglomerate.

The Personal Data Act contains strict rules regarding processing of sensitive data, such as information on race or ethnic origin, criminal act committed or punishment received, state of health, sexual orientation, social welfare needs or social welfare assistance received as well as political or religious affiliation or trade union membership. Sensitive data may be disclosed only by an express consent of the person concerned or on certain other grounds, as specified in the Personal Data Act.

Furthermore, a bank may disclose confidential information contained in its customer register, except for sensitive data, to a Finnish or foreign entity belonging to the same financial consortium with the bank, provided that such consortium is subject to the above or similar confidentiality obligation. The Credit Institutions Act does not include a definition of the 'entity belonging to the same financial consortium'.

The right of a bank to disclose information to such entity is to be determined on a case-by-case basis, taking into consideration such issues as mutual ownership, commercial interdependence and nature of co-operation between the entities in question. However, because the recipient of confidential information is required to be subject to the statutory confidentiality obligation, the disclosure of confidential information is in practice limited to, inter alia, credit institutions, investment firms, insurance companies and asset management companies for mutual funds, as well as to corresponding foreign entities subject to similar confidentiality obligations.

Interests of the banking system

A disclosure of certain confidential information is justified in the interests of securing the operation of the banking system. The Instructions on Bank Confidentiality issued by the Finnish Bankers' Association deal with some of such circumstances.

It is considered that, generally, when a credit card or debit card is presented for the purposes of making payment, the bank is allowed to disclose to the recipient of the payment whether there is sufficient balance/credit limit available to cover the payment, although the actual amount of the balance/credit limit must not be disclosed. Disclosure of the name and address of the holder of the account is allowed in case there is no sufficient balance/credit limit, provided that the bank has made sure that the receipt is duly signed. The same rights to obtain information are enjoyed by the drawee of a cheque. However, cheques are no longer used for domestic payments in Finland.

Similarly, in connection with electronic money transfers between the banks, certain information which is necessary for implementing the transfer may be exchanged. If a transfer has gone astray, certain information may be disclosed for tracing the funds and directing them to the correct recipient.

Credit reference agencies and personal data protection

Pursuant to the Credit Institutions Act, a credit institution may carry on credit reference services as part of its business. Credit information is primarily to be collected and recorded for the bank's own use.

However, the Credit Institutions Act expressly provides that a bank has the right to disclose certain information to external credit reference agencies. Such right has been deemed appropriate because lenders are, generally, responsible for controlling, as far as possible, the capability of the borrowers to service their loans. In this respect the possibility of lenders obtaining information for the evaluation of the creditworthiness of a potential customer is most helpful, if not often mandatory. In addition, third party interests (such as the interests of the guarantor of a loan) benefit from the possibility of obtaining credit reference information on the solvency of the borrower or on any previous defaults.

Although the operation of a credit reference agency is not subject to a licence, the dealing with information passed on to a credit reference agency is subject to restrictions as set out in the Personal Data Act.

The provisions of the Personal Data Act regulate, for instance, the extent of the registration and release of information contained in credit reference registers. The Personal Data Act applies only to information on private persons, including personal credit information, and thus, the registration and release of information on legal entities by credit reference registers is unregulated by law. As regards information on such legal entities, a bank has a certain discretion in deciding to which credit reference agencies information is released by the bank. With regard to credit information on private persons, in addition to the name and the contact information, information on defaults in payments or performances may be stored in a credit reference register, as specified in the Personal Data Act. In addition, information may be recorded in a credit reference register, inter alia, on the entries contained in the register of debt administration, on the placement of a person under guardianship and on the appointment of a trustee to administer the financial affairs of a person.

The Personal Data Act expressly provides that personal credit information may be disclosed only to a credit reference agency and to an entity which needs the information for purposes of granting credit or credit monitoring, or for another comparable purpose. Furthermore, the Personal Data Act includes special provisions, inter alia, on deletion of information from a credit reference register, notifying a registered person of the information recorded in the credit reference register, registered person's right of access to the information on him in the credit reference register and secrecy obligation. A breach of the provisions of the Personal Data Act may constitute a criminal act which is punishable by a fine and/or imprisonment, generally, for a maximum period of one year.

The authorities supervising the maintenance of appropriate data protection are entitled to obtain information from or inspect the records of the banks with respect to matters related to data protection, the registers and the use of such registers. As the Personal Data Act only applies to information on private persons, registers containing information on legal entities do not fall under the supervision of the data protection authorities.

Furthermore, under the provisions of the Act on Guarantees and Third Party Collateral of 1999, a lender (for example, a bank) must provide a private guarantor or third-party pledgor of collateral with information on debts and related costs falling within the scope of the guarantee or collateral in question, the conditions on the basis of which the guarantor's or pledgor's performance may be demanded, as well as with other information that essentially affects the position of the guarantor or pledgor. Private guarantors and pledgors must also be provided with information on the commitments and financial standing of the underlying borrower which information may be relevant to the guarantor or pledgor. Such information is considered to include, inter alia, details of income, property, employment and any defaults relating to other credits granted. A lender must also comply with certain continuing obligations to provide the guarantor and pledgor with certain information. Moreover, certain information must be provided upon request of the guarantor or pledgor.

Scientific research

Despite the duty of non-disclosure, a bank may disclose confidential information for the purposes of scientific research, provided that the disclosed documents are more than 60 years old. In addition, the recipient of confidential information must assure in writing that the information will not be used to hurt the persons or infringe the rights of the persons affected by such documents.

Legal proceedings

Legal proceedings involving the bank as a party

Despite the duty of non-disclosure, a bank may disclose to the court confidential information in connection with legal proceedings conducted by the customer against the bank or initiated by the bank against the customer (for instance, proceedings for collecting the moneys owed by the customer to the bank). However, the disclosure is only allowed to the extent necessary in respect of each particular case.

If the bank litigates against its customer, the employee or official of the bank may, without the consent of such customer, as a witness disclose confidential information relating to such customer. In addition, other information subject to bank confidentiality may be disclosed if it is necessary for solving the matter.

Legal proceedings involving third parties

In addition, a bank may be involved in legal proceedings, for example, where the customers of the bank or a third party and the customer of the bank are parties to such proceedings.

The Procedural Code provides that a witness, like an employee of the bank, has the right to refuse to disclose information to the court in connection with civil or criminal proceedings if such disclosure may lead to prosecution against the witness himself or persons close to him, as specified in the Procedural Code. The Procedural Code further provides that a witness has a right to refuse to disclose information related to a business or trade secret, unless 'fundamentally significant reasons' require such disclosure. In practice, such fundamentally significant reasons may be deemed to exist in cases where, for example, an innocent person would be convicted for a crime without disclosure of such information. Thus, it is unlikely that the witness's right to refuse to disclose a business or trade secret would be overridden in civil proceedings by application of such 'fundamentally significant reason' test.

The witness is, furthermore, entitled to disclose confidential information if the customer has consented thereto. Before giving the testimony, the witness must declare that he is under the bank confidentiality obligation.

Under the Procedural Code, if a witness refuses to make the disclosure as described above, he must give pertinent grounds for the refusal. This, however, may sometimes mean that when explaining the reasons for the refusal, the witness would then release confidential information.

If the court orders the witness to disclose confidential information, it may decide that the witness shall be heard behind closed doors. In case of a closed hearing, the court may declare that the trial documents which contain confidential information shall be kept secret for a fixed period of time.

The above applies also in cases where a confidential document is to be presented to the court or the employee or official of the bank is to be heard as an expert in a court proceeding.

Arbitration proceedings

Under the Act on Arbitration Proceedings of 1992, the arbitrators can hear the parties, witnesses and experts (however, without taking an oath) and receive documents that may have relevance as evidence in an arbitration proceeding. Nevertheless, the arbitrators are not vested with the power to impose conditional fines or use coercive measures in order to force the persons to testify or present evidence. The court of arbitration may, however, seek assistance from the ordinary courts. Where the parties, witnesses or experts are heard or evidence is presented before the ordinary courts in connection with arbitration proceedings, the above general rules that apply to the disclosure of confidential information in ordinary court proceedings also apply to the disclosure in arbitration proceedings.

Disclosure to authorities

Tax authorities

According to the provisions of the Act on Taxation Procedure of 1995, the Finnish tax authorities enjoy extensive rights to obtain, for the purposes of assessing the taxes, confidential information on payments or transfers made by a person, the identity of the recipient of such payments and transfers and the grounds for such payments and transfers. Specific disclosure provisions apply, inter alia, to securities intermediaries as to the trades made and the derivative contracts concluded, to credit and financial institutions as to loans granted and interest paid, and to collective investment funds as to units owned by a person or the units redeemed.

Furthermore, the obligation to disclose information applies, generally, to third parties, like the banks, as regards such information which may be relevant for the tax assessment or dealing with the tax appeal and which information can be identified on the basis of a name, bank account details, an identified banking transaction or other similar means of identification. This obligation is based on a specified request made by the tax authorities and covers all such information which is in the possession or otherwise known to a person, except for such information which the person is entitled under the provisions of the Procedural Code not to disclose.

In addition, a number of provisions in various specific tax statutes further specify the right of the tax authorities to obtain information. The scope of the information to be disclosed thus may depend on the particular tax statute which is applied to the individual case. However, information may only be disclosed to the extent necessary for the tax authorities to discharge their duties in connection with the taxation under the specific tax statute.

The tax authorities must make the request for the information in writing and the bank must not give any information orally. The request must be signed by such authority which is authorised to do so under the provisions of the relevant tax statute.

In certain circumstances the bank is obliged to refuse the disclosure of information to various authorities. This duty of refusal applies to the customer's business and trade secrets, unless special circumstances require the disclosure of such information. Such special circumstances could, for instance, involve reasonable suspicion of criminal conduct in relation to tax or bookkeeping matters in which the tax authority needs the information for the purposes of proof. Information on the financial standing of a customer must, nevertheless, always be given to tax authorities upon request.

The tax authorities can also, pursuant to specific provisions in various tax statutes, obtain information by using the right to inspect documents controlled or in the possession of the bank that may contain the information required. Such right to inspect documents can be the only means of obtaining information, and, thus, it is not necessary that the tax authorities request the disclosure of the information by the bank first. The tax authorities must, however, present their authorisation for the inspection of the documents as well as identify the object and extent of the inspection in each case.

Certain provisions in various tax statutes entitle the tax authorities to carry out an inspection of documents solely for the purpose of collecting information which is to be used for comparing a person or entity with other persons or entities in connection with taxation. However, such inspection for the purposes of comparison cannot be carried out in respect of information held by a licensed credit institution or a branch in Finland of a foreign credit institution. Nevertheless, if a tax inspection has been carried out on a credit institution or a branch of a credit institution, information received in connection therewith can be used in connection with the taxation of another person or entity.

The information to be disclosed by the bank must cover as long a period as the tax authority requests, provided that the bank still has the access to such information. As a rule, the bank has no right to refuse to disclose the information on the grounds, inter alia, that the time limit for the assessment of that particular taxation has lapsed.

Foreign tax authorities

A bank in Finland is not, generally, obliged to disclose any information to the authorities for the purposes of taxation in a country other than Finland. However, Finland is a party to a number of multilateral and bilateral tax conventions and treaties regarding mutual exchange of information and provision of assistance by the tax authorities of the convention/treaty countries.

Under a convention between the Nordic countries concluded in 1989, and effected in Finland in 1991, tax authorities in Nordic countries (ie Finland, Sweden, Denmark, Norway and Iceland) have agreed to assist each other in obtaining information. Such assistance to other Nordic tax authorities will be provided by the Finnish tax authorities in accordance with the provisions regulating the right by the Finnish tax authorities to obtain such information for domestic purposes. Further, in April 1995 Finland entered into a Convention on Mutual Administrative Assistance in Tax Matters between OECD and EC member states concluded in 1988. Currently, the member states to the OECD/EC Convention are, in addition to Finland, The Netherlands, Sweden, Denmark, Norway, Iceland, Poland, Belgium and the US. A request by the relevant authority of a member state shall always be delivered to the relevant Finnish authority and will then be addressed to the relevant bank by the Finnish authority.

Under the OECD/EC Convention, the member states agreed to provide exchange of information and administrative assistance to each other in tax matters. A member state must, upon request, provide another member state with information concerning a particular person or transaction. If the information available in the tax files of the requested state is not sufficient to enable it to comply with the request for information, that state must take all relevant measures to provide the applicant state with the information requested. However, the member state is not under an obligation to carry out such measures which would not be allowed under its own laws or administrative practice or such measures which it considers to be contrary to public policy or essential interests. Further, any trade, business, industrial, commercial or professional secrets need not be disclosed.

Furthermore, Finland has concluded a number of bilateral tax treaties which typically contain provisions on exchange of information and mutual assistance in tax matters. However, matters covered by bank secrecy may have been excluded in some bilateral treaties.

Police and other criminal investigation authorities

Under the provisions of the Credit Institutions Act, a bank is obligated to disclose confidential information to the public prosecutor, police authorities and other pre-trial investigation authorities, such as Finnish Customs and Finnish Border Guard Service, for the purposes of solving a crime.

The request by the police and other pre-trial investigation authorities to the bank must be in writing and signed by such person who under the law is authorised to do so. The request must be specified including the grounds for and the extent of the request.

If a person employed by the bank or otherwise subject to the bank confidentiality obligations is being questioned as a witness in pre-trial investigation, this person must declare that he is under the confidentiality obligation. Such witness has the right to refuse to give information on a business or trade secret of a customer, unless special circumstances otherwise require, and he must give pertinent grounds for the refusal.

According to the Police Act of 1995, the police authorities are entitled to obtain confidential information for the purposes of crime investigation and prevention. The request for information must also be in writing and signed by the police official who under the Police Act and Police Decree is authorised to do so. Such request must include the same information as described above.

The Police Act also provides that the police authorities are entitled to obtain confidential information in connection with a non-criminal investigation carried out by the police (for instance, locating a missing person) if an important public or private interest so requires. Again, the request must fulfil the same requirements as described above.

In addition, the prosecuting, police, customs and border guard authorities have the right to receive information on the book-entry accounts from the Finnish Central

Securities Depository Plc. In cases where the information requested is not available, the Finnish Central Securities Depository Plc directs the request to the relevant bank.

In connection with a criminal investigation, funds and assets of a suspect person may be seized for the purposes of, inter alia, securing the payment of damages and the collection of profits of the criminal act which are to be confiscated. Additionally, documents may be seized to prevent such documents being lost or destroyed.

Mutual assistance in criminal matters

Finland has ratified the European Convention on Mutual Assistance in Criminal Matters of 1959, subject, however, to a number of reservations which may exclude assistance in circumstances where the subject crime is under investigation in Finland or in a third country, or the person who is prosecuted in the country requesting assistance has been sentenced or currently is being prosecuted in Finland or in a third country, or prosecution or investigation against the person has been dropped or suspended in Finland or in a third country, or the prosecution of the crime or the enforcement of the sentence would be time-barred under Finnish law. Further, assistance is excluded in cases referred to in art 11 of the Convention.

In addition, the Act on International Assistance in Criminal Matters of 1994 deals with assistance to be provided, generally, by Finnish authorities in criminal matters. Pursuant to the Act, Finland may provide assistance to foreign authorities for various purposes, like hearing of witnesses, production of documents or securing the enforcement of confiscation orders. The relevant authority to deal with requests for assistance is the Ministry of Justice to whom any requests should be addressed by the relevant foreign authority.

A properly compiled and presented request should lead to the assistance being provided, in accordance with and subject to the restrictions of Finnish law, 'without delay', as stated in the Act.

However, assistance must be refused if the assistance would breach the sovereignty or would endanger the security of Finland or her essential interests. The assistance must also be refused if such assistance would be contrary to the principles of human or civil rights or the principles of Finnish law. Further, assistance may be refused, inter alia, if the underlying criminal act is a political or military offence, if pursuant to provisions of Finnish criminal law no prosecution could be mounted because of time-bar or other similar circumstances, or if the matter is pending before the pre-trial investigators, prosecutor or a court in Finland or in a third country, or if the costs for the assistance in relation to the offence concerned would be unreasonable.

When hearing a witness for the purposes of providing assistance to authorities in a foreign country, the witness shall enjoy the rights to refuse to disclose the information as enjoyed under Finnish law or under the laws of the country requesting assistance. Furthermore, despite the duty of non-disclosure provided by Finnish law, confidential documents may be transferred for the purposes of proof in foreign criminal proceedings, unless Finnish law prohibits or restricts the use of confidential information or document as proof or the transfer of confidential information or document to a foreign country.

Supervisory and regulatory authorities

The supervisory and regulatory authorities of the banking industry enjoy very wide powers to receive from a bank (which definition in this chapter has a very wide definition indeed) information that is necessary for the authority to discharge its supervisory duties. According to the Act on Financial Supervision Authority of 1993, the FSA is thus entitled to obtain from banks all information as well as to inspect any documents concerning the relevant bank and its customers, including data processing systems, held by banks which it deems necessary for the fulfilment of its supervision duties.

Further, the FSA is entitled to obtain information from any entity which is controlled by the bank, including a foreign branch or subsidiary (ie branch located outside Finland) of a Finnish bank under its supervision, or any entity which controls the Finnish bank. Such an authority can, naturally, lead to a conflict situation if, under the local laws, such foreign branch of a Finnish bank would not be in a position to disclose the information requested by the FSA.

Notwithstanding the confidentiality obligation referred to in the Act on Publicity of the Operations of Public Authorities, the FSA is entitled to disclose information on the financial standing or business or trade secrets of a person or entity or on private circumstances of a person to another supervisory authority of the financial markets, or to an institution which in its home country, by virtue of law, performs a duty similar to that of the FSA. Furthermore, the FSA may disclose information to, inter alia, pre-trial and prosecuting authorities for the purposes of solving a crime as well as to other authorities, as specified in the Act on Financial Supervision Authority.

A bank must also disclose to the Bank of Finland, upon request, all information and documents which are necessary for the carrying out by the Bank of Finland of its responsibilities as central bank or for statistical purposes.

Foreign supervisory bodies

The Act on Operations in Finland of a Foreign Credit and Financial Institution provides that, despite the duty of non-disclosure set forth in the Credit Institutions Act, a branch or a representative office in Finland of a foreign credit or financial institution has the right to disclose to the supervisory or other authorities or auditors of the credit or financial institution of the relevant home country such information which in accordance with the home country statute or pursuant to an appropriate home country order is to be disclosed.

Under the Act on Financial Supervision Authority, a supervisory authority of a country within the EEA is entitled to carry out (or have a third party carry out on its behalf) an inspection in a branch in Finland of a credit or financial institution of that EEA country, subject to a prior notification to the FSA. Upon request by a supervisory authority of an EEA country, the FSA may within its competence carry out an inspection in a branch in Finland of a credit or financial institution from such EEA country or verify otherwise information regarding such branch.

Execution/enforcement officials

Under the Execution/Enforcement Act, the execution/enforcement officials (bailiffs) have the right to obtain information on the debtor from a third party, including the banks, in areas such as whether:

1   the third party possesses property belonging to the debtor and the nature of such property;
2   the third party has a receivable from the debtor and the grounds thereof and the amount of such receivable; and
3   the third party has made an agreement or arrangement with the debtor that is significant in relation to the execution/enforcement procedure and the terms of such an agreement or arrangement.

The execution/enforcement officials may, if necessary, oblige the third party to disclose such information subject to a fine in case of non-compliance.

The execution/enforcement officials' right to obtain information corresponds to that enjoyed by the police and tax authorities. The execution/enforcement officials are also entitled to receive information from other authorities on, inter alia, the financial standing of the debtor. Furthermore, the execution/enforcement officials are entitled to obtain information on the book-entry accounts from the Finnish Central Securities Depository Plc. In cases where the information requested is not available, the Finnish Central Securities Depository Plc directs the request to the relevant bank.

In connection with the enactment of the Act on Publicity of the Operations of Public Authorities in 1999, the Execution Act of 1895 was also amended to include a provision which provides the execution/enforcement officials with the right to disclose confidential information in certain cases. Inter alia, confidential information may be disclosed to other execution/enforcement authorities and, in case there is any reason to suspect that the debtor may have committed a crime, also to prosecuting and pre-trial authorities.

Other authorities

Various specific statutes in Finnish law entitle certain other authorities to obtain confidential information from the banks. For instance, in connection with the supervision of bankrupt estates, the supervisory authority for bankruptcies has rights similar to those of the debtor of the bankrupt estate to receive information with respect to such bankrupt estate.

Consumer protection authorities have under provisions of the Consumer Protection Act of 1978 a right to obtain certain information from the banks. Further, competition authorities and, for instance, social security authorities have certain rights to obtain information as well.

Money laundering

In January 1998, provisions on money laundering, previously scattered over a number of separate statutes, were consolidated in the Money Laundering Act.

The objective of the Money Laundering Act is to enhance the prevention of money laundering by synchronising the mechanism for reporting suspicious transactions and by concentrating the investigation of all suspected money laundering cases to a single authority, a special unit of the Central Criminal Police titled the Money Laundering Clearing House (the Clearing House). In addition to banks, a large number of entities are under the obligation to report suspected money laundering. The Money Laundering Act includes provisions on, inter alia, customer identification, duty to keep records, detection and reporting of unusual or suspicious business transactions, due diligence to be observed and procedures to be applied to protect the financial system against criminal abuse.

The Money Laundering Act provides that a bank must always verify the identity of its regular clients. The expression 'regular client' refers to a client with a long-term business relationship (for example, opening an account or entering into a loan agreement). The identity of an individual (not regular) client must be verified if the total value of a single transaction or several connected transactions exceeds the equivalent of €15,000. However, the identity of a customer, whether regular or not, must always be verified if there is any reason to suspect the lawful origin of the funds or other property in the transaction. Further provisions concerning customer identification are included, inter alia, in the Credit Institutions Act and the Money Laundering Regulation issued by the Ministry of the Interior. The FSA has in 1998 issued a statement on non-face-to-face identification, which contains principles for the identification by the bank of remote customers, for example, when providing banking services via the Internet. The Credit Institutions Act provides that the banks must be familiar with the nature of their clients' business operations and the reasons for the clients' need for services provided by the banks. Similar duty to exercise due diligence is laid down in the Money Laundering Act.

As regards exemptions from the identification obligation, customer identification is not necessary if payment is made from the customer's account in a bank licensed in a member state of the EEA or in a branch office located within the EEA of a bank not licensed in a member state of the EEA. If it is likely that a customer is acting on behalf of another person (a principal), for example, on the basis of authorisation, the identity of the principal should also be verified by applying all available means to do so. However, there is no need to verify the identity if the customer is a credit or financial institution, an investment firm or a life insurance company licensed in a member state of the EEA or a branch office located within the EEA of a credit or financial institution, an investment firm or a life insurance company not licensed in a member state of the EEA.

Banks must keep records of customer identification data in a reliable manner for a period of at least five years after the termination of each business transaction or business relationship.

Under the Money Laundering Act, negligence in customer identification or record keeping constitutes a criminal offence and is sanctioned with criminal liability of a fine or imprisonment for up to six months.

On the other hand, in case of unfounded reporting to the Clearing House, suspension of a business transaction or refusal to effect a business transaction, a bank may become liable to compensate for the possible financial loss incurred by the customer. Liability for the loss does not arise if the bank or its employee has exercised reasonable diligence before taking the measures in question.

Under the Penal Code, money laundering covers, inter alia, the deliberate concealment by a third party, like a bank, of the origin of assets that have been obtained through criminal activities, and thus constitutes a criminal offence. The maximum penalty for such offence constitutes imprisonment for up to six years or if the act is minor, the penalty may comprise a fine. Where the offence has been committed by a person acting as the legal representative or member of the management of a legal entity, corporate fines may apply.

As a result of the ratification of the International Convention for the Suppression of the Financing of Terrorism in June 2002, the banks' obligation to report suspicious transactions to the authorities was extended to include possible financing of terrorism. Pursuant to the new provisions in the Penal Code, financing of terrorism is a criminal offence. The maximum penalty for such an offence constitutes imprisonment for up to eight years.

The Money Laundering Act and the Penal Code were amended as of 1 April 2003. Pursuant to such amendments, money laundering is now a separate category of financial crime under the Penal Code. Also a new offence of negligent money laundering was introduced. The financial crimes legislation is expected to undergo further reform in the course of 2003 as, *inter alia*, the category of persons subject to the diligence and reporting obligations will be extended to cover accountants, auditors and legal practitioners.

Mutual assistance in civil matters

Finland has ratified a number of multilateral conventions to the effect of facilitating legal proceedings of international character, including the Hague Convention on the Taking of Evidence Abroad in Civil and Commercial Matters of 1970. However, when incorporated in Finnish law, the application of the pre-trial discovery of documents procedure as set out in art 23 of the Convention was excluded, to the extent that such procedure would obligate someone to identify the documents in his possession which are relevant to the subject matter or to deliver documents other than those expressly named in the request which documents can be assumed, with reason, to be in his possession.

The authority in Finland which deals with requests by foreign authorities under the Convention is the Ministry of Justice. The Convention contains, in art 12, the grounds on which a formally appropriate request for assistance may be refused. There are only two grounds for such refusal, ie the measure for which assistance is requested is beyond the powers of the authority in Finland and Finland considers that the requested measure would be a breach against her sovereignty or security.

Similarly, Finland has also ratified, inter alia, the Hague Conventions of 1954 and 1965, although the earlier Conventions have been largely replaced by the Convention of 1970.

A convention between the Nordic countries which covers, inter alia, assistance in obtaining testimony or other evidence was entered into in 1974 and became law in Finland in 1975.

An Act on the Co-operation between Finnish and Foreign Authorities in Court Proceedings and Enforcement of Judgments in Certain Cases was enacted in 1921.

Enforcement of foreign judgments and arbitral awards

As a rule, a foreign judgment is not enforceable in Finland unless a specific EU regulation or a bi- or multilateral treaty or convention otherwise provides.

Enforcement in Finland of a foreign judgment or an arbitral award may also involve a bank confidentiality dimension if, for example, a customer of a Finnish bank obtains a court judgment or arbitral award outside Finland which orders the bank to release a document to the customer.

In case of a judgment given by a foreign court in an EU or EEA state, such judgment may be enforceable under the provisions and subject to the restrictions of the Lugano Convention, the Brussels Convention or the EC Regulation on jurisdiction and the recognition and enforcement of judgments in civil and commercial matters.[3] Further, the provisions of the Convention between the Nordic Countries on the Recognition and Enforcement of Judgments in Civil Matters and the bilateral Convention between Finland and Austria on the Recognition and Enforcement of Judgements in Civil Matters may be relied on in relation to matters to which the above Council Regulation does not apply. The EC Regulation on cooperation between the courts of the Member States in the taking of evidence in civil or commercial matters,[4] which has been in force since 1 July 2001, will become fully applicable on 1 January 2004.

Foreign arbitral awards are recognised and enforceable in Finland under the provisions of the Act on Arbitration Proceedings and the New York Convention of 1958.

FINANCIAL MARKETS

Inside information

The Securities Market Act contains a prohibition on misuse of inside information. Furthermore, provisions on misuse of inside information are contained in the Penal Code, which was amended in 1999 to include provisions on securities market crimes. The Penal Code defines inside information as information relating to publicly traded securities (whether listed on the Helsinki Stock Exchange or other public market place) or standardised options and futures that has not been published or that otherwise is not publicly available and that may materially affect the price or value of the securities or standardised options or futures in question.

3   Council Regulation 44/2001/EC.
4   Council Regulation 1206/2001/EC.

The Penal Code defines the misuse of inside information as use of inside information by dealing in securities or by providing advice, whether direct or indirect, in order to achieve financial benefit for oneself or for another person. Misuse of inside information through wilful misconduct or gross negligence constitutes a criminal offence that may be sanctioned with a fine and/or imprisonment for a maximum period of two years or, in case of a gross misuse, four years. In addition, an attempt to misuse inside information constitutes a criminal offence.

The provisions on misuse of inside information apply to all persons, irrespective of their position or the manner in which they have received inside information. In the case of an offence committed by a legal entity, such as a bank, criminal sanctions may be imposed on the physical persons that have acted on behalf on the legal entity. In addition, corporate fines may be imposed on the legal entity. Further, both legal entities and physical persons may incur civil liability for any loss or damage caused, and any profit made may, under the general principles of criminal law, be confiscated.

Conflict of interests/Chinese Walls/separate businesses

A bank operating in Finland may often find itself in a difficult and, indeed, delicate situation as confidential information is continuously obtained by the various departments/subsidiaries of the bank. For example, a department/subsidiary of the bank may be advising on a contemplated merger of a company whilst another department/subsidiary of the bank is simultaneously providing broker/dealer services on the securities issued by the company, or perhaps asset management services involving shares in the company or, indeed, the bank may be doing proprietary trades in the shares. Considering the relatively small number of commercial banks and investment banks operating in Finland (although, especially, London and New York-based commercial banks and investment banks are also often engaged in mergers and acquisitions and capital market transactions involving Finnish companies) situations with a potential conflict aspect are not rare for the banks.

Questions relating to the segregation of securities business functions, ie the so-called Chinese Wall, have not been expressly regulated in Finnish law. However, guidance may be sought in the conduct of business rules which a securities intermediary (which definition for the purposes of this chapter is equivalent to the definition of the bank used herein) must observe as well as in the Guideline on Segregation of Securities Business Functions, issued by the FSA in 1998.

According to the conduct of business rules included in the Securities Market Act, a securities intermediary is under an obligation to execute the orders diligently, in the interests of the customer and without undue delay. Furthermore, a securities intermediary must aim at avoiding conflicts of interest and, in case they occur, treat its customers fairly and equally. The own interests of the securities intermediary or the interests of a customer or an issuer must not affect the advice given by the securities intermediary to another customer or the way of effecting the order.

Accordingly, a potential conflict situation may arise not only between the bank and the customer but also between the customers of the bank.

The Guideline on Segregation of Securities Business Functions is applicable to credit institutions and investment firms licensed in Finland or having a branch in Finland. According to the Guideline, due segregation of functions presupposes measures to be taken to limit the transmission of information relating to financial instruments and customers within the firm or the group. The purpose of arranging business functions in a segregated manner is, according to the Guideline, to allow the firm to engage in several business activities without giving rise to conflicts of interest between the firm and its customers or between the customers. Further, the segregation of functions serves to prevent misuse of inside information.

The Guideline provides that firms shall obtain a confidentiality undertaking to be signed by all individuals with access to confidential information, and that those undertakings be renewed at appropriate intervals. In conjunction with renewals of such confidentiality undertakings, the personnel shall be appraised of the applicable statutes and legal sanctions concerning breaches of secrecy. Furthermore, access to parts of internal computer networks should be limited so that only individuals handling securities functions on behalf of customers have access to the relevant customer files.

The Guideline requires that at least the following functions be segregated:

1   any activities dealing with inside information, such as investment banking and financial advice services;
2   asset management functions;
3   proprietary trading on the bank's own account (including market making);
4   intermediary trading on behalf of customers; and
5   safe custody and the maintenance of a book-entry register.

The solution applied by the Finnish banks to deal with the above requirements has been, primarily, separation (on physical, organisational and personnel level) of those operations where the cross-distribution/access of confidential information obtained by the bank could endanger a customer's interests in relation to the bank or to another customer of the bank or could expose the bank to allegations of insider dealing, ie a Chinese Wall arrangement. Such measures may have meant, in practice, restricted access by the members of the staff to premises or to IT systems of the bank other than those required for their duties, clear definitions of the areas of responsibility for the managers and directors of the bank and also, generally, advising, training and supervising the staff in the relevant matters.

Some banks have transferred their investment banking, securities intermediation, asset management and proprietary trading operations into separate subsidiary companies with their own personnel, which companies may also operate from premises entirely separate from the banking premises. In certain cases, the potential problem may be avoidable by a disclosure to the customer of the existence of the potential conflict. By obtaining the customer's consent the bank can conduct the business as disclosed.

FURTHER REGULATIONS

Data protection

The processing of files comprising personal data is regulated by the Personal Data Act, which implements the EC Data Protection Directive[5] in Finland. The scope of application of the Personal Data Act is limited to the processing of personal data in cases where the 'controller' of files is established in Finland or otherwise is subject to Finnish law. A controller is defined as a person or body for the use of whom a personal data file is set up and that is entitled to determine on the use of the said file.

Under the Personal Data Act, personal data is defined to mean any personal information or any information on personal characteristics or personal circumstances, based on which an individual person (the data subject) or the members of the family or the household of the data subject can be identified. The processing of personal data is defined as, inter alia, collection, recording, storage, use, combination and transfer of personal data.

The personal data to be collected and recorded must be limited to such data that is relevant for the operations of the collector (the *connection requirement*) and necessary for the purpose of the file in question (the *necessity requirement*). In the absence of the explicit consent of the data subject, under the connection requirement, personal data may be collected and recorded only provided that a relevant connection based on a customer-, service-, membership- or other similar relationship exists between the data subject and the operations of the collector. Strict rules apply to the processing of personal identity numbers and sensitive personal data.

The personal data may be disclosed if the data subject unambiguously has consented to the same. In the absence of the explicit consent of the data subject, under the above connection requirement, personal data may be disclosed only if such disclosure is a regular feature of the operations concerned and if the purpose for which the data is disclosed is not incompatible with the purposes of the processing and if it can be assumed that the data subject is aware of such disclosure. Furthermore, personal data may be transferred to a country outside the EU or EEA only in specific cases, inter alia, if the data subject has unambiguously consented to the transfer of his personal data or if the country in question guarantees an adequate level of data protection, as from time to time resolved by the European Commission.

According to the Personal Data Act, furthermore, a controller is under an obligation to compile a description of the personal data file indicating, inter alia, the controller's contact information, the purpose of the processing of the personal data, a description of the group of persons the data of which shall be recorded, including a description of the information to be collected, the regular destinations of disclosed data and whether data are transferred to countries outside the EU or the EEA and a description of the principles in accordance to which the data file has been secured. As a general rule, the above description must be submitted to the Finnish Data Protection Ombudsman and, also be kept publicly available.

5   Council Directive 95/46/EC.

Reform of the legislation on Finnish Financial Supervision

Proposals for the new Act on the FSA and the amendments to the related legislation have been presented to Parliament and are expected to enter into force in June 2003. To increase the efficiency of supervision on the Finnish financial markets, the new Act would, inter alia, widen the scope of the FSA's supervisory functions. Under the proposed legislation, the FSA's supervisory authority would be extended to cover some of the authority currently exercised by the Ministry of Finance, such as the granting and withdrawal of the licences for credit institutions and investment firms. However, the current provisions regarding the FSA's right to inspect and the right to obtain and disclose information, including confidential information, would remain largely unchanged.

11   France

Jean-François Adelle

THE NATURE AND EXTENT OF THE BANKER'S DUTY OF CONFIDENTIALITY

Source

The banker's duty of confidentiality has already undergone a long evolution, starting as early as 1810 with art 378 of the Penal Code, which imposed sanctions upon persons such as physicians or all other persons in possession, by virtue of their ... profession of secrets confided to them and who revealed such these secrets.

For more than a century, even if a tendency grew in favour of the application of the duty of confidentiality, it remained doubtful whether this provision could apply to bankers. In 1922, it was considered that this provision applied to stockbrokers. A step forward was then made in 1973 by the law on the Banque de France, which specified that the agents and employees of the Banque de France were bound by a duty of confidentiality and that the sanctions of art 378 of the Penal Code would apply in the event of breach of such duty.

In 1984, when the entire organisation of banks in France was revised, it was made clear that art 378 applied to 'any member of a board of directors, and, if any, of a supervisory board and any person who in whatever capacity takes a part in the management or in the operation of a bank or is employed by a bank' (art 511-33 of the Monetary and Financial Code). It should be noted that, in 1994, art 378 of the Penal Code was replaced by art 226-13 of the New Penal Code, but the new wording of this article does not entail any modification of the definition of the offence. However, the applicable penalties have been increased.

The duty of confidentiality is justified by the protection of private life and patrimonial interests of clients and also by the protection of the financial markets and security of transactions because the disclosure of confidential information may bring about insider dealings and affect the trust of investors in the market.

Therefore, the duty of confidentiality regulates both the disclosure of confidential information and the abuse of confidential information.

The banker's duty of confidentiality has been limited by a number of exemptions defined by case law or statute.

271

In particular, it is limited by powers of supervising authorities and, since 1990, the legislation on the fight against money laundering.

It should be noted that the Law of 2 July 1996, which implemented the EC Directive on investment services,[1] requires credit establishments and investment enterprises to provide for obligations regarding the circulation of confidential information in internal regulations. However, the notion of confidential information referred to in the said Law is not the same as the notion of duty of confidentiality which applies exclusively to banks.

The scope of the duty of confidentiality

With respect to the information

The duty of confidentiality applies to non-public information confided to the bank by its client or a third party or which the bank has knowledge of in the course of its professional activity.

However, it does not apply to any and all information which banks may receive.

Although the law does not distinguish, it appears that only information relating to bank operations is subject to the duty of confidentiality. The following operations are considered as bank operations: the reception of funds, the granting of loans and the management of means of payment.

It is, however, unclear whether information relating to ancillary operations (exchange, custody or distribution of securities, assistance and advice in portfolio management, financial engineering) are covered by the banker's duty of confidentiality.

Criminal courts tend to consider the said information to be subject to the bank's duty of confidentiality.[2] The commercial judge considered information disclosed with respect to a company to a potential purchaser as not being of a banking nature.

Furthermore, according to French law, the duty of confidentiality of banks only covers specific information with respect to the amount shown by an account or transactions carried out by the client or the client's financial statements, as opposed to general information relating to the client's solvency (for example, regular payments, protests, non-compliance with maturity dates, cheques returned unpaid etc). In accordance with a bank usage, banks may therefore provide general information to clients or other banks asking for 'references' with respect to the financial situation of a company with which one is intending to do business. But they have no obligation to respond.

However, the bank could be held liable if it does not communicate information in accordance with the reservation, objectivity and the rules in usage in the profession (in particular, the banker would be liable if he negligently communicated inaccurate information).

1   Council Directive 93/22/EEC.
2   Cass Crim, 25 January 1977.

The communication of a list of clients with their names, addresses and account numbers could be seen as a breach of the duty of confidentiality.[3]

With respect to the persons subject to the confidentiality obligation

The confidentiality obligation applies to members of the board or supervisory board of a financial institution or to any person involved in any respect in the direction or management of a financial institution or employed by such a person.

With respect to the persons entitled to confidential information

The banker's duty of confidentiality aims at protecting the client against disclosure of confidential information. Therefore, the client is admitted to share confidential information. He is entitled to receive all information regarding transactions carried out with the bank. However, as regards cheques, banks may refuse to disclose the back of the cheque which contains information on the presenting bank and the account number of the payee.

Neither the members of the client's family (including a spouse) nor his creditors have access to such information.

However, by way of an exception to the above-mentioned rule, a few other persons are allowed to share the confidential information confided by a client to his banker, ie:

1 When the client is an individual:
    (a) the heirs of such individual;
    (b) the legal guardian; and
    (c) the co-holders of a joint bank account.
2 When the client is a legal entity:
    (a) its legal representative;
    (b) the members of the board of directors or of the managing board and the supervisory board. However, it is generally considered that they should act jointly. Nevertheless some authors deny them any right to share confidential information because they do not represent the company;
    (c) the statutory auditors; and
    (d) shareholders having unlimited liability for the corporate debts. Such shareholders are entitled to receive information on the corporate financial situation. Shareholders with limited liability have no right to share confidential information.

The company administrator will have the same rights as the legal representative if the court decision appointing him entrusts him with management powers. During the observation phase of bankruptcy proceedings, the receiver in bankruptcy (*administrateur judiciaire*) does not represent the company. But if the bankruptcy court orders the liquidation, the liquidator represents the company.

---

3 Rennes, 13 January 1992.

Moreover, there is no breach of the duty of confidentiality when the information is disclosed to a person who is bound by a duty of confidentiality such as another banker (ie according to art L 513-33 of the Monetary and Financial Code any officer of the board of directors, of the managing board and the supervisory board and any other person who by reason of his office participates in the administration or management of the bank or is employed by it) or an employee of a supervisory authority such as the Banque de France.[4]

On the other hand, when the information is disclosed to a person outside the bank, there is breach of the duty of confidentiality.

Criminal sanctions

Article 226-13 of the New Penal Code now sets out the sanctions applicable to the breach of the duty of confidentiality formerly provided for by art 378 of the Penal Code.

Accordingly, the breach by a bank of its duty of confidentiality is a criminal offence and may be punished by a one-year imprisonment and by a fine of up to €15,000.

There are very few examples of criminal proceedings having been initiated against bankers.

Remedies

Should the breach of the duty of confidentiality cause the claimant to suffer a loss, the latter may claim damages. The general rules of tortious liability provided for at art 1382 of the Civil Code would apply. Accordingly, the claimant would have to establish that there has been a fault, a damage and a causal link between the fault and the damage.

EXCEPTIONS TO THE BANKER'S DUTY OF CONFIDENTIALITY

The exceptions to the banker's duty of confidentiality are several and of various kinds.

The client's consent

While criminal courts still seem to refuse to admit that a professional may be released from his duty of confidentiality by his client, civil courts have adopted diverging views on this issue and held that the banker's duty of confidentiality was only aimed at the client's protection and that, accordingly, the client could waive such protection.

Most often the issue arises in connection with actions brought by a court-appointed receiver of a bankrupt company before the President of a Commercial Court on the basis of art 145 of the New Code of Civil Procedure – which allows measures to be

---

4   Thus, a bank who reports bad cheques to Banque de France in compliance with art L 333-4 of the Consumer Code does not breach its duty of confidentiality.

ordered to obtain various documents from third parties prior to any trial – to obtain from banks the disclosure of documents relating to the granting of loans to the debtor (for instance, balance sheet analysis and the minutes of the credit board meetings), in order to establish that the bank unduly and irregularly sustained its ailing client.

Until a Commercial Chamber of the Supreme Court (Cour de Cassation) 1995 precedent, disclosure could be ordered in favour of the court-appointed creditors' representative.[5] However, that solution was reversed by a 2002 decision of the Plenary Chamber of the Commercial Court, which held that the notion of the client consenting to the disclosure must be construed strictly in the context of a bankuptcy proceeding and does not benefit the sale plan commissionner (commissaire à l'exécution du plan) who represents the general interest of creditors.[6] As a result, banks are released of their duty of confidentiality only vis-à-vis the administrator (administrateur judiciaire) and the liquidator (liquidateur judiciaire) who represent the bankrupt debtor.

Compulsion of law

Criminal and civil proceedings

A banker may not invoke his duty of confidentiality when requested to provide evidence before a criminal court, including requests made by investigating magistrates or by police officers acting upon the instructions of such magistrates.[7] However, when a banker appears before a civil or a commercial court, a distinction must be made between whether the banker is requested to testify either as a witness or as a party to the trial.

Before a civil or a commercial court, a banker may, as a witness, only testify or disclose documents concerning his client, if his client agrees.

There are, however, three exceptions to this rule:

1 In the case of liquidation of matrimonial property (art 259-3 of the Civil Code).
2 In the case of conciliation, insolvency or bankruptcy proceedings, the commercial court or the supervising judge (juge commissiaire) may request information from banks on the financial situation of the debtor (arts L 611-3, L 621-55 of the Commercial Code). Upon instructions from the commercial court the supervising judge may request similar information on the patrimony situation of the managers of the debtor. In the case of an insolvent individual, the Over-indebted Indviduals Commission (Commission de surendettement des particuliers) may also request information from banks on the financial situation of the debtor (art L 331-3, para 8 of the Consumer Code).
3 In the case of the attachment of an account (saisie-attribution or saisie conservatoire) by a client's creditor, where the bank is bound to declare the amount of money on the client's account on the day when the attachement is

5 Cass Com, 11 April 1995.
6 Cass Com, 10 December 2002.
7 Cass Com, 27 April 1994.

carried out (art 44 of Law no 91-650 of 9 July 1991) and cannot raise its duty of confidentiality.[8]

On the contrary, when a banker is a party to a trial before a civil or a commercial court, such banker may testify or disclose information to the extent that such information is likely to be helpful for his defence.

However, he may not rely on his duty of confidentiality for his own benefit as an excuse for refusing to provide information.[9]

Regulatory authorities

The banker's duty of confidentiality will not prevail either against inquiries from the Commission Bancaire, which is the regulatory authority for banking institutions, or against the Banque de France (art 511-33 of the Monetary and Financial Code), or the Comité des Etablissements de Crédit et des Entreprises d'Investissement (CECEI) which is competent to approve and strike from the list investment companies and credit institutions and to take individual decisions), or the Conseil des Marchés Financiers (CMF) which has control and disciplinary powers over investment enterprises and credit institutions or the Commission des Opérations de Bourse (COB), the French securities markets regulatory authority (art L 621-11 of the Monetary and Financial Code).

All these authorities have access to all accounting documents, including particulars of any client's account. The fact that the information relates to an account held outside France is not relevant provided that the information is available in France.

The agents of these authorities are themselves subject to a duty of confidentiality vis-à-vis the judicial authority acting in the course of criminal proceedings, the European Commission, foreign authorities subject to reciprocity and to their being bound by confidentiality obligations, Parliament and investigation commissions speakers, certain courts and other regulatory authorities.

The Competition Council (Conseil de la Concurrence) has access to all books, accounts and professional documents. However, banks are not authorised to disclose to it confidential information except if a visit of Competition Council agents has been authorised by the President of the Civil Court.

The National Institute for Statistics and Economic Studies (Institut National des Statistiques et des Etudes Economiques, INSEE) and the National Commission of Computer Sciences and Liberties (Commission Nationale Informatique et Libertés, CNIL) also have access to banks' information. However, they cannot obtain precise data on clients' accounts or operations.

---

8   Cass 2nd Civ, 1 July 1999. Note that the creditor who has obtained an enforceable judgment and needs to know the names and addresses of the banks where accounts have been opened in the debtor's name in order to carry out the attachment of those accounts may ask the Public Prosecutor to obtain such information from the relevant banks.
9   Cass Com, 19 June 1990.

Certain supervisory authorities are expressly authorised to communicate to each other all information necessary for the accomplishment of their duties : the Banque de France, the CECEI, the Commission Bancaire, the Insurance Control Commission (Commission de contrôle des assurances), the COB, the Social Security Control Commission, the Deposits Guaranty Fund, the Insurance Guaranty Fund, the CMF, the Disciplinary Council of Financial Management, market enterprises and clearance companies. All data so transmitted are subject to a duty of confidentiality in the conditions applicable both to the sender and the recepient of the information.

Tax and customs authorities

Bankers have the obligation to declare to the authorities the opening and closing of accounts of any and all natures (art 1649 A of the French Tax Code) and the date and the amount of sums transferred outside France by individuals, associations and non-commercial companies.

The French tax authorities, furthermore, have a right of access to the books of the banks.

Customs authorities enjoy similar rights provided, however, the documents requested resort to current or exceptional powers of the customs authorities.[10]

However, the French social security administration has no right to the banks' confidential information.

Police and other criminal investigators

Prior to the 1984 Banking Law, police officers were not entitled to conduct investigations within banks. Article L 511-33 of the Monetary and Financial Code states that the duty of confidentiality will not justify non-disclosure to 'the judicial authority acting in the course of criminal proceedings'. The question therefore arose as to whether police officers may be regarded as a judicial authority. Article 75 of the Code of Criminal Procedure provides that officers and agents of the 'police judiciaire' (who are defined at art 20 of the Code of Criminal Procedure) are authorised to conduct preliminary investigations either upon the Public Prosecutor's instructions or upon their own initiative. Such investigations are, in both cases, conducted under the control of the Public Prosecutor, who is a judicial authority.

The view is thus taken by some legal commentators that police officers are now authorised to request information from banks. Others think that police officers may be regarded as a 'judicial authority' only when acting upon the Public Prosecutor's instructions. In practice, it is advisable for the bank to request the officer or agent to sign a declaration specifying his role and whether or not he is acting upon the Public Prosecutor's instructions. Deputy police agents are not regarded as judicial authorities.

---

10 Cass Crim, 3 May 2001.

The fight against money laundering

The most recent exception to the banker's duty of confidentiality is related to the fight against organised crime and drug trafficking. French rules applicable to money laundering are set out in Law no 90-614 of 12 July 1990 on the 'Participation of financial institutions in the fight against money laundering and drug trafficking', subsequently amended by Law no 93-122 of 29 January 1993 on 'the prevention of corruption and the transparency of economic life and public proceedings', Law no 96-392 of 13 May 1996 on the 'fight against money laundering and drug trafficking and international cooperation relating to attachments and the confiscation of proceeds of crime', Law no 2001-420 of 15 May 2001 on 'New economic regulations' and Law no 2001-1062 of 15 November 2001 on 'Daily safety', as well as in the Decrees of 13 February 1991, 25 September 2001, 2 February 2002 and 22 March 2002. All such texts are codified under Livre VI of the Monetary and Financial Code.

The participation of banks in the fight against money laundering takes three forms:

1   the declaration of suspicions;
2   the duty of vigilance; and
3   the duty to check the identity of the clients and to keep information relating to clients.

A bank may be subject to disciplinary sanctions if following a default of gross vigilance or a default in its internal procedures of control it has failed to comply with its obligations.

THE DECLARATION OF SUSPICIONS

Article L 562-2 of the Monetary and Financial Code compels banks to disclose any sum or transaction which may result from drug trafficking or from organised crime, as well as any and all transactions carried out where the identity of the operator or of the beneficiary remain doubtful despite the care taken under art 563-3 of the Monetary and Financial Code (duty of vigilance, see below) or transactions effected with individuals or legal entities including their subsidiaries or branches, acting as or on behalf of fiduciary funds or any management entity of a trust (patrimoine d'affectation) when the identity of the persons setting up the trust or of the beneficiary is unknown.

This declaration is made to a department placed under the authority of the Ministry of Economy – called the TRACFIN (Traitement du renseignement et action contre les circuits financiers clandestins) – set up in 1990 and composed of civil servants duly authorised by the minister.

The TRACFIN collects and assesses all relevant data and information contained in the declarations[11] and requests financial institutions to forward the statements of the

---

11   The most recent data provided by the TRACFIN reveals an impressive increase in the number of declarations of suspicions:
   – 1,244 declarations of suspicions were made in 1998;
   – 1,655 declarations of suspicions were made in 1999;
   – 2,537 declarations of suspicions were made in 2000;
   – 3,598 declarations of suspicions were made in 2001; and
   – it is estimated that between 6,500 and 7,000 declarations of suspicions will be made in 2002.

accounts of the relevant persons. If the collected information is likely to reveal money laundering activities, the TRACFIN will provide such information to the Public Prosecutor.

The declarations may be oral and the identify of their author is not recorded in the file.

Any information likely to modify the appreciation made by the TRACFIN or the bank at the time of the declaration must be immediately disclosed to the TRACFIN (art L 562-3 of the Monetary and Financial Code).

THE BANKER'S DUTY OF VIGILANCE

Pursuant to art 563-3 of the Monetary and Financial Code, the bank has a duty to check carefully any transaction which, although it may not seem to result from drug trafficking or organised crime, cumulatively meets the following three tests: (i) the transaction is for an amount of more than €150,000 and exceeds the amount of transactions usually carried out by the agent; (ii) the transaction appears to be unusually complex; and (iii) appears not to be economically grounded or not to have a lawful purpose.

The bank must request from its client the details of the origin and destination of these funds, as well as the purpose of the transaction and the identity of the beneficiary. The banks then records the details of the transaction that it is in a position to forward the relevant documents, upon request, either to TRACFIN or to the control authority.

In a decision of 2 March 2002,[12] the Paris Court of Appeal ruled that the unusual complexity must be assessed in concreto. Sarl Moon had stolen a letter sent by another company to the tax authorities including a cheque for an amount of FRF 1,559,909 payable to the said authorities and then withdrew the amount of FRF 700,000 in several bank cheques. The court considered that the presentation of a cheque of FRF 1,559,909 and the withdrawal of FRF 700,000 in one day by means of bank cheques was unusually complex and without economic justification because the bank account of Sarl Moon had never recorded any deposit or debit in excess of FRF 100,000 and the company had never requested any bank cheques. The court therefore sentenced Crédit Lyonnais to indemnify the company which had issued the stolen cheque.

THE BANKER'S DUTY TO KNOW HIS CLIENTS

The bank has an obligation to:

1   Check the identity of its clients whether existing or new clients and to keep a copy of an official document (such as the client's national identity card or passport).
2   Check the identity of its occasional clients (someone not yet a client of the bank) or clients who wish to remain anonymous who wish to carry out

---

12   CA Paris 15, no 2001/03509, *SA Crédit Lyonnais v Sarl Moon et autres*.

transactions of an amount exceeding €8,000, or who wish to rent safety deposit boxes;

3   Inquire about the identity of the persons who are beneficiaries of the transactions carried out, when the individuals who act do not seem to act on their own behalf (except when the transaction is effected through another financial institution). This includes not only the French and EU institutions, but also institutions in countries outside the EU which inspire confidence by their status.[13]

So as to promote the fight against money laundering, banks are also required to keep any documents relating to the identity of their usual or occasional clients for a period of five years as from either the date of closing of the client's account or as from the date of termination of their relationship.

The TRACFIN as well as the supervisory authority may (also at any time and proprio motu) require the disclosure of any documents which are likely to help in analysing a transaction which is declared as being suspicious pursuant to art L 562-2 or carefully checked pursuant to art L 563-3 of the Monetary and Financial Code so as to determine whether this transaction is lawful.

Banks which take part in the fight against money laundering benefit from a double protection. Provided they have acted in good faith, they may neither:

1   be sued before the criminal courts on the basis of art 226-13 of the New Penal Code;

2   be held liable before a civil or commercial court for breach of their duty of confidentiality – this means that should a client suffer a loss, the bank will not have to indemnify the said client, it is the government who is liable for indemnification; nor

3   be subject to professional sanctions.

The bank's clients also benefit from a protection. Thus, the rights of disclosure developed for the benefit of the TRACFIN may not be used for the benefit of any other administration such as the tax administration (art L 563-5 of the Monetary and Financial Code).

Such provision is very important in that it tends to protect clients and to safeguard the mutual confidence which constitutes the basis of the banker/client relationship.

EXTRA-TERRITORIAL ASPECTS

French law provides for the co-operation between various control authorities for the exchange of any and all information necessary for the enforcement of their decisions.

The rules outlined above are rules provided for by French domestic law. However, rules of international law will have to be taken into account if, for example, a foreign authority seeks to obtain information or if, conversely, a French authority seeks to obtain information outside France.

13   Note that the EU Parliamentary Conference of 7–8 February 2002 envisaged a systematic declaration with the TRACFIN of transactions carried out with fiduciary or assimilated funds in case the economic beneficiary cannot be identified.

Foreign authorities seeking information in France

Information sought from a bank

The professional duty of confidentiality may override claims from a foreign authority, except possibly if such authority relies on an international treaty such as a bilateral tax treaty or the 1970 Hague Convention on the obtaining of evidence abroad. The Hague Convention provides that evidence may be obtained either through diplomatic or consular agents, who do not, however, have any compulsion power, or through the French Ministry of Foreign Affairs (which conveys the request to the Ministry of Justice, which itself conveys the request to the Public Prosecutor who, in turn, conveys it to the competent French court). But even in this case, it is doubtful whether a French judge would accept evidence where this would constitute a breach of a professional duty of confidentiality under French law.

In addition to the professional duty of confidentiality, a banker may invoke the provisions of art 1 or 1bis of Law no 68-678 of 26 July 1968 with respect to modified disclosure of economic, commercial, industrial, financial or technical documents and information to foreign individuals or legal entities.

Article 1 provides that the act of providing economic, commercial, industrial, financial or technical information to foreign public authorities is a misdemeanour where the communication of such information could interfere with the sovereignty, security, essential economic interests of France or with French public order. This applies to any and all individuals of French nationality or residing in France, as well as to any and all managers, representatives, agents or employees of a corporation having its registered office or a branch in France. This provision would therefore apply to any and all managers or employees of foreign banks having a branch in France.

Article 1bis provides that when commercial or financial information is requested from any person with a view to producing evidence for any judicial or administrative proceedings abroad, the request and the communication of such information are misdemeanours.

The prohibition applies to 'any person'. Therefore, if a French national who resides in France visits a foreign country and discloses information for the purpose of judicial proceedings in that country, Law no 68-678 would probably apply, if the information was obtained in France.[14]

Both articles apply subject to international treaties and therefore may not be invoked if the procedure provided for by the 1970 Hague Convention is followed.

Information sought from a supervisory authority

A foreign authority seeking information in France may request its French counterpart to provide it with such information. For instance, the American Federal Bank Examiners or the SEC could request the French Commission Bancaire or the Banque

---

14   Response to written question no 4356, Official Journal, Senate Debate, 4 June 1987, p 390.

de France or the COB to provide it with information concerning a US bank having a branch in France. The Conseil des Marchés Financiers, the Commission Bancaire, the Banque de France and the COB may obtain such information, notwithstanding any duty of confidentiality to which may be subject the bank (arts L 621-21 and L 632-1 of the Monetary and Financial Code).

The question, however, arises as to whether the French authority may be in breach of its own duty of confidentiality when providing the information to the foreign authority.

As regards the Commission Bancaire and the Banque de France, the information may be given to the foreign authorities in charge of the surveillance of credit establishments, provided that reciprocity exists and subject to the condition that these authorities are themselves bound by a professional duty of confidentiality with the same guarantees as in France. As regards the COB (art L 621-21 of the Monetary and Financial Code) and the CMF (art L 632-1 of the Monetary and Financial Code), they may provide information to either any analogous authority of another member state of the EU or of the EEA which is bound by a professional duty of confidentiality or to any analogous body of a foreign state, provided that reciprocity exists and that the foreign authority is bound by a professional duty of confidentiality with the same guarantees as in France.

Article L 621-21 of the Monetary and Financial Code restricts the forwarding of information to foreign authorities by providing that the COB must refuse to provide the information to the foreign analogous authority if the conveyance of such information is likely to interfere with the sovereignty, the security, the essential economic interests or with the public order in France, or when any criminal proceeding has been instituted in France on the basis of the same facts and against the same persons, or when these persons have already been subject to a final judgment on the same facts.

French authorities seeking to obtain information from a bank outside France

It should be pointed out that in France, at least in non-criminal matters, courts do not play an active part in the process of producing evidence. As a consequence, issues which arise in some countries as regards, for instance, subpoenas and contempt of court, are not relevant in France.

When criminal proceedings have been initiated, the investigating judge (juge d'instruction) may issue letters rogatory by virtue of the Hague Convention or of a bilateral treaty on judicial assistance.

Finally, French supervisory authorities may obtain information through foreign analogous authorities relying on EU rules. In addition, the COB is entitled to enter into agreements with foreign analogous entities.

REGULATED MARKETS

Regulatory authorities

In France, the main regulatory authorities for regulated markets are the CMF, and the COB. The function of the COB is to protect savings, investments and information on investors, as well as the sound operation of regulated markets. In order to carry out such a mission, the COB has broad powers, (ie to investigate transactions, to issue injunctions to stop practices which are contrary to the COB regulations and to issue sanctions). The objective of the CMF includes a disciplinary role over market enterprises and investment services providers.

Insider dealing

Employees or managers of banks or financial institutions can be tempted to use the information they collect to their own benefit or to the benefit of related persons.

Insider dealing may be punished both by criminal sanctions and by administrative sanctions.

The criminal offence of insider dealing is governed by arts L 465-1 to L 465-3 of the Monetary and Financial Code.

The administrative breach of privileged information is governed by the COB regs 90–08 related to the use of privileged information. It has a much larger scope than the penal law.

The criminal offence of insider dealing

It has been a criminal offence since 1970 for the managers of a company or persons who obtain information with respect to a company in the course of their profession to use such information before it has become public in order to carry out transactions for their own benefit. This was extended to all persons by a law of 15 November 2001.

We will examine in turn:

1   the persons who may be liable;
2   the nature of the relevant information;
3   what is meant by the 'abuse' of such information;
4   the intention which must be established; and
5   the sanctions imposed upon offenders.

Persons who may be liable

Law no 2001-1062 of 15 November 2001, which implements the European Directive on market's abuse[15] and amends art L 465-1 of the Monetary and Financial Code, enlarges the scope of the insider dealing as to the persons who may be liable. Insider dealing used to be aimed at 'persons finding themselves in possession of privileged information in the course of their profession or of their duties'. It was therefore necessary that the information be obtained by reason of the exercise of the profession or duties and not by mere luck or through friendly or family relationships.

---

15   See now Council Directive 2003/6/EC.

Since the Law of 15 November 2001, 'any person that is in possession of an insider information, even if it is not in the course of his profession or of his duties, may also be sentenced for using or revealing such information'.

Bank managers and employees are obviously in a privileged position to obtain information with respect to the transactions that their clients contemplate, and there are many examples of bank managers using such information for their own benefit. In 1978, a bank manager, who was in charge of the supervision of the personal bank account of a client, took cognisance of the fact that the said client intended to take over a company if the results of the parliamentary elections were what he expected. The bank manager bought for his own account 90 shares of the said company after a meeting with the said client and 155 shares of the said company on the day following the elections. He was sentenced to three-months' imprisonment with remission of sentence and to a fine of FRF 20,000 (€3049).[16]

The nature of the information

Article L 465-1 of the Monetary and Financial Code does not set forth any particular conditions as to the accuracy of the information. The contents of the information have been very broadly defined by case law as 'any information relating to the forecast or the situation of an issuer or on the likelihood of evolution of securities or of a futures contract'.

The Supreme Court has ruled that the privileged nature of information must be assessed on an objective basis.[17]

'Abuse' of the information

The abuse must take the form of a transaction completed on the market. Therefore, if a bank advised and led a lending syndicate for a company purporting to make a take-over bid for one of the bank's clients, there will be no offence of insider dealing, although there may be a breach of the duty of confidentiality.

The offence of insider dealing is however defined broadly in that (i) it is not necessary to establish a causal link between the information and the transaction completed, and (ii) it is an offence for a person in possession of privileged information not only to complete a transaction directly or through an intermediary, but also to enable a third party to complete a transaction.

The prohibited transactions may be carried out by the privileged person directly or, more often, through a 'dummy' who is often a non-resident company (often located in a tax haven). The COB has therefore called for the conclusion of international treaties.

Co-operation between the appropriate national authorities is obviously necessary, although confidentiality should be ensured. The COB is at present authorised to provide information to its EC counterparts and also to foreign authorities outside

16   Trib Corr, Paris, 13 January 1978.
17   Paris 9ème Ch, 12 March 1993.

the EC, provided that the assistance is reciprocal and the foreign authority is subject to a duty of confidentiality with the same guarantees as in France. Similar provisions apply to the Commission Bancaire, the Banque de France and the CMF.

We have seen that it is an offence for a privileged person to enable a third party to complete a transaction. This 'third party' may be a client or an employee of the same financial institution. Thus, a bank manager having privileged information regarding a company who advises its client to deal on such company's securities or who uses this information when managing its clients' securities will be liable. Similarly, a bank employee dealing with the account of a client who passes some information onto another employee dealing with the management of securities accounts falls within the ambit of arts L 465-1 to L 465-3 of the Monetary and Financial Code.

Intention

Where the person in possession of privileged information completes a deal himself or through an intermediary, such person will be liable if he was aware of the fact that the information had not yet been disclosed to the public. Where the information is passed on by the privileged person to a third party, it must be established that the informer knew that the third party would act upon it.

The Supreme Court considers that there is insider dealing if the manager of the company uses the privileged information for a compelling reason dictated by the corporate interest. It is unclear as to how the banker may benefit from the corporate interest.

Penalties

The penalties provided for by the art L 465-1 of the Monetary and Financial Code differ according to whether:

1 the person in possession of confidential information, whether or not obtained in the course of his profession or his function, carried out, or knowingly allowed the realisation, either directly or through an intermediary, of one or several transactions before the information was brought to the knowledge of the public; or
2 the person in possession of confidential information disclosed such information to a third party, outside the usual course of his profession or duties.

In the first case, offenders may be sentenced to two years' imprisonment and a fine of up to €1,500,000. However, the fine may not be for an amount inferior to the profit made and may reach ten times the amount of such profit. In the second case, offenders may only be sentenced to one year's imprisonment of one year and a fine of up to €150,000.

Note that pursuant to arts L 465-1 and L 465-3 of the Monetary and Financial Code, legal entities may now also be sentenced to sanctions in compliance with the conditions set out in art 121-2 of the New Penal Code, for the offences defined in art L 465-3 of the Monetary and Financial Code.

Article 421 of the Penal Code, as modified by the Law of 15 November 2001, provides that the offence of insider dealing can be held as a terrorist action if the offence is committed intentionally in relation to an individual or collective enterprise aiming to disturb public order through the means of intimidation or terror. In such case, the procedure and the penalties are different. This amendment was enacted in reaction to the terrorist attacks of 11 September 2001.

Criminal sanctions are cumulative with administrative sanctions applied by the COB under reg 90-08. However, the judge may impute the financial penalty on the penal fine.

COB reg 90-08 relating to the use of privileged information

The COB reg 90-08, adopted by the COB in 1990, is more precise and broader than the law in that it defines four categories of insiders :

1   *Primary internal insiders.* Persons who, by their professional activities or by their duties and in their capacity as members of administrative, managing or supervisory bodies, obtain confidential information. These persons shall refrain from using such information.
2   *Primary external insiders.* Persons who obtain confidential information in order to prepare and carry out a financial transaction. These persons shall also refrain from using such information on their own behalf or on behalf of others.
3   *Secondary insiders.* Persons who, during the course of their professional activity or duties (such as journalists or lawyers), obtain confidential information should also refrain from using such information for other purposes.
4   *Tertiary insiders.* Persons who knowingly obtain confidential information either directly or indirectly from one of the persons defined in 1 to 3 above.

Third parties also fall within the scope of insiders and can therefore be held liable as parties to a transaction.

Except for tertiary insiders, the communication of privileged information is also prohibited unless it is justified by professional reasons.

The breach of privileged information requires that the insider must either provide an undue benefit, distort the operation of the market, breach the equality of information and treatment of investors or have issuers or investors benefit from information obtained from intermediaries' in breach of the obligations of the latter.

Regulation 98-08 applies to French financial markets only. Sanctions can amount to €150,000.

Professional rules of conduct

Large financial institutions raise a specific problem which is partly due to the variety of services they now provide, including dealing with securities owned by their clients. Moreover, they often carry out transactions on their own behalf and so do their employees. Conflicts of interests may therefore arise between several clients, as well as between the financial institution itself and its clients.

The main base reflection was produced by a working committee at the end of the 1980s (Commission Brac de la Perrière 1989 and Commission sur la déontologie boursière, chaired by Mr Pfeiffer). The purpose was to make recommendations for professional rules that should be included in ethical norms of financial markets.

These rules and codes aimed to go further and do better than the law. They are typical of the period in which the state disengaged and left the professionals with a duty to draft the codes. However, the responsibility for the implementation of the rules belonged to the government. For example, art 6 of reg 90-08 of the COB provides that issuers of securities traded on a regulated market and financial intermediaries must take all appropriate measures to avoid the undue use of circulation of privileged information. The implementation of the Investment Services Directive,[18] which includes certain professional rules, brought about codification. Most of the rules are codified by art 533-4 of the Monetary and Financial Code, which applies to all investment services providers including investment and credit establishments.

These rules pursue several goals, including the protection of market integrity and the prevention of an undue circulation of confidential information in every investment services provider.

Investment services providers must ensure that all employees abide by the following rules, set forth by art 533-6 of the Monetary and Financial Code. These internal regulations must provide for:

1   conditions under which employees make negotiations on financial instruments for their own account;
2   conditions under which employees must, in such case, inform their employer; and
3   obligations to avoid the undue circulation of confidential information.

The General Regulation of the CMF authorises investment services providers to restrict the potential for employees performing sensitive functions to complete transactions for their own account. Sensitive functions include functions exposed to the holding of confidential information, responsibility for the arrangement of financial transactions, counselling, trading on markets, financial analysis, transactions on capital structure, industrial strategy and M & A.

Employees who have information on financial instruments must not act as traders and must not complete any transaction on the said financial instruments.

Finally, compliance with professional rules of conduct is entrusted to a compliance officer. The compliance officer's functions are exclusive. He controls transactions completed by employees for their account and establishes a surveillance list of financial instruments on which the investment services provider or its employees have sensitive information. He also establishes a prohibition list, which lists all financial instruments on which the employee must abstain from negotiating for his own account, distributing financial analysis or recommending negotiation to clients. Such list is disclosed to all employees.

---

18   Council Directive 93/22/EEC.

Article 3-1-6 of the General Regulation of the CMF (1998) has imposed the implementation of the 'Chinese Wall' principle in order to ensure that confidential and privileged information remains confidential.

In practice, this procedure consists in a material organisation that allows the separation of the activities that are likely to create conflicts of interests in the financial institution's premises. This procedure is also used in order to provide for the conditions under which the compliance officer can authorise the transmission of confidential information from one department to another or the assignment of an employee to a department different from the one to which he belongs (art 3-1-7).

APPENDIX

Legal provisions

New Penal Code

ARTICLE 226-13

The disclosure of any secret information by any person who, by reason of his or her status or profession or temporary duties or mission, holds secret information, shall be sentenced to a one-year imprisonment and to a fine amounting to €15,000.

Monetary and Financial Code

ARTICLE L 142-9

The agents of the Banque de France are bound by a professional duty of confidentiality. They may not acquire or receive any and all participations or interests or remuneration whatsoever in consideration either of worker counsel in private, public, industrial, commercial or financial companies, unless otherwise authorised by the governor. The said provisions do not apply to the production of scientific, literary or artistic works.

ARTICLE L 465-1

The managers of any company referred to at Article L 225-109 of the French Commercial Code and the persons who, by reason of their professional activities or duties, are in possession of privileged information in relation to the forecasts or to the situation of an issuer, whose securities are traded on a regulated market, or to the evolution of a financial instrument listed on a regulated market, and who carry out or knowingly allow the carrying out, either directly or through a nominee, of one or several transactions prior to the information being made available to the public, shall be sentenced to a two-year-imprisonment and a fine of €1,500,000, the total amount of which may be increased up to ten times the amount of the profit, if any, possibly earned, without the fine being lower than the amount of the said profit.

Any person who, by reason of his or her professional activities or his or her duties, is in possession of confidential information in relation to the likely evolution or to the situation of an issuer, whose securities are negotiated on a regulated market, or to the forecast of a financial instrument listed on a regulated market and who discloses such information to a third party beyond the scope of his or her usual professional activities or duties, shall be sentenced to a one-year imprisonment and a fine of €150,000.

Any person, other than those referred to in the two paragraphs hereinabove, who possesses in full knowledge inside information related to the forecasts or to the situation of an issuer, whose securities are traded on a regulated market, or to the evolution of a financial instrument listed on a regulated market, and who carries out or knowingly allows the carrying out, either directly or through a nominee, of a transaction, or who communicates the said information to a third party prior to the information being made available to the public, shall be sentenced to a one-year imprisonment and a fine of €150,000, the total amount of which may be increased up to ten times the amount of the profit, if any, possibly made, the fine not to be lower than the amount of the said profit. When the information at stake pertains to the perpetration of a crime or an offence, the sanction incurred will be increased up to seven years of imprisonment and to a fine of €1,500,000, if the amount of the profit earned is lower than the said sum.

Any person who, by any process or means whatsoever, knowingly forwards false or misleading information related to the likely evolution or to the situation of an issuer, whose securities are negotiated on a regulated market, or to the forecast of a financial instrument listed on a regulated market, which are likely to influence listings, shall be sentenced to the same penalties as those provided for in paragraph 1.

ARTICLE L 465-2

The fact, for any and all persons, to carry out or to attempt to carry out, directly or through an intermediary, steps aimed at affecting the due operation of a market or financial instruments by misleading a third party, shall be punished by the sanctions provided for in the first section of Article L 465-1.

ARTICLE L 465-3

Legal entities may be held liable from a penal point of view under the conditions provided for at Article 121.2 of the New Penal Code, for any offence defined at Articles L 465-1 and L 465-2.

Penalties incurred by legal entities include:

- fines, pursuant to the terms and conditions provided for at Article 131.38 of the French Penal Code;
- the penalties mentioned in Article 131.39 of the French Penal Code.

The prohibition provided for in paragraph 2 of Article 131.39 of the French Penal Code refers to the activity in the course of which the offence was committed.

ARTICLE L 511-33

Any and all officers of a Board of Directors and, as the case may be, of a Supervisory Board (conseil de surveillance) and any and all other persons, who by reason of their office, participate in the administration or management of a credit establishment or are employed by the said credit establishment, are bound by a professional duty of confidentiality, under the conditions and the penalties provided for at Article L 571-4.

ARTICLE L 561-1

Persons others than those specified at Article L 562-1 who, in the conduct of their business, execute, monitor or give advice on transactions resulting in capital movements, must report to the Public Prosecutor (Procureur de la République) transactions of which they are aware and which involve sums that they know derive from one of the offences provided for at Article L 562-2.

Having made such a report in good faith, the said persons shall benefit from the provisions of Article L 562-8 of the said Law. They must comply with the obligations provided for at Article L 574-1. The Public Prosecutor shall inform the department stated in Article L 562-4, which shall provide him with all relevant information.

ARTICLE L 562-1

The provisions of this chapter apply to:

1   undertakings governed by the provisions of title I of this section;
2   the Banque de France, the Institut d'émission des départements d'outre-mer and the Institut d'émission d'outre-mer;
3   undertakings referred to at Article L 310-1 of the French Insurance Code and insurance and reinsurance brokers;
4   bodies, which fall within the scope of Article L 111-1 of the French Mutuality Code;
5   investment companies, members of regulated markets of financial instruments and legal entities mentioned in Articles L 421-8 and L 442-2;
6   money changers;
7   persons which carry out, supervise or advise transactions on the purchase, sale, transfer or rental of real estate properties;
8   legal representatives and managers in charge of casinos;
9   persons, whose usual activity is commercial or who organise the sale of precious stones or materials, antiquities and works of art.

For purposes of this section, persons mentioned at Articles 1 to 6 shall be referred to as financial undertakings.

ARTICLE L 562-2

The financial undertakings and persons referred to at Article L 562-1 must report to the department mentioned at Article L 562-4, under the conditions specified by this section:

1   deposits of funds in their books which may result from drug trafficking or from organised crime;
2   transactions involving funds which may result from drug trafficking or from organised crime.

Financial undertakings must also report to the said department:

1   transactions, in which the identity of the operator or beneficiary remains uncertain, in spite of the care carried out in compliance with Article L 563-1;
2   operations carried out by financial undertakings on their behalf or on behalf of third parties, both individuals and legal entities, including their subsidiaries or entities,

Financial organisms are also compelled to declare to the above-mentioned service:

1   any and all transactions in which the instructing parties' identity or the beneficiary's identity remains doubtful, in spite of the precautions carried out pursuant to Article L 563-1;
2   any and all operations carried out by financial organisms on their behalf or on behalf of third parties with natural or legal persons, including with the subsidiaries and establishments of the said legal persons, acting under the form or on behalf of trust funds or of any and all instruments of management of allocation estate in which the identity of constituents or beneficiaries is unknown.

A decree may extend the obligation of declaration provided for in the first paragraph to the transactions carried out on one's own behalf or on behalf of third parties and carried out by financial organisms with individuals or legal entities, including the subsidiaries or establishments of the said legal entities and domiciled, registered or established in any of the states or territories, the legislation of which is recognised as insufficient, or the practices of which are considered as being an obstacle to the fight against money laundering carried out by the international instance of consultation and co-ordination as regards the fight against money laundering. The said decree shall provide for the minimum amount of operations subject to declaration.

ARTICLE L 562-4

A department placed under the authority of the Minister for Economic Affairs and Finance must receive the report provided for at Article L 562-2. The said department consists of the State civil servants that the Minister endows with specific powers, under the conditions established by a Decree approved by the Conseil d'Etat. The said department collects and compiles all information, which helps determine the origin of funds or the types of transactions covered in the report. As soon as the information received evidences funds likely to result from drug trafficking or from organised criminal activity, the department shall submit it to the Public Prosecutor and shall inform him, where applicable, that the matter has been referred to the Customs Authority, so that the latter may initiate an investigation to establish an offence pursuant to Article 415 of the French Customs Code.

ARTICLE L 562-5

Without prejudice to the provisions of Article L 562-6, the department established pursuant to Article L 562-4 shall acknowledge receipt of the aforementioned report. The acknowledgement of receipt, which may be accompanied by an injunction, shall be issued prior to the deadline for execution of the transaction.

The injunction forces execution to be delayed for up to 12 hours at the most. If the acknowledgement of receipt is not accompanied by an injunction, or if the financial undertaking or the person referred to at Article L 562-1 has not obtained any decision from the President (presiding judge) of the Tribunal de Grande Instance of Paris or, where appropriate, from the investigations magistrate (Juge d'instruction), it may execute the transaction at the end of the period to which the injunction applies.

The report shall deal with transactions already completed if delaying execution proves impossible, which is also the case if it has become obvious, upon execution of the transaction, that the sums appear to result from drug trafficking or from organised criminal activity. The department established pursuant to Article L 562-4 shall acknowledge receipt of the said reports.

Upon consultation with the Public Prosecutor of the Tribunal de Grande Instance of Paris, the presiding judge of the Tribunal de Grande Instance of Paris may, upon request of the department established pursuant to Article L 562-4, extend the period provided for in the first paragraph of this Article or order temporary sequestration of funds, accounts or securities covered by the report. The Public Prosecutor of the Tribunal de Grande Instance of Paris may present a request for the said purpose. The order, which accedes to the request, shall be immediately enforceable as against the person concerned to whom the report is notified.

ARTICLE L 562-6

The report may be oral or written. The undertaking may request that the department established pursuant to Article L 562-1 does not acknowledge receipt of the report. In the event that the said department refers the matter to the Public Prosecutor, the report drawn to his attention, shall not be contained in the summary.

The declaration may be either written or oral. The financial organism or the person provided for at Article L 562-1, may request that the department established pursuant to Article L 562-4 does not acknowledge receipt of the declaration. In the event that the said department should refer the matter to the Public Prosecutor, the declaration, of which the latter is informed, shall not appear in the file of the procedure.

The department established pursuant to Article L 562-4 may, upon request of the financial organism or of the person having carried out a declaration in compliance with Articles L 562-2, L 563-1, L 563-1-1 and L 563-4, indicate whether it has referred the matter to the Public Prosecutor, on the grounds of the said declaration.

ARTICLE L 562-7

If, either as a consequence of a serious lack of vigilance or of a shortcoming in the organisation of its internal procedures of control, a financial undertaking or a person referred to at Article L 562-1 fails to make a report as provided for in this section, the disciplinary authority in charge shall initiate proceedings on the grounds of professional or administrative rules and regulations and inform the Public Prosecutor thereof.

ARTICLE L 562-8

With respect to sums or transactions covered by the report referred to at Article L 562-2, no proceedings under Articles 226-13 and 226-14 of the French Penal Code shall be initiated against managers or employees or any and all persons referred to at Article L 562-1 against financial undertakings who carry out the report in good faith.

No proceedings under civil law shall be instituted, nor shall any professional sanctions be imposed against a financial undertaking, its managers or employees or any person referred to at Article L 562-1, which carry out the report referred to at Article L 562-2 in good faith. Should such a report entail any direct damage, the state shall be liable for the damage suffered.

The provisions of this Article shall be applicable even if no evidence has been provided that the nature of the facts on which the report is founded is that of a criminal offence or if the facts have resulted in a nolle prosequi order, discharge or acquittal.

If the transaction is executed as provided for at Article L 562-5 and unless there is collusion with the owner of the funds or the initiator of the transaction, the financial undertaking shall be relieved from any and all liabilities, and in such event, no penal proceedings may be initiated against its managers or employees under Articles 222-34 to 222-41, 321-1, 321-2, 321-3 and 324-1 of the French Penal Code or Article 415 of the French Customs Code. The other persons referred to at Article L 562-1 shall also be relieved from all liabilities.

ARTICLE L 563-1

Before opening an account, financial undertakings as referred to at Article L 562-1 must determine the true identity of the account holder by obtaining evidence in writing. The said financial undertaking shall apply the same conditions so as to determine the identity of occasional clients who request the financial undertaking to carry out transactions of a nature and threshold amount specified in a Decree.

They shall ascertain the true identity of the persons for whom an account is opened or a transaction executed, when it appears to them that the persons asking for an account to be opened or a transaction to be carried out, might not be acting on their own behalf.

ARTICLE L 563-2

The provisions of Article L 563-1 shall be applicable to the assets and securities referred to at Article 990 A of the French Tax Code.

The tax status of the said assets and securities shall be maintained.

The provisions of the second paragraph of Article 537 of the French Tax Code shall not preclude the application of Article L 563-1. Nevertheless, the information to which the said Article refers shall be recorded in a register separate from that established pursuant to Article 537 of the French Tax Code.

Once a client has declined to authorise the financial undertaking to disclose his identity and his domicile provided, for tax purposes, to the tax authorities, the right to forward information pursuant to Articles L 83, L 85, L 87 and L 89 of the Tax

Procedures Manual shall apply neither to the register thus established by the present Article nor to the documents evidencing identity, as referred to in the first paragraph of Article L 563-1 presented for the transactions in bills, securities and assets referred to at Article 990A and in the second paragraph of Article 537 of the French Tax Code.

ARTICLE L 563-3

Any large-scale transaction involving sums which, individually or in total, exceed a threshold prescribed by a Decree approved by the Conseil d'Etat and which, without being covered by Article L 562-2, occurs under complex and unusual conditions and which has no apparent economic or visible lawful purpose, must give rise to a special investigation conducted by the financial undertaking. In such case, the financial undertaking shall question the client with respect to the origin and destination of the said funds as well as to the purpose of the transaction and the payee's identity.

The particulars of the transaction shall be written down and the records kept by the financial undertaking, under the conditions provided for at Article L 563-4. Only the department established pursuant to Article L 562-4 and the supervisory authority may be provided with the said elements with the documents in relation thereto.

Financial undertakings must ensure that the obligations specified in the preceding paragraph are applied both by its foreign branches and subsidiaries, unless precluded by local law, in which case it shall inform the department established pursuant to Article L 562-4.

ARTICLE L 563-4

Without prejudice to the provisions requiring more strict measures, financial undertakings shall keep records relating to the identity of their usual or occasional clients for a period of five years at least upon closing of the said clients' accounts or upon termination of their business relations. They shall also retain documents relating to transactions made by the above clients for a period of five years further to the execution of transactions.

For purposes of the present section, the department established pursuant to Article L 562-4 and the supervisory authority may request that the documents be forwarded to them for the purpose of reconstructing, in their entirety, the transactions carried out by an individual or legal entity and in connection with a transaction dealt with in a report referred to at Article L 562-2 or with a special investigation provided for at Article L 563-3, with the aim of providing information to the departments of other states having similar skills, under the conditions provided for at Article L 564-2.

ARTICLE L 563-5

Without prejudice to the application of Article 40 of the French Code of Penal Procedure, the information obtained by the department established pursuant to Article L 562-4 and by the supervisory authorities in accordance with Articles L 562-2, L

563-2 to L 563-4 must not be used for purposes other than those provided for by this section.

The disclosure of the said information is prohibited. Except where this information is related to the facts referred to at Article L 562-2, the department established pursuant to Article L 562-4 is authorised to forward the information it has collected to officers of the Criminal Investigation Department (Police judiciaire) which is appointed by the Minister of the Interior under the conditions specified by a Decree approved by the Conseil d'Etat, as well as to the supervisory authorities. It may also transmit the information to Customs. It is also authorised to obtain the information it requires, with a view to the carrying out of its tasks, from officers of the Criminal Investigation Department and from supervisory authorities.

ARTICLE L 563-6

If, either as a consequence of a serious lack of vigilance or of a default in the organisation of its internal procedures of control, a financial undertaking has failed to meet the obligations imposed thereupon under this Chapter, the authority having disciplinary power may act on its own initiative under the conditions provided for in professional or administrative rules and regulations.

ARTICLE L 574-1

Without prejudice to the application of the penalties incurred with respect to one of the offences provided for at Articles 222-34 to 222-41 of the French Penal Code and 415 of the French Customs Code, the managers or employees of financial undertakings or any and all persons referred to at Article L 562-1, which knowingly inform the owner of the funds or the initiator of one of the transactions referred to at Article L 562-2 of this Law, of the existence of the report made to the department established pursuant to Article L 562-4, or transmit confidential information related to any and all proceedings initiated on the basis of the said report, may be punished by a fine of €22.500.

ARTICLE L 613-20

I   Any and all persons who participate or have participated in the control of the persons mentioned at Articles L 613-1, L 613-2 and L 613-10, under the conditions provided for in this chapter, are bound by a professional duty of confidentiality, subject to the penalties provided for at Article 226-13 of the French Penal Code.

II The said duty may not be invoked against the judicial authority acting in the course of criminal proceedings.

It may not be invoked in the event of a hearing within the context of a committee of inquiry, in the conditions provided for in the fourth paragraph of section II of Article 6 of ordinance no 58-1100 of 17 November 1958 relating to the running of Parliamentary Assemblies.

III   Notwithstanding the provisions of the Law no 68-678 of 26 July 1968, the banking committee (Commission Bancaire) may provide information to the authorities in charge of the persons, mentioned in section I, in other countries, provided that reciprocity exists and that the said authorities are themselves bound by a professional duty of confidentiality with the same guarantees as in France.

ARTICLE L 621-10

In order to ensure the performance of its mission, the commission for stock market transactions (Commission des Opérations de Bourse) may act through agents whose powers are granted by its chairman, in accordance with a decree approved by the Conseil d'Etat.

The agents may obtain any and all documents, under any form whatsoever (Law no 2001-1276 dated 28 December 2001), 'including data files kept and processed by telecommunications operators within the scope of Article L 32-3-1 of the Code des postes et télécommunications and by service providers mentioned at Articles 43-7 and 43 of the Law no 86-1067 dated 30 September 1986 on the freedom of communication', and may obtain a copy thereof. They may convene and interview any and all persons in possession of information. They have access to all professional premises.

ARTICLE L 621-11

Any and all persons summoned to appear before the commission are entitled to be assisted by a counsel of their choice. The terms of this summons and the conditions under which such right is exercised is determined by decree. [Decree no 71-615 dated 23 July 1971, Article 4: 'These summons are addressed to the relevant person concerned by registered letter no later than eight days prior to the hearing. If the person summoned wishes to be assisted by a legal counsel, he must provide the said counsel's identity and position to the Commission des Opérations de Bourse no later than eight days prior to the holding of the hearing']. Except for judicial auxiliaries, no one may invoke a professional duty of confidentiality against agents of the commission.

The officers and agents of the commission are bound by a professional duty of confidentiality in respect of the facts, acts and information that they may have obtained because of their functions, under the conditions and penalties set out at Article 378 of the Penal Code.

ARTICLE L 621-21

The Commission may, under the same conditions, procedures and sanctions as those provided for in the said code, with a view to the performance of its mission, conduct investigations upon request of foreign authorities performing analogous powers, provided that reciprocity exists, except in the event of a request made by an authority of a member state of the European Communities, or by any other member state to the Treaty on the European Economic Area.

The professional duty of confidentiality provided for at Article L 621-11 does not prevent the Commission des Opérations de Bourse from conveying the information that it has in its possession or that it has obtained upon request from authorities of other member states of the European Communities (or from any other member state to the Treaty on the European Economic Area performing analogous powers and bound by the same professional duty of confidentiality), to the said authorities.

The Commission des Opérations de Bourse may also convey information that it has in its possession or that it has obtained upon request of authorities of other states performing analogous functions, to the said authorities, provided that reciprocity exists that such foreign authorities are bound by a professional duty of confidentiality with the same guarantees as in France.

The assistance requested by a foreign authority performing analogous functions with a view to the procedures of investigation, or the disclosure of information that the Commission has or has obtained, shall be refused by the commission when the performance of the said request may interfere with France's sovereignty, security, essential economic interests or public order, or when any penal proceeding has been initiated in France on the basis of the same facts and against the same persons, or when the latter have already been subject to a final judgment on the same facts.

The Commission des Opérations de Bourse may, in order to comply with the foregoing paragraphs, enter into agreements organising its relations with foreign authorities performing analogous functions.

The Commission must approve the said agreements, under the terms and conditions provided for in Article L 621-3. They are published in the Journal Officiel.

Commercial Code

ARTICLE L 621-55

The supervising judge (juge commissaire) may, notwithstanding any contrary legal or regulatory provisions, obtain any information allowing him to set out accurately the debtors' economic and financial situation, from the statutory auditors, the members and representatives of personnel, from public administrations and organisations, social security and state insurance organisations, credit establishments, as well as from departments in charge of centralising banking risks and defaults in payments.

12 Germany

Thomas Schulz
Joachim Preussner

SOURCE OF SECRECY OBLIGATION

Current German law does not define in any statute the obligation of secrecy incumbent on banks, although the concept has a very long tradition and has been subject to public regulation. For example, a decree by Friedrich the Great stated in 1756 that all banks had to maintain secrecy on the wealth of their customers and had to take that information to the grave with them.[1] Despite the long tradition, the source of the secrecy obligation has not been clarified.

Constitution

In particular, it is still uncertain whether, as some authors argue,[2] bank confidentiality as such is guaranteed by the German Constitution, the Grundgesetz (GG) and, if so, to what extent.

The right to determine the use of one's personal data is part of the right of privacy[3] which is laid down in art 2, para 1 and art 1, para 1 of the GG. Since this right covers all personal data, it covers information that is subject to the secrecy obligation as well. In this respect the secrecy obligation shares the constitutional protection of the customer's right to determine the use of his personal data. The bank, however, does not participate in this protection, but it enjoys the protection of its right to choose and perform its profession as guaranteed in art 12, para 1 of the GG.[4]

But the protection offered by those provisions is relatively weak, since in most cases the information on a customer will not be of a private or intimate nature. Already, the Constitution allows a number of limitations to the secrecy obligations if the

---

1   'Art 19 des Reglements der Königlichen Giro- und Lehn-Banco' quoted in Claussen *Bank- und Börsenrecht* (2nd edn, 2000) p 181.
2   Overview given by Bruchner in Schimansky, Bunte and Lwowski *Bankrechts-Handbuch* (2nd edn, 2001) p 742.
3   ORR Koberstein-Windpassinger 'Wahrung des Bankgeheimnisses bei Asset-Backed-Securities-Transaktionen' (1999) WM 473 at 475.
4   Kümpel *Bank- und Kapitalmarktrecht* (2nd edn, 2000) p 60.

limitations pursue a legitimate public interest, are based on a statute and respect the principle of appropriateness.

Consequently, the secrecy obligation may conflict with the legislation only in small measure, which can also be deduced from the number of exceptions to be discussed in Banking information below.

Clause 2 of the General Business Conditions

In any case, bank confidentiality derives from contractual origins: The highest German court in civil matters, the Bundesgerichtshof (BGH), held as early as 1953 that the secrecy obligation was an implied contractual duty of the bank due to the special relationship between a bank and its customer which requires (and is therefore particularly shaped by) mutual trust.[5] Hence, there is no need for any particular agreement between bank and client on a secrecy obligation.

Since 1 January 1993 this has also been expressly provided for in cl 2 of the General Business Conditions of German banks, which apply to all orders of a bank customer, no matter whether a single order or various orders during a longer contractual relationship between the bank and its customer. Those general conditions are used by virtually all banks doing business in Germany and, as regards the secrecy obligation, they have taken over the development that bank confidentiality has undergone so far. Therefore, the scope and limits of the secrecy obligations can be shown by referring to cl 2 of the General Business Conditions.

Protected persons

The first person to be protected is the customer, ie every person with whom a bank enters into a contractual relationship.[6] Since in principle a contract does not require a certain form according to German civil law, the contract is formed when bank and customer have exchanged offer and acceptance.

Under certain circumstances even third persons – for example, spouses or the customer's company – who are not party to a banking contract can benefit from the secrecy obligation. This is the case when the third person is affected by the bank's performance of its contractual duties.

Information subject to secrecy obligation

Clause 2, para 1 of the General Business Conditions states that the bank has to maintain secrecy about any customer-related information and that no differentiation is to be made between factual information and evaluations by the bank. The obligation regarding evaluation is not limited to those evaluations based on information that is known only to the bank.

---

5   BGH in BB 1953 S 993.
6   Bruchner, n 2 above, p 745

However, the bank must have obtained knowledge of the information during the contractual relationship. Through which channels the bank acquired the knowledge is irrelevant.[7]

Of course, the secrecy obligation exists only if the person wants the information to remain secret. The customer's wishes prevail, even if contrary to his own interests or common sense. If his wishes are not known to the bank and cannot be established, the bank has to deduce them from all circumstances that may give indications concerning the actual wishes.[8]

Duration of secrecy obligation

Bank confidentiality covers all phases of the contractual relationship between bank and customer from the start of negotiations throughout the duration of the contract. Even after termination of the contractual relationship, the bank will be bound by its contractual duty not to reveal the protected information – as laid down in the decree issued by Friedrich the Great.

Limitations

Clause 2 of the General Business Conditions also shows the limitations on bank confidentiality: information may be disclosed if it is required by law, if the customer has consented hereto or if the bank is authorised to disclose banking affairs. The latter is more clearly defined in cl 2, paras 2, 3 and 4 and is an instrument of information exchange between banks which was established to allow the creditworthiness of a business partner to be verified. Under what prerequisites one of these three exceptions limits the secrecy obligation will be discussed in further detail in The exceptions to the secrecy obligation below.

Remedies for breach of secrecy obligation

If certain information falls within the scope of the secrecy obligation and none of the limitations allows disclosure, then the bank is obliged not to pass that information to third persons outside the bank or to employees of the bank whose knowledge of the information is unnecessary for the purpose of fulfilling the customer's orders.[9] Should the bank reveal the information in breach of the secrecy obligation, this has the following legal consequences.

DAMAGES

In the first instance, the disclosure constitutes a breach of contract which will entitle the customer to claim damages if the bank acted deliberately or negligently. Any fault on the part of employees or the bank's executive organs will be attributed to the bank. The damages that may be claimed cover the loss caused by the breach;

7   Kümpel, n 4 above, p 62.
8   Bruchner, n 2 above, p 744.
9   Claussen, n 1 above, p 188.

German civil law does not allow for punitive damages. There is no causation where a customer has to pay taxes after discovery of a tax evasion, since he was obliged to pay those already before the breach was committed.

Under special circumstances a customer may also claim damages according to tort law, but the provisions of tort law are unfavourable to the customer since the burden of proof regarding the bank's fault – contrary to damages deriving from breach of contract – lies with the customer and the attribution of the employee's fault may be excluded.

INJUNCTION: S 935 OF THE CIVIL PROCEDURE CODE

If a customer learns that his bank is about to disclose information he may move for an injunction: the client has to substantiate that the bank is under a contractual obligation not to reveal the information and that the passing on of information is imminent. Due to the apparent difficulty of knowing in advance what a bank will do, no such cases are known.[10]

TERMINATION OF BANKING RELATIONSHIP

Since the customer relies on the bank keeping his information secret, a breach of that obligation constitutes an important reason according to cl 18, para 2 of the General Business Conditions, entitling the customer to terminate the banking contract with immediate effect.

LEGAL CONSEQUENCES REGARDING THE EMPLOYEES

The bank's employees are under a contractual obligation, deriving both from their individual employment contract and from the collective agreements, to maintain bank confidentiality and to protect their employer's interests. This holds true even after the employment is terminated. In case of a breach, the bank may claim damages and in serious cases terminate the employment for good cause.

CRIMINAL LAW

There is no criminal law provision regarding the violation of bank confidentiality except in some cases of limited scope: for instance, s 93 of the Stock Corporation Act applying to board members and s 203 of the German Criminal Code applying to organs of banks incorporated according to public law. If the list in s 203, para 2 of the Criminal Code were interpreted in a manner so as to also include banks incorporated according to civil law,[11] this would not be compatible with the clear wording of that provision and would therefore be contrary to the principle 'nullum crimen sine lege' guaranteed in art 103, para 2 of the GG.

---

10   Bruchner, n 2 above, p 785.
11   Schünemann in *StGB – Leipziger Kommentar* (11th edn, 2001) s 203 Rn 71.

Privacy of data

The law on protection of data privacy is a corresponding field with a scope similar to bank confidentiality and has evolved very rapidly over the last years, showing the growing concern for privacy of data. In order to understand how these two matters influence each other it is necessary to establish how they are related. It will be shown that the bank has primarily to respect the provisions of the obligation of secrecy and apply the provisions of the Federal Data Protection Act (BDSG) only when the rules of bank confidentiality fail to ensure a minimum standard.

Scope of the Federal Data Protection Act

In s 1, para 1 of the BDSG the aim of the statute is defined as being the protection of the right of privacy, which is identical to the individual's right to determine the use of his personal data,[12] ie the right to decide when and to what extent his personal information is made known to others.[13] This already reveals one fundamental difference: while the secrecy obligation aims at ensuring confidentiality towards third parties, the BDSG aims at protecting a customer against other kinds of improper use of personal data through the customer's bank.

In keeping with the nature of the right of privacy, the Federal Data Protection Act provides only for the protection of natural persons and not of legal entities: s 3, para 1 of the BDSG. However, the protection of legal entities is granted when information permits conclusions with regard to personal data on the people constituting the entity.[14]

According to s 1, para 2, n 3 of the BDSG, inquiries regarding personal data as well as processing and use of such data for professional purposes are subject to the provisions of the Act. Section 3, para 1 gives the definition of personal data: it is single information about personal and factual circumstances relating to a determinable person. As with cl 2 of the General Business Conditions, this includes both factual information and evaluations; information that is already generally known falls under both definitions. However, there is a difference regarding the processing of data: non-public legal entities have to comply with the provisions of the Federal Data Protection Act if they use methods of automated data processing, which also covers methods of more traditional record-keeping.[15]

Having partially the same scope as other obligations of secrecy, s 1, para 3, sent 2 of the BDSG states that special obligations of secrecy are left unaltered; this includes bank confidentiality,[16] while the Federal Data Protection Act ensures the minimum standard of data protection. Therefore, a bank has to ensure that it meets not only the requirements under the contractual secrecy obligation, but also must check whether in a given case the standards set by the Federal Data Protection Act are met. The latter holds especially true for the use of personal data within the bank.

12   Gola in Gola and Schomerus *Bundesdatenschutzgesetz* (7th edn, 2002) s 1 Rn 6, BVerfGE 65 p 1ff.
13   Gola, n 12 above, s 1 Rn 7.
14   Gola, n 12 above, s 3 Rn 11.
15   Gola, n 12 above, s 3, Rn 15.
16   Gola, n 12 above.

Limitations on the protection of data

The basic principle for the treatment of personal data is laid down in s 4, para 1 of the BDSG: it allows inquiries for data processing and use of data in accordance with the provisions of any statute, including the BDSG, or if the person to whom the data relates has consented to the treatment. The first exception to data protection is identical to the limitation on the secrecy obligation. The Federal Data Protection Act itself allows in s 28, paras 1, 2 and 3 certain uses of data in non-governmental entities for professional purposes, for the protection of the entity's legitimate interests and for purposes of assistance in criminal prosecution. These provisions correspond for the most part with the limitations on bank confidentiality.

However, a difference exists regarding the customer's consent. There is no obligation for the consent relating to the bank's secrecy obligation to be given expressly, since an implied consent would suffice; the Federal Data Protection Act requires express consent in written form allowing only few exceptions (s 4a of the BDSG). This means that the protection provided by the secrecy obligation is weaker than that under the Federal Data Protection Act; therefore – applying the principle of s 1, para 2 of the BDSG – the contractual provisions should be overruled.

But even implied consent is possible[17] since the bank pursues a legitimate interest of its own when fulfilling its obligation under the contract in providing the service the client requested and thus acting in the interest of the client as well.

Finally, it remains to be stated that the practical consequences of differences between secrecy obligations and the law of data protection are of little importance. Nevertheless, the bank has to ensure that the provisions of the Federal Data Protection Act are followed, since violation may constitute a criminal or administrative offence according to ss 43 and 44 of the BDSG.

THE EXCEPTIONS TO THE SECRECY OBLIGATION

As shown above, cl 2, para 1 of the General Business Conditions lays down three main exceptions to the bank's secrecy obligation: customer's consent, request of banking information and disclosure that is required or permitted by law.

Customer's consent

Since the actual wish of the bank's client is decisive with regard to what information shall be kept secret, he is obviously free to release the bank from its secrecy obligation. He may do so for a particular case or may grant the release generally in advance; the release may be complete or restricted to certain types of information. Whether the consent has been given to the bank directly or to a third person is of no importance. Even an implicit release which can be deduced from the customer's behaviour will suffice.

---

17   ORR Koberstein-Windpassinger, n 3 above, at 477, 481.

If the customer did not consent expressly or where the bank has no knowledge of circumstances giving indications regarding the customer's actual wish, the bank may assume that the customer's actual wish corresponds to the hypothetical wish of a reasonable average customer.[18]

In the particular case of outsourcing of data processing work or other tasks to third entities, it is advisable to obtain the customer's consent in advance. The applicability of ss 11 and 27 of the BDSG, which generally allow for the transfer of data processing and the transfer of processing tasks without the customer's consent, is disputed heavily in its details.[19]

Another particular case in which the customer's consent has been given generally in advance concerns the so-called SCHUFA. The SCHUFA is an entity set up by banks and other enterprises that regularly give credit to their customers. From its partners and from public registers, the SCHUFA collects information regarding the creditworthiness of persons. The partners are obliged to transmit information about their customers to the SCHUFA in a standard format and containing formalised factual information about the customer relationship. The information given to and received by the SCHUFA does not contain any information about the wealth of a person or an evaluation of his creditworthiness. The SCHUFA passes on information relating to a certain person if the partner who requested it has demonstrated a legitimate interest in that information and the person has agreed to the collection of his information. The customer of a bank will be asked to declare his consent to that procedure generally in advance when, for example, a banking contract is concluded.

Banking information

Definition

Banking information is an instrument that has been developed between banks to share reliable information about the creditworthiness of their business partners. According to the contract, one bank must furnish to another bank true and complete information it possesses about its clients;[20] in case of negligent violation of this duty it will be liable for damages. It is important to state that according to cl 2, para 4 of the General Business Conditions, banking information will be provided not only to other banks, but also to clients of a bank.

What kind of information may be provided is defined in cl 2, para 2 of the General Business Conditions? Covered are general statements and comments as to the economic situation relating to the bank's customer. Unlike the SCHUFA system, the information here will not contain specific data but comprises comments on the banking relationship, on bank account movements and an evaluation of

---

18   Bruchner, n 2 above, p 747.
19   Steding and Meyer 'Outsourcing von Bankdienstleistungen: Bank- und datenschutzrechtliche Probleme der Aufgabenverlagerung von Kreditinstituten auf Tochtergesellschaften und sonstige Dritte' (2001) BB 1693.
20   BGH in ZIP 1999 p 275.

creditworthiness. The only exception to this rule is when a bank possesses information concerning cheques returned unpaid and protest of bills.[21]

The bank is obliged only to transmit the information currently available; a duty to conduct further investigation does not exist. When passing on information the bank has to do so concisely, revealing no unnecessary information.

Preconditions of disclosure

Clause 2, para 2 of the General Business Conditions lays down different requirements for two types of bank clients: business persons and others. Business persons are all legal entities and natural persons registered in the Commercial Register and their banking relationship can be attributed to the professional sphere. Regarding these customers, banking information is considered a trade custom; business persons are assumed to know of and to have consented to the disclosure through implied conduct. However, a business person might prove the contrary, and will then be treated like a non-business person.

Release of information about non-business persons always requires their express consent, which may also be given generally in advance. For both types of clients, the requirements are the existence of a credible legitimate interest in the information and the assumption that no legitimate interest of the customer contrary to the disclosure exists. An example of an interest of the bank requesting information may be its intention to avoid the risk of entering into business relations with insolvent debtors, while, on the customer side, banking information itself limits his legitimate interest in keeping financial information secret. The bank therefore has the obligation to apply a balancing test in which it has to consider which interest prevails. Should the outcome of that balancing test not clearly favour the disclosure, it is advisable to seek the specific consent of the customer concerned.

Statutory exceptions

Generally speaking, statutory exceptions can regularly be found when state authorities require banks to furnish information necessary for the achievement of public functions, for example, in a broad variety of administrative procedures. But under certain circumstances disclosure of confidential information is also allowed when statutory provisions govern the resolution of conflicts among private persons.

Tax proceedings

Confidentiality in tax proceedings is one of the most controversial issues since the provision acknowledging the existence of secrecy obligation (s 30a of the Tax Procedure Act) is widely considered to be unconstitutional. While during a normal procedure of tax assessment such an issue – only the Federal Constitutional Court may decide on the unconstitutionality of a statute – has no practical impact, it gives rise to problems regarding investigations on tax evasion.

21   Bruchner, n 2 above, p 792.

TAX ASSESSMENT

In principle, banks are to furnish information to the competent tax authorities about their customers and to produce the relevant documents as if the secrecy obligation did not exist (s 93, para 1 and s 97, para 1 of the Tax Procedure Act) and, in fact, bank confidentiality is not a professional secret in the sense of s 102 of the Tax Procedure Act. However, banks are considered a 'special kind of information source'[22] and therefore s 30a of the AO has been introduced to demonstrate the respect for the particular relationship between the bank and its customer, as s 30a, para 1 makes clear.

According to s 30a of the Tax Procedure Act, information from a bank may not be required for purposes of general supervision, merely a repetition of the principle of due course of law,[23] according to which investigations commenced out of the blue are unlawful. While paras 3 and 4 do not apply to the procedure of tax assessment, para 5, sent 1 states the applicability of s 93 of the Tax Procedure Act where in para 1, sent 3 the principle of subsidiarity is laid down. Consequently, information may be requested from a bank only if it cannot be obtained from the taxpayer himself. Furthermore, the request has to be both necessary and appropriate with respect to the assessment of taxes;[24] which information and the scope in which it is requested must be stated in detail.

In practice, the tax authorities assume that the taxpayer's declaration of income is true and complete.[25] Lack of personnel prevents them from requesting information from banks even where it would be possible.[26] Therefore, further investigation will take place only in the presence of aggravating circumstances when, for instance, systematic or large-scale tax evasion and active collaboration by the bank is suspected.

When the bank receives a request from the tax authorities it is obliged to verify whether the requirements for a lawful request have been satisfied – otherwise the bank must refuse to disclose the information since an unlawful request does not release the bank from its secrecy obligations. If the request is lawful the bank has to provide the requested information truthfully and completely.

Where the unlawfulness of the request is in doubt both bank and customer may file a petition for administrative review and if the petition is denied they may initiate proceedings before a fiscal court. Bank employees are obliged to testify before a fiscal court: s 84 of the Fiscal Procedure Act and s 102 of the Tax Procedure Act.

Finally, even with respect to foreign authorities, the secrecy obligation proves too weak: a request for information made by a foreign authority will be fulfilled by its German counterpart provided that the requirements of the Tax Procedure Act are met.[27]

---

22 Carl and Klos *Bankgeheimnis und Quellensteuer im Vergleich internationaler Finanzmärkte* (1993) p 33.
23 Metzner in Beermann 'Steuerliches Verfahrensrecht – AO, FGO, Nebengesetze – Kommentar' AO, s 30a, Rn 41.
24 Carl and Klos, n 22 above, p 34.
25 Metzner, n 23 above, AO, s 30a, Rn 38.
26 Ehrhardt-Rauch and Rauch 'Ist der Schutz von Bankkunden nach §30a AO auch künftig noch haltbar? – Neue Wege bei der europäischen Zinsbesteuerung' (2002) DStR 57 at 58.
27 Carl and Klos, n 22 above, p 70.

INVESTIGATION IN RESPECT OF TAX EVASION

The investigation regarding fiscal fraud has a different objective (s 208 of the Tax Procedure Act: discovering tax evasion, investigation of cases where taxes have not yet been assessed), but it is conducted by the same authorities and basically follows the same rules.

According to s 208, para 1, sent 3 of the Tax Procedure Act, the principle of subsidiarity of s 93, para 1, sent 3 of the Act is not generally applicable within the investigation procedure, thus enlarging the competence of the tax authorities. But s 30a, para 5, sent 2 of the Tax Procedure Act re-establishes the applicability of that principle. Furthermore, s 30a, paras 2 and 3 of the Act limit the powers of the tax authorities. Therefore, the protection of the confidential information depends on whether or not the provision of s 30a the Act is constitutional.

Prior to the introduction of s 30a of the Tax Procedure Act, tax authorities based their activities on a regulatory order with almost identical contents; it was declared unconstitutional by the Federal Constitutional Court in 1991.[28] Instead of creating the potential to assess taxes equally and abolishing s 30a of the Tax Procedure Act, the legislator raised the tax-free allowance tenfold, ensuring equal taxation of all capital gains within that allowance. A pragmatic solution. The fact that s 30a still constituted an obstacle to investigations was no longer considered a problem. The provision itself was not brought before the Federal Constitutional Court.

In 1999 the allowance was been cut by 50% and constitutional concerns are growing once more.[29] Moreover, in 1997 the eighth senate of the Federal Fiscal Court held that the provision had to be construed along the guidelines set out by the verdict of the Federal Constitutional Court and could therefore be saved from unconstitutionality.[30] Contrary to this, the seventh senate of the Federal Fiscal Court held in 2000 that the eighth senate's interpretation of s 30a of the Tax Procedure Act was compatible neither with the wording of that provision nor with the will of the legislator. The seventh senate made clear that it considered the provision unconstitutional but was unable to submit the question to the Federal Constitutional Court for procedural reasons. The practical consequences were: according to the first opinion, a tax inspector inspecting the bank may pass on information to other authorities regarding customers of that bank if he reaches the conclusion (based on fact) that taxes might not have been assessed correctly, while according to the second opinion, the protection of the secrecy obligation would prevail. The question remains open.

On the horizon the next challenge is already visible – the EC is currently elaborating a Directive aiming at harmonisation of taxes on capital gains.[31] In January 2003, 12 member states, including Germany, decided to set up a systematic exchange of information between the tax authorities of all member states of the EU. Under this system banks in Germany would be obliged to transmit information about non-

28 BVerfG in ZIP 1991 p 1123.
29 Blesinger 'Materielle Steuerpflicht von Zinseinkünften nach §20 I Nr. 7 EStG und Ermittlungsbefugnisse der Finanzbehörden – Zum latenten Konflikt um die Auslegung des §30a AO durch den 7. und 8. Senat ds BFH' (2001) NJW 1459 at 1460.
30 BFH in NJW 1997 p 2067.
31 Blesinger, n 29 above, at 1463.

German customers to the German tax authorities which would then pass on the information to the competent tax authority abroad. That system could leave s 30a of the Tax Procedure Act unaltered since it applies to German taxpayers. But automatically the question arises whether such provision is compatible with the prohibition against discrimination of European citizens contained in art 12 EC (Treaty of Amsterdam) and with the guarantees of free movement of services and capital within the European Single Market.[32] While a reasonable justification for the discrimination of taxpayers is conceivable, the provisions regarding the single market could be violated by leaving s 30a unchanged.[33] In any case, it is desirable that German legislation acts with more sense of responsibility and more far-sightedness than in the past.

PENAL PROCEEDINGS FOR TAX OFFENCES

The prosecution can be carried out either by the tax authorities themselves or by the office of public prosecution. Both have the same powers, based on the Criminal Procedure Act instead of the Tax Procedure Act; therefore problems regarding s 30a of the Tax Procedure Act will not occur. Against the measures both the bank and the customer may file a complaint before a court of ordinary jurisdiction: s 23 Introductory Act to the System of Judicature Act.

SPECIAL INFORMATION DUTIES

According to s 45d of the Income Tax Act, banks are obliged to disclose to the tax authorities to what extent a single customer has made use of his tax-free allowance of capital gains.

Section 33 of the Inheritance Tax Act imposes on banks the duty to inform the tax authorities regarding all goods of deceased customers which the bank holds in its possession, as well as all claims.

Being special regulations in relation to s 30a of the Tax Procedure Act, the latter provision is never applicable in these circumstances.[34]

Criminal proceedings

NO RIGHT TO REFUSE TO GIVE EVIDENCE

Section 53 of the Criminal Procedure Act enumerates the professional secrets enjoying protection in criminal proceedings. Unlike auditors, banks and their employees are not included in the list. Interpretation enlarging the scope of the provision is universally rejected both by courts and commentators,[35] based on the argument that even the legislator has to respect certain limits in order to maintain the efficiency of criminal proceedings.

32 Ehrhardt-Rauch and Rauch, n 26 above, at 63.
33 Ehrhardt-Rauch and Rauch, n 26 above, at 64.
34 Metzner, n 23 above, AO, s 30a, Rnn 68, 73.
35 Dahs in Löwe and Rosenberg *Die Strafprozeßordnung und das Gerichtsverfassungsgesetz* (25th edn, 1999) s 53, Rn 4.

PRELIMINARY INVESTIGATION

The secrecy obligation is not protected during preliminary investigation, but no person is obliged to make any statements concerning the subject of the investigation unless he is being questioned by a district attorney: s 161a, para 1, sent 1 of the Criminal Procedure Act.

If concrete factual information gives reason to believe the bank might be in possession of objects that could be seized according to s 94, para 1 of the Criminal Procedure Act because they constitute evidence, the office of public prosecution has power to search the facilities of the bank: s 103, para 1, sent 1 of the Criminal Procedure Act. General experience or mere speculation are not sufficient.[36] For example, the Federal Constitutional Court upheld the constitutionality of measures against several subsidiaries of a bank based on the suspicion that one subsidiary had helped its customers evade taxes.[37] The judgments have been widely criticised but, so far, courts regard similar searches as lawful.[38]

If the bank has no right to refuse to provide evidence, the bank also has no right to object to the seizure of documents or objects according to s 97, para 1 of the Criminal Procedure Act. Evidence regarding further criminal acts that was found by chance may be seized as well, but prosecutors are not competent to search for anything that is not covered by the objectives of the search order.

In principle, search orders have to be issued by a judge of proper jurisdiction (s 105 of the Criminal Procedure Act) and it is only in rare cases of emergency (for example, a bank employee being suspected of having aided in the criminal act) that a search order issued by the office of public prosecution will suffice. The search order must name the investigated offence specifically and may be carried out only during hours of daylight unless there are particular circumstances: s 104 of the Criminal Procedure Act.

Often, the public prosecutor will ask the bank deliberately to provide the information requested, thus rendering a search and seizure of documents superfluous. Of course, the bank is not obliged to hold back the information for as long as possible and as long as the formal requirements are not evaded it may pass on the information. But it is important to emphasise that unless all requirements are met (including the search order issued by a judge) the bank is not obliged to produce any documents.

Therefore, the bank is also obliged to check whether or not the request for information is lawful. To protect itself and its customers' interests it may request the decision of a judge when the search has been conducted by virtue of an order from the office of public prosecution issued in an emergency, or it may file a complaint against the judicial order.

INTERNATIONAL CO-OPERATION IN CRIMINAL MATTERS

The application of the German Act on International Assistance in Criminal Matters (IRG) is broad: assistance meaning every part of the criminal proceedings from

---

36 Kleinknecht and Meyer-Goßner *Strafprozeßordnung* (44th edn, 1999) s 94, Rn 8, s 152, Rn 4.
37 BVerfG in WM 1994 p 691; and BVerfG in WM 1995 p 234.
38 Bielefeld in WM 2000 p 239.

preliminary investigation to execution of a sentence, irrespective of whether the assistance is requested by a foreign court or other authority (s 59, abs 2 of the IRG).

Section 59ff of the IRG, in particular, interfere with the bank's secrecy obligation as they allow assistance basically in accordance with the German provisions on investigative measures and criminal proceedings: s 59, para 3 of the IRG. That means that the same requirements as stated in ss 94ff and 103ff of the Criminal Procedure Act for seizure of documents and searches of bank premises must be met[39] if German authorities are to lend assistance to foreign authorities.[40]

Within the field of application of the European Convention on Mutual Assistance in Criminal Matters – provided the Federal Republic of Germany and the country of the requesting authority have both ratified the Convention – international co-operation differs only slightly from the IRG's provisions, since Germany has declared a reservation regarding art 5, para 1, lit a and c of the Convention, establishing the prerequisite that the crime investigated be punishable in both countries and the investigation compatible with German law.

The ratification of the Convention on Money Laundering, Search, Seizure and Confiscation of the Proceeds of Crime on behalf of Germany has brought no changes to the previously existing legal situation.

Other proceedings

CIVIL PROCEEDINGS AND OTHER JUDICIAL PROCEEDINGS

Contrary to the situation during criminal proceedings, the secrecy obligation is protected according to s 383 para 1, n 6 of the Civil Procedure Act and the bank's employees are obliged under the banking contract with their customer to refuse to give evidence.[41] However, the customer may release the bank from this obligation; the bank employees are then obliged to testify as are all normal witnesses: s 385, para 2 of the Civil Procedure Act.

The bank is entitled to refuse testimony if giving evidence would lead to economic losses (s 384, n 1 of the Civil Procedure Act), for example, giving rise to liability on the part of the bank for damages for a breach of its secrecy obligation.[42] The customer's consent will not overrule the right to refuse testimony, but excludes the possibility of liability for damages.

Both provisions may be invoked where German judicial organs act upon request by foreign courts within the scope of the Hague Convention on the Taking of Evidence Abroad in Civil and Commercial Matters (art 11 para 1, lit a). Furthermore, they apply before labour courts, in insolvency proceedings (s 4 of the InsO), in proceeding of voluntary jurisdiction (s 15 of the FGG); in proceedings before administrative (s 98 of the VwGO) and social courts (s 118, para 1 of the SGG).

---

39   Lagodny in Schomburg and Lagodny *Internationale Rechtshilfe in Strafsachen* (3rd edn, 1998) p 208.
40   Lagodny, n 39 above, p 318.
41   Greger in Zöller *Zivilprozeßordnung* (22nd edn, 2001) p 1088.
42   Damrau in *Münchner Kommentar zur Zivilprozeßordnung* Pt 2 (2nd edn, 2000) s 174.

DECLARATION OF THIRD-PARTY DEBTOR

A judgment against a bank's customer might be enforced by attaching the customer claims against the bank, such as his bank account. In these cases the bank is obliged – just like any other third-party debtor – to give the declaration of a third-party debtor according to s 840, para 1 of the Civil Procedure Act. The declaration comprises the statement as to whether the bank recognises the claim and whether other creditors have already claimed or even attached it. No further information regarding other claims of the customer or private facts is to be revealed.

ADMINISTRATIVE PROCEDURE

Participants (s 13 of the VwVfG) in administrative procedures are not generally obliged to reveal information, but some special regulations do apply concerning social welfare law.

For instance, if a bank's customer has applied for unemployment benefits the bank is under a duty to pass on information about the financial situation, not only of the applicant but also of his spouse or partner if that information cannot be obtained otherwise – in particular where the statements made by the applicant are not credible: s 315, para 2 of the SGB III.

If a customer has requested public welfare the bank itself is not obliged to disclose information, but s 60, para 1, n 1 of the SGB AT imposes a requirement to release the bank from its secrecy obligation.

Since the second edition of this book, the number of contracting parties to the European Convention on Mutual Assistance in Administrative Matters has risen to six – the Convention is still of only little practical importance.

SUPERVISION OF SECURITY EXCHANGES

The trade of securities in Germany is subject to special supervision aimed at preserving the integrity of the financial market, first, through control of the institutions participating in the exchange and, secondly, through control of the trade itself, with particular respect to insider trading. The secrecy obligation may come under the provisions regarding insider trade in two instances: first the bank may be requested by the competent supervision authority (Federal Corporation for Supervision of Financial Services, BAFin) to supply information or the bank might be tempted to use insider information to their own or their clients' advantage.

Obligations of disclosure regarding insider trading

The competence of supervision is limited by the definition of the concepts of insider, insider information and insider securities.[43] The latter covers stocks, bonds, stock options and others (s 2, para 1 and s 12, para 2 of the Securities Trading Act), while insider information is all information not publicly known relating to the issuer and

---

43   Assmann and Schneider *Wertpapierhandelsgesetz* (2nd edn, 1999) above s 12, Rn14.

capable of influencing the price of the security. It is evident that the secrecy obligation covers more protected information than the prohibition of insider trading; in other words not all information falling under bank confidentiality is insider information. Of both types of insiders – a primary insider (s 13, para 1 of the Securities Trading Act) or a secondary insider (s 13, para 2) – the bank's organs and employees will in nearly all cases be the primary insider, for they regularly obtain insider information in performance of their profession or a specific task.[44] Section 14, para 1 of the Securities Trading Act sets up an interdiction for primary insiders to trade in securities on the basis of their insider knowledge, to pass on the insider information and to recommend the purchase or sale to third parties.

To ensure that these interdictions are respected, the BAFin has been given certain powers. First, all institutions offering services relating to the exchange of securities are obliged according to s 9, para 1 of the Securities Trading Act to furnish particular information on every single exchange made by them. This information comprises data to identify the securities traded, date and time of sale, price and number of traded securities and – added by the 4th Financial Market Promotion Act – distinguishing marks for the depot holder and, if not identical, the principal. If this information gives reason to believe that a violation of the regulations on insider trading has been committed, the BAFin may require the bank according to s 16, para 2, sents 1, 3 and 4 of the Securities Trading Act to give detailed information about the trading, including the information necessary to identify the principal, as well as the production of documents relating to the trading. Finally, the bank in such cases has to acquiesce to a search of its premises.[45]

The information obtained in this manner may be communicated by the BAFin to similar authorities in other member states of the EU according to s 19 of the Securities Trading Act; the refusal of transmission is allowed only in very few cases (s 19, paras 3 and 4 of the Securities Trading Act). The co-operation with authorities of other states is provided for in s 19, para 5. Germany has not signed the European Council Convention on Insider Trading.

Advising investors

Without the slightest doubt, it is forbidden for the bank to use any insider information it has obtained in the course of a banking relationship with a client for its owns sales and acquisitions of securities. But when a bank advises one of its customers regarding his investments, it is obliged to provide complete and true information regarding the investment, as well as to render competent services.[46] Does this contractual duty exempt the bank from the interdiction on disclosing insider information and to not recommend transactions based on such information? It does not, because a contractual provision cannot constitute grounds sufficient to justify a violation of statutory provision.[47] Therefore, information subject to the secrecy obligation which at the

---

44   Assmann 'Insiderrecht und Kreditwirtschaft' (1996) WM 1337 at 1343.
45   Assmann and Schneider, n 43 above, above s 12, Rn 28.
46   Assmann, n 44 above, at 1352.
47   Assmann, n 44 above, at 1351.

same time amounts to insider information may not be disclosed to other customers of the bank. Whether this holds true also for information not falling under the definition of insider information remains to be seen (see Collision of duties below).

The matter will be divided into two parts: here the provisions of the German Banking Act will be discussed, while some recent amendments will be discussed more thoroughly at the end of the chapter.

The supervision of banks and similar institutions aims to prevent damage to the banking structure and – being a key function[48] – to the economy as a whole, as well as to avoid losses to individual customers.[49] The BAFin was only established in 2002 and now centralises all supervisory competence regarding financial services and also exercises control both of the inner structure of banks and of their business practices. To accomplish these tasks the BAFin is authorised to request information from all banks and similar institutions (s 1, para 1 of the German Banking Act) on every part of their business and without any special cause,[50] for example, on the development of income and expenditure, large loans and even information regarding a single customer relationship. It is, however, not entitled to request information incompatible with the control of structure and conduct of business and, furthermore, the request must be both necessary and appropriate to the accomplishment of said tasks.[51]

If those requirements are met, the authority also has power to request documentation from the bank and carry out an audit. According to s 44a of the German Banking Act, the BAFin assists foreign authorities in the supervision of German banks when the principles mentioned above are respected.

Criminal law and money laundering

SECTION 261 OF THE CRIMINAL CODE

The purpose of this long and complicated provision is to fight money laundering, ie the introduction of money or goods deriving from criminal acts, such as tax evasion, theft, burglary, and dealing in illegal drugs, into the legal circulation of money. It punishes the concealment of such goods, covering up their origin, endangering prosecution as well as acquiring or keeping such goods for somebody else. This criterion is already fulfilled when a bank accepts money to deposit or transfer it. Sufficient to commit the offence is, according to s 261, para 5 of the Criminal Code, the recklessness of the person accepting the proceeds from crime. Obviously, according to principles of rule of law, a bank employee is not obliged to denounce himself if he fears that he has committed the offence of money laundering, but such self-denunciation does constitute grounds for mitigation of sentence (s 261, paras 9

---

48   Boos and Bock *Kreditwesengesetz* (2000) p 107.
49   Begründung zum KWG in BT Drs. III/ 114 as quoted in Boos and Bock, n 48 above, p 107.
50   Boos and Bock, n 48 above, p 900.
51   Boos and Bock, n 48 above, pp 891, 899.

and 10 of the Criminal Code), thus exercising considerable pressure on bank employees to do so.

THE ACT ON THE DETECTION OF PROCEEDS FROM SERIOUS CRIMES

This Act (in short, the Money Laundering Act) contains provision in order to obtain information on money laundering especially from banks and is therefore an implementation law with regard to s 261 of the Criminal Code. It imposes on banks duties to identify its customers thoroughly, to report any suspicious movement of money and to keep records of transactions. If a bank violates these duties, it may constitute negligent conduct in the sense of s 261, para 5 of the Code. It always constitutes a minor offence: s 17 of the Money Laundering Act.

The obligation to identify a customer comes into existence when the customer requires a transaction exceeding certain limits: ss 2 to 5 of the Money Laundering Act. If the bank notices suspicious behaviour by its clients it is under the duty to give notice of this suspicion to the competent prosecution authorities according to s 11 of the Money Laundering Act. The obligation requires that all information leading to the suspicion a certain transaction amounts to money laundering be disclosed. The suspicion may be based on striking details of a certain transaction or on deviations from normal conduct. It is not necessary for the bank to suspect that the money originates from a criminal act.

In contrast to s 261 of the Criminal Code, which lays down the punishments for individuals, s 11 of the Money Laundering Act imposes the duty on the bank itself. The bank is required to ensure the respect of the provisions of the Money Laundering Act through measures such as the appointment of a money laundering officer and the adoption of procedures for the detection of money laundering. The pressure put on the individual bank employees is therefore lessened because if a bank employee reports a suspicion to the competent officer he will not be punishable for negligence.

A recent amendment to s 14, para 2 of the Money Laundering Act poses new problems and will be discussed at the end of the chapter.

Civil law

CHEQUES AND BILL OF EXCHANGES, DEBIT ENTRY

Before making a demand for payment, the payee usually asks the bank if it deems the cheque payable. The positive answer is that the bank considers the drawer's bank account sufficient to the payment on the cheque. The bank is entitled to reveal this information since drawing a cheque implies that the drawer reveals both the existence of a bank account and a certain sum on its bank account.

If the bank does not pay on the cheque, the bank is entitled to disclose any information on the drawer necessary for the collection of the debt. That is grounded on the assumption that the drawer has tacitly consented to disclosure guaranteeing smooth traffic of his cheques.[52]

---

52   Bruchner, n 2 above, p 749.

On the other hand, the permission to perform debit entries does not include an implied consent to answer a request on the bank account – while the cheque has been drawn on a certain sum the permission to perform debit entries is generally given for several debit entries in advance and depends furthermore on the submissions of accounts prior to the transaction.[53]

GUARANTEES AND OTHER THIRD-PARTY SURETIES

If a third party guarantees for a bank's claim against a bank customer, the bank may in particular circumstances be obliged to furnish information regarding the customer to the guarantor, for example, if the bank has learned that the customer is not creditworthy, if it was plain to the bank that the guarantor acted erroneously or the customer himself caused the guarantor to bind itself.[54]

After a guarantor has satisfied the obligation, the claim against the debtor is automatically transferred to him: s 774 of the Civil Code. The guarantor then is entitled according to ss 412 and 402 of the Code to obtain all information necessary for collection of the debt, but does this right release the bank from its secrecy obligation? Since s 402 of the Code only covers the legal relationship between assignee and the bank, in this case it may not justify the violation of third-party interest.[55] Therefore, the bank has in principle to keep its customer's information secret. There are various solutions to this problem: the bank may decide not to pass on information relating to the client and to work as a service agent collecting the debt for the assignee or it may seek the consent of the client to disclosure of information. Regarding certain types of assignments, the consent is presumed, for instance, when the assignment forms part of a structure to share the risk originating from the claim or generally if the claim is assigned to another bank that itself is subject to a secrecy obligation.[56] Commentators argue that the consent of a customer to sureties by third parties always contains the implied release of the bank from its secrecy obligation as far as information relating to the secured claims is concerned.[57]

If the bank reveals information, it will be facts such as the identity of the debtor, the amount of the claims and the delivery of existing deeds. Information irrelevant to the collection has to be rendered illegible.

ASSIGNMENT OF CLAIMS AND EXECUTION OF OTHER SURETIES

This category applies to cases where the customer has assigned a claim to his bank – the assignment itself does not have to be disclosed to the debtor: on the contrary, very often the client will expressly wish the assignment to be kept confidential. If payment of the assigned claim is delayed, the bank may disclose the assignment in order to try to collect the debt. Usually, this will be provided for expressly in the

---

53 Bruchner, n 2 above, p 750.
54 Bruchner, n 2 above, p 750, with Rspr-Nachweisen.
55 ORR Koberstein-Windpassinger, n 3 above, at 478.
56 Früh 'Abtretungen, Verpfändungen, Unterbeteiligungen, Verbriefungen und Derivate bei Kreditforderungen vor dem Hintergrund von Bankgeheimnis und Datenschutz' (2000) WM 497 at 503ff.
57 OLG Oldenburg (1985) WM 748.

contract underlying the assignment, especially when an instalment plan exists. The extent to which information may be disclosed is determined again by the necessities of debt collection.

ASSET-BACKED SECURITIES

Asset-backed securities transactions involve the assignment of a bank's claim against its customer to a legal entity (a so-called 'special-purpose vehicle') which has been created to issue securities to investors using the assigned claims as back-up. Those transactions are undertaken by banks to limit their need for proprietary capital.[58] Regarding bank confidentiality, two problems occur: the bank is obliged to furnish information about the debtor (its customer) to the assignee according to s 402 of the Civil Code and the investors of the special-purpose vehicle will want to examine the financial reliability of the claims backing their investment.

As explained above, s 402 of the Civil Code does not hinder the assignment of claims, but disclosing information will breach the secrecy obligation.[59] In most cases the bank will operate as a service agent of the special-purpose vehicle.

To ensure the success of asset-backed securities transactions, investors must be granted the opportunity to scrutinise the financial standing of the special-purpose vehicle and, in particular, the assigned claims. Therefore, they must also have knowledge of information that relates to individual customers. The bank, though, has the opportunity to present the information in anonymous and aggregate form.[60] Information regarding the historical development of the pool of claims and the classification of debtors will enable rating agencies to check sufficiently the financial reliability of the claims underlying the securities issued by the special-purpose vehicle. The identity of a debtor which necessarily forms only a very small part of the pool of claims is irrelevant.

INSOLVENCY PROCEEDINGS

Upon appointment of an administrator in insolvency, a legal entity or a natural person loses his power of disposal to the administrator. Consequently, the administrator is entitled to obtain all information about the financial situation from the bank as long as the information concerns the insolvency procedure. Regarding other information, such as facts from the private sphere, the secrecy obligation prevails.

INHERITANCE

The heirs of a deceased bank customer step automatically into the banking relationship. As the new customer of the bank the heir is entitled to all information relating to the banking relationship, such as the existence of bank accounts, deposits, claims and so on. Courts, however, have set up a barrier to the disclosure of information

58   ORR Koberstein-Windpassinger, n 3 above, at 473.
59   Conclusion from s 407 of the Civil Code: ORR Koberstein-Windpassinger, n 55 above, at 474.
60   Früh, n 56 above, at 502ff.

regarded a personal secret of the deceased, protecting his right to privacy[61] and subsisting even after the death of a person.

Persons entitled to a compulsory portion of the inheritance and legatees are not entitled to receive information from the bank – they may only invoke such right against the heir: s 2314 of the Civil Code.

ESCROW ACCOUNTS

Banks set up accounts for certain professions, such as notaries, lawyers and auditors, that accept money in a third party's name, administrate the money and transfer it to the third party. Regarding this type of account, only the trustee has power of disposal and is solely entitled to information. Therefore, a bank is not obliged to answer a request by the trustor and if it did so it would be liable towards the trustee. Not even the aforementioned principle of the inclusion of a person in close relation to the bank's customer applies since the contracts regarding escrow accounts expressly exclude such protection.[62]

SELF-DEFENCE

The bank is entitled to disclose information under the provision of s 227 of the Civil Code if disclosure of the information is necessary to prevent any damage arising from illegal acts committed by the bank itself or other people (such as employees, customers and other third persons). Refusal to pay will not amount to unlawful conduct, which has to interfere with a particularly protected interest of the bank or the third person. Furthermore, self-defence is only an appropriate measure when the unlawful act is either about to begin or still endures and has not been completed.

COLLISION OF DUTIES

This exception designates a very broad category of which only individual cases have been expressly laid down in statutory provisions (such as s 227 of the Civil Code). It applies in cases where a bank is under contractual duties towards two (or more) customers and those duties collide, ie the fulfilment of one duty excludes the fulfilment of the other. A typical example is when a secrecy obligation collides with the bank's duty to warn a second customer of risks relating to business with the first customer. In these cases the principle that a bank is not obliged to warn customers about the risks relating to their business partners is universally recognised.[63] The situation changes though when a bank learns that one client is attempting to deceive the second customer. Whether the duty to warn prevails over the secrecy obligation is a question the bank has to consider very carefully: it has to perform a balancing test similar to the one mentioned regarding banking information in order to find out which of the concrete interests involved proves stronger.[64]

---

61   OLG Stuttgart in MDR 1983 p 236.
62   Bruchner, n 2 above, p 755.
63   BGH in WM 1978 p 1038; WM 1987 p 1546; WM 1989 p 1409.
64   BGH in WM 1991 p 85.

PURSUIT OF LEGITIMATE INTERESTS

Where interests of customers may conflict, a conflict of interests of a customer with interests of the bank is also conceivable. The justification of a disclosure by overriding interests of the bank would be the general principal underlying self-defence in the sense of s 227 of the Civil Code. However, the applicability of that principle has been recognised only relating to the setting up of the SCHUFA system (see Customer's consent above).[65] General applicability to other cases must be denied since then the respect of the secrecy obligation would merely depend on a balancing test – carried out by a bank knowing their own interest is at stake.[66] Exceptions to this principle may be made in single cases where a customer has acted contrary to loyalty and good faith, causing damage to the bank – for instance, a customer may not invoke the secrecy obligation in a lawsuit against the bank.

LEGISLATION IN REACTION TO THE TERRORIST ATTACKS OF 11 SEPTEMBER 2001

The terrorist attacks aimed at the World Trade Center in New York and the US Ministry of Defense have been followed by the adoption of measures with which the German Parliament seeks to provide the competent authorities with appropriate instruments to react effectively to the newly discovered threats.[67] With two packages of security measures the Bundestag has enacted amendments to facilitate the investigation, prosecution and prevention of crimes relating to terrorism. Particular importance was attributed to the discovery of financial sources and, therefore, the drafts of amendments to the Money Laundering Act and the draft of the Fourth Financial Market Promotion Act have been revised in this respect. The Fourth Financial Market Promotion Act entered into force on 1 July 2002, while the amendments to the Money Laundering Act entered into force on 15 of July 2002.

In particular, a request repeatedly made by the former supervising authority for banking affairs, BAKred, now a department of the BAFin, which met with considerable opposition from the banks, seems to have been satisfied: the authority demanded that an obligation be imposed on the banks to monitor transactions not only when suspicions arise but generally and without particular cause. The banks refused to comply with that request, which lacked a foundation in statutory law, because they feared that they would be unduly burdened with the undertaking of primarily public tasks and also feared that they would lose the confidence of their clients.[68] It is the opinion of several commentators that the wish of the authority has been translated

---

65   BGH in WM 1978 p 999.
66   Bruchner, n 2 above, p 757.
67   Overview legislative activities: Jahn 'Verschärfte 'Finanzkontrollen nach Terroranschlägen' (2002) ZRP 109.
68   Dittrich and Trinkaus 'Die gesetzlichen Regelungen der Geldwäsche und ihre Reform – eine Praxisanalyse' (1998) DStR 342 at 347; Fülbier and Aepfelbach *GwG – Kommentar zum Geldwäschegesetz* (4th edn, 1999) s 14, Rn 123; Herzog 'Der Banker als Fahnder? Von der Verdachtsanzeige zur systematischen Verdachtsgewinnung – Entwicklungstendenzen der Geldwäschebekämpfung' (1996) WM 1753.

into law, especially in s 14, para 2, n 2 of the Money Laundering Act and s 25a, nr 4 of the German Banking Act.[69]

Criminal law – amendments to the Money Laundering Act

Underlying the new provisions in the field of banking regulation[70] and extended to the Money Laundering Act are the guidelines set up by the Basle Committee on 'Customer due diligence for banks'.[71] The new s 14, para 2, n 2 of the Money Laundering Act requires the development of internal principles and the adoption of appropriate security measures relating to transactions and clients to prevent money laundering and financing of terrorist groups. The method proposed by the BaFin is to analyse the patterns of money laundering, to gather the available information on every customer relationship and to search that data for circumstances similar to the patterns of money laundering. If this so-called screening leads to a suspicion that there might be a case of money laundering, the bank is obliged under s 11 of the Money Laundering Act to notify the authorities. It is still not clear if the approach suggested by the authorities is founded on statutory provisions.

A legal basis for screening cannot be seen in s 14, para 2, n 2 of the Money Laundering Act and the very similar provision of s 25a, n 4 of the German Banking Act (corresponding to n 15 of Basle Committee guidelines) because the provisions do not determine with sufficient clarity and certainty which measures are to be taken[72] but leave the choice of how the rights of the bank's customers are limited to the discretion of the banks. Some banks, therefore, have declared that they will not translate the proposed method of screening into action.[73]

The amendments have also led to the creation of a new department within the Bundeskriminalamt, a federal investigative authority which will be competent from now on regarding the collection of notices according to s 11 of the Money Laundering Act. It will have the task of devising schemes to detect money laundering, make them available to banks and will also analyse in further detail cases of suspicion before passing them on to the competent prosecution offices.[74]

Changes in securities and banking regulations

The changes to the Securities Trading Act have been secondary: the reporting requirement according to s 9 has already been mentioned and the ban on price manipulation inserted in s 20a was to be found previously in s 88 of the Stock Exchange Act. According to the new s 20b of the Securities Trading Act, the BAFin

69 Jahn, n 67 above; SOWIE Bergles and Eul.
70 Hutter 'Das 4. Finanzmarktförderungsgesetz aus Unternehmenssicht' (2002) NZG 649 at 652.
71 Bergles and Eul '"Rasterfahndung" zur Geldwäschebekämpfung – ein Konflikt mit dem Datenschutz?' (2002) BKR 556 at 558, 559.
72 Escher 'Bankaufsichtsrechtliche Änderungen im KWG durch das Vierte Finanzmarktförderungsgesetz' (2002) BKR 652 at 661.
73 Bergles and Eul, n 71 above, at 562.
74 Jahn, n 67 above.

may request information as to manipulation in the sense of s 20a from banks and institutions offering services relating to security trading.[75]

At the time the government presented its draft of the Fourth Financial Market Promotion Act, s 24c of the German Banking Act provided for the setting up of a register of all bank accounts and depots in Germany.[76] After protest from banks the moderated new s 24c obliges banks to create the facilities enabling online access of the BAFin to the data of banks.[77] The online access will release the authority from the necessity to issue an individual request to each of the nearly 3,000 banks in Germany and will enable the BAFin to control 'with which institutions a certain person or a certain organisation maintains banking relationships'.[78] Even more than the desire of the authorities that banks may screen their customer's data, this provision is bound to impair the trust of the customers in bank confidentiality since the authority may pass on the data collected (bank account number, date of opening and closure, name and date of birth) to other authorities enumerated in s 24c, para 3 if it is required for their purposes.[79]

The newly introduced s 25b of the German Banking Act obliges banks and similar institutions to collect a set of data on identity, the bank account number and the address of customers wishing to transfer money to a country other than a member state of the EU. It must also transmit the information to the bank receiving the transferred funds.

Summing up the latest developments regarding the secrecy obligation of banks in Germany, it can be said that the once high standard[80] has been considerably limited in the last months regarding the powers of public authorities to request information from banks.

---

75   Hutter, n 70 above, at 651.
76   Former §24c KWG-E. See also Möller 'Das Vierte Finanzmarktförderungsgesetz – Der Regierungsentwurf' (2001) WM 2405 at 2413.
77   Jahn, n 69 above, at 110.
78   Federal Ministry of Finance, press release, 19 June 2002.
79   Escher, n 72 above, at 658.
80   Carl and Klos, n 22 above, p 32.

13   Greece

Marios Bahas

INTRODUCTION

This chapter deals with the issues relating to bank secrecy and confidentiality under Greek law. Such rules are included in the Greek Constitution of 1975, the Penal Code and statutes regulating the pertinent issues.

The statutes in question address, in particular, the nature of the obligation of confidentiality; the remedies available for breach thereof, as well as for breach of bank secrecy; the exceptions to the rule; the scope of the exceptions; and the question of how foreign investigatory and supervisory bodies can gain access to confidential information in Greece.

Following this line of thought, this chapter will examine some practical examples related to such access, and address the pertinent questions arising therefrom. Subsequently, examples concerning the tracing of funds both in Greece and abroad are discussed. The last part of the chapter addresses various areas of the law that are worthy of examination, such as insider dealing, cross-selling, the use of information stored as data and protection thereof. Finally, examples relating to conflict of interest and take-overs are discussed in the light of existing Greek legislation. In the latter case a differentiation is made between financing through public subscription and private placement and the role of the bank is clarified accordingly.

OVERVIEW OF BANK SECRECY LAW

The rules of Greek law relating to bank secrecy are included in the Greek Constitution, the Penal Code and statutes. A brief analysis of the relevant rules is therefore necessary.

Greek Constitution

Article 19 of the Constitution of 1975 stipulates the principle of protection of communication and correspondence. Such protection also embraces foreign persons, as according to art 4 both Greek citizens and foreign nationals enjoy the same civil rights. Consequently, the constitutional protection in question includes both bank secrecy and the duty of confidentiality for Greek and foreign nationals alike.

Penal Code

Article 371, para 1 of the Penal Code provides that the penalties of a fine or of up to one year's imprisonment be imposed upon doctors, lawyers, notaries and other persons (such as bankers and bank officials) and their assistants confided with private secrets in the exercise of their profession who reveal such secrets to third parties in any manner whatsoever. The article in question embraces both Greek and foreign persons without distinction.

Article 371, para 2 provides that criminal proceedings are not suspended in the case of the death of the person confided with such a secret and that proceedings continue against the person who acquires possession of the documents and notes related thereto.

Article 371, para 3 stipulates that an act is not unjust and remains unpunishable if the person responsible thereof aims at the fulfilment of a duty or at the protection of a lawful or otherwise justified substantial interest, either public or of his own or of a third party, that could not be otherwise protected.

THE BANKS' DUTY OF CONFIDENCE

Banks

Article 1 of LD 1059/1971 provides that all deposits with Greek banks are secret, thereby excluding foreign banks from its ambit of protection. However, the controversy was settled by art 10 of L 1858/1989, which has substituted the term 'Greek banks' with the broader term 'financial institutions' thereby embracing foreign banks as well.

The principle of the secrecy of bank deposits includes deposits of any kind, for example, deposits in money and claims deriving from bonds, bank transfers and the like. Therefore, the disclosure by a bank of any information in any way as regards the deposits made with it is prohibited.

Remedies

Where there is a breach of bank secrecy and confidentiality as laid down in art 1 of LD 1059/1971, the liability of the violator is both criminal, as mentioned above, and civil.

Civil liability is based on art 914 of the Civil Code, which provides that 'whoever unlawfully and intentionally has caused damage to another is liable to pay compensation'. Particularly in the case of the breach of bank secrecy, the act in question is unlawful because it infringes art 914 of the Civil Code. However, the damage, the unlawfulness of the act, the intention and the adequate connection between the act and the damage must be proven.

The person liable is obligated to redress the damage and pay compensation that includes positive damage and loss of profits.

Finally, an injunction to restrain publication is a remedy available under art 682ff of the Code of Civil Procedures to any person having a lawful interest thereto.

THE EXCEPTIONS TO THE DUTY OF NON-DISCLOSURE

Article 2, para 2 of LD 1059/1971 provides that the consent of the person protected by the secrecy does not change the criminal character of the offence. This is a literal translation of the law, which seems to suggest that a criminal offence is committed even when the customer consents.

An exception, however, is one dictated by reasons of public interest. In particular, art 3 of LD 1059/1971 provides that the disclosure of information concerning bank deposits is lawful subject to the following requirements:

1 it must result from a duly reasoned order or application or decision of an investigating organ or judgment of a Greek court; and
2 such information must be absolutely necessary for the identification and punishment of actions characterised either as crimes committed in Greece or violations of the national currency legislation.

Greek courts hold the view that, among other cases, the secrecy is inapplicable to the case of a bankruptcy receiver of a foreign company lawfully established in Greece who seeks relevant information from a bank.

Other exceptions have been introduced by statutes and administrative decisions. In particular:

1 Article 2 of L 1325/1972 waives bank secrecy in cases of cheques returned unpaid.
2 Decisions 213/19-1-1983 and 1132/1-9-1987 of the Governor of the Bank of Greece (being the Central Bank) establish the right of control of auditors appointed by the Bank of Greece.
3 Article 40 of L 1806/1988 waives bank secrecy as regards some persons appointed by the Bank of Greece in the exercise of its powers related to the supervision and control of the banking system.
4 Article 27, paras 1 and 2, sub-paras a and b of L 1868/1989 waive bank secrecy as regards crimes characterised as felonies vis-à-vis the Bank of Greece.
5 Article 38 of L 1828/1989 waives the right of bank secrecy vis-à-vis the Bank of Greece in case of appointment of a Commissioner to a bank by the Governor of the Bank of Greece.
6 Article 44 of L 2065/1992 provides that bank secrecy is waived:
   (a) in cases of tax evasion where the difference in the taxable amount exceeds 300 million drachmae; and
   (b) in cases where an amount exceeding 50 million drachmae deriving from deducted taxes, duties and contributions has not been rendered to the Greek state.

7   Article 25, para 1 of L 2214/1994 waives bank secrecy and stipulates that there exists an obligation to furnish the requested information to the director of the competent tax authority. Compliance with this obligation cannot be evaded by the invocation on the part of the interested party of the secrecy of bank deposits that is waived for the facilitation of tax control. However, for such a waiver a joint decision of the tax authority inspector and of the director of the tax authority is necessary. Moreover, bank secrecy is waived as regards cheques issued in favour of the Greek state provided they exceed the amount of 1 million drachmae.

8   Article 66, para 1 of L 2238/1994 stipulates that bank secrecy can be waived only by means of a decision of the appropriate tax authority carrying out the audit, or by a joint decision of the director of the competent tax authority and the Director of the Internal Revenue Service. However, in cases of identified tax evasion, the waiver of bank secrecy embraces also those deposits kept in the name of the President and the Managing Director of the Board as well as those kept in the name of the administrators of limited liability companies or general partnerships, in addition to the blocking of deposits kept in the name of the company.

9   Articles 4, 5, 7 and 8 of L 2331/1995 and Circular 2/1997 of the Governor of the Bank of Greece regulate cases related to money laundering. Credit institutions are required to ask for evidence relating to the identity of the person in question for every transaction of €15,000 or more. Moreover, credit institutions should not make transactions for which they know or have valid suspicions that transactions are related to the legalisation of proceeds deriving from criminal activity, unless the immediate realisation of the transaction is urgently required, as well as in cases where the non-realisation of the action is likely to make difficult the disclosure of evidence or persons involved in the legalisation of such proceeds. Where an investigation is carried out with regard to the legalisation of proceeds deriving from criminal activity, the investigator, after a concurrent opinion of the prosecutor, may prohibit the use of the accounts, provided that valid suspicions exist that the accounts in question contain moneys deriving from the legalisation of proceeds related to criminal activity. The disclosure of information in such cases is allowed, provided it is made in good faith, and may be used in court. Finally, the committee established by art 7 accepts, evaluates and investigates any information related to transactions for the legalisation of proceeds deriving from criminal activities and transmitted to it by foreign agencies with which it co-operates for the provision of every possible assistance.

10   Article 14 of L 2523/1997 reiterates, completes and explains with more clarity the process of implementation of the measures set by the dispositions of art 92 of L 2.238/1994 and, more specifically:

     (a) Paragraph 1, provides that:
          a.   In cases of detected tax infringements concerning non payment to the tax authorities of sums more than €146,305.77, then:
                a.a. With respect to the public sector, bank confidentiality of deposits, accounts, joint accounts, safe-deposits etc of the taxpayer is suspended.
                a.b. 50% of the above-mentioned is blocked.
          b.   The above measures may also apply against the following:

b.a. In the case of Greek SAs, against the chairmen of the board of directors, the managing directors or the authorised directors, the governors, the general directors, the directors and any person authorised to the management of the SA.

b.b. In the case of partnership or joint-stock companies, against the partners or their managers.

b.c. In the case of limited liability companies, against their managers.

b.d. In the case of co-operatives, against their presidents, secretaries, or their treasurers or their managers.

b.e. In the case of joint ventures, societies, civil, participating or sleeping companies, against their representatives.

b.f. In the case of foreign businesses and organisations, against their directors, or their representatives or their agents in Greece.

(b) Paragraph 2 provides procedural matters.

(c) Paragraph 3 determines that, within a month from the notification of the above-mentioned persons, these persons may request the removal of the prohibitive measures after petition to the Minister of Finance.

(d) Paragraph 4 determines the process of obligatory removal of the above-mentioned prohibitive measures when the liable taxpayer pays an amount over the 70% of the owing to the public sector sums.

11 Article 2 of Law 2.713/1999:

(a) Paragraph 2 provides:

a.a. That the dispositions of art 3 of LD 1.059/1971 apply to crimes of corruption of police officers, determined in this law.

a.b. The process of removal of confidentiality (mentioned above) regarding the removal of confidentiality of bank accounts.

(b) Paragraph 2 also provides:

b.a. The process and the conditions that pertain to prohibition of use of the accounts or the safe-deposits.

b.b. That the public sector is entitled to proceed to the confiscation of any property belonging to police officers, if the acquisition of this property is a result of the perpetration of crimes described in this law.

12 Article 24 of Law 2.915/2001 provides that:

'The confidentiality of any kind of accounts ... is not valid against the creditor who has the right to confiscate the property of the beneficiary of the account. The confidentiality may only be removed with respect to the amount that is required in order to satisfy the creditor.'

CONFIDENTIAL INFORMATION

As regards the issue of the access of foreign investigatory bodies and foreign supervisory bodies to confidential information in Greece, some distinctions may be drawn. In the first place, branches of foreign banks established in Greece are governed by Greek law. In order, however, for such bodies to have access to information in Greece, we must inquire whether a bilateral treaty of judicial assistance is in force between the two states involved (for example, cases between the governments of the US and the UK, on the one hand, and the government of Greece on the other). If no such treaty is in force between the two states involved (for example, US-Greece, UK-Greece), art 3 of LD 1079/1971 applies which, as stated above, requires a duly reasoned order or application or decision of the investigating organ or judgment of a Greek court and that such information must be absolutely necessary for the identification and punishment of actions characterised either as crimes committed in Greece or violations of the national currency legislation.

Indeed, such bilateral treaties of judicial assistance have been signed between Greece and the US and between Greece and the UK, and have been ratified by L 5554/1932 and L ΔΛΑ/1912 respectively. Therefore, the provisions of these two treaties shall be applicable in cases where the disclosure of confidential information is requested by the Chief Executive Officer of the bank in the US, in the first example, and the Securities and Investments Board, in the second example.

The issue of whether the Greek criminal or supervisory authorities, who are undertaking the investigation and trying to compel the bank established in Greece to disclose information held by a branch or wholly owned subsidiary in the UK are entitled to do so shall be decided on the basis of whether a bilateral treaty of judicial assistance is in force between Greece and the UK. In the contrary case, English law shall be the applicable one. However, as mentioned above, a bilateral treaty of judicial assistance is in force between the two states and, therefore, the provisions of the treaty shall apply to the case in question.

As regards the process of tracing funds, we shall address first the case where our client in Greece has been defrauded of large sums of money by some of its employees who have vanished. Assume that the funds have been traced from our client's bank account to various other accounts of banks in Greece. Recipient banks can be compelled to disclose whether or not they still hold the funds on the basis of art 5, para 5 of the Brussels Convention on International Jurisdiction and Execution of Judgments in Greece providing that: 'A person domiciled in the territory of a contracting party may be sued in another contracting state ... as regards disputes related to the exploitation of a branch, agency or any other kind of establishment, before the court of their seat.' In view of the fact that the US and the UK, on the one hand, and Greece, on the other, have signed the Convention, its provisions apply and, therefore, the recipient banks may be compelled to disclose whether they still hold the funds and whether they sent them to any party having a lawful interest on the basis of the procedure related to injunctions: art 682ff of the Code of Civil Procedures.

Assume that orders have been obtained obliging the banks to disclose where the money went and that the banks report that the funds have been transferred abroad to other banks which they name, in countries which again they name, for the account of named customers or to numbered accounts. In such a case, the banks of such foreign destinations cannot be compelled to help our client to trace the funds further because the foreign law of the country of final destination shall be the applicable one. The position would not be different if the foreign bank were a branch or a subsidiary of one of the banks against whom the tracing order had been obtained in Greece. Again, the foreign law of the home country would apply.

If one reverses the facts and assumes that the foreign lawyer or client has obtained orders in his own country revealing that the stolen funds have reached a particular bank in Greece, the provisions of the Brussels Convention mentioned above would apply.

REGULATION OF FINANCIAL MARKETS

Insider dealing

Insider dealing is assimilated to fraud pursuant to art 386 of the Penal Code. The elements of the offence are:

1   the damage to another person's property;
2   an unlawful benefit at the expense of another person's property;
3   intention;
4   intentional presentation of untrue facts as true or unlawful concealment thereof; and
5   persuasion upon another person to an act, omission or tolerance.

Moreover, civil liability against the person responsible may be established on the basis of arts 914 ff of the Civil Code.

In Greece the inter-bank network, TEIRESIAS, serves the needs of the banks for information related to cheques and bills of exchange; however, for bank secrecy to be waived a duly reasoned court decision would be the necessary condition as mentioned above.

Cross-selling

Cross-selling between companies which are members of the same group does not give rise to liability, criminal or civil. Banks are also allowed to pass each other credit information about customers, but not to their client companies, because in such a case they would breach the provisions of Greek law mentioned above related to bank secrecy and confidentiality.

Data protection

In Greece a Data Protection Act has recently been introduced in Parliament and awaits endorsement.

However, art 42 of L 2121/1994 does not allow the reproduction, translation, adaptation, or any other change of a computer program without a licence. Article 43 of the same law specifies that reverse engineering, decompilation and disassembly are allowed to the licensee only in order to enable the latter to collect the necessary information and secure the networking of an independently created computer program with other programs, provided that such information is not easily and quickly accessible to the licensee and is restricted to the parts of the original program necessary for the accomplishment of the networking thereof.

Conflicts of interest

Where a bank or one of its subsidiaries has financial information about a customer as a result of acting as its banker, it is not entitled to advise other customers in the stockbroking business on the benefits of buying or selling its customer's shares, nor is the bank itself entitled to deal in the customer's shares, even if it separates the two businesses. This is because in acting in such a way the bank breaches its duty of confidentiality and commits the offence mentioned in art 371 of the Penal Code as discussed.

If the bank knows that its customer is in financial difficulties, while another part of the bank is simultaneously advising its clients to buy the customer's shares, the bank again breaches its confidentiality duty, while a civil liability pursuant to the provisions of art 914ff of the Civil Code related to tortious liability cannot be ruled out.

Take-overs

Where a bank organises financing for a take-over bid, some distinctions must be drawn. In the first place, such financing is governed by Decision no 1955/2-7-91 of the Governor of the Bank of Greece, as amended, which stipulates that financing for the purchase of shares is also allowed in cases where the borrower maintains or increases his shareholding in the undertaking in whose share capital the participation is effected.

If the increase of the share capital is effected by means of a public subscription, the underwriter, the borrower and the bank in question are involved. The bank, however, as a lender is responsible only to check the details pertaining to the financing, creditworthiness and viability of the project and to approve the loan following an approval of the share capital increase by means of a public subscription by the Capital Market Committee. Liability arises only for the underwriter in cases where the information related to the share price included in the prospectus is inaccurate, where the issuing company and the underwriter are jointly liable.

Where the increase of the share capital of the borrower company is effected by means of a private placement of shares, the bank acts simply as an intermediary for the financing and, therefore, no liability of the bank may arise.

CONCLUSION

Bank secrecy cannot be waived except in cases specified in the statutes addressing the issue, in particular in cases of tax evasion, facilitation of the control exercised by the Bank of Greece in the frame of its supervisory role assigned to it under Greek law, or in case of crimes committed in Greece and characterised as felonies.

14 Hungary

Péter Köves
Gábor Felsen

INTRODUCTION

It is generally true to say that with respect to the regulation of banking secrecy, the fundamental conflict is one between the personal interests or rights of the client of the bank and the public interest of society as a whole.

Banking is a relationship based on mutual trust and confidence and this generates the need for banking secrecy.

As a general rule, in Hungary all information concerning clients and their bank accounts is confidential and may only be disclosed by the bank or financial institution in exceptional circumstances.

In practice, laws on banking secrecy are typically stricter in those countries where the citizens have less faith in their state institutions. In Hungary, for example, before the reforms there were traditionally strict regulations, limiting the ability of a Hungarian bank to disclose information to third parties, which reflected the lack of confidence in the communist regime.

However, as a practical matter, even though the laws on banking secrecy were strict during the communist era, the fact was that the Hungarian state and its various organs and agencies could obtain whatever information on a Hungarian client that they wanted from a Hungarian bank (almost all of which were then in the exclusive ownership of the Hungarian state).

Over the last ten years, a dominant trend in Hungarian law and regulation has been a move from strict banking secrecy towards limited access to confidential banking information in specific circumstances. The principal reasons for this trend include the growing demand to fight international money laundering effectively and the desire of Hungary to adopt a legal and regulatory regime compatible with that of the EU.

HISTORICAL BACKGROUND

Until the beginning of the 1990s, banking secrecy in Hungary was strictly, but not clearly, regulated. The State Finances Act of 1979 provided that: '... the employees of a financial institution shall keep and maintain all banking secrets that they become aware of during the course of their work. An exemption may be granted as to this confidentiality by a statute or the person (institution) to whom the secret related.'

However, there were no general regulations defining banking secrets or the consequences of an unauthorised disclosure of such banking secrets. Confidential information was determined on an individual case-by-case basis. During 1991, Hungarian financial institutions, in line with general banking practice, only disclosed information of any kind with the authorisation of the client or as provided for in law.

In the case of saving deposits, for example, there were statutory provisions whereby information could be disclosed if a court judgment ordered the confiscation of property or ordered the payment of damages to the Hungarian state.

The commencement of the reform process, with privatisations and the demands of a growing number of multinational companies, brought to light the lack of available banking information regarding the situation and solvency of Hungarian companies.

As a general rule, Hungarian banks have been fairly conservative and have always sought to protect themselves in the event that a dispute were to arise and consequently, in the absence of clear regulations, have always tended to adopt a cautious approach and, officially at least, maintain tight banking secrecy.

THE PRINCIPAL CHANGES IN THE STATUTORY REGIME

Act LXIX of 1991 on Financial Institutions and Financial Activity

The roots of the current regulatory regime go back to the Act LXIX of 1991 on Financial Institutions and Financial Activity (the 1991 Banking Act). In order both to increase the confidence that clients had in banks and to provide information required for the smooth operation of the market economy, the 1991 Banking Act contained detailed provisions regulating bank secrecy.

The 1991 Banking Act stipulated the scope of banking secrets and regulated the obligation to keep banking secrets, extending the obligation to keep and maintain banking secrets to all persons who acquired confidential information in the course of their work or activity, and reinforce the protection of banking secrets.

However, the 1991 Banking Act recognised the need for there to be clearly regulated exceptions to the doctrine of banking secrecy, with recognition of the legitimate interests of those engaged in business and those organisations 'acting in the interest of society'.

The 1991 Banking Act provided that a banking secret could only be disclosed to a third party if:

1   the client (or his/its representative) gave his/its express consent to the release of the information specified in the consent;
2   there was a written request of the Hungarian Banking Supervisory Authority, duly performing its statutory functions;
3   there was a written request of the National Bank of Hungary (NBH), duly performing its statutory functions;
4   a public notary was duly executing a will;
5   the Public Prosecution Office was duly acting in criminal proceedings;

6   a Hungarian court was acting in criminal or insolvency, liquidation proceedings;
7   the Hungarian tax, customs or social security authorities were seeking to establish the enforceability of overdue tax, customs duties or social security payments; or
8   there was drug trafficking or terrorism involved.

Act CXII of 1993

The regulation of banking secrecy under the 1991 Banking Act was widely criticised in Hungary, principally because it was felt that it was too restrictive and that, in certain key areas, it did not allow for the assertion of justifiable economic and other public interests.

Act CXII of 1993 sought to rebalance the rights and interests of individuals with those of the society as a whole and reflect international practice in this area.

Act CXII of 1993 amended the 1991 Banking Act in several areas, including that of banking secrecy. Principal amendments included:

1   enabling owners of a financial institution to establish the actual value of the financial institution's portfolio – thereby facilitating the establishment of a share price and the privatisation process;
2   enabling criminal investigators to obtain sufficient information;
3   enabling financial institutions to disclose information where a valid claim had been made against their client; and
4   enabling, in certain circumstances, bodies such as the Hungarian National Deposit Insurance Fund, the Hungarian Office of Economic Competition, the intelligence/security services, a receiver in a bankruptcy procedure and a liquidator in a liquidation procedure to gain access to banking secrets.

At the same time, Act XCII of 1993 also amended the Criminal Code and a person found to be violating the banking secrecy regulations could be held criminally liable.

Act L of 1995

Act L of 1995 further amended the 1991 Banking Act and the Hungarian State Audit Office was added to the institutions to which banking secrets could, in certain circumstances, be disclosed.

1996: Hungary joins the OECD

One of the prerequisites for Hungary joining the OECD in 1996 was the requirement to amend the regulations governing banking secrecy. These amendments were carried out in the first half of 1996, by way of Act XII of 1996.

Act XII of 1996

Act XII of 1996 amended further the provisions of the 1991 Banking Act governing bank secrecy. The purpose of these amendments was to try to ensure that persons possessing bank secrets are only obliged to disclose such information in clearly defined cases and upon the written request of a specified body.

In addition, in order to reassure banking clients that unauthorised persons could not gain access to their banking secrets, Act XII of 1996 stipulated that information provided under the terms of the banking legislation could only be used for the purposes indicated in the relevant written request, and confirmed that there is no time limitation on the keeping of bank secrecy, ie the obligation is 'open-ended'.

The overall effect of these amendments was to increase the ease with which Hungarian state institutions entrusted with the collection of taxes and other public contributions can gather the information necessary to facilitate such collection.

At this time in Hungary, it was estimated that the so-called 'black economy' typically ranged from 25% to over 40% of GDP. The economic distortions of such a large black economy and the resultant effect on state finances were obvious in the mid 1990s.

The Act had four new paragraphs. The obligation of banking secrecy did not apply in cases where the taxation authority requested information in writing from the financial institution in order to fulfil a written request from a foreign authority, in accordance with an international agreement. This allows the taxation authorities of countries with which Hungary has a treaty on the avoidance of double taxation. According to further supplements, the written request had to indicate the client and the bank account of which the banking secret was requested, together with the type of data and the purpose of the request. The Act also stipulated that anybody who was in possession of banking secrets was obliged to maintain secrecy, except for the use for the indicated purpose, without time limitation. The bodies requesting the disclosure of bank secrets should keep record of the request made and prepare internal rules on the handling of data.

The amending regulation did not grant the right to the financial institutions to refuse a written request of an authorised body for the disclosure of data on the grounds of the obligation of banking secrecy. Furthermore, the financial institution was prohibited from notifying the client of the disclosure of data when the request was made by the intelligence service, the National Security Service or in relation to money laundering.

The amendment repealed the sections dealing with banking secrets contained in the Customs Act and in the Act of Rules of Taxation.

ACT CXII OF 1996 ON CREDIT INSTITUTIONS AND FINANCIAL UNDERTAKINGS – THE PRESENT REGULATION

Act CXII of 1996 on Credit Institutions and Financial Undertakings (the 1996 Banking Act) came into force on 1 January 1997. Although it has not made any fundamental changes in the principles regulating banking confidentiality, the relevant provisions are more detailed and accurate. The 1996 Banking Act has been modified several times since 1996; it was complemented by provisions concerning issues such as the central credit information system, the conflict of interests and insider trading.

According to the 1996 Banking Act, a 'banking secret' is any fact, information, solution or data at the disposal of a financial institution, which relates to the clients' personal details, data, property status, business activity, economic administration, owner's or business connections, as well as to the accounts (balance and turnover) maintained by a financial institution, and contracts concluded between clients and a financial institution, ie a fairly wide and comprehensive definition.

In addition, the 1996 Banking Act provides that any person receiving financial services from financial institutions is to be considered to be a 'client' of a financial institution.

The 1996 Banking Act, as amended defines four cases where a financial institution is allowed to disclose confidential information to third parties:

1   Where the client of a financial institution, his/its legal representative so requires or gives authorisation to that end. Such authorisation has to identify precisely (in a document executed as a notarial deed or in a private document with full legal effect) the scope of the bank secret that may be disclosed to third parties.
2   Where the interest of a financial institution itself necessitates the use of the relevant information, for the purpose of selling of its claim arising under an arrangement with a client or for the recovery of its overdue claim.
3   Where the 1996 Banking Act expressly grants exemption from the obligation of keeping banking secrecy. These exemptions are listed in s 2, para 51 of the 1996 Banking Act:
    (a)   the National Deposit Insurance Fund, the NBH, the State Audit Office, the Office of Economic Competition, the Hungarian Financial Supervisory Authority (the Supervisory Authority), the voluntary institution protection and deposit insurance funds when discharging their functions, the Government Control Office controlling the conformity to rules and expediency of the use of central budgetary funds;
    (b)   the notary public when executing a will, as well as the public guardianship authority when discharging its functions;
    (c)   the receiver, liquidator, bailiff, financial guardian or final accountant acting in bankruptcy proceedings, winding-up proceedings, court execution procedures, debt settlement proceedings of self-governing bodies or final accounts proceedings;
    (d)   the investigating authority (ie the police) and/or the Public Prosecution Office acting in criminal proceedings in processing or completing the complaint;
    (e)   in criminal proceedings and civil actions related to inheritance, and the court in proceedings concerning bankruptcy or winding up, as well as in the framework of proceedings of debt settlement of self-governing bodies;
    (f)   the bodies authorised to use intelligence service tools and collect secret information subject to conditions specified under separate legislation;
    (g)   the National Security Service discharging its functions subject to the authorisation for individual cases of the general director;
    (h)   the Minister of Interior and the Minister of Finance in the case of targeted subsidy and appropriation to the local self-governing bodies;
    (i)   the taxation authority, the customs authority and the social security body in proceedings concerning the examination of compliance with obligations

with respect to taxation, customs and social security, as well as in proceedings related to the enforcement of an enforceable document establishing such debts;

(j)   the taxation authority when fulfilling the written request of a foreign authority pursuant to the provisions of an international treaty provided that the request contains a confidentiality clause signed by the foreign authority;

(k)   Hungarian authorities involved in criminal proceedings when fulfilling the written request of a foreign authority involved in criminal proceedings pursuant to the provisions of an international treaty provided that the request contains a confidentiality clause signed by the foreign authority; and

(l)   the Supervisory Authority and the National Bank of Hungary in the course of supervision made according to statutory regulations or the NBH's decree.

In addition, there is a specific regulation designed to prevent the Hungarian financial system from being used for the purposes of money laundering which complies with the EC Money Laundering Directive.[1] The effect of this regulation is to make it easier to obtain an exemption from the rules of bank secrecy where information comes to light to the effect that a bank account or bank transaction is related to drug trafficking, terrorism, illegal trade in arms, money laundering or organised crime. In such a case, the financial institution must not inform the client concerned of the request or of the transfer of data. There is no obligation on a financial institution to report to its client the request for information or the transfer of such information in cases of criminal proceedings, data collection carried out with the help of intelligence service tools and proceedings carried out by the National Security Service. In all other cases, the client must be notified by the financial institution of the request for data. The 1996 Banking Act includes several guarantees as to the means of disclosing such confidential information, for example, the financial institution must be referred to in writing, the client must be identified together with the bank account concerned and the type of information requested, and the purpose of the request must also be specified.

In order to take part in the international efforts against money laundering and the financing of terrorist activities, the Hungarian Parliament has ratified the International Convention for the Suppression of the Financing of Terrorism (the Convention) adopted by the General Assembly of the United Nations on 9 December 1999. To comply with the obligations under the Convention, Government Decree 2286/2002 ordered the setting up of a committee co-ordinating the implementation of necessary changes of relevant Hungarian laws. The proposals of the committee remain to be seen, but the spirit of the Convention suggests that bank confidentiality and information delivery rules will be subject to further scrutiny and the scope of reporting obligations of credit institutions to authorities regarding suspicious direct and indirect transactions will in all likelihood be widened.

4   The 1996 Banking Act lists those cases, which are not considered to be a violation of banking secrecy and where disclosure of certain classes of information is not prohibited. It is not a violation of bank secrecy:

(a)   to supply aggregate data from which the personal or business data of individual clients cannot be identified;

(b)   to supply data concerning the name and number of the current account of the client;

1   Council Directive 91/308/EEC.

(c) for financial institutions, legal entities exclusively underwriting guarantee and suretyship and investment service providers (Credit Data Providers) to supply data to the central credit information system, established and operated by them or from that system to the financial institution, in accordance with the rules of the system;

(d) to provide data to an auditor, a legal or other expert authorised by the financial institution, as well as to an insurance company providing insurance coverage for a financial institution to the extent necessary for discharging an insurance contract;

(e) to provide data, at the written consent of the Board of Directors of a financial institution, to an owner with a qualifying holding in that financial institution, with such data being made available to a person (company) intending to acquire such holding (or to the auditor, legal or other expert authorised by such owner or prospective owner);

(f) to present the sample of signatures, on request of a Hungarian court, of those having the right of disposal over the bank account of a party to the legal action;

(g) to provide data suitable for individual identification of credit institutions supplied by the Supervisory Authority – with respect to the rules concerning bank secrecy – to the Central Statistical Office for the purposes of statistics or the Ministry of Finance for the purpose of the analysis of the processes of the national economy and the planning of the central budget;

(h) for a financial institution to disclose data to a foreign financial institution, provided that the client has previously consented in writing and the foreign financial institution's (data receiver) procedure complies with the requirements of the Hungarian statutory regulations concerning data management and the foreign country has adequate statutory regulations on data protection;

(i) to disclose data to the supervisory authority of a foreign financial institution necessary for its supervision according to the provisions of the co-operation agreement between the supervisory authorities providing the confidential management and usage of the information and the Supervisory Authority's consent to the processing of data to foreign authorities involved in criminal proceedings;

(j) to disclose data to a business association discharging outsourced activity;

(k) to disclose data within a banking group, a financial holding company or a mixed-activity group in order to comply with the regulations concerning consolidated supervision; and

(l) to disclose data suitable for individual identification of credit institutions supplied by the Supervisory Authority to the Economic Competition Office when performing its functions.

In these cases, the data of a particular client cannot be ascertained, as there are mainly aggregate data, or an interest of another kind, mainly that of the owner or the financial institution, justifies such use of bank secrets.

All who become aware of business or banking secrets in the course of performing their duties or performing an assignment are obliged, without time limitation, to keep all business and bank secrets, not use them outside their scope of activity or disclose them to third persons unless the 1996 Banking Act so authorises them. The 1996 Banking Act strictly prohibits the disclosure of business information to third parties or making use of it personally in order to gain business advantage and/or using it to the detriment of the financial institution or the clients of the financial institution.

MISCELLANEOUS

Data of public interest

Public information (information of public interest) means any data managed by a public authority or agency, government or local and other bodies attending to public duties specified by law. Public accessibility to data of public interest may not be restricted by reasons of bank secrecy in cases where such data that is directly connected to financial services and auxiliary financial services in relation to the following:

1   suretyship or other guarantee undertaken by the central budget;
2   targeted subsidy and appropriation to the local self-governing bodies; and
3   the budget of central or local government bodies.

The central credit information system

The central credit information system was established by an amendment of the 1996 Banking Act as of 1 January 2001. The central credit information system retains data obtained from the Credit Data Providers on their clients. The central credit information system aims at setting up a database regarding defaulted debtors. It implemented a different mechanism for natural persons and corporate entities.

Natural persons

The central credit information system collects and manages key data relating to specific debtors, who failed to fulfil their respective contractual obligations under a credit agreement for more than 90 days after the due date. Such overdue obligation has to exceed the applicable minimum wage amount in order for a debtor to be listed in the database. Data about such debtor will include personal details and details of the default of the credit agreement.

The central credit information system collects and manages key data (including personal details and details of the nature and the violation of the respective obligation) concerning credit card holders or cheque holders in the following cases:

1   where the credit card claimant/holder or cheque holder provided untrue data or data of another person to the Credit Data Provider;
2   uncovered use of credit card (exceeding the applicable minimum wage amount) or transaction with a cancelled credit card;
3   unfounded complaints occurring a minimum of three times a year;
4   criminal proceedings in connection with the credit card; and
5   where the credit card holder failed to fulfil his contractual obligation for more than 60 days after the due date (exceeding the applicable minimum wage amount).

The central credit information system cannot retain or manage any identifying data for more than five years after the debt has been paid in full.

Corporate entities

The central credit information system manages key data of corporate entities, who have a queue of payments of at least 1 million Hungarian forints to be debited from a bank account for more than 30 days after the due date.

Insider trading

Regulations concerning insider trading were enacted by the 1996 Banking Act. Insider dealing involves the utilisation of unpublished price-sensitive information obtained through a privileged relationship to gain profit or avoid loss. The regulation aims to prohibit any transaction connected with insider information. Insider information relates to the actual financial, economic or legal position of the financial institution or its client, or the expected changes in such position, which could be materially affected by the public disclosure of that information. A person has information as an insider in the following cases:

1   a person who is an executive officer or qualifies as a manager or an executive officer under the 1996 Banking Act or the internal rules of the financial institution;
2   a person acting as an official or an expert and having access to insider information in the course of his activity at the financial institution;
3   the close relatives of the persons mentioned above;
4   any person who has obtained insider information, including the manager and the employees of a foreign financial institution.

According to s 59 of the 1996 Banking Act, persons defined as insiders cannot use their position or the insider information obtained through that position, and cannot convey such information to acquire advantage, either directly or indirectly, for themselves or for any third person or to cause disadvantage to the financial institution or its client. It is prohibited to conclude any deal or give an order to any transaction or to provide an investment advice with the utilisation of insider information that results in financial advantage to the insider person, his close relative or any third person or causes damage to a third person.

Conflicts of interests

The new Act CXX of 2001 on Capital Markets (in force as of 1 January 2002) implemented an important regulation in connection with the management of conflict of interests in a credit institution (Chinese Wall legislation). Credit institutions providing investment and auxiliary investment services besides financial services must guarantee in their internal rules that the two units are separated in order not to influence the transactions between their clients, the credit institution divisions, the credit institutions and other participants. The internal rules must determine precisely the way data is conveyed between the units, and bank secrets should be available exclusively for those who need them for performing their tasks. The internal rules have to be submitted to the Supervisory Authority.

Legal consequences of breach of bank secrecy obligation

Civil law

The violation of bank confidentiality constitutes an infringement of .personal rights. These rights (and also the remedy in case of violation) can only be exercised or enforced personally. According to Act IV of 1959 on the Civil Code (the Civil Code) there are a number of remedies available to the injured party. It may submit a claim to the relevant court requesting for:

1   a declaration of the infringement;
2   the cessation of the infringement and ordering the other party to restrain from further infringement;
3   remedy in the form of a statement or by other adequate means;
4   the cessation of the injurious status and the restoration of the previous status; and
5   damages under general provisions of the Civil Code.

In relation to point 5, we note that in order to obtain damages, the burden of proof lies with the client to prove that he suffered a loss or detriment as the consequence of the breach of bank secrecy (for example, unlawful disclosure). In the absence of damages, the court can only make a declaration as to the unlawful conduct, the infringement of rights and restraint.

Concerning the banks' ability to limit claims for breach of confidentiality, Hungarian regulation is based on both the specific regulation of the Banking Act dealing with bank secrecy and the general rules on liability of the Civil Code.

As discussed above, the persons acquiring any business or bank secrets must keep them confidential without any time limitation. As the protection of consumers' interest is of utmost importance under Hungarian legislation, the obligation of keeping business or bank secrets confidential is based on law, and is usually also referred to in banking contracts. According to the Civil Code, as a general rule, the liability of a bank for a breach of contract cannot be excluded or restricted.

Criminal law

The Act IV of 1978 on the Criminal Code penalises the infringement of bank secrets. A bank officer who becomes aware of bank secrets in the course of performing his tasks and discloses the bank secrets to any third person (unless duly authorised) commits a misdemeanour and can be sentenced to imprisonment (up to two years') or public labour or a fine. The punishment is more serious (imprisonment of up to three years) if the crime was committed to acquire unjustified advantage or to cause detriment to the financial institution or someone else.

Administrative law

In the event of the violation of any of the provisions set out in legal regulations and any NBH's decree concerning financial and auxiliary financial services (including the violation of bank secrecy), the Supervisory Authority can impose fines and penalties (along with other measures in serious cases). When determining the amount of the fine, the Supervisory Authority shall consider the following:

1   the extent of damage caused by the intentional or negligent violation of the statutory regulations;
2   whether the responsible persons fully co-operated with the Supervisory Authority and the National Deposit Insurance Fund;
3   good or bad faith of the person affected by the measure, the advantage acquired by the violation and the intention to mitigate the damage;
4   suppression of data, facts and information needed to decide on the type of measure; and
5   recurrence or frequency of the violations.

Jurisdictional issues in relation to electronic payment and information systems

In line with the relevant recommendation of the Supervisory Authority, credit institutions and financial enterprises are required to adhere to general data protection and bank confidentiality laws in the process of setting up the contractual framework and settlement of electronic payments. The service providers may not take advantage of the specific features of electronic payment to hide their relevant company information from their customers or to evade consumer protection regulations.

Outsourcing

The outsourcing of certain administrative activities of credit institutions and financial enterprises, where data handling, processing or filing is carried out, is strictly regulated. Outsourcing some of such activities is subject to the approval of the Supervisory Authority, which must be requested at least 30 days before the execution of the outsourcing agreement. Credit institutions must attach to such request a certification proving that the legislative rules on data protection have been adhered to and the credit institution's statement that the supplier undertaking to perform the outsourced activities fulfils the criteria set by the internal control of the credit institution. The supplier, if carrying out activities for more than one credit institution in parallel, is very strictly obliged to protect and handle all the data and information received from the individual credit institutions separately from each other.

Confidentiality in the process of securitisation

In the process of transfer of a loan portfolio of a credit institution, confidential information relating to the borrowers will also be transferred to the transferee. The Banking Act allows such disclosure of confidential information by the transferor (ie originator) if (i) the borrower of the underlying loan consents to the transfer of its loan or (ii) the interest of the transferor so requires. It is market practice in the consumer loan market that credit institutions reserve the right in the credit agreements to assign their claims, which is consented to and accepted by the borrower in the agreement.

CONCLUSION

The Hungarian financial markets have, in recent years, undergone rapid growth and evolution. Now that Hungary is a member of the OECD and has been accorded an investment-grade rating by the major rating agencies, the rapid pace of change is ongoing and looks unlikely to slow in the foreseeable future.

Hungary is a civil law jurisdiction and it should be noted that, generally speaking, save for certain decisions of the Hungarian Supreme Court, a court decision in the Hungarian lower courts is not binding on subsequent courts. Unlike common law jurisdictions, Hungarian courts base their decisions predominantly on written law rather than case law. Case law precedents (especially decisions of the Supreme Court) may nevertheless have an influence on court rulings. This means that it can sometimes be difficult to advise on areas of Hungarian law and regulation that are innovative and/or contentious.

So far as banking confidentiality is concerned, the bad news is that, in relative terms, the regulatory framework is more or less new and as yet untested.

The good news is that:

1   the legal and regulatory framework is based on the model adopted by the EU;
2   the evolutionary process of Hungarian law governing banking secrecy demonstrates the focus placed on this issue by the legislators; and
3   as Hungary continues its integration into the various international bodies, such as the OECD and possibly the EU, the pace of legislation is likely to continue along the right lines.

The challenge for lawyers in Hungary will be to guide banking clients sensibly and practically through the potential legal and regulatory pitfalls that are inevitable where laws are evolving and frequently being amended or reinterpreted.

15   Ireland

William   Johnston

INTRODUCTION

Irish law imposes a duty of confidentiality on a bank in relation to dealings with its customers. This obligation derives, for the most part, from the common law which implies a duty of confidentiality on the bank in a contract which governs the relationship between a bank and its customer, unless the terms of the contract otherwise provide. The parameters of the common law duty of confidentiality are unclear in many respects. In addition, there is no substantial body of Irish case law on a bank's obligation; the Irish courts when considering the obligation have often relied on relevant decisions of the courts in other common law jurisdictions, in particular, the decisions of the English courts. It should be noted, though, that decisions of English courts are not binding in Ireland but, particularly where there is an absence of Irish precedence, English decisions are of persuasive authority in Irish courts.

COMMON LAW DUTY

The starting point in considering a banker's duty of confidentiality is the English Court of Appeal's decision in *Tournier v National Provincial and Union Bank of England Ltd*.[1] This decision affirmed the common law duty of confidentiality which exists between a banker and his customer. Thus, confidentiality is an implied term in a contract in Ireland between a banker and his customer. This duty though is not absolute, but qualified. In *Chestvale Properties Ltd and Hoddle Investments Ltd v Glackin*,[2] the High Court stated: 'It is common case that the customary and contractual right of a client to confidentiality from his banker is and always has been subject to a very wide range of exceptions.'

The qualifications to the duty can be classified under the four heads as outlined in *Tournier*:

1   [1924] 1 KB 461.
2   [1993] 3 IR 35.

1   where disclosure is required by law;
2   where there is a duty to the public to disclose;
3   where the interests of the bank require disclosure; and
4   where the disclosure is made by the express or implied consent of the customer.

In addition to the common law duty of confidentiality, a statutory duty of confidentiality applies in certain instances.

STATUTORY DUTY

Every officer and employee of the banking regulator, currently the Central Bank of Ireland, is precluded from disclosing any information concerning the business of any person or body which comes to his knowledge by virtue of his office or employment (unless such disclosure is to enable the Central Bank to carry out its functions). Each officer and employee at the time of his appointment is required to acknowledge that he has been informed and understands his secrecy obligations. The implications of, and rationale for, the secrecy obligations of the Central Bank's officers and employees were highlighted in *Cully v Northern Bank Finance Corpn Ltd*,[3] where the High Court upheld the objections of the Central Bank to disclose information following the service of a subpoena. The court indicated:

> '... the provisions of s 31 of the Central Bank Act 1942 [now replaced by s 16(3) of the Central Bank Act 1989], give rise to a claim of privilege on grounds of public policy from disclosure of any information of the type referred to in the oath of secrecy. S 6(1) of the same Act provides that in relation to part, at least of the functions and duties of the Central Bank "the constant and predominant aim shall be the welfare of the people as a whole." This gives some indication for the justification for granting an exceptional degree of protection to the confidentiality of the bank's transactions, as a matter of public interest.'

These non-disclosure requirements have been made subject to a number of exceptions as outlined in reg 19 of the European Communities (Licensing and Supervision of Credit Institutions) Regulations 1992;[4] reg 7 of the European Communities (Consolidated Supervision of Credit Institutions) Regulations 1992;[5] reg 28 of the European Communities (Deposit Guarantee Schemes) Regulations 1995;[6] and s 49 of the Investment Intermediaries Act 1995.

Statutory exceptions (under the Central Bank Act 1989, as amended) to the prohibition of disclosure by the Central Bank, include:

1   disclosure required by a court in criminal proceedings;
2   disclosure made with the consent of the person to whom the information relates and of the person from whom the information was obtained;
3   disclosure to the principal where the Central Bank is acting as agent; and

3   [1984] ILRM 683.
4   SI 395/1992.
5   SI 396/1992.
6   SI 168/1995.

4   disclosure where the Central Bank considers it necessary for the common good
made to a person charged with the supervision of financial institutions.

An example of the third exception can be seen from the courts' decisions in *Desmond
and Dedeir v Glackin, The Minister for Industry and Commerce of Ireland and The
Attorney General.*[7] In that case, Glackin was appointed by the Minister for Industry
and Commerce as an inspector for the purpose of investigating the affairs of two
companies. The inspector requested the minister to obtain information from the
Central Bank through the Minister for Finance concerning transactions of a related
company. The Central Bank had relevant information arising out of its duties under
the Exchange Control Act 1954. It was held in the High Court, and affirmed by the
Supreme Court, that (i) as the Central Bank was acting as agent of the Minister for
Finance in relation to its functions under the Exchange Control Act 1954, it was
bound to divulge the relevant information to its principal, the Minister for Finance,
(ii) the Minister for Finance was not bound by any duty of confidence under the
Central Bank Act 1989 and (iii) the public interest required all the information
which the inspector needed for the purposes of his investigation to be made available
to him, and that there was no countervailing public interest of equal or near equal
weight in denying the inspector access to the information emanating from the Central
Bank.

The public interest requirement referred to in the judgments and, indeed, the fourth
'common good' exception may mean that even where the Central Bank is acting as
principal and not agent, as it does in its supervisory and licensing functions, it
should disclose information to an inspector.

Each bank in Ireland is required to provide the Central Bank with 'such information
and returns' concerning its business as the Central Bank may specify from time to
time, or request in writing, being information and returns which the Central Bank
consider to be necessary for the performance of its statutory functions.

The statutory function of the Central Bank includes the licensing and supervision of
banks. Accordingly, a bank must comply with a request to provide information to
the Central Bank, even where the bank's customer has obtained an injunction
restraining disclosure. Since the legislation governing the functions of the Central
Bank overrode the duty of confidence, it must also override inter parties orders made
on that basis, otherwise the Central Bank could not properly discharge its public
duty of supervision.

Chinese Walls

The Central Bank's Licensing and Supervisory Requirements and Standards for
Credit Institutions set out non-statutory requirements of the Central Bank in relation
to the licensing and supervision of banks and other financial institutions, under
which each bank must satisfy the Central Bank with regard to resolution of conflicts
of interest arising in the conduct of different types of activity under its control and
that adequate arrangements have been made to protect the interest of its customers.

7   [1993] 3 IR 67.

The Requirements and Standards state that the Central Bank will require all banks to comply with codes of conduct which are issued by it. One such code of conduct provides that a bank shall ensure that there are effective Chinese Walls in place between the different business areas of the bank, and between the bank and its connected parties in relation to information which could potentially give rise to a conflict of interest or be open to abuse. All procedures relating to the maintenance of Chinese Walls must be in writing and notified to all relevant officers and employees of the credit institution.

Data protection

The Data Protection Act 1988 regulates the collection, processing, keeping, use and disclosure of certain information relating to living individuals which is processed automatically. The 1988 Act gives effect to the Council of Europe Convention for the Protection of Individuals with regard to Automatic Processing of Personal Data, Strasbourg, 1981 (the Strasbourg Convention). The Act has been amended in part by the Data Protection (Amendment) Act, 2003, which gives effect to Council Directive 95/45/EC of 24 October 1995. Essentially, the 1988 Act provides as follows:

1   it imposes certain obligations on persons who keep or process personal data;
2   it confers rights upon persons concerning whom data is kept/processed;
3   it creates the office of the Data Protection Commissioner and outlines the Commissioner's powers, functions and duties; and
4   it provides for compulsory registration with the Commissioner under the 1988 Act of certain data controllers (including banks) and data processors and deals generally with the implications of registration.

Only individuals, as opposed to body corporates, are conferred with rights under the 1988 Act. The Act requires banks to register as data controllers with the Commissioner. A data controller who is required to register must not keep personal data unless he is registered. A registered data controller is prohibited from:

1   keeping or using personal data for a purpose other than the purpose or purposes described in the registered entry;
2   disclosing personal data to a person who is not described in the entry (other than a person to whom disclosure is authorised under s 8 of the 1988 Act); or
3   directly or indirectly transferring such data to a place outside Ireland other than one named or described in the entry.

The 1988 Act requires a data controller or data processor to protect the privacy of individuals with regard to personal data kept by it. These obligations include not allowing personal data to be used or disclosed in any manner incompatible with the lawful purpose specified in the registration, and taking appropriate security measures against unauthorised access to, or alteration, disclosure or accidental loss of personal data.

The 1988 Act provides that a data controller or data processor, so far as regards the collection of personal data or dealing with such data, owes a duty of care to the relevant subject of the data. However, the Act disapplies restrictions imposed under the Act in relation to the disclosure of personal data by data controllers or data processors, including where the disclosure is required:

1   for the purpose of safeguarding the security of the State in the opinion of a senior police or army officer;
2   to prevent, detect or investigate offences, apprehend or prosecute offenders or assess or collect taxes or other moneys owed to the State;
3   in the interests of protecting the international relations of the State;
4   by or under any enactment or by a rule of law or order of a court; and
5   for the purpose of obtaining legal advice or for the purpose of legal proceedings in which the person making the disclosure is a party or witness.

The restrictions are disapplied also where the disclosure is made to the subject of the data or his agent, or where the disclosure is made at the request or with the consent of the subject of the data or a person acting on his behalf. In relation to the latter, standard bank documentation often contains provisions entitling the bank to make disclosures for the purposes of the 1988 Act.

Powers of enforcement are conferred on the Commissioner in relation to breaches of the 1988 Act by means of issuing enforcement notices. Non-compliance with an enforcement notice is a criminal offence. The Act enables the Commissioner to prohibit the transfer of personal data abroad where the Commissioner is of the opinion that the transfer is likely to lead to a contravention of the basic principles for data protection contained in the Strasbourg Convention.

DISCLOSURE REQUIRED BY LAW

Legal proceedings

The Bankers' Books Evidence Act 1879 provides that:

> 'On the application of any party to a legal proceeding a court or judge may order that such party be at liberty to inspect and take copies of any entries in a banker's book for any of the purposes of such proceedings.'

The expression 'banker's book', initially defined by s 9 of the 1879 Act but amended by the Bankers' Book Evidence (Amendment) Act 1959 and subsequently expanded by the Central Bank Act 1989, now 'includes any records used in the ordinary business of a bank' including microfilm, magnetic tape and other records in any non-legible form capable of being reproduced in a permanent legible form. The expression 'used in the ordinary business of the bank' does not mean that the book must be in use each day, but a book which was used and now kept for reference purposes. It should be noted that the meaning of 'banker's book' as defined is not all inclusive and, following amendment by statute in 1989, it may include any record in a bank, however recorded, provided it is done so in the ordinary business of the bank.

The courts have adopted a cautious approach in permitting this Act to be used. In *L'Amie v Wilson*,[8] Andrews J stated:

---

8   [1907] 2 IR 130.

'Such caution is requisite, even when the inspection applied for is of the account of a party to the action; but when the account is that of a third party, still greater caution is necessary; and before granting an inspection of a third party's account, the Court or Judge, ought to be satisfied that there are good grounds for believing that there are entries in the account material to some issue to be tried in the action, and which would be evidence at the trial for the party applying for the inspection.'

In *Staunton v Counihan*,[9] Dixon J began his judgment by saying:

'The jurisdiction to order inspection of entries in a banking account conferred by s 7 of the Bankers' Books Evidence Act 1879, must be exercised with extreme caution even where it is the account of a party to the action.'

It should be noted, however, that the Bankers' Books Evidence Acts and the meaning of a banker's book do not limit the power of a court to order discovery or inspection of an item which may not be a banker's book.[10]

An example of the constraints of the application of s 7 can be seen from the decision in *Staunton v Counihan*.[11] In that case the plaintiff sued the defendant as guarantor of a debt for £12,000 incurred by a company owned by the defendant's son, who was a co-guarantor. The plaintiff applied to inspect the company's account in a Dublin bank for the purpose of proving that the debt existed. In refusing the application, Dixon J approached the principles of the legislation on two grounds:

1   'The jurisdiction was intended really to extend only to accounts which were in form and substance those of a party to the action.'
2   'The entries must be material to some issue in the action and, if they are so, must be admissible in evidence on behalf of the applicant.'

Dixon J found, on the first issue, that the account was not in any sense in form and substance the defendant's account, nor was it so closely connected with her that it could be regarded really as her account in another name and, on the second issue, the plaintiff's proof does not essentially depend on the entries in the company's bank account and therefore at this stage the entries were not clearly and necessarily admissible in evidence. These two grounds were applied by Carroll J in granting an order for inspection of bank accounts in Dublin.[12]

Where a bank is not a party to proceedings, notice of an application for inspection need not be served on the bank. In *Staunton v Counihan*, Dixon J considered notice on the party whose account was to be inspected was sufficient; in *Larkins v National Union of Mineworkers and Bank of Ireland Finance Ltd*,[13] an order for inspection was granted ex parte; but in *L'Amie v Wilson*[14] Andrews J thought notice of the application should be given.

---

9   (1957) 92 ILTR 32.
10   *Larkins v National Union of Mineworkers and Bank of Ireland Finance Ltd* [1985] IR 671.
11   (1957) 92 ILTR 32.
12   See *Chemical Bank v McCormack* [1983] ILRM 350, where the order was not granted for foreign accounts.
13   [1985] IR 671.
14   [1907] 2 IR 130.

Banks with foreign offices

As already seen, s 7 of the Bankers' Books Evidence Act 1879 applies to records used in the ordinary business of a bank. Any bank which holds a banking licence from the Central Bank comes within the ambit of the Act. However, it has been decided that the records or other entries in a 'banker's book' should not apply to the books of a foreign branch of a licensed bank. In *Chemical Bank v McCormack*,[15] the High Court held:

'There are no clear words in the 1879 Act or the amending 1959 Act which would support the interpretation of an intention to have extra territorial effect

...

R v Grossman[16] appears to be authority for the making of an order addressed to AIB as a company incorporated within the jurisdiction to make available for inspection in this country the account of the defendant ... in the Park Avenue branch of the bank in New York.

However, even if it is, I do not propose to make such an order in case there would be a conflict of jurisdiction, which should be avoided in the interest of the comity of courts.'

Foreign banks with offices in Ireland

It would seem that a bank with its head office outside Ireland would not be subject to the jurisdiction of the Irish courts so far as producing records which were kept outside the jurisdiction of Ireland, but only such records kept in Ireland relating to the bank's branch. In this regard the courts are likely to follow the English decision of *MacKinnon v Donaldson Lufkin & Jenrette Securities Corpn.*[17]

Discovery

The rules of discovery can be found in order 31 of the Rules of the Superior Courts 1986,[18] as amended by the Rules of the Superior Courts (No 2) 1993,[19] and as further amended by Rules of the Superior Courts (No 2) (Discovery) 1999.[20] Rule 12 provides:

'(1) Any party may apply to the Court by way of notice of motion for an order directing any other party to any cause or matter to make discovery on oath of the documents which are or have been in his or her possession or power, relating to any matter in question therein. Every such notice of motion shall specify the precise categories of documents in respect of which discovery is sought and shall be grounded upon the affidavit of the party seeking such an order of discovery which shall:

---

15 [1983] ILRM 350.
16 [1981] Crim LR 396
17 [1988] 1 All ER 653.
18 SI 15/1986.
19 SI 265/1993.
20 SI 233/1999.

> (a) verify that the discovery of documents sought is necessary for disposing fairly of the cause or matter or for savings costs ;
>
> (b) furnish the reasons why each category of documents is required to be discovered.
>
> (2) On the hearing of such application, the Court may either refuse or adjourn the same, if satisfied that such discovery is necessary, or not necessary at that stage of the cause or matter …

> (3) An order shall not be made under this rule if and insofar that the Court shall be of the opinion that it is not necessary either for disposing fairly of the cause or matter or for saving costs.'

Rule 29 provides:

> 'Any person not a party to the cause or matter before the Court who appears to the Court to be likely to have or have had in his possession custody or power of any documents which are relevant to an issue arising or likely to arise out of the cause or matter or is likely to be in a position to give evidence relevant to any such issue may by leave of the Court upon the application of any party to the said cause or matter be directed by order of the Court to answer such interrogatories or to make discovery of such documents or to permit inspection of such documents.'

The distinction between party and non-party discovery was explained and highlighted by the Chief Justice in *Allied Irish Banks plc and Allied Irish Banks (Holdings & Investments) Ltd v Ernst & Whinney and the Minister for Industry & Commerce*,[21] where the Chief Justice indicated:

1   That whereas an order for discovery under r 12 should only be refused or adjourned if the party resisting discovery discharged the onus of establishing that discovery was not necessary at all or at the time for disposing fairly of the cause or matter or for saving costs; by contrast an order for discovery under r 29 should only be made where the applicant discharged the onus of establishing that the notice party was likely to have or to have had documents in his possession, custody or power relevant to an issue arising or likely to arise out of the cause or matter.

2   That whereas the court's discretion under r 12 was confined to its being satisfied that the order was not necessary; by contrast, under r 29, even assuming that the applicant has established the likelihood of the notice party having or having had relevant documents, the court had a further discretion which related to the oppression or prejudice which would be caused to the notice party and which would not be capable of being adequately compensated by the payment of the costs of making discovery.

3   That whereas an order for discovery under r 12 was sufficient if it directed discovery of a particular category of documents or of all documents relevant to the issues arising in the action, since the person making discovery would be a party to the action and would know the issues arising; by contrast, an order for

---

21   [1993] 1 IR 375.

discovery under r 29 was directed to a stranger to the action, who would not have such knowledge and who could not reasonably be expected to investigate the pleadings or to engage a lawyer to do so for him; so that an order for discovery under r 29 should in some simple form, either by annexing of pleadings or by a schedule to the order, identify the issues, by reference to the pleadings, to which an alleged relevance occurred.

Similar orders for discovery may be made by Tribunals of Inquiry under the Tribunals of Inquiry (Evidence) Act 1921 and the Tribunals of Inquiry (Evidence) (Amendment) Act 1979 as applied by Geoghegan J in *Bailey, Bovale Developments Ltd and Bailey v Flood and Bank of Ireland.*[22]

An example of where the courts are willing to order discovery, even where the action does not directly affect the account holder, can be seen in the decision of *Flynn v RTE, Bird and Howard.*[23] In that case, the High Court ordered discovery of names of bank account holders in an action for defamation brought by a former employee of a bank who claimed the defendants defamed her in claiming she had induced customers to participate in a scheme aimed at evading tax.

Where a mareva injunction is granted and the assets the subject of the injunction include moneys in a bank account the court may, if it decides that the claimant is entitled to discovery of the balance in the account, exercise its powers under the Bankers' Books Evidence Act 1879 to order that the claimant may inspect and take copies of entries in the banker's books.

Subpoena

A bank which is compelled by subpoena to produce to a court bank statements will not breach its contractual duty of confidentiality by doing so without obtaining the customer's consent. This may pose problems for a bank in deciding whether or not it should inform its customer, as it may be entitled, for its own protection or compelled by public duty, to refrain from informing its customer.

Subpoenas from other jurisdictions

A foreign court may issue a subpoena on an international bank for the purpose of obtaining information in relation to an Irish branch. This raises issues of conflicts of law and respect for the comity of nations. Where the international bank has a branch or place of business in the jurisdiction where the subpoena is issued, the subpoena may be enforceable as a practical matter in that jurisdiction. However, where the revelation of information by a branch in Ireland in relation to dealings with its customers would be in breach of the bank's duty of confidentiality, the issue arises whether an Irish court would issue an injunction restraining the disclosure. There is no Irish case law directly on the point, but it is likely that an Irish court would follow

---

22 (15 May 1998, unreported), HC.
23 [2000] 3 IR 344.

the position taken by the English courts in *X A-G v A Bank*[24] and restrain such a disclosure, in particular, in circumstances where compliance with the injunction in Ireland would not result in the bank being in contempt of the foreign court which granted the subpoena. This conclusion is consistent with the approach taken by the High Court in *Chemical Bank Ltd v McCormack*.[25]

Obtaining evidence abroad for use in Irish proceedings

Subpoena

The usual means of securing the presence of a witness at a trial is by the service on him of a subpoena ad testificandum. To secure documents to be put in evidence, a subpoena duces tecum is served on the person in possession of them, requiring him to produce the documents in court. If the person on whom it is wished to serve the subpoena is out of the jurisdiction, no subpoena may be issued by the court. Where documents are held out of Ireland, but there is a person within Ireland in whose control they are, it would appear that there is power to compel that person to produce the documents. In *Chemical Bank Ltd v McCormack*,[26] the High Court held in relation to the Bankers' Books Evidence Act 1879 that while the court had an inherent jurisdiction to make an order compelling a bank incorporated in Ireland to produce an account maintained outside the jurisdiction for inspection, this should not be done as it would involve 'a conflict of jurisdiction, which should be avoided in the interest of the comity of courts'. It was also held that as the 1879 Act could not be interpreted as having extra-territorial effect, the High Court had no jurisdiction to order an inspection under the 1879 Act outside Ireland.

Evidence by commission

Where a person is abroad but consents to give evidence or produce evidence, the High Court may permit the taking of evidence abroad by commission under an inherent jurisdiction which is recognised by the Rules of the Superior Courts and has been exercised for a long time.[27] The courts are reluctant to exercise this jurisdiction and will generally only do so in rare cases where it is necessary in the interests of justice.[28] Circumstances which have justified the use of the procedure on occasion include a witness not having sufficient financial resources to travel to Ireland.[29]

Letters of request

Letters of request may be issued in accordance with the Rules of the Superior Courts to a foreign court or judicial authority requesting the oral examination of a witness

24   [1983] 2 All ER 464.
25   [1983] ILRM 350.
26   [1983] ILRM 350.
27   *Carbery Divorce Bill* [1920] 2 IR 345.
28   *Neil v Silcock* (1903) 38 ILTR 5.
29   *Keane v Hanley* [1938] Ir Jur Rep 16.

before the court or other competent authority in respect of the examination of witnesses. Where an order is made for the issue of a request to examine a witness in a foreign country with which a convention with Ireland exists, the procedure may be varied.

Obtaining information from banks in Ireland for use in foreign civil proceedings

Letters of request

Ireland has not yet ratified the 1968 Hague Convention on the Taking of Evidence Abroad in Civil and Commercial Matters (although the Law Reform Commission has recommended ratification). The position where letters of request are received in Ireland from a foreign court is covered by the Foreign Tribunals Evidence Act 1856, which provides that:

> 'Where, upon an application for this purpose, it is made to appear to any court or judge having authority under this Act that any court or tribunal of competent jurisdiction in a foreign country, before which any civil or commercial matter is pending, is desirous of obtaining the testimony in relation to such matter of any witness or witnesses within the jurisdiction of such first-mentioned court, or of the court to which such judge belongs, or of such judge, it shall be lawful for such court or judge to order the examination upon oath, upon interrogatories or otherwise, before any person or persons named in such order, of such witness or witnesses accordingly; and it shall be lawful for the said court or judge, by the same order, of such court or judge, or any other judge having authority under this Act, by any subsequent order to command the attendance of any person to be named in such order, for the purpose of being examined, or the production of any writings or other documents to be mentioned in such order, and to give all such directions as to the time, place, and manner of such examination, and all other matters connected therewith, as may appear reasonable and just.'

The proceedings, which are the subject of the letters of request, must be civil or commercial. The 1856 Act provides that the giving of a certificate by a diplomatic agent or consul is evidence that the relevant matter pending before the foreign court is a civil or commercial matter. The letters of request must require testimony from named persons within Ireland. Any person duly authorised by the foreign court or tribunal may apply to the High Court to have evidence taken. There are two possible routes. Letters of request may be forwarded by a foreign embassy to the Department of Foreign Affairs. The Department transmits them to the Chief State Solicitor who in turn makes an application to the High Court who will normally direct the examination to take place before a District Court judge with questions put by counsel briefed by the Chief State Solicitor. The second procedure (and the one which may in practice be more expeditious) involves the sending of a letter of request to solicitors in Ireland who, acting as agents of the parties to the foreign proceedings, apply ex parte on affidavit to the High Court for an appropriate order directing that a specified witness attend to give evidence before an examiner, again, normally a District Court judge.

The court has a discretion in relation to the production of documents. In general, it must be satisfied that the documents are relevant to the proceedings. The witness' evidence is given under oath and the normal rules of evidence apply.

In *Re Chomutov Savings Bank*,[30] the Supreme Court reversed the High Court and made an order requiring a witness to be examined notwithstanding the fact that the defendant to the foreign action had not yet been served with proceedings.

Obtaining information from banks in Ireland for use in foreign criminal proceedings

Request for assistance

Under the Criminal Justice Act 1994, where the Minister for Justice receives 'a request for assistance' from a foreign court, tribunal or other authority in obtaining evidence in Ireland in connection with criminal proceedings in the foreign state, and the Minister is satisfied that an offence under the law of the foreign state has been committed (or that there are reasonable grounds for suspecting that such an offence has been committed) and that proceedings or an investigation into that offence is being carried out, he may nominate a judge of the District Court to receive such of the evidence (including documents and other articles) to which the request relates as may appear to the judge to be appropriate to give effect to the request.

A typical summons would require a bank manager to attend the District Court to give evidence as to all bank accounts held legally and/or beneficially in the name of the person under investigation and any related accounts in the name of subsidiaries. The bank manager would typically be required to attend the court with:

1   copies of all bank statements and vouchers including ledgers, documents evidencing electronic fund transfers (for example, SWIFT transactions), pay cheques, debit advices, pay in slips and other credit advices for the said account/ accounts;
2   copies of all customer files, customer records cards, statement inquiry cards, account opening fees, records showing authorised signatory and all correspondence between either the bank and the account holder, the bank and third parties and internal bank correspondence and other records maintained by the bank relating to the monitoring of the said accounts from the date of opening to the present time; and
3   copies of all documents held by the bank on computer or in hard copy in respect of the use of these said accounts.

The summons typically provides that the provisions of the Bankers' Books Evidence Act 1879 must apply to the documents, namely that the book or documents or microfilm was at the time of making the entry one of the ordinary books of the bank and that the entry was made in the usual and ordinary course of business of the bank and the books are in the custody or control of the bank.

---

30   [1957] IR 355.

Sequestration of bank deposits

Not applicable for enforcement of foreign penal law

The courts will not enforce a foreign sequestration order on the grounds that the courts will not be used to enforce a penal law of a foreign state as decided in *Buchanan Ltd v McVey*.[31] The reason for this approach is that the courts are not competent to arbitrate on the justice or injustice of the penal laws of foreign states. An example of the application of these principles arose in the case of *Larkins v National Union of Mineworkers and Bank of Ireland Finance Ltd*,[32] which attracted much publicity at the time (the principal officers of the union concerned, who were trustees of its funds, were Arthur Scargill, Michael McGahey and Ernest Heathfield). English courts appointed the first four plaintiffs sequestrators following the failure of the first defendant (the union) to pay a fine. The sequestrators sought an interim order from the High Court claiming that the union had transferred funds of approximately £8,000,000 from its account in the UK to bank accounts with the second defendant (the bank). The sequestrator claimed possession of the funds and they needed to establish the whereabouts of the funds with a view to preventing them from leaving the Irish jurisdiction. The Irish High Court made an interim order providing, inter alia, that:

1   the union and the bank and their servants and agents and 'any bank or financial institution' within the Irish jurisdiction be restrained from disposing of or otherwise dealing in any manner with any monies held to the union's account; and
2   the bank (or any financial institution or bank in Ireland served with notice of the order) produce for inspection 'the bankers' books including correspondence or computer printouts from electronic recordings' relating to any account of the union held by the bank.

At the trial of the action (where it was held that the sequestrators were not entitled to the funds on deposit on the grounds that the court would not enforce a penal law or process of a foreign state), Barrington J gave his reasons for his 'very far reaching order':

'In the normal course a freezing order would have been sufficient to maintain the status quo and there would have been no justification for making an inspection order such as this, ex parte. The necessity for the ex parte order arose from the fear that a portion of the funds had already been transferred to other financial institutions in Ireland, the identity of which was unknown to the sequestrators [as it transpired funds had been transferred not to other financial institutions in Ireland but to banks in New York, Luxembourg and Switzerland].'

Consumer affairs

An authorised officer, appointed by the Minister for Enterprise, Trade and Employment or by the Director of Consumer Affairs, may for the purpose of obtaining information

31   [1954] IR 89.
32   [1985] IR 671.

to enable the Director of Consumer Affairs to carry out her functions under the European Communities (Unfair Terms in Consumer Contracts) Regulations 1995:[33]

> '(a) at all reasonable times enter premises at which any business or any activity in connection with a business is carried on ...
> (b) require any person who carries on such business or activity and any person employed in connection therewith to produce to the authorised officer any books, documents or records relating to such business or activity which are in that person's power or control and to give the officer information in regard to any entries in any books, documents and records,
> (c) inspect and take copies from such books, documents and records,
> (d) require any such person to give to the authorised officer any information the officer may require in regard to the persons carrying on such business or activity ...
> (e) require any such person to give to the officer any other information which the officer may reasonably require in regard to such business or activity.'

These powers are certainly intrusive, but it should be borne in mind that they are only to enable the Director of Consumer Affairs to carry out her functions under the Regulations and therefore should not in the normal course involve opening accounts to the officer, but rather procedures adopted by banks in its dealings with consumer customers generally.

Company investigations

The Companies Act 1990 provides that in certain circumstances a company may have an inspector appointed to it to investigate its affairs. Subject to the court's approval, an inspector appointed to investigate the affairs of a company may investigate also the affairs of any other body corporate which is related to such company.

The Companies Act 1990 requires all officers and agents of a body corporate whose affairs are being investigated to produce to the inspectors all books and documents relating to the body corporate. Section 10(2) provides:

> 'If the inspectors consider that a person other than an officer or agent of the company or other body corporate is or may be in possession of any information concerning its affairs, they may require that person to produce to them any books or documents in his custody or power relating to the company or other body corporate, to attend before them and otherwise to give them all assistance in connection with the investigation which he is reasonably able to give; and it shall be the duty of that person to comply with the requirement.'

The problem that this statutory provision poses for banks was highlighted in the correspondence leading up to the application of *Chestvale Properties Ltd, Hoddle Investments Ltd v Glackin and Ansbacher Bankers Ltd, Noel Smyth and Partners and the A-G.*[34] Following the request to the bank from the inspector to deliver certain

33   SI 27/1995.
34   [1993] 3 IR 35.

documents relating to the applicants, the applicants' solicitors wrote to the bank's solicitors stating:

'If your client [the bank] now complies with the demands and it is subsequently deemed that your client [the bank] was not obliged to do so then our clients [the applicants] would have an appropriate remedy.'

The unenviable predicament for bankers was highlighted a month later by Murphy J in *Chestvale Properties Ltd & Hoddle Investments Ltd v Glackin*,[35] when he said:

'Obviously the Bank and the Solicitor are in an awkward position; if they neglect to produce books or documents which should properly have been produced they expose themselves to the risk of penalties which might be imposed on them for contempt of court. On the other hand, if they hand over books or records which do not fall within the terms of the Act they may be liable to their clients for damages for breach of contract.'

The impact of this predicament was felt by the bank a month later in *Re Chestvale Properties Ltd and Hoddle Investments Ltd, Glackin v Trustee Savings Bank and McInerney*.[36] When the bank was requested by the inspector to supply documents, it contended that without their customer's consent, or a High Court order, it could not comply with the inspector's request without breaching the duty of confidentiality which it owed to its customer. The court held that not only did the bank have to supply the documents but also to pay the inspector his costs of the hearing.

When considering s 10 of the Companies Act 1990 the words of Mr Justice Costello in *Re Chestvale Properties Ltd and Hoddle Investments Ltd, Glackin v Trustee Savings Bank and McInerney* should be heeded. He stated:

'It seems to me that the bank has misunderstood its statutory duty … It is a duty to give assistance if requested to do so under s 10, sub-s 2 of the Act of 1990. It is not permitted to refuse assistance, because of a contractual arrangement with a customer which may have involved a term of confidentiality. The Oireachtas [Parliament] has made perfectly clear, to my mind, what people … are required to do. They are required to assist the inspector. They are not entitled to obstruct him and they must observe his requests. They are not entitled to ask their customer whether or not the customer objects. Whatever contractual arrangement there has been between the bank and the customer has been clearly over-ridden by the provisions put into this section by the Oireachtas and the manner in which it should comply with the request has been made clear by Mr Justice Murphy. They are to give assistance to the inspector when requested to do so.'

The reference by Mr Justice Costello to Mr Justice Murphy was a reference to his decision in *Chestvale Properties Ltd & Hoddle Investments Ltd v Glackin*. Mr Justice Murphy indicated in the course of his judgment that under s 10 of the Companies Act 1990 there are two classes of obligation imposed on agents or former agents of a company whose affairs are being investigated, namely:

35 (10 March 1992, unreported), HC.
36 [1993] 3 IR 55.

'first of all an obligation to produce books and documents and secondly an obligation to attend and give viva voce evidence ... those words "all assistance in connection with the investigation" illuminate fully the nature of the obligation imposed upon an addressee with regard to not merely information but also to the production of books and records. In my view the nature of the obligation which is imposed upon officers or agents can indeed be expressed in terms comparable to that of the obligation imposed upon a person of whom discovery is sought ... All the persons to whom the demand is addressed can do is to produce books and records which in their honest opinion may be of assistance to the inspector.'

Section 10 of the 1990 Act was challenged in a case involving the investigation of improper charging of interest and fees by a licensed bank, on the grounds that it removed the privilege against self-incrimination. In *Re National Irish Bank Ltd (No 1)*,[37] the Supreme Court held (unanimously) that

1   the right to silence was not absolute but could in certain circumstances give way to the exigencies of the common good, provided that the means used to curtail the right were proportionate to the public object to be achieved;

2   if there were grounds for believing that there was malpractice or illegality in the operation of the banking system, it was essential, in the public interest, that the public authority had the power to investigate the matter fully;

3   the powers given to the inspectors under s 10 of the 1990 Act were no greater than those which the public interest required; and

4   the interviewees were not entitled to refuse to answer questions put to them by the inspectors.

Dormant accounts

Under the Dormant Accounts Act 2001 the proceeds of accounts with banks which have been dormant for 15 years must, unless reactivated by the account holder following notification to it (at its last known address), be transferred to the Dormant Accounts Fund of the State. A bank which transfers money to the Fund is required not to refer to the account holder by name or in any manner by which the account holder could be identified.

Deposit Interest Retention Tax

The Finance Act 1986 introduced a concept commonly referred to as DIRT – Deposit Interest Retention Tax. A bank when making a payment of interest in respect of a deposit is required to deduct from that payment the standard rate of tax. The bank is required to make a return to the Collector-General of the relevant interest paid by it and of the appropriate tax in relation to the payment of that interest (but it is not required that such return contain details of the recipients of the interest payments).

---

37   [1999] 3 IR 145.

Where the beneficial entitlement to interest on a deposit is held by a person who is not ordinarily resident in Ireland, tax is not to be deducted by the bank on the interest payable provided the beneficial owner declares, in such form as is prescribed by the Revenue Commissioners, that he is not ordinarily resident in Ireland. The declaration will include details of the name of the depositor, the address of his principal place of residence and the name of the country in which he is ordinarily resident. The declaration must be kept by the bank for the longer of six years, or three years after the deposit is repaid. The bank is required to make the declaration available to the inspector of taxes as and when required.

Deduction of deposit interest retention tax is not required in respect of interest on a deposit which is beneficially owned by a company within the charge to corporation tax or a pension scheme or a charitable body. As a result of the Finance Act 2002 such bodies are required to provide banks paying deposit interest to them with their reference numbers. A bank is then required to return these numbers to the Revenue Commissioners together with details of the names and addresses of such bodies to whom they have paid interest without deduction of DIRT.

A deposit account opened before 6 April 2001, may be designated by the bank holding the deposit as a 'special savings account' provided the depositor is an individual beneficially entitled to the interest, who does not hold another special savings account and the amount of the deposit does not exceed €63,500. The individual must make a declaration in such form as may be prescribed by the Revenue Commissioners. The declaration must include details of the name and address of the individual beneficially entitled to the interest. The bank is required to keep such declarations and make them available to the inspector of taxes as required.

Disclosure required by the Revenue Commissioners

A bank may be required to disclose details of a customer's account with it by the High Court on the application of an inspector or other duly authorised officer of the Revenue Commissioners. The High Court must be 'satisfied that there are reasonable grounds for the application being made'. The grounds on which an application may arise are set out in s 908(2) of the Taxes Consolidation Act 1997, as amended by the Finance Act 1999, which states:

> 'An authorised officer [of the Revenue Commissioners] may, subject to this section, make an application to a judge for an order requiring a financial institution, to do either or both of the following, namely—
> (a) to make available for inspection by the authorised officer, such books, records or other documents as are in the financial institution's power, possession or procurement as contain, or may (in the authorised officer's opinion formed on reasonable grounds) contain information relevant to a liability in relation to a taxpayer,
> (b) to furnish to the authorised officer such information, explanations and particulars as the authorised officer may reasonably require, being information, explanations and particulars that are relevant to any such liability
> and which are specified in the application.'

The Act enables the High Court to prohibit any transfer or dealing with any assets or moneys in the custody of the financial institution at the time the order is made. This provision was first introduced by s 18 of the Finance Act 1983. In the first reported decision on s 18,[38] Murphy J stated:

'Undoubtedly any order made under the section would involve an invasion of the traditional bond of confidentiality between a banker and his customer.'

In the Supreme Court in the same case the Chief Justice stated:

'Section 18 can be summarised with regard to its purpose and effect as giving to the High Court wide and entirely novel powers of forcing a bank to reveal the affairs of a customer and in addition, under certain circumstances, vests in the High Court a discretion to freeze the bank account of a taxpayer.'

Disclosure was granted under this section in *Liston v G O'C and A O'C*.[39] In that case, an inspector of taxes in the Investigation Branch of the Revenue Commissioners formed the view that the taxpayers maintained an account or accounts at specified branches of Allied Irish Banks and Bank of Ireland and that the books of both banks were likely to contain information regarding the taxpayers financial affairs leading to the conclusion that returns of income made by them were false. Following an ex parte application by the inspector of taxes, an order was made by the High Court (pursuant to the section) requiring the banks to furnish the inspector of taxes with particulars of all accounts held by the taxpayers at specified branches during a two-year period, as well as details of all lodgements and withdrawals into or out of the accounts for that period and any mandates or other instructions relating to the operation of the accounts.

The High Court's decision was upheld by the Supreme Court. In giving the judgment of the Court, Keane J explained the scope of the section:

'the role of the inspector under the section is a purely investigative one. His belief that the information which he seeks from the bank will indicate that there have been significant omissions from the taxpayers' return of income may prove to be erroneous. The clear object of the provision is, however, to enable the Revenue Commissioners to obtain information of this nature in order to ensure that all taxpayers pay the tax which by law they are required to pay. That object would be seriously frustrated if an onus was imposed on the applicant to satisfy the court that the information sought would in fact disclose that false returns had been made. However, an order made under the section seriously abridges the right of confidentiality which every person dealing with a bank enjoys and it is for that reason that the Oireachtas not merely stipulated that the inspector must have reasonable grounds for his belief but provided the additional and valuable safeguard that a High Court Judge must be satisfied that such reasonable grounds exist before the institution concerned can be required to furnish the information sought.'

---

38 *Re JB O'C v PCD and A Bank* [1985] IR 265.
39 [1996] 1 IR 501.

Transfer of assets abroad

A further head under which the Revenue Commissioners may require disclosure arises under s 808 of the Taxes Consolidation Act 1997. Under this section, the Revenue Commissioners may require any person to furnish such particulars as they think necessary in connection with the transfer of assets abroad by persons ordinarily resident in Ireland. However, the banker-customer confidentiality relationship is respected by the exclusion of a bank from such disclosure requirement of 'any particulars of any ordinary banking transactions between the bank and a customer carried out in the ordinary course of banking business' save in limited circumstances specified in s 808(6). Whether a transaction is one carried out in the ordinary course of banking business will depend upon the ordinary business of 'that type of banking institution' and not whether it is in the ordinary course of banking business generally.

This provision was first introduced by s 59 of the Finance Act 1974. In considering its application, it might be noted that the High Court in *The Royal Trust Company (Ireland) Ltd and Whelan v The Revenue Commissioners*[40] applied the judgment of Megarry J in *The Royal Bank of Canada v Inland Revenue Comrs*.[41] This latter case involved the application of s 414(5) of the English Income Tax Act 1952, the relevant portion of which is identical to s 808(4) of the 1997 Act. In the course of his judgment, Megarry J stated:

'Questions as to the ambit of the term "ordinary banking transactions" are not made easier by the circumstances that at least on some views there are many different types of bank ... A transaction that to one type of bank may be ordinary may to another type be exceptional ... I certainly do not accept that every transaction lawfully carried out by a bank is a "banking transaction". Furthermore, even if they were "banking transactions" I cannot regard them as being "ordinary" banking transactions. I do not think it is for counsel for the commissioners to establish that they were "unusual" or "extra-ordinary" or whatever is the appropriate antithesis to "ordinary"; it is for counsel for the bank to show that they were "ordinary" ... nothing will suffice him save a sufficient demonstration of ordinariness.'

In *The Royal Trust Company (Ireland) Ltd and Whelan v The Revenue Commissioners* the High Court held that one type of transaction came within the exclusion, but that the second type did not, 'as there has not been what Megarry J described as "sufficient demonstration of ordinariness" with regard to them'.

Section 890 of the 1997 Act requires every person in receipt of money belonging to a chargeable person to prepare and deliver, when required to do so, a list in a prescribed form containing (i) a statement as to the money, (ii) the name and address of every person to whom it belongs and (iii) a declaration whether such person is, inter alia, of full age, or resident in Ireland.

40   [1982] ILRM 459.
41   [1972] 1 All ER 225.

Tax arrears

A bank may be required to disclose to the Revenue Commissioners the amount standing to the credit of its customer in the event of the bank being informed by the Revenue Commissioners that the customer is in arrears of its tax payments. A bank will be obliged to make a disclosure where it has received written notification from the Revenue Commissioners (under s 1002 of the Taxes Consolidation Act 1997) that the bank's customer has defaulted, and not made good the default, 'in paying, remitting, or accounting for, any tax, interest on unpaid tax, or penalty to the Revenue Commissioners'.

The written notification (notice of attachment) will direct the bank:

1   to deliver to the Revenue Commissioners within ten days a written return specifying:
    (a) whether or not any debt is due by the bank to its customer; and
    (b) the amount of the debt, or where the debt is equal to or greater than the notified tax arrears, the amount of the so notified tax arrears, and
2   to pay to the Revenue Commissioners the lower of the amount of the debt or the amount of tax arrears notified.

Where the deposit is held in the bank by more than one party for their joint benefit, the bank must inform the depositors of the notice of attachment and that the deposit is deemed to be held for the benefit of the depositors equally unless evidence to the contrary is produced to the satisfaction of the bank within ten days. Unless such evidence is produced within ten days, the bank is required to pay to the Revenue Commissioners the amount of the deposit deemed to be held by the defaulting taxpayer (or, if lower, the amount stated in the notice of attachment). It can be seen that this requirement imposes on the bank a duty to disclose to one of its customers the fact that another customer has tax arrears of a specified amount.

Once a notice of attachment has been delivered to a bank, the bank is precluded from paying monies to the depositor except to the extent that such monies will not reduce the deposit below the amount specified in the notice. The legislation is silent as to whether a bank is still required to comply with an attachment notice where a security interest whether by way of assignment or charge is created over the depositor in favour of the bank itself or a third party. It is considered a bank will not be required to comply with an attachment notice in respect of a deposit over which there is a security assignment or over which it has a fixed charge (provided it is a blocked account). However, a floating charge over an account is unlikely to maintain priority over such a notice.

A further infringement of the relationship of confidentiality between a banker and customer arises on the service of a notice by the Revenue Commissioners on a bank under s 1001 of the 1997 Act. This provision, first introduced by s 115 of the Finance Act 1986, may affect any bank which has a fixed charge over the book debts of a taxpayer who has defaulted in its PAYE or VAT payments to the Revenue Commissioners. Following service of the notice, any subsequent monies received by the bank from the taxpayer must be paid out to the Revenue Commissioners to discharge the tax due to them.

Money laundering

Every bank, including their directors, employees and officers, is required under the Criminal Justice Act 1994 to report to the Garda Siochána where they 'suspect' that a money laundering offence in relation to the business of that bank has been or is being committed. A bank is required also to report to the Garda Siochána where it suspects that an offence in relation to drug trafficking or other criminal activity has been or is being committed and that the services offered by the bank have been used to launder the proceeds of that offence. Furthermore, where the suspicion is that a transaction involves the proceeds of tax evasion, it should be reported. A banker's difficulty in deciding whether to make a disclosure and run the risk of breaching its duty of confidentiality where it transpires there has been no offence is alleviated by the statutory provision that disclosure made in good faith in the course of making the report is not regarded as a breach of statutory or common law duty of confidentiality.

A bank (its directors, officers and employees) which discloses to its customer that it has made a report to the Garda Siochána in respect of funds in its customer's account will commit an offence under the 1994 Act if such disclosure 'is likely to prejudice any investigation arising from the report into whether an offence has been committed'. Thus, a bank is required to inform on its customer without alerting its customer to the fact of its disclosure. Guidance Notes for credit institutions issued by the Department of Finance with the approval of the Money Laundering Steering Committee (updated in November 2001) require banks to designate an officer at management level with responsibility for the bank's obligations in relation to money laundering and to provide continuing training programmes for their employees. The role and duties of the money laundering reporting officer are set out in the Guidance Notes. Banks are required to have in place adequate arrangements and procedures to prevent and detect the commission of a money laundering offence.

The 1994 Act has been amended in part by the Criminal Justice (Theft and Fraud Offences) Act 2001. This Act updates and expands the ambit of money laundering, as well as giving effect to provisions of the Convention of the European Communities' Financial Interests (Brussels, 26 July 1995) and the three Protocols to that Convention. The Act provides that the Minister for Justice may designate 'any state, or territorial unit within a state, that in his or her opinion has not in place adequate procedures for the detection of money laundering'.

A bank (including any director, employee or officer) is required to report to the Garda Siochána any transaction with a state or territorial unit that has been so designated by the Minister for Justice. The Act specifically provides that a disclosure made in good faith shall not be treated as a breach of any restriction on the disclosure of information or involve the person making the disclosure in liability of any kind.

Proceeds of crime

The Proceeds of Crime Act 1996 enables a court to make an order, following an ex parte application, by a member of the Garda Siochána not below the rank of Chief Superintendent or by an authorised officer of the Revenue Commissioners, prohibiting a person from disposing of or otherwise dealing with property, including money, where the property constitutes, directly or indirectly, proceeds of crime or where the property was acquired in whole or in part with or in connection with property that, directly or indirectly, constitutes proceeds of crime. Such an order may be made for an interim period of 21 days.

During this interim period, an interlocutory order may be sought extending the effect of the interim order. To discharge the order, the applicant needs to show that the property does not constitute proceeds of crime or was not acquired with or in connection with property that constitutes proceeds of crime.

The order will expire unless a forfeiture order or confiscation order is made under the Criminal Justice Act 1994 or a forfeiture order made under the Misuse of Drugs Act 1977. The Act specifically provides that no action or proceedings shall lie against a bank or any other person in any court in respect of any act or omission done or made in compliance with an order under the Act.

Criminal Assets Bureau

The Criminal Assets Bureau Act 1996 established the Criminal Assets Bureau and sets out its extensive functions and powers in relation to criminal and related activities. The broad objectives of the Bureau are stated to be:

1   the identification of assets, wherever situated, of persons which derive or are suspected to derive, directly or indirectly, from criminal activity;
2   the taking of appropriate action under the law to deprive or to deny those persons of the assets or the benefit of such assets; and
3   the pursuit of any investigation or the doing of any other preparatory work in relation to any proceedings arising from the objectives mentioned in paragraphs 1 and 2 above.

The 1996 Act allows a judge on application by a Bureau member who is a Garda Siochána to issue a search warrant for the search of any place or person in that place, if the judge is satisfied that there are reasonable grounds for suspecting that evidence of or relating to assets or proceeds deriving from criminal activities, or to their identity or whereabouts, is to be found in that place. A similar power to grant a search warrant is conferred on a Bureau officer who is a member of the Garda Siochána, not below superintendent level, in cases of urgency.

Funds of an unlawful organisation

Under the Offences Against the State (Amendment) Act 1985 a bank is required on receipt of a document, 'purporting to be signed by the Minister for Justice', which states that in the opinion of the minister moneys described in the document and held by the bank are the property of an unlawful organisation, to pay the moneys so specified into the High Court. This statutory requirement runs for periods of three months and if not renewed lapses until renewed. The consequences of a bank failing to comply with such a requirement are heavy fines and/or imprisonment for directors or officers of the bank, including the manager or other official of a branch of the bank.

As well as the bank being required to pay moneys into the High Court, it may be required by the court 'to produce and prove to the court all or specified documents that are relevant to the payment of the moneys or part of them into or out of the bank or to the opening, maintenance, operation or closing of any account at the bank in respect of the moneys or part of them'. Statutory protection is given to a bank which complies with a requirement of the minister.

A person claiming to be the owner of such moneys paid into the High Court may within six months apply to the court seeking an order that the moneys be returned with interest. The court will make the order if it is satisfied that the applicant is the owner of the moneys and the moneys do not belong to an unlawful organisation.

Prosecution of criminal offences

Under s 299 of the Companies Act 1963 (as amended by S 51 of the Company Law Enforcement Act, 2001) , if it appears to the liquidator in the course of a voluntary winding up that any past or present officer or member of the company has been guilty of any offence in relation to the company for which he is criminally liable, he shall report the matter to the Director of Public Prosecutions and the Director of Corporate Enforcement. In the event of a liquidator not making such a report, a person interested in the winding up may apply to the court seeking a court direction for such a report to be made. Similarly in the case of a winding up of a company by the court, the court may direct the liquidator to refer any offence to the Director of Public Prosecutions and the Director of Corporate Enforcement.

Following such report, if the Director of Public Prosecutions or the Director of Corporate Enforcement institutes proceedings, it is the duty of every past and present banker to the company 'to give all assistance in connection with the prosecution which he is reasonably able to give'.

Where it appears to the stock exchange that a person has committed an offence under Pt V of the Companies Act 1990, the exchange must make a report to the Director of Public Prosecutions. If the Director issues proceedings following such report, it is the duty of every person who appears to the Director to have relevant information, 'to give all assistance in connection with the prosecution which he or they are reasonably able to give'. In applying the principles outlined by Costello J in *Re Chestvale Properties Ltd and Hoddle Investments Ltd, Glackin v Trustee Savings Bank and McInerney*,[42] a bank would be required to disclose details of such accounts as are required by the Director of Public Prosecutions in the course of his proceedings for unlawful dealing.

Application of Garda Siochána and Director of Corporate Enforcement

The legislature has endeavoured to assist the Garda Siochána, and more recently the Director of Corporate Enforcement in bringing to justice persons who may have

42   [1993] 3 IR 55.

committed a criminal offence by permitting them access to documentation held in a bank. The Bankers' Books Evidence Act 1879, as amended by the Central Bank Act 1989, the Disclosure of Certain Information for Taxation and Other Purposes Act 1996 and the Company Law Enforcement Act, 2001, provides:

> 'If, on an application made by a member of the Siochána not below the rank of Superintendent or the Director of Corporate Enforcement a court or judge is satisfied that there are reasonable grounds for believing—
> (a) that an indictable offence has been committed; and
> (b) that there is material in the possession of a bank specified in the application which is likely to be of substantial value (whether by itself or together with other material) to the investigation of the offence
> a court or judge may make an order that the applicant or another member of the Garda Siochána, or officer of the Director of Corporate Enforcement nominated by the Director, as the case may be, be at liberty to inspect and take copies of any entries in a banker's book, or inspect and take copies of any documentation associated with or relating to an entry in such book, for the purposes of investigation of the offence (the word "documentation" is deemed to include "information kept on microfilm, magnetic tape or in a non-legible form (by use of electronics or otherwise) which is capable of being reproduced in a permanent legible form").'

DUTY TO THE PUBLIC TO DISCLOSE

The second qualification to a banker's duty of confidentiality referred to in *Tournier v National Provincial and Union Bank of England*[43] is where there is a duty to the public to disclose. There has been a dearth of precedent or case law to illustrate this principle until the Supreme Court's decision in *National Irish Bank Ltd and National Irish Bank Financial Services Ltd v Radio Telefís Eireann.*[44] In that case, the defendants sought to publish information showing that certain named customers of the plaintiffs had, at the suggestion of the plaintiffs, used their moneys on deposit (with the plaintiffs) for the purpose of investing in an Isle of Man company, Clerical Medical Insurance, the result of which the defendants alleged, enabled the return on such moneys to evade tax which would otherwise have been payable on the deposit accounts. Although it was not proved that the customers intended to evade tax and the plaintiffs denied it was the intention of the scheme to evade tax, the Supreme Court held by a three to two majority that the defendants could disclose to the public at large the information which they possessed including the names of individual customers (albeit at the risk of a claim for defamation from the customers).

The principle of this exception to the duty of confidentiality was set out by Lynch J in his majority judgment, where he said:

> 'There is no doubt that there exists a duty and a right of confidentiality between banker and customer as also exists in many other relationships such as for

43   [1924] 1 KB 461.
44   [1998] 2 IR 465.

example doctor and patient and lawyer and client. This duty of confidentiality extends to third parties into whose hands confidential information may come and such third parties can be injuncted to prohibit the disclosure of such confidential information. There is a public interest in the maintenance of such confidentiality for the benefit of society at large. On the other hand there is also a public interest in defeating wrong doing and where the publication of confidential information may be of assistance in defeating wrong doing then the public interest in such publication may outweigh the public interest in the maintenance of confidentiality.'

In applying the principle in the case, Lynch J held:

'... the allegation which [the defendants] make is of serious tax evasion and this is a matter of genuine interest and importance to the general public and especially the vast majority who are law abiding tax payers and I am satisfied that there is a public interest that the general public should be given this information.'

The lack of proof by the defendants of any wrong doing, but simply an allegation of wrong doing, made the majority decision somewhat surprising (although the editorial of *The Irish Times* at the time of the decision stated: 'Perhaps we should not be unduly surprised. The Supreme Court has a proud and distinguished record of affirming individual rights and liberties' – no mention was made of the rights of customers to have their affairs kept confidential). In his dissenting judgment, Keane J (now Chief Justice) with whom the then Chief Justice Hamilton concurred, pointed out that the details of the scheme were already the subject of inquiries by the Revenue Commissioners and the Central Bank. Keane J stated:

'The authorities ... made it clear that where someone is in possession of confidential information establishing that serious misconduct has taken place or is contemplated, the courts should not prevent disclosure to persons who have a proper interest in receiving the information. RTE accordingly, should not be restrained in this case from disclosing to the Revenue Commissioners the confidential information in their possession which, they say, establishes that this scheme has been availed of in order to evade the payment of tax.'

Thus, according to the Supreme Court, disclosure to the public at large is in the public interest not just where there is wrong doing, but also where there is a suspicion of wrong doing.

INTERESTS OF THE BANK TO DISCLOSE

Where disclosure is justified under this exception, it must be restricted to that which is strictly necessary to protect the bank's interest. The classic example of this exception is where the bank discloses information in relation to its customer in order to enforce its rights against the customer by legal proceedings. The exception should also cover disclosure for the purpose of protecting the bank's business reputation in circumstances where it is brought in to question by actions of the customer.

In relation to the relevance of this exception to disclosures between separate legal entities within a banking group, it would not be safe for a bank to assume such disclosures are permitted under this exemption.

This intra-group disclosure issue was raised in *Kennedy v Allied Irish Banks plc*,[45] where disclosure between two members of an Irish banking group was at issue. The judge did not find it necessary to resolve the issue in the particular circumstances but, in passing, stated that this is an 'interesting and important point for all banking groups'. The better view is that, as a general rule, express consent is necessary for such disclosure and the decision of the English Court of Appeal in *Bank of Tokyo Ltd v Akron*[46] that each company in a group is to be regarded as a separate entity for disclosure purposes would probably be followed if the issue were to be considered by an Irish Court. Some banks include in their standard documentation express consents to intra-group disclosures.

The question whether the bank's interest exception covers disclosure of information in relation to customers to credit bureaux has not been considered by the Irish Courts. In the case of disclosure of information relating to customers who are not in default, it is unlikely that the exception would apply and the bank should have the consent of the customer before disclosing information in such circumstances.

CONSENT OF THE CUSTOMER

The duty of confidentiality of a bank in respect of its customers' affairs may be disapplied where the customer consents to the disclosure in question. A consent for this purpose may be express or implied. In the case of implied consent, it is difficult to determine the scope of the exception and whether it applied will depend on the particular circumstances of each case. One circumstance in which implied consent to disclosure usually inferred is where the customer provides a third party with the name of the bank for the purpose of it providing a reference in relation to the customer. The customer's implied consent will not protect the bank if it is negligent when providing information when giving a reference.

Some banks now insert express provisions in their mandates and application forms permitting them to make, in relation to dealings with customers, intra-group disclosures, disclosures to regulators (including regulators outside of Ireland) and, in a few cases, disclosures to other third parties.

Standard home loan mortgage documentation usually contains a consent by the customer to disclosure for the purpose of a securitisation. The Code of Practice issued by the Central Bank for such transactions provides:

(1) A loan secured by the mortgage of residential property may not be transferred without the written consent of the borrower. When seeking consent from either an existing or a new borrower the lender must provide a statement containing sufficient information to enable the borrower to make an informed decision. This statement, which must be cleared in advance with the Central Bank of Ireland, must include

45   (18 May 1995, unreported), HC, Murphy J.
46   [1986] 3 All ER 468.

a clear explanation of the implications of a transfer and how the transfer might affect the borrower. The borrower must be approached on an individual basis and given reasonable time to give or to decline to give his consent.

(2) When seeking a consent and where there is to be or where there may be an arrangement under which the original lender will service the mortgage as an agent of any transferee, the lender will confirm that the transferee's policy on the handling of arrears and in the setting of mortgage interest rates will be the same as that of the original lender, and that the original lender will handle arrears as its agent.

(3) Where the lender in the ordinary course of business would no longer have control in relation to
   (a) the setting of interest rates, <u>and/or</u>
   (b) determining the conduct of relations with borrowers whose mortgage payments are seriously in arrears
   the lender must seek the borrower's consent to a transfer notwithstanding any previous consent which a borrower has given.

(4) When seeking the borrower's consent to the transfer of his mortgage, as described in paragraph 3 above, the lender will provide the borrower with the following information:
   – the name and address of the intended transferee, and of any holding company, if applicable;
   – the relationship, if any, between the lender and the transferee;
   – a description of the intended transferee and of its business, including details of how long it has been in operation, and of its experience in the management of mortgages;
   – an explanation of the policy and procedures which will apply for the setting of the mortgage interest rate and for making repayments if the transfer takes place;
   – confirmation that in the absence of a specific consent the existing arrangements will continue to apply.

(5) The terms of the transfer agreement shall require the transferee
   (a) to allow transferred mortgages to be redeemed without charging a redemption fee (unless approved under s 28 of the Central Bank Act 1989).
   (b) to continue any existing mortgage protection insurance arrangements;
   (c) to allow the borrower arrange his own house insurance;
   (d) to provide to the authorities the mortgage statistics previously provided by the original lender;
   (e) to comply with this code of practice in relation to any future transfer of these mortgages.

QUALIFICATIONS

The foregoing qualifications to the common law duty of confidentiality, as outlined in the *Tournier*[47] decision, may apply also to the statutory duty of confidentiality. As of now, decisions of the courts on this are awaited.

---

47   *Tournier v National Provincial and Union Bank of England* [1924] 1 KB 461.

16   Italy

Marcello Gioscia
Giuseppe de Falco

SOURCES OF THE BANK'S DUTY OF CONFIDENTIALITY

Introduction

The bank's duty of confidence, that is, the bank's duty not to reveal to third parties the existence and the nature of its relationships with its clients (and that which is confided by those clients to it), has still not been expressly recognised or codified under Italian law. Therefore, given the recognised need for banks to maintain the confidentiality of transactions entered into with their clients, it is necessary to identify the legal sources which give rise to the banks' obligation to maintain confidentiality.

Customary practice

Some legal writers have maintained that the obligation of confidentiality in relation to banking transactions is based on the Italian Constitution, art 47 which provides that 'the Republic encourages and protects savings in any form'. The obligation to maintain confidentiality in banking transactions is, therefore, seen to constitute one of the elements essential for the encouragement and protection of savings.

The existence of an obligation to maintain confidentiality in banking transactions is undoubtedly implicitly supported by various provisions of Legislative Decree 385 of 1 September 1993, as amended by Legislative Decree 333 of 4 August 1999 (the Banking Law), which will be discussed in more detail below.

Nevertheless, the legal source which more directly gives rise to the obligation of confidentiality in relation to banking transactions is generally considered by legal writers and judicial authority to be 'customary practice', which is a source of law consisting of the repetition of uniform behaviour carried out in the conviction that such behaviour is in the nature of the performance of legal obligations.[1]

---

1   Gianfelici *Il segreto Bancario* Milan (1996) p 2; see Cass 18 July 1974, n 2147, in *Massimario* (1974) p 514.

Such customary practice, which imposes the said obligation of confidentiality on the banks, assumes importance in relationships between banks and their clients, and assumes the nature of a contractual obligation owed by the banks to their clients, by virtue of the fact that the banking contract is supplemented by various implied terms. In fact, art 1374 of the Italian Civil Code requires the parties to a contract to act not only according to the terms of the contract, but also in accordance with the consequences that derive from law or, in the absence of law, common practice and equity.

Obligations of fairness and good faith

According to some legal writers, the obligation owed by banks to maintain the confidentiality of banking transactions is based on legal norms embodying general principles of fairness and good faith.

Therefore, the banks' obligation of confidentiality, rather than arising from individual contracts between banks and their clients, constitutes a specific application of the obligation – owed by a debtor and creditor in any given transaction – to act in accordance with norms of fairness,[2] with specific reference both to pre-contractual negotiations[3] and the subsequent performance of the contract.[4]

The Banking Law

As mentioned above, the obligation to maintain confidentiality of banking transactions is implicitly confirmed by various provisions of the Banking Law.

First, art 7 of the Banking Law – which replaces art 10 of Royal Decree 375 of 12 March 1936 (the Old Banking Law) – provides as follows:

'1. All notices, information and data in the possession of the Bank of Italy by virtue of its supervisory activities are covered by official secrecy also in respect of public administrative bodies, except for the Minister of the Treasury as Chairman of the Credit Committee. Professional secrecy may not be invoked with respect to judicial authorities when the information requested is needed for investigations or proceedings involving violations subject to criminal sanctions.

2. The officers and employees of the Bank of Italy, in exercising their supervisory functions, are public officers and are obliged to refer exclusively to the Governor all irregularities ascertained, even when such irregularities may constitute an offence.

3. Officers and employees of the Bank of Italy are bound by official secrecy.'

---

2   Civil Code, art 1175.
3   Civil Code, art 1337.
4   Civil Code, art 1375.

Although it has been argued that the secrecy obligation contained in art 10 of the Old Banking Law applies solely to the Bank of Italy and its personnel, it has also been argued, on the other hand, that this obligation constitutes a confirmation (albeit indirect), of the existence of a general obligation owed by banks to maintain confidentiality of banking transactions.[5]

The above theory is founded primarily on two considerations. First, the obligation regards and covers all information concerning the banks, and does not provide for nor permit a distinction to be drawn between information relating to credit institutions and information relating to individual clients.

Secondly, art 135 of the Banking Law, which deals with corporate offences, provides that certain provisions of the Civil Code relating to corporate offences apply to those persons within the bank who perform functions of an administrative, managerial or supervisory nature. Among such provisions there is art 2622 of the Civil Code, according to which 'the directors, officers, statutory auditors and liquidators who, without just cause, for their own profit or for the profit of others, make use of or reveal information obtained by them by reason of their position, are punishable ...' Since art 135 of the Banking Law expressly provides for the protection of information relating to the banks, it is considered that the above-mentioned art 7 of the Banking Law cannot have as its sole and exclusive object such protection, but rather must be seen to establish the obligation to maintain confidentiality in relation to all information relating to both the bank and its individual clients.

Further, art 87, para 5 of the Banking Law (which replaces the last paragraph of art 78 of the Old Banking Law), in protection of bank secrecy, provides that the list of unsecured creditors – a summary of which must be produced by the receiver in proceedings for the compulsory winding up of the bank – 'is not to be made available', that is, it is not provided with the statement of creditors to be included in the court documents thereby avoiding the possibility that third parties may view it.

It is possible to infer from the above article (although also in this case indirectly) further confirmation of the existence of the banker's duty to maintain confidentiality. Nevertheless, we note that art 87, para 5 of the Banking Law has, on the one hand, strengthened the protection of the bank confidentiality in relation to the specific bank's bankruptcy proceedings (liquidazione coatta amministrativa). On the other hand, it has eliminated any express reference to the principle of bank confidentiality (while art 78 of the Old Banking Law was clearly based on the principle of the protection of bank confidentiality).[6] In any case, the principle of the protection of bank confidentiality during the liquidazione coatta amministrativa has been supported by the Italian Constitutional Court.[7]

5   Bricola *Commento sub art 10 lb* in AA VV *Codice commentato della Banca* Milan (1990) vol I, p 134ff.
6   Galanti *Commento sub artt 87 e 88 Legge Bancaria* in *Commentario al Testo Unico delle leggi in materia bancaria e creditizia Padova* (1994) p 87ff.
7   Corte Costituzionale, 14 January 1977, n 26, in *Giurisprudenza Costituzionale* (1977) I, p 80ff.

Criminal law

There is an old judicial trend, now considered outdated, according to which the source of the banker's duty of confidentiality is also seen to be founded in criminal law.

In particular, this trend relied on art 622 of the Italian Criminal Code, which punishes 'whoever, having knowledge of a secret by reason of his position, office or profession, reveals that secret, without just cause, or uses it for his own profit or the profit of others, if such behaviour can cause damage'.

Nevertheless, according to the majority of the more recent case law and legal theory, bank secrecy is not founded on criminal law principles. In particular, art 622 could not be applied to cases of breach of the banker's duty of confidentiality, given that (i) the information provided to the bank by its clients is not a 'secret' of the type contemplated by art 622, and (ii) banking services – far from constituting individual professional services – are performed by corporate entities and are of a commercial nature.

Likewise, art 326 of the Criminal Code – which punishes public officials or persons entrusted with public service who, in violation of the duties inherent in their position or service, or in any event abusing their position, reveal official information which should remain secret, or in any way facilitate the communication thereof – cannot be applied to cases of the nature in question, as the information known by the banks relating to the clients does not constitute a 'secret' as contemplated by this article.

EXCEPTIONS TO THE PRINCIPLE OF BANK SECRECY

Exceptions to duty of confidence in relation to the powers of tax authorities

With the entry into force of Law 413 of 30 December 1991, containing in Pt III the 'Provisions for transparency of relationships between tax authorities and taxpayers', bank secrecy in relation to the tax authorities was substantially reduced by means of profound modifications to numerous provisions contained in Decree of the President of the Republic (DPR) 600 of 29 September 1973 (in relation to assessment of income tax), and DPR 633 of 26 October 1972 (in relation to VAT).[8]

In particular, the area in question is regulated by art 32 of DPR 600/1973 and art 51 of DPR 633/1972, as amended by art 18 of Law 413/1991. These articles confer wide powers of audit on the tax authorities which may be exercised in requesting information and documentation (provided that it is relevant from a tax point of view) both directly from the person the subject of the tax audit and indirectly from third parties (including credit institutions) which have conducted relationships of an economic nature with that person.

With specific reference to the powers of the tax authorities to request information and documents from the banks relating to their clients, it is necessary first to specify

---

8   Gianfelici, n 1 above, p 16ff.

that the tax authorities may obtain from the banks copies of the accounts of the client under investigation, with details of all transactions connected with such accounts. Once the requested documentation is obtained, the tax authorities may also request the bank to provide further information of a more specific nature by requesting them to respond to questionnaires.

There are no prerequisites provided for the exercise of this power. The relevant tax authorities make the request to the bank exclusively on the basis of their own discretional evaluation that such request is necessary, subject to authorisation by the regional director or by the area commander of the relevant tax authorities.

If the tax authorities have not received the requested documentation from the bank within the time limit fixed by the tax authorities (which cannot, in any event, be less than 60 days after the date of notification of the request to the bank) or if the tax authorities have established reasons to doubt the correctness or the authenticity of the information received, they may, subject to authorisation by the regional director or area commander, gain access to the bank's premises to obtain the relevant information directly in accordance with the procedures prescribed by Decree of the Finance Minister.

For the protection of the bank's client who is subject to the tax investigation, the bank is obliged to provide the client with immediate notice of the request for information received from the tax authorities and, further, all data and information collected by the tax authorities is covered by secrecy, violation of which is punishable by specific administrative sanction (unless such violation constitutes a criminal offence and apart from any internal disciplinary actions).

Finally, it is necessary to note in this respect that art 3, paras 177 and 178 of Law 549 of 28 December 1995 (in relation to the rationalisation of public finance) helps to render the power of the tax authorities, referred to above, more effective, providing that the tax authorities, in the performance of their duties, may request the person subject to the tax investigation to give a declaration containing the details of the nature of, and essential data relating to, their relationships with credit institutions, the post office, trust companies and all other domestic and foreign financial intermediaries.

Exceptions to bank secrecy in relation to criminal judicial authorities

The protection of bank secrecy in respect of criminal judicial authorities is principally regulated by arts 248 and 255 of the new Criminal Procedure Code.[9]

Article 248, in relation to searches ordered by a criminal judicial authority, provides that, if the object of the search is to find a specific item, the judicial authority may ask the holder to deliver it, thereby avoiding the search (unless it is considered useful to proceed with the search for the completion of the investigation). Further, in order to locate the items to be seized or to ascertain other useful facts for the purposes of the investigation, the judicial authority or officers of the judicial police may

9   Conso-Grevi *Profili del nuovo codice di procedura penale* Padova (1993) p 238.

examine documents and correspondence in the bank's possession (both Italian banks and foreign banks operating in Italy) and search such items in the event of a refusal by the bank.

Article 255 of the Criminal Procedure Code, in relation to seizures from banks (Italian banks and foreign banks operating in Italy), grants to the judicial authority the power to seize documents, instruments, valuable goods, funds deposited in accounts and all other items, even if contained in a safe deposit box, when such authority has established reasons to consider that those items are pertinent to the offence, even if they do not belong to the accused and they are not registered in his name.

From art 248 of the Criminal Procedure Code it is understood that the concerned bank does not have any right to refuse to comply with the judicial authority's request. Banks generally comply with informal requests from the criminal judicial authorities to receive specified information, in order to avoid any personal intervention by the magistrate at the banks' offices for the retrieval of the relevant documentation. Such behaviour by the banks, at least in the cases in which a direct response is given by letter by the banks to the criminal magistrate, on the one hand, appears to be consistent with a relatively common practice of co-operation between banks and criminal magistrates, and, on the other, is considered by the case law as lawful behaviour which does not constitute a violation of the duty of confidentiality.

In the case in which the bank fails to observe the orders of the criminal judicial authority, criminal sanctions are applicable. In particular, reference is made to art 650 of the Criminal Code, which, in relation to the failure to observe the orders of the authority, expressly punishes those who do not observe an order made legally by the competent authority by reason of justice, public security, public order or hygiene. The provisions in issue are applicable only in cases not involving a more serious crime: in fact, the failure to observe the order of a criminal magistrate by a bank may constitute a more serious offence – for example, aiding and abetting, receiving stolen goods or money laundering – with the consequent application of the more severe criminal sanctions relating to such offence.

The bank is required to verify the authenticity of the order by the judicial authority, the adequacy of the relevant grounds or motives and the limits of any delegation of the judicial authority to the judicial police officers, as such delegation cannot be of a generic nature, but must be precisely detailed both from a subjective and objective point of view. However, the bank does not have any power to challenge or question the legitimacy of an order by a criminal magistrate.

In relation to the issue of notifying the client of the investigation by the criminal authority, contrary to that provided by the tax legislation in relation to tax investigations, the bank – from a civil point of view – is under no obligation to inform its client of the request for information made by the criminal magistrate, and – from a criminal point of view – the bank may not reveal such information to the client, being under an obligation of criminal secrecy provided for by art 329 of the Criminal Procedure Code.

Nonetheless, if the request by the criminal magistrate has as its object not information relating to the bank-client relationship, or documentation concerning the client or the production or seizure of documentation concerning the bank-client relationship, but rather the seizure of sums or assets held by the bank on an agent basis, the obligation on the bank not to notify the client of the request by the judicial authority no longer exists. In fact, such a seizure affects the right to deal with those assets and therefore the bank is obliged to notify the principal of the seizure.

Exceptions to bank secrecy in relation to the powers of civil judicial authorities

The civil magistrate has the power to issue orders for the inspection of documents in the bank's possession or to require the bank to provide documents or information which is relevant to the outcome of civil proceedings pending between third parties.[10]

In particular, in accordance with art 118 of the Civil Procedure Code, the judge may order the parties to the civil proceedings or third parties to allow items in their possession to be inspected where essential for ascertaining the facts relating to the proceedings, provided that this would not involve serious damage for the parties or for third parties.

It is considered, however, that the bank may avoid the inspection of its clients' documents on the grounds that allowing the inspection and the consequent violation of the duty of confidentiality could involve damage to the bank, arising from the loss of its clients' trust. Further, if the bank has doubts about the existence of the conditions for the admissibility of the evidence, it is under a duty to make a claim to the court objecting to the order for the inspection.

If the magistrate does not accept the bank's grounds for refusal, or where the said claim to the court is rejected, the bank must thereafter comply with the magistrate's order (according to art 118 of the Civil Procedure Code, a failure to so comply may be considered by the judge in evaluating the behaviour of the party). On the other hand, such order exempts the bank from all civil liability in respect of its client as it would constitute just cause for the banker's disregard of the duty of confidentiality.

Further, in accordance with art 210 of the Civil Procedure Code, the civil judge, upon request by the counterparty, has the power to order the other party or a third party to produce in the proceedings documents or other items which he considers necessary for those proceedings, within the same limits within which such documents may be ordered to be subject to inspection. In such a case, if the judge does not accept the justification of serious damage on which the bank's objection is based, the bank must comply with the civil magistrate's order, being exempt from all civil liabilities in respect of its client.

Regarding the relationship between protection of bank secrecy and the obligation to testify, employees of the bank called to testify in civil proceedings may not fail to comply with the obligation to testify about facts and circumstances of which they have knowledge by reason of their employment, since the right of abstention from

---

10   Finocchiaro *Ispezione giudiziale (dir proc civ)* in *Enc Dir* Milan (1972) p 948ff.

giving testimony is accorded by law in exceptional cases, of which this is not considered one.

Finally, a bank which has been notified of an act of seizure or attachment of items held by it on behalf of a client is obliged to make a third-party declaration of seizure or attachment in accordance with art 547 of the Civil Procedure Code, according to which the third party (holder of assets belonging to the party against whom the seizure or attachment has been ordered by the civil judge) must specify which items and sums are in its possession and when delivery must be made.

Exceptions to bank secrecy in relation to monetary regulations

Following the entry into force of a law containing the new monetary regulations (DPR 148 of 31 March 1988, as subsequently amended and added to), the movement of capital between Italian residents and residents of other EU member states was liberalised in accordance with the relevant regulations.[11]

Following this legislative initiative, the Italian Exchange Office (UIC), which was previously responsible for exchange control in the monopoly system, has retained only a supervisory role in respect of the credit institutions authorised to conduct exchange transactions and operate on the monetary market on their own behalf and in their own name.

UIC in its supervision of compliance with monetary regulations, has, amongst others, the right to carry out inspections at the premises of banks and others where it has reason to believe that there are relevant documents on those premises and has the right to request production of relevant account books, documents and correspondence (availing itself of the co-operation of the tax authorities and the national institute for foreign trade). In respect of parties subject to the supervision of the Bank of Italy, UIC may proceed to carry out the inspection directly using the inspection services of the Bank of Italy.

Further, UIC – for survey and statistical purposes in relation to economic relationships with foreign entities – is also authorised to request the banks entitled to carry out transactions in foreign currency to send information concerning the foreign exchange transactions in which those banks are in any way involved (excluding, however, transactions for less than €12,500).

UIC's officers and all other persons performing monetary supervisory functions are considered to be public officers and are bound by official secrecy in relation to information obtained in the performance of their duties.

Regarding the existing relationship between bank secrecy and monetary regulations, it is necessary to deal with the issue of the so-called 'tax monitoring', introduced into Italian law by Law 227 of 4 August 1990 containing the regulations for monitoring, for tax purposes, of transfers over a certain amount of cash, financial instruments and securities into and out of Italy.

---

11   Council Directive 88/361/EEC. See Gianfelici, n 2 above, p 151ff.

In particular, art 1 of Law 227 of 1990, as amended by Legislative Decree 461 of 21 November 1997, establishes that the banks authorised to carry out monetary transactions must maintain records of the transfer from or to a foreign entity of cash, instruments or securities of an amount greater than €12,500,[12] effected on behalf of or in favour of physical persons, non-commercial entities and certain other entities – expressly indicated in art 1 – which are resident in Italy. Such records, which are to contain the details of the transactions including name/business name, residence, tax code of the Italian resident on whose behalf or in favour of whom the transfer is effected and the identifying particulars of any accounts of destination, must be kept available to the tax authority for a period of five years, and sent to the competent authority in accordance with specific terms and procedures established by Ministerial Decree.

These obligations are also applicable to the sale and purchase of foreign instruments and securities effected by the persons referred to above if an Italian authorised bank is involved in the transaction.

Exceptions to bank secrecy in relation to the powers of the Bank of Italy

The Banking Law confers on the Bank of Italy wide powers to request information from banks for the performance of its supervisory functions. In particular, arts 51, 53 and 54 of the Banking Law govern the supervisory role which the Bank of Italy has in respect of banks subject to its control.[13]

With specific reference to the supervisory role, banks involved in an investigation conducted by the Bank of Italy are obliged to produce to the Bank of Italy's inspectors all documentation as those inspectors consider appropriate.

It should be noted that, in accordance with art 7 of the Banking Law, all information obtained by the Bank of Italy through its supervisory activities is covered by official secrecy, including those in respect of public administrative bodies, other than in cases provided for by law relating to the investigation of criminal violations. Further, the employees of the Bank of Italy – in the performance of their supervisory duties – are considered to be public officers bound by official secrecy and they are obliged to refer all irregularities exclusively to the Governor of the Bank of Italy, even where there is an offence involved. The Governor then must refer information to the criminal judicial authority if the elements of a criminal offence can be made out in the facts referred to him by the inspectors.

---

12   This threshold has been fixed by the Legislative Decree 290 of 17 October 2002, issued by the Ministry of the Economy and Finance, published in the Official Gazette of the Republic of Italy on 11 December 2002.

13   Berionne *Commento sub art 51* in *Commentario a cura di Capriglione*, p 262ff; Trequattrini *Vigilanza sulle banche* in *La nuova legge bancaria, Commentario a cura di Ferro-Luzzi e Castaldi* Milan (1996) p 775ff.

Exception to bank secrecy in relation to the client's consent

Confidentiality in banking transactions is the right of the bank's client and such right may be expressly or implicitly waived by the client.

Consequently, from a civil liability point of view (contractual and non-contractual), communication of client information to third parties (in particular, in relation to the solvency of the client) cannot be considered a violation of the duty of confidentiality if the client has requested the bank to make such communication in the interests of the client or where the client has otherwise authorised the communication of the information.

From a criminal law point of view, this conclusion is also valid even if it is sought to make out an offence in accordance with art 626 of the Criminal Code in relation to the violation of the duty of confidentiality. In fact, art 50 of the Criminal Code expressly excludes the liability to punishment of whoever prejudices or endangers a right with the consent of the person who may validly dispose of that right.

Exceptions to bank secrecy in relation to anti-money laundering regulations

With reference to the offence of money laundering it should be noted that, in accordance with art 648 of the Criminal Code, whoever substitutes or transfers money, assets or other profits which are the proceeds of crime or performs other transactions in order to hinder the identification of criminal proceeds, shall be punished. Further, it should be added that art 648 of the Criminal Code punishes whoever makes use of, in economic or financial activities, money, assets or other profits which are the proceeds of crime.

Amongst the provisions aimed at combating the crime in question (so called anti-money laundering regulations), Law 197 of 5 July 1991 is of particular significance. Article 1 of this Law prohibits: (i) the transfer of money, cash or instruments:

> 'to the bearer in lire or foreign currency in the case in which the value of the transfer is greater than Euros 12,500[14] (the transfer may be performed only through authorised intermediaries, including banks); (ii) to issue bank cheques and bank drafts in favour of third parties for amounts greater than Euros 12,500 without including the details of the beneficiary and the non-assignment clause; (iii) to issue "to the bearer" savings books for amounts greater than Euros 12,500'.[15]

Article 2 of this Law provides that whoever performs transactions involving the transfer of money or other valuables of whatever nature which are of an amount greater than €12,500 with a bank or other expressly listed entity must be identified by the bank and must indicate in writing its own complete details or those of the

---

14 This threshold has been fixed by Legislative Decree 290 of 17 October 2002, issued by the Ministry of the Economy and Finance, published in the Official Gazette of the Republic of Italy on 11 December 2002.

15 Turone *Le tecniche di contrasto del riciclaggio* in Cass pen mass amm (1993) 1790 p 2692.

party on whose behalf the transaction was undertaken. All the details of the transaction are archived and must be retained for a period of ten years. In addition, such identification shall also be made when, owing to the nature and procedures of the transactions set up, it appears that several transactions effected at different times within a certain period of time, even if individually below the aforesaid threshold amount, constitute parts of a single transaction.

With direct reference to the issue of bank secrecy, art 3 of Law 197 of 5 July 1991 provides that the person responsible for the branch office or other operative point of the authorised intermediary – amongst which are the banks – is under an obligation to notify to the responsible superior of that bank or other authorised intermediary every transaction that, by its nature or due to other circumstances, gives rise to a suspicion, based on the available facts, that the money, assets or profits the object of the transaction may derive from any of the types of criminal offences referred to in art 648 of the Criminal Code (receiving stolen goods).[16]

The responsible superior must examine such notice and, if he finds it to be founded, must transmit it without delay electronically or by other means to the UIC without any indication of the name of the person making the report, which may exercise the powers conferred on it by the monetary regulations in order to examine the notification in further depth.

Further, it is expressly provided that such notifications do not constitute violations of the secrecy obligation, and do not therefore involve any liability of any kind. It is, in fact, expressly prohibited for those persons obliged to give notice, and anyone else having knowledge of such notice, to reveal the contents to parties other than those indicated above.

Finally, art 5 of Law 197 of 5 July 1991 places the authorised intermediaries under an obligation – and therefore also the banks – to notify the Minister of the Treasury within 30 days of becoming aware of any notification of the violation of the prohibitions contained in art 1 of the Law.

Still on the subject of money laundering, the Bank of Italy in November 1994 compiled and circulated a so-called 'Manual' containing the 'Guidelines for the notification of suspect transactions', a manual addressed to bankers and containing suggestions aimed at facilitating the work of the banking and finance system in the battle against money laundering.

Such guidelines provide, amongst other things, specific 'signs of anomaly' relating to transactions and conduct which could possibly involve violations of the anti-money laundering regulations and to which the authorised intermediaries – including the banks – must have regard in the performance of their notification obligations referred to in art 3 of Law 197/1991.

16   Santacroce *La segnalazione di operazioni sospette dopo la legge 9 agosto 1993, n. 328: Novità e prospettive di riforma in Banca, borsa e titoli di credito* (1995) I, p 165ff.

Exceptions to bank secrecy in relation to anti-terrorist acts regulations

The bank's duty of confidentiality is also derogated from in the recent legislation issued in order to detect, prevent and suppress the financing of terrorism and terrorist acts.

In light of the importance of taking action to combat the financing of terrorism and of the general rule set forth under art 270bis of the Criminal Code (as repealed by art 1, para 1 of Legislative Decree 374 of 18 October 2001), pursuant to which whoever finances, directly or indirectly, terrorist organisations shall be punished, Legislative Decree 369 of 12 October 2001 and the Instructions of the Italian Exchange Office of 9 November 2001 imposed certain obligations on banks and on the other financial institutions subject to anti-money laundering provisions in order to counter terrorism.

In particular, banks and the other financial institutions subject to anti-money laundering obligations are asked to take all the relevant measures to freeze funds and other assets of terrorists, whose personal data are entered in special lists made available by the Italian Exchange Office.

In addition, they shall report promptly the adopted measures to the Italian Exchange Office, specifying the involved subjects, the amount of the funds, as well as all the transactions and relationships, which, according to the available information, can be considered linked to or related to, directly or indirectly, the financing of the terrorist acts or organisations.

Exception to bank secrecy in relation to anti-mafia regulations

Law 575 of 31 May 1965, as subsequently modified and containing anti-mafia provisions, is also of relevance in relation to bank secrecy as it confers on the criminal judicial authorities and the police the right to request from banks information and documentation considered useful for the purposes of mafia investigations.[17]

In particular, art 2bis of Law 575/1965 provides that the judicial authorities may request – either directly or through officials and agents of the judicial police – any official of the public administration and any credit entity, including enterprises, corporations and other types of entity, to provide information and copies of documentation considered useful for the purposes of investigations of persons against whom preventive measures are proposed in that there is reason to suspect that those persons belong to a mafia-style organisation.

Further, the judicial police officials, subject to authorisation by the criminal judicial authority, may seize from the banks documents considered relevant in accordance with the terms and procedures provided in arts 253, 254 and 255 of the Criminal Procedure Code.

17   Gianfelici, n 1 above, p 225ff.

Exceptions to bank secrecy in relation to powers of foreign judicial authorities

The protection of bank secrecy does not exist in relation to specific decisions or requests by a foreign criminal judge, as an Italian criminal judge, following such decisions and requests, may order a bank to testify or produce certain documents relating to the bank's relationship with its clients.

The European Convention on Judicial Assistance in Criminal Matters, signed at Strasbourg on 20 April 1959, was ratified by Italy with Law 215 of 23 February 1961 and provides for the gathering of evidence by judicial authorities in one signatory state at the request of judicial authorities of another signatory state. In addition, the procedure applicable to international requests of this nature is specifically regulated by art 723 of the Criminal Procedure Code.

In relation to civil matters, any possible order by a civil magistrate requiring a bank to testify or produce certain documents in relation to its existing relationships with its clients is based, on the one hand, on the Hague Convention on Civil Procedure of 1 March 1954 and numerous bilateral agreements on civil procedure to which Italy is a signatory, and, on the other, on art 64 of Law 218 of 31 May 1995, containing the reform of international private law (in particular, art 69 of that law governs the gathering of evidence by foreign judges).

INSIDER TRADING

Unauthorised use of inside information (insider trading) is regulated in Italy mainly by arts 180–187 (except for art 181) of Legislative Decree 58 of 24 February 1998 (the Consolidated Act on financial matters), which, having confirmed the criminal nature of the related penalties introduced by Law 157 of 17 May 1991, has, however, made important amendments in respect of the persons to whom such provisions apply, the behaviour forbidden, as well as the investigation powers granted to the Italian Commission for Corporations and the Stock Exchange (CONSOB).

In particular, art 180 of Legislative Decree 58/1998 has replaced the prohibition to carry out transactions on securities when a person avails himself of the possession of inside information (originally envisaged under art 2 of Law 157/1991), with the prohibition to act (making purchases or sales or carrying out other transactions, directly or through a nominee, involving financial instruments) on the basis of inside information possessed by virtue of holding an interest in a company's capital or exercising public or other duties, a profession or an office.

Article 180 of Legislative Decree 58/1998 punishes any person who, possessing inside information by virtue of holding an interest in a company's capital or exercising public or other duties, a profession or an office (the so-called insiders) or who, having obtained directly or indirectly inside information from the insider (the so-called tippee):

1   purchases or sells or carries out other transactions, directly or through a nominee, involving financial instruments on the basis of such information; or
2   divulges such information to others without justified reason or advises others, on the basis thereof, to carry out any of the transactions referred to above.

In other words, the acts forbidden to the insiders are:

- the carrying out of transactions on listed instruments (trading);
- the communication of the inside information to third parties (tipping); and
- the transmission of an investment advice to third parties on the basis of the privileged information or pushing third parties to trade (tuyautage).

Pursuant to art 180, para 3 of Legislative Decree 58/1998, inside information means 'any specific information having a precise content concerning financial instruments or issuers of financial instruments that has not been made public and that, if made public, would be likely to have a significant effect on the price of such instruments'.

The offence is committed by virtue of the use of such particular information and not because of its simple possession.

As to the scope of application of the provision, art 183 of Legislative Decree 58/1998 establishes that the offence is committed where the trading is carried out in respect of financial listed instruments:

1 in Italy, even if the instruments are traded in EU-regulated markets; and
2 abroad, provided that the instruments are traded in Italian regulated markets.

In particular, the legal scholars[18] deem that art 183, para 1 of Legislative Decree 58/1998 makes reference both to the hypothesis pursuant to which the offence is committed abroad in respect of financial instruments traded in an Italian regulated-market and to the hypothesis where the offence is committed abroad in respect of financial instruments traded in a foreign-regulated market, provided that such instruments are also traded in an Italian-regulated market (in particular, in this case, even if the activity is performed abroad by foreign persons on instruments belonging to foreign companies).

However, according to Principle 3 set forth in the 'Guidelines on the information to the market' issued in June 2002 by the Italian Stock Exchange Authority (Borsa Italiana SpA), certain information, such as letters of intent and negotiations, are disclosed to the market where both the following events occur:

1 duties of confidentiality are not fulfilled by whoever has obtained such information; and
2 there are grounded reasons to deem that the relevant transactions, of which such information represent the initial step, will be carried out.

According to such Guidelines, there is no breach of confidentiality duty if the issuers disclose inside information, by virtue of their office duty, to third parties legally or contractually bound to keep them confidential.

As to CONSOB investigation powers, art 185, para 2 of Legislative Decree 58/1998 sets forth that CONSOB shall investigate the violations using the powers attributed to it with respect to the persons subject to its supervision, by requiring information, data or documents from and hearing anyone who appears to be acquainted with the facts,

---

18 Marchetti and Bianchi *La disciplina delle società quotate* Milan (1999) vol II p 2022; Cottino *La legge Draghi e le società quotate in borsa* Torino (1999) p 418.

establishing the time limits for the related communication and drafting minutes of such hearings. In addition, CONSOB can avail itself of the co-operation of governmental bodies and have access to the information system of the taxpayer register.

In this respect, it shall be noted that pursuant to art 3.4.2 of the Regulation of the markets adopted on 29 April 2002 by Borsa Italiana SpA and approved by CONSOB on 9 July 2002, where in the course of market surveillance the Borsa Italiana SpA acquires evidence suggesting that acts of insider trading may have been committed, it shall immediately report such evidence to CONSOB.

According to some authoritative legal scholars,[19] the regulation of insider trading is additional to and separate from the regulation of bank secrecy. In fact, the regulation of bank secrecy places a limit on the communication of confidential information obtained by banks in order to protect the interests of third parties to whom such information refers; the banks, however, retain the freedom to use information subject to the duty of confidence for their own purposes.

On the contrary, the regulation of insider trading censures the conduct of holders of information who use or divulge it or, on the basis of it, carry out the relevant transactions for their own benefit, where the element which characterises the conduct as an offence is the active conduct of the insider/tippee who uses such information in order to realise an advantage.

As regards the general rule concerning information held by banks, it is useful to emphasise the difference between information requested from the bank by third parties and information which is exchanged between banks. In the first case, a specific authorisation is required from the concerned party, whilst in the second case it is generally considered permissible for banks to exchange information between themselves.

It has been stated that the practice of information exchange between banks may be considered permissible when it confirms the known position of the company, the subject of the information, but not when the information could be of interest to the bank with specific reference to a transaction in progress from which the bank could obtain an undue advantage.[20]

This is the natural consequence of the fact that, in the opinion of the majority of legal writers, insider trading constitutes a violation of a temporary secrecy, that is, confidential information is obtained and used by a person before the time in which the information is distributed and known, attempting in this way to anticipate the effect which in time would be produced by the spreading of the information.[21]

In the absence of case law on insider trading, some authors have even considered that unfavourable information transmitted by banks in relation to a certain party is spread so rapidly that a violation of the temporary secrecy is not even conceivable.[22]

---

19   Buonuomo in *Banca, Borsa e Titoli di Credito* (1995) I, p 137ff.
20   Porzio *Insider Trading ed ordinamento bancario in AA VV Il dovere di riservatezza nel mercato finanziario: 'l'insider trading'* p 321.
21   Carriero *Il problema dell'Insider trading* in *Foro Italiano* (1988) V, p 146.
22   Mazza *La repressione dell'Insider trading nel quadro della tutela del mercato azionario* in *Banca, Borsa e Titoli di Credito* (1988) I, p 673.

In conclusion, it has to be noted that Legislative Decree 58/1998 imposes a series of detailed obligations on the issuer of securities to provide information in relation to the company's activities, which could affect the price of the shares or the financial situation of the issuer, in an attempt to reduce the level of concealed information which could be exploited by insiders.

CONFLICTS OF INTEREST

In considering bank secrecy and use of privileged information, one must necessarily consider the issue of conflict of interest, in which a bank could easily find itself involved. All financial information converges at the bank by virtue of its role as the centre of all monetary economic transactions.

By virtue of the varied activities of the bank, it may occur, for example, that the bank uses information, relating to a client, for the purposes of advice which it is providing to another client for an acquisition, or may exploit its knowledge of amounts held on deposit by its clients in order to advise other clients to invest or not invest in the first client.

The problem has arisen, in particular, from the time when banks were authorised in Italy to operate as securities brokers in accordance with Law 1 of 2 January 1991. Law 1/1991 was abrogated by Legislative Decree 415 of 23 July 1996, which puts into effect Council Directive 92/22/EEC of 10 May 1993 relating to investment services in the securities sector, which in turn was repealed by Legislative Decree 58/1998, whose provisions on intermediaries were implemented by CONSOB Regulation 11522 of 1 July 1998 (the Regulation on Intermediaries).

In particular, according to art 18 of Legislative Decree 58/1998, the provision of investment services to the public on a professional basis is reserved to investment firms and banks.

Article 21 of Legislative Decree 58/1998 replaces art 17 of Legislative Decree 415/ 1996, which regulated the behaviour to be followed by banks in the performance of investment services by confirming the same criteria. In particular, it states that banks (as well as all the authorised subjects), shall:

(a) act diligently, correctly and transparently in the interests of customers and the integrity of the market;
(b) acquire the necessary information from customers and operate in such a way that they are always adequately informed;
(c) organise themselves in such a way as to minimise the risk of conflicts of interest and, where such conflicts arise, act in such a way as to ensure transparency and the fair treatment of customers;
(d) have resources and procedures, including internal control mechanisms, likely to ensure the efficient provision of services; and
(e) conduct an independent, sound and prudent management and make appropriate arrangements for safeguarding the rights of customers in respect of the assets entrusted to them.

As to the risk of conflict of interests provided for by (c) above, it should be noted that this was already regulated by art 16 of Law 1/1991, and the Regulation of the

Bank of Italy of 2 July 1991 (the Regulation 1991), which, in implementing the said art 16 and in order to guarantee the reduction of risk of conflict of interest, established the adoption of separation of accounting and organisation (Chinese Walls) thereby burdening the organisational structure of investment companies and banks.

The current formulation, confirming the wording of Legislative Decree 415/1996, seems less concerned with providing the means for avoiding conflict of interest and more interested in reducing the risk of such conflict as far as possible.[23] In particular, from the analysis of art 21 it appears that the existence of conflict of interests is considered unavoidable in the performance of investment services; in consequence, such situations shall be regulated by making them transparent through an adequate information to the client, a criterion which is already set forth under art 1374 of the Civil Code.

Article 27, para 2 of the Regulation on Intermediaries specifies that transactions with or on behalf of the clients in conflict of interest can be carried out only where the banks have previously informed the investor in writing of the nature and extent of their interest in the transaction and the investor has expressly agreed in writing to the carrying out thereof. Where the transaction is concluded by telephone, compliance with the foregoing information requirements and the issue of the related authorisation by the investor must be evidenced by a recording on magnetic tape or an equivalent medium.

As to the contract, art 23 of Legislative Decree 58/1998 establishes that it shall be reduced to writing and a copy given to customers. In case of failure to comply with the prescribed form, the contract shall be null and void.

It is worth noting, in conclusion, the provisions of art 21(e) of Legislative Decree 58/1998, according to which the banks (like all other investment enterprises) must conduct an 'independent, sound and prudent' management and adopt 'appropriate measures for safeguarding rights pertaining to deposited financial instruments and funds'.

DATA PROTECTION ACT

Law 675 of 30 December 1996 came into force in Italy on 8 May 1996 and deals with the protection of physical and legal persons and other subjects in relation to the treatment of personal data. It applies to the treatment of all personal data, even if the data is kept overseas.

Law 675/1996 established an Authority (the Garante) to which anyone intending to deal with data must give notice, in each case, indicating for what purposes it is intended to deal with such personal data.

---

23   Miola and Piscitello *Commento sub art 17, in Eurosim Commentario al D Lgs 23 luglio 1996*, n 415, a cura di Campobasso, p 117ff.; Recine *Svolgimento dei servizi di investimento in Il Testo Unico dell'intermediazione finanziaria* a cura di Rabitti Bedogni C, Milan (1998) p 183ff.

The controller, which is the person competent to determine the purposes and the methods of the processing of personal data can appoint a processor, who shall be a person having adequate knowledge, experience and reliability so as to ensure thorough compliance with the provisions in force applying to processing, and shall abide by the instructions given by the controller in carrying out this processing and inform the data subject of the way in which it is intended to deal with the personal data. In fact, the consent of the data subject is required; consent which may not be necessary in some cases including, for example, where the information must be provided in fulfilment of a contractual obligation owed by the data subject or when the data derives from public documents.

On this point, the Italian Banking Association (ABI) clarified in a circular, LG/5499 of 14 August 1997, that there is a category of subjects, which carry out an activity linked to the exercise of banking, to which personal data can be communicated, such as issuers of credit cards, companies which administer means of payment etc.

In particular, it must be noted that information relating to the collection of personal data shall always be provided to the data subject, even if his consent is not required.

By virtue of art 13 of Law 675/1996, the data subject enjoys a series of rights including, by way of example, the right to obtain the cancellation of or block on data dealt with in violation of the law, the updating or amendment of data, the right to object to the treatment of personal data for commercial or advertising purposes or to the sale of that data.

The violation of these rights results in an obligation to pay compensation for damage which the controller must pay, unless he is able to demonstrate that he has adopted all appropriate measures for avoiding the damage.[24]

Law 675/1996 also provides the terms, conditions and limits according to which the personal data so dealt with may be distributed. In relation to the banks, art 20.1(h) is of particular relevance, according to which the personal data which has been dealt with may be communicated within the bank group, as defined in art 60 of the Banking Law, when this communication is undertaken for the same purposes for which the data were collected. On the contrary, as a matter of principle, and unless the data subject has expressed its consent, it is prohibited to distribute such data to the public.

The data subject may avail himself of his rights either before the ordinary judicial authority or before the 'Authority for the protection of persons and other subjects in relation to the handling of personal data' established by Law 675/1996.

Finally, it is worth noting that Law 675/1996 was amended by Legislative Decree 467 of 28 December 2001, which came into force in February 2002, and in this respect important new measures have been introduced. According to these measures, for example, the data subject's consent is not required when the processing of personal data is necessary for the performance of obligations resulting from a contract to which the data subject is a party.[25] By the end of 2003, the Garante is expected to issue a new regulation, where such measures and simplifications will find a clearer discipline.

---

24   Art 2050 of the Civil Code.
25   See art 12, para 1(b).

17   Luxembourg

Pit Reckinger

INTRODUCTION

It is traditionally admitted that a banker receiving private information from or on his client owes his client a duty of confidence. Whereas in most jurisdictions this duty of confidence is merely a civil law obligation,[1] Luxembourg bank confidentiality originates from, and is based on, criminal law provisions. Together with Switzerland, Luxembourg therefore has the strongest bank confidentiality laws, constituting one of the pillars of its banking system.

Despite the lack of express legal provisions before 1981, the existence of a rule of confidence imposed on bankers has never been challenged in Luxembourg. Indeed, it is generally accepted that a democratic legal and political system must endeavour to protect the individual vis-à-vis his fellow citizens as a whole and to preserve his intimacy and private life. Those are the objects, the raison d'être, of the duty of confidence.[2]

Discussions among authors and practitioners become more lively when they try to establish the legal basis and nature of bank secrecy in Luxembourg and when they try to set the limits of bank confidentiality. Torn between the conflict created by private interests (pursuant to which confidence must be safeguarded, discretion be guaranteed) and public interests and the social order (which justify to a certain extent a transparency vis-à-vis the authorities), solutions are found on a case-by-case basis, each time further defining what is the scope of the duty of confidence of the banker.

A recent example may be found in the discussion within the EU on the introduction of harmonised taxation of interest for physical persons (proposed European Directive on Taxation of Savings). The basic principle of this proposed Directive is an exchange of information among the member states on details of payment of interest or similar income paid by a person to an individual resident in another member state. Given

---

1   Belgium: Com Namur (4 ch) 29 June 1995, JT 1996 p 328; England: see R N S Grandison in *Bank Confidentiality* (2nd edn, 1997) ch 8; France: Cassation Civ 1, 2 June 1993, Bull Civ I no 197.
2   R Hoffmann 'Réflexions sur le fondement du secret professionnel' Bull Droit et Banque n° 2, page 3ff

that under current laws the Luxembourg tax authorities are not allowed to obtain such information because of the rules of bank confidentiality, the implementation of such proposed Directive would require the introduction of a legal exemption to the obligation to secrecy and would constitute a partial erosion of the current strength of bank confidentiality in Luxembourg.[3]

'Confidentiality' (French: confidentialité) is defined as 'what must remain secret'.

'Secrecy' itself does not need to be defined – every child knows what a secret is: anything most hidden, most intimate, shielded from other people's view or knowledge.[4]

Swiss authors on bank secrecy[5] have used a descriptive definition of bank secrecy which is a useful start to an analysis of bank confidentiality laws in Luxembourg:

'Bank secrecy consists in the discretion which bankers have to apply to personal or financial information relating to their clients or third parties of which they have knowledge through the exercise of their profession.'

The last words of this definition 'through the exercise of their profession' introduce the concept of the banker being the 'necessary confident'[6] (French: confident nécessaire), such as a priest or a doctor. The banker is also considered in our society as a person with whom one ineluctably has to share intimate and confidential information. Basic principles of a right to privacy and protection of private life governing our systems must lead to making those confidents subject to a duty of confidence: by qualifying the banker as a 'necessary confident' in our society we will later justify the criminal nature of the laws governing his duties of confidence.

From very early on, Luxembourg authors have insisted on the dual feature of bank confidentiality. It is not only the duty of confidence of the banker in respect of information which he receives. It is also the right of the client to the confidentiality of such information.[7]

---

3   For this reason Luxembourg (together with Austria and Belgium) has maintained its position at the Council of Economics and Finance Ministers of 21 January 2003 that it will after the transitional period (ending at the latest on 1 January 2010) implement an automatic exchange of information with the other EU tax authorities if and when the EU enters into agreements with certain non-member states (in particular, Switzerland) by which these countries commit themselves to an exchange of information upon request as defined in the OECD Agreement on Exchange of Information on Tax Matters. As long as no such agreements are reached, paying agents in Luxembourg will retain a withholding tax (15% as from 1 January 2004, 20% as from 1 January 2007 and 35% as from 1 January 2010) on interest payments to be made to natural persons resident in a EU member state, but there will be no exchange of information: OECD Agreement on Exchange of Information on Tax Matters, available at www.int/tax.com/TREATIES/OECD%20Model%20TIEA.pdf.

4   Although there is a general tendency in Luxembourg to use the term 'bank secrecy' one may interchangeably speak of 'bank confidentiality' or 'bank secrecy'.

5   M Auber, P A Béguin, P Bernasconi, J Graziano-Von Burg, R Schwob and R Tréuillaud *Le secret bancaire suisse 'Ed Staempfli + Cie SA'* (3rd edn,1995) p 43.

6   These words do equally transpire from the Luxembourg Code Pénal (art 458) which refers to the professional secrecy of the medical profession but on which bank secrecy is based (see below).

7   A Dondelinger 'Le Secret Bancaire' Pasicrisie 23 page 1.

Starting from this dual feature, authors, judges and practitioners try to establish the limits of bank confidentiality by determining when and by whom the banker may be authorised or forced to reveal secrets. The answer to those questions requires the prior analysis of the nature and origin of the basic rule of bank confidentiality.

NATURE AND ORIGIN OF THE DUTY OF CONFIDENCE

Under Luxembourg law the duty of confidence of a banker, as well as of his supervisory authority, stems from art 458 of the Code Pénal[8] which is as follows:

> 'Doctors, surgeons, health officers, pharmacists, midwives and all other persons who, through their function or profession, are entrusted with secrets and who, except in instances where they are called upon to testify in court and in instances where they are compelled by law to reveal such secrets, divulge such secrets, shall be punished by imprisonment from 8 days to 6 months and to a fine from 500 Euros to 5,000 Euros.'

While the existence of bank confidentiality in the sense of a civil law obligation of the banker to such confidentiality, was never challenged under Luxembourg law,[9] authors have for considerable time discussed the question whether a breach of the rule would be a criminal offence.[10] The non-exhaustive list of art 458 of the Code Pénal does not explicitly mention the banker. This raised the question whether the banker is one of those persons 'who, through their function or profession, are entrusted with secrets'.

Prominent doctrine traditionally insisted on the 'contractual basis' of bank secrecy (such as in England, where 'it is often an implied term of the contract between bank and customer, no more and no less'[11]) and thus concluded that a breach thereof could not trigger criminal sanctions.

Modern doctrine (adopted in particular by the banks' supervisory authority, then called the Institut Monétaire Luxembourgeois (IML) and the corporate association for banks in Luxembourg, Association des Banques et Banquiers Luxembourgeois (ABBL)), however, emphasised the 'public role' of the banking profession and qualifies the banker as 'the necessary confident in the exercise of his profession'. Similarly, in France eminent authors agree that the banker is the 'ineluctable confident'[12] of his client. Indeed, clients are in fact by contract or by law obliged to resort to the services offered by banks. The latter thus contribute to public service in

---

8   Code of Criminal Law.
9   C Schmit and A Dondelinger 'Le Secret Bancaire dans la CEE et en Suisse' in *Le Secret Bancaire en Droit Luxembourgeois* (1973) p 140.
10   For a contractual basis: T Biever and R Weber 'Le secret professional des banques en droit luxembourgeois', Feuilles de liaison de la Conference St Yves, 1959, Luxembourg, ed J Guill, nos 4–5, p 99ff; L Schaus 'Le secret professionnel devant la loi', Conference given on 22 February 1938 for the Young Bar Association, Luxembourg St Paul, p 27. For a criminal law basis: A. Dondelinger, n 7 above; Association des Banques et Banquiers, Luxembourg (ABBL) 'Avis au projet de loi portant réforme de l'impôt sur le revenu', Doc parl nos 571–578, session ordinaire de la Chambre des Députés 1956–57.
11   RNS Grandison, footnote n 1 above, ch 8.
12   Ch Gavalda and J Stoufflet 'Le Secret Bancaire en France' Colloque organised at the Sorbonne, October 1971, cited in Dondelinger, footnote n 7 above.,

the interest of the community, which establishes the public order feature of bank secrecy. The logical consequence thereof was to include bankers in the non-exhaustive list of professions enumerated in art 458 of the Luxembourg Code Pénal.

The Luxembourg legislator in 1981 put an end to this now academic discussion. By the banking law of 23 April 1981 it was indirectly affirmed that a breach of the confidentiality rule under Luxembourg law was a criminal offence and that art 458 of the Luxembourg Code Pénal would apply to the banker upon such breach.[13]

The criminal nature of bank secrecy in Luxembourg was thereafter confirmed by the Luxembourg legislator through the banking law of 17 November 1984 and is currently governed by article 41 of the Law of 5 April 1993 on the financial sector (hereafter the Banking Law). The Banking Law directly and expressly sets forth the positive legal duty of confidence of banks, as well as settlement agents, central counterparties, clearing houses, foreign operators of systems designated as such in Luxembourg and all other professionals of the financial sector, ie any person exercising professionally an activity of the financial sector,[14] and provides that a breach thereof is a criminal offence:

'(1) Directors, members of managerial and supervisory bodies, managers, employees and all other persons employed by credit institutions, other professionals of the financial sector, settlement agents, central counterparties, clearing houses, and foreign operators of systems designated as such in Luxembourg, referred to in part I of the present law are obliged to keep secret all information entrusted to them in the course of their professional activities. The act of revealing such information shall be punished pursuant to article 458 of the Code Pénal.

(2) The obligation to secrecy ceases when the disclosure of information is authorised or imposed by or under the terms of a legal provision, even if the implementation of such legal provisions shall have preceded the present law.

(3) The obligation to secrecy shall not apply vis-à-vis national and foreign authorities in charge of prudential supervision acting within their powers and for the purpose of such supervision, and provided the information communicated is covered by the professional secrecy of the supervisory authority receiving it. The transmission of necessary information to a foreign authority for the purposes of prudential supervision must be made through the parent company or the shareholder or the member itself subject to such supervision.

(4) The obligation to secrecy shall not apply vis-à-vis shareholders or members, who themselves are a condition for the authorisation of the institution concerned, provided that the information communicated to these shareholders or members is necessary for the purposes of sound and prudent management and does not directly reveal the institution's

13   J Guill and J N Schaus 'La nouvelle loi bancaire luxembourgeoise du 23 avril 1981', Feuilles de liaison de la Conférence St Yves, 1981, no 51, p 6.
14   The main professions concerned are financial advisers, brokers, commissioners, fund managers, distributors of investment funds, professional depositaries of securities, underwriters, market makers etc.

      commitments towards a customer other than a professional of the financial
      sector.

(5) Subject to the rules applicable pursuant to the Code Pénal, information
referred to in paragraph (1), once revealed, shall only be used for the
purposes for which the law permitted their disclosure.

(6) Anyone who is bound by the obligation to secrecy referred to in paragraph
(1) who has legally revealed information covered by such an obligation
shall not by the sole fact thereof have committed a civil or criminal
offence.'

Turning to the dual feature of bank confidentiality as a duty of the banker and a right
of the client, the criminal nature of bank confidentiality undoubtedly strengthens
the legal view that the secrecy must be analysed first of all as an obligation of the
banker. Furthermore, bank confidentiality belongs to the rules of public order to
which only the law may grant exemptions.[15] Indeed, as set out above, bankers serve
public interest, are part of public service and thus the duty of confidence is a matter
of public order.[16]

To the extent that banks form part of public service and that bank secrecy is a rule of
public order, the right of the client is thereby limited and the power to trigger disclosure
of information covered by bank secrecy may be at least partially withdrawn from the
power of the client.[17]

This is definitely the position which has been adopted by the banks' supervisory
authority, today called the Commission de Surveillance du Secteur Financier (CSSF).
Despite doctrinal debates,[18] the public order character of Luxembourg bank secrecy
was recently confirmed by the courts.[19]

The right and duty of confidence are not hard-and-fast rules, but are limited in scope
pursuant to exemptions set up by art 458 of the Code Pénal and by art 41 of the
Banking Law. It is therefore legitimate to raise[20] the question whether art 41 of the
Banking Law creates a new duty of confidence, thus replacing the existing obligation
firmly established on the basis of art 458 of the Code Pénal. In other words, is bank
confidentiality today still one element of a single professional secrecy based on art
458 of the Code Pénal or has the Banking Law created a specific duty of confidence
for banks to which the existing solutions derived from the application of art 458 of
the Code Pénal may not be applied? Parliamentary documents which accompanied
the introduction of the Banking Law firmly put aside any hesitations which one

15   Doc parl no 3600, Commentaires des articles, p 8.
16   This view is shared by a large majority of authors as referred to herein; contra, see D
    Spielman 'Le Secret Bancaire et l'Entraide Judiciaire Internationale Pénale au Grand-Duché
    de Luxembourg' (1999) 20 Les dossiers du Journal des Tribunaux at 36ff.
17   See below, The banker as a witness in civil courts.
18   D Spielmann 'Le secret bancaire et l'entraide judiciaire international penale', 1999, Les
    dossiers du Journal de Tribunaux, no 20.
19   Cour d'Appel, Saverys, Struye de Swieland c/Kredietbank Luxembourg SA, 2 April 2003,
    no 26050 du Role; Cour d'Appel, Hosdain, Soupart c/Kredietbank Luxembourg SA, 2 April
    2003, no 26256 du role.
20   J Schroeder 'Le Secret Bancaire au Luxembourg' in 'Le Secret Professionnel', Conférence
    EFE 26/27, November 1996, Luxembourg.

might have.[21] Doctrine adheres to this theory of continuity of the bank secrecy obligation in Luxembourg.[22] We may therefore conclude that art 41 of the Banking Law translates, incorporates and confirms the long-existing bank secrecy based on art 458 of the Code Pénal, although it introduces certain additional exemptions.

SANCTIONS TO A BREACH OF BANK CONFIDENTIALITY[23]

Criminal sanctions

Article 41(1) of the Banking Law provides that disclosure of any information which is subject to bank confidentiality is punished by sanctions provided for in art 458 of the Luxembourg Code Pénal.

Article 458 of the Code Pénal provides for imprisonment of up to six months or a fine (in current terms[24]) between 500 Euros and 5,000 Euros or both.

Pursuant to general rules of Luxembourg criminal law a breach of bank secrecy may only constitute a criminal offence if a 'material (tangible) element' and an 'intentional element' coexist.

1   *Tangible element*: The breach of secrecy must be duly evidenced.
      The banker must have revealed to another person or to the public in general secret information which he shares through, or by reason of, the exercise of his profession. The disclosure could be oral or written or derived from a positive or even negative (abstention) behaviour.

2   *Intentional element*: The breach of secrecy must have been made 'intentionally'. Would a mere negligence therefore not constitute a criminal offence if the breach was done without the banker being conscious that he was communicating an information covered by secrecy?[25]
      The interpretation of what is 'intentional' at the time of disclosure is left to the courts and varies according to the different criminal offences existing under Luxembourg law. In terms of breaches of bank secrecy the intention is sufficiently evidenced if the banker committed the breach of secrecy 'knowing that he was committing a criminal offence regardless of the intention or the goal for which the breach was committed'.[26] It is thus not required by court cases to commit a 'strictly speaking intentional' breach but, acting 'knowingly' (en connaissance de cause), will be sufficient to characterise the breach as a criminal offence.

---

21   Doc parl no 3600, Commentaires des articles, p 8, re art 41(1): '[art 41] recalls the obligation to professional secrecy'; and Doc parl no 3600–3601, avis IML, p 15, re art 41(1): 'there may currently no longer be any doubts on the continued existence of professional secrecy imposed on the professional of the financial sector.'
22   Inter alia, J Kauffman and A Steichen, cited in J Schroeder, n 20 above.
23   For an in-depth study on sanctions of breaches of professional secrecy see T Hoss 'L'avocat et le réviseur d'entreprises: confidents nécessaires en droit luxembourgeois et en droit communautaire', mémoire de DEA, 1 June 1996, Paris; and, in particular, on bank secrecy see P Mousel and C Feipel 'Les sanctions du secret bancaire', Conférence EFE 26/27, November 1996, Luxembourg.
24   Following enactment of various laws increasing the amounts of the fines set out in the original Code Pénal of 1879.
25   T Hoss, n 21 above, nos 282 and 283.
26   J S G Nypels, cited in P Lambert *Le Secret Professionnel* (1985) p 133.

It should be noted that general provisions regarding criminal law such as mitigating circumstances or excuses may apply.

Criminal sanctions do not apply to corporate entities, but only to natural persons.

To the extent that the person who has committed the breach and thus the offence has been identified, he will be personally subject to criminal sanctions.

The problem is more delicate if the actual person within the corporate entity who committed the breach remains unidentified. According to authors and court cases, 'the managers of the corporate bodies must be actioned in court in their own name and be sentenced accordingly'.[27] It is therefore likely that in such case managers of the bank or even the bank's managing director or directors would be subject to court action.[28]

Civil sanctions

The obligation of confidence is also a civil law obligation. Disclosure of a secret may undoubtedly cause prejudice to a client. Such prejudice gives rise to a liability action against the person who committed the breach and/or the bank (ie his employer).

Vis-à-vis the person having committed the breach, it is an action in tort.

Vis-à-vis the bank, the action will be based on the contractual relationship between the client and the banker.

The Luxembourg court of appeal recently specified the regime applicable to the civil liability of bankers for breach of bank secrecy.[29] The motivation of these decisions, which may be criticised in various respects, is clear:

> 'It is normal that the [client] information shared with the bank at the time of entering into the contract is kept secret. There is no particular hazard that this result, which is part of what the parties to the contract anticipated and what is protected by law through criminal sanctions, is not achieved.
>
> The secrecy obligation of the bank is therefore an obligation to achieve a result [French: obligation de résultat].
>
> In case of breach of the obligation to achieve a result, the debtor of the obligation is presumed to be liable without need for any proof from the claimant of a fault or wrongdoing from the debtor'

This recent court case conflicts with our prior understanding that the obligation to ensure confidentiality of the information transmitted to the banker was an obligation for the banker to do its best compared to a normally prudent professional (French: obligation de moyens) as opposed to an obligation to achieve a result. Indeed, the confidentiality obligation is part of the section of the Banking Law dealing with professional obligations of the bank together with know-your-customer rules and

---

27   S Stefani, G Levasseur and B Bouloc 'Droit Pénal Général' 14-d Précis Dalloz no 311.
28   P Mousel and C Feipel, n 21 above.
29   Cour d'Appel, 2 April 2003, no 26050 et 26256 du role (at the time of publication the delay to make a recourse in fron of the supreme court had not elapsed).

rules of conduct. Such other obligations are all indisputably characterised as 'obligations de moyens'. The decision to qualify bank confidentiality as an obligation to achieve a result is even more surprising knowing that a Luxembourg bank may have to share confidential data with outside service providers (in particular in respect of IT maintenance and development) and that there may be situations where the access to data by any such third party cannot be avoided (circulaire IML 96/126 relating to central administration – item 4.5.2.1.(f)).

As a consequence of these court decisions bankers may only avoid their liability by evidencing that the breach of bank secrecy is due to a force majeure event or due to an action of a third party. They may no longer prove to have acted properly and thus avoid liability.

These decisions take a conservative view of the obligation of bank secrecy in line with the consistent characterisation that the obligation is a matter of public order. It should be stressed however that such decisions are still subject to recourse in front of the Cour de Cassation (supreme court) and the judicial interpretation of the regime of civil liability for breaches of bank secrecy as set out therein is likely to change at least in certain aspects (in particular as to the extent of 'moral damages' awarded to the claimants).

The civil sanction to repair the damage caused clearly constitutes a remedy in monetary terms to any person who suffered from the breach. Under Luxembourg law a court could not award penal (unless so provided for by an agreement between the parties concerned), multiple or punitive damages.

Disciplinary sanctions

Banks are subject to supervision by the CSSF.

The CSSF may following any breach of bank secrecy issue injunctions against the bank concerned on the basis of art 59 of the Banking Law. To the extent that the bank would not follow any such injunction, its managers may be subject to a suspension from the exercise of their function. Any such injunction aimed at getting the bank to remedy an existing situation will, however, most certainly not be the sole measure taken by the CSSF. Indeed, at such time the breach of law will have been committed and the prejudice caused. The CSSF will no doubt take additional measures directly aimed at the management of the bank concerned.

Luxembourg Banking Law provides in art 7 that the approval of the credit institution in Luxembourg is subject to the professional reputation of its management. If the managers have committed criminal offences they would no longer qualify for the purposes of such condition of reputation and one of the conditions for approval of the credit institution concerned in Luxembourg no longer exists. Such bank could therefore be subject to withdrawal of its banking licence.

In summary, the strength of Luxembourg bank secrecy rules results from the criminal sanctions attached to a breach thereof. The victim is generally less concerned by the fact that the person who committed the breach is made criminally liable and prefers to see his damage duly repaired on a civil basis. For bankers, the criminal sanction plays an essential but moral role.[30] It will have an immediate effect on the exercise of their profession. It may also affect their bank by civil and disciplinary sanctions and, finally, it may affect their reputation.

SCOPE OF THE EXEMPTIONS TO BANK CONFIDENTIALITY

The purpose of this section is to determine the scope of exemptions to bank secrecy and thereby evidence the strength of Luxembourg bank secrecy which is only levied in the course of criminal investigations (including fiscal criminal investigations).

As indicated in the introduction, it is not possible to proceed by theoretical reasoning only. Solutions are found and limits are set on a case-by-case basis envisaging possible situations which a banker may face.

For this reason, the following subsections will deal with the various situations where the banker is confronted with different entities, authorities and persons in day-to-day life on a national basis, while analysing the international situations in a separate and last section:

1   Bankers and judges.
2   Bankers and tax authorities.
3   Bankers and shareholders.
4   Bankers and supervisory authorities.
5   Bankers and financial market.
6   Bankers and clients.
7   Bankers party to a court action.
8   Bankers and international investigations.

Bankers and judges

Unlike the section below which specifically deals with situations where the bank is a party to a court action, this section deals with situations where the banker as a 'third party' is confronted with judicial investigatory measures, including, in particular, where he is asked to testify or where his premises are subject to an arrest or searches or seizures of documents relating to its clients and their accounts .

Civil law proceedings

THE BANKER AS A WITNESS IN CIVIL COURTS

This first exemption to the duty of confidence is mentioned in art 458 of the Code Pénal and repeated by art 41(1) of the Banking Law where disclosure is 'authorised by law'. Pursuant to art 406 of the Luxembourg Nouveau Code de Procédure Civile, any person is obliged to testify under oath in a civil investigation unless he has a legitimate reason to refuse to testify.

---

30   A Bruyneel 'Le Secret Bancaire en Belgique après l'arrêt du 24 octobre 1978', observation sous Cass belge 25 October 1978 (1979) JT at 371, no 18, cited in Mousel and Feipel, n 21 above.

Bank secrecy constitutes such a legitimate motive and may be opposed in response to a request to testify. Since 1957 court cases have decided that any person subject to professional secrecy may testify in court but cannot be compelled to do so.[31] While called as a witness, the banker may speak or remain silent at his discretion.[32]

Although a banker may also have received confidential information regarding third parties, he will most frequently be called to testify in a court case involving his client. Thus he may receive the client's consent or even be under firm instructions from the client to testify. He will, however, never be bound to follow his client's request but shall only be guided by his conscience.

OTHER CIVIL LAW INVESTIGATORY MEASURES

Pursuant to the provisions of Luxembourg procedural law, a person may on the basis of a judgment or another authentic document of title or, pursuant to an authorisation granted by the President of the District Court in Luxembourg,[32] put an arrest on bank accounts maintained with Luxembourg banks. In connection with any such procedure the banker will be compelled to make a declaration (déclaration affirmative) setting out exactly what assets and rights are held for, or on behalf of, his client. Any such declaration has to be made only as and when the proceedings validating the arrest have been successfully concluded. In other words, the client must have been definitively ordered to a certain obligation and the arrest procedure must have been definitively validated. Then, but only then, will the banker have to disclose details of all assets and rights held by and for the person subject to the arrest. He may even have to disclose details of previous accounts held by the person concerned, which may have since been closed.[33]

Thus the civil arrest procedure is an exemption to bank secrecy. Bank secrecy is safeguarded as the banker will only be obliged to disclose any information if the claim of the person instigating the arrest is adjudged to be justified by the court and the arrest is validated. In such case he has the right to receive information on the claim which he then 'owns' by judicial contract. It is only where information on previous accounts and transactions is disclosed that there is a real exemption to bank secrecy.

In addition, the question has to be analysed whether a person could with the help of other investigatory measures available under civil procedural law receive information from banks. In particular, art 350 of the Luxembourg Nouveau Code de Procédure Civile is of interest and provides that:

> 'If there is a legitimate motive to preserve or establish before any judicial proceedings evidence of facts which may determine the solution of a dispute, investigatory measures, legally permitted may be ordered at the request of an interested person in summary proceedings.'

31 Cour Supérieure de Justice (Cassation Criminelle), 21 March 1957, Pasicrisie 17 page 43.
32 L Schaus, n 10 above.
33 Cour d'Appel, 5 February 1992, no 12949 du rôle.

For the same reasons as set out above, in civil matters any such measure (which could include production of documents or testimonies) may only be authorised provided that bank secrecy would not be breached.[34]

Criminal law proceedings

THE BANKER AS A WITNESS IN CRIMINAL COURTS[35]

When called upon to testify in criminal proceedings, the question of exempting the banker from his obligation to secrecy no longer concerns private interests only, but also touches public interest. On this basis some authors have concluded that a banker could not keep secret his knowledge of criminal offences.[36]

Indeed, how could a banker call upon his conscience to keep criminal offences silent? On what grounds could he justify in his mind to keep a criminal unpunished?

Looking at medical secrecy, equally based on art 458 of the Code Pénal, judges have consistently ruled that doctors are free to reveal their secrets or bury them forever, even in front of criminal courts in relation to criminal offences.[37]

The same solution applies to lawyers, the professional secrecy of whom is also based on the same legal provisions.[38]

From a strictly legal point of view, the same solution shall apply to the banker as the origin or basis of the professional secrecy is the same, ie art 458 of the Code Pénal.[39] It is therefore generally admitted that the legal solution applicable in front of civil courts must be transposed into criminal law.[40]

In this respect in a recent court case[41] the Luxembourg courts had the occasion to recall the obligations of a Luxembourg banker vis-à-vis investigating magistrates. The terms used in the judgment seemed to imply that a banker is always under the obligation to furnish information to a judge. In this respect the author commenting the decision criticises the decision of the judge and confirms the position set out above that the banker remains free to decide to speak or remain silent.[42]

Mr Jacques Kauffmann, however, summarises the limited interest of this strict legal position as follows:

'In practice banks have to measure the opportunity to testify in light of the right of search and of arrest or seizure of documents which is given to the

---

34 Court cases confirming this principle see Cour d'Appel (référé), 28 November 2000, no 19224 du rôle; ordonnance de référé, no 1157/97, 2 December 1997.
35 For the money laundering offence where an obligation or denounciation exists, see Bankers and the financial markets, below.
36 A Dondelinger 'Le secret bancaire' speech given on 29. May 1972 on invitation of the Conference of the Young Bar.
37 Cour Supérieure de Justice (Appel Civil), 6 June 1961, 18 Pasicrisie at 351.
38 T Hoss, n 21 above, no 211.
39 L Schaus, n 10 above; J Kauffman .
40 Contra: see D Spielman, n 16 above, p 45.
41 Tribunal d'Arrondissement, 8 June 2000, no 1326/2000.
42 A Hoffmann Bull Droit et Banque no 31 at page 36.

investigating magistrate. As any information would have to be disclosed as part of such investigating powers of the investigating magistrate it is difficult to imagine why and on what basis a banker could refuse to testify in front of criminal courts.'

OTHER CRIMINAL LAW INVESTIGATORY MEASURES

While carrying out an investigation, the investigating magistrate may conduct searches on the premises of a bank or the domicile of bank employees, seize documents and put arrests on bank accounts with Luxembourg banks. Pursuant to art 88 of the Code d'Instruction Criminelle (Criminal Procedural Code), in Luxembourg a banker does not have the power to oppose any such proceedings and will have to disclose any information requested by the investigating magistrate.

In the course of criminal investigations, there is no doubt that a banker does not have any possibility to oppose bank secrecy to those investigatory measures.

Bankers and tax authorities[43]

Direct taxes

In respect of direct taxes (mainly income tax) a grand-ducal decree of 24 March 1989[44] provides that the competent tax authorities in charge of income tax (Administration des Contributions Directes) are not authorised to request from credit institutions individual information on their clients:

> 'The fiscal authorities are not authorised to request from credit institutions individual information on their clients ...'

This grand-ducal decree is to be regarded as a mere confirmation of a long-existing situation, ie that bank secrecy is not to be levied vis-à-vis investigations of income tax authorities in Luxembourg.

This principle, however, only applies in respect of the determination of the taxation and no longer during the phase of recovery against the taxpayers, where the rights of the tax administration as a creditor are the same as any other ordinary creditor, in particular in relation to arrests over bank accounts.[45]

Indirect taxes and inheritance taxes

The law of 28 January 1948, on the correct and proper collection of the taxes, however, compels the banker to provide information and documents to the tax authorities in charge of the indirect taxes (Administration de l'Enregistrement et des Domaines) in relation to assets and accounts held by a deceased resident.

---

43 For an in depth study see A Lutgen 'Secret Bancaire, délit d'initié et fraude fiscale', Conference EFE, 27–28 November 1996, and A Steichen 'Le secret bancaire face aux autorités publiques nationales et étrangères' (1995) Bull Droit et Banque no 24.
44 Mémorial A 1989, p 181.
45 see Tribunal d'Arrondissement, no 554/99.

Any information so provided to the Administration de l'Enregistrement et des Domaines can in theory be used by the Administration des Contributions Directes (the authority responsible for direct income tax) in order to assess liability to income tax. Surprisingly, according to certain authors, the exchange of information does not occur[46] or takes place only in cases of fiscal fraud.[47] Experience shows that this tends to be a general practice and information circulates between those authorities. The general prohibition applicable to direct taxes (above) thus seems partly circumvented through the exemption applicable to indirect taxes even if the legality thereof could be discussed and eventually challenged in a court.[48]

Criminal fiscal law

Luxembourg income tax laws[49] traditionally contained three types of offences in tax matters:

1   breach of fiscal regulation (German: Steuerordnungswiedrigkeit) (AO, para 413);
2   non-intentional fiscal fraud (German: Steuergefährdung) (AO, para 402); and
3   intentional fiscal fraud (German: Steuerhinterziehung) (AO, para 396).

These offences, which are punishable by a fine, are deemed to be fiscal offences only and not proper criminal offences.[50] Thus the banker may not divulge any information which might be requested by the tax authorities. The general position remains unchanged.

By a law of 22 December 1993 the Luxembourg legislator introduced a further degree of intentional fiscal fraud which involves (i) a fraud (ii) over 'significant amounts', (iii) committed by 'systematic use of fraudulent manoeuvres', (iv) in order to hide pertinent evidence to the authorities or to convince it about untrue facts. This expanded offence of fiscal fraud is generally referred to in French as 'escroquerie fiscale'.

The above criminal offence does not create a particular regime as regards bank secrecy in respect of criminal offences in general. Bank confidentiality rules do not apply in investigations concerning escroquerie fiscale. It may give rise to testimonies, searches and arrest procedures under criminal law by the competent investigatory authorities.

The subject will be of particular interest in international matters, which is dealt with below.[51]

46   A Steichen, 43 above, at 36.
47   C Schmit and M P Weides-Schaeffer 'Le Secret Bancaire en Droit Luxembourgeois' (1984) Cahiers de la BIL, no 5/84 at 36.
48   A Steichen, 43 above, at 37.
49   The laws on indirect taxes mentioned above and the laws on value added taxes contain other fiscal criminal offences.
50   A Steichen, 43 above, at 46.
51   See below Bankers and international investigations.

Bankers and shareholders

In the interests of the shareholders of a bank an exemption to bank secrecy has been expressly introduced under Luxembourg law since 1981 vis-à-vis the main shareholders of a bank, ie 'those who directly or indirectly hold the majority of the shares or a participation allowing them to exercise a significant influence on the affairs of the bank concerned'. In such capacity those shareholders are subject to authorisation by the CSSF. Their approval is one of the constituent elements of the issuance of the banking licence.

As those shareholders bear the ultimate risk of the management of the bank, it is normal that they are put in a position to obtain such information as is necessary properly to determine the measure of their liability. The Banking Law, however, limits this exemption to the duty of confidence by excluding from the allowed disclosure any information which is privy to the assets of individual clients which are not professionals of the financial sector. In practice, this exemption allows, inter alia, the assessment of risks of a banking group at group level, while the Luxembourg entity may forward general information on its exposure without forwarding the names, identities and assets of individual clients.

A particular situation arises where foreign banks have established a branch in Luxembourg as opposed to a subsidiary. However, no distinction is made between a branch or a subsidiary. The same secrecy has to be observed by the branch vis-à-vis its parent company as that observed by the subsidiary vis-à-vis its main shareholders. In this respect it should be noted that although the branch will be subject to prudential supervision by a foreign authority, the CSSF keeps a residual authority to supervise branches, in particular, in relation to banking secrecy.

Bankers and supervisory authorities

Being the second legal exemption provided for by the Banking Law, this exemption concerns requests for information originating from national or foreign authorities in charge of prudential supervision of a bank or another professional of the financial sector authorised in Luxembourg.

In Luxembourg, the CSSF is entrusted with prudential supervision of banks, stock exchanges, investment funds and other professionals of the financial sector. Banks have the obligation to collaborate with the CSSF in its investigations. Any such investigation is valid only to the extent that the CSSF acts within the scope of its mission determined by the law of 23 December, 1998 relating to the creation of the CSSF. The CSSF has general investigatory powers (art 53 of the Banking Law) but is itself subject to professional secrecy (art 44 of the Banking Law).

Information given to the CSSF may be forwarded to foreign authorities provided that:

1   the principle of reciprocity is observed – the foreign authority will only receive information to the extent that it also forwards information to the CSSF upon its own request;
2   the information is necessary for the purpose of prudential supervision; and

3   the information is covered by professional secrecy of the receiving foreign authority.

In respect of the last condition, it is interesting to note that there is no requirement regarding the stringency of the professional secrecy to which the foreign authority is subject and which varies from one country to another.

Upon requests from foreign supervisory authorities, the CSSF may either carry out the investigation itself and then forward it to the foreign authorities or authorise an intermediary or the foreign authority itself to proceed with the investigation.

A particular situation arises in connection with consolidated supervision where a subsidiary or a branch of a foreign bank is included in the consolidated supervision by a foreign authority. In such case the investigations are made by the foreign authority in charge of supervision but through the parent company, ie the foreign bank, which in turn has to request the relevant information from the Luxembourg subsidiary. The foreign authority upon receipt of any information is free to request confirmation of such information by the CSSF.

Bankers and the financial market

Money laundering

Luxembourg has, over the years and prior to the Banking Law, established legislation regarding money laundering.[52] Those rules initially aimed at the prevention of transactions which might involve drug money laundering were extended and cover today money laundering derived from criminal offences relating to professional and organised crime in general (including, in particular, terrorism), as well as arms traffic, prostitution, corruption and kidnapping of persons under age. They oblige banks to make thorough checks and controls in order to identify the origin of funds, the identity of their clients (including the beneficial owner) and suspect transactions and prohibit (through abstention) the banker to enter into certain transactions. In order to allow and oblige banks to denounce facts which might constitute acts of money laundering, a legal exemption to bank secrecy was required and therefore introduced in art 40 of the Banking Law which provides that:

(1) Credit institutions and other professionals of the financial sector are required to give full co-operation and as complete a response as possible to any legal request addressed to them by the competent law enforcement authorities in the exercise of their duties.

(2) Credit institutions and other professionals of the financial sector, their management and employees shall co-operate fully with the Luxembourg authorities responsible for combating money laundering:

---

52   Law of 19 February 1973 regarding the sale of medical substances and the fight against drug addiction, as amended; arts 506-1–506-7 of the Luxembourg Code Pénal; law of 15 April 1993 regarding the financial sector; numerous circulars of the CSSF (see www.cssf.lu) and various international conventions such as the United Nations Convention of Vienna of 20 December 1988 against illegal drug traffic and the summit creating the Financial Action Task Force on Money Laundering in June 1989.

 – by furnishing those authorities, at their request, with all necessary information, in accordance with the procedures established by the applicable legislation;

 – by informing the public prosecutor (Procureur d'Etat) at the District Court in Luxembourg, on their own initiative, of any fact which might be an indication of money laundering.

The information referred to in the first paragraph shall be forwarded by the person or persons designated by the credit institutions and other professionals of the financial sector in accordance with the procedures provided for in paragraph (5). Information supplied to the authorities, other than legal authorities, in accordance with the first paragraph, may only be used in connection with the combating of money laundering.

(3) Credit institutions and other professionals of the financial sector shall refrain from carrying out transactions which they know or suspect to be related to money laundering until they have informed the public prosecutor referred to in paragraph (2). The public prosecutor may give instructions not to execute the operation. Where such a transaction is suspected of giving rise to money laundering and where to refrain in such manner is impossible or is likely to frustrate efforts to pursue the beneficiaries of a suspected money-laundering operation, the institutions concerned shall inform the authorities immediately afterwards.

  The terms for the application of the present paragraph may be the object of a Grand-Ducal Regulation.

(4) Credit institutions and the other professionals of the financial sector, their management and employees may not inform the client concerned or to third parties that information have been given to the authorities pursuant to paragraphs (2) and (3) or that an investigation on money laundering is taking place.

(5) Credit institutions and the other professionals of the financial sector are obliged:

 (a) to set up adequate internal control and communication procedures in order to foresee and prevent the realisation of money laundering operations in Luxembourg;

 (b) to take appropriate measures to focus their employees on the provisions contained in the present section. These measure shall comprise the participation by the employees concerned to special training programs allowing them to better recognise operations which may be connected to money laundering and to teach them on the way to proceed in such case.

The banker has thus become subject to an obligation of denunciation imposed by law and in this respect exempted by law from bank secrecy vis-à-vis the criminal investigating authorities in Luxembourg. It is important to stress that the obligation of denunciation encompasses facts relating to money which is effectively the proceeds of crime and also which is the object of crime, ie used to finance any of the above activities.

Insider trading

By a law of 3 May 1991 on insider dealing (the Insider Dealing Law) Luxembourg implemented Council Directive 89/592/EEC of 13 November 1989.

This law prohibits certain persons having knowledge of inside information to deal in the securities of the issuer concerned.

A breach of the prohibitions to use insider information set out in the Insider Law is a criminal offence and is punishable by imprisonment of one to five years and a fine up to 1,239,467.62 Euros (being the equivalent of 50,000,000 Luxembourg Francs).

The Insider Dealing Law differentiates the following:

1   the management body of the issuer concerned (directors, managers, employees etc);
2   important shareholders; and
3   those persons who 'by reason of the exercise of their profession, their profession or their functions get inside information'.

The banker obviously plays an important role in cases which are likely to give rise to prosecutions involving insider dealing.

In this respect it is interesting to note that 'Chinese Walls' are currently not yet requested to be set up by law or regulation.

It may be held that this lack of regulation is less of a concern in Luxembourg, where banks tend to specialise in private banking and do not, with few exceptions within the same entity, hold capital market arms or similar advising departments. However, banking entities tend to be smaller and different decisions are therefore likely to be taken by the same persons. This does though create the problem of introducing Chinese Walls within one's own mind.

One interesting scenario in respect of insider dealing is where a bank employee merely follows decisions made by one of his clients. Normally, following another person's movements on the stock market does not constitute a breach of the Insider Dealing Law. If such client is an important investor and his order may have an effect on the price of the shares he is buying or selling, then merely following this client might well constitute insider trading.[53]

The authority responsible for the enforcement of the Insider Dealing Law is the CSSF. The CSSF has full investigatory powers and has the right to forward the information to a foreign authority within the EU, provided that the information transmitted is only used for the purpose for which it is requested in relation to the insider dealing. In principle, specific information on the identity of the client should not be transmitted if such foreign authority does not already have knowledge thereof.[54] In case of a request from a foreign authority from outside the EU, the CSSF is free to decide whether it will collaborate and make an investigation and eventually transmit the information.

53   A Lutgen, n 43 above.
54   D Spielman, n 16 above, at 26.

Bankers and clients

In respect of a possible authorisation by, or instruction from, the client to disclose 'secret information' the 'public order character' inherent to Luxembourg bank confidentiality regains importance. Applied to private interests, the idea of 'public order' raises the question whether the client has the absolute right or power to relieve his bank from the obligation to secrecy. Is the client the 'master' of the secret?

The CSSF, endorsing the dominant opinion among authors, insists on the public order character of bank secrecy and the severe consequence of the client not being in a position to force the bank to levy bank secrecy at its own discretion. Other authors add that describing the duty of confidence as a mere right of the client would be contrary to the text of art 41 of the Banking Law, pursuant to which secrecy may only be levied by law, ie not by instructions from or pursuant to a contract with a client.[55]

In this context authors generally point to one Luxembourg court case[56] which firmly stated that:

> 'Vis-à-vis himself [the client], the banker does not have an own right. He must follow instructions from the latter [the client]. Professional secrecy may not turn against interests of the clients. The banker may not be put in a position to judge what is, and what is not, in the interests of his client.'

While commenting on this decision, an author[57] recalls the context in which this decision was taken. A banker effectively refused to furnish certain documents to heirs of a deceased client. It is a generally accepted principle that heirs 'continue the life' of the deceased client and therefore have the right to receive full information on the accounts of the client and request all documents in respect therewith. In this case the position of the bank to refuse to deliver documents was clearly unjustified. Put in this context, Mr Kauffman concludes that the general principle of the banker not having to follow the client's instructions definitely remains valid. The present writer entirely concurs with this view.[58]

The conclusion drawn is that the banker is never forced to follow an authorisation or even a firm instruction from his client to disclose certain information, but his behaviour will have to be dictated by his conscience, bearing in mind the interest of the client.[59]

55 D Kolbach 'Le Secret Bancaire au Luxembourg' mémoire de DEA, Droit des Affaires, 1 June 1995, Université de Paris, p 37.
56 Tribunal d'Arrondissement, 24 January 1991.
57 J Kauffman 'Le Secret Bancaire en Droit Luxembourgeois – Aspects Actuels et Perspectives', Droit Bancaire et Financier au Grand-Duché de Luxembourg 10th anniversaire de l'Association Luxembourgeoise des Juristes de Banques, vol 1, ed Larcier (1994) p 525.
58 Contra: D Spielmann in 'Le secret bancaire et l'entraide judiciaire internationale pénale' (1999) 20 Les Dossiers du Journal des Tribunaux page 36: the author comments on the same court decision and based on Belgian doctrine pleads in favour of an absolute right of the client over the secrecy obligation of the bank.
59 J Kauffman 'Le Secret Professionnel du Banquier en Droit Luxembourgeois' (1996) 2/96 Les Cahiers de la BIL at 40.

Similarly, the banker is not under an obligation to provide negative confirmations that a person is not a client of the bank. Even if it can be argued that vis-à-vis such person who by definition is *not* a client there cannot be any secrecy obligation and thus nothing should prevent a banker to answer such request, the banker may never undertake any action which is likely to put his confidentiality duty vis-à-vis the clients at risk. Precisely by giving "negative confirmations", there may be situations where implicitly such negative confirmation entails confirmation on the situation of other clients of the bank which are thereby put at risk.

Looking at it from another angle, could the banker be in breach of bank secrecy laws while choosing to follow an authorisation or instruction from his client?

Authors agree that a banker would not be allowed to reveal information on the basis of a general unlimited authorisation from the client and consequently could thus be subject to the criminal offence of breaching secrecy laws. In this sense bank secrecy laws are meant to protect the client 'against himself'. In the interest of the client, where the banker is not knowingly breaching bank secrecy laws, it is admitted, however, that he may follow specific instruction to disclose certain information to third parties.[60] Any other solution would be detrimental to the client and unworkable in practice. In such a case the banker is not in breach of secrecy laws. This solution therefore validates a generalised practice where banks or other professionals of the financial sector are being given a specific authorisation to transfer client information to other group companies or even specified third party service providers in order to enhance servicing of clients. This is done frequently to allow clients to access their information in different places of the world or to allow banks to successfully set up outsourcing projects. As a condition the waiver or authorisation needs to be specific and justified by proper reasons.

A banker as party in a court action

A different situation arises where the banker is one of the parties to a court case and would deem it to be in his own interest to reveal certain information for his defence which falls under his obligation to bank secrecy. Such a court case could involve his client or any third party. This question has been very clearly decided by the courts.

The legitimate interest of the banker permits disclosure of certain information.[61] Organising his own defence is most certainly a legitimate interest. Deciding the contrary would be highly prejudicial to the banker who would, in a court case against his clients, be prohibited from putting forward arguments for his own defence. Interestingly in order to justify this exemption the Luxembourg decision expressly refers to the famous *Tournier* case in England,[62] which constitutes the basis of bank confidentiality under common law.

Judges have, however, drawn limits on the scope of this exemption. Any such disclosure may only occur in cases involving 'financial interests' of the banker and

60   J Kauffman, footnote n 59 above.
61   Tribunal d'Arrondissement, 26 June 1981, no 27163 du rôle.
62   *Tournier v National Provincial and Union Bank of England* [1924] 1 KB 461.

with respect to information strictly necessary for the purposes of the defence. Where an action could entail a 'moral prejudice' for the banker only, disclosure would not be permitted. In practice, however, it will be extremely difficult to draw the line between cases involving only moral prejudice and those which also carry patrimonial interests.

An interesting problem has arisen in labour law matters. Luxembourg law obliges the employer who wishes to terminate an employment contract to set out very precisely the motives on which a dismissal of an employee is based. Regardless of the question whether the motives given by the employer justify the termination or not, if they are not indicated with sufficient precision in the letter to the employee, the dismissal will be declared to be abusive (irregular in form only) as the employee and the judge were not put in a position to determine on the basis of those imprecise motives whether the dismissal was justified. There is virtually no possibility to provide further evidence during the course of a possible court action.

Depending on the motives for the dismissal the banker may, however, have to refer to precise files or precise clients where the employee purportedly acted wrongly. In fact, bank secrecy may prohibit him to reveal such details. Therefore, while having to observe his duty of confidence, court cases have held that the dismissal of an employee was abusive to the extent that the letter of termination did not give enough indications as to the motives for the dismissal,[63] for instance, by referring to the name of the customer and the details of the transactions incriminated.

To solve this paradox it appears that only the legislator could introduce a solution by law.

Bankers and international investigations

The next question concerns the obligation to bank secrecy at an international level already partly referred to above.

In Luxembourg extra-territorial aspects mainly involve requests for assistance from foreign authorities to Luxembourg authorities or, more particularly, to Luxembourg courts in order to obtain information or documents or to arrest assets.

Luxembourg legal provisions basically deal with international co-operation at a judicial level.

However, the situation of insider dealing has to be included and has been dealt with above. The duty of assistance has to be analysed under the double taxation treaties and, in particular, the European Directives.

In principle, double taxation treaties to which Luxembourg is a party contain provisions which cover transmitting of information between the competent tax authorities.

However, the traditional language to be found in the double taxation treaties contains reservations that none of the contracting parties is obliged to take any measures

---

63 *RNB c/Goldstein* Tribunal de Travail, 21 April 1997, no 2124197 du rôle.

which (i) would be inconsistent with its administrative practice, or (ii) may not be obtained under its national financial legislation or, indeed, (iii) which may be contrary to applicable professional secrecy. Any request to obtain information from Luxembourg banks would be barred by any of the three conditions.

There is also among the member states of the EU a Directive (Council Directive 77/799/EEC) providing for transmission of information. A law of 15 March 1979 has introduced the obligations of this Directive into Luxembourg law. It again refers to the reservation that no tax administration is bound to make investigations or transmit information which law or practice do not empower the administration to do at a national level. Moreover, the express reservation of bank secrecy is again to be found in the regulation of 15 March 1979 issued under law.

Finally, reference may be made to a Convention between the member states of the EU which attempts to eliminate double taxation also between affiliated parties.[64]

Information may be communicated to a commission which has to solve any issue of double taxation. However, the members of such commission which comprise representatives of the various tax administrations concerned are bound by secrecy pursuant to art 9, para 6 of the Convention of 23 July 1990.

With respect to the judicial proceedings, it is necessary to distinguish between civil law and criminal law proceedings.

Civil law proceedings

LETTERS ROGATORY

Letters rogatory, or 'letters of request', involve a request for evidence made by the foreign court which is seeking the information to the court in the place where records are maintained in order to obtain the information without directly or indirectly infringing the sovereignty of another country.[65] Similarly, as in England, the use of such letters rogatory is regulated in Luxembourg by the Hague Convention on the Taking of Evidence Abroad in Civil or Commercial Matters of 1970. This Convention was approved in Luxembourg by a law of 19 March 1977.

The importance of this Convention for the purpose of investigations with a Luxembourg bank is extremely limited for two reasons.

Article 11 of the Convention provides that a letter rogatory is not executed to the extent that the person to whom it is addressed may invoke an exemption or a prohibition to testify. Bank secrecy constitutes a legal impeachment to testify. It is interesting to note that art 11 expressly refers to testimony and not to other investigation procedures such as arrests or searches. To the extent, however, that at the national level a banker may invoke secrecy in civil matters and refuse to hand over or produce documents, the same applies internationally. A report established by a commission comprised of representatives of the Ministry of Finance, the Ministry

64 Signed in Brussels on 23 July 1990.
65 RNS Grandison, n 1 above, p 197

of Justice, the Foreign Affairs and the ABBL very clearly states that it is the duty of the Luxembourg authorities to make sure that requests for taking evidence are only granted to the extent that they aim to search for and determine criminal offences.

More particularly, art 1 of the law of 19 March 1977 approving the Hague Convention of 1970 contains a reservation whereby Luxembourg declares that it will not continue any request under a letter rogatory in respect of 'pre-trial discovery of documents' in countries of common law.

SUBPOENA FROM OTHER JURISDICTIONS

Luxembourg banks receive subpoenas mainly issued by US courts whereby they are ordered to produce documents to be used in proceedings in a foreign country. In the absence of any particular convention, Luxembourg banks must oppose on the grounds of bank secrecy and are prevented from producing documents as requested.

Criminal law proceedings[66]

LETTERS ROGATORY

International letters rogatory are governed by the law of 8 August 2000 on international judicial co-operation in criminal matters (the 2000 Law) and are generally based on the following Conventions:

1   the European Convention regarding extradition of 13 December 1957 (the 1957 Convention);
2   the European Convention regarding judicial co-operation in criminal matters of 20 April 1959 (the 1959 Convention);
3   the Convention on extradition and judicial co-operation in criminal matters between the Benelux countries of 27 June 1962 (the 1962 Convention); and
4   the Treaty regarding judicial co-operation in criminal matters between the Grand-Duchy of Luxembourg and the United States of America of 13 March 1997 (the 1997 US Treaty).

It is important to separate tax matters from other criminal law aspects.

LETTERS ROGATORY IN FISCAL MATTERS

Until 1997, under both the 1959 Convention and the 1962 Convention co-operation for criminal offences of a fiscal nature was not allowed. Although not expressly excluded by the text of these Conventions, authors unanimously concluded that the exclusion of fiscal matters is based on their art 2(b) as a waiver of bank secrecy in this respect would be against 'public order or other essential interests of the country'.[67]

However, by a law of 27 August 1997, Luxembourg adopted an additional protocol (Protocol I) to the 1959 Convention. Pursuant to this law, international co-operation

---

66   For an in-depth study see D Spielmann, n 16 above.
67   A Steichen, n 43 above, at 24; J Kauffman, footnote n 59 above, at 29.

(at a judicial level only) pursuant to the 1959 Convention is granted for the criminal offence of expanded fiscal fraud (escroquerie fiscale) as defined by the law of 22 December 1993.[68]

Luxembourg made express reservations to specify that co-operation will not be granted for so-called 'fiscal offences'[69] and that any information transmitted may only be used for the purpose of investigation of criminal offences (including escroquerie fiscale) for which judicial aid was requested (principe de spécialité).

The 2000 Law specifically confirms that except as otherwise provided in international conventions every request for co-operation will be refused for offences related to direct or indirect taxes applicable pursuant to Luxembourg law.

The situation under the 1997 US Treaty is specifically referred to in art 1, item 5 thereof and follows the principle agreed upon in Protocol I.[70] The text of this 1997 US Treaty provides that judicial co-operation for fiscal offences will be granted in case the facts underlying the request allow to establish a 'reasonable presumption' that the criminal offence of expanded fiscal fraud exists. Discussions have arisen on the wording of the 1997 Treaty combined with an exchange of letters between the US and Luxembourg which could be deemed to soften the interpretation of what would constitute the offence of escroquerie fiscale for which co-operation is granted. Authors in Luxembourg agree however that the interpretation of the 1997 US Treaty must be such that co-operation will be granted only if the facts analysed constitute the criminal offence of expanded fiscal fraud as set out by Luxembourg law.[71]

LETTERS ROGATORY IN GENERAL CRIMINAL MATTERS

In general criminal matters, co-operation will be granted if the following conditions are fulfilled.

The facts which give rise to the letter rogatory must constitute a criminal offence in both the requesting and the requested state.

The request will be refused when an offence is a political offence, or is connected with a political offence or where the request is likely to prejudice the sovereignty, security, public order or other essential interests of the country.

Pursuant to the 1959 Convention, a letter rogatory is first transmitted through diplomatic channels to the Ministry of Justice, which has an overriding discretion to refuse to provide assistance. The most important duty of the Ministry of Justice is to ensure that any preliminary request in relation to a criminal offence would not be a 'façade' for investigating other offences, mainly in fiscal matters. The request if authorised passes to the public prosecutor, who again has the power to authorise the request or refuse it and then transmit it only to the investigating magistrate. On the basis of an order of the investigating magistrate, the letter rogatory will be executed.

---

68 See above, Bankers and tax authorities.
69 See above, Bankers and tax authorities.
70 In fact, the reason why it took two-and-a-half years to ratify the 1997 Treaty with the US was that this should be simultaneous to the same extension at a European level.
71 P Santer 'L'approbation du traité d'entraide judiciaire en matière pénale entre le Luxembourg et les Etats-Unis du 13 mars 1997' (2000) 14/2000 Codex at 359. Doc p 4599, pp 20 and 21.

It is only at that stage that the parties concerned receive knowledge of the letter rogatory. The parties concerned and any interested parties have ten days following the day the investigating measure is notified to the person where it is executed to appeal the decision of the investigating magistrate in Luxembourg. There is controversy in Luxembourg on the point whether for this purpose the bank which merely holds the accounts is an interested party and as such may itself exercise recourse against these decisions.

TESTIMONIES

If a banker is called upon to testify before Luxembourg authorities (even on the basis of a foreign letter rogatory) the national situation explained above equally applies; the banker has a right to testify or may refuse to testify in civil as well as in criminal matters invoking bank secrecy laws.

The question of a banker being called upon to testify in a foreign court is extremely delicate. This raises the question of the extra-territorial effect of confidentiality law. The Banking Law provides in art 41(2) that the obligation to bank confidence ceases where the disclosure of an information is 'authorised or imposed by law'. Traditional doctrine held that the legislator could only have meant a 'Luxembourg' law.

The 1959 Convention allows a person from a requested state to be called as a witness in the requesting state. If a Luxembourg banker is called upon to testify before a foreign court, he will thus have to refuse since the lifting of bank secrecy is only provided for in favour of Luxembourg courts. Obviously, the foreign court may well not accept this position under its own laws. A witness may therefore be faced with the dilemma that he will suffer imprisonment and fines whether he testifies or not.

An interesting decision recently shed some light on this question.[72] A Dutch national residing in Luxembourg and employed by a Luxembourg bank was the subject of criminal proceedings in Belgium for certain actions carried out in Belgium and related to his activity as employee of a Luxembourg bank. There is no evidence the employee concerned acted in violation of Luxembourg law. When the employee concerned was interrogated by the Belgian judicial authorities on the manner he approached clients and on other aspects of services rendered for them in Belgium, he refused to answer and justified his refusal through his obligation to bank confidentiality in Luxembourg.

As part of a prejudicial question discussed before the European Court of First Instance in Luxembourg, the Luxembourg government set out its own interpretation on the effects of bank secrecy. The Luxembourg government first indicated that the Luxembourg laws on bank secrecy have indeed an extra-territorial effect in the sense that such laws would be ineffective if bankers were allowed to disclose any information outside Luxembourg. Conversely, exceptions to the bank secrecy laws equally have to be given an extended effect and the concept of judicial authorities contained in article 458 of the Code Penal not only covers Luxembourg judicial

---

72   Arrêt de la Cour CJCE, 10 décembre 2002

authorities but also those of other member states. However, such exceptions must find their origin in the provisions of Luxembourg law. As a consequence, where art 458 of the Luxembourg Code Pénal provides that the bank secrecy obligation ceases when a person is called upon to testify before judicial authorities, this does not only cover Luxembourg judicial authorities but also similar authorities of other countries. Therefore, if a Luxembourg banker is called upon to testify before foreign courts he would be authorised to disclose facts subject to bank confidentiality. If the banker talked he would not be the subject of criminal proceedings in Luxembourg. It is to be expected that this official governmental interpretation shall prevail in the future.

The downside of this interpretation is that unlike a situation in which the banker is called upon to testify in front of Luxembourg courts where he has the right to remain silent or to talk, foreign legislation may well not recognise that bank secrecy is a legitimate motive not to provide information. When confronted with the fact that not talking would expose him to criminal sanctions in the country where the banker is interrogated, he might have little choice left.

CONCLUSION

Outside Luxembourg, bank secrecy laws are envied by some, hated and vilified by others. Within Luxembourg, they constitute, together with all the other professional secrecies, an inherent element of the social and economic order of society. Over the years, men of law and men of finance have learned to live with bank secrecy. They modelled it on a case-by-case basis bearing in mind the basic principles of a democratic system and balancing public and private interests.

This chapter shows that bank secrecy in Luxembourg, although strongly protective of the private life and sphere of intimacy of individuals, is not a means to keep crimes undiscovered. Bank secrecy is levied in order to 'make justice'.

Under current law no document is shielded from bank secrecy. In criminal proceedings bankers must always produce documents following seizure or searches. It is only where a confidence is an oral confidence that bank secrecy might remain inviolable.

Planned legal reforms go in the direction of extended international co-operation, in particular for those areas where combined efforts of all nations are required to combat international organised crime. Thus the traditional concept of protection of private life into which only a judge could authorise interference is largely being eroded.

18 Mexico

Thomas S Heather

INTRODUCTION

As with many other emerging market economies, bank secrecy in Mexico has evolved from simply being a traditionally unregulated relationship of confidentiality between financial institutions and their clients to becoming a standard of banking practice within Mexican law. This topic has earned particular attention in recent years as regulators have attempted to determine the corresponding responsibilities and obligations of financial institutions and their clients to, on the one hand, bolster public confidence in the Mexican banking system and, on the other, avoid certain criminal activities, such as money laundering and other white-collar crimes.

In this chapter, we will briefly examine (i) the principles of bank secrecy, (ii) the general legal and conceptual framework, (iii) anti-money laundering provisions, (iv) reporting criteria, requirements and confidentiality and (v) remedies against disclosure of bank secrets as they are applicable under Mexican banking law. Throughout the chapter, we will take a particular interest in the applicability of bank secrecy to tax evasion and money laundering-related issues.

PRINCIPLES OF BANK SECRECY

The principles which surround the concept of bank secrecy are found in both customary banking practices and the positive law that regulates such practice. These principles, many of which derive from precepts of the Political Constitution of the United Mexican States, include:

1   the institution of private property itself, and the financial information gathered by financial entities;
2   the right to privacy (attributed to the individual client and, arguably, to the financial institution itself);
3   the professional obligation of a financial institution to maintain client information secrecy;
4   the contractual relationship between a bank and its client, whereby the dissemination of client information is prohibited; and

411

5   the legal consequences for disseminating a client's financial information without due cause, ie the extra-contractual responsibility under Civil and Criminal Law.

The principals of bank secrecy have been cornerstones to promote a basic confidence in financial institutions in Mexico, early on in their inception, and have come to embody an inseparable public trust in such financial services.

GENERAL LEGAL AND CONCEPTUAL FRAMEWORK

The legal framework of Mexican banking secrecy and confidentiality provisions are contained in:

1   the Credit Institutions Law (Ley de Instituciones de Crédito), as published on 18 July 1990, and as amended thereafter (the Law);
2   the Anti-Money Laundering Rules (the Rules), as published on 10 March 1997, defining certain rules to prevent money laundering activities utilising banking services provided by Mexican financial institutions (the Financial Institutions); and
3   The Credit Bureau Law (Ley para Regular las Sociedades de Información Crediticia), as published on 15 January 2002.

The Law, the Rules and the Credit Bureau Law are collectively referred to herein as the 'Bank Secrecy Statutes'. The Bank Secrecy Statutes work both to define which practices are akin for maintaining the institution of bank secrecy and provide the regulatory oversight functions concerning bank secrecy to the Ministry of Finance and Public Credit (Secretaría de Hacienda y Crédito Público – SHCP) and the National Banking and Securities Commission (CNBV).

A Financial Institution must request and keep on file a significant amount of information with respect to each corporate and individual client. Pursuant to art 117 of the Law, confidential information (Confidential Information) is considered all information with respect to deposits, services or any other type of operations of a client, as well as the relevant personal information for the client itself or those authorised signatories relating thereto. For individuals, this information includes, primarily, personal identification, tax registration numbers and proof of domicile. For companies, this information can be sensitive in nature and includes, most importantly, the corporate byelaws and the names of legal representatives and company directors and/or administrators. Foreign individuals are required to present a valid passport and legal authorisation of their immigration to Mexico and foreign entities must present their respective charter and incorporation documentation.

Financial Institutions are prohibited from releasing Confidential Information to any person other than a party with a direct interest with said Confidential Information, such as the depositor or account holder or relevant beneficiary, including legal representatives thereof.

The exception to the foregoing is adopted when such information is requested by (i) a judicial authority pursuant to a resolution adopted in a legal procedure where the account holder or beneficiary is acting as defendant or otherwise, and/or (ii) by the federal tax authorities, through the National Banking and Securities Commission, in connection with tax related matters. Concerning the former, amendments of 17 November 1995 to the Law (and other related regulations) have given powers to the SHCP to issue general rules and regulations to prevent and detect acts or operations in which funds of illicit origin are used and where the occurrence of a crime is suspected. Additionally, the CNBV, a decentralised agency of the SHCP, can provide confidential information to foreign financial authorities if treaties of reciprocity and information sharing are valid between Mexico and the foreign signatory nation.

As an exception to the foregoing rule, Mexican banks may reveal Confidential Information in connection with the sale of their portfolio to prospective purchasers thereof. In such case, the prospective purchasers must sign a confidentiality agreement undertaking not to reveal or disclose the Confidential Information. Additionally, as provided in the Credit Bureau Law, credit bureaux can release Confidential Information to other similar credit bureaux, Financial Institutions who have been designated as bureau service users and the proper administrative authorities, upon official request, as provided by regulatory jurisdictional powers attributed thereto in oversight matters without violating the bank secrecy provisions of the Law.

ANTI-MONEY LAUNDERING PROVISIONS

The topic of money laundering has been the focus of many of recent legal reforms, first to the Mexican Tax Code and later to the Criminal Code. The Mexican Tax Code (Codigo Fiscal de la Federación) first typified the act of money laundering in 1989, and these provisions were finally incorporated to reforms in the Criminal Code in 1996. Additionally, in 1993, the then National Banking Commission (Comisión Nacional Bancaria) issued a guide to prevent money laundering by banks, in accordance with the provisions issued by the Basel Commission, the 40 Recommendations of the Financial Action Task Force on Money Laundering (FATF) of the Organization for Economic Development (OECD) and the Model Regulation for money laundering of assets related to illicit drug trafficking of the Organization of the American States (OAS). The purpose of the guide was to design a public-private partnership between the Mexican government and regulated financial institutions to combat both national and cross-border money laundering.

On 13 May 1996, art 400bis of the Federal Criminal Code (Código Penal para el Distrito Federal en Materia de Fuero Común y para toda la República en Materia de Fuero Federal) was amended to classify money laundering as a federal crime. The reforms were directed towards those individuals and companies that participate in activities involving the acquisition, sale, administration, deposit, investment, transport, transfer within Mexico or abroad of funds of any nature with knowledge that such funds originate from an illegal activity and have the purpose of disguising or falsifying the true origin of said funds.

The new provisions in the Criminal Code also provide that those employees of financial institutions who aided or assisted their clients who originally perpetrated and undertook such crimes with malice intent are guilty of the same crime and therefore may be punished equally. Prison terms have been set at five to 15 years for each act of money laundering and all those who are prosecuted are denied any form of provisional bail during trial. Perhaps just as important, stricter penalties, such as additional years in prison and public discharge, are levied against public servants and officials who participate in money laundering activities. On 7 November 1996, the collaboration of individuals in money laundering activities was defined as atypical of organised crime under the new Federal Law Against Organized Crime (Ley Federal contra la Delincuencia Organizada).

These reforms are also significant since they provide for an increased technical and administrative collaboration among Mexican banking and criminal authorities. Currently, if money laundering involves a Financial Institution, the SHCP, through the assistance of the relevant decentralised agencies (ie CNBV), must file the prosecutorial complaint with the Public Prosecutor (Ministerio Publico) in accordance with the provisions of art 115 of the Law.

REPORTING CRITERIA, REQUIREMENTS AND CONFIDENTIALITY

By issuing the Rules in 1997, regulators attempted to design reporting mechanisms that would not violate the concept of bank secrecy and confidentiality. As a result, the following Financial Institutions, as defined under the Law, must co-operate to combat money laundering:

1   banks and credit institutions;
2   insurance and bonding companies;
3   general depositories;
4   financial leasing companies;
5   savings and loan institutions;
6   credit unions;
7   collection agencies;
8   broker dealers and other stock market intermediaries;
9   currency exchangers;
10   special purpose financial institutions (SOFOLES);
11   retirement fund administrators (AFORES); and
12   any other financial intermediary.

These Financial Institutions are now obligated to report certain transactions as a means of assisting the SHCP detect suspicious activities, defined as 'Unusual Operations'. According to the Rules, Financial Institutions are required to file reports with the SHCP and with the CNBV as soon as they become aware of suspicious transactions or of any other transaction in excess of US$10,000. Some of the criteria used to target suspicious transactions include:

1   specific client characteristics, such as profession, commercial business and licit activity;
2   historical evolution of activity concerning funds, relative to aforementioned client characteristics;
3   unusual banking activities, particularly those transactions which are not related to the economic purpose of the account holder; and
4   refusal by account holder or potential client to provide proper identification as required by the Financial Institution upon developing a client profile.

Those transactions solely in excess of US$10,000 are also routinely reported as 'Relevant Operations'. The practices, used by Financial Institutions for detecting Unusual and Relevant Operations, must be defined within a procedural manual (an Anti-money Laundering Manual) and registered with the SHCP and the CNBV before undertaking such extra-administrative supervisory activities.

REMEDIES AGAINST DISCLOSURE OF BANK SECRETS

As mentioned above, pursuant to art 117 of the Law, Financial Institutions cannot reveal Confidential Information, with the exception of information required by authorities in the prosecution of public crimes, ie tax evasion or money laundering.

The reporting requirements ultimately provide certain data classified as Confidential Information to authorities. To safeguard the Confidential Information, according to s 12 of the Rules, the officers from the SHCP and the CNBV, as well as the employees, officers, directors, statutory and external auditors of the Financial Institutions, must maintain strict confidence in respect to the reports and information required to be delivered under the Rules, and must abstain from releasing such privileged information to any third party other than the financial authorities. Any information that is not classified, as Confidential Information in accordance with the Anti-money Laundering Manual, cannot be required to be delivered to the relevant Financial Institutions.

Material penalties are in place to punish those public officials who release the information without due cause. Likewise, the board of directors, statutory auditors, external auditors, officers and employees of a Financial Institution which divulges Confidential Information to an authority, other than those officially designated to receive such Confidential Information, shall be found in violation of the confidentiality requirements and fined, in accordance with the Bank Secrecy statutes. Again, if in fact an authority does file a complaint to prosecute any act of money laundering, all information provided in such a criminal procedure is also considered confidential and cannot be revealed by a court of law.

The Rules also provide that Financial Institutions will not held liable for violating their contractual obligations, thereby giving rise of damages under civil and commercial law, for revealing Confidential Information to authorities as part of the reporting requirements.

CONCLUSIONS

Traditional practices in bank secrecy in Mexico have been sustained as a hallmark of Financial Institutions. Although new safeguards have arisen to detect illegal activities such as tax evasion and money laundering, a developing legal framework continues to distinguish between relevant information for prosecutorial purposes and the respected right to maintain certain information confidential by Financial Institutions and even banking authorities. Although bank secrecy and confidentiality provisions have been increasingly regulated, globalisation and the economic integration of Mexico will undoubtedly continue to define and redefine the lines between public access and private domain of Confidential Information.

19 The Netherlands

Victor P G de Serière

INTRODUCTION

There is no statutory law in The Netherlands on the duty of confidentiality owed by banks to their customers. There are certain statutory rules which deal with aspects of bank secrecy:

1   Article 10 of the Constitution of The Netherlands lays down the principle of protection against disclosure of personal data.
2   Article 64 of the Banking Act provides for the confidential treatment of data obtained by the Dutch Central Bank (de Nederlandsche Bank NV) in the course of its supervisory duties.
3   Article 31 of the Securities Transactions Supervision Act contains similar provisions in respect of data available to the Securities Board of The Netherlands (de Autoriteit Financiële Markten or AFM, formerly known as the Stichting toezicht effectenvcerkeer, STE), the governmental watchdog over stock exchanges and securities transactions in The Netherlands.
4   Article 272 of the Criminal Code makes it a criminal offence to disclose data if confidentiality is required because of the nature of the function or profession of the person holding such data or on the basis of an express provision of the law.
5   The 2000 Act on the Protection of Personal Data provides for detailed regulations applicable in all cases where personal data relating to individuals are compiled and used.

These are examples of specific statutory provisions relating to certain instances of bank confidentiality. However, a general statutory rule on bank confidentiality does not exist; the duty of confidentiality which under Dutch law a bank generally owes its customer is based on the contractual relationship between the bank and its customers.

There is currently no discussion in The Netherlands on the question whether such general statutory rules ought to be introduced. The arguments in favour of introducing legislation on this subject are:

1   the scope of the duty of confidentiality based on the contractual relationship between customer and the bank is unclear;

2   there are numerous exceptions to the duty, which are not in any way co-ordinated and for this reason inconsistent with one another; and

3   there is uncertainty as to the territorial scope of the duty of confidentiality and on the effect of foreign law and judgments as constituting exceptions to the duty.

These arguments, which are in themselves convincing, have so far not led to any debate on the need for regulation of this subject matter in The Netherlands. The main reason for this is that the system, based on a contractual general duty to a certain measure eroded by various statutory disclosure obligations, is generally deemed to work satisfactorily both from the banks' and the customers' point of view. In addition, the drafting of a law on this subject will be a complex task, requiring many existing statutory rules in different Acts to be amended; why embark on this if there is no certainty that the result will be any better than the current situation?

THE BANK'S DUTY OF CONFIDENTIALITY

The duty of confidentiality under civil law

Under Dutch law, there undoubtedly exists a duty of banks to maintain confidentiality towards their customers. This duty is generally deemed to be based on the contractual relationship between the bank and its customers. This relationship more often than not is governed by the General Bank Conditions (Algemene Bankvoorwaarden). Banks in The Netherlands will invariably endeavour to ensure that these General Bank Conditions are part of the contractual relationship. The General Bank Conditions provide in art 2:

'The bank shall exercise due care in providing services. It will thereby to the best of its ability take into consideration the interests of the customer, provided however that it is not required to use information which is available to it but which is not in the public domain, including information which may affect quoted prices of securities.'

The phrases 'to exercise due care' and 'to the best of its ability take into consideration the interests of the customer' are considered, inter alia, to contain the duty to maintain customer data confidentiality.

The proviso in art 2 that the bank is not required to use non-public information available to it is curious; essentially, it relates to the dilemma that a bank may be confronted with when the investment advisory departments of the bank are providing investment advice (or research reports) to its customers whilst in other departments of the bank (for example, the credit department or the corporate finance department) data are available which are confidential but which are certainly relevant to the investment advice to be given. This problem will be addressed later in the chapter.

The duty of care and the duty to take into consideration the interests of customers would apply to the relationship between a bank and its customer even if they had not been expressed in the General Bank Conditions. These duties are generally considered applicable on the basis of the principle of reasonableness and fairness which is a cornerstone of the Dutch law of contract. See arts 6:2 and 6:248 of the

Civil Code. The question arises whether the General Bank Conditions, by explicitly referring to this duty of care and this duty to take into consideration the interests of the customers, impose on banks obligations that are more far reaching than the obligations imposed by the principles of reasonableness and fairness of arts 6:2 and 6:248. In Dutch legal doctrine, it is sometimes argued that this is indeed the case; however, without specification as to what such extended duty may in practical terms mean.

The General Bank Conditions do not contain any specific provision on the extent of the duty of confidentiality. Questions such as which data must be kept confidential and which data may without consent of the customer be disclosed must be solved on an ad hoc basis by application of the general principles, each time taking into account the specific circumstances in which the question arises. The General Bank Conditions likewise contain no provisions on exceptions to the general principle.

Surprisingly perhaps, there is in The Netherlands virtually no case law on the extent of the duty of confidentiality based on art 2 of the General Bank Conditions. This absence of case law appears to indicate that, in practice, few occasions arise where there is a dispute between bank and customer in the application of the duty of confidentiality. A more down to earth reason for the absence of case law may be that the very reason why a customer is interested in a bank's strict adherence to rules of confidentiality often also constitutes a very good reason for that customer not to litigate on the issue.

There is one judgment of the District Court in Zwolle that perhaps deserves to be mentioned here.[1] In this case, the bank had advised a third party of the precarious financial condition of one of its customers. The third party was also doing business with this customer, and providing it with financial facilities. Although it could be argued that it was logical and defensible for the bank to provide information to the third party, particularly given the context of discussions that had been conducted between all parties involved, the bank was nevertheless held liable. The judgment is of a lower court, and therefore perhaps not too much weight should be given to it. Nevertheless, the judgment provides a clear warning that implied consent of a customer should not be easily assumed. Additionally, the judgment seems to indicate that also in (the early stages of) restructuring exercises, especially where lenders are not protected by commonly applicable disclosure provisions in the credit documentation, one should be careful about the exchange of information that is not specifically condoned by the borrower in distress.

What happens if the General Bank Conditions are not applicable? In certain contractual relations, for example, often in transactions between banks inter se and sometimes in transactions between banks and large corporate customers, applicability of the General Bank Conditions is excluded. In addition, it is noted that the General Bank Conditions will not apply in relationships between customers and the foreign offices of the bank (see art 1 of the General Bank Conditions); in other words, applicability is territorially limited. When, for instance, a Dutch customer does business with a Dutch bank acting through its London branch, they will not apply.

---

1   JOR 2000/130, dated 22 December 1999.

Where application of the General Bank Conditions is contractually excluded, the duty of confidentiality would, in the present writer's view, still fully apply on the basis of the principles of reasonableness and fairness (assuming, of course, that Dutch law applies). There is no logical justification for discriminating between these situations and those where art 2 applies. But where application is excluded for reasons of territoriality, a different approach must be taken: first, it must be determined, using the relevant conflicts of laws rules, which law applies to the contractual relationship concerned, and whether a duty of confidentiality exists and what such duty entails must then be determined according to the applicable law.

The duty of confidentiality under criminal law

Article 272 of the Dutch Criminal Code provides:

'He who deliberately discloses a secret of which he should know or reasonably be aware that such secret should not be disclosed because of function, profession or statutory provision, or because of a previous function or profession, will be punished …'

Article 273 provides:

'(1) He who deliberately discloses information relating to a trading or industrial or service enterprise with which he works or has worked, concerning which information a duty of secrecy has been imposed on him, or (2) he who discloses or uses non public information which was obtained in the commission of a crime from automated data relating to a trading or industrial or service enterprise and such disclosure and use may damage such enterprise, will be punished …'

It will be clear from the text of these two articles, that while art 272 addresses the breach of a general duty not to disclose confidential information acquired by a person in the performance of his function or profession, the scope of art 273(1) is rather more limited: it only relates to information concerning the enterprise where the person in question works or has worked. In other words, an employee of a bank would not necessarily be in breach of art 273(1) if he disclosed information about a customer rather than about the bank itself.

This chapter will not expand on the meaning of these provisions of criminal law, except to note the following. In its judgment of 18 December 1974,[2] the Amsterdam Court of Appeal determined with respect to art 272 that the profession of a banker is not of such confidential nature that a duty of secrecy in relation to information which is obtained in the exercise of his profession may be considered to exist. This judgment is, of course, principally relevant in the criminal law context. The judgment has been criticised on the grounds that the underlying reasoning appeared to address the question whether a banker could excuse himself from acting as a witness in legal proceedings (this relates to the privilege of refusal to testify, or *verschoningsrecht*) rather than to answer the question whether a duty of secrecy exists per se with respect to the profession of a banker even though there is no statutory basis for such

---

2   NJ 1975, 441.

duty of secrecy. The decision of the Court of Appeal was not submitted to the Supreme Court. Although the reasoning may be suspect, the decision itself is nevertheless approved in the legal doctrine: the nature of the profession of a banker is not such that a secrecy duty towards third parties should be deemed necessarily inherent in that profession. This duty to maintain secrecy thus denied to bankers, is generally deemed to apply to, inter alia, notaries, lawyers, tax advisers, external accountants, doctors and psychiatrists. It should be noted with respect to these categories of professionals, that the fact that they are subject to a duty of secrecy pursuant to the provisions of art 272 does not mean that they for that reason have the privilege of refusal to testify pursuant to the provisions of arts 218 and 191 of the Code of Criminal Procedure; whether this privilege applies depends basically on whether a statutory basis for such privilege can be construed; this statutory basis must demonstrate that the legislator deemed the critical importance of confidentiality to outweigh the serious disadvantage of possible obstruction of justice.

The duty of confidentiality pursuant to certain specific statutory provisions

There are numerous statutes which provide for specific duties of confidentiality to be maintained. This chapter will not discuss all of these statutes, but will mention the following.

The Dutch Banking Act

Article 64 of the Dutch Banking Act (Wet toezicht kredietwezen 1992) provides for the confidential treatment of data assembled by the Dutch Central Bank in the course of its supervisory duties. These provisions enact the requirements on this subject imposed by the Second Banking Directive.[3]

The duty of confidentiality imposed on the Dutch Central Bank may, however, not prevent the Dutch Central Bank from using such data wherever necessary to perform its duties under the Dutch Banking Act. In this connection, one could think of the duty to assess whether an institution is subject to bank licence requirements, investigations as to the solvency or liquidity of a bank, the imposition of sanctions, the need for defence in cases of legal proceedings in which the Dutch Central Bank is involved, the exchange of information with other Central Bank authorities in other countries etc. Article 64(5) of the Dutch Banking Act does allow the Dutch Central Bank to publish data acquired in the course of the exercise of its duties, provided these data are anonymous (that is to say, the identity of the financial institution involved cannot be deduced from the data published).

The Second Banking Directive leaves it to the domestic legislation of the member states to determine whether Central Bank officials have the privilege of refusal to testify in (criminal or civil) legal proceedings. Article 64 of the Dutch Banking act provides that this privilege is not available in the case of criminal or civil proceedings.

4   Council Directive 89/646/EEC.

The privilege is, however, available to bank officials for those cases where they have been involved in an attempt at financial restructuring of a bank: see art 64(4) of the Dutch Banking Act.

Article 65 of the Dutch Banking Act, finally, provides for the disclosure of data to governmental agencies (both in The Netherlands and abroad). This disclosure is subject to restrictions and covenants which are not discussed here, but which are principally designed to prevent – to the extent practically feasible – the abuse of such data.

The Dutch securities laws

Article 31 of the 1995 Securities Transactions Supervision Act (Wet toezicht effectenverkeer 1995) provides that data obtained by the Securities Board of The Netherlands may not be published and are secret. The provisions of art 31 are clearly derived from those of art 64 of the Dutch Banking Act. With respect to the privilege of refusal to testify, the same system as described above applies. It is to be noted that art 31(5) of the Securities Transactions Supervision Act allows the Minister of Finance to publish information, provided such information cannot be attributed to individual enterprises or institutions. This provision corresponds with art 64(5) of the Dutch Banking Act, described above. In addition, corresponding with art 65 of the Dutch Banking Act, art 33 of the Securities Transactions Supervision Act allows the disclosure of data to governmental agencies both in The Netherlands and abroad, subject to basically the same restrictions and caveats mentioned above. Article 32 of the Securities Transactions Supervision Act does allow for the disclosure to the public of certain data if disclosure is necessary for or enhances the proper functioning of the securities markets. These data include refusals to grant licences, withdrawals of licences, the names and particulars of institutions that operate without licence etc. It is noted that there is no corresponding provision in the Dutch Banking Act.

The Act on the Protection of Personal Data

The Act on the Protection of Personal Data (Wet bescherming persoonsgegevens) aims to protect the right to privacy of individuals concerning whom data are compiled in data systems. This Act serves to implement Council Directive 95/46/EC, dated 24 October 1995 and entered into force on 1 September 2001. The Act imposes certain obligations on those who wish to compile and use personal data (the so-called 'controller'). These obligations include the following:

1   Personal data may be collected only for specified, explicit and legitimate purposes.
2   Personal data may be processed only if (a) the subject has unambiguously given his consent, or if this is necessary in the context of (b) the performance of a contract to which the individual concerned is a party, (c) the fulfilment of statutory duties or public functions, (d) vital interests of the data subject or (e) processing is necessary for the purposes of legitimate interests pursued by the controller, except where such interests are overridden by privacy interests.
3   Data may only be used if this is done in a manner compatible with the purposes for which they were compiled.

4   If the purposes for which data were compiled have been achieved, the data may, in principle, no longer be maintained in a manner where the identity of the individuals concerned may still be determined. There is an exception for continued maintenance of data for statistical and academic purposes.

5   It is prohibited to compile and use data relating to religion, race or ethnic origin, political opinions, health, sexual life and membership of trade unions, unless one of the statutory exemptions apply.

6   Technical and organisational measures must be taken to protect personal data against accidental or unlawful destruction or accidental loss, alteration, unauthorised disclosure or access and the personal data must be accurate and kept up to date.

The Act contains elaborate statutory provisions requiring disclosure of the data to the individual concerned, and protecting the legitimate interests of the individual concerned. These statutory provisions will not be further described in this chapter.

The Act allows for a certain measure of self-regulation. Thus, in certain sectors of the economy, organisations of persons or entities that wish to set up data systems may develop and adopt codes of conduct. These codes of conduct can be submitted to the supervisory authority (College bescherming persoonsgegevens), which will then determine whether or not they comply with the requirements of the Act. It is clear that the Act applies to the data processing relating to customers maintained by banks in The Netherlands. The Privacy Code of Conduct for the Banking Industry was originally developed and issued by the Dutch Banking Association on 29 March 1989. It has since been revised. The supervisory authority has meanwhile confirmed that the revised Code is in line with the requirements of the Act.

THE EXCEPTIONS TO THE DUTY OF NON-DISCLOSURE

Express or implied consent of the customer

An exception to the bank's duty of confidentiality exists if the customer consents to disclosure.

Express consent

If the customer issues its express consent to the bank, the bank is discharged from its duty of confidentiality. The express consent can be given in any form: in writing or verbally. Verbal consents may in the event of subsequent disputes give rise to evidentiary problems; banks are well advised to have consents properly documented. It is generally not advisable for banks to use a system whereby the bank requests a consent under the condition that if the customer does not respond consent will be deemed to have been given.

Implied consent

A customer may issue an implied consent. If, for instance, a customer instructs or mandates a bank to carry out a certain transaction, it may generally be assumed that this instruction or mandate includes an authorisation for the bank to do all such things as are necessary to implement such instruction or mandate, including disclosure of data concerning the customer concerned. Should it, however, be uncertain whether the customer understands or reasonably ought to understand that disclosure is necessary to carry out the instruction or mandate, it will be prudent for the bank to double-check with the customer. The judgment of the Zwolle District Court,[4] discussed above, corroborates this.

Consent Directives

In respect of the US practice of Consent Directives, the following comments from a Dutch law perspective are made. There is no doctrine or case law on this issue. However, if there is a Consent Directive signed by a customer on the basis of a US court order to sign, a bank in The Netherlands would, in the present author's view, in principle treat such consent as a valid consent to disclose. Whether a Consent Directive constitutes a valid consent should arguably be determined in accordance with principles of Dutch law, which govern the relationship between bank and customer. If such consent is given under coercion (bedreiging; see art 3:44(2) of the Dutch Civil Code), the consent would be subject to nullification by the customer concerned. But a US court order cannot of itself constitute a coercion under Dutch civil law. This is because coercion is, under Dutch law, recognised only if such coercion is 'illegal' (onrechtmatig), and, of course, a court order cannot by definition be illegal. The question arises whether by considering such Consent Directive a proper consent under Dutch law, The Netherlands would unjustifiably grant extra-territorial effect to a foreign judgment, which is not in itself enforceable in The Netherlands. The answer to this question must, in the present writer's view, be negative: if the fact that the consent is obtained by way of the threat of fines or imprisonment in the US does not in itself constitute coercion, the circumstance that a US court order underlies the Consent Directive should not be relevant from a Dutch law point of view.

Disclosure in the interests of the bank

Disclosure in the interest of the bank is not under Netherlands law expressis verbis considered a valid exception to the rule of non-disclosure. However, when a bank is suing to recover from a customer overdue indebtedness, it goes without saying that such bank may make such disclosures as are necessary to protect its position. The same undoubtedly applies if a bank is a defendant in a suit brought by its customer. Nobody will argue that the defences of the bank would in such a case be curtailed by its duty of confidentiality.

This being said, the question arises as to what is the legal basis for this exception to the rule of confidentiality. Must the customer be deemed to have given an implied consent to the bank when the credit facility concerned was granted to him to disclose in case of his default? In the second instance, must the customer be deemed to have

---

4 Judgment of 18 December 1974, NJ 1975, 441.

given his implied consent when he commenced litigation? This, it seems, can be convincingly argued. Furthermore, the argument could be made that the right of the customer to confidentiality in such cases must be deemed inferior to the more fundamental and therefore stronger right to substantiate one's position in legal proceedings.

The situation becomes somewhat more difficult, however, if the bank is involved in litigation with third parties where the bank would be better off if it could disclose details of transactions with other customers. Could the bank in such a situation make such disclosures without being exposed to liability towards such other customers? In these situations, the bank should generally not have the right to disclose without the customer's consent.

Disclosure within the banking group

A distinction must be made here between disclosure from one legal entity to another and disclosure by one department to the other within the same entity.

In so far as disclosure between one legal entity and another, both belonging to the same banking group, is concerned, the correct position must be that the legal concept of a group is not relevant in this context. A customer has a contractual relationship with one particular legal entity, and that contractual relationship does not by implication or otherwise extend to other legal entities belonging to the same group. In practical terms, of course, this position is rather difficult to implement. Consider the situation where a bank decides to discontinue extending credit to a customer because of the customer's threatened insolvency: if this customer then applies for a leasing transaction with a leasing subsidiary of the bank, may the bank inform its subsidiary of the increased credit risk? Or will a duty of confidentiality be breached by such action? The answer to this question is unclear. In the Dutch banking practice, intra-group sharing of information is probably commonly done. The legal basis for this practice is likely to be implied customer consent.

In so far as disclosures between different departments within the same legal entity are concerned, there are no specific statutory or contractual restrictions to the flow of confidential information. There may be restrictions on the basis of Chinese Walls. But Chinese Walls are voluntary restrictions, and it is unclear to what extent customers of banks may claim the benefit of these restrictions (or could assert a damages claim if banks fail to adhere to these voluntary restrictions). The concept of Chinese Walls is discussed further at the end of the chapter.

Credit reference agencies

There are many credit reference agencies operating in The Netherlands. They are not subject to specific regulatory constraints. The banks are prevented, by virtue of their duty of confidentiality, to contribute to the data compiled by these agencies. There is no exception from this duty based on the general notion that disclosure is 'in the public interest', or on the basis that banks could by disclosing credit risk to such agencies legitimately protect their own positions. The banks are not statutorily restricted in using the data compiled by these agencies.

There is one agency, known as the BKR, which is a dominant force in this area. The Foundation for the Registration of Credit Data has been established by banks and financial institutions to prevent the occurrence of payment defaults. A bank of financial institution can become a participant by payment of an annual fee. Each participant is required to obtain information from the system if it intends to extend credit to a customer. The system is very popular and is widely used for the purpose of checking credit data when extending loans or consumer credits to individual customers. More than 20,000 credit checks are routinely carried out daily. There are elaborate internal rules governing the provision of information to participants and third parties, and providing for protection of the Foundation's data banks. Clearly, the operations of the Foundation are subject to the detailed requirements of the Act on the Protection of Personal Data, discussed above.

Disclosure required by law

A distinction can be made between disclosures required by court judgments on the one hand, and disclosures required by statutory provisions on the other.

Compulsion by court judgment

Here, a distinction could be made between various categories of court judgments and court orders. A very generalised attempt at such categorisation is made below (but note that the resulting scheme somewhat simplifies the issues):

1   a final domestic court judgment;
2   a domestic court judgment where a remedy is still available;
3   a domestic arbitral award; and
4   a domestic binding advice (bindend advies).

In 3 and 4, again a distinction could be made between the situation where remedies are still available and the situation where this is not the case but this will lead to an undesirable level of detail. A similar distinction could be made for foreign judgments, awards and advices:

1   a final foreign court judgment, order or subpoena not enforceable in The Netherlands;
2   a foreign court judgment where a remedy is still available, not enforceable in The Netherlands;
3   a foreign court judgment that has become enforceable in The Netherlands;
4   a foreign arbitral award, not enforceable in The Netherlands; and
5   a foreign arbitral award that has become enforceable in The Netherlands.

In the Dutch context, the question whether a judgment, order, subpoena or award will set aside the duty of confidentiality must always be considered from the viewpoint that this duty is a contractual duty, which is not in any way specifically worked out in the contractual relationship between the bank and its customer. Thus the answer to this question will very much depend on what should be considered reasonable and fair in the circumstances. This leads to an unfortunate uncertainty as to what the right position in a given case ought to be. The Dutch banking community could, by promulgating rules on this subject (which rules could be made part of the General Bank Conditions or could be a separate code which the banks could, for instance, apply except where deviating contractual arrangements are made with customers), clarify their (and their customers') position, but no initiative has (yet) been taken to this end.

A FINAL DOMESTIC COURT JUDGMENT

Here, there is no question that compliance with the judgment will be a justified exception to the duty of confidentiality. It is difficult to perceive any argument on the basis of which compliance with the court judgment could be denied. The only conceivable area of contention would be the interpretation of the meaning and extent of the court judgment.

A DOMESTIC COURT JUDGMENT WHERE REMEDIES ARE STILL AVAILABLE

In this situation, the question arises whether the judgment is as from its rendition enforceable. If so, again it would be difficult to construe any argument for non-compliance. Under certain circumstances, one could imagine that a bank could convincingly take the position that it ought to wait until the judgment has become final. This position would normally be the logical position to adopt, if the judgment concerned is not immediately enforceable.

DOMESTIC ARBITRAL AWARDS AND ADVICES

In these instances, there are no compelling reasons under Dutch law to take any other position than that described above with respect to judgments. With respect to binding advice, however, a bank may argue that it is entitled to refuse disclosure until the advice is confirmed by a court judgment to be enforceable.

FINAL FOREIGN COURT JUDGMENTS, ORDERS OR SUBPOENAS NOT ENFORCEABLE IN THE NETHERLANDS

Here, the position is difficult. To the present writer's knowledge, there is no dependable case law. Could a bank reasonably argue that it may comply with such final court judgment even if it is not (yet) enforceable in The Netherlands? Is it, to put this question in a slightly different perspective, under all circumstances justified that the formality of obtaining an 'exequatur' or a confirming domestic court judgment must first be taken care of? It is at first sight perfectly acceptable for a bank to take the position that it wishes to comply with a final foreign court judgment, even if it is not enforceable. But then, if the bank so complies, it effectively deprives its customer from the remedies which such customer might have if the claimant concerned were to seek recognition of its judgment in The Netherlands. It is difficult to argue that a bank should be entitled to do this.

FOREIGN COURT JUDGMENTS WHICH ARE NEITHER FINAL NOR ENFORCEABLE

Here the bank would under ordinary circumstances be ill-advised to follow the foreign judgment. The argument that the bank by doing this will deprive the customer from (at least) two opportunities to employ remedies appears conclusive. The foregoing does not provide an answer for those cases where foreign courts serve a disclosure order or subpoena on the local branch office of a bank. In such cases, the bank is faced with the dilemma that a refusal to comply will expose it to sanctions in the foreign jurisdiction concerned, whilst compliance may entail a violation of its duty of confidentiality at home. In instances where there is doubt as to the correct position, a solution could be for the bank or for the customer concerned to obtain a court order in The Netherlands in preliminary relief proceedings. The question will then arise, of course, whether a Dutch judgment upholding the duty of confidence would constitute sufficient excuse for the foreign court concerned to allow non-compliance.

FOREIGN COURT JUDGMENTS WHICH HAVE BEEN MADE ENFORCEABLE IN THE NETHERLANDS

The position is the same as discussed above with respect to final domestic court judgments.

FOREIGN ARBITRAL AWARDS

With these, again, there are no compelling reasons to take any other position than as described above with respect to foreign court judgments.

The question how a court judgment becomes enforceable in The Netherlands will not be dealt with in extenso in this chapter. But, as stated above, the question is relevant for determining whether a bank is justified in complying with a judgment which is not enforceable in The Netherlands.

Generally, judgments will be enforced in accordance with the EU Regulation of 22 December 2000 on Jurisdiction and Recognition and Enforcement of Judgments in Civil and Commercial Matters,[5] if such judgments are rendered in a country covered by the Regulation. It is to be noted that this Regulation only allows for extremely limited grounds on which enforcement of a foreign judgment can be denied: see arts 27 and 28 of the Regulation. A review of the merits of the case is under no circumstances permitted: see art 29 of the Regulation.

Judgments obtained in countries that are not covered by the Regulation may become enforceable under the terms of the 1988 Lugano Convention on Jurisdiction and the Enforcement of Judgments in Civil and Commercial Matters (this is the Convention which aims to extend the original EU Convention that the Regulation has now replaced to EFTA member states). If neither the Regulation nor the Convention applies, there may be an applicable bilateral convention. The Netherlands does not have bilateral conventions with the US or Japan. If not, the claims in question must be re-litigated. In that case, if certain conditions are met, ie:

1   the foreign court in question has jurisdiction according to internationally accepted standards,

6   Council Regulation 44/2001/EC.

2   the judgment results from proceedings compatible with Dutch concepts of due process, and

3   the judgment does not contravene Dutch public policy,

then the foreign judgment will be recognised by the Dutch courts and the Dutch courts will give the same relief as the foreign judgment, without re-litigation of the merits. The above general description as to the enforcement of judgments in The Netherlands is relevant to the extent that it demonstrates that under certain (but generally quite limited) circumstances the procedures which must be fulfilled to enforce a foreign judgment will give the defendant (or the bank's customer as intervening third party) an opportunity to oppose. For banks which are inclined to conform to foreign judgments which are not enforceable in The Netherlands, this raises the question, discussed above, whether they are authorised to deprive the defendant (or intervening customer) from such an opportunity.

In looking at the position of banks when confronted with court judgments or court orders, one always has to remember that banks might wish to argue in different directions depending on the case at hand. To illustrate this point, consider a bank that is faced with a foreign court order to allow discovery. Obviously, the bank would fervently wish to be able to ignore this court order. But if the bank is faced with an order to freeze certain deposits, the position could be different; it may then conceivably be favourable for the bank concerned to be compelled to maintain the deposit accounts concerned until the matter in dispute is resolved.

Compulsion by statute

There are numerous statutory provisions requiring disclosure. This chapter will not attempt to deal with these exhaustively. However, some of the statutory provisions which are practically the most important are the following.

ASPECTS RELATING TO THE COLLECTION OF TAXES

The General Act on State Taxes (Algemene Wet Rijksbelastingen) contains in art 47ff elaborate provisions on the duty to disclose data to the tax authorities. These duties not only relate to data on the basis of which the tax obligations of the disclosing party can be determined, but also those enabling the determination of tax obligations of third parties: see art 53. The Act provides in art 51 that no exception from this duty to disclose is allowed on the basis that the person concerned has a legal duty of secrecy. In other words, in principle, not only contractual but also statutory duties not to disclose will be set aside for the purpose of tax collection. Where there is a duty to disclose information concerning third parties, only religious professionals, notaries, lawyers, doctors and pharmacists are entitled to invoke their duty of secrecy: see art 53A. Tax advisers may not invoke their duty of secrecy. As a consequence of these legal provisions, in principle, banks will need to disclose information on customers to the tax authorities. The tax authorities themselves are only allowed to disclose information made available to them in the course of their duties to the extent that disclosure is necessary to implement the tax laws and to arrive at proper tax assessment or collection: see art 67(1). The Minister of Finance has the authority to grant dispensation from this duty of confidentiality. Article 67(1) does not in any way restrict the grounds on which such dispensation may be given; accordingly, there is some measure of discretion here.

The judgment of the Supreme Court of 10 December 1974[6] may be of interest here. In an attempt to refuse to disclose information to a tax inspector (who had for obvious reasons asked an insurance company to disclose to him all the names of persons who had taken out insurances on pleasure boats), the insurance company, Stad Rotterdam, argued that the relevant provisions of the General Act Concerning State Taxes are in violation of art 8 of the European Convention on Human Rights, which provides that each individual's private life, family life, home and correspondence should be respected. This argument was not accepted by the Supreme Court, on the basis that art 8(2) of the Convention permits restrictions to the extent that the same are 'necessary in a democratic society in the interests of the economic well being of the country'.

Inter alia, in consequence of the above Supreme Court judgment, the tax authorities and the Dutch banks have deemed it necessary to clarify their mutual relationship in a Code of Conduct, which is the product of co-operation between the Ministry of Finance and an ad hoc committee representing the banks. The Code was established in 1984, but has since been amended. The Code regulated the provision of information relating to customers by banks in The Netherlands to the tax inspectorate. The Code has meanwhile been replaced in 1998 by Resolution of the Director General of the Tax Administration, amended and restated by Resolution of 18 March 2002.[7] The following features of this Resolution are worth noting:

1   As of 2001, banks are obliged to provide information on their own accord relating to individual customers on, inter alia, savings balances, share deposits, interest and dividend receipts, annuities and endowment assurances.
2   Tax inspectors, when issuing a request for information, are not required to state the reasons for issuing such request, other than to state that the information may be of interest in connection with tax assessments or tax collection against or from third parties. As a consequence, banks are, practically speaking, not in a position to argue in a given case that a request was unduly made.
3   Tax inspectors should first try to obtain information from the taxpayers themselves before making requests for information to the banks. This rule aims to prevent unnecessary infringement of the duty of confidentiality which banks owe their customers. The rule does not apply if addressing the taxpayer will prejudice the position of the tax authorities.
4   Information requests must be made in writing, specifying the legal basis for the request.
5   Tax inspectors are entitled to ask non-individualised information relating to interest payments made by banks (whether as principal or as intermediary), certain payments on bonds, dividend stripping activities and activities of subsidiaries of banks that engage in banking business.
6   In addition, certain other information may be requested on a non-individualised basis, provided the Minister of Finance has explicitly authorised this. This

---

6   *Re Stad Rotterdam* NJ 1975, 178.
7   Stcrt 2002, 58.

authority, together with the authority described in 5 above will, to a certain extent, allow 'fishing expeditions' by the tax inspectorate.

7   Banks are not entitled to subject access to information to the prior consent of the customer concerned. Banks are not specifically prohibited from disclosing to their customers that an information request has been made by the tax authorities. Conversely, banks have no duty to make such disclosure, and customers do not have the right to be informed thereof by their bank or by the tax authorities.

8   The tax authorities also have the right to obtain information from banks in The Netherlands in connection with non-Dutch tax assessments or collections, but this right must be exercised pursuant to provisions of international conventions.

There is some doubt whether taxpayers can themselves invoke the benefit of the terms of this Resolution. In a judgment of the Supreme Court dated 23 May 1990,[8] a limited right to involve these terms was recognised, and this was confirmed by decision of the Dutch national ombudsman dated 21 March 2000.

In the area of tax collection in the international context, the provisions of the 1986 Act on the Provision of International Support for Tax Assessments (Wet op de internationale bijstandverlening bij de heffing van belastingen) are relevant. This Act was promulgated pursuant to the provisions of Council Directive 77/799/EEC, dated 19 December 1977. It provides that the Minister of Finance will provide information to the competent authorities of another state (being an EU member state or another state with which a tax treaty has been conducted by The Netherlands), either at the request of such authorities or at the minister's own initiative: see arts 5, 6 and 7 of the Act. According to art 8 of the Act, the Minister of Finance may instruct an investigation to be conducted by tax officers. Such investigation could, for instance, be made in respect of books and records of banks. In the implementation of the provisions of the Act, the Dutch tax authorities are subject to the same duties of confidentiality which are imposed by art 67 of the General Act Concerning State Taxes. On certain grounds set out in art 13 of this Act, the Minister of Finance may refuse to co-operate. These grounds include situations where considerations of Dutch 'public order' are at stake, or where disclosure would lead to the revelation of commercial, industrial or professional secrets. In addition, the Act provides that the Minister of Finance may not provide information to competent authorities of another country if there is no duty of confidentiality imposed on the tax authorities of such other country. This reciprocity principle is set out in art 14 of the Act. There is a fair amount of case law on the manner in which the provisions of this Act are implemented. This case law will not be discussed in this chapter.

ASPECTS RELATING TO EVIDENCE IN CIVIL COURT PROCEEDINGS

The duty of confidentiality of banks may be set aside on the basis of the rules of evidence in legal proceedings in civil matters. The rules of evidence under Dutch law are set out in art 149ff of the Code of Civil Procedure. It is important to note that there is no provision in Dutch procedural law for discovery or disclosure of documents

8   BNB 1990/240.

either before or during court proceedings. An important means of proof is the examination of witnesses. This may be done during the court proceedings, at the initiative of one of the parties or at the initiative of the court itself (see art 166 Code of Civil Procedure), and also in preliminary hearings. These preliminary hearings (see art 186ff) are permitted to be held according to special procedural rules designed to avoid unnecessary court proceedings based on mistaken legal proceedings, to extract information from counterparties unwilling to provide evidentiary documents or information voluntarily. Additionally, use is sometimes made of this procedural facility in the context of 'fishing expeditions'.

Article 165 of the Code of Civil Procedure provides that persons who are bound by a duty of secrecy in respect of information provided to them, in view of their function or profession, have the privilege of refusal to testify. The privilege applies both in testimonies taken during court proceedings and in preliminary hearings of witnesses. The privilege does not extend to employees of a bank. There are various (lower) court judgments confirming this. In the context of criminal proceedings, see the judgment of the Amsterdam Court of Appeals dated 18 December 1974, discussed above.

In this context, reference should also be made to the Supreme Court judgment of 22 July 1986.[9] In that judgment, which related to the duty of secrecy imposed by statute (ie, the Dutch Banking Act), the Supreme Court held the view that in certain circumstances the statutory duty of secrecy could be set aside depending on whether the fundamental need that justice be done outweighs the requirement that secrecy be maintained; whether this is the case should be determined by the Dutch courts on an ad hoc basis. Legal writers have argued, on the basis of this Supreme Court judgment dated 22 December 1989,[10] which judgment will not be discussed in this chapter, that even in cases where there is no *statutory* duty, this determination must still take place.[11] It seems, in the present writer's opinion, that this view is correct only to the extent that the courts in taking witness testimonies should always consider whether questions put to a witness are relevant in the context of the evidence being sought.

Whenever testimonies are required to be taken abroad, this may be done by way of letters rogatory (rogatoire commissies), either on the basis of an applicable treaty (The Netherlands is a party to the Convention dated 18 March 1970 on obtaining evidence in civil and commercial matters) or, in the absence of a treaty, on the basis of art 176 of the Code of Civil Procedure. The member states of this Convention include a number of European states and the US. Note that art 11 of the Convention deals with the question of the privilege of refusal to testify; it appears from this article that the Convention allows the privilege to be invoked not only if it is accorded by the law of the country which requests the testimony to be taken, but also if it is accorded by the law of the country where the testimony is to be taken, thus potentially expanding the legal basis for the refusal to testify. Note further that The Netherlands

---

9   NJ 1986, 823.
10   NJ 1990, 779.
11   See P W Bartelings 'Het Bankgeheim staat of valt bij de wet: enkele opmerkingen over het bankgeheim in Nederland, Zwitserland en Luxemburg' (1991) 91/3 TVVS at 59.

has declared under the Convention that it will not execute letters of request issued for the purpose of obtaining the type of pre-trial discovery of documents known in common law countries.

Finally on this subject, a brief word on civil law attachments. According to art 718 of the Code of Civil Procedure, attachments may be effected on goods and claims. Credit balances on current account bank accounts and on deposit accounts are 'claims' against the bank which may be attached. If attachment is made under a bank, the bank will need within four weeks from the date of the attachment to make a declaration of the amount of the 'claims' which are the subject of the attachment. The declaration must contain various details relating to the 'claims', as set out in art 476a of the Code of Civil Procedure. The bank, under which the attachment is made, is not entitled to invoke its duty of confidentiality towards the customer concerned. If the bank does not issue the required declaration, it may be forced to do so on penalty of payment of the amounts for which the attachment is effective: see art 477a(1). According to art 477a(2), the party who has effected the attachment has the right to contest the accuracy of the bank's declaration.

ASPECTS OF THE LAW OF CRIMINAL PROCEDURE

The Code of Criminal Procedure contains various provisions on the basis of which investigating authorities may seek information and data from banks. The following statutory provisions are mentioned without being exhaustive, and without discussing these provisions in any detail.

Article 94ff of the Code of Criminal Procedure permits the attachment of all assets which 'may serve to expose the truth or to demonstrate illegally obtained gains'. Assets which can be attached include financial assets held by suspects with banks. According to art 98, attachment may not be made on correspondence or other documents held by persons who have been granted the statutory privilege of refusal to testify. As discussed above, bank employees do not have this privilege.

Article 126ff allows the conduct of a 'criminal financial investigation', in those cases where it is suspected that illegal financial gains are obtained in the course of the commitment of a crime, in order to arrive at dispossession. The principle of dispossession of illegally obtained gains is set out in art 36e of the Criminal Code. In this 'criminal financial investigation', banks may be required to disclose which assets (including moneys and securities) are held or have in the past been held by it for the account of suspects. Assets so disclosed, including documents, may be attached. Banks and bank employees involved in this special type of investigation cannot refuse to co-operate on the basis of their duty of confidentiality towards customers.

Article 150 permits the public prosecutor, and art 192 permits the investigating judge (rechter commissaris), to enter premises and to review items (including books and records). Although these provisions are designed principally to allow the inspection of the locus delicti, they may be employed in a broader context.

Article 213 provides for witnesses to be heard. Articles 217 and 218 contain provisions on the privilege of refusal to testify. As discussed above, bank employees have no right to invoke this privilege.

THE ACT ON IDENTIFICATION WHEN PROVIDING SERVICES

The Act on the Determination of the Identity when Providing Financial Services was promulgated on 19 May 1988, principally in an attempt to prevent tax frauds. Pursuant to Council Directive 91/308/EEC, of 10 June 1991, this Act was replaced by the 1993 Act on Identification when Providing Financial Services (Wet identificatie bij financiële dienstverlening 1993), which has the broader goal of also preventing money launderers from using banks and financial institutions on an anonymous basis. The 1993 Act was recently replaced by a new, broader Act, the 2002 Act on Identification when Providing Services (Wet identificatie bij dienstverlening 2002). The Act imposes identification duties on 'financial institutions', which term is defined in the Act and its implementing regulations as including banks, brokers, investment funds, insurance companies, insurance brokers, securities houses, and other categories of businesses designated from time to time as such by regulation. The term 'financial services' as used in the Act includes, inter alia:

1   custody services for moneys, securities and other valuables;
2   opening of money and securities accounts;
3   the letting of safe deposit boxes;
4   payment of coupons on bonds (and similar debt instruments);
5   conclusion of and providing intermediary services in respect of life insurance contracts if the premium to be paid exceeds a certain amount;
6   payments under life insurance contracts;
7   provision of services in financial transactions which exceed a certain threshold (or when the value of a financial transaction is not known); and
8   provision of other kinds of services designated from time to time as such by regulation.

The Act imposes the duty to determine the identity of a customer prior to providing financial services as described above. Article 3 of the Act provides for the procedures to be followed for identification. If the (legal) person so identified is acting for a third party, such third party also will need to be identified in accordance with the provisions of the Act. There are certain exemptions from the above statutory requirements, which will not be discussed in this chapter. The data which the financial institutions compile in the implementation of the Act must be properly filed and maintained for not less than five years. Non-compliance with the provisions of the Act constitutes a criminal offence.

The Act contains no specific provisions on making the data compiled available to the authorities. Neither does the Act contain any provisions by virtue of which the financial institutions concerned are to keep the data compiled confidential. For these matters, the legislator relies on the other laws discussed in this chapter.

THE ACT ON THE NOTIFICATION OF UNUSUAL TRANSACTIONS

The Act on the Notification of Unusual Transactions (Wet melding ongebruikelijke transacties) came into force on 1 February 1994, again in the context of the implementation of Council Directive 91/308/EEC, of 10 June 1991. It has been amended on several occasions, most recently in December 2001. Essentially, the Act imposes a duty to notify to a specific agency all unusual transactions. The Act applies to whoever provides services in the conduct of a business or profession, including banking and insurance services, but also including other services that may be engaged in order to achieve effective money laundering (such as transactions involving ships, cars, antiques, jewels etc). As soon as an unusual transaction is proposed or effected, the financial institution involved is required to notify the same to the agency set up to implement the Act (centrale meldpunt). The notification includes:

1   the identity of the client;
2   the type and registration number of the identification papers of the client;
3   the nature, volume, time and place of the transaction;
4   the reason why the transaction is deemed unusual;
5   if applicable a description of the assets involved; and
6   other data designated as such from time to time by regulation.

Whether a transaction is to be characterised as unusual must be determined according to guidelines (indicatoren-lijst) of the Minister of Finance. These guidelines are published regularly, at no fewer than six-monthly intervals.

What happens after notification? The agency will register and analyse the transaction concerned, and the data may be used for prosecution purposes. The agency is entitled to request the financial institution who has made a notification for additional information: see art 10 of the Act. The financial institution cannot invoke a duty of confidentiality.

The financial institution which makes a notification may not disclose this to the customer concerned: see art 19. The Act provides that all persons entrusted with duties in connection with its implementation are subject to a duty of non-disclosure, except to the extent disclosure is necessary to perform such duties: see art 18.

Naturally, banks and other financial institutions are concerned that they may incur civil liabilities towards third parties in connection with notifications made pursuant to the Act. For this reason, art 13 provides that notifying persons may not be held liable for notifications made unless it is proved that given the circumstances of the case notification should reasonably not have been made. The party who wishes to hold a notifying person liable is thus faced with a rather difficult burden of proof.

In addition to the civil law indemnity described above, financial institutions have the benefit of a criminal law indemnity: see art 12. Basically, the data which a financial institution provides on the basis of the Act may not be used for the prosecution of such a financial institution for fencing (heling). This perhaps requires some explanation. A bank which accepts moneys from a customer in the knowledge or reasonable suspicion that such moneys were obtained in the commission of a crime commits the criminal act of fencing (receiving stolen property). If the transfer of such moneys to the bank is notified in accordance with the requirements of the Act, the information thus supplied may not be used by the prosecution. But this does obviously not constitute a complete indemnity; the bank concerned may still be prosecuted on the basis of other evidence than that notified under the Act. Additionally, the provisions of art 12 only provide relief in the context of the criminal offence of fencing, and not in case of other crimes. Accordingly, art 12 only provides a rather limited criminal law indemnity to banks and other financial institutions subject to the Act.

Most banks in The Netherlands have developed quite elaborate compliance manuals in order to ensure that the provisions of the Act (and of the Act on Identification when Providing Services) are complied with, and have installed compliance officers who monitor, and can be consulted about, the implementation of the Act. Since the Act does contain various provisions pursuant to which banks and other financial institutions have to use their own judgment as to whether or not to notify and as to the timing of a notification (and sometimes as to whether (and when) to notify subject to agreement with the agency as to how the matter will further be dealt with), there is an obvious need for such internal guidelines.

A duty to the public to disclose

Other than in Anglo-Saxon jurisdictions, which appear to recognise an exception to the duty of confidentiality in situations where a duty to disclose is in the public interest, for example, if there is knowledge of a crime being committed or fraud is deemed to exist, Dutch law does not explicitly recognise such exception. However, the principle that a statutory duty of confidentiality must give way to the overriding principle that justice must be done, appears very similar in concept and effect: see the Supreme Court judgment dated 22 July 1986, discussed above. Moreover, it can be convincingly argued that if there is knowledge or a strong indication of crime, the contractual duty of confidentiality will not prevent the bank from disclosing the same, because the principles of reasonableness and fairness would dictate that a customer cannot enforce his contractual rights vis-à-vis the bank in the context of a criminal cover up. The Act on the Notification of Unusual Transactions (discussed above) has obviously largely taken away the need to provide for a general statutory duty to disclose in the public interest.

REGULATION OF FINANCIAL MARKETS

Powers of regulatory bodies to require disclosure

Pursuant to the Dutch Banking Act

The Dutch Central Bank (DNB), has powers to require disclosure under art 53ff of the Dutch Banking Act. Pursuant to art 53, DNB is entitled to obtain information from institutions which it suspects are subject to bank licence requirements. Under art 54, DNB has all the investigative powers required to fulfil its supervisory duties. Article 55 requires credit institutions to comply with elaborate periodic reporting obligations. Article 56 obliges credit institutions to make ad hoc reports if they no longer comply with DNB's directives on solvency, liquidity or administrative organisation. The investigative powers of DNB in relation to credit institutions are extended by virtue of art 57 to certain other group companies of the credit institution concerned. This applies to group companies both within and outside of The Netherlands.

In addition to the above-described powers, arts 60 and 61 provide for procedures to be followed in cases where DNB requires information to be verified from companies in other EU member states, and vice versa if a Central Bank in another EU member state wishes DNB to verify information concerning companies in The Netherlands.

All of the foregoing comprise investigative powers conferred on DNB in the context of its supervisory duties under the Dutch Banking Act, and there is nothing unusual about these powers.

Pursuant to Dutch securities laws

The Securities Board of The Netherlands, the AFM, has similar investigative powers in the context of its supervisory functions in respect of stock exchanges and securities transactions. Under art 29 and following of the Securities Transactions Supervision Act (Wet toezicht effectenverkeer 1995, the STSA), the AFM may obtain, or cause to be obtained, all the information which is reasonably necessary for the proper performance of the duties and responsibilities vested in the AFM under the STSA and in order to ascertain whether the statutory provisions are being complied with. This information may be obtained, inter alia, from securities institutions, other group companies of securities institutions, stock exchanges and offerors of securities.

There is uncertainty as to whether the AFM also has the right to inspect cash accounts of clients of a bank or documents which do not relate to broker-dealer activities or portfolio management activities of a bank. An interesting judgment was rendered in 1996 in a case brought before the President of the Council for Appeals for Business Enterprises (College van Beroep voor het Bedrijfsleven, CBB).[12] In this case, the STE (as the AFM was then called) had announced in a letter to ABN AMRO Bank NV that it would collect data and information at ABN AMRO in order to be able to ascertain whether the provisions of the STSA relating to insider trading had been complied with in a certain case. In its letter, the STE had asserted that the bank was under an obligation to extend to officials charged by the STE with supervisory duties every co-operation which they may reasonably require in the performance of their duties. At the request of the bank, the STE clarified that it also intended to inspect cash accounts of clients of ABN AMRO. The bank understandably objected vigorously to this extension by the STE of its investigative powers; these investigative powers were alleged by the STE to cover not only the securities business of the bank, but also the actual banking business. The President of the CBB considered that the position of the STE was incorrect to the extent that it also covered inspection by the STE of other cash accounts than those which directly relate to the securities transactions effected by ABN AMRO to the order of the customer in respect of whom the suspicion had arisen. In other words, the President of the CBB did allow the investigative powers of the STE to extend to specific cash accounts, but did not allow these powers to be used in a more generalised manner.

12   *ABN AMRO/STE* CBB 15 October 1996, No 96/0033/113/226.

Pursuant to the Act on the Supervision of Investment Institutions

Article 19(1) of the Investment Undertakings Supervision Act (Wet toezicht beleggingsinstellingen) provides that DNB may seek information from or conduct or cause to be conducted on its behalf an investigation:

1   an applicant for a licence as an investment institution;
2   an existing investment institution (including an investment institution operating from another EU member state under the UCITS Directive);
3   a custodian or depository company used by an investment institution; and
4   an organisation with which an investment institution is affiliated, if an exemption from the licence requirement under the Act applies which is based on such affiliation.

The term 'investment institutions' in the Act includes all sorts of open-end and closed-end type funds, whether or not incorporated. It also includes funds established abroad, of which participations or shares are offered for sale or traded in The Netherlands.

The investigation may be carried out to verify compliance with the requirements of the Act. The person from whom information is requested must furnish the same within a period to be determined by DNB. The person who is the object of an investigation must give DNB access to all books and documents relating to the investment institution or, where applicable, the custodian or depository company and shall give all assistance necessary for the proper completion of the investigation. Any third party who keeps books and records is required to submit these books and records to DNB at its request.

Individualised information in respect of enterprises, institutions and depositaries obtained by DNB may not be published and must be kept secret: see art 19(5) of the Act. In addition, according to art 24, data compiled by DNB pursuant to the Act may not be disclosed or used other than for the purposes of the implementation of the Act.

The provisions of the STSA on insider trading

The provisions relating to insider trading were introduced in the Dutch Criminal Code on 16 February 1989, and were moved to the STSA effective as of 18 July 1992. Article 46 of the STSA sets out the principal insider trading prohibitions, and currently reads as follows:

'1.   It is prohibited for any person who has prior knowledge to commit or bring about any transaction in or from within the Netherlands in respect of
   a.   securities listed on a securities exchange authorised under Article 22 of the Securities Transactions Supervision Act, or on an officially authorised stock exchange established outside of the Netherlands, or securities that are likely shortly to be admitted to any such stock exchange;
   b.   securities of which the value is in whole or in part determined by the value of securities as described under a.

2. Prior knowledge is knowledge of any particulars of the legal entity, company or institution to which the securities relate, or concerning the trade in the securities:
    a. which has not been made public;
    b. the disclosure of which may reasonably be expected to have an effect, whether positive or negative, on the quoted price.
3. The prohibition of the first and second subsection is not applicable
    a. to the broker who, having prior knowledge with respect to the trade only, acts in accordance with the rules of good faith to carry out customers' orders;
    b. the legal entity, company or institution of which the employees involved in committing or bringing about transactions in the securities, have prior knowledge only of the trade; and
    c. the person who commits or brings about transactions to fulfil an enforceable obligation that already existed at the moment such person obtained the knowledge about the particulars referred to in paragraph 2.
4. Certain categories of transactions may be exempted by regulation from the prohibition of paragraph 1. In such exemption, distinctions may be made with respect to the persons who commit or bring about transactions, and the circumstances under which such transactions are committed or brought about.
5. With respect to criminal transactions as meant in the first subsection, the District Court of Amsterdam in first instance has exclusive jurisdiction.'

Subsection 4 provides for the possibility of exemptions. By a Regulation of 17 December 1998, six categories of transactions were given the benefit of exemptions, including (in each case subject to certain restrictive conditions which are not described here) the granting of options and similar instruments in the context of ESOP's, the exercise of such options and similar instruments, transactions necessary to fulfil existing obligations to transfer shares or depository receipts, stabilisation transactions, underwriting commitments and the issue of stock dividends. Clearly these exemptions are quite restrictive, and the Regulation has been heavily criticised by practitioners arguing that quite a few categories of transactions that are perfectly legitimate (for example, share redemption programs of public companies) ought also to have been included.

Article 46(a) contains a prohibition to 'tip off'. There is an exemption for persons acting in the normal course of their function or duties. There is also an exemption for entities where the employees that advise on securities trades do not have the insider knowledge that the entity itself could be deemed to have; this is clearly a statutory facility that allows banks and securities houses to provide securities investment advice, provided adequate Chinese Wall arrangements are put in place.

Until 1999, the insider trading rules in The Netherlands did not include a duty for insiders to notify transactions. As of 1999, this duty to notify is imposed on certain categories of insiders. This is provided in art 46(b) and (c) of the STSA, complemented by the Regulation of the Minister of Finance dated 29 June 1999. Notifications must be made to the Securities Board of The Netherlands, the AFM. The AFM maintains a public register of such notifications. The categories of insiders concerned comprise (subject to certain qualifications and exceptions which are not detailed here) quoted companies themselves, directors and supervisory directors of these quoted companies, directors and supervisory directors of certain other companies belonging to the same group, certain shareholders (and the directors and supervisory directors of such shareholders), certain family members of insiders and, finally, members of works councils of the quoted companies concerned. Clearly, the circle of insiders on whom the duty to notify is imposed is quite wide, in fact, significantly wider than in many other jurisdictions, including the US and the UK.

Since 1987, the Amsterdam Stock Exchange required quoted companies to have a Model Code. Effective as of 1 January 1999, there is now a statutory duty for quoted companies to have an internal regulation, set out in art 46(d) of the STSA. The internal regulation must comply with the rules set out in an implementing Regulation of the Minister of Finance dated 15 December 1998. These rules provide, inter alia, for the installation of a 'central officer', a compliance officer, in each quoted company and for the restrictions to be imposed on employees and other deemed insiders. The internal regulation should also provide for 'open' or 'closed' periods, and for the registration of transactions in securities issued by the quoted company in question.

Pursuant to art 2 of the Economic Offences Act (EOA) violation of the insider trading prohibitions of the STSA constitutes a criminal offence (misdrijf). The Economic Surveillance Department (Economische Controle Dienst, ECD) is authorised to investigate possible violations of art 46 of the STSA. The investigative powers based on the EOA are more extensive than those based on the Dutch Criminal Procedure Code. It will be clear that banks cannot invoke any duty of secrecy in relation to these investigations. Furthermore, the AFM has also been granted extensive investigative powers pursuant to the STSA, as well as the authority to apply administrative sanctions and measures.

In furtherance of its powers and duties under the STSA, the STE (as the AFM was then called) promulgated a so-called Further Regulation on the supervision of securities trade of 28 April 1992 (Nadere regeling toezicht effectenverkeer, the Further Regulation), containing, inter alia, rules of conduct to be observed by securities institutions. The current version of the Further Regulation is dated 17 July 2002.[13] Article 22 of the Further Regulation states that securities institutions must have an internal regulation containing a code of conduct for dealing with price sensitive data. Article 23 of the Further Regulation, in addition, requires securities institutions to have a code of conduct for securities transactions carried out by employees for their own account. Each securities institution must have a supervisor (a compliance officer) who reviews compliance with the terms of these two codes.

Chinese Walls

The Dutch association of banks (Nederlandse Vereniging van Banken) has promulgated a specific code of conduct concerning Chinese Walls, to which banks

---

13   Stcr 2002, 136.

in The Netherlands are expected to conform. This Code is dated 8 November 1990. It has not since been modernised or adapted to current thinking on Chinese Walls.

The Code prescribes that the institutions concerned must establish a procedural distinction between their credit business, underwriting business and brokerage business. The existence of these Chinese Walls must also be notified to customers; in addition, customers will need to be informed that if the institution concerned has price-sensitive information, such information will not be passed on to customers and will not be used in giving investment advice to clients. Banks and securities institutions are furthermore required to appoint within their organisation a so-called 'supervisor' (toezichthouder) whose function will be to effect compliance control. The code not only imposes obligations on the institutions, but also on the individual employees of such members. Employees must observe certain rules relating to the handling of price-sensitive information. They are prohibited from trading in securities or advising on investments in securities while they have inside information on such securities. This prohibition does not apply if the insider information relates to the 'trade in securities' (as opposed to insider information relating to the company to which the securities in question relate) and the members concerned act in good faith on the instructions of clients.

One of the principal aims of Chinese Walls is to ensure that sensitive knowledge available to one or more persons working on a particular matter is only legitimately used for that particular matter and is not divulged to others working in the same firm where such sensitive information may be used for other purposes. Is the establishment of an effective Chinese Wall sufficient to avoid application of the insider trading prohibition of art 46 of the STSA? There is no case law on this issue, and Dutch legal doctrine is not uniform in its answer to the question. The problem here is that grounds for disculpation will have to be found by application of general principles of criminal law, which as such are ill-suited to cope with questions of this kind. In relation to this, it is interesting to note that in the explanatory notes (Memorie van toelichting) relating to the 1999 amendments to the insider trading provisions in the STSA, the Minister of Finance made the comment that the mere existence of Chinese Walls would not be sufficient to exculpate a bank, but that it would need to be demonstrated that the Chinese Walls concerned actually work.[14]

The existence of Chinese Walls raises a number of legal questions, mainly in consequence of the fact that the above-mentioned Code is insufficiently clear as to what a Chinese Wall actually is, for which purposes exactly it is being erected and in which instances information is nevertheless permitted to cross. The Code, in the present writer's view, insufficiently recognises that, depending on which departments they are erected between, these Walls have different functions and purposes. It also does not effectively address the reality that most banks operate various of their banking and related activities through group companies. The Dutch Association of Banks would be well-advised to amend the Code so as to become less abstract, and more modern and practicable. The principles to be applied are quite clear. There are, however, two complex issues which need careful consideration: (i) the formulation of the exceptions to the principles; and (ii) how to ensure that the rules together with

---

14   See *Kamerstukken* II (1996–97) 25095, p 3, n 6.

their exceptions have the desired external effect (so that banks have an adequate measure of protection against third-party civil liability).

Further Dutch developments in relation to enhancement of financial integrity and the combat of terrorist financing

In consequence of the terrorist attacks in the US of 11 September 2001 and the ensuing actions of, amongst others, the Financial Action Task Force, the Dutch Ministers of Finance and Justice on 16 November 2001 issued a Memorandum on the integrity of the financial sector and the combat of terrorism (Nota integriteit financiële sector en terrorismebestrijding). The Memorandum contemplated further amendments to existing financial laws and regulations, which included stronger integrity requirements imposed on financial institutions that are subject to licence requirements; supervision of trust companies and finance companies (both categories of institutions had hitherto not been subject to specific supervision, since they could effectively avail themselves of exemptions from the Dutch Banking Act and STSA licence requirements); the strengthening of the supervision of money transfers; widening the scope of the requirement to identify customers when providing financial services to them; and the requirement to notify unusual transactions. A number of other areas of concern were noted in the Memorandum: the need to counter the possible abuse of physical bearer securities (principally by moving towards complete dematerialisation of bearer securities); the need to make money laundering a separate criminal offence; the need to counter the abuse of corporate entities; the need to enhance the exchange of information between Central Banks and supervisory authorities; the need to enhance the investigative powers of the public prosecutors and police (especially financial investigations); and so forth.

A number of these concerns have, meanwhile, already led to amendment of the financial regulatory regime. Examples of this are the now more stringent provisions of the Act on Identification when Providing Services and the Act on the Notification of Unusual Transactions, both discussed above. On several other issues, new legislation is being prepared or has recently been adopted. These new (draft) Acts are not listed here comprehensively, but note that the following Acts are in the process of being promulgated or have over the past few months come into force:

1   A draft Act whereby the Code of Criminal Procedure will be amended so as to increase the powers of investigators to demand information from financial institutions. This is in furtherance of the Luxembourg Protocol of 16 October 2001.

2   A draft Act whereby various financial acts (including the Dutch Banking Act and the STSA) will be amended so as to enhance the flow of information between supervisory authorities in The Netherlands and authorities and agencies in other countries. This draft act implements Council Directives 2000/12/EC and 2000/64/EC, dated 7 November 2002.

3   A draft Act amending the STSA, whereby the supervision of securities transactions is extended to all parties that are active on the securities markets (rather than just to specifically described institutions that are subject to licence requirements).

4   A draft Act updating and harmonising the existing financial laws.

5   An Act on money transfer institutions (geldtransactiekantoren); this Act has meanwhile, in July 2002, been promulgated.
6   An Act, also promulgated in July 2002, amending the Dutch Banking Act so as to introduce supervision over so-called electronic money institutions (instellingen voor electronisch geld).
7   A draft Act amending the 1977 Sanctions Act, whereby, amongst others, increased regulatory powers are given to the Minister of Finance, including the right to require financial institutions to provide information on request.
8   A draft Act submitting trust offices to government supervision.
9   Regulations dated 1 July 2002 of the Minister of Finance whereby finance companies are subject to more stringent registration requirement and whereby the scope of the exemptions regime is significantly narrowed.

The sense of urgency that some of these initiatives had in the immediate aftermath of 11 September 2001 has now to a certain degree been replaced by a more mature approach to the monumental task that the Dutch legislator has set itself. The complexity of these exercises is increased by other developments that are taking place at the same time: (i) the need, perceived by the Minister of Finance and the financial regulators, to arrive at a complete overhaul of the statutory supervisory regime applicable to the financial sector in The Netherlands (the Ministry of Finance is reportedly still aiming to have this new regime in place in 2005); and (ii) the need to reorganise the financial supervisory structure whereby a 'functional' approach is introduced (ie in summary, the prudential supervision, on the one hand, and the supervision of conduct rules, on the other, are entrusted to different supervisory agencies). This latter reorganisation is now well underway in The Netherlands.

20 Norway

Terje Sommer

INTRODUCTION

Bank confidentiality rules were introduced in Norwegian legislation as early as in 1924 when the two first Banking Acts were passed by Stortinget (the Norwegian Parliament). There was one act for savings banks and one act for commercial banks. Two new acts were passed in 1961 and the scope of the confidentiality rules from 1924 was carried on into the new legislation and also into a new Finance Activity Act 1988, which supplements the two Banking Acts.

The rules have always aimed at protecting bank customers against the bank giving confidential information about them or their relationship with the bank to others. The obligation to keep customer information confidential is directed to the individual officer and employee of the bank, not at the bank itself. Any breach of the rules is a criminal offence. This model has been used for newer confidentiality rules in the Securities Trading Act 1997, the Insurance Activity Act 1988 and the Stock Exchange Act 2000.

Although over time confidentiality provisions have been introduced in a number of pieces of financial legislation, the effect of the rules has at the same time been diluted by exemptions for the benefit of, inter alia, tax authorities, police, competition authorities, the Banking Insurance and Securities Commission, the stock exchange and even spouses under certain circumstances. Last, but not least, rules implementing the EC Money Laundering Directive[1] oblige individual officers and employees working within the financial community under certain circumstances to give otherwise confidential information of their own accord to central prosecution authorities.

The traditional Norwegian confidentiality provisions do not regulate how financial institutions shall collect and store information about customers. Such rules are laid down in the Personal Data Act 2000, which implemented the EC Personal Data Protection Directive.[2] In contrast to the confidentiality rules in the financial legislation, the Personal Data Act only applies to information about physical persons.

1   Council Directive 91/308/EEC.
2   Council Directive 95/46/EC.

The current confidentiality provisions were made for a quite different society and appear not to be well suited in all respects for today's society, and there is therefore a need for modernising the rules. A public commission, the Banking Law Commission (the Commission), is reviewing the financial institutions and credit legislation, aiming to modernise, co-ordinate and revise it. In its Sixth Report,[3] the Commission discusses, among other things, confidentiality of customer particulars and proposes new rules. While primarily the current legislation will be discussed herein, references will also be made to the Commission's proposal where relevant.

CONFIDENTIALITY RULES – PERSONAL DATA RULES

As mentioned above, the bank confidentiality rules in Norway are directed to the individual officer and employee of the bank and not at the bank itself. Bank confidentiality rules protect all customers, both physical persons and legal entities.

Although Norway is not a member of the EU, it has, as a party to the EEA agreement, undertaken to implement the various EU/EC Directives.

The Personal Data Act implements Council Directive 95/46/EC. The Directive only protects physical persons, and the Act regulates the collection and treatment of personal information and imposes restrictions on the delivering of such information to others.

According to the Personal Data Act, financial institutions are under certain conditions allowed to collect and process personal data about customers being physical persons. Disclosure of such information can only take place to the extent allowed under the Act. These restrictions come in addition to restrictions imposed in confidentiality rules elsewhere in the legislation, so that the strictest rule will always apply. Today, there is some inconsistency between the general rules in the Personal Data Act and the specific confidentiality rules elsewhere in the legislation. This will be addressed by the Commission.

BANK CONFIDENTIALITY RULES

The present confidentiality rules can be found in the Commercial Bank Act 1961 and the Savings Bank Act 1961. Section 18 of the Commercial Bank Act (which is similar to the corresponding provision in the Savings Bank Act) reads as follows:

> 'Elected officers, employees and auditors of a commercial bank are obliged to treat as confidential any information which comes to their knowledge by virtue of their position concerning the bank or a customer thereof, or another bank or its customer, unless they are obliged to disclose information pursuant to this or any other Act. The duty of confidentiality does not apply to information which the board of directors or anyone authorised by the board discloses on behalf of the bank to another bank.
> Notwithstanding this provision, the bank may carry on credit reference activity in accordance with the laws applying thereto.'

3   NOU 2001:23.

In principle, the confidentiality obligations apply to all matters which officers, employees and auditors receive knowledge of in their position in the bank. 'In connection' means that the person must have received the information in his capacity as employee, officer or auditor, irrespective of whether he actually received the information at the time when he was working. The duty of confidentiality extends only to information which was not publicly known or available at the time, but, for example, was made available through newspaper, television, radio, the Internet or because it was available upon search of public registers.

The duty of confidentiality extends in principle to any disclosure of such information, also internally in the bank, except that information can be given on a 'need to know'- basis. In particular, confidential information can not freely be given to other legal entities within the same financial group: see 'Information exchange within group' below.

The confidentiality rules in the Banking Acts do not deal with the question of outsourcing or use of external consultants such as lawyers etc. It has in practice been accepted that confidential information can be disclosed to external consultants, but the Banking, Insurance and Securities Commission (BISC, which supervises banks, insurance companies and investment firms) has in its above-mentioned circular stated that they would regard such consultants as being directly subjected to the confidentiality rules in the Banking Acts. It will be the obligation of the outsourcing entity to ensure that such consultants undertake to keep information received confidential.

In late 2002, Stortinget approved the government's proposal for new rules for securitisation. Under these rules, financial institutions wishing to assign a loan portfolio to a non-financial institution must notify the borrowers, who must object within a time of not less than three weeks. Under the Financial Contracts Act 1999, a financial institution may transfer a loan to another financial institution without the borrower's consent. The borrower shall, however, be notified about the transfer. Neither of these sets of rules authorise the release of confidential information about the borrower(s), and specific consent must therefore be obtained. In the preparation documents for the new securitisation rules, the Ministry of Finance expressly states that when the seller is going to act as a service provider/manager of the sold loan portfolio, the seller may not disclose confidential customer information to the purchaser without customer consent, although it is acknowledged that the purchaser may have a legitimate interest in such information. The rules only apply to financial institutions.

A bank can of course disclose information about a customer to the customer. Under the Personal Data Act, a customer will also have a right to demand to see information registered on him. Norwegian banks (and other financial institutions) generally follow a strict practice when it comes to disclosing confidential information about customers to a person who purports to act on the customer's behalf. In many cases, for example, for companies, deceased persons and customers subject to bankruptcy proceedings, the relevant legislation will give the necessary directions. Problems may, however, arise when the customer is a non-resident of Norway: see the discussion starting at Extra-territorial aspects below.

Breach of the confidentiality rules in the Banking Acts is a criminal offence (also when committed through negligence) and is punished by fines or, in particularly aggravating circumstances, by imprisonment not exceeding three months.

The Commission proposes to introduce a two-tier system, with one set of rules directed towards the individual officer, employee or auditor and another set of rules directed to the institution itself. Also nder the proposal, those who carry out work for the institution will be directly subjected to these rules. BISC (the supervisory authority) may under the proposal dispensate from or suspend the confidentiality rules, in whole or in part, in respect of a finance institution. It is not known when the Commission's proposal will be put before Stortinget. The proposal, which will then be made by the government, may look different in many aspects.

OTHER FINANCIAL CONFIDENTIALITY RULES

The most important other confidentiality rules in the financial legislation are the following:

- the Finance Activity Act 1988, which contains a confidentiality rule for finance companies and mortgage institutions;
- the Insurance Activity Act 1988, which contains rules for both life and non-life insurance companies as well as pension funds;
- the Securities Trading Act 1997, which regulates investment firms (STA); and
- the Investment Fund Act 1981 (IFA).

In broad terms, the provisions in these acts are similar to the rules in the Banking Acts.

The confidentiality rules in STA and IFA go further than those in the Banking Acts and the Insurance Activity Act. In STA and IFA, 'neutral' customer information such as name and address is also comprised by the confidentiality rules and an investment firm or an investment fund manager may not disclose, even to other members of a group to which it belongs, that someone is a customer.

The Commission's proposal will result in one Act that will basically apply to all types of financial undertakings, including insurance companies. Investment firms and investment funds will still be subject to separate legislations.

INFORMATION EXCHANGE WITHIN GROUP

The wording of the confidentiality rules described above should in principle mean that customer information cannot be exchanged with other companies in the same financial group. BISC has, in a circular of 17 April 2000, accepted that 'neutral' information about customers, such as name and address, is not confidential information within a group. A bank or an insurance company may therefore under these rules disclose the name and address of a customer to other members within the group. Such information will, however, fall under the Personal Data Act and, for physical persons, a joint register would therefore need to be set up in accordance with, and with the appropriate approval, under the Personal Data Act. Following strong objections from the Norwegian Financial Services Association to this interpretation, BISC accepted in a letter of 27 April 2001 that general information about the customer relationship, such as the type of products provided to the customer, may also be exchanged within the group. More detailed information such as balances on accounts or loans will, however, be protected by the confidentiality rules and cannot be included in a 'group register' without an explicit consent from the customer.

Under the Banking Acts and the Finance Activity Act, finance institutions within a group must consolidate their exposure to customers. For this purpose, customer information must be exchanged.

It is important to note that if a financial group includes an investment firm or an investment fund manager, even 'neutral' customer information will be protected and cannot be included in a group register without the explicit consent of the customer.

RELEASE OF INFORMATION BY CUSTOMER CONSENT

A customer may also consent to disclosure of confidential information. Such consent should be informed and explicit. It will not suffice if a bank notifies its customers that, unless the customer objects, certain information will be disclosed to a third party. In particular, if the consent is of general nature, this must be very clearly spelled out. Of course, in certain cases a consent must be regarded as implicit, typically when a customer asks his bank to transfer money to a third party, or when he uses a bank card, since the bank then confirms that there are sufficient means for the payment in question.

BISC has, in the letter of 27 April 2001 referred to above, accepted that a 'passive' consent is sufficient where a fund management company in a group wishes to inform other group members about the fact that a customer is a shareholder in a particular fund.

EXCEPTIONS

Disclosure to other financial institutions

Under the Banking Acts and the Finance Activity Act, information can be disclosed to other finance institutions. Although the wording of the relevant paragraphs are quite wide, the right to disclose confidential customer information is probably limited to situations where a finance institution needs to discuss the customer with other finance institutions because of a special situation, for example, where the situation around the customer is such that an institution is exposed to a loss.

Under the Banking Acts and the Finance Activity Act, such disclosure shall be authorised by the board of directors.

To the extent a bank can disclose information under this rule, the bank should also be allowed to share the information with foreign finance institutions, provided that such institutions themselves are subject to a high standard of confidentiality.

Money laundering rules

Norway has implemented the EC Money Laundering Directive[4] in the Finance Activity Act, and will also have to implement the Second EC Money Laundering Directive.[5]

4   Council Directive 91/308/EEC.
5   Council Directive 2001/97/EC.

Under the money laundering rules, financial institutions must ensure that they know their customers and there are strict requirements regarding proof of identity for new customers.

In addition, as set out in the Directive, under certain circumstances employees of a financial institution are obliged to report suspected criminal acts to a special agency – the National Authority for Investigation and Prosecution of Economic and Environmental Crime in Norway ('ØKOKRIM'). The customer in question or an involved third party must not be informed about the report; Norwegian law is somewhat stricter on this point than the provisions in the Directive.

A person or an institution that wilfully does not comply with the above disclosure obligation is considered to be committing a criminal offence, which is punishable by fines or imprisonment for up to one year.

Actions against terrorism

Norway has implemented the UN Convention Against the Financing of Terrorism of 9 December 1999 and the UN Security Council Resolution 1373 of 28 September 2001 in a provisional decree of 2001.

If a bank or another financial institution is suspicious of a transaction being directly or indirectly connected with a terrorist act, the institution is obliged to report to ØKOKRIM information about all circumstances which may indicate such a connection. This obligation is also imposed on the officers and employees of the institution.

A person or an institution that wilfully does not comply with the above disclosure obligation is considered to be committing a criminal offence, which is punishable by fines or imprisonment for up to one year.

Court proceedings

Both in criminal and civil cases, the court can decide that employees of a financial institution shall give evidence of matters that normally would be subject to the confidentiality obligation.

Tax authorities

An important exception from the confidentiality rules is the right of the tax authorities to require detailed information about customers' accounts, and Norwegian financial institutions must annually report electronically details about customers' accounts which, among other things, includes balance and interest statements.

Banking, Insurance and Securities Commission Act

BISC carries out its activity in accordance with the Banking, Insurance and Securities Commission Act 1956 (BISC Act). The Act gives BISC wide authority to require all kinds of information from financial institutions, insurance companies, investment firms and investment fund managers which is necessary for their supervision.

Stock Exchange Act

Under the Stock Exchange Act 2000, a Norwegian stock exchange has a right to require information about transactions from its members. The Act states that stock exchange members, unhindered by confidentiality rules, are obliged to give information that is necessary if the stock exchange is to fulfil its legal obligations.

Competition Act

Under the Competition Act 1993, the competition authorities have the right to require information unhindered by confidentiality rules.

Marriage Act

Spouses have, under the Marriage Act 1991, the right to demand information about financial matters concerning each other from financial institutions and insurance companies unhindered by confidentiality rules.

The above list does not purport to be exhaustive, but it seeks to deal with the main issues.

EXTRA-TERRITORIAL ASPECTS – OVERVIEW

Identifying the problems

Separate problems concerning disclosure of information subject to confidentiality rules arise when extra-territorial aspects are involved. If, for example, a US branch of a Norwegian bank is asked by a US court or regulator to supply information maintained with its head office in Oslo, or a foreign bank's head office is requested by that country's courts or regulator to provide information regarding a customer's dealings with branches or subsidiaries in Norway, questions of sovereignty and confidentiality have to be addressed.

If a Norwegian bank or a branch or subsidiary of a foreign bank complies with the order of a foreign court or regulator, it may breach its duty of confidence to its customer. This may again give rise to legal action being commenced by the customer. On the other hand, failure to comply may leave the officers of the bank open to criminal charges, for instance, if a New York court finds the officer of the US bank in contempt of court because he cannot or will not provide information located in Norway.

There are a number of rules under Norwegian law that address such extra-territorial matters. However, not all problems are satisfactorily solved by these rules.

Law Courts Act

The Law Courts Act 1915 contains general regulations, applicable both to civil and criminal matters, with respect to legal requests from foreign courts and similar requests from a Norwegian court to a foreign authority with respect to taking of evidence.

Requests from foreign courts or other foreign authorities must be forwarded through the relevant Norwegian ministry (the Ministry of Justice or the Foreign Department, as the case may be) and will be passed on to the local city court. The court will initially resolve the matter of whether it has the competence to carry out the request or not. The request will be treated subject to Norwegian law.

Similarly, a Norwegian court may decide that a matter before it can be investigated abroad by requests for hearing of evidence by foreign authorities and courts.

Treaties and conventions

Norway is party to the Hague Convention on the Taking of Evidence Abroad in Civil or Commercial Matters of 1 March 1954. The Convention was ratified by Norway and came into force in 1958. Furthermore, Norway has ratified the Lugano Convention of 1988.

The incorporation of the Lugano Convention into Norwegian law is to be understood in such a manner that the regulations of the Convention, as lex specialis, supersede contradictory regulations, for example, in the Civil Procedures Act 1915.

The Lugano Convention is concerned with civil matters, and does not, for instance, include matters of tax or bankruptcy.

Norway entered into a treaty with the UK regarding Civil Procedures on 30 January 1931. The treaty has a separate section with respect to the taking of evidence. The treaty is no longer of any great importance, since the UK joined the Treaty on Taking Evidence of 18 March 1970 and the Convention on Service of Process of 15 November 1965, to which Norway is also a party.

Scandinavian Witness Act

Persons living in the Scandinavian countries, ie Denmark, Finland, Iceland, Sweden and Norway, are according to the Scandinavian Witness Act 1975 obliged to give evidence before each respective national court where a matter is being treated.

A Norwegian court may summon Scandinavian persons and command them to appear as witnesses before the courts of Norway. The courts may only summon a witness when it is important that the witness gives his explanation in Norway and his explanation must be deemed to be important for the matter at hand. When making this evaluation the court shall consider the importance of the case and whether the summons would greatly inconvenience the witness. Normal procedural regulations are followed with respect to the examination of the witness.

This law has effect with respect to both civil and criminal matters.

Likewise, Norwegian citizens or persons having their domicile in Norway, Denmark, Finland, Iceland or Sweden have the same obligation to meet and give witness before the courts in these countries in accordance with the rules governing such procedures in each respective country and which in principle conform with the regulations in the 1975 Act.

OBTAINING INFORMATION FROM NORWEGIAN BANKS FOR USE IN FOREIGN CIVIL PROCEEDINGS

Introduction

A Norwegian court may issue an order for the obtaining of evidence in civil proceedings in courts of other countries upon request from that court, provided that the evidence requested relates to a matter which is being tried before the foreign court. The letter of request shall set forth the nature of the matter and shall be accompanied by a list of the questions which are to be asked of the witness, or contain precise instructions or information with respect to the matters about which the witness is to testify before the Norwegian court. The letter of request for a hearing before the Norwegian court can be denied if the courts of Norway find that the request would impair its sovereignty or security or is considered to be contrary to public interest.

Generally, it can be said that a person shall not be compelled to give any evidence which he could not be compelled to give in civil proceedings instituted under Norwegian law. The extent of disclosure to a foreign court shall not exceed that which would be available in Norwegian proceedings.

Subpoenas from other jurisdictions

If a foreign court serves a subpoena on an international bank in order to obtain information relating to its overseas branches or subsidiaries, and the bank makes a request or gives an order to its Norwegian branch to provide the same, the Norwegian officers of the bank may not breach their duty of confidence to customers by obeying and thus infringing the confidentiality laws of Norway where the information is maintained. Such information can only be made available through a decision made by the Norwegian courts as previously outlined.

The duty to appear before and give evidence to a Norwegian court

Regulations with respect to the duty to give witness before the courts are regulated in the Civil Procedures Act 1915. Certain categories of people have no right to explain themselves to the court without permission from the person who has the right of confidence. This principle extends, for instance, to lawyers and defence lawyers in criminal cases.

Bank officers and employees do not fall under this category. However, a witness may refuse to answer questions if he cannot reply without disclosing a commercial or operative secret, or on the principle of self-incrimination. Disclosure of secrets means matters which it is important to keep secret for competitive reasons. A legal duty of confidence with respect to other business matters does not exempt from the duty to appear as witness before the courts. In a case of disclosure of secrets, the court must evaluate each party's interest, and it will be essential how important the explanation is as evidence in the case. The court will also take into account how important the matter is to the parties involved.

These evaluations will be made when a witness refuses to answer a question and the other party demands that he shall explain himself notwithstanding the principle stated above. In such cases the court may oblige the witness to explain himself when after an evaluation of the two parties' interests it finds it is required. In such cases the court may decide that the explanation only shall be given to the court and the parties in closed hearings and under order of confidentiality.

Applied to a bank or another financial institution, its officers and employees, it could be of importance to the court when making its evaluation if the officer explains that in giving a reply he would be in violation of his duty of confidentiality under the financial laws. As explained above, a Norwegian court may, however, lift the duty of confidentiality and require a bank witness to testify.

Generally, a Norwegian court will not be able to ask for information which would be in violation of a bank's duty of confidentiality in the foreign country, unless the court has the power and is willing to lift the duty of confidentiality.

OBTAINING EVIDENCE ABROAD FOR USE IN NORWEGIAN CIVIL PROCEEDINGS

Introduction

In addition to the reverse situation of that described above, it may well be that a party that has brought proceedings in the Norwegian courts may wish to obtain evidence from, amongst others, foreign banks which are not a party to the proceedings. Where a claimant alleges that the defendant has misappropriated funds belonging to him and has transferred them through various banks in order to cover his tracks, the claimant may wish to obtain information of this nature. In such situations, Norwegian courts may at their discretion apply to the court in the country in which the relevant bank is situated for the requested information.

Letters of request

A Norwegian court can issue letters of request to obtain information from parties situated abroad. The success of such a request depends to a large extent on whether the country concerned is a party to a convention or treaty with Norway. As discussed above, Norway has passed an Act in 1975 with respect to witnesses from the other Scandinavian countries (the Scandinavian Witness Act) and, in addition, bilateral treaties exist (among others) between Norway and the UK and Norway and the Federal Republic of Germany. In addition, Norway is a party to the Hague Convention on the Taking of Evidence Abroad in Civil and Commercial Matters of 1970. Under the Hague Convention, a witness may be compelled to provide information in certain cases. Such information is not limited to oral evidence, but may require the witness to provide documentary evidence as well.

In relation to non-convention countries, a letter of request may still be issued by the Norwegian court, but whether the foreign court will assist or not is a matter of local law.

The Hague Convention 1970

Under the Hague Convention, when receiving a letter of request, the authority which executes a letter of request shall apply its own law as to the methods and procedures to be followed. However, it shall do its best to oblige the request as stated, if this is not impossible because of that country's internal practice and procedures or declared contrary to public interest.

In a declaration to the Hague Convention, Norway has stated that it will not execute letters of request issued for the purpose of obtaining pre-trial discovery of documents as known in common law countries. Furthermore, a letter of request shall not be used to obtain evidence which is not intended for use in proceedings; commenced or contemplated.

In executing a letter of request, the requested authority shall apply the appropriate measures of compulsion to the same extent as are provided by its internal law for the execution of orders issued by the authorities of its own country or all requests made by parties in international proceedings.

The Lugano Convention

As mentioned above, Norway is a party to the Lugano Convention, and there is nothing to prevent a claimant who has brought proceedings in Norway from bringing proceedings for disclosure of documents in the courts of the country in which the bank in question is based. Whether the foreign court will grant such an order will, of course, depend on local law.

OBTAINING EVIDENCE IN NORWAY FOR USE IN FOREIGN CRIMINAL PROCEEDINGS

Norway ratified the European Convention on Mutual Assistance in Criminal Matters 1959 in 1962. Norwegian authorities, when requested to do so by a letter rogatory from a foreign criminal court, may nominate a court in Norway to receive such of the evidence referred to in the request as appears to them to be appropriate, taking Norwegian law into account.

The Norwegian authorities must be satisfied that a criminal offence under the law of the country or territory in question has been committed, or that there are reasonable grounds for suspecting that such an offence has been committed; and proceedings in respect of that offence have been instituted in that country or an investigation into the offence is being carried out there.

OBTAINING EVIDENCE ABROAD FOR USE IN NORWEGIAN CRIMINAL PROCEEDINGS

As a reverse situation to that described above, a Norwegian court may issue a letter rogatory requiring assistance from another government to obtain evidence outside Norway, if an offence has been committed or there are reasonable grounds to suspect that an offence has been committed; and proceedings in respect of that offence have been instituted or the offence is being investigated by the Norwegian courts upon request from either the police, ØKOKRIM, BISC or any other appropriate authority.

When, for example, ØKOKRIM is investigating a possible criminal act, it may ask Norwegian courts to issue a letter rogatory to a court in another country and ask for investigation to be carried out before that court.

OTHER RELEVANT PROVISIONS

Money laundering rules

The money laundering rules mentioned above apply also to Norwegian branches of foreign banks as regards services provided in Norway. These rules are based on the EC Money Laundering Directive,[6] but are on some points somewhat stricter than the Directive. It is assumed that the specific Norwegian rules do not apply if a bank or another financial institution in an EEA state outside Norway provides services directly from its main office.

Cross-border activities

A foreign bank or other financial institution might provide services in Norway directly from its main office. If the institution is located in an EEA state, the Norwegian confidentiality rules shall apply according to a regulation of 1994 by the Ministry of Finance.[7] The ministry has the authority to make exceptions from this provision and let the law of the foreign state prevail. As for foreign institutions outside EEA, Norwegian rules and regulations apply in full.

Norwegian law does not have explicit rules of confidentiality for Norwegian banks or other financial institutions providing services directly in another country. It is assumed that the law of the foreign state applies in such cases, both inside and outside the EEA.

Banking, Insurance and Securities Commission Act

The members and officers of BISC are bound by an obligation of confidentiality. According to the BISC Act and regulations by the Ministry of Finance, the confidentiality rules do not, however, apply when it comes to supplying information to supervisory authorities that executes banking or other financial supervision in

---

6   Council Directive 91/308/EEC.
7   Regulation 7 July 1994 as amended, most recently 9 September 1998.

other countries, both inside and outside the EEA. BISC has made agreements about information exchange with a number of foreign supervisory authorities, but such agreements are not sufficient in order to demand information from private institutions or persons.

Disclosure obligation upon stock exchange members

As mentioned above, stock exchange members are obliged, unhindered by confidentiality rules, to give the stock exchange of which they are members information that is necessary to fulfil the legal obligations of the stock exchange. Firms with main offices outside Norway, but within the EEA, have the right to become stock exchange members, presupposing that they have the authority to provide investment services. The disclosure obligation applies also to foreign members, including banks and other financial institutions.

Foreign exchange regulations

In accordance with the Foreign Exchange Act 1950 and regulations given by the Ministry of Finance, banks and other financial institutions are obliged to report to the Central Bank on a monthly basis about the establishment of accounts in foreign banks used for business purposes and payments and settlements with foreigners. Furthermore, Norwegian banks have reporting obligations to the Central Bank when Norwegian residents transfer money abroad.

CONCLUDING REMARKS

In conclusion, it is fair to say that the obligation of bank confidentiality has been more or less eroded in several areas of national and international finance, both for control purposes and because of the internationalisation of the financial market. As has been shown, however, in other areas, especially with regard to securities trading, the principle of confidentiality has been further enhanced in several aspects of such business. Furthermore, the basic principle and obligation of confidentiality between a bank and its customer is still in force, apart from those specific laws and regulations which have been enacted contrary to that principle.

21 Panama

José Agustín Preciado Miró

OVERVIEW OF BANK CONFIDENTIALITY

As is the case with many long-recognised legal institutions, there is no single and generally accepted definition of what constitutes 'bank confidentiality' in Panama, but rather a wide spectrum of definitions that will depend on, among other things, the juridical nature under which the issue is analysed.

As for its regulatory basis, there is no specific body of law that encompasses and regulates bank confidentiality as a whole; one is able to find provisions related to it in a varied range of codes, laws, executive (presidential) decrees and regulatory dicta.

Several legal provisions have regulated – in one way or another – bank confidentiality in Panama, of which the following are worth mentioning:
- the Constitution of the Republic of Panama, on the inviolability of private correspondence and records;
- Law 18 of 1959, on numbered accounts;
- arts 88 and 89 of the Commerce Code, on general confidentiality safeguard principles for commercial activities in general;
- art 170 of the Criminal (Penal) Code, on professional secrecy; and
- Law 1 of 1984, on trusts.

The widely recognised principle on which bank confidentiality is structured in Panama is that banks are allowed to disclose information on their customers and their operations only if: (i) the customer duly authorises such disclosure; or (ii) if a competent authority in a criminal or tax-related investigation requests such information.

Panama's legal system has traditionally recognised as 'competent authorities' the Attorney - General Office (Procurador General de la Nación or Ministerio Público) and the judicial criminal courts, although recent Supreme Court rulings recognise as 'competent authority' the Ministry of Economy and Finances on tax evasion investigations and other criminal tax-related issues.[1]

---

1   See *Banco Continental de Panamá v Regional Revenue Administration* in 'Recent relevant court rulings'.

Information cannot be disclosed to foreign criminal authorities if such information is not requested formally through competent Panamanian officials and the order is deemed enforceable in the Republic of Panama.

Although several laws have been passed and international treaties adopted by Panama's Legislative Assembly, mostly on issues related to the illegal drug trade, corruption of government officials and money laundering, it is safe to say that the general principle on bank confidentiality has remained basically unchanged.

Panama's Banking Law (Law Decree no 9 of 1998) provides mechanisms under which any bank or the Superintendence of Banks may reveal information concerning the banks' clients. The Superintendence may only reveal information obtained in the exercise of its regulatory authority, regarding individual clients of a bank, to the competent authority through the mechanisms established by law within a criminal procedure initiated in Panama.

The Superintendence of Banks, and its officials, must guard the secrecy and confidentiality of all the information provided gathered within the scope of their functions. Reports or other documents, which pursuant to the banking legislation must be disclosed to the public, are exempt from this prohibition. Public officials must also remain bound by the secrecy provisions in the exercise of their functions, even after ceasing their office.

Any infraction of these provisions may be punished with fines of up to US$100,000, without prejudice of any civil and criminal sanctions which may be imposed.

Under art 337 of the Criminal Code, any public officer who discloses or publishes the documents or information that he possesses for reason of his job or office and which had to kept confidential may be sanctioned with imprisonment for between six and 18 months, or with 25 to 75 days-fine.[2]

INTERNATIONAL TREATIES AFFECTING BANK CONFIDENTIALITY ADOPTED BY THE REPUBLIC OF PANAMA IN RECENT YEARS

Inter-American Convention Against Corruption

By means of Law 42 of 1998, the Republic of Panama adopted the Organization of American States' (OAS) Inter-American Convention Against Corruption (Convención Interamericana Contra la Corrupción).

Among its basic principles, the Convention cites the following:
1   The fact that corruption undermines the legitimacy of public institutions and strikes at society, moral order and justice, as well as at the comprehensive development of peoples.

---

2   Art 48 of the Panamanian Criminal Code defines the concept of days-fine (día-multa) as: 'The obligation to pay a sum of money to the State, which shall be determined in accordance with the person's economic situation, and subject to his wealth, income, means of subsistence, expenses and other elements deemed appropriate by the Court.' It basically consists of a fine to be paid daily for up to 360 days. Failure to pay at any point results in imprisonment of the offender for a number of days corresponding to half the number of unpaid day-fines.

2   That representative democracy, an essential condition for stability, peace and development of the region, requires, by its nature, the combating of every form of corruption in the performance of public functions, as well as acts of corruption specifically related to such performance.
3   That fighting corruption strengthens democratic institutions and prevents distortions in the economy, improprieties in public administration and damage to a society's moral fibre.
4   That corruption is often a tool used by organised crime for the accomplishment of its purposes.
5   That, in some cases, corruption has international dimensions, which requires co-ordinated action by states to fight it effectively.

As stated in art II of the Convention, its purposes are:
1   to promote and strengthen the development by each of the states parties of the mechanisms needed to prevent, detect, punish and eradicate corruption; and
2   to promote, facilitate and regulate co-operation among the states parties to ensure the effectiveness of measures and actions to prevent, detect, punish and eradicate corruption in the performance of public functions and acts of corruption specifically related to such performance.

Article XIV of the Convention, relating to matters of assistance and co-operation, provides that states parties, always in accordance to their own laws, shall afford one another mutual assistance by processing requests from authorities that:

'in conformity with their domestic laws, have the power to investigate or prosecute the acts of corruption described in this Convention, to obtain evidence and take other necessary action to facilitate legal proceedings and measures regarding the investigation or prosecution of acts of corruption.'

The states parties, according to **art XIV** of the Convention, 'shall also provide each other with the widest measure of mutual technical co-operation on the most effective ways and means of preventing, detecting, investigating and punishing acts of corruption'.

Article XV, relating to measures regarding property, dictates that 'States Parties shall provide each other the broadest possible measure of assistance in the *identification, tracing, freezing, seizure and forfeiture of property or proceeds obtained, derived from or used in the commission of offenses established in accordance with this Convention*' (emphasis added).

The Republic of Panama made a reservation to this measure in that it will not consider itself bound to extend the actions of seizure of forfeiture of property envisaged under art XV of the Convention, to the extent that such actions violate the provisions of art 30 of the Constitution of the Republic, which prohibits the seizure of property as a penalty.

The specific issue of bank confidentiality **is addressed in art XVI:**
'1.   The Requested State shall not invoke bank secrecy as a basis for refusal to provide the assistance sought by the Requesting State. The Requested State *shall apply this article in accordance with its domestic law,* its

procedural provisions, or bilateral or multilateral agreements with the Requesting State .

2. The Requesting State shall be obligated not to use any information received that is protected by bank secrecy for any purpose other than the proceeding for which that information was requested, unless authorized by the Requested State.' (emphasis added).

It is clear that the text of the Convention in no way affects the long-standing Panamanian tradition regarding bank confidentiality, since the Convention specifically conditions its enforcement to be in accordance with the applicable domestic laws of the state parties and the relevant treaties or other agreements that may be in force between or among them.

Central American Convention for the Prevention and Persecution of Laundering of Money and Assets Related to the Illegal Drug Trade

In September 1998 the Republic of Panama adopted the Central American Convention for the Prevention and Persecution of Laundering of Money and Assets Related to the Illegal Drug Trade (Law 51 of 1998).

The Convention is based on the premise that the laundering of money and assets related to the illicit drug trade and connected crimes is a social plague that must be forcefully combated. It also recognises that the monies generated by these activities produce economic distortions to the local economies of each of the Central American nations and that the ultimate objective of money laundering is the legitimisation of monies.

Issues such as jurisdiction, seizure of assets, 'bona fide' third parties and treatment of seized assets are addressed by the Convention.

A provision reflecting modern 'Know Your Customer' practices is included in art 11, where it is mandated that, in those state parties where numbered, anonymous or any other accounts operated under representation are allowed, financial entities must know the real identity of their client in the event that such information is ever requested. Financial entities must use adequate means to verify the client's identity by means of passport or any other valid identification. In the event that the financial entity, for any reason, has doubts that the person they regard as their client is not the beneficial owner of the account, they must proceed by any means at their disposal to determine the identity of the actual beneficial owner.

Article 12 of the Convention decrees that all entities involved in financial intermediation must comply with any information request submitted to them by competent authorities.

Bank confidentiality principles remain unaltered by the provisions of this Convention, since it will only be applicable by competent authorities acting on criminal procedures. Article 19 states that no internal provisions of any of the state parties will be deemed as an impediment to comply with the Convention as long as the information is requested or shared by a competent authority in accordance to each party's laws.

RECENT LEGISLATION ON BANK CONFIDENTIALITY

Law Decree no 9 of 1998

In February 1998, Law Decree no 9 of 1998 replaced the outdated Cabinet Decree 238 of 1970 as the regulatory basis for the Panamanian banking system. Among several important innovations, Law Decree no 9 replaced the Banking Commission with the Superintendence of Banks as the regulatory entity for the banking system.

The traditionally accepted principles of bank confidentiality are recognised under arts 84, 85 and 86 of Law Decree no 9 of 1998.

Article 84 provides that information obtained by the Superintendence in pursuance of its duties related to individual clients may only be disclosed to a competent authority under legal provisions in force, within the scope of criminal procedures.

In addition, in accordance with the general principle stated above, art 85 provides that banks may only disclose information about their clients or their operations with their consent or attending the request of a competent authority as prescribed by law.

Infringements of these confidentiality principles will be penalised with fines of up to US$100,000 in addition to civil liability and imprisonment penalties imposed by the Penal Code (ten months' to two years': art 170).

Law 41 of 2000

By means of Law 41 of 2000, several modifications are entered into the Penal Code. It is important to point out for the purposes of this analysis that Law 41 doubles the prison term contemplated in art 170 of the Penal Code (cited above) if the violator of the secrecy principles is a public official that has obtained access to information in pursuit of a measure destined to prevent money laundering activities.

Decree no 163 of 2000

Decree no 163, issued by the President of the Republic of Panama on 3 October 2000, modifies the structure and some functions of the office of Financial Analysis Unit (Unidad de Analisis Financiero).

The Financial Analysis Unit was created by Decree no 136 of 1995 with the main purpose of identifying transactions that may be involved in money laundering operations.

Decree no 163 expands the authority of the Financial Analysis Unit to gather information from public and private entities, analyse such information, keep statistics, exchange general information with foreign offices and supply information to the Attorney-General's Office and the Superintendence of Banks related to activities that may be linked to money laundering operations.

Article 3 of Decree no 163 maintains the confidentiality principle by stating that, apart from the disclosure of information to competent authorities as authorised by the Decree, officials must maintain complete confidentiality and reserve in regard to the information they handle.

Law 42 of 2000

Law 42 of 2000 mandates a series of measures that seek to prevent the use of financial transactions for money laundering purposes. These measures are directed to banks, trust companies, money exchange and transfer entities, loan providers, co-operatives, stock exchanges and other institutions of similar nature dedicated to provide financial services and intermediation.

By means of Law 42 of 2000, the financial services entities to which it is directed must:

1 Properly identify their clients. They must require from their clients all business references and certifications evidencing the good standing of their corporations, identity of the directors, valid powers of attorney, legal representatives and any other evidence required to ascertain the identity of the beneficial owner of the account, be it direct or indirect.
2 Issue a declaration, and require from their clients all necessary information when executing transactions, or series of transactions above US$10,000. These declarations shall be submitted to the Financial Analysis Unit (Unidad de Analisis Financiero).
3 Review with special attention any transaction deemed suspicious and to communicate such transaction to the Financial Analysis Unit. The financial services entity must not reveal to the client nor to third parties the fact that it has disclosed information to the Financial Analysis Unit.

It is deemed by art 3 that any information disclosed to the Financial Analysis Unit will not constitute a violation to the professional secrecy principles, being added in art 4 the obligation that has any official, who by virtue of this law has received information, to maintain strict confidentiality. Violations to Law 42 of 2000, including the disclosure of privileged information by public officials, will be penalised with fines of up to US$1,000,000 in addition to other penalties applicable.

General Resolution SB no 02-2002

The Bank Superintendence approved, on 18 July 2002, General Resolution no 02-2002, which contains a Code of Ethics for the officials of the Superintendence.

For the purposes of this analysis, it is important to highlight art 16 of the Resolution, where special attention is given, once again, to the confidentiality issue, by stating that all Superintendence officials must keep secret facts and information they may have knowledge of because of their official duties. Furthermore, arts 34 and 35 of the Resolution place restrictions, based on the principles of confidentiality, professional secrecy and privileged information, on the handling of information by Superintendence officials.

RECENT RELEVANT COURT RULINGS

Banco Continental de Panamá v Regional Revenue Administration[3]

The Regional Revenue Administration of the Province of Panama, during the course of a *tax evasion investigation*, requested from Banco Continental de Panamá, SA (a Panamanian bank) information related to transactions performed by some of the bank's clients.

In this case, Banco Continental de Panamá, SA argued before the Supreme Court that the Regional Revenue Administration may not be deemed a 'competent authority' and therefore it was not obligated to surrender the requested information, since such request violated the inviolability of private documents recognised by art 29 of the Constitution of the Republic of Panama.

The Supreme Court ruling recognised that the banking secrecy and confidentiality principles are not absolute, as excluded from such principles are information that banks must disclose to competent authorities in tax-related criminal investigative processes. The Supreme Court ruled that since the Regional Revenue Administration is in charge of investigating and prosecuting tax-related criminal cases, it is, for these purposes, a competent authority.

Banco Exterior, SA v General Revenue Administration[4]

The General Revenue Administration, during the course of an *audit* (non-criminal tax investigation), requested from Banco Exterior, SA (the Panamanian branch of a Spanish bank) information related to transactions performed by some of the bank's clients.

It was successfully argued by Banco Exterior, SA that the General Revenue Administration was not authorised to request information to banks during the course of non-criminal tax audits.

The Supreme Court ruled that banks are not obligated to disclose information related to its clients to the General Revenue Administration or any other tax authority, unless such tax authority issues an order to request information during a tax-related criminal investigation.

Vladimiro Montesinos: request to lift bank confidentiality made by the Republic of Peru[5]

A request by the Government of the Republic of Peru was made to the Republic of Panama petitioning the disclosure of information related to former Peruvian official, Vladimiro Montesinos. Some of the information requested was related to Montesinos' accounts in banks in Panama.

3   13 May 1997.
4   22 June 1998.
5   21 February 1998.

By virtue of art 101 of Panama's Judicial Code, the Supreme Court must rule on the legality of a foreign authority request before it may be enforced in the Republic of Panama.

In this case, the Supreme Court ruled that the request was enforceable in the Republic of Panama, and that any request of information made to banks must be satisfied by them. The Supreme Court based this ruling on the fact that the request was being made by a Peruvian competent authority investigating a criminal matter which is also regarded as a crime in Panama.

CONCLUSIONS

As many recent developments in several areas of the law in the Republic of Panama have important links to the issue of bank confidentiality, two realities become apparent in this analysis:

1   that the efforts to combat crimes such as government corruption and the illicit drug trade, and connected crimes such as money laundering, have led the way on domestic and international legislative initiatives on issues affecting bank confidentiality; and
2   that the general principle on bank confidentiality that has ruled for decades in the Republic of Panama (ie that banks may only disclose information on their customers and their operations if the customer has authorised such disclosure or if a competent authority in a criminal or tax-related investigation requests the information) has remained unscathed.

It is this fine line between aggressively prosecuting and punishing crimes and criminals and at the same time safeguarding the intimacy of the legitimate investor, businessperson or account holder, which public officials, lawyers, accountants, bankers and other professionals find themselves walking on a daily basis in Panama.

It is fair to say that the Panamanian banking community has taken a leading role in working with government officials and legislators in order to adopt whatever measures are needed to prevent the use of the Panamanian banking system for money laundering purposes. These measures, along with a stern self-regulation imposed by the banks, have been key factors in allowing authorities to prevent and persecute money laundering and other financial crimes while preserving the long recognised and enforced bank confidentiality principles.

22 Poland

Tomasz Wardyñski

INTRODUCTION

The transformation of the Polish economy which started in 1989 and the attendant increasing number of commercial entities and the rapid development of their activities, has meant that information possessed by banks about their customers has become very useful to a number of bodies who, therefore, have expressed a need for it. Criminal investigative authorities, judicial bodies, tax authorities, banking supervisory bodies and common commercial entities have also been attempting to convince banks that they should have access to information about bank customers.

At the same time as the restrictions imposed on commercial activity by the previous regime were being eased, a number of spectacular financial dealings of a dubious, if not fraudulent, nature surfaced, indicating, quite clearly, the absence of a well-developed system of controls of the marketplace and, of course, banking, such as may be expected in a developed market economy.

The provisions of the Banking Act of 31 January 1989 did not regulate bank confidentiality satisfactorily and precisely, and those matters were not satisfactorily clarified until 1997.

Poland's aspiration to accede to the EU required Polish legislation and practice to be adjusted to that of the EU.

On 1 February 1994, the Europe Agreement, establishing an association between the European Communities and their member states, of the one part, and the Republic of Poland, of the other part, came into force, which by arts 69 and 83 obliges Poland to approximate, among others, its banking legislation to European standards.

Moreover, it must be stressed that the obligation to keep banking details confidential falls under art 8, cl 1 of the European Convention on Human Rights, concerning the right to privacy.

THE RULE OF CONFIDENTIALITY UNDER POLISH LAW

Source and scope

The concept of bank confidentiality arises from art 104 of the Banking Act, dated 29 August 1997.

The provisions of that article significantly improved the regulations under the previous banking law of 1989 and reflect art 16 of the Second Banking Directive[1] of 15 December 1989 on the co-ordination of the laws, regulations, administrative provisions relating to the taking up and pursuit of the business of credit institutions and amending Council Directive 77/780/EEC.[2]

Article 104 defines banking confidentiality in three dimensions: persons, who are responsible for maintaining banking confidentiality; the ambit of information which is subject to the rule; and the time within which information is to be kept confidential.

Banks are subject to the requirement of confidentiality, and art 104 also extends that obligation directly to bank employees and the persons entrusted with implementing actions by banks.

The provision applies to the following information:

1   any information concerning bank activities and parties to agreements, obtained during negotiations and connected with conclusion of an agreement with a bank and performance, thereof, except for information the disclosure of which is indispensable for the proper performance of the agreement by a bank;
2   any information about the persons, who are not parties to the agreements referred to above, but who performed specific actions in connection with the conclusion of such agreements, except for those situations where legislation anticipates disclosure of such actions; and
3   any information to be provided to the police under the conditions specified in art 20, paras 4 to 10 of the Police Act of 6 April 1990, and concerning notification which is referred to in art 20, para 13 of that Act. Under art 20, para 3, to be read in conjunction with para 5, the police are entitled to use the information processed by the banks which is subject of bank secrecy, upon the consent granted by a relevant district court.

A literal interpretation of art 104, para 1 of the Banking Act suggests that bank confidentiality does not cover the information on persons who have not concluded an agreement (with the bank). Legal opinion, however, rejects that interpretation, arguing that bank confidentiality arises at the time when the bank is provided with the information covered by the scope of the article, regardless of whether an agreement is concluded or not. It seems a judicial ruling is required finally to decide the matter.

Information which falls within the scope of the list above is to be kept confidential indefinitely.

The law allows disclosure in only two situations: upon the request of institutions, or persons, specified by law; or with the written consent of the person whose information

---

1   Council Directive 89/646/EEC.
2   Currently, it is art 30 of the EC Banking Directive, Council Directive 2000/12/EC, on taking up and pursuit of the business of credit institutions.

is covered by the provision. Such consent has to specify the information and a person to which the information can be disclosed.[3]

Criminal and civil liability

Disclosure of confidential banking information constitutes a criminal offence in Poland.

Article 171, para 5 of the Banking Act states that anyone who, being obliged to keep banking information confidential, discloses or uses such information in breach of the authorisation specified in the legislation, shall be punishable by a fine of up to PLN 1,000,000 and imprisonment for up to three years.

The criminal sanctions cover both bank employees and persons entrusted to carry out actions by the bank, who are mentioned in art 104, para 1 of the Banking Act, as well as persons to whom such information is disclosed, upon their request, under art 105, para 1 of the Banking Act, which will be discussed further below.

Provisions of the Banking Act also regulate some aspects of civil liability for breach of the rule of bank confidentiality.

Article 105, para 5 indicates who is to be liable and make good the loss resulting from breach of the rule. By that article, the bank is to be liable for the loss resulting from disclosure and use of such information inappropriately.

Article 105, para 5 is not a separate legal basis for bank liability, and needs to be read in conjunction with art 471 or 415 of the Civil Code, depending on whether the claim for loss is based on liability for breach of an obligation (statutory or contractual) or in tort.

Bank liability is excluded if the loss results from disclosure by the persons, or institutions, authorised by legislation to require banks to provide them with the information which otherwise is to be confidential.[4]

Remedies for breach of the duty of confidentiality

Article 104, para 1 of the Banking Act imposes a statutory obligation on the bank, bank employees and the persons entrusted to carry out actions by the bank to keep information concerning persons being a party to an agreement (with a bank) and the persons, who are not parties to such agreements but who performed certain actions in connection with conclusion of such agreements, confidential.

When the duty of confidentiality arises from an obligation (statutory or contractual), the person whose information is to be kept confidential may claim damages from a bank for breach of the obligation, unless the disclosure of the information is a consequence of circumstances for which the bank, its employees and the persons entrusted to carry out actions on behalf of the bank are not responsible.[5] The burden of proof that such disclosure is due to such circumstances lies with the bank.

The civil liability of a bank for breach of the obligation not to reveal confidential banking information can be limited by a contract concluded between a bank and a

3   Banking Act, art 104, para 2.
4   Banking Act, art 105, para 6.
5   Art 105, para 5 of the Banking Act, read in conjunction with art 471 of the Civil Code and art 104, para 1 of the Banking Act.

customer. Under art 473, para 1 of the Civil Code, a bank cannot, however, exclude liability for loss caused to a customer intentionally.

Limitation of bank civil liability to a customer for disclosing confidential information does not release a bank, bank employees and the persons entrusted to carry out actions by the bank from the criminal liability specified in art 171, para 5 of the Banking Act.

A person whose information is to be kept confidential by the bank can also seek damages in tort from a bank, provided that the person is able to prove that the disclosure was caused by the negligence of a bank, its employees or the persons entrusted to carry out actions by the bank, that losses were incurred and that a causal link exists between the two.

If it is decided by a court that bank confidentiality only covers persons who conclude an agreement with a bank, then those who provide a bank with the information which is covered by art 104, para 1 of the Banking Act, but who do not conclude an agreement, can claim for damages for disclosure on the doctrine of culpa in contrahendo, under art 415 of the Civil Code.

A claim for damages for disclosure of confidential information by an institution, or a person authorised by legislation to request that the banks provide them with confidential information can be based, depending on the circumstances, on one of the legal bases mentioned above, ie liability for breach of an obligation, tort or culpa in contrahendo.

Although it is not possible under Polish law to apply for an injunction to restrain a bank from disclosing confidential information on the basis of showing a mere intent of a bank to do so, an interim injunction may be possible when disclosure has already occurred and further disclosure is intended by a bank. For this to be possible, grounds for the claim would have to already exist, such a claim would have to be credible and the absence of an order for an interim injunction could make it impossible to satisfy the claim. An interim injunction is temporary relief and, therefore, a court will oblige a successful claimant to instigate proceedings against a bank for satisfaction of a secured claim within a specified period of time, which cannot be longer than two weeks.

Under art 18 of the Act on Combating Unfair Competition of 16 April 1993, which sets out the civil remedies for an act of unfair competition,[6] a customer (ie engaged in commercial activity)[7] may demand from a bank, if his interest has been threatened or infringed, that the bank:

1   Ceases to disclose the customer's business secrets.
2   Eliminates the effects of the disclosure of such secrets.
3   Issues, or publishes, one or more statements, with appropriate contents, and in a defined form.

---

6   An act of unfair competition is defined as the activity which is contrary to the law or good morals, if it constitutes a threat or infringes the interest of another undertaking or a customer (Act on Combating Unfair Competition, art 3, para 1). The act of unfair competition is, among others, a delivery, disclosure or making use of another person's information constituting secrets of a person engaged in commercial activity, or purchase thereof from a non-authorised person (Act on Combating Unfair Competition, art 11, para 1).
7   Act on Combating Unfair Competition, art 2.

4   Redresses any losses by paying damages, under general principles (ie under art 471 or 415 of the Civil Code).

5   Surrenders unjustified benefits to the customer, under general principles; this demand is based upon arts 405 to 414 of the Civil Code, by which any party who, without legal grounds, has gained a material benefit at the expense of another party shall be obliged to surrender that benefit (to the latter party) in kind and, if that is impossible, to surrender an equivalent monetary value. The duty to surrender the benefit includes not only any benefit gained directly, but also anything which in the case of sale, loss or damage, has been gained in exchange for that benefit, or as a redress of such loss or damage. This provision could be of particular use for benefits gained by the bank as a result of the use of confidential information concerning a customer for cross-selling.

6   Pay an appropriate amount of money to a specified social purpose connected with supporting Polish culture, or protection of national heritage – if such act of unfair competition was committed.

It is also possible to argue that the banking information is a personal asset, and as such is protected by the provisions of arts 23 and 24 of the Civil Code in the same way as personal correspondence, creative and scientific works and inventions.

On that basis it could be possible to seek an injunction because, in certain circumstances, revealing banking details could be detrimental to a person's social or commercial position and situation and could lead to the disclosure of other matters. Moreover, a customer can require a bank which has divulged confidential information, which constitutes a personal asset, to perform acts necessary to remedy the effects of such disclosure and, in particular, make or publish a statement with appropriate content and in a defined form. Irrespective of a customer's right to seek damages, under the general rules of the Civil Code a customer can require pecuniary damages for intangible harm inflicted (krzywda – this can include, for example, the psychological distress suffered, or the damage to the reputation of an individual, or a commercial entity). The amount of damages is set by the court.

EXCEPTIONS TO THE RULE OF BANK CONFIDENTIALITY

Article 105 of the Banking Act constitutes an exception to the principle of non-disclosure to third persons.

It provides for a wide range of persons or institutions which have ex lege access to confidential information. Banks, state bodies and persons to whom confidential bank information has been disclosed are obliged to use such information exclusively within the limits of the authorisation specified in para 1 of art 105.[8] This means that the confidential information received from a bank under art 105, para 1 or 2 of the Banking Act cannot be disclosed further to other persons or institutions, including those listed in that article, unless provisions of law provide otherwise.

Information exchanged between banks and provided to the National Bank of Poland

Article 105, para 1, point 1) of the Banking Act states that a bank shall be obliged to disclose confidential information to other banks and – on the basis of reciprocity –

---

8   Banking Act, art 105, para 3.

other institutions authorised by legal act to give credit, on debts and on bank account turnover and balances, to the extent necessary to give credit, make loans, bank guarantees and suretyships and with foreign exchange operations, and also in connection with consolidation of financial statements.

A bank shall also disclose confidential information to the National Bank of Poland needed for control and collection of data necessary to prepare a balance of payments and of foreign debt, and foreign obligations of the state, as well as to other banks which are authorised to act as an agent in execution of transfer of money abroad by residents and to make settlements in the country with non-residents, within the scope specified in the Act of 27 July 2002 on Foreign Exchange Law.[9]

Information disclosed to the Commission for Banking Supervision

A bank is also obliged to disclose the confidential information at the request of the Commission for Banking Supervision within the scope of supervision exercised under the Banking Act and the Act on the National Bank of Poland of 29 August 1997 inspectors of banking supervision, who are referred to in art 139, para 1, point 2 of the Banking Act, and the persons authorised by a resolution of the Commission for Banking Supervision within the scope specified in such authorisation:[10] art 105, para 1, point 2)a) of the Banking Act.

The obligation to disclose the confidential information to the above-mentioned persons is directly connected with the statutory supervisory tasks imposed on the Commission for Banking Supervision under art 25, para 2 of the Act on the National Bank of Poland and art 133 of the Banking Act.

In order for the Commission for Banking Supervision to fulfil such tasks, it is vested with wide control over banks. For instance, art 139, para 1, point 2) of the Banking Act states that the banks, as well as branches and agencies of foreign banks in Poland, shall be obliged to enable authorised persons to perform supervisory tasks specified in art 133, para 2 and, in particular, to make books, balance sheets, registers, plans, reports and other documents accessible to them, and enable them, upon a written request, to make copies of such documents and other carriers of information, and provide them with any explanations requested by such persons.

Information disclosed to courts, public prosecutors and court executive officers

Confidential information is to be disclosed, if requested, by:

9 Banking Act, art 105, para 1, point 3).
10 The following persons can be authorised on the basis of a resolution of the Commission for Banking Supervision to request a bank to provide them with the confidential information: (i) an auditor who examines a bank upon an order issued directly by the Commission for Banking Supervision (Banking Act, art 135, para 2), (ii) persons authorised in connection with performance of the consolidated supervision to perform on-the-spot checks in undertakings (ie among others, the banks) to which a bank, which is referred to in art 141f, para 1, point 1, is a dominant undertaking, or which have a close links with that bank, and in the undertakings which are a part of holding companies, referred to in art 141f, para 1, point 2-3 (Banking Act, art 141h) and, eventually, (iii) other persons authorised to perform the activities of the banking supervision, which are specified in art 133, para 2 of the Banking Act, and tasks of the Commission for Banking Supervision, specified in art 25, para 2 of the Act on the National Bank of Poland.

1   a court, or public prosecutor, in connection with criminal proceedings, or fiscal penal proceedings pending against the holder of an account being a natural person or in connection with application for legal aid made by a foreign country entitled to request for providing information being a bank secrecy, under an international agreement ratified by Republic of Poland;[11]
2   a court, or public prosecutor, in connection with criminal proceedings, or fiscal penal proceedings pending for an offence committed in connection with activities conducted by a legal person or an organisational unit having no legal personality – within the scope of bank accounts and banking operations performed by that legal person or unit;[12]
3   a court in connection with inheritance proceedings, or proceedings for division of marital property or lawsuit for maintenance or alimony payment pending against a natural person being a party to a contract;[13]
4   a court executive officer in connection with pending execution proceedings.[14]

Information disclosed to the directors of customs offices

Article 105, para 1, point 2)e) of the Banking Act states that a director of customs office shall be provided with the confidential information, upon request, if it is in connection with:

1   a criminal case or fiscal penal case pending against a natural person, being a party to a contract concluded with a bank;
2   a criminal case or fiscal penal case pending concerning an offence committed within the scope of activity of legal person, or organisational unit having no legal personality, who are holders of an account.

Under art 7, para 2 of the Customs Code of 9 January 1997, the banks are obliged to provide a director of customs office, upon request, with information on turnovers and balance of the bank accounts in connection with fiscal penal case pending:
1   against the holder of a bank account, being a natural person;
2   concerning an offence committed within the scope of activity of a legal person, or organisational unit having no legal personality, where such person or organisational unit are holders of a bank account.

The request of a director of customs office shall identify the holder of the account and the time for which the information is relevant.[15] The customs organs, in order to perform their statutory tasks, are entitled to collect and use the information, including personal data, and process it within the meaning of the provisions on protection of the personal data, also without the knowledge and consent of a person this data relates to. Administrator of such data is obliged to make it accessible on the basis of the individual authorisation issued by a custom organ, presented by a custom official together with an official identity card. Information on making such data available is protected in accordance with the provisions on protection of confidential information.[16]

11   Banking Act, art 105, para 1, point 2)b).
12   Banking Act, art 105, para 1, point 2)c).
13   Banking Act, art 105, para 1, point 2)d).
14   Banking Act, art 105, para 1, point 2)l).
15   Customs Code, art 7, para 3.
16   Customs Code, art 7, para 4.

Information disclosed to the President of the Supreme Chamber of Control

Article 105, para 1, point 2)f) of the Banking Act states that the President of the Supreme Chamber of Control shall be provided, upon his request, with confidential information (by the bank) to the extent necessary to carry out control proceedings specified in the Act of 23 December 1994 on the Supreme Chamber of Control.

The Supreme Chamber of Control is authorised, among others, to control the activity of the state and municipal legal persons, as well as activity of other organisational units and entities carrying out commercial activity within the scope they use state or municipal assets or resources and fulfil their financial obligations to the state.[17]

Banks covered by art 2 of the Supreme Chamber of Control Act are obliged, upon the request of the Supreme Chamber of Control, to deliver all, or any, documents and materials which are necessary to prepare and conduct the control, subject to the provisions on confidential information protected by legislation.[18] Authorised representatives of Supreme Chamber of Control are entitled, among others:

1   to have access to all, or any, documents connected with the activity of the controlled entity, collect and secure the documents and other evidence, subject to the provisions on secret information protected by legislation;[19]
2   to demand from the employees of an entity being inspected delivery of written and oral explanations.[20]

Information disclosed to the Chairman of the Securities and Exchange Commission

Confidential information shall be delivered to the Chairman of the Securities and Exchange Commission, upon request, by a bank within the scope of supervision under the Act of 21 August 1997 on Law on Public Trading in Securities.[21]

The Securities and Exchange Commission shall, among others, supervise the observance of the rules of fair trading and competition in public trading in securities and supervise the provision of public access to reliable information on the securities market.[22] In connection with the implementation of the tasks specified in art 13, para 1, point 1), the Commission, or its authorised representative, shall have access to confidential information and information being subject to professional secrecy in possession of those obliged to keep it secret (for instance, banks conducting the brokerage activity).[23]

Information disclosed to the President of the Board of Management of the Banking Guarantee Fund

The President of the Board of Management of the Banking Guarantee Fund is entitled to receive confidential information from a bank, to the extent specified in the Act of 14 December 1994 on the Banking Guarantee Fund.[24]

17   Act on the Supreme Chamber of Control, art 2.
18   Act on the Supreme Chamber of Control, art 29, point 1).
19   Act on the Supreme Chamber of Control, art 29, point 2)b).
20   Act on the Supreme Chamber of Control, art 29, point 2)e).
21   Banking Act, art 105, para 1, point 2)g).
22   Law on Public Trading in Securities, art 13, para 1, point 1).
23   Law on Public Trading in Securities, art 161, para 1.
24   Banking Act, art 105, para 1, point 2)h).

Under art 38, para 6 of the Act on the Banking Guarantee Fund, banks, which are covered by an obligatory deposit guarantee scheme, are obliged to provide the Banking Guarantee Fund with all information other than that provided to the National Bank of Poland which is necessary to fulfil the fund's tasks. The scope of such information is specified by the President of the National Bank of Poland, upon the motion of the Banking Guarantee Fund.[25] The tasks of the Fund cover, among others:

1   within the scope of operation of the mandatory and voluntary guaranteed deposit scheme, analysis of the information about entities covered by the deposit guarantee scheme;[26]
2   within the scope of giving the assistance to the entities covered by deposit guarantee scheme, control of appropriate use of the repayable financial assistance given to such entities in case of danger of insolvency, or for the purpose of purchase of the shares of the banks.[27]

Information disclosed to auditors

A bank is obliged to provide confidential information to a certified auditor, upon request, authorised to examine the financial statements of a bank, under a contract concluded with a bank.[28]

Information disclosed to the Retirement Pension Funds Supervisory Office

Confidential information is to be delivered by a bank, upon request, to the Retirement Pension Funds Supervisory Office, for supervision of the performance of a bank as a depositary under the Act of 28 August 1997 on Organisation and Operation of Retirement Pension Funds.[29]

Art. 204, para 2, point 2) of the Act provides that the person authorised by the supervisory body (ie Retirement Pension Funds Supervisory Office) is entitled to have access to the premises of a depositary to check whether activity connected with holding the assets of the funds complies with the law and the agreement on holding of the assets of the fund. The person carrying out the inspection has the right, among others, to: (i) check all books, documents and other sources of information; (ii) demand preparation and delivery of copies of such documents and sources of information; and (iii) require information from the members of the executive bodies and employees of the controlled entity.[30]

Information disclosed to the trustee and his deputy

According to art 105, para 2 of the Banking Act, the confidential information is to be also disclosed to a trustee and his deputy within the scope and according to the rules specified in the Act of 29 August 1997 on the Lien's Letters and the Mortgage Banks.

25   Act on the Banking Guarantee Fund, art 38, para 7.
26   Act on Banking Guarantee Fund, art 4, para 1, point 3).
27   Act on Banking Guarantee Fund, art 4, para 2, point 2), read in conjunction with point 1).
28   Banking Act, art 105, para 1, point 2)i).
29   Banking Act, art 105, para 1, point 2)j).
30   Act on Organisation and Operation of Retirement Pension Funds, art 204, para 3, points 1)–3).

Trustee and his deputy are appointed for each mortgage bank by the Commission for Banking Supervision. They cannot be the employees of a bank and their obligation is to control a mortgage bank[31] within the scope provided for in art 30 of the Act.

According to art 30 of the Act, the trustee is obliged to verify whether:

1   the obligations deriving from lien's letters being in circulation are secured by a mortgage bank in accordance with the provisions of the Act,
2   a bank-mortgage value of a real estate adopted by a mortgage bank has been established in accordance with by-laws, which are mentioned in art 22, para 2 of the Act,
3   a mortgage bank complies with the limits specified in art 18 of the Act (ie a total amount of nominal values of the mortgage lien's letters being in circulation),
4   a manner in which a mortgage bank runs a register for security of the lien's letters complies with the conditions of this Act,
5   a mortgage bank provides, in accordance with this Act, a security for planned emission of the lien's letters and control, whether the appropriate records have been made to the register for security of the lien's letters.

In order to fulfil his tasks, which are referred to in art 30 of the Act, a trustee is entitled to check at any time the accounting books, registers, plans and other documents of a bank.[32] The bank is obliged to provide a trustee and his deputy, in connection with performance of their duties and within the scope specified in para 1, with the confidential bank information.[33] Under, art 32, para 1b of the Act, a trustee and his deputy are obliged not to disclose the information, which they received during performance of their duties.

Information disclosed to the Social Insurance Institution

The banks are obliged, upon written request from Social Insurance Institution, to prepare and deliver information concerning numbers of the bank accounts of the

---

31   The activity of a mortgage bank covers, among others:
   1   granting the credits secured by a mortgage,
   2   granting the credits not secured by a mortgage, which are referred to in art 3, para 2 (ie credits which are granted to or which are partly secured by the National Bank of Poland, the governments or central banks of the member states of the European Union, OECD and the local authorities),
   3   purchase of the receivables of other banks deriving from the credits granted by those banks, which are secured by a mortgage, and the receivables deriving from the credits not secured by a mortgage, which are referred to in point 2,
   4   emission of the mortgage lien's letters the basis of which constitutes the receivables of a mortgage bank:
     –   deriving from the granted credits secured by a mortgage, and
     –   deriving from the purchased receivables of other banks to which those banks are entitled to due to the credits, which were granted by those banks and secured by a mortgage.
   5   emission of the public lien's letter the basis of which constitutes:
     –   the receivables of a mortgage bank deriving from the credits which are not secured by a mortgage, which are referred to in point 2,
     –   the receivables of other banks purchased by a mortgage bank deriving from the credits granted by those banks and not secured by a mortgage, which are referred to in point 2. (Act on the Lien's Letters and the Mortgage Banks, art 12).
32   Act on the Lien's Letters and the Mortgage Banks, art 32, para 1.
33   Act on the Lien's Letters and the Mortgage Banks, art 32, para 1a.

payers of insurance premium and to deliver details which allow identification of the holders of such bank accounts.[34]

Information disclosed to the institutions authorised to collect and provide information to the banks and other institutions authorised to grant credit

Under art 105, para 4 of the Banking Act, banks are entitled, jointly with bank commercial associations, to establish institutions authorised to collect and provide to the banks and other institutions authorised by legal act to give credits the information on debts and on bank account turnover and balances, to the extent to which such information is necessary to grant credit, loans, bank guarantees and suretyships.

Information disclosed to the Commercial Information Office

On 25 April 2003, the Act of 14 February 2003 on Making Accessible Commercial Information came into force amending, among others, provisions of the Banking Act.

The new Act details the principles and procedures for commercial information to be made available on the repayment credibility of other undertakings and consumers, in particular, information on delays in performance of pecuniary obligations to third parties who or which are not specified at the moment this information is made available.[35]

Under art 105, para 4a) of the Banking Act, the institutions established on the basis of art 105, para 4 of the Banking Act are entitled to provide the commercial information office, operating on the basis of the Act on Making Accessible Commercial Information with the information within the scope and upon the conditions defined in that Act.

Banks are entitled to provide offices, which are mentioned in art 105, para 4a) of the Banking Act, with information on obligations arising from the contracts connected with performance of the banking acts, if such contracts include a clause informing on possibility to provide such offices with such information.[36]

Under art 2 of the Act, commercial information is to mean information:

1   *With relation to a legal person or an organisational unit having no legal personality*: firm name, registered office and address, number under which the undertaking is registered in the appropriate register and indication of a register court, tax identification number, REGON number (ie statistical number), name and surnames of the persons being the members of the executive bodies, proxies of the undertaking or unit, main subject of the commercial activity.

2   *With relation to a natural person*: name and surname, nationality, residence, identification number, information concerning identity card, or other document confirming identity of a person, date of birth and, additionally, in relation to a natural person engaged in commercial activity, firm name, registered office and address, tax identification number, REGON number, number under which the

---

34   Banking Act, art 105, para 2a.
35   Act on Making Accessible Commercial Information, art 1.
36   Proposed art 105, para 4b) of the Banking Act.

undertaking is registered in the appropriate register and indication of a register court, name and surnames of the proxies, if any, and main subject of the commercial activity.

3   *On pecuniary obligation*: legal title, amount and currency, due amount, date of arising of amount due, state of proceeding concerning obligation, including information on court decisions, information on questioning by a debtor of the obligation in whole, or in part, date of sending of a call for payment, including warning on intention to provide the information to the office and a firm and registered office of such office, other information – delivered in the course and on conditions specified in art 10 of the Act.

Under art 14, para 4 of the Act on Making Accessible Commercial Information, the office shall disclose the commercial information on a consumer's obligations only to: (i) the undertaking, which has concluded with the office a contract on making such information accessible; (ii) other offices, or institutions, established on the basis of art 105, para 4 of the Banking Act, to comply with the motions requesting disclosure of such information; and (iii) entities specified in art 16, para 1 of the Act, ie National Prosecutor, Main Chief of the Police, Chief of the Government Security Office, General Inspector of the Fiscal Control, General Inspector of the Financial Information, directors of the fiscal offices, directors of the fiscal control offices, General Inspector of Banking Supervision, President of the Supreme Chamber of Control and the courts.

An undertaking, which concluded a contract on making commercial information accessible, and has been authorised by the consumer to request such information, is entitled to request that the commercial information on that consumer's obligations be disclosed to it within 30 days from a day such authorisation has been granted.[37]

If a consumer refuses to grant the authorisation mentioned above, an undertaking is entitled to refuse to conclude a contract on consumer credit or conclude such contract upon conditions less favourable for the consumer.[38]

A person or unit which received commercial information from the office is obliged to erase it within 90 days from the day it was received. A person or unit receiving the commercial information concerning a consumer is not permitted to disclose it to other persons. The obligations deriving from the last two sentences do not apply to the entities listed in art 16, para 1 of the Act on Making Available Commercial Information.[39]

Information disclosed to the state security service and the police

Under art 105, para 1, point 2)k) and l) of the Banking Act, a bank, upon request, is obliged to deliver confidential information to:

1   the state security services and, holding written authorisation, their officials or soldiers, within the scope necessary for conducting verification proceedings pursuant to provision of non-public information; and

2   the Police, if it is necessary for effective crime prevention, detection thereof, or for determining the perpetrators thereof, and obtaining evidence under the rules

---

37   Act on Making Accessible Commercial Information, art 15, para 1.
38   Act on Making Accessible Commercial Information, art 15, para 2.
39   Act on Making Accessible Commercial Information, art 17.

and procedure referred to in art 20 of the Police Act of 6 April 1990. Under art 20, para 3, in conjunction with para 5 of the Police Act, the police are entitled to use the information processed by the banks, which is subject of bank secrecy, upon the consent granted by a relevant district court.

Information disclosed to the issuers of electronic payment instruments

The Act on the Instruments of Electronic Payments adopted on 12 September 2002 (to come into force in October 2003) introduces an amendment to art 105, para 1, point 2) of the Banking Act which lists institutions and persons to whom a bank is obliged to disclose confidential information.

Under art 105, para 1, point 2)m), a bank is obliged to provide confidential information to the issuers of electronic payment instruments, which are not the banks, within the scope specified by the Act on the Instruments of Electronic Payments.

The issuers of electronic payment instruments are, among others,: (i) the issuers of the payment cards; and (ii) the banks and the electronic money institutions, issuing the electronic monetary instruments (ie an electronic device on which money is stored electronically, in particular, an electronic card loaded to a specified amount).[40]

Banks and electronic money institutions which have concluded a contract on electronic money instrument are obliged to guarantee safety within the scope of transferring of electronic money, by implementing measures which make impossible deformation or collection by non-authorised persons of the information on actions and settlements carried out with a holder [41] (ie natural person, legal person or any other person who or which on the basis of a contract on electronic payment instrument executes on his behalf and account the operations specified in a contract[42]).

Issuers of the electronic payment instruments are entitled to exchange between each other information on the holders who or which improperly perform their obligations deriving from a contract on electronic payment instrument. Such information covers: (i) for natural persons: name and surname, PESEL record number, residence and description of an improper performance of a contract; and (ii) for non-natural persons: name (firm), registered office and address, tax identification number and description of an improper performance of a contract.[43]

The above information can be also collected and disclosed to the issuers by institutions which are referred to in art 105, para 4 of the Banking Act.[44]

Under art 10, para 3 of the Act on the Instruments of Electronic Payments, the obligation not to disclose the information concerning a holder or user to a non-authorised person was also imposed on a settlement agent (ie bank, or other legal person, which had concluded with an acceptor a contract on acceptance of a payment made by use of the electronic payment instrument).

---

40   Act on the Instruments of Electronic Payments, art 2, point 6.
41   Act on the Instruments of Electronic Payments, art 62, para 1.
42   Act on the Instruments of Electronic Payments, art 2, point 11.
43   Act on the Instruments of Electronic Payments, art 68, paras 1–3.
44   Act on the Instruments of Electronic Payments, art 68, para 4.

Money laundering and counteracting the financing of terrorism

Provisions aimed at the prevention of money laundering and financing of terrorism are also an exception to the rule.

Article 105, para 2 of the Banking Act states that the scope of and the rules concerning disclosure of information held by the banks which is to be disclosed to the General Inspector of Financial Information is to be regulated by separate legislation.

The relevant provisions are included in the the Act as of 16 November 2000 on counteracting introduction to the financial circulation of assets coming from illegal, or undisclosed sources, and on counteracting financing of terrorism (Act of 16 November 2000).

On the basis of art 8, para 1 of the Act of 16 November 2000, the 'obliged institutions' (ie, among others, banks, branches of banks, banks carrying out brokerage activities), performing transactions upon the order of a client, which value exceeds €10,000,[45] both where the transaction comprises one operation or a few operations, if the circumstances indicate that they are connected to each other, are obliged to register such transaction.

The above obligation also applies if the circumstances indicate that the material values may come from an illegal or undisclosed source regardless of the value and type of the transaction.[46]

In order to fulfil the registration obligations, banks are to identify customers each time a disposition is filed or order to perform a transaction is made on the basis of documents presented upon filing a disposition, or an order to perform transaction or upon conclusion of an agreement.[47]

The identification includes the personal details of a customer, such as name, surname (firm), citizenship, residential address (address of a registered office seat of a legal person, or organisational unit having no legal personality), details of a document on the basis of which identity of a person was confirmed (extract from the court register, or other document indicating organisational form of a legal person, identity card, or passport of a natural person), organisational form of a legal person, or organisational unit having no legal personality, document confirming authorisation to act on behalf of the legal person, or an organisational unit having no legal personality.[48] Identification also includes the beneficiaries of the transaction and covers establishment and record of their identity (name, surname, firm) and address.[49]

Information on a registered transaction is to be passed to the General Inspector of Financial Information.[50] Such information is to include:

1 date and place of execution of the transaction;
2 name, surname, citizenship, address, PESEL record number or code of a country and features of document on the basis of which the person executing the transaction was identified;
3 amount, currency and type of the transaction;

45 From 1 January 2004, this amount will be increased to €15,000.
46 Act of 16 November 2000, art 8, para 3.
47 Act of 16 November 2000, art 9, para 1.
48 Act of 16 November 2000, art 9, para 2.
49 Act of 16 November 2000, art 9, para 3.
50 Act of 16 November 2000, art 11, para 1.

4   number of the bank account which was used in order to execute the transaction and information concerning the owner, or person, who uses that bank account;

5   information concerning a natural person, legal person or organisational unit having no legal personality, on behalf of which the transaction was made;

6   name, surname, or firm, and address of the beneficiary of the transaction and, if such address cannot be established, name (firm) of his bank;

7   justification in case of delivery of information on transactions which are referred to in art 8, para 3 of the Act.[51]

The information listed in points 1 to 6 above is to be delivered to the General Inspector of Financial Control by a bank, where a bank was filed with a disposition or an order to perform a transaction or is to perform a transaction, with relation to which a reasonable suspicion exists, that may be connected with commencement of an offence stipulated in art 299 of the Penal Code.[52]

Under art 16a, para 2 of the Act of 16 November 2000, a bank is obliged immediately to inform the General Inspector of Financial Control of a bank account for a person with relation to whom or which a reasonable suspicion exists that he or it is connected with commencement of a terrorist act, and each transaction to which such a person is a party.

A bank is also obliged, immediately, to make accessible information concerning transactions covered by the provisions of the Act upon the written request of the General Inspector of Financial Information. This includes the following: providing information on the parties to the transaction; content of the documents, including balance and turnovers on the bank account; and delivery of certified copies of such documents, or making appropriate documents available to the authorised employees of the appropriate unit of the Ministry of Finance to make notes on or copies of such documents.[53]

Fulfilment of the obligations imposed by the Act of 16 November 2000 is supervised by the General Inspector.[54]

Control is performed by employees of the appropriate unit of the Ministry of Finance, who are authorised by the General Inspector.[55] Upon the request of an inspector, a bank is obliged to provide him with all the documents and materials necessary to carry on the inspection, which is referred to in art 21, para 1 of the Act, with exception of documents and materials including information covered by state secrecy.[56]

Control, which is referred to in para 1, is also performed, within the scope of performed supervision or control, in the course of and on the basis of rules specified in other provisions, by:

1   the Commission for Banking Supervision with relation to the banks and branches of foreign banks;

2   the Securities and Exchange Commission with relation to the banks conducting the brokerage activity and the banks running the securities accounts.[57]

51   Act of 16 November 2000, art 12, para 1.
52   Act of 16 November 2000, art 16, para 1.
53   Act of 16 November 2000, art 13a, para 1.
54   Act of 16 November 2000, art 21, para 1.
55   Act of 16 November 2000, art 21, para 2.
56   Act of 16 November 2000, art 22, para 1.
57   Act of 16 November 2000, art 21, para 3.

All the information collected and passed on by organs of financial information under the Act are subject to the protection specified in the provisions of a separate Acts.[58]

Provisions preventing money laundering are also included in art 106 of the Banking Act. Under art 106, para 1, a bank is to counteract the abuse of its activity for purposes connected with offences referred to in art 299 of the Penal Code, or with intention to conceal criminal activity. A bank is also obliged, under art 106, para 4, to register all financial payments exceeding a specified amount and details of persons making such payments. Procedures, which are to be followed by the banks, as well as the minimum amount which is to be registered and the conditions of regulating the register, were established by the Resolution of the Commission for Banking Supervision no 4/98 dated 30 June 1998.

According to para 2, point 1 of the Resolution no 4/98, the banks are obliged to run in their branches the separate registers of financial payments which value exceeds an equivalent of €10.000. Also subject to registration shall be, among others, any cases where the circumstances indicate that the material values may come from, or are connected with, money laundering, regardless of the value and type of the transaction.[59]

In cases of justified suspicion that the transaction, which is referred to in para 2, points 1 and 5, is connected with money laundering, the banks are obliged to inform the appropriate prosecutor office immediately and confidentially about it.[60]

Fiscal incursions into banking confidentiality

A wide scope of information, including that of confidential nature, which is in possession of banks also has to be disclosed to the tax authorities and fiscal control authorities.

Article 105, para 2 of the Banking Act states that the scope of and the rules concerning disclosure of information held by the banks which is to be disclosed to tax authorities or to fiscal control authorities is to be regulated by separate legislation.

Those Acts are the Tax Ordinance Act of 29 August 1997 and the Fiscal Control Act of 28 September 1991.

Under these Acts, in certain circumstances, the tax and fiscal control authorities were given almost unlimited access to the information possessed by banks about their customers.

Under art 82, para 2 of the Tax Ordinance Act, banks are to prepare and provide to the revenue offices monthly information concerning opened and closed bank accounts of undertakings engaged in commercial activity. The information indicates the number of bank account, particulars enabling identification of the holders of such account and a date when a bank account has been opened or closed.

Banks are also subject to tax inspections by the tax authorities.

58 Act of 16 November 2000, art 30.
59 Regulation no 4/98, para 2, point 5.
60 Regulation no 4/98, para 5 point 1.

The inspectors, to the extent authorised, are entitled, in particular, to request access to records, account books and all documents connected with the purpose of the inspection and to make copies, extracts and notes.[61]

Under arts 33 and 33a of the Fiscal Control Act, banks are obliged to supply the confidential details of customer accounts upon the written request of the General Inspector of Fiscal Control, or of a director of a fiscal control office, but only in the following circumstances:

1 In connection with the preparatory proceedings initiated in a penal case and offence, or a fiscal penal case, or fiscal offence.[62]
2 In connection with an inspection (initiated by an inspector under issued authorisation) after the prior summons of a tax payer by the inspector to provide information in that field or to authorise the financial institutions to pass on the said information, but only where a tax payer:
   (a) has not given consent to the information being disclosed;
   (b) has not authorised the fiscal control office to apply to the financial institution (ie a bank) for the said information to be passed on; or
   (c) has not, within the time limit specified by the fiscal control office, provided information, or authorisation mentioned above.[63]

The General Inspector of Fiscal Control, or a director of a fiscal control office, can request the following information concerning the suspected customer:

1 bank accounts or savings accounts operated, amount of such accounts, as well as the turnover and balance thereof;
2 pecuniary or securities accounts owned by him, amount of such accounts, as well as the turnover and balance thereof;
3 credit contracts or loan contracts concluded, as well as deposit contracts;
4 state treasury shares or state treasury bonds acquired through the banks, as well as trading in these securities;
5 trading in the deposit certificates issued by the banks or in other securities.[64]

In the course of the penal, or offence, proceedings and fiscal penal, or offence, proceedings by an inspector, or control proceedings by a director of the fiscal control office, or General Inspector of Fiscal Control, access to the information referred to in art 33 is to be given exclusively to the inspector conducting the proceedings and appropriate organs of fiscal control. The information has to be kept in at the premises duly secured in compliance with the provisions on the protection of confidential information and upon completion of proceedings removed from the case files and lodged in a safe.[65] The information collected and processed in a course of fiscal control constitutes a fiscal secret. The following persons are obliged to observe a fiscal secret: (i) employees of the offices of fiscal control; (ii) the General Inspector of Fiscal Control and employees of the Ministry of Finance, referred to in art 10, para 3; and (iii) persons who, on the basis of separate provisions, do professional traineeship in the offices of fiscal control.[66]

61 Tax Ordinance Act, art 286, para 1, point 4).
62 Fiscal Control Act, art 33, para 1.
63 Fiscal Control Act, art 33a, para 1.
64 Fiscal Control Act, art 33, para 1.
65 Fiscal Control Act, art 33b, para 1-3.
66 Fiscal Control Act, art 34, para 1 and 2.

Files containing such confidential details are only accessible to:

1 The minister responsible for public finances, the General Inspector of Fiscal Control, or a fiscal chamber – in the course of tax proceedings, or fiscal penal and fiscal offence proceedings.
2 The General Inspector of Financial Information – under the provisions on counteracting the involvement in financial dealings of the assets coming from illegal or undisclosed sources.
3 Revenue offices or other fiscal control authorities – in connection with the tax proceedings initiated under the decision issued earlier, or in connection with the initiated control proceedings, or penal and offence, or fiscal penal, or fiscal offence proceedings.
4 The administration court – in case a party has filed a complaint.
5 The Minister of Justice, First President of the Supreme Court, President of the Supreme Administrative Court – in connection with the examination of the case in order to lodge an extraordinary appeal, and also the Citizen's Rights Ombudsman in connection with such a submission by a party.
6 The General Public Prosecutor:
   (a) in connection with the examination of a case to lodge an extraordinary appeal;
   (b) on the motion of a competent public prosecutor;
      – in the cases specified in Section IV of the code of Administrative Procedure;
      – in connection with the participation of a public prosecutor in the proceedings held before the administrative court.
7 The Supreme Court – in connection with examination of an extraordinary appeal.
8 State security services and its authorised in writing officers or soldiers within the scope necessary to perform control proceedings on the basis of provisions on protection of confidential information.[67]

Provisions of the Tax Ordinance Act and Fiscal Control Act introduced a concept of fiscal confidentiality which concerns, inter alia, information obtained by tax authorities, or fiscal control authorities, from banks and indicates authorities and officials obliged to maintain such confidentiality, whilst providing criminal penalties for any breach, thereof, as such details acquire the character of official secrets by the Penal Code.

The Citizen's Rights Ombudsman found that these provisions infringed the right to privacy and confidentiality of correspondence provided in the Polish Constitution, and subsequently asked the Constitutional Tribunal to adjudicate upon the conformity of these regulations with the Constitution. On 24 June 1997, the Constitutional Tribunal held that the rights of fiscal authorities to demand information from the banks were in conformity with the Constitution.[68]

Amendment to the Fiscal Control Act

Significant amendments to the Fiscal Control Act currently before the Polish Parliament aim at strengthening the powers of the fiscal control authorities.

---

67 Fiscal Control Act, art 34a, para 1.
68 Constitutional Tribunal, K.21/96.

Under the new proposals, it is planned that the authorities be able to investigate the sources and content of the assets of the persons performing public duties, within the meaning of the Act on restricting the commercial activity of public officials (this Act is subject to pending legislation procedure), as well as parliamentarians from the upper and lower Houses of Parliament.[69]

Under art 35k, para 1 of the Fiscal Control Act, the director of the fiscal control office is entitled to make a written application to financial institutions (ie among others, the banks) which may be in possession of the information necessary to verify the factual state with data deriving from the property declaration filed by the public officials and parliamentarians, in order to confirm such data.

Moreover, upon a request in writing by the General Inspector of Fiscal Control, or director of the fiscal control office, issued in connection with an investigation which has commenced, financial institutions referred to in art 33, paras 1 to 3 (ie among others, banks) are obliged to prepare and provide the information concerning public officials including spouses in joint ownership of assets within the scope referred to in art 33, para 1, points 1 to 5.[70]

Slight changes are also envisaged in relation to art 33a, para 1 of the Fiscal Control Act, which transfers the powers, stipulated in that article, from the fiscal control office directly to a fiscal inspector.

Under the proposed version of art 33a, para 1 of the Act, banks are obliged to supply the confidential details within the scope specified by art 33, para 1[71] upon the request of the General Inspector of Fiscal Control or of a director of the fiscal control office, and also in connection with an investigation initiated by an inspector under the authorisation issued only after a taxpayer first being required by the inspector to provide such information or to authorise the fiscal inspector to apply to the financial institution for the such information, has:

1   not consented to the information being disclosed;
2   not authorised the fiscal inspector to apply to the financial institution (ie the bank) for the said information to be provided; or
3   not, within the time limit specified by the fiscal inspector, provided such information, or authorisation, which is referred to in points 1 or 2.

Additional amendments are envisaged by a proposal for an Act on establishment of the Voiwodship Fiscal Councils and on amendment of some Acts regulating tasks and competences of bodies and the organisation of units subjected to a minister appropriate for public finances.

In art 33a, para 1 mentioned above point 4 is going to be added with the following content:

4   delivered the information, which requires to be completed or compared with information provided by a financial institution (ie among others, a bank).

According to proposed new version of art 33b, para 1 of the Act on Fiscal Control, access to the information, which is referred to in art 33, is to be extended also to the inspector's superior.

---

69   Proposed art 35i of the Fiscal Control Act.
70   Proposed art 35t, para 1 of the Fiscal Control Act.
71   See note 64, above.

Some amendments are envisaged with relation to art 34, para 2 of the Act on Fiscal Control. Under the proposed version of the article, the following persons are obliged to observe a fiscal secret: (i) inspectors and employees of the offices of fiscal control; (ii) persons, who are referred to in art 13, para 4 (ie persons authorised on the basis of international agreements ratified by Poland, representatives of the EU bodies in case of control of means provided to Poland by EU institutions); (iii) the General Inspector of Fiscal Control, inspectors and employees employed in the office of minister appropriate for public finances; and (iv) persons, who on the basis of separate provisions do professional traineeships in the offices of fiscal control.

Exceptions to the rule of confidentiality, other than those listed in art 105 of the Banking Act

The list included in art 105 of the Banking Act does not include all the exceptions to the principle that the confidential information should not be revealed to third persons.

Other exceptions can be found in art 144, para 2 of the Banking Act and art 27 of the Banking Guarantee Fund Act.

Access to confidential information is granted to a supervisor for simplification of the recovery programme by the bank.[72] Under art 144, para 2 of the Banking Act, the supervisor shall have a right to participate in the sessions of the bank's bodies and obtain any information necessary to perform his duties.

Information possessed by the bank shall be also accessible to the receiver, who within 30 days from the day the bank was declared bankrupt shall, among others, establish on the basis of the records of the bank and provide in written form to the Bank Guarantee Fund a list of depositors, indicating the guaranteed amounts due to each depositor, prepared in accordance with sample specified by the Bank Guarantee Fund Act.[73]

The customer's consent

Consent of the customer to disclosure of information constitutes an exception to the rule of confidentiality, under the principle volenti non fit injuria.

The rule of confidentiality can be modified by the person whose information should be kept confidential by the bank, within an unrestricted scope. The consent of the customer can be of a general nature and release the bank from all obligations deriving from art 104, para 1 of the Banking Act. It can be also restricted to the particular person(s), information and/or time within which the confidential information is to be kept secret.

---

72 Under the Banking Act, art 142, para 1, if a bank incurs a balance sheet loss or there is a threat of such loss or a risk of insolvency by a bank, the management board of the bank is obliged immediately to notify the Commission for Banking Supervision and present to it a recovery programme for the bank with a confirmation of its implementation. The Commission for Banking Supervision may adopt a decision on appointment of a supervisor for implementation of the recovery programme by the bank: Banking Act, art 144, para 1.
73 Act on Bank Guarantee Fund, art 27, para 1, point 1).

Consent of the customer to a bank revealing wholly or in part confidentiality is to be given in writing to the bank, and to indicate precisely the scope of such release. Article 104, para 2 of the Banking Act states that the information is not to be disclosed to third parties (by the bank), with the exception of cases specified in art 105 of the Banking Act, and also where a person being a party to the contract authorises the bank, in writing, to disclose certain information to a person indicated by that party.

ACCESS TO INFORMATION BY FOREIGN AUTHORITIES

Foreign state institutions, such as courts and prosecuting or fiscal authorities, may also, in certain circumstances, request legal assistance and the delivery of information which is normally protected by banking confidentiality.

There are three instances in which a foreign institution or state can request legal assistance and the delivery of information from an institution or bank in Poland:

1   In the case of a crime, or an offence or a civil matter handled by a foreign court, confidential banking information can be revealed to foreign courts or prosecuting authorities if there is an international treaty concerning legal assistance in criminal or civil cases, and only where reciprocity exists. Poland has concluded bilateral treaties concerning legal assistance in criminal and civil cases with a number of countries. Poland is also a signatory to the following treaties concerning legal assistance in civil cases:
    (a) the Hague Convention on Civil Procedure of 17 July 1905;
    (b) the Hague Convention on Civil Procedure of 17 March 1954.
        However, for Polish investigatory authorities to require the disclosure of such confidential information, a legal basis must exist under the Banking Act. They cannot simply do this on the basis of request from abroad. Such a legal basis constitutes art 105, para 1, point 2)b) of the Banking Act, which states that the bank shall be obliged to disclose information subject to bank secrecy to, and at the request of a court or a prosecutor in connection with an application for legal aid made by a foreign country entitled to request information which is a bank secret under an international agreement ratified by the Republic of Poland. In addition, one can envisage a certain informal and unofficial exchange of information between investigative authorities of countries on a quid pro quo basis, especially in cases of organised crime, drugs trafficking etc.
2   In the absence of an international treaty concerning legal assistance a court, or other institution, of a foreign country may seek legal assistance from a Polish court in accordance with the procedures provided in the Civil Procedure Code and in the Penal Procedure Code.
        In principle, foreign courts and institutions need to communicate with the Polish courts and institutions through the Ministry of Justice.
        Under art 1131, para 2 of the Civil Procedure Code, courts will refuse to render legal assistance if:
    (a) the action requested would be contrary to the basic principles of legal order in Poland, or would infringe the country's sovereignty;
    (b) carrying out the requested activity is not within the jurisdiction of a Polish court;
    (c) the state which files the application for a legal aid refuses legal aid to the Polish courts.

Under art 588, para 2-3 of the Penal Procedure Code, the Polish court and prosecutor are also entitled to refuse legal assistance if:

(a) the requested action would be contrary to the basic principles of legal order in Poland, or would infringe the country's sovereignty;

(b) performance of a requested action does not fall within the scope of the court's, or prosecutor's, activity under the Polish law;

(c) the state which filed the motion requiring the legal assistance does not guarantee reciprocity in this respect;

(d) the motion requiring legal assistance concerns an act which is not an offence under Polish law.

3   This area of information interchange relates to the treaties on prevention of double taxation and tax evasion. All these treaties anticipate this interchange and it is possible that tax authorities authorised to acquire information for their own purposes could pass on such information. In addition, the minister responsible for public finances, or his authorised representative, is authorised to demand confidential information from the banks if a request for this is submitted by foreign tax authorities within the scope of and according to the rules provided in the treaties on the prevention of double taxation and tax evasion and other international agreements ratified by Poland.[74]

TRACING OF FUNDS

All the measures and procedures described above may in principle be applied to tracing funds held in banks.

Access to funds in local banks

Funds kept in bank accounts are the most available assets for creditors if a debtor defaults.

It is possible for a creditor to obtain an interim injunction securing a claim by way of sequestering assets held in an account. Polish law obliges trading entities to quote their bank account numbers on their business stationery. The main difficulty, however, is the fact that a creditor does not have access to any information concerning the balance held on the debtor's account and, therefore, the creditor's efforts may well be in vain as accounts that are frozen may be empty of funds.

As mentioned above, a bank is under an obligation to disclose to a court executive officer bearing an executory title confidential information concerning a debtor. Such information may cover bank accounts that are held by a debtor, turnover as well as balance held on his accounts. This obviously assists executory proceedings.

However, a court executive officer is able to freeze financial resources held by a party in a given bank without even indicating the number of the account. This is effected by a simple notice served by the court executive officer in accordance with art 889 of the Civil Procedure Code.

In the case of claims pertaining to foreigners, Polish courts have jurisdiction if the debtor's assets comprise financial resources kept in bank accounts in Poland. Thus,

---

74   Tax Ordinance Act, art 82, para 3, as of 29 August 1997.

foreign entities may act as claimants and, as such, enjoy all of the rights granted by the Civil Procedure Code. Consequently, when granted an executory title they may, by using a Polish court executive officer, seize the debtor's funds.

Subpoena from foreign courts

Any subpoenas ordering disclosure of information by Polish banks or foreign banks situated in Poland can be enforced in Poland only after the requirements of the Civil Procedure Code are fulfilled.

The enforceability of subpoenas and the execution of judgments of a foreign court in Poland would be subject to the provisions of art 1150 of the Civil Procedure Code. This provides that judgments of a foreign court issued in civil cases which are subject to court proceedings in Poland and which are enforceable through execution proceedings, constitute executory titles and are enforceable in Poland on condition of reciprocity, provided that such judgments are enforceable in the country of issue and subject to additional requirements as defined in art 1146, para 1 of the Civil Procedure Code.

Those are:

1   the judgment must be final in the country of its origin;
2   the subject matter of the judgment must not belong to the exclusive jurisdiction of Polish courts, or the court of the other country;
3   a party must not have been deprived of the possibility of his defence and, in cases where he does not enjoy an ability to take the actions before court, appropriate representation;
4   the judgment must not be inconsistent with the basic principles of Polish legal order;
5   there must not have been prior final judgment rendered by a Polish court;
6   there must not have been any court proceedings launched in Poland before the judgment of the foreign court became final and if in rendering a judgment Polish law should have been applied, then such law is actually applied, unless the foreign law applied in the case does not materially differ from the applicable Polish law.

Tracing of funds abroad

Once funds have been transferred to a foreign bank, the chances of tracing such funds depend on the policy on banking confidentiality in the jurisdiction that the bank is situated in. Even on the assumption that one was aware which bank the funds were transferred to and had obtained an injunction, or other form of judgment in Poland, enforceability would entirely depend upon whether such an injunction or judgment is recognised in that jurisdiction.

MISCELLANEOUS

Insider trading

Insider trading is an offence under the Act on Public Trading in Securities punishable by six months' to five years' imprisonment and a fine up to five million PLN (approximately US$1,250,000).[75] The Securities and Exchange Commission can submit applications to a prosecutor that an investigation be conducted, who, in turn, can require that stockbrokers and banks divulge details of relevant transactions.

This is possible under the provisions of art 105, para 1, point 2)b) or c) of the Banking Act that enable the prosecutor to require information in relation to criminal proceedings pending against an account holder. As in any jurisdiction, such offences are difficult to detect and prove. However, under criminal law, the penal provisions of the Act on Public Trading in Securities are unusually draconian and the absence of jurisprudence could lead to improper application. It must be stressed that confidential information is any information which is not publicly known and which could significantly affect the value of securities.

Criminal investigatory bodies must also be given access to bank details whenever bank accounts are being used for the preparation of crimes or concealment of ill-gotten gains.

Personal Data Protection Act

The Personal Data Protection Act of 29 August 1997 defines the rights and responsibilities of persons and institutions maintaining databases and the rights of persons whose personal details are kept in such databases.

The Act guarantees the protection of the rights of individuals and their freedoms. Under the provisions, the processing of personal data should not infringe the rights of the person to whom they pertain, and persons whose details are being processed have the right to know where such data is to be held, by whom and for what purpose. Supervisory rights within the scope of processing personal details in accordance with the provisions of the Personal Data Protection Act have been vested in the General Inspector for the Protection of Personal Data.

Provisions of the Personal Data Protection Act constitute a separate legal basis for protection of personal data of the customers being natural persons which has been collected by the bank. Disclosure of the data under the above Act may be effected only in accordance with the conditions specified in it. From provisions of the Personal Data Protection Act, personal data can be processed (ie, among others, disclosed) by the banks in the following situations, specified in art 23, para 1 of the Personal Data Protection Act, subject to the provisions of art 104 of the Banking Act:

1 a person, whose data are concerned, gives his consent, unless the processing actions are aimed at removal of his details;
2 provisions of law allow for that;
3 it is indispensable to fulfil the obligations deriving from the agreement, if a person to whom the data relates is a party to such agreement or if it is indispensable to take the necessary actions before the agreement is concluded;
4 it is indispensable to perform tasks specified by law which are performed for the public good;
5 it is indispensable to fulfil the legally justified purposes of the administrators of data, who are referred to in art 3, para 2, or third persons to whom such data is

---

75   Act on Law on Public Trading in Securities, art 174, para 1.

delivered – and processing of data does not infringe the rights and freedoms of the person to whom such data relates.

In order to secure the safety of the personal details processed by the administrator of such data, the administrator of personal data was obliged, under art 36 of the Personal Data Protection Act, to apply technical and organisational measures which guarantee protection of processed personal data; in particular, he needs to secure such data from being disclosed to unauthorised persons or being taken by the unauthorised person, processed in breach of the Act, amended, lost, damaged or destroyed.

Cross-selling

So-called cross-selling, which involves the divulging of any confidential information by a bank, is prohibited. In the light of arts 104 and 105 of the Banking Act, the fact that an account of a particular person is held at a particular bank will only be disclosed to a party that has a justifiable legal right to know. Cross-selling is not a practice that has become a problem in Poland in relation to banks, who treat confidentiality seriously.

Conflict of interest

It is a general rule in Polish civil and commercial law that a person or entity taking care of the affairs of another cannot act to the detriment of such a party.

Therefore, if a bank conducts the financial affairs of a customer in a manner which could affect the interest of another customer, it would become essential for the bank to construct a so-called Chinese Wall. Otherwise, the bank might expose itself to liability for damages vis-à-vis both of its customers, and evidence would have to be produced to prove that access given to information concerning the interests of both of its customers was not used to the detriment of either of them. In practice, if ever such a conflict of interests is identified, both customers need to be advised on the fact.

CONCLUSION

The evolution of laws aimed at limiting bank confidentiality is, increasingly, becoming an intrusion into the personal privacy of citizens.

Attempts have been made to justify this on the basis of the necessity to protect the fiscal interests of the state. Bearing in mind the lack of clarity of Polish tax laws and the aptitude of tax authorities to interpret these provisions by only taking into account the interests of the state, one has to say that the area of abuse is becoming greater than ever.

23 Portugal

Manuel P Barrocas
Margarida Caldeira

INTRODUCTION

The Portuguese Constitution[1] provides in art 26 for the protection of privacy.[2] It is generally understood that the bank confidentiality obligation falls within the scope of this constitutional protection.[3]

In addition, the bank confidentiality legal regime is established in several statutory provisions, as follows:

1   The Banking Law (more specifically, the 'Legal Regime for the Credit Institutions' as laid down in Decree Law no 298/92, dated 31 December, amended by Decree-Law 201/02, dated 26 September).

   This Law sets forth a detailed regime of the bank confidentiality obligation which is understood as a part of the rules of conduct of banks and their directors and employees. Also, the conflict of interests between the activity of banks vis-à-vis the public and particularly their customers and their private interests is covered by the Law.

2   The Criminal Code (Decree Law no 48/95, dated 15 March) and other criminal law legislation, including the Criminal Procedure Code.

3   The Civil Code (Decree Law no 47344, dated 25 November 1966).

4   Data protection legislation (Law 67/98, dated 26 October).

5   Other.

---

1   The Portuguese Constitution is dated 2 April 1976 and its last revision is dated January 1997.
2   The text of this provision is following:
   'Everyone is entitled to personal identity, civil capacity, citizenship, good name and reputation, image, free expression and privacy.'
3   Only a small number of tax law commentators have held the opinion that the need of the tax authorities to obtain information for tax purposes does not allow constitutional protection to the bank confidentiality obligation. However, this is not only a minority view, but also highly controversial.

LEGAL REGIME OF BANK CONFIDENTIALITY OBLIGATION

Bank confidentiality in the Portuguese legal system and brief reference to some major issues

Bank confidentiality is, in sum, defined in the law as the secrecy which the banks, their directors, employees and other people working or providing services to a bank must keep as to the customer's business or activity, ie the economic, financial and personal data concerning the customer which have been acquired by virtue of their activity.

One of the first references to bank confidentiality in Portuguese law dates back to the nineteenth century, more particularly, the Law of 1881 ruling the activity of the Bank of Portugal. Since then, bank confidentiality has always been laid down in Portuguese law concerning banking activity. The purpose of the law has always been the protection of customer's investments and savings, thus accomplishing the public economic interest of creating a climate of confidence in investment. Bearing in mind that the customer's right to bank confidentiality is connected to the constitutional protection of the privacy right, it has always been understood that the customer is not only someone who enters into any particular transaction with a bank, but also someone who has initiated contacts with the bank with a view to entering into any possible transaction. Therefore, information and personal data about a prospective customer of the bank who, with a view to entering into a negotiation, has supplied the bank with some personal data without, however, reaching any final agreement is covered by bank confidentiality.

Thus, the matter of bank confidentiality may be relevant within the scope of pre-contractual liability.

But, bank confidentiality gains a special importance during any transaction with the bank and after it has been concluded.

A classic question in bank confidentiality concerns the limits of bank confidentiality vis-à-vis the interests of criminal investigation. Until 1994, banks, the police and criminal courts faced this problem, and often the banks refused to provide any information about customers to police or criminal courts. However, Act no 36/94, dated 29 September, on measures against corruption and economical and financial crimes, amended by Law 5/02, dated 11 January 2002, implemented new legislation to oblige the banks to provide confidential information whenever the criminal investigation is related to bribery and certain defined financial and economic crimes (generally, so-called white-collar crimes) as well as, since the latest amendment, terrorism and certain forms of trafficking. Bearing in mind the importance of this law, a special reference shall be made below.

The Banking Law and the scope of bank confidentiality

One of the major purposes of the Banking Law is to define and keep banking activity within the codes of professional conduct and consider the customer as a consumer of services.

Banking legislation is applied to:

1   banks;
2   investment companies, leasing, factoring and hire-purchase companies, electronic currency institutions; and
3   any other entities that the law considers as similar to banks for some specific purposes, which are herein referred to, in general, as banks even though, technically, the entities indicated in 2 and 3 are not, strictly speaking, banks.

This broad application of the Banking Law to all those entities is an important factor of protection of customers' rights. The supervision of all banking activities in Portugal is conducted by the Bank of Portugal.

The first relevant provision of the Banking Law (art 78) on the confidentiality obligation reads as follows:

'1.   The board of directors members and the supervisory board members of credit institutions, its employees, proxies and all other people who provide them services, permanently or not, shall not disclose or use information on facts relating to the activity of the institution or its relations with customers which have been obtained exclusively during the performance of their functions or the provision of services.
2.   Bank confidentiality covers, among others, the customers' names, the deposit accounts and all other banking operations.
3.   The confidentiality obligation does not end on the termination of contractual relations.'

Consequently, the following persons are, within and in addition to the banks, obliged to keep confidentiality and abide by the bank confidentiality legislation:

1   the members of the board of directors and supervisory board of banks;
2   bank employees and proxies; and
3   any other person or entity providing services to a bank on a permanent or occasional basis.

The confidentiality obligation includes:

1   the duty of non-disclosing,
2   the duty of non-using,

any information upon facts or data concerning the bank activity relating to customers, provided that they have acquired them by virtue of the exercise of their functions.

Those confidentiality duties do not terminate with the termination of their functions or employment in the bank.

The infringement of those duties is a crime.

Exceptions to the bank confidentiality obligation

These exceptions are laid down both in the Banking Law and other legislation.

Article 79 of the Banking Law reads that:

'1. The facts concerning the relationship between the customer and the bank may be disclosed in case of customer's consent.

2. Beyond this case, the facts covered by confidentiality obligation may only be disclosed:
   a) to the Bank of Portugal;
   b) to the Securities Board;
   c) to the Guarantee of Deposits Fund and the System of Indemnities to Investors;
   d) under the provisions of criminal law;
   e) where there is another legal provision that expressly provides for a limitation to the confidentiality obligation.'

Exceptions provided for in the Banking Law

CUSTOMER'S CONSENT

In order to understand the content of the customer's consent, it is of use to point out that what does not require the customer's consent is information which has become known by the public and so lost its secret nature.

On the other hand, there are some persons who are authorised by the customer or the law to have access to confidential information kept by the bank. Such is the case for, inter alia:

1 the guarantors of some commercial papers in possession of a bank, such as bills of exchange, who need to know the information covered by confidentiality concerning those documents in order to exercise their rights or duties;
2 proxies;
3 third parties representing the bank's customer by operation of law (for instance, a representative of a minor etc); and
4 bankruptcy trustees.

There is no legal requirement that the customer's consent should be given in writing, even though this is the most advisable way to communicate with the bank.

Information provided to some entities authorised by law

In addition to the entities to whom the customer's affairs may be disclosed under the paragraphs above, the following entities may also receive confidential information under certain limited conditions:[4]

1 the Bank of Portugal (as the central bank), for instance, in connection with the sanctions to apply to the practice of crimes for the issuance of cheques returned unpaid;
2 the Securities Board in connection with its function of supervising the securities market;

---

4 The Banking Law does not set out a duty of co-operation between banks and tax entities as an exception to bank confidentiality.

3   the Guarantee of Deposits Fund; and
4   entities authorised to have access to bank data under certain special legislation which will be mentioned below.

Exceptions provided for in other legislation

THE CRIMINAL CODE

The Criminal Code provides in art 195 that:

> 'whoever, without permission, discloses a secrecy related to a third party which has been obtained by virtue of his profession, status or employment is subject to a one year imprisonment penalty or, in alternative, to a maximum fine of 240 days.'[5]

On the other hand, art 196 establishes that:

> 'whoever, without permission, takes advantage or benefit from a confidential information concerning the commercial, industrial, professional or artistic activity of a third party by virtue of his profession, status or employment is subject to a one year imprisonment penalty or, in alternative, to a maximum fine of 240 days.'

The Criminal Code considers as a reason that may exclude criminal liability the protection or satisfaction of an interest which is clearly more important than the interest protected by the bank confidentiality rules, which, therefore, may be overridden.

Moreover, the Criminal Code establishes an exception based on necessity (art 34):

> 'An act is not illegal which has been practised as the adequate way to remove a threat to the legitimate interests of someone or of a third party, provided that (cumulatively):
>
> (I)   the threat has not been voluntarily created by it;
> (II) there is a reasonable superiority of its interest in relation to the interest which can be offended by the threat; and
> (III) it is reasonable to impose upon the third party the loss or damage of its interest taking into consideration the nature or the higher value of the interest threatened.'

As a consequence, in criminal law matters other interests may prevail over bank secrecy.

The Criminal Procedure Code

This provides that credit institutions may invoke bank confidentiality to prevent them having to make depositions or statements in criminal investigation procedures.

---

5   Under art 47 of the Criminal Code, the amount of a criminal fine defined in terms of days is fixed by the judge case by case between €1 and €498,80 per day.

If the judge, however, has doubts about the confidential nature of the information required from a bank, he shall decide about the disclosure duties after consultation with the professional or banking association representing the persons under the disclosure duty.

Article 135 of the Code provides:

'1. Priests, lawyers, doctors, journalists and members of credit institutions and other people allowed or obliged by law to keep professional confidentiality may refuse to make any statements or provide information covered by the confidentiality duty.
2. If the court has reasonable doubts about the validity of the refusal, it may take all necessary measures to solve the doubt. If the Court concludes that the refusal is not legally valid, it may order that the statement be produced.'

In this last case, the entity which represents the professional involved (union, association etc) would also be heard in order to help the court to decide on whether the confidentiality obligation should be overridden or not.

In addition, the Criminal Procedure Code regulates in art 182 the presentation to the court of documents or objects that the above indicated professionals and, therefore, also credit institutions have in their possession. According to this legal provision, the credit institutions must present to the criminal authorities, at their request, any documents or objects held by them which may be seized. The credit institution may refuse in writing and then the criminal authority will decide whether the protection is to be accepted or not. As noted above, the criminal authority may override the confidentiality obligation where such is considered necessary to assure the protection of interests of higher value or importance.

Furthermore, the Criminal Procedure Code also allows (art 181) the seizure of money, documents or other things deposited in a credit institution (even in a bank private safe box) if they are connected with the commission of any crime and are of great importance to the development of the investigation. It is not necessary that the documents or other things be owned by any suspect involved in a criminal investigation.

Paragraph 2 of art 181 establishes that the criminal investigation judge may inspect any correspondence in possession of banks or other banking documentation with a view to deciding which goods are to be seized.

The judge and all people who have co-operated with him are subject to a strict duty of confidentiality in relation to the information obtained under such conditions.

The inspections and searches made at credit institutions should be preceded by an express court decision, of which a copy must be previously sent to the bank, except in special cases, for instance, suspicion of terrorism, violent crimes etc where the criminal inspection or search may be conducted by the police before an authorisation is granted by the court, which should, in any case afterwards, confirm the validity of such investigations.

OTHER LEGISLATION

Bribery and certain crimes of a financial and economic nature (white-collar crimes) have a special legislation allowing the police duly authorised by the criminal investigation judge to have access to bank confidential information.

In addition, an important bill about criminal investigation concerning the production, preparation or trade of narcotics and funds connected with that illegal activity (Decree Law no 15/93, dated 22 January, amended by several bills, the most relevant to this matter being Law 45/96, dated 3 September) authorises the access to information covered by bank confidentiality and the duty of credit institutions to provide such information to the authorities.

This bill establishes (art 60) that by virtue of the needs of the criminal authorities, the competent court may request any information and the presentation of documents relating to assets, bank deposits and the like which belong to individuals who are suspects or accused of having committed crimes relating to the production, preparation or trade of narcotics. In case such request respects to banking entities, or financial or equivalent entities, the request may be addressed by the Bank of Portugal. The requested entities, both public (including tax authorities) and private (including all credit institutions), cannot refuse to provide the authorities with such information or documents.

USE OF CREDIT INSTITUTION TO LAUNDER MONEY

The use of credit institution to launder money has also a special legal regime following Council Directive 91/308/EEC, dated 10 June 1991. The implementation of that Directive implied the promulgation of new legislation (Decree Law no 313/93, dated 15 September) which provides:

1 Credit institutions are obliged to inform the criminal authorities whenever they suspect that any funds or transactions are connected with money laundering. The information provided by such credit institutions may only be used in the investigation and punishment of those crimes. The criminal authorities which receive the information requested must guarantee the anonymity of the credit institution. On the other hand, the credit institutions cannot disclose to their customers or third parties that they have provided the criminal authorities with the said information, not even when a criminal proceeding or investigation is taking place.

2 Credit institutions are obliged not to follow or perform any customer's instruction whenever they suspect that they are connected or related to money laundering and to inform the criminal authorities at once. If it is impossible for the credit institution to abstain from executing the instructions given by the customer or if the abstinence would prejudice the investigation by the criminal authorities, the banks are allowed to execute the customer's instructions, but must immediately after that inform the criminal authorities.

TAX LEGISLATION

Exceptions concerning tax matters are also established in the law. They can be materialised through the following powers given to tax authorities, inter alia:

1   the banks are obliged to give access to private safe boxes and inform the tax authorities of the contents of them in connection with inheritance tax;

2   failure of payment of taxes where the taxpayer has used cheques returned unpaid, when the tax authorities may inquire of banks about the respective accounts; and

3   information about funds which have not been drawn during 15 years under certain conditions.

As briefly mentioned above, certain tax law commentators hold that the above-quoted provision of the Constitution related to the protection of privacy of citizens does not always cover information falling within the scope of bank confidentiality.

Their view is based on the fact that the above-mentioned provision of the Constitution refers only to basic rights of citizens connected with human dignity and spiritual values such as philosophical or religious convictions or sexual inclinations. Therefore, the financial situation of individuals would fall outside the scope of protection given by the Constitution. Consequently, under this point of view, where the information kept by banks relates to the above basic rights, bank confidentiality is effective; if such is not the case, it may be overridden for tax purposes, particularly with a view to obtaining information on the financial situation of bank customers.

Moreover, the same commentators hold that the duty corresponding to the public interest of obtaining tax information has higher value than the interests protected by bank confidentiality. Therefore, the banks should provide information covered by the bank confidentiality obligation in order to allow the tax authorities to have information on the real incomes of companies, taking into account that the principle of taxation of the truthful income is also laid down in the Constitution as a right of taxpayers.[6] In addition, according to the same legal commentators, the bank customers will not be affected by such measures once the tax authorities are subject to the duty of tax confidentiality which covers precisely the information obtained about the financial situation of taxpayers.[7] However, the majority of legal commentators have argued that such understanding would, in fact, jeopardise the value of bank confidentiality. Indeed, it is almost consensually understood that this confidentiality obligation falls within the constitutional protection and that there is no exception in favour of tax authorities. Furthermore, other authors who disagree with the opinion of those tax commentators have pointed out that the activities of tax authorities, when carrying out an investigation into the financial situation of individuals, may

6   This principle is set out in art 104, para 2 of the Constitution, which states that 'taxation over companies shall be applied on the real income'.

7   Notwithstanding, even those commentators agree that a search made by tax authorities in the house or premises of the taxpayer, particularly companies, as set out in art 125 of the Corporate Income Tax Code, can only be made with the previous authorisation of a court if the taxpayer does not agree to it voluntarily.

be punished under criminal law. As regards the duties of the employees of the tax authorities, it should be noted the amendment provided by Law 5/02, dated 11 January, on measures against corruption and economical and financial crimes, detailed below.

There are more exceptions including, inter alia:

1 The right of the civil courts to receive information from the banks. This includes:
    (a) information concerning funds or assets owned by debtors (bank customers) in civil actions for money which is in the possession of banks;
    (b) in connection with the enforcement of letters of request addressed by foreign authorities or foreign courts to Portuguese civil courts under international conventions; and
    (c) for obtaining legal aid.
2 In certain cases, the Parliament's commissions of investigation may request information from private entities.
3 The bank's customer's spouse may request information from the bank in cases where:
    (a) the customer is not able to manage the bank account because of being at an unknown place and provided that no power of attorney has been granted to anyone; or
    (b) the customer provides the spouse with a general proxy for the administration of assets.
4 In addition, as seen below on case law, the department of inspection of a bank may inspect the accounts of its employees who are suspected of having committed irregular or dishonest acts.

As mentioned above, the supervising authorities are also subject to a duty (art 80 of the Banking Law) as follows:

'1. Everyone who is carrying or has carried out functions in the Bank of Portugal, or the ones who are rendering or have rendered services, both on a permanent or occasional basis, are subject to the confidentiality obligation about the facts which knowledge has been obtained exclusively by virtue of the exercise of their functions or services and may not disclose or use the information so obtained.'

The facts covered by the confidentiality obligation may only be disclosed in the following cases:

1 through the customer's consent given to the Bank of Portugal;
2 in pursuance of provisions of criminal law or criminal procedure law;
3 in connection with court proceedings of bankruptcy or winding up of companies under certain conditions; and
4 the disclosure of certain data is allowed for statistical purposes provided that does not include the identification of people or institutions.

Co-operation with regulatory entities and other entities

In pursuance of art 81 of the Banking Law, the Bank of Portugal may exchange information with other entities which, however, must keep it confidential as follows:

1   with the Securities Board under certain limited conditions;
2   the Insurance Institute (the regulatory and supervising entity of the insurance activity) and the Central Institute for Credit to Agriculture;
3   other banking supervisory authorities of the EU member states in compliance with EC Directives; and
4   co-operation agreements entered into with supervising authorities of credit institutions with a registered seat in Portugal and of institutions of equivalent nature with a registered seat abroad.

This information may be supplied on an individual or consolidated basis.

The co-operation agreements with countries outside the EU as set out in art 82 of the Banking Law may only be executed where such countries provide for a guarantee of confidentiality at least equivalent to the one granted by the Portuguese Banking Law.

Under art 83 of the Banking Law, credit institutions are allowed under the bank confidentiality rules to establish a system whereby they exchange and maintain a central register of information about banking business risks.

Remedies for breach of the bank confidentiality obligation

Article 84, in its turn, relates to the remedy for the infringement of the bank confidentiality obligation. This provision reads that:

'Without prejudice to other penalties which may be applicable, the infringement of bank confidentiality is subject to the Criminal Code.'

Therefore, there is the possibility of cumulating civil liability with criminal liability. Civil liability, particularly liability in contract for breach of the confidentiality obligation, is governed by the general regime of civil liability. The law does not specify what damages cannot be claimed. Thus, the damages that may be claimed are those which, under the general regime of civil liability, could have been caused by any unlawful act.

Special reference to the Data Protection Act

Data protection legislation is covered by Law 67/98, dated 26 October, implementing in the Portuguese legal system Council Directive 95/46/EC of 24 October 1995 relating to the protection of individuals concerning the treatment of personal data and the free circulation of such data. This law incorporates, therefore, the EU regime of transfer of personal data within the EU and to third countries. The national supervising entity, which may also issue opinions, is an administrative independent entity named, as before, the National Commission for Data Protection.

The scope of application of this law is the following: the treatment of personal data, by means totally or partially automatic, as well as the non-automatic treatment of personal data, contained in manual files or destined to such files (except treatment made by individuals to their exclusively personal or domestic activities) either (i) within the scope of activities of the establishment responsible for the treatment located in Portuguese territory; or (ii) outside national territory in a place where Portuguese law is applicable by virtue of international law; (iii) where the responsibility for the treatment of data is not established in the EU but has recourse to means, automatic or not, located in Portuguese territory, save if such means are only used to traffic throughout the EU.

Article 3 of Law 67/98 provides for several definitions, among which the following:

'Personal Data' is defined as 'any information of whatever nature and irrespectively of its vehicle including sound and image, relating to an individual identified or identifiable ("the owner of the personal data")'; it is considered as identifiable the person that may be identified directly or indirectly, namely by means of a reference to an identification number or to one or more specific elements of its physical, physiological, psychic, economic, cultural or social identity.

'Treatment of Data' is defined as 'any operation or aggregate of operations about personal data, made with or without recourse to automatic means, such as the collection, the registry, organization, conservation, adjustment or alteration, the recovery, consulting, use, communication through transmission, broadcast or any other form of making available, with comparison or interconnection, as well as the blockage, erasure or destruction'.

'Consent of the owner of personal data' is defined as any free, specific and informed expression of intentions, under which the owner accepts that its personal data are treated.

Beyond regulating the manner of treatment of such data and principles that must be complied with, this law establishes, in art 6, the conditions under which the treatment of data is lawful. Such treatment can only be made if the respective owner of the data had provided clearly its consent or if the treatment is necessary for:

1   the execution of contracts where the owner of data is part of, or of previous diligences to, the formation of the contract or declaration of the intention to contract made at its request;
2   the compliance of a legal obligation to which the responsibility for the treatment is subject to;
3   the protection of vital interests of the owner of data if the latter is physically or legally incapable of providing its consent;
4   the execution of a task of public interest or in the exercise of public authority in which quality the responsible for the treatment is acting or a third recipient of such data; or
5   the carrying out of lawful interests of the responsibility for the treatment or of a third recipient of the data, provided that the rights or freedom or guarantees of the owner of the data shall not prevail.

Article 7 governs the treatment of sensitive data, forbidding the treatment of personal data referring to philosophical, political or religious beliefs, private life or racial or ethnical issues, as well as health and sexual life, including genetic information. In case of legal permission or authorisation of the National Commission for Data Protection, the treatment of this data may be carried out if, due to an important public interest, such treatment is necessary to the exercise of statutory functions of its responsibility or where the owner of data has provided its express consent to such treatment (in both cases with compliance of certain rules).

The treatment of this kind of data is also allowed when:

1   it is necessary to protect vital interests of the owner of data or of another person and the owner is physically or legally prevented from expressing its consent;
2   it is carried out with the consent of the owner to certain non-profitable entities of political or ideological nature, within certain rules;
3   it relates to data clearly made public by its owner, provided that it may lawfully conclude from its declarations that consent is being given in relation to such treatment; or
4   it is necessary to the declaration, exercise or defence of a right in a court procedure and is made exclusively with that purpose.

According to art 17 of Law 67/98, the entities responsible for the treatment of personal data, as well as all those who, in connection to the exercise of their functions, become aware of treated personal data, are obliged to maintain professional secrecy even after the termination of their functions. This does not exclude the duty of supply of compulsory information under the legal terms, except where such information is contained in files organised for statistical purposes.

Law 67/98 also contains a provision on the treatment of data and organisation of files, made by the competent authorities, relating to suspicions of illegal activities.

Special reference to the bona fide principle

The Portuguese Civil Code is strongly influenced, as far as contractual relations are concerned, by the bona fide principle.[8]

Indeed, this principle is laid down in art 227 of the Civil Code on guilt on the formation of contracts (in general) which reads as follows:

'1.   Whoever negotiates with a third party to the completion of a contract must, both in the preliminary actions and in the formation of the contract, act under the rules of bona fides, otherwise such person is liable for the damage caused with guilt to the other party.'

In this provision, there is a reference to the distinction between the two stages precedent to the contract: (i) the so-called negotiation stage, consisting of the preparation of the contents of the agreement; and (ii) the so-called decision stage, where each of the parties issue a declaration to contract, more precisely the proposal and its acceptance.

---

8   A large number of legal essays have been written about the principle of bona fides, eg António Menezes Cordeiro 'Da Boa Fé no Direito Civil' in Coimbra (ed) (1985) vols I and II; António Menezes Cordeiro 'Banca, Bolsa e Crédito' in Almedina (ed) *Estatutos de Direito Comercial e de Direito da Economia* (1990) vol I.

Throughout the Portuguese legal system there are various applications of this principle in several areas of the law.

Consequently, whenever there is no specific rule concerning any particular point of bank confidentiality, the banks, in performing their functions or discharging their contractual duties vis-à-vis their customers, must act towards the protection of the customers' interests using loyalty and due diligence, including informing the customers about any matter concerning their interest.

Of course, the duty of confidentiality does not authorise the bank to use any information concerning a customer to protect another customer in a conflict of interests situation. The bona fide principle is, however, of use to discipline the position of banks towards their customers and limit their use of information contrary to their duty of protection of the customer's interests, including any customer which has a conflict of interests with another customer of the same bank.

It is an application of this principle that art 74 of the Banking Law reflects in providing:

> 'the bank directors and employees must proceed diligently in their relations with the customers, being loyal and discrete and dealing conscientiously with the interests of the customers that have been entrusted to them.'

It is, therefore, of importance to point out that, where conflict of interests is concerned, both the law and banking practice in Portugal do not require from the banks the duty to provide their customers with advice implying the infringement of bank confidentiality obligations concerning another customer or any protected data held by a bank. In other words, the banks are not allowed to provide such information to any customer, even where they are engaged to advise him on a business matter, if this may infringe the confidentiality obligation owed to another customer. The principle of bona fides is also reflected in Law 67/98, dated 26 October (the Data Protection Legislation; see above), as a general principle to the treatment of such data (art 5, 1.a) of this law).

A special reference to legislation on measures against corruption, economical and financial crimes, terrorism and certain types of traffic crimes

Act no 36/94, dated 29 September, on measures against corruption and economic and financial crimes was amended by Law 5/02, dated 11 January. The scope of application of this law, providing for breaches of secrecy (as well as a special regime of collection of evidence and loss of goods in favour of the state); is now the following, according to art 1 of Law 5/02:

1   traffic of narcotics;
2   terrorism and terrorist organisations;
3   traffic of guns;
4   certain forms of corruption and peculation;
5   money laundering;
6   criminal association;

7   illegal commerce (contraband);
8   traffic and illegal alteration of stolen vehicles;
9   traffic of minors and certain connected types of crimes; and
10   counterfeiting of currency and titles equivalent to currency.

Article 2, no 1 of Law 5/02, on breach of secrecy states the following:

> 'In the stages of enquiry, production of evidence and trial of procedures relating to the crimes set forth in art 1, the professional secrecy of members of corporate bodies of credit institutions and financial companies, and of its employees and persons who render services to such institutions, as well as the secrecy of employees of the tax authorities, shall cease if there are reasons to believe that the respective information have interest to the finding of the truth.'

The extension of the scope of the breach to employees of the tax authorities has been an important amendment provided in Law 5/02 which did not exist in Law 36/94, especially taking into account that the list of crimes covered by this law has been also expanded.

Article 2 contains in addition the following provisions which are herein quoted due to their major importance:

'2.   To the purposes of this law, the regime laid down above depends only on the decision, duly justified, of a court in charge of such procedure.

3.   The decision referred to in the previous number must identify the people covered by the measure and shall specify the information that must be provided and the documents that must be requested; such decision may have a generic formulation to each of the people covered where the mentioned specification is not possible.

4.   If the person or people who own the accounts or the intervenient in the transactions are not known, it is considered sufficient the identification of the accounts and transactions in relation to which information is required.

5.   In case of information relative to an accused person in a criminal procedure or a collective entity, the decision referred to in number 2 above shall always have a generic formulation comprising:

   a)   Tax information;

   b)   Information relative to bank accounts and the respective movements that the accused or the collective entity is the owner or co-owner, or in relation to which such person or the collective entity has the power to make movements;

   c)   Information relative to banking and financial transactions where the accused or the collective entity is an intervenient;

   d)   Identification of the other intervenients in the operations referred to in items b) and c);

   e)   Supporting documents of the information referred to in the previous numbers.

6.   In order to comply with the provisions contained in the previous numbers, the courts and the criminal police with competence to the investigation shall have access to the data base of the tax authorities.'

On the other hand, art 3 of Law 5/02 regulates the procedure, subsequent to the steps laid down in art 2 quoted above, applicable to credit institutions or financial companies. Basically, it provides for the request, made either by a court or – through the delegation of the latter – a criminal authority competent to the investigation, to the credit institutions or financial companies for all information and supporting documents considered relevant.

Such entities are obliged to provide the authorities with the requested documents within certain deadlines, established in Law 5/02, otherwise (or if the authorities suspect that certain documents or information have not been duly disclosed) the court in charge of the procedure shall enforce the attachment of such documents.

If the credit institutions or financial companies mentioned above are not known, the court in charge of the procedure shall request the Bank of Portugal to broadcast the request for documents and information.

Moreover, art 4 of the same bill governs the 'control of bank accounts' as follows:

Such control obliges the credit institution to transmit to the court or the criminal police information on any movements concerning the bank account within the subsequent 24 hours.

The control of the bank account may be either authorised or imposed, depending on the circumstances of the case, by the decision of a judge where there is a great interest of this procedure to the finding of the truth. This decision shall identify:

1 the bank account(s) covered by the measure;
2 the respective period of duration; and
3 the court or entity of the criminal police responsible for the control of the bank account.

The said decision may also include the obligation of suspension of the movements specified therein, where such is necessary to prevent crimes of money laundering.

It should be noted that the persons referred to in art 2, no 1, quoted above, ie the members of corporate bodies of credit institutions and financial companies, their employees and those who render services and employees of the tax authorities, are bound to the justice secrecy in relation to the above-described procedures, if they become aware of those, and cannot disclose the knowledge of such procedures to the persons whose accounts are controlled or about which there has been a request for the provision of documents and information.

If any of these people fail to comply with the provision of information and documents without justified cause, or supply false information or documents, the penalties are imprisonment from six months to three years or a corresponding fine of not less than 60 days (art 13 of Law 5/02).

CASE LAW

Criminal law cases

Case law on bank confidentiality has mainly focused on criminal, civil and labour cases, and a reasonably large amount of case law has been adjudicated.

Most concern the classical issue relating to the protection of bank confidentiality towards an order given by criminal authorities to the bank, requiring the latter to disclose private information for the purpose of helping the investigation of a crime.

Even when the law was not so clear on the limits of bank confidentiality as it is now, the Courts of Appeal have held that bank confidentiality must be overridden by the higher interest of criminal investigation and criminal justice.[9] This position has also been sustained in other judgments, for instance, by the Courts of Appeal of Coimbra (dated 31 October 1990, 6 July 1994 and 17 April 1996) and Évora (dated 5 November and 12 May 1992) as discussed in detail below.

Let us consider in particular some of the most important case law.

Judgment of the Court of Appeal of Coimbra dated 31 October 1990

The court applied in this case the Criminal Code in force at the time on the duty of disclosure of information about a person suspected of having stolen and used valuables belonging to a third party. The court based the judgment on the assumption that the 'interest of good administration of justice is clearly of higher value than the interest of obtaining and maintaining a climate of confidence of the clients with the banks', despite this being also a very important value.

The court, therefore, decided that the bank should disclose the information requested by the criminal authorities where such disclosure is the right way to make justice.

The principle stated by the court in this judgment, which has been repeated in other similar case law, provides for a clear option about the conflict of interests in question, that is, the conflict between the interest of the banks' customers to keep trust in the banking system and the interest of the community in reaching criminal justice.

The same understanding was held in the following judgments.

The Court of Appeal of Coimbra, dated 31 January 1990

This case also concerned a theft of valuables. The court decided that the bank should disclose the identity of the person who received from the bank the amount of the stolen value.

The Court of Appeal of Évora, dated 5 November 1991

The court had in mind that, in the context of a criminal investigation, any relevant information should be disclosed by the bank where the criminal authorities consider that the requested information is 'necessary and adequate for the purpose of accomplishing the public interest'.

---

9   Eg the judgment of the Court of Appeal of Oporto, dated 11 November 1991.

The Court of Appeal of Évora, dated 12 May 1992

Also dealing with investigation in a criminal case, the court decided that 'the purpose of investigation of the facts is clearly higher than the ground on which the bank confidentiality obligation is based; in case of a conflict between the public interest of the state in acting against everyone who violates the criminal law and the right to privacy of the citizens, the former should prevail over the latter'.

The Supreme Court of Justice, dated 12 November 1986

The Public Prosecutor should start criminal proceedings even where the facts that may qualify as a crime have been brought to his knowledge through a breach of the bank confidentiality obligation.

The Court of Appeal of Coimbra, dated 6 July 1994; the Supreme Court of Justice, dated 4 November 1981; and the Court of Appeal of Évora, dated 11 October 1994

The first two of these judgments were given in the context of the criminal investigation of cheques returned unpaid; the third related to joint bank accounts.

All judgments concluded that the interest of criminal investigation should override the duty of bank confidentiality. The Supreme Court of Justice decided that 'in case of unpaid cheques, bank secrecy cannot prevail over the right of the court to arrest the necessary documents to obtain evidence of the crime'.

The Court of Appeal of Coimbra, dated 17 April 1996

In this judgment, the court reinforced former decisions when it said: 'It is legal to override the bank confidentiality obligation when it is necessary for the criminal investigation.'

This judgment, therefore, established in a strict way (ie not depending on particular circumstances of the case) the priority of one interest over the other.

This priority is not applicable if the purpose of the investigation is not the defence of a public interest or if such investigation does not necessarily require the disclosure. Where there is no public interest, bank confidentiality may not be overridden without a specific legal provision allowing it. This was established, for instance, in the judgment of the Supreme Court of Justice, dated 21 May 1980. The court decided that:

> 'If there is no specific legal provision that authorises banks to disclose information to criminal authorities about certain data of the client, the bank confidentiality obligation should maintain and the bank has the right to refuse any request for disclosure under such conditions.'

Similarly, the judgment of the Supreme Court of Justice, dated 20 October 1988, concluded that the bank confidentiality obligation promotes the creation of a climate of confidence with banks and may only be overridden when the law allows a derogation.

Judgment of the Court of Oporto, dated 9 January 2002

The court concluded that the directors and employees of the tax administration are bound to keep secrecy about the facts relative to the tax situation of the taxpayers; however, such duty of secrecy ceases under the applicable provisions of the Penal Code and the Criminal Procedure Code.

Civil law cases

Similarly to the above case law in which the priority of the interest of the criminal investigation over bank confidentiality is concerned, the courts have adjudicated decisions acknowledging that *certain private interests* must prevail over bank confidentiality.

Such has been the case of the attachment of funds in actions for money. In these actions the court may need to obtain the co-operation of banks to obtain information which may facilitate the identification of funds to attach. The courts have decided in these cases that it is not fair that, based on bank confidentiality rules, someone may avoid the attachment of their own funds which are responsible for the compulsory payment of a debt.[10]

Particularly, in the judgment of the Court of Appeal of Lisbon, dated 22 June 1995, the court decided that all banks are obliged to execute the order given by a court as to the attachment of funds in actions for money and, moreover, the bank must inform the court in the event that the amount of money in the customer's account is less than the amount that the court requested to be attached.

More recent case law, for example, the judgment of the Court of Lisbon, dated 20 January 2000, focused on the breach of bank confidentiality in case of attachment of the accounts further to the court claim filed by the creditor who faced limitations of its own knowledge in the identification of the bank accounts.

However, in some cases where there is a *mere interest of a party to prove a fact in a lawsuit based on a bank information*, the courts have not agreed to set aside the bank confidentiality obligation.

For example, the Supreme Court of Justice delivered a judgment, dated 10 April 1980, in a civil matter, according to which it considered that, as a general rule, anyone, even one who is not a party to an action, has the duty to co-operate in the search for truth. However, the refusal of co-operation is legitimate if the co-operation would imply a breach of the bank confidentiality obligation which binds all directors and employees of banks.

In addition, the bank confidentiality obligation was not overridden in the judgment of the Supreme Court of Justice, dated 8 February 1990. The court concluded in this case that a court may not override the confidentiality obligation of a bank by ordering

---

10   Judgments of the Court of Appeal of Coimbra, dated 7 November 1989; the Court of Appeal of Lisbon, dated 22 June 1995 and 8 October 1996; the Court of Appeal of Oporto, dated 12 June 1995; and the Court of Appeal of Évora, dated 18 June 1996.

an inspection of the bank with a view to investigating accounts for tax purposes which are not expressly allowed by law.

This judgment is very interesting because it brings face-to-face the public interest relating to the payment of taxes and the public interest of bank confidentiality.

The factual background was as follows. The Public Prosecutor, in a judicial action for distribution of an inheritance estate, sued the heirs on the ground of failure to file with the tax authorities the list of the whole estate. According to the Public Prosecutor, this was an attempt to infringe the payment of the inheritance tax rules. The heirs maintained that, in fact, there were bank accounts forming part of the estate, which were not identified. The tax authorities notified the bank, which refused to indicate the accounts. The heirs did not identify the accounts. The Public Prosecutor then asked the court to send a court clerk to the bank's premises to check there the documents needed to identify the bank accounts. The bank maintained its refusal.

The first instance court found acceptable the position of the heirs based on the bank confidentiality obligation.

The Court of Appeal, however, decided in favour of the Public Prosecutor, considering that, since there was a lack of information from the heirs which would allow the determination of the values on which the inheritance tax would be applied, the inspection at the premises of the bank was necessary. Moreover, the court held that an order given by a court must always be executed either by public or by private entities, including banks.

The heirs filed an appeal to the Supreme Court of Justice and maintained that bank confidentiality could only be overridden if there is a specific legal provision allowing an exception to such duty of confidentiality, which was not the case.

The Court of Justice adjudicated in favour of the heirs. It pointed out that, although there was a conflict of two public interests, that is, the public interest of payment of taxes and the public interest of keeping bank confidentiality, the latter should be protected and prevail over the former whenever there is no legal provision providing for an exemption to the confidentiality obligation.

The court concluded that the bank was entitled to refuse the disclosure of information and considered that the bank confidentiality obligation in this case was a lawful limit to the duty of banks to co-operate with authorities in the search for truth.

This was also the conclusion of a judgment of the Court of Appeal of Oporto, dated 21 October 1996, on a labour law matter.

This appeal was filed by a worker against his employer after, from the point of view of the worker, he had been unfairly dismissed. During the production of evidence in the court of first instance, the issue was raised concerning the conflict between bank confidentiality and the necessity of disclosure of information kept by banks in order to support the worker's defence at court. The Court of Appeal of Oporto decided:

> 'In labour matters, bank confidentiality must prevail against the general duty of co-operation with courts in order to provide evidence which may be relevant to settle the dispute.'

In another context, the judgment of the Court of Appeal of Lisbon, dated 5 July 1989, also on a labour law matter, decided that there is no breach of bank confidentiality in a case where the Internal Inspection Department of a bank investigated the accounts of its workers who were suspected of having committed irregular and dishonest acts.

Similarly, the Supreme Court of Justice delivered a judgment of 29 May 1991, according to which:

> 'the bank is entitled to make all the necessary investigations as to the defence of its interests, including examining the bank account of the worker who is suspected of having committed irregular acts. For this purpose, the worker does not acquire the quality of a bank's customer when irregular acts were committed by him.'

The judgment of the Court of Oporto, dated 21 May 20001, decided, as to the scope of bank confidentiality, that it does not qualify as breach of bank secrecy the right of the employee to request from the employer, a bank, that the latter discloses to the court internal audits made in the bank (since the worker needed to extract from such documents evidence to support a particular claim against the employer), provided that the names of the clients and identification of the accounts is not disclosed.

More recently, the Court of Lisbon issued on 14 November 2000 and 28 February 2002 judgments stating that the right of the owner of the bank account to obtain information on the movements of such an account shall be transmitted to the respective heirs who, therefore, shall become the beneficiaries of the duty of bank confidentiality. Consequently, a bank cannot refuse such information to the heirs (after evidence is produced on the death of the owner) on the basis of bank confidentiality.

CONCLUSIONS

Bank confidentiality is ruled in Portugal by several legal provisions, including the Banking Law, which assures the bank customers (and also those who have provided banks with some personal information with a view to entering into any agreement which was not concluded or for any other purpose) that their affairs will not be disclosed to third parties, except in those limited cases laid down in statutory provisions.

Bank confidentiality is considered by law a professional duty and, therefore, more than just a contractual obligation. As a consequence, its infringement is punished as a crime and may give rise to an imprisonment charge and civil liability for bank directors, employees and suppliers of services to the banks. The criminal sanction is expressly laid down in the law, both in the Banking Law and in the Criminal Code. Civil liability is governed by the Civil Code. Banking law does not establish any limitation as to the damages that can be claimed from a bank in such cases.

The most significant exception to bank confidentiality relates to criminal investigation. The search for truth in a criminal action has a higher value than bank confidentiality. However, it is necessary that the criminal investigation judge authorises previously, and expressly, the banks to disclose the information protected by the confidentiality rules.

Some case law regarding civil matters has also been established to the effect that the banks must co-operate with the courts about the attachment of funds of a bank customer who owes money to a third party who has applied to the court for the attachment of such funds in an action for money.

To the contrary, in civil matters of a different nature, including labour matters, the breach of the bank confidentiality obligation should be allowed only by a court in exceptional and duly justified circumstances.

The data protection legislation is very detailed and follows the EU regime.

Banks may be, under international conventions, obliged to co-operate with other foreign banks, criminal authorities and others in supplying information about their clients.

The service of a writ of summons in connection with actions pending in foreign courts and addressed to a national court in order to be served on a bank, for instance, to request the disclosure of information, is governed both by domestic law and by international conventions.

Of special importance in this respect is legislation on measures against organised crimes and economic-financial crimes, which covers money laundering, the unlawful production of and trade in narcotics, white collar crimes and, since the latest and very recent amendment, terrorism, terrorist organisations and certain types of trafficking, including that of minors and of guns. This very recent amendment gains particular importance since it has expanded (i) the scope of crimes where breach of secrecy duty is required and (ii) the scope of the breach of secrecy, since it now covers also the professional secrecy of employees of tax authorities, thus allowing for more efficiency in this area within the international and EU trend of actions against these kind of crimes.

24 Singapore

Alvin Yeo
Joy Tan

INTRODUCTION

Singapore as a financial centre of international importance

Over the past couple of decades, Singapore has developed into an international financial centre, rivalling, and in some sectors even surpassing, more traditionally renowned financial hubs like Tokyo and Hong Kong. In the *Global Competitiveness Report* (2001–2002), compiled by the Swiss-based World Economic Forum, Singapore was ranked as the tenth most competitive nation, ahead of Hong Kong (ranked eighteenth) and New Zealand (ranked twentieth). In the *World Competitiveness Yearbook* (2002), compiled by the International Institute for Management Development, Singapore was ranked in fifth place, after the US.

Certainly, within the South-East Asian region, Singapore is the pre-eminent financial centre, with 118 commercial banks (five of which are local) as at September 2002, 54 merchant banks, 53 representative offices of banks and merchant banks, and eight international money brokers. Of special importance in recent years is the emergence of the Asian Dollar Market, centred in Singapore, which as at the end of 2001 consisted of a pool of market resources of some US$471.4 billion.

Singapore's success as a financial centre has been achieved partly through building on its position at the crossroads of international trade. So, for instance, one writer opined that Singapore's strategic location on traditional international trade routes has resulted in her present importance to international trade, transportation and finance.[1]

This success has also been achieved partly by design, in that the government has identified financial services as an integral part of the economy and promulgated various measures to help the sector grow. As one senior government leader described this at the Second Reading of the Banking (Amendment) Bill of January 1984:

---

1   Dennis Campbell *International Bank Secrecy* (1992 edn) p 578.

'Since the introduction of the Banking Act in 1971, Singapore has developed into a financial centre of international importance. This is indicated by the presence of a large number of financial institutions of international standing and reputation, the advent of new financial instruments, the rapid development of the Asian Dollar Market, the extensive nature of the financial transactions entered into and the numerous financial services that are now being provided.'[2]

Singapore's financial sector is regulated by the Monetary Authority of Singapore (MAS), which is regarded as the de facto central bank.

Banker-customer relationship under the 2001 new statutory regime

In the Singapore chapter in the previous edition of this book, the axiomatic principle arising from the English landmark case of *Tournier v National Provincial and Union Bank of England*[3] that a bank would be under a contractual duty not to divulge information concerning its customer's account to third parties, which duty is implied by virtue of the banker-customer relationship, was discussed. Within Singapore's legal framework, under the Banking Act (Cap 19), the bank would also be under a statutory obligation not to make unauthorised disclosure.

It was concluded therefore that, in Singapore, the duty of the banking confidentiality stemmed from two sources:

1   the English common law contractual duty of confidentiality as received in Singapore; and
2   a statutory duty imposed by s 47 of the Banking Act (hereinafter s 47).

In the present writer's view, this *general* position – that the contractual duty owed at common law runs parallel with the statutory duty enforced by criminal statute – has not changed despite the recent material and far-reaching amendments to the Banking Act which came into force in June 2001, well after the previous edition of this publication. However, the amendments which were introduced by way of the Banking (Amendment) Bill 2001 (hereinafter the 2001 amendments) substantially revised the structure of the s 47 bank confidentiality provisions, and does away with the exceptions to bank confidentiality owed at common law, such that much of the previous edition's chapter would no longer reflect the current position on bank confidentiality in Singapore.

The timeliness of this new edition allows the present writers to update the chapter on Singapore law and to discuss the new statutory regime introduced by the 2001 amendments.

The reception of English common law in Singapore

As will be discussed in detail below, the new statutory regime raises questions as to the extent to which the English common law position (and, in particular, the common law exceptions to the duty of confidentiality) continues to apply in Singapore.

---

2   Parliamentary Debates, 17 January 1994, at the 2nd Reading of the Banking (Amendment) Bill by the then First Deputy Prime Minister Goh Keng Swee.
3   [1924] 1 KB 461.

Nevertheless, the previous brief outline of the way English common law is received in Singapore is still relevant as a starting point to this discussion.

The reception of English law in Singapore was effected by the Letters Patent issued on 27 November 1826. This was more commonly referred to as the Second Charter of Justice that established the Court of the Judicature of the Prince of Wales, Singapore and Malacca (the Straits Settlements). Thereafter, English law and equity, as it stood in England in 1826, became part of the law of the Straits Settlements.[4] Section 5 of the Civil Law Act was later enacted, providing that, in relation to commercial issues not governed by any Singapore statute, the relevant law applicable in England (covering both common law and statute) would apply.

In 1993, to overcome the difficulties in applying s 5 of the Civil Law Act, the Singapore Parliament passed the Application of English Law Act 1993 which provided, inter alia, for the continuing reception of the English common law of Singapore, in so far as:

1   it was part of the law of Singapore immediately before the commencement of this Act; and
2   it is applicable to the circumstances of Singapore and its inhabitants and is subject to such modifications as those circumstances may require.[5]

The Act also lists the specific English statutes which are deemed to be part of Singapore law, save where provided otherwise by Singapore statutes.

BASIC RULE OF CONFIDENTIALITY PRIOR TO THE 2001 AMENDMENTS

Nature of the Singapore banker's obligation

Prior to the 2001 amendments to the Banking Act, it was generally accepted that the common law duty of confidentiality applies to civil liability, while s 47 creates a statutory obligation, the breach of which would constitute a criminal offence.[6]

The English contractual duty under *Tournier*

The English landmark case of *Tournier v National Provincial and Union Bank of England*[7] laid down the principle that the banker's obligation to keep particulars of a customer's account confidential is an implied term that arises out of the banker-customer contractual relationship.

As there was no other provision made by any law having force in Singapore imposing a contractual duty of secrecy, and since this was treated as part of the law of Singapore immediately before the commencement of the Application of English Law Act in

4   Campbell, n 1 above, pp 580–581. See also Walter Woon *The Singapore Legal Systems* (1989).
5   Section 3 of the Application of English Law Act. This Act repeals the previous s 5 of the Civil Law Act, which was the relevant law that had provided for the continuing reception of the common law.
6   Poh Chu Chai *Law of Banker and Customer* (4th edn, 1999) p 572.
7   [1924] 1 KB 461.

1993, this common law principle continued to be in force in Singapore, at least until the 2001 amendments.

The scope of this common law contractual duty under *Tournier* has been extensively covered in ch 9, England. In brief, under the duty, the bank is obliged under an implied term of the contract between itself and its customer not to divulge information as to the state of the customer's account, any of the customer's transactions with the bank or any information relating to the customer acquired through the keeping of this account to third parties.

This is, however, a qualified obligation. The bank may release the above-stated information when:

1   an order of court compels the bank to disclose;
2   the disclosure is necessitated by a duty to the public;
3   the protection of the bank's interests requires disclosure; or
4   there is an express or implied consent of the customer.

Since the Application of English Law Act, English authorities are now not strictly binding on Singapore courts, but nevertheless considered highly persuasive.

The former statutory duty of confidentiality: comparison with contractual duty

In Singapore, the former statutory duty of confidentiality, imposed by the old s 47, provided for a general prohibition against disclosure of the affairs of the customer's account, which was then qualified by various exceptions. The general prohibition against disclosure was contained in the old s 47(3). This duty was not merely imposed on bank 'officials',[8] but also covered any person who has any means of access to the records of the bank by reason of his capacity or office, and on any person in a 'professional relationship' with the bank (for example, wide enough to cover solicitors and accountants who were engaged by the bank).

The old s 47(4) provided for certain exceptions to this general prohibition.

The Singapore chapter in the previous edition of this book discussed and sought to compare in detail the common law exceptions to the duty of confidentiality with the then statutory exceptions, and to examine the overlap between the specific local statute and the common law which stems from Singapore's legacy as a former English law jurisdiction.

Pre-amendments, the differences between the two regimes lay not so much in the general rule of confidentiality but rather in the exceptions to the general rule.

Similarities and differences in the exceptions under the old regime

It would appear that some of the defences available to a bank at common law were different from those under the former s 47. In theory, this would mean that the banks

---

8   The former s 47(11) defined 'official' of the bank to include a director and an employee of the bank.

would be able to rely on the common law exceptions as defences in civil actions brought against them by their customers whereas, if prosecuted, they and their employees would be confined to the statutory exceptions under s 47.

The first exception to the contractual duty, whereby the disclosure may be made under compulsion of law, found a parallel of sorts under the old s 47(4)(d) and (e).

The second exception to the contractual duty, whereby a disclosure may be made under a duty to the public, had no corresponding provision under the statutory duty.

The third exception under the contractual duty of confidentiality is to allow disclosure to be made in the interests of the bank. This was mirrored in the old s 47(4)(b) and (c).

Finally, the exception that disclosure may be made under the express or implied consent of the customer does not find an exact parallel enacted under the statutory duty of confidentiality – the former s 47(4)(a) provided that nothing less than a *written* consent by the customer or his personal representatives would suffice to lift the prohibition.

The differences in the exceptions raised the issue of whether the public interest and implied consent exceptions applies under the statutory regimes. It was argued by one writer that the then s 47 was not exhaustive since this would result in a narrow interpretation.[9] In the previous edition, it was opined that that the common law duty and the statutory duty supplemented each other and s 47 was not exhaustive as it would not be in keeping with the legislative intent if the common law exceptions, which would constitute a valid defence to civil liability, were not also available as a defence in respect of the more onerous criminal liability. It was noted that the issue had then yet to be resolved by the Singapore courts.

It would appear, however, that the legislature had seen fit to take up the resolution of the issue themselves, with the enactment of the 2001 amendments. It now seems clear, under the new statutory regime, that the exceptions to the statutory duty stated in the Banking Act are intended to be *exhaustive* and the common law exceptions are not to apply.

THE 2001 AMENDMENTS: THE NEW STATUTORY DUTY OF CONFIDENTIALITY

On 16 May 2001, the Singapore government introduced in Parliament the Banking (Amendment) Bill, which revised various provisions of the Banking Act. Focussing on prudential oversight issues, the Bill was expressed to reflect the MAS' new risk-focused supervisory approach that enhanced its oversight on banks without increasing their cost of regulatory compliance. In the words of the Deputy Prime Minister (and concurrent Chairman of the MAS) in moving the Bill:

'[MAS'] objective of ensuring financial stability is unchanged. But in order to have a more dynamic and vibrant financial sector, we have shifted emphasis

---

9   Myint Soe 'Changes in the Law Relating to Banking Secrecy, the Banking (Amendment) Act 1983' [1983] 25 Mal LR 387.

from regulation to supervision. We have moved away from one-size-fits-all laws and regulations, towards tailored supervision of individual institutions according to each institution's financial strength, risk management capability and risk profile.'[10]

In line with this policy, s 47 was amended to provide for a revised banking secrecy regime whereby banks would be given greater operational flexibility in handling customer information while still being subject to sufficient safeguards to ensure that the confidentiality of customer information is not compromised.

The Deputy Prime Minister described this as follows:

'Tight banking secrecy is important to maintaining the confidence of customers in our banking system. However, our present banking secrecy provisions have impeded banks wanting to take advantage of potential operational benefits and savings. For example, banks find it difficult to securitise mortgage loans, or to outsource data processing to third parties ... We have considered both the operational requirements of the banks and the need to preserve customer confidentiality. The measures set out in the section 47 strike a careful balance between these two sets of considerations.'[11]

Overview of the new section 47 and exceptions

The new s 47 enacts a more extensive set of circumstances under which banks can disclose customer information, and the terms of such disclosure, which is now separately set out in the Sixth Sch to the Banking Act (the Sixth Sch). The Sixth Sch contains two parts – Pt I, which contains many of the old exceptions in existence under the previous statutory regime, and Pt II, which contains most of the new exceptions.

Both Schedules contain a first, second and third column, which contain, in relation to each exception, the purpose of the permitted disclosure (lawful purpose), the person or class of persons to which that disclosure may be made (lawful recipient) and certain conditions which must be complied with in relation to that disclosure (conditions), respectively.

The new s 47(2) provides that a bank may, for a lawful purpose, disclose customer information to the corresponding lawful recipient, and in compliance with any applicable conditions (primary disclosure).

In relation to the exceptions in Pt I, the lawful recipient of information, not just the bank itself, is permitted to make further disclosure of the information (secondary disclosure) without penalty. However, under a new s 47(5), the lawful recipient of information furnished pursuant to any of the exceptions in Pt II is not permitted to

---

10   Parliamentary Debates, 16 May 2001, at the 2nd Reading of the Banking (Amendment) Bill, col 1684. (An example of this policy is the enactment of the new s 9A, which reduces the paid-up capital requirement for banking subsidiaries of local banks which have met the former S$1.5 billion capital requirement, to S$100 million. This was to facilitate the setting up of banking subsidiaries that adopt new business models such as Internet banking.)
11   Parliamentary Debates, n 10 above, col 1689.

make secondary disclosure, except as authorised under the Sixth Sch or if required to do so by an Order of Court. A breach of this section would constitute an offence.

The new s 47 applies not only to banks but to merchant (and investment) banks, subject to the notifications set out in the Third Sch to the Banking Regulations 2001, which were operative from 18 July 2001. The Merchant Bank Directive 12 on Banking Secrecy, issued under the former regime, has been revoked.

Subject matter of the new statutory duty: customer information

The new s 47(1) prohibits a bank in Singapore (the bank) or any of its officers from disclosing customer information except as expressly provided in the Act.

Under section 40(A), 'customer information' (in relation to the bank) means—

'(a) any information relating to, or any particulars of, an account of a customer of the bank, whether the account is in respect of a loan, investment or any other type of transaction, but does not include any information that is not referable to any named customer or group of named customers; or

(b) deposit information, which means any information relating to—
   (i)   any deposit of a customer of the bank;
   (ii) funds of a customer under management by the bank; or
   (iii) any safe deposit box maintained by, or any safe custody arrangements made by, a customer with the bank,
   but does not include any information that is not referable to any named customer or group of named customers.'

Under the former s 47(3), the statutory duty of confidentiality only applied to 'information regarding the money or other relevant particulars of the account of [the] customer'. The subject matter of the common law duty is wider than this – for instance, in *Tournier*,[12] the bank had made disclosure to a third party of the fact that the customer had diverted the proceeds of a cheque to a bookmaker, which information neither related to the money in the customer's account nor is it a particular of his account.

This anomaly was raised in the previous edition, and it was suggested that the narrower scope of the duty as per the statute should apply, on the principle of statutory interpretation that a penal statute be narrowly construed.

The new definition of 'customer information', therefore, brings the statutory duty of confidentiality more in line with the *Tournier* common law position, and does away with the anomaly.

It should be noted that this new position is also now consistent with the position in Malaysia, where the equivalent provision prohibits the disclosure of 'any information or document whatsoever relating to the affairs or account' of a customer.

The issue of what constituted customer information was addressed in the recent local case of *PSA Corpn v Korea Exchange Bank*.[13] In that case, PSA commenced

---

12   *Tournier v National Provincial and Union Bank of England* [1924] 1 KB 461.
13   [2002] 3 SLR 37.

action against Korea Bank for payment under two guarantees of a contractor, CY Singapore. Korea Bank's main defence was that PSA did not open an account with CY Singapore as required under the contract, but with its Korean affiliate, CY Korea. PSA sought discovery of account opening documents between Korea Bank and non-parties CY Singapore and CY Korea. Korea Bank admitted the documents sought were relevant but said it was precluded by s 47 of the Act from giving discovery.

PSA's main argument regarding confidentiality was that the documents did not contain protected 'account information', and that the old definition of protected information under the former s 47 was unchanged by the 2001 amendments.

Rejecting PSA's argument, the High Court held that the new, wider definition of customer information under s 47 protected the documents, and refused to make the discovery order sought against Korea Bank.[14]

The new exceptions

Much of the attention generated by the 2001 amendments centred on the new exceptions to the general rule on bank secrecy (which are largely to be found in Pt II of the Sixth Sch), which did not exist under the original regime. These new exceptions were by and large welcomed as necessary developments in the law to reflect the current practice and needs of banks in the climate of internationalisation, specialisation and competition in the new millennium.

Part I of the Sixth Sch mainly contains the exceptions set out in the old s 47(4). Some of the 'new' Pt I exceptions will be briefly discussed before turning to the Pt II exceptions.

PART I, ITEMS 3 AND 4: PROCEEDINGS IN CAMERA UNDER SECTION 47(3)

Items 3 and 4 relate to disclosure made in connection with bankruptcy/winding up of the customer, and with proceedings between the bank and customer(s) (with the exception of item 4(c), which is dealt with below). It is to be noted that under the new s 47(3), in cases involving such disclosure, a court is empowered to direct that the proceedings be held in camera and make other orders necessary to ensure confidentiality of the customer information.

The High Court opined obiter in *PSA Corpn v Korea Bank* that the current s 47(3) was too narrow, and should not be confined to items 3 and 4. This was because there are other exceptions which may require the court's assistance to ensure confidentiality, for example, items 6 and 7 of the Sixth Sch, which pertain to garnishee proceedings and a court order pursuant to Pt IV of the Evidence Act (Cap 97).[15]

PART I, ITEM 4: DISCLOSURE IN CONNECTION WITH CONDUCT OF PROCEEDINGS OVER PROPERTY OF BANK

The previous exception under s 47(4)(c) was where disclosure was made with a view to instituting or conducting civil proceedings between the bank and its customer or

14 [2002] 3 SLR 37 at 43.
15 [2002] 3 SLR 37 at 44.

guarantor relating to the customer's banking transaction, or in an interpleader situation. Item 4 substitutes 'guarantor' with the more encompassing 'surety', dispenses with the qualification 'civil', thus arguably expanding the exception to arbitration proceedings, and adds the following situation:

> '(c) between the bank and one or more parties in respect of property, whether movable or immovable, in or over which some right or interest has been conferred or alleged to have been conferred on the bank by the customer or his surety.'

This exception permits the bank to rely on customer information in order to prove its title or right to property, which property is the subject of litigation between the bank and third parties (who may not be the customer), as distinct from the interpleader situation. Conversely, this also permits the third parties to obtain discovery against the bank in order to challenge such title. This is a welcome addition to the limited 'litigation' exceptions under the former regime.

However, it is submitted that these exceptions should have even wider scope, as was noted in *PSA Corpn v Korea Exchange Bank*. The High Court, in holding that a court could not order disclosure from a bank if none of the Sixth Sch exceptions applied, had the following comments:

> 'It may well be that the present case calls for further amendments to be made to the Act to include an exception which allows disclosure in litigation between a bank and the beneficiary of an instrument issued by the bank. Indeed, there are many instances of banks issuing instruments like guarantees, performance bonds and letters of credit. It seems to be incongruous that where there is litigation between, say, a bank and a surety relating to the banking transaction of a customer, discovery of relevant documents pertaining to `customer information` is allowed but yet where a beneficiary sues a bank on any of the instruments I have mentioned, such disclosure is not allowed. Since the dispute between the beneficiary and the bank relates to an instrument which must have been issued at the request of the customer, the customer should not be in a position to complain if information relating to his account is disclosed so long as it satisfies the test of relevance in the litigation. In addition, the current s 47(3) can be expanded to allow the court to make such directions and orders it thinks fit to ensure confidentiality where this exception, if available, applies.
>
> ...
>
> However, it is for Parliament to decide whether any further exception to banking secrecy or confidentiality is required and whether the current s 47(3) should be expanded.'[16]

It remains to be seen if Parliament does act to expand the 'litigation' exceptions to bank secrecy.

---

16   [2002] 3 SLR 37 at 43–44.

PART I, ITEM 7: DISCLOSURE PURSUANT TO PART IV OF THE EVIDENCE ACT

Under Pt I of the Sixth Sch, the exception under item 7 permits primary disclosure in order to comply with an Order of Court pursuant to the powers conferred under Pt IV of the Evidence Act – relieving banks from the necessity of attending and producing their books in court.

This is not strictly a new exception – under the former s 47(4)(d), banking secrecy obligations would not apply to the officials of any bank who by compulsion of any written law in force in Singapore (including Pt IV of the Evidence Act) are required to give information to the police or a public officer who is duly authorised under that law to obtain that information or to a court in the investigation or prosecution of a criminal offence under any such law. However, s 47(4)(d) addressed entirely criminal matters, and did not cover the situation of disclosure orders made by the court under Pt IV of the Evidence Act in civil cases. This was a loophole in the drafting that was addressed by the 2001 amendment.

The main section in Pt IV of the Evidence Act is s 175(1), which provides that:

'On the application of any party to a legal proceeding, the court or a Judge may order that such party be at liberty to inspect and take copies of any entries in a banker's book for any of the purposes of such proceedings.'

'Bankers' book' is defined in s 170 of the Evidence Act as follows:

'"Bankers' books" includes ledgers, day books, cash books, account books and all other books used in the ordinary business of the bank.'

The recent unreported case of *Anthony Wee Soon Kim v UBS AG*[17] clarifies that the exception under item 7 *only* applies to orders made under Pt IV of the Evidence Act, and if disclosure of confidential banking documents is being ordered via some other means, an order under Pt IV of the Evidence Act would have to be sought as well. In the *Anthony Wee* case, defendants who had applied for and obtained subpoenae duces tecum against other banks to produce banking documents relating to the plaintiff, were ordered to take out an application under s 175 of the Evidence Act to enable the banks to make the disclosure pursuant to the subpoena. It seems clear from this decision (which has been appealed against) that a disclosure order under s 175 would be necessary before a bank would be exempted under this item from its duty of confidentiality, notwithstanding that an order under some other provision for disclosure had already been obtained.

This does, however, create some difficulty, as an additional 'exempting' application under s 175 might be difficult to obtain in relation to disclosure orders to trace funds of fraudsters under the principle set out in *Bankers Trust v Shapira*[18] – the scope of such orders are often wider than the orders for inspection of bankers' books pursuant to s 175.

Further, s 175 contemplates an existing legal proceeding, and an 'exempting' application cannot be brought in a pre-action situation, for instance in relation to disclosure pursuant to a *Norwich Pharmacal*[19] order, or even pre-action Mareva injunction orders.

Formerly, despite this, banks would, as a matter of practice, comply with such disclosure orders rather than risk being in contempt of court. (Previously, the wider *Tournier* exception of disclosure pursuant to compulsion of law might have applied to this situation.) It remains to be seen, after the *Anthony Wee* decision, how this lacuna will be addressed in practice by banks, especially now that the s 47 exceptions would appear to be exhaustive.

PART II, ITEM 1: DISCLOSURE IN CONNECTION WITH PERFORMANCE OF DUTY

As a matter of practice in Singapore, as well as elsewhere, bank officers already often disclose customer information to their colleagues in Singapore, as well as in overseas branches and to their professional advisers. The new item 1 has formally recognised this practice as an exception to the duty of bank secrecy.

The scope of the exception is as follows. A bank officer may disclose customer information to his fellow bank officer in Singapore, or to an officer designated in writing by the head office overseas, in connection with the performance of duty on the part of both parties. The lawful recipient in this case does not however include bank officers from overseas branches and subsidiaries (who have not been so designated by the head office).

Another lawful recipient of such information would be the bank's auditor, lawyer, consultant or other professional adviser appointed or engaged by the bank under a contract of service.

PART II, ITEM 2: CONDUCT OF INTERNAL AUDIT AND RISK MANAGEMENT

Pursuant to this exception, in connection with the conduct of internal audit or risk management, a foreign bank in Singapore may now disclose customer information to (i) its head office or parent bank, (ii) an overseas branch designated by the head office and (iii) a designated 'related corporation' (ie its subsidiaries or affiliates). A local bank may disclose to its parent bank or any related designated corporation.

Several writers[20] have mentioned the lacuna in the old regime, where disclosure is permitted under the previous s 47(4)(f), to a bank's head office (of information relating to credit/foreign exchange details), under s 47(4)(k) to a bank's local parent bank (of information relating to credit facilities) and s 47(4)(l) to a bank's head office and branch (for the purposes of collating and processing of information). It appeared that while disclosure could be made to a branch of a bank and a parent bank, no disclosure could be made to a subsidiary. Now, at least for the purpose of this exception, a subsidiary can finally be made (by designation) a lawful recipient of customer information.

---

19   Norwich Pharmacal Co v Customs & Excise Commissioners [1974] AC 133.
20   Eg Tan Sin Liang 'Banking Secrecy – legal implications for banks in Singapore under the Banking (Amendment) Act 2001' [2001] Straits Lawyer, August, at 28.

PART II, ITEM 3: OUTSOURCING OPERATIONAL FUNCTIONS

This is a particularly welcome exception which allows a bank to outsource its operational functions and thereby disclose customer information to 'any person including the head office of the bank or any branch thereof outside Singapore' who is engaged to perform the functions.

It has become increasingly more commercially expedient for banks in Singapore to outsource many of their operational functions such as processing of credit cards to third parties, who might enjoy greater economies of scale in that particular function than the banks themselves. This enabled banks to focus on their core banking business in the value chain. However, such activities were not strictly authorised under the former banking secrecy regime – instead, approval from the MAS on a case-by-case basis under the old s 47(12) was necessary before such outsourcing activities could take place. This has now been addressed by the new exception in item 3.

The new exception draws a distinction between local and domestic outsourcing. If the outsourced function is to be performed outside Singapore, the MAS may impose conditions on the outsourcing contracts, as compared with domestic outsourcing, where no such conditions are imposed. This appears from the parliamentary debate at the Second Reading of the Banking (Amendment) Bill to have been done to safeguard against the foreign lawful recipient wrongfully disclosing customer information. While that foreign service provider would have committed an offence under s 47(5) by so doing, the penalties for this would be difficult to enforce extra-territorially. For that reason, before it would permit a bank in Singapore to disclose customer information overseas, the MAS therefore desired a certain level of standing in proposed foreign outsource service providers, and in the legal and regulative framework of its home jurisdiction.[21]

PART II, ITEM 4: MERGERS AND ACQUISITIONS

This new exception permits a bank to disclose customer information in connection with a merger or acquisition, or proposed merger or acquisition, of the bank or its financial holding company, to any person participating or otherwise involved in the merger/acquisition or proposed merger/acquisition (including his lawyers and other advisers), whether or not the merger/acquisition is subsequently entered into or completed.

Obviously, one of the big challenges in the merger or acquisition of a bank is in overcoming the banking secrecy issue. Since not all banks would have provided for a consent to such disclosure in their account opening forms in anticipation of a merger or acquisition, a bank may have to undertake the onerous and commercially inexpedient task of corresponding with its million (or more) customers to obtain their consents prior to making disclosure.

It is to be noted that contemporaneously with the coming into effect of this exception in July 2001, there was a rash of merger and acquisition activity in the banking sector in 2001. This exception no doubt facilitated such activity as the banks involved

---

21 Parliamentary Debates, n 10 above, cols1709–1710, per the Deputy Prime Minister, BG Lee Hsien Loong.

were able to share and exchange information freely in negotiations and due diligence exercises without having to engage in the time-consuming exercise of obtaining customer consents.

This new exception permits a bank to disclose customer information in connection with the restructure, transfer or sale (or proposed restructure, transfer or sale) of credit facilities of the bank, to any transferee, purchaser or person participating or otherwise involved (including his lawyers and other advisers), whether or not the restructure/ transfer/sale is subsequently entered into or completed. There is a caveat that only information relating to the relevant credit facilities may be disclosed (and not deposit information relating to funds in the customer's account).

This exception was enacted to make it easier for banks to take advantage of potential benefits in dealing with existing credit facilities, in particular, with regard to securitising mortgage loans and engaging in asset securitisation generally. Prior to this, there was obvious difficulty for a bank to engage in transactions for the transfer or sale of its credit facilities when the identity of the borrowers could not be disclosed without being in breach of bank secrecy. Now, a bank would be entitled to disclose customer information in connection with transfers or assignments of its loans, for instance, via novation agreements, participation agreements and assignment agreements, as well as in asset securitisation and loan mortgage securitisation. Further, customer information may be disclosed in connection with restructuring of credit facilities – although this term is not defined, this would in all likelihood include rescheduling of loans and private 'work-outs'.

This new exception paves the way to establishing a Credit Bureau in Singapore, which would allow banks to obtain credit evaluations regarding certain customers and obtain information about 'delinquent' customers which they would wish to avoid. The exception permits the sharing of certain customer information between a member bank and the Bureau and between fellow members of the Bureau.

Under item 7, a Bureau member bank can disclose certain customer information to the Bureau and to fellow members for the purpose of 'assessing the creditworthiness of the customers of banks'. This is subject to two caveats. First, no deposit information is to be disclosed. Secondly, secondary disclosure to one member by the Bureau of information disclosed by another member is to be regulated by the MAS.

The Bureau (known as the Consumer Credit Bureau) has recently been formally constituted. At the date of writing, it has yet to be gazetted by the MAS and to commence operations, although it is envisaged that this will happen shortly. The preliminary feedback from the consumer public regarding the Bureau has been mixed – while many acknowledge the benefit to the banking sector, most appear concerned about the risk to privacy and the potential inroads into the confidentiality of their bank information.

PART II, ITEM 9: CROSS-MARKETING

This new exception facilitates the extension of cross-marketing capability to promote financial products and services in Singapore of any local financial institution which is licensed or regulated by MAS to customers of the bank. As banks in Singapore may not be experts across the entire spectrum of financial products, cross-marketing was seen as desirable to help broaden consumer choice.

In the parliamentary debates during the Second Reading of the Banking (Amendment) Bill, the issue of increased customer demand for rapid Internet processing and epayments was mentioned, together with the examples of Citigroup's successful use of the MSN portal and the emergence of PayPal in competition with credit card companies.[22] Cross-marketing was seen to cater for perceived growing customer demand, both for new products which may not be not offered by more traditional banks, and a one-stop 'banking-cum-services' centre. Additionally, in the face of increased competition, banks were under pressure to enter into mutual alliances and tie-ups with other financial institutions to cross-market their own products and services and to provide a one-stop financial centre.

To address the concern about the potential invasion of customers' privacy regarding unsolicited approaches by allied third-party institutions such as insurance providers and credit card companies, banks are only permitted to disclose the customer's name, identity, address and contact numbers. No deposit information or credit or investment information, for example, the amount of funds in a customer's account and his investment profile, which might be very useful for the cross-marketing party, may be disclosed. Further, cross-marketing of non-financial products and services, cross-marketing with a party who is not a MAS-regulated financial institution and cross-marketing of financial products and services outside Singapore would not come under the exception.

APPLICABILITY OF, AND COMPARISON WITH, COMMON LAW UNDER THE NEW REGIME

Status of the exceptions

As mentioned above, the Singapore chapter of the previous edition of this book took the position that the common law duty of confidentiality and the *Tournier*[23] exceptions thereto would still be implied in the Singapore civil law context, notwithstanding the 'co-existing' statutory regime under s 47. The chapter then discussed the differences between the two regimes (for instance, 'negative' consent is an exception under *Tournier*, but s 47 requires actual written consent).

The new s 47(1) now provides:

> 'Customer information shall not, in any way, be disclosed by a bank in Singapore or any of its officers to any other person *except as expressly provided in this Act*' (emphasis added).

---

22 Parliamentary Debates, n 10 above, col 1699.
23 *Tournier v National Provincial and Union Bank of England* [1924] 1 KB 461.

The amendment seems to clarify that there is now little scope for arguing that the common law exceptions can be implied in the Singapore context.

So while the common law regarding the existence of an implied contractual duty of confidentiality should still subsist, it is now unlikely that *Tournier* common law exceptions would still apply even as defences to civil action for breach of contract by the customer, since that would lead to the anomalous situation that an exception might be a good defence at civil law but not under criminal law.

This approach seems to be consistent with the High Court's decision in *PSA Corpn v Korea Exchange Bank*,[24] discussed above. Woo JC concludes his judgment with the strong statement that s 47 sets out the general prohibition against disclosure, and the (only) exceptions to this are to be found in the Sixth Sch (and, implicitly, not under the common law).[25]

Of further note is the new s 47(8), which states that nothing in s 47 shall prevent a bank from entering into an express agreement with a customer for a *higher* standard of confidentiality than that contemplated by the new statutory regime. There was no corresponding provision in the former s 47.

It is submitted that the existence of this new section does recognise (if by implication only) that the common law contractual duty of 'civil' confidentiality exists side by side with the statutory 'criminal' duty. Further, the new section would seem to clarify that the common law position is (now) the same as the statutory position, ie under common law the terms that will be implied into the bank-customer contract would be *the same provisions* under s 47, save where these are modified to impose a higher standard by an express term of the bank-customer contract.

Contractual obligation on the bank v criminal liability on bank officials

As noted above, the common law duty imposes a contractual obligation on the bank itself. Previously, the former s 47 imposed a statutory prohibition on the bank's *officials* and any other person with access to the bank's records, the breach of which would result in the commission of a criminal offence, and not strictly the bank itself.

This distinction was criticised, and one writer[26] pointed out that the prohibitions set out in s 47 would, in practice, apply equally to the bank just as much as to its officials.

Further, the scope of the former s 47 was very wide, also covering 'any person who by reason of his capacity or office has any means of access to the records'. Thus it was not restricted to a person rendering professional services to the bank, but could in theory include the junior clerk or messenger boy who may have means of access to the bank's records.

Both these aspects have now been amended in the new s 47(1), which now clarifies that the duty of confidentiality (and criminal penalties for a breach thereof) lies on the bank as well as its officers. ('Officers' is defined in s 2 of the Banking Act and includes a director, secretary, employee, receiver, manager and liquidator of the

---

24   [2002] 3 SLR 37.
25   [2002] 3 SLR 37 at 43.
26   Chai, n 6 above, pp 578–579.

bank, and, although it does not expressly say so, would seem to exclude the junior clerk or messengers of the bank.)

Further, the s 47(1) primary duty is not now extended to any person other than the bank and its officers (for example, the bank's professional or other advisers) at the first instance. Instead, where customer information was disclosed to lawful recipients, under an exception in the Sixth Sch which does not permit secondary disclosure, only then is a secondary duty not to disclose further imposed on those lawful recipients under the new s 47(5).

The new provisions bring the statutory duty of confidentiality in line with the position at common law.

The respective remedies/penalty for breach of confidentiality

As stated earlier, it is generally accepted that if a bank, its officers and any lawful recipient under a Pt II exception breach their duty of confidentiality, they will find themselves faced with both a civil claim by the customer and a prosecution by the state for the commission of a criminal offence.

Under the contractual duty of confidentiality, the customer can avail himself of two remedies:

1   *Injunction.* It is generally accepted that when a customer discovers that his bank intends to or has breached its duty of confidentiality without his consent, he can apply to the court for an order to restrain the bank from breaching or further breaching its duty. The grant of an injunction will be according to the general principles in the leading case of *American Cyanamid Co v Ethicon Ltd*.[27]

2   *Damages.* The customer has the option of withdrawing his mandate by closing his account with the bank and thereafter suing the bank for damages for breach of contract. Damages will be assessed in accordance with the general rules relating to measurement of damages under contract law.

In practice, the damage is done when the disclosure is made and would be difficult to quantify in monetary terms, which means that the injunction (if the customer is aware of the proposed disclosure in time) remains the most effective remedy.

Under the statutory duty of confidentiality, the new s 47(6) provides that an individual may be punished with a fine not exceeding S$125,000 or imprisonment for a term not exceeding thee years, or both. In the case of a corporation, a fine not exceeding S$250,000 may be imposed.

It is further provided in s 66 of the Banking Act that any director, managing director or manager of the bank who had wilfully failed to take any reasonable steps to secure compliance with the provisions of the Banking Act shall be liable to a fine of up to S$125,000 or imprisonment for a term of up to three years, or to both such fine and imprisonment. This means that the senior management in the bank cannot simply avoid liability by a subordinate breaching the duty of confidentiality, but must show that they had taken reasonable steps to ensure such compliance.

27   (1975) AL 396.

Duration of the duty of confidentiality

Contractual duty

The English Court of Appeal in *Tournier* were of the view that the duty of secrecy commenced once the contractual relationship has been entered into, and that it continued even after the termination of the banker-customer relationship, whereby the customer closed his account with the bank.

Statutory duty

Under the former regime, the stated persons were prohibited from disclosure during the employment in or professional relationship with the bank or after the termination of such employment or relationship. This position is preserved in the new s 47(7)(b). Nothing is said about the status of the *customer's* relationship with the banks. In the circumstances, it would appear from a literal reading of the section that there is no duty to preserve the confidentiality of someone who used to be a customer *after* he has closed his account with the bank.

Although 'bank' and 'banking business' are defined in the Banking Act, there is no definition of a 'customer'. *Halsbury's Laws of England* defines customer as 'someone who has an account with a bank or who is in such relationship with the bank that the relationship of banker-customer exists, even though at this stage he has no account'.[28]

It is submitted that the statutory duty should continue even after the cessation of the banker-customer relationship. As pointed out by one writer,[29] this interpretation would be consistent with the contractual duty of confidentiality and in the interests of any customer. A further argument canvassed by the same writer is that although the statutory provision does not deal with the customer's rights in themselves, it prohibits the disclosure by the stipulated persons *even after* the termination of their employment by or professional relationship with the bank. Seen in this light, the legislative intent must have been that the customer's right of confidentiality be protected perpetually.

CONCLUSION

It can be seen that the duty of confidentiality in Singapore is an onerous one because the banks owe a contractual duty to their customers and, at the same time, they are also subject to a statutory duty of confidentiality which carries with it a criminal liability. As criminal liability would attach, no bank in Singapore would deliberately flout their banking secrecy obligations simply because the customer would not find out or be able to sue them thereafter.

The confidentiality provisions in the Banking Act have undergone considerable amendments since the 1971 legislation, the most recent being the 2001 amendments. This is a commendable effort on the part of the legislature in ensuring that there is

---

28   3(1) *Halsbury's Laws* (4th edn, reissue) para 148.
29   Cheong May Fong 'Banking Secrecy in Malaysia' (1993) 20 JMCL 157 at 166, in relation to the Malaysian provisions on secrecy, which is similarly silent on the issue.

sufficient supervision of the banks by the MAS, yet at the same time in seeking to address the public interest of pursuing criminal and civil remedies and the private concerns of commercial and lay persons that the banks should not be over-regulated to the extent of practical unworkability. This ongoing effort to strike the right balance is particularly conspicuous in the area of bank confidentiality.

APPENDIX

BANKING ACT (CAP 19)

Interpretation of this Part

40A. In this Part—

'customer' , in relation to a bank, includes the Authority or any monetary authority or central bank of any other country or territory, but does not include any company which carries on banking business or such other financial institution as may be designated by the Authority by notice in writing;

'customer information', in relation to a bank, means—

(a) any information relating to, or any particulars of, an account of a customer of the bank, whether the account is in respect of a loan, investment or any other type of transaction, but does not include any information that is not referable to any named customer or group of named customers; or
(b) deposit information;

'deposit information', in relation to a bank, means any information relating to—

(a) any deposit of a customer of the bank;
(b) funds of a customer under management by the bank; or
(c) any safe deposit box maintained by, or any safe custody arrangements made by, a customer with the bank,

but does not include any information that is not referable to any named person or group of named persons;

'funds of a customer under management' means any funds or assets of a customer (whether of the bank or any financial institution) placed with that bank for the purpose of management or investment;

'parent bank' , in relation to a bank, means a financial institution which is able to exercise a significant influence over the direction and management of the bank or which has a controlling interest in the bank;

'parent supervisory authority' , in relation to a bank incorporated outside Singapore, means the supervisory authority which is responsible, under the laws of the country or territory where the bank or its parent bank is incorporated, formed or established, for supervising the bank or its parent bank, as the case may be.

Banking secrecy

47.—(1) Customer information shall not, in any way, be disclosed by a bank in Singapore or any of its officers to any other person except as expressly provided in this Act.

(2) A bank in Singapore or any of its officers may, for such purpose as may be specified in the first column of the Sixth Schedule, disclose customer information to such persons or class of persons as may be specified in the second column of that Schedule, and in compliance with such conditions as may be specified in the third column of that Schedule.

(3) Where customer information is likely to be disclosed in any proceedings referred to in item 3 or 4 of Part I of the Sixth Schedule, the court may, either of its own motion, or on the application of any party to the proceedings or the customer to which the customer information relates—

(a) direct that the proceedings be held in camera; and
(b) make such further orders as it may consider necessary to ensure the confidentiality of the customer information.

(4) Where an order has been made by a court under subsection (3), any person who, contrary to such an order, publishes any information that is likely to lead to the identification of any party to the proceedings shall be guilty of an offence and shall be liable on conviction to a fine not exceeding $125,000.

(5) Any person (including, where the person is a body corporate, an officer of the body corporate) who receives customer information referred to in Part II of the Sixth Schedule shall not, at any time, disclose the customer information or any part thereof to any other person, except as authorised under that Schedule or if required to do so by an order of court.

(6) Any person who contravenes subsection (1) or (5) shall be guilty of an offence and shall be liable on conviction—

(a) in the case of an individual, to a fine not exceeding $125,000 or to imprisonment for a term not exceeding 3 years or to both; or
(b) in any other case, to a fine not exceeding $250,000.

(7) In this section and in the Sixth Schedule, unless the context otherwise requires—

(a) where disclosure of customer information is authorised under the Sixth Schedule to be made to any person which is a body corporate, customer information may be disclosed to such officers of the body corporate as may be necessary for the purpose for which the disclosure is authorised under that Schedule; and
(b) the obligation of any officer or other person who receives customer information referred to in Part II of the Sixth Schedule shall continue after the termination or cessation of his appointment, employment, engagement or other capacity or office in which he had received customer information.

(8) For the avoidance of doubt, nothing in this section shall be construed to prevent a bank from entering into an express agreement with a customer of that bank for a higher degree of confidentiality than that prescribed in this section and in the Sixth Schedule.

(9) Where, in the course of an inspection under section 43 or an investigation under section 44 or the carrying out of the Authority's function of supervising the financial condition of any bank, the Authority incidentally obtains customer information and such information is not necessary for the supervision or regulation of the bank by the Authority, then, such information shall be treated as secret by the Authority.

(10) This section and the Sixth Schedule shall apply, with such modifications as may be prescribed by the Authority, to a merchant bank approved as a financial institution under section 28 of the Monetary Authority of Singapore Act (Cap 186) as if the reference to a bank in this section were a reference to such merchant bank

SIXTH SCHEDULE

Section 47

PART I

FURTHER DISCLOSURE NOT PROHIBITED

First column	Second column	Third column
Purpose for which customer information may be disclosed	**Persons to whom information may be disclosed**	**Conditions**
1. Disclosure is permitted in writing by the customer or, if he is deceased, his appointed personal representative.	Any person as permitted by the customer or, if he is deceased, his appointed personal. representative	
2. Disclosure is solely in connection with an application for a grant of probate or letters of administration in respect of a deceased customer's estate.	Any person whom the bank in good faith believes is entitled to the grant of probate or letters of administration.	
3. Disclosure is solely in connection with—	All persons to whom he disclosure is necessary for the purpose specified in the first column.	*Note: Court may order the proceedings to be held in camera [see section 47 (3) and (4)].*
(a) where the customer is an individual, the bankruptcy of the customer; or (b) where the customer is a body corporate, the winding up of the customer.		
4. Disclosure is solely with a view to the institution of, or solely in connection with, the conduct of proceedings—	All persons to whom the disclosure is necessary for the purpose specified in the first column.	*Note: Court may order the proceedings to be held in camera [see section 47 (3) and (4)].*
(a) between the bank and the customer or his surety relating to the banking transaction of the customer; (b) between the bank and 2 or more parties making adverse		

First column	*Second column*	*Third column*
Purpose for which customer information may be disclosed	**Persons to whom information may be disclosed**	**Conditions**
claims to money in an account of the customer where the bank seeks relief by way of interpleader; or (c) between the bank and one or more parties in respect of property, whether movable or immovable, in or over which some right or interest has been conferred or alleged to have been conferred on the bank by the customer or his surety.		
5. Disclosure is necessary for— (a) compliance with an order or request made under any specified written law to furnish information, for the purposes of an investigation or prosecution, of an offence alleged or suspected to have been committed under any written law; or (b) the making of a complaint or report under any specified written law for an offence alleged or suspected to have been committed under any written law.	Any police officer or public officer duly authorised under the specified written law to carry out the investigation or prosecution or to receive the complaint or report, or any court.	
6. Disclosure is necessary for compliance with a garnishee order served on the bank attaching moneys in the account of the customer.	All persons to whom the disclosure is required to be made under the garnishee order.	
7. Disclosure is necessary for compliance with an order of the Supreme Court or a Judge thereof pursuant to the powers conferred under Part IV of the Evidence Act (Cap 97).	All persons to whom the disclosure is required to be made under the court order.	
8. Where the bank is a bank incorporated outside Singapore, the disclosure is strictly necessary for compliance with a request made by its parent supervisory authority solely in connection with the supervision of the bank.	The parent supervisory authority of the bank incorporated outside Singapore.	(a) No deposit information shall be disclosed to the parent supervisory authority. (b) The parent supervisory authority is prohibited by the laws applicable to it from disclosing the customer

First column	Second column	Third column
Purpose for which customer information may be disclosed	**Persons to whom information may be disclosed**	**Conditions**
		information obtained by it to any person unless compelled to do so by the laws or courts of the country or territory where it is established.
9. Disclosure is in compliance with the provisions of this Act, or any notice or directive issued by the Authority to banks.	The Authority or any person authorised or appointed by the Authority.	

PART II
FURTHER DISCLOSURE PROHIBITED

First column	Second column	Third column
Purpose for which customer information may be disclosed	**Persons to whom information may be disclosed**	**Conditions**
1. Disclosure is solely in connection with the performance of duties as an officer, or a professional adviser of the bank.	Any— (a) officer of the bank in Singapore; (b) officer designated in writing by the head office of the bank; or (c) auditor, lawyer, consultant or other professional adviser appointed or engaged by the bank under a contract for service.	
2. Disclosure is solely in connection with the conduct of internal audit of the bank or the performance of risk management.	In the case of— (a) a bank incorporated outside Singapore— (i) the head office or parent bank of the bank; (ii) any branch of the bank outside Singapore designated in writing by the head office of the bank; or (iii) any related corporation of the bank designated in writing by the head office of the bank; or (b) a bank incorporated in Singapore— (i) the parent bank; or (ii) any related corporation of the bank designated in writing by the head office of the bank.	
3. Disclosure is solely in connection with the	Any person including the head office of the bank or any	If any out-sourced function is to be performed outside

First column	Second column	Third column
Purpose for which customer information may be disclosed	**Persons to whom information may be disclosed**	**Conditions**
performance of operational functions of the bank where such operational functions have been out-sourced.	branch thereof outside Singapore which is engaged by the bank to perform the out-sourced functions.	Singapore, the disclosure shall be subject to such conditions as may be specified in a notice issued by the Authority or otherwise imposed by the Authority.
4. Disclosure is solely in connection with— (a) the merger or proposed merger of the bank or its financial holding company with another company; or (b) any acquisition or issue, or proposed acquisition or issue, of any part of the share capital of the bank or its financial holding company, whether or not the merger or acquisition is subsequently entered into or completed.	Any person participating or otherwise involved in the merger, acquisition or issue, or proposed merger, acquisition or issue, including any of his lawyers or other professional advisers (whether or not the merger or acquisition is subsequently entered into or completed).	
5. Disclosure is solely in connection with the restructure, transfer or sale, or proposed restructure, transfer or sale, of credit facilities (whether or not the restructure, transfer or sale is subsequently entered into or completed).	Any transferee, purchaser or any other person participating or otherwise involved in the restructure, transfer or sale, or proposed restructure, transfer or sale, including any of his lawyers or other professional advisers (whether or not the restructure, transfer or sale is subsequently entered into or completed).	No customer information, other than information relating to the relevant credit facilities, shall be disclosed.
6. In the case of a customer who has been issued with a credit or charge card by a bank in Singapore, disclosure is strictly necessary for notification of the suspension or cancellation of the card by the bank by reason of the customer's default in payment to the bank.	Any financial institution in Singapore which issues credit or charge cards.	No customer information, other than information relating to the following, may be disclosed: (a) the customer's name and identity; (b) the amount of the debt outstanding on the customer's credit or charge card; (c) the date of suspension or cancellation of the customer's credit or charge card, as the case may be.

First column **Purpose for which customer information may be disclosed**	Second column **Persons to whom information may be disclosed**	Third column **Conditions**
7. Disclosure is strictly necessary— (a) for the collation, synthesis processing of customer information by the credit bureau for the purposes of the assessment of the credit-worthiness of the customers of banks; or (b) for the assessment, by other members of the credit bureau specified in the second column, of the credit-worthiness of the customers of banks.	Any— (a) credit bureau of which the bank is a member; (b) other member of the credit bureau that is— (i) a bank or merchant bank; or (ii) a person, or a person belonging to a class of persons, recognised by the Authority, by notification published in the *Gazette*, as authorised to receive the information, where that member receives such information from the credit bureau.	(a) No deposit information shall be disclosed. (b) The disclosure by any credit bureau to any person referred to in paragraph (b) of the second column shall be subject to such conditions as may be specified in a notice issued by the Authority or otherwise imposed by the Authority.
8. Disclosure is strictly necessary for the assessment of the credit-worthiness of the customer in connection with or relating to a bona fide commercial transaction or a prospective commercial transaction.	Any other bank or merchant bank in Singapore.	No customer information, other than information of a general nature and not related to the details of the customer's account with the bank, shall be disclosed.
9. Disclosure is solely in connection with the promotion, to customers of the bank in Singapore, of financial products and services made available in Singapore by any financial institution specified in the second column.	Any financial institution in Singapore which is licensed or otherwise regulated by the Authority.	No customer information, other than the customer's name, identity, address, and contact number shall be disclosed.

PART III
INTERPRETATION

In this Schedule, unless the context otherwise requires—

'appointed personal representative', in relation to a deceased person, means a person appointed as executor or administrator of the estate of the deceased person;

'credit bureau' means a credit bureau recognised as such by the Authority by notification in the *Gazette* for the purposes of this Schedule;

'lawyer' means an advocate and solicitor of the Supreme Court of Singapore, or any person who is duly authorised or registered to practise law in a country or territory other than Singapore by a foreign authority having the function conferred by law of authorising or registering persons to practise law in that country or territory;

'merchant bank' means a merchant bank approved as a financial institution under section 28 of the Monetary Authority of Singapore Act (Cap. 186);

'public officer' includ- es any officer of a statutory board;

'specified written law' means the Companies Act (Cap. 50), the Criminal Procedure Code (Cap. 68), the Goods and Services Tax Act (Cap. 117A), the Income Tax Act (Cap. 134), the Internal Security Act (Cap. 143), the Kidnapping Act (Cap. 151) and the Prevention of Corruption Act (Cap. 241);

'surety' , in relation to a customer of a bank, includes any person who has given the bank security for the liability of the customer by way of a mortgage or a charge.

25 South Africa

Angela Itzikowitz

BANKER-CUSTOMER RELATIONSHIP

This chapter examines the legal aspects of the relationship between a bank and its customer and, in particular, the banker's duty of secrecy to his client under South African law.

The relationship between a bank and a customer is based on contract and is one of debtor and creditor in terms of which the bank becomes owner of the money deposited in the customer's current account and is obliged to pay cheques drawn on it by the customer.[1] The contract founding this relationship is not one of agency nor of the Roman law of depositum or mutuum since not all its consequences can be explained under these contracts of loan. Because of the complexity of the relationship it has been classified as one sui generis.[2]

In so far as the contract between the bank and the customer obliges the bank to render certain services, the so-called services de caisse, to the customer on his instructions, it has been classified as a contract of mandatum. The bank-customer relationship is based on a comprehensive mandate in terms of which the customer lends money to the bank on current account, the bank undertakes to repay it on demand by honouring cheques drawn on it and to perform certain other services for the customer, such as the collection of cheques and other instruments, and the keeping and accounting of his current account. The fact that the customer lends money to the bank, or the bank, in the case of an overdraft, to the customer, does not determine the nature of the contract between them; these loans facilitate the execution of the comprehensive mandate between the parties.[3]

---

1   See *London Joint Stock Bank Ltd v McMillan and Arthur* 1918 AC 777(, HL); *Standard Bank of South Africa Ltd v Oneanate Investments (Pty) Ltd* 1995 4 SA 510 (C) at 530 ff; *GS George Consultants and Investments (Pty) Ltd v Datasys (Pty) Ltd* 1988 (3) SA 726 (W); and *ABSA Bank Ltd v Standard Bank of South Africa LimitedLtd* [1997] 4 ALL SA 693 (SCA).
2   A contract sui generis is a contract of its own kind. *GS George Consultants and Investments (Pty) Ltd v Datasys (Pty) Ltd* 1988 3 SA 726 (W) at 735–736; and *Comr of Customs and Excise v Bank of Lisbon International Ltd* 1994(1) SA 205(N) at 213–214. See generally F R Malan and J T Pretorius *Malan on Bills of Exchange, Cheques and Promissory Notes* (4th edn, 2002) ch 16 (Malan) on which I have relied heavily.
3   Malan, n 2 above, p 336.

THE DUTY OF SECRECY

There is perhaps no more hallowed a custom than that of a banker to preserve confidentiality or privacy in regard to his customers' affairs.[4] Notwithstanding this confidential relationship between the bank and its customer, there has never evolved in South African banking law a legal privilege such as that which exists between an attorney and his client.[5] It has, however, been argued that a bank has a limited privilege under s 236(4) of the Criminal Procedure Act 1977[6] in so far as this section entitles the bank to withhold disclosure unless expressly ordered by a court. A similar provision is contained in s 31 of the Civil Proceedings Evidence Act 1965.[7]

The duty of secrecy was first recognised in *Abrahams v Burns*[8] and has subsequently been recognised in a number of decisions.[9] Banking secrecy is founded on legislation, contract and the protection of privacy. Several legislative enactments apply to bank secrecy and expressly or impliedly give recognition to it. Examples of such statutes are set out below.

The Promotion of Access to Information Act 2002[10] gives effect to the constitutional right of access to information held by the state, and any information that is held by another person and that is required for the exercise or protection of any rights. In terms of s 64(1) of the Act, access to certain information is limited. The head of a private body, for example, a bank, must refuse a request for access to a record of the body if the record contains, amongst other things, financial, commercial, scientific or technical information, a disclosure of which would be likely to cause harm to the commercial or financial interest of the customer. Section 65 provides that the head of a private body such as a bank must refuse a request for access to a record of that body if its disclosure would constitute an action for breach of duty of confidence owed to a third party in terms of an agreement. Such information could only be procured by a subpoena (writ) served on the bank to disclose.

Section 33 of the Reserve Bank Act 1989[11] provides that no director, officer or employee of the bank may disclose to any person, except to the minister or the Director-General: Finance, or for the purpose of the performance of his duties or functions or when required to do so before a court of law or under any law, any information relating to the affairs of the bank, a shareholder or client of the bank, acquired in the performance of his duties or functions or other information pertaining to the activities of the bank.

Where the information relates to the client of the bank, it may only be disclosed with the written consent of the minister and the governor, after consultation with the client concerned.

---

4   C Smith 'The Banker's Duty of Secrecy' (1979) Modern Business Law 24.
5   Smith, n 4 above.
6   Act 51 of 1977.
7   Act 25 of 1965. See W G Schulze 'Big Sister is Watching you: Banking Confidentiality and Secrecy under Siege' (2001) 13 SA Merc LJ 601.
8   1914 CPD 452.
9   *GS George Consultants and Investments (Pty) Ltd v Datasys (Pty) Ltd* 1988 (3) SA 726(W); *Sasfin (Pty) Ltd v Beukes* 1989 (1) SA(A); *Cywilnat (Pty) Ltd v Densam (Pty) Ltd* 1989 (3) SA 59(W); and *Densam (Pty) Ltd v Cywilnat (Pty) Ltd* 1991(1) SA 100 (A).
10   Act 2 of 2002.
11   Act 90 of 1989.

Section 87(2) of the Banks Act 1990[12] prohibits the husband of a depositor with a banking institution from obtaining, save with her written consent, any particulars concerning any deposit she has with that institution.

These statutes proceed from the assumption that a bank is under a duty to keep its clients information confidential without indicating what the basis of that duty is.[13] Generally, bank secrecy is said to have a contractual foundation and a bank's duty to keep its customer's information confidential is seen as an express or implied term of the banker-customer contract.[14] In so far as this contract can be classified as one of mandate, the bank's duty of secrecy can be characterised as an example of a mandatary's duty to perform his mandate in good faith.[15] In this sense, banking secrecy is not a peculiar institution but is similar to the duty of secrecy resting on other professionals.

However, in so far as a bank is obliged to keep all information concerning a customer confidential, including the fact that he was a customer,[16] contract alone does not provide the foundation of banking secrecy.

The Code of Banking Practice,[17] a self-regulatory mechanism which sets guidelines relating to the relationship between banks and their customers, deals, among other things, with issues of confidentiality. Section 4 provides that the bank will treat the customer's personal information (such as his name and address) as private and confidential even when the customer ceases to be customer. It states further that no information about the customer's account will be disclosed to anyone, including other companies within the banking group, other than in circumstances permitted by law.

Moreover, banks are obliged to keep all confidential information secret whether it relates to a customer or to any other person. A bank is under a duty to respect the financial and personal privacy of its customers and other members of the public and not to injure their creditworthiness or personal integrity by disclosing confidential information.[18]

This duty is, however, not absolute and there are circumstances justifying disclosure. In South African law as in English law, the oft-cited *Tournier v National Provincial and Union Bank of England* forms the cornerstone of bank secrecy.[19] *Tournier* recognised four qualifications to this duty:

1   where disclosure is under compulsion of law;
2   where there is a duty to the public to disclose;
3   where the interest of the bank require disclosure; and
4   where the disclosure is made with the express or implied consent of the customer.

---

12   Act 94 of 1990.
13   Malan, n 2 above, p 378 and see n 245.
14   1991(1) SA 100 (A).
15   Malan, n 2 above, p 379 and nn 250–252.
16   *Tournier v National Provincial and Union Bank of England* [1924] 1KB 461 at 485.
17   The Code, which has no force of law, is to a large extent based on the Banking Code (3rd edn, March 1997) of the British Bankers Association. The Code became effective on 3 April 2000.
18   Malan, n 2 above, p 380.
19   For a discussion of the facts, see ch 9, England, p 219 above.

THE QUALIFICATIONS TO THE DUTY

Where disclosure is under compulsion of law

This exception arises where a bank has to give evidence in a court of law or is obliged by a court order or statute to disclose information. At the time of the *Tournier* judgment,[20] compulsion by law on banks to release confidential information about their customers was unusual. Besides the Bankers Book Evidence Act 1897 cited by Banks LJ in *Tournier*, the only other instance was under s 5 of the Extradition Act 1873. The picture today under both English and South African law is very different. In South Africa, the last decade has seen the promulgation of a plethora of statutes obliging or permitting banks to disclose confidential information.

Income Tax Act 1962

Sections 74 and 74A of the Income Tax Act 1962[21] provide that the Commissioner for Inland Revenue may, for the purposes of the administration of the Act, in relation to any taxpayer, require such taxpayer or *any other person* to furnish to the Commissioner such information, documents or things as he may require. For the purposes of an inquiry contemplated in s 74C, any person may, by written notice issued by the presiding officer, be required to appear before him in order to be questioned under oath or solemn declaration.

The question that arises in this regard is whether the Commissioner will be able to rely on s 74A to obtain information from banks about their customers without a court order compelling it to do so. It has been argued that in so far as s 74A does not expressly authorise or compel banks to disclose information about their customers, they would not be permitted to do so. It is a well-established rule of the interpretation of statutes, so the argument goes, that there is a presumption that the legislature does not intend to alter the common law any more than is necessary.[22] Any legislative provision that aims at infringing a common law fiduciary relationship should therefore state so unambiguously. If ss 74 and 74A were to be interpreted in such a way so as to allow banks to disclose information to the Commissioner, the Commissioner could effectively go on fishing expeditions relating to the financial affairs of the bank's customers. The argument to the contrary is that in so far as a bank is *any person* these provisions apply also to it.[23]

National Prosecuting Authority Act 1998

Section 28(1) of the National Prosecuting Authority Act 1998[24] provides that if the investigating director has reason to suspect that an offence has been or is being committed or that an attempt has been made to commit an offence, he may hold an

---

20   *Tournier v National Provincial and Union Bank of England* [1924] 1KB 461.
21   Act 58 of 1962.
22   Schulze, n 7 above, at 611.
23   Malan, n 2 above, p 379.
24   Act 32 of 1998.

inquiry. The investigating director may, for purposes of the inquiry, summon *any person* whom he believes is able to furnish any information on the subject to appear before him and be questioned by him. The director may also summon *any person* who is believed to have any book, document or other object relating to the subject of inquiry, to be questioned or to produce such book, document or object. The question which has yet to be answered by our courts is whether this provision would permit a bank to disclose information relating to the affairs of its customer. In so far as a bank is any person it would seem to apply to a bank (see s 74 of the Income Tax Act 1962, discussed above). There is, however, an argument that the bank would be able to rely on s 236(4) of the Criminal Procedure Act 1977 and withhold disclosure of any document, book or object unless production is ordered by a court.[25]

Criminal Procedure Act 1977

In terms of s 236(4) of the Criminal Procedure Act 1977, no bank shall be compelled to produce any books of account (including any ledger, daybook or cashbook) at any criminal proceedings unless the court concerned orders that such book be produced. Section 31 of the Civil Proceedings Evidence Act 1963 contains a similar provision. Information obtained under a compulsion of court order is always subject to an implied (and sometimes express) undertaking that it will only be used for the purposes of the action. The undertaking applies to all documents disclosed under specific orders, as well as documents produced under discovery.

Attorneys Act 1979

Section 78(13) of the Attorneys Act 1979[26] obliges a bank to furnish to the Council of the Law Society a certificate indicating the balance of an attorneys trust, savings or other interest bearing account if the Council requires it.

Money laundering legislation

The statutes regulating money laundering are the Prevention of Organised Crime Act 1998[27] (POCA) and the Financial Intelligence Centre Act 2001[28] (FICA). Regulations promulgated under these Acts clarify and amplify the various obligations and provide for certain exemptions.[29] In the main, POCA contains the substantive money laundering provisions while FICA provides the administrative framework. In addition, regs 47 and 48 promulgated under the Banks Act 1990 require banks to establish independent compliance functions as part of their risk management and to implement and maintain policies and procedures to guard against the bank being

---

25 Schulze, n 7 above, at 612.
26 Act 53 of 1979.
27 Act 121 of 1998.
28 Act 38 of 2001.
29 GN R416 of 1 April 1999, GN R850 of 1 September 2000 and GN 24176 of 20 December 2002.

used for purposes of market abuse, including money laundering. Chapter 3 of the Anti-terrorism Bill 2002 deals with the reporting of terrorist-related activities.

Prevention of Organised Crime Act 1998

POCA applies to proceeds of unlawful activity, which is far wider than proceeds of crime. 'Proceeds of unlawful activity' is defined in s 1 of POCA to mean:

> 'any property or any service, advantage, benefit or reward which was derived, received or retained, directly *or* indirectly, in the Republic or elsewhere, at any time before or after the commencement of this Act, in connection with or as a result of any unlawful activity carried on by any person, and includes any property representing property so derived.'

(Property is widely defined in s 1(1) to include money.)

> 'Unlawful activity' means 'any conduct which constitutes a crime or which contravenes any law whether such conduct occurred before or after the commencement of the Act and whether such conduct occurred in the Republic or elsewhere'.

Section 2 of the Interpretation Act 1957[30] defines the term 'law' as meaning:

> 'any law, proclamation, ordinance, Act of Parliament or other enactment having the force of law.'

'Unlawful activity' as defined would thus include the commission of common law crimes, contraventions of statutes, regulations and possibly even unlawful contracts.

Both definitions provide for retrospectivety and for extra-territoriality. In other words, the proceeds were and will continue to be proceeds of unlawful activities no matter when or where they were received or retained. It should be pointed out, however, that it is the definitions and not the Act itself that operate retrospectively. In *National Director of Public Prosecutions v Basson*,[31] the Court of Appeal held that in South African law there is a presumption against the operation of a statute retrospectively. The court held further that a statute that operates retrospectively will offend against s 35(3)(l) and (n) of the Constitution Act 1996.[32]

Furthermore, s 1(1)(xv), as set out above, makes the connection between the 'proceeds' and the 'unlawful activity' a fairly loose one (not necessarily restricted by the element of causation as was the position prior to the amendment of this section) by including any property or benefit which was 'derived, received or retained ... in connection with or as a result of any unlawful activity'. As a result, the definition of 'proceeds of unlawful activity' is very wide ranging.

On the assumption, that the money is retained in connection with unlawful activity, the Act restricts the definitions of the offences relating to proceeds of unlawful activities to situations where the person 'knows or ought reasonably to have known',

---

30   Act 33 of 1957.
31   [2002] 2 All SA 247.
32   Act 108 of 1996.

or, in the case of s 29 of FICA, suspects or knows that the property is the proceeds of unlawful activities. Unless the requisite state of mind is present on the part of the accused, he cannot be successfully prosecuted under the relevant laundering offences.

For purposes of the Act, a person has knowledge of a fact if he actually knew or if the court is satisfied that he believed there to be a reasonable possibility of the existence of that fact and then failed to obtain information to confirm the existence of that fact.[33]

Furthermore, a person who negligently fails to appreciate the criminal nature of the money or property and engages in a transaction involving such money or property commits an offence under POCA.

Negligence is defined in s 1(3) of the Act as follows:

'[f]or purposes of this Act a person ought reasonably to have known or suspected a fact, if the conclusions that he ought to have reached are those which would have been reached by a reasonably diligent and vigilant person having both –
(a) the general knowledge, skill, training and experience that may reasonably be expected of a person in his or her position; and
(b) the general knowledge, skill, training and experience that he in fact has.'

Section 1(3), goes further than the common law test for negligence, in that it directs the court to examine both the actual and the expected general knowledge, skill, training and experience of a person in the accused's position, as opposed to the common law where the court only goes beyond the accused's actual circumstances when the accused professes to have a certain skill or holds a position which indicates that the has such a skill.

Section 4 of POCA deals with the offence of money laundering, s 5 with assisting another to launder the proceeds of unlawful activity and s 6 with the acquisition, use or possession of proceeds of unlawful activities.

Financial Intelligence Centre Act 2001

FICA applies to 'accountable institutions' (defined in Sch 1), supervisory bodies (set out in Sch 2), reporting institutions (defined in Sch 3) and persons. Different obligations are imposed on the different institutions, bodies or persons, with the most onerous of these being imposed on accountable institutions. The list of accountable institutions covers most of the players in the financial services or financial market arena. Among others, banks, long-term insurers, investment advisors, dealers in foreign exchange and money remitters are listed as accountable institutions. The Minister of Finance, in consultation with the Money Laundering Advisory Council (constituted in terms of the Act), is empowered by notice in the Gazette to add to or delete from this list of accountable institutions and to exempt an institution from compliance with all or some of the provisions on conditions for the period determined in the notice.[34]

---

33 POCA, s 1(2).
34 FICA, ss 73 and 74.

Money laundering control measures applicable to accountable institutions are as follows.

In terms of s 21(1) of FICA, an accountable institution may not establish a business relationship or conclude a single transaction with a client or prospective client unless it has taken the prescribed steps to establish and verify the identity of the client or prospective client, as the case may be. Identification of the 'principal' and 'agent' and proof of authority are required where the client is acting on behalf of another or someone is acting on his behalf.

An accountable institution that enters into a transaction or conducts a business relationship, either new or existing, without identifying the person will be guilty of an offence.[35]

RECORD KEEPING

The duty to keep records will arise when an accountable institution establishes a business relationship or concludes a single transaction with a client.[36] Records must be kept in respect of the following: the identity of the client, of the person on whose behalf the client is acting and of any person acting on behalf of the client; the authority to act where a 'principle and agent' relationship is involved; the manner in which the identity of the relevant person was established; the nature of the business relationship or transaction; the amounts involved and the parties to the transaction, as well as all accounts at the institution that are involved in the transaction or business relationship. The name of the person who obtained the information must also be recorded. Records relating to the establishment of a business relationship must be kept for a period of at least five years from the date on which the business relationship was terminated and, in the case of a single transaction, five years from the date on which the transaction was concluded.[37] These records may be kept in electronic form, stored centrally or contracted out to a third party.[38]

The Centre can access records kept by or on behalf of the accountable institution and where these records are not by nature public records, access can be obtained by a warrant issued in chambers.[39]

REPORTING

In terms of s 27 of FICA, the Financial Intelligence Centre (the Centre) established in terms of the Act may request a bank (or any other accountable institution) to state whether a specified person is or was a client of the bank or whether a specified person is acting or has acted on behalf of any client of the bank.

---

35   FICA, s 46.
36   FICA, s 22.
37   FICA, s 23.
38   FICA, s 24.
39   FICA, s 26.

FICA provides for a hybrid reporting system – a combination of threshold and suspicion-based reporting. Accountable institutions will, within a prescribed period, have to report cash transactions paid out and received above a limit to be prescribed by the Centre.[40] The threshold will be prescribed by regulation and different thresholds may be prescribed for different institutions (at the time of writing, no thresholds had been prescribed).

The duty to report suspicious and unusual transactions is more widely cast. It applies not only to accountable institutions, but to any person who carries on business.

Section 29(1) provides:

'A person who carries on a business or is in charge of or manages a business or who is employed by a business and who knows or suspects that –
(a) the business has received or is about to receive the proceeds of unlawful activities;
(b) a transaction or series of transactions to which the business is a party –
  (i) facilitated or is likely to facilitate the transfer of the proceeds of unlawful activities;
  (ii) has no apparent business or lawful purpose;
  (iii) is conducted for the purpose of avoiding giving rise to a reporting duty under this Act; or
  (iv) may be relevant to the investigation of an evasion or attempted evasion of a duty to pay any tax, duty or levy imposed by legislation administered by the Commissioner for the South African Revenue Service; or
(c) the business has been used or is about to be used in any way for money laundering purposes.
must, within the prescribed period after the knowledge was acquired or the suspicion arose, report to the Centre the grounds for the knowledge or suspicion and the prescribed particulars concerning the transaction or series of transactions.'

Transactions in respect of which inquires were made but which were not concluded must also be reported if they may have caused any of the consequences set out in s 29(1) above.[41]

Failure to comply with the reporting obligation to keep records and to verify identity, constitutes an offence for which a person is liable to a fine not exceeding R10 million or to imprisonment for a period not exceeding 15 years.[42]

Any person, accountable institution or reporting institution required to report under the Act [43]may continue with that transaction unless directed otherwise by the Centre.[44]

---

40   FICA, s 28.
41   FICA, s 29(2).
42   FICA, s 68(1).
43   FICA, ss 28 and 29.
44   FICA, s 33.

The duty to report overrides any duty of secrecy or confidentiality or any other restriction on the disclosure information save for the common law right to professional privilege between an attorney and the attorney's client.[45]

No action whether criminal or civil will lie against a person (including a bank) who reports in good faith as required by the Act.[46] The immunity granted seems to be a general one in so far it contains no qualification that it applies exclusively to crimes established under FICA. To hold otherwise would expose the person who has reported in good faith, to the risk of prosecution under other statutes such as the Income Tax Act 1962 or the Exchange Control Regulations promulgated in terms of the Currency and Exchanges Act 1933.[47] Thus, provided that the defence is related to information contained in a report to the Centre, such person would be protected from prosecution under FICA and any other statute. If the immunity is a limited one confined only to FICA, this provision, s 38 and the reporting provision, s 29, would be subject to a constitutional challenge on the basis that they unjustifiably violate the right against self incrimination in s 35(3)(j) of the Constitution.

A person who reports will be a competent but not a compellable witness. Unless the broker testifies at the criminal proceedings no evidence concerning his identity is admissible.[48]

The Centre must be informed if an accountable institution through electronic transfer sends money into or out of South Africa above a limit to be prescribed, where the institution is acting on behalf or on the instruction of another person.[49]

INTERNAL COMPLIANCE

Accountable institutions are obliged to formulate and implement internal rules concerning the establishment and verification of the identity of persons who must be identified and of the records to be kept.[50]

An accountable institution must provide training to employees and must appoint a person responsible for compliance by the employees with the provisions of FICA and internal rules.[51]

Failure to formulate and implement internal rules and to provide training or appoint a compliance officer will constitute an offence. On conviction a person will be liable to imprisonment not exceeding five years or to a fine not exceeding R1 million.[52]

THE FINANCIAL INTELLIGENCE CENTRE

All reports must be made to the Centre. The Centre is a juristic person outside the public service, but within the public administration as envisaged by s 195 of the Constitution, and is accountable to the Minister of Finance.[53]

45   FICA, s 37.
46   FICA, s 38(1).
47   Act 9 of 1933.
48   FICA, s 38(2).
49   FICA, s 31.
50   FICA, s 42.
51   FICA, s 43.
52   FICA, s 68(1).
53   FICA, s 2.

Functions of the Centre include the collection, analysis and interpretation of all information disclosed to it.[54] The Centre will also disseminate information to the relevant investigating authorities, intelligence and the South African Revenue Services and provide advice and assistance to such authorities. Information may also be exchanged with international counterparts of the Centre.[55] The Centre does not, however, have investigative powers.

The next hurdle is, of course, the successful implementation of the legislation. Creating a culture of compliance within the financial services industry will not be easy and the questioning of customers' legitimacy and integrity conflicts with established practice. The effectiveness of costly and burdensome requirements imposed on accountable institutions must be routinely reviewed by the financial industry, the enforcement authorities, politicians and the legislature to ensure that they continue to be justified in deterring money launderers.

Duty to the public to disclose

An explanation of this qualification was given by Banks LJ in *Tournier*[56] as follows:

> 'Many instances of this [exception] might be given. They may be summed up in the language of Lord Finlay in *Weld-Blundell v Stephens*[57] where he speaks of cases where there is a higher duty than the private duty involved, as where "danger to state or public duty may supersede the duty of the agent to its principal".[58]
>
> The scope of this duty remains undefined by South African case law and is probably the most difficult of the exceptions, the dividing line between a state or public duty and a private duty being hard to define. It is for this reason that the view has been advanced that the licence to disclose by reason of such a duty should not be too highly assumed.'[59]

It is interesting to note in passing that when the South African government appointed a Commission of Enquiry into the Rapid Depreciation of the Rand (The Myburgh Commission) banks would not disclose information to the Commission without a subpoena first having been issued, compelling disclosure, thereby bringing it within the exception 'disclosure under compulsion of law'. Arguably, the documents could have been disclosed without a subpoena, under the exception 'duty to the public disclose', but the banks were not willing to take this risk.[60]

---

54 FICA, s 3.
55 FICA, s 4.
56 *Tournier v National Provincial and Union Bank of England* [1924] 1KB 461.
57 [1920] AC 956 at 965.
58 [1924] 1KB 461 at 473, per Bankes LJ, referred to in a paper by R Grady 'Privacy Law Issues Reform Proposals and their Impact on the Financial Industry' presented at the Fourteenth Annual Banking Law and Practice Conference, 22 May 1997.
59 M Megrah, F R Ryder and A Bueno *Paget's Law of Banking* (9th edn, 1982) p 54, cited by P Latmer 'Liability in Defamation and Negligence Following Breach of Banking Secrecy' (2000) 8 J Financial Crime 2 at 150. See in this regard *Libyan Arab Foreign Bank v Bankers Trust Co* [1989] QB 728, referred to in ch 9, England.
60 See in this regard *Price Waterhouse v BCCI Holdings (Luxembourg) SA* [1992] BCLC 583, referred to in ch 9, England.

Disclosure in the bank's interest

This exception would come into play where a bank sues a customer for repayment of an overdraft. Details of the amount will obviously be disclosed in the summons. Similarly, when a guarantor is sued, details of the guaranteed account must be disclosed.

In *GS George Consultants of Investments (Pty) Ltd v Datasys (Pty) Ltd*[61] (*GS George*), the court had to consider whether a bank could cede[62] (transfer) its claim against its customer to a third party. The bank purported to cede to the respondent its rights against the applicants arising from the granting of overdraft facilities to the latter. The applicants argued that the rights were not cedable since such a cession would constitute a breach of the bank's duty of secrecy. The court accepted this argument and concluded that a banker cannot cede or, by necessary implication, pledge his personal rights against his customers. Stegman J held that in the absence of agreement to the contrary, the contract of a banker and customer obliges the banker to guard information relating to his customer's business with the banker as confidential, subject to certain exceptions, none of which in his opinion were relevant. The court held further that such duty of secrecy imports the element of delectus personae into the contract, and that the banker's claims against his customer were not cedable without the consent of the customer.[63]

At first blush the judgment seems correct. However, a disclosure of information which necessarily flows from the exercise of its rights by the bank, even though it is an indirect exercise of this right, involving a sale and a cession is justified. The existence of a duty of secrecy does therefore not provide sufficient reason for finding that the bank's rights were not cedable.[64]

In *Cywilnat (Pty) Ltd v Densam (Pty) Ltd*,[65] Goldstein J rejected the *GS George* judgment and stated that 'if a bank wishes to sue its customers for an overdraft, it may do so revealing the amount of the overdraft to the world. I cannot see why the interposition of a cessionary should change the principle'. In *Densam (Pty) Ltd v Cywilnat (Pty) Ltd*,[66] the court of appeal confirmed the decision of the trial court that a banker could validly cede monetary claims owed to it by its customer. Botha JA was of the view that it was reasonable and proper for a bank to further its own interests in regard to collecting an overdraft, by ceding its claim to a third party.[67] In response to the appellant's suggestion that a bank may want to cede its claim for an ulterior purpose, unrelated to the furtherance of its own interest, Botha JA stated that the mere fact that a bank has ceded its claim would raise a prima facie inference, if nothing appeared to the contrary, that the bank had decided to dispose of its claim to realise and liquidate its own interest.[68] But the court did not consider it necessary to

---

61   1988(3) SA 726 (W).
62   In South African law, the terms 'cede' and 'cession' is used to denote a transfer of rights. Unlike English law, the term 'assignment' denotes a transfer of rights and obligations.
63   1988(3) SA 726 (W) at 737E–F and 739D–E.
64   See *Sasfin v Beukes* 1989(1) SA 1 (A), where Van Heerden JA in his minority judgment expressed doubt as to the correctness of the *GS George* judgment.
65   1989(3) SA 59 (W).
66   1991(1) SA 100 (A).
67   1991(1) SA 100 (A) at 110–111.
68   1991(1) SA 100 (A) at 111B–C.

pursue this point any further. Consequently, the court held that the application of principles laid down in *Tournier* to the facts of the case before it led to the conclusion that the bank was not precluded from ceding its claim against the appellant to the respondent.[69]

Botha JA also disagreed with Stegman J's view that the duty of secrecy which a banker owes its customer imports the element of delectus personae into the contract. He stated that Stegman J had based his view with regard to the element of delectus personae only on the banker's obligation to maintain confidentiality; the nature of the customer's obligation to pay the amount of the banker's claim had not been mentioned. This approach was, in Botha JA's view, contrary to principle and authority. The question whether a claim was not cedable on the basis that a contract involved a delectus personae fell to be answered with reference not to the nature of the cedent's obligations vis-à-vis the debtor, which remained unaffected by the cession, but rather to the nature of the debtor's obligations vis-à-vis the cedent, which was the counterpart of the cedent's right, the subject matter of the transfer comprising the cession.[70]

Applying the principle that, unless the contract is so personal in its character that it can make any reasonable or substantial difference to the other party whether the cedent or cessionary is entitled to enforce the performance of the obligation the right of action can be freely ceded, the court found that it would make no difference at all to the appellant whether it was the bank or the respondent who exercised the right to enforce payment.[71] Accordingly, the court held that the bank's claim against the appellant had been cedable.

Parties can, of course, stipulate that the rights cannot be ceded, by the inclusion of a so-called pactum de non cedendo into the contract.

Disclosure to other companies within the group[72]

An area of concern is the growing perception that banks can release confidential information about their customers, without their consent, to other companies – both banking and non-banking entities – within the group. Banks argue that such an exchange of information is in their interest and is necessary to protect the group. This information may, however, be released not only for the protection of the bank's interest, but also for marketing purposes, particularly in the light of the diversification of banks' business interests. In practice, banks usually rely on the implied consent of their customers for disclosure 'in the interest of the bank'. There is thus an evident connection between disclosure 'in the bank's interest' and disclosure 'with the express or implied consent of the customer'. The giving of information to other companies within the group cannot, however, without more, be said to be with 'the implied

---

69 1991(1) SA 100 (A) at 111E–F.
70 1991(1) SA 100 (A) at 112A–B.
71 See S Scott 'Can a Banker Cede his Claims Against his Customers?' (1989) 1 SA Merc LJ 248.
72 'Group' is defined in s 6.7 of the Code as 'a holding company as defined in the Companies Act 61 of 1973 and its wholly owned subsidiaries'.

consent of the customer' as a customer may not be aware of the practice. A customer intends to bank with a bank, not a group, and the contract, where the duty of secrecy is a naturalia of such contract, is with a particular bank and not the banking group.

It is interesting to note that s 4 of the Code of Banking Practice provides that 'the bank's interest will not be used to disclose information about a customer (including the customer's name and address) to any other company in the group for marketing purposes'.

The marketing of services is dealt with in s 2.8 of the Code. It provides that the bank may give certain information about existing customers to other subsidiaries within the banking group for marketing purposes where it informs the customers of its intention. While the customer may withhold his consent to the dissemination of such information, the Code provides that if the customer does not withhold consent, it will presume that the customer has agreed to the bank continuing the practice. Quiescence will be taken to amount to consent in this case. Whether the banks can assume implied consent in this way is doubtful, but the issue has not yet been pertinently raised. As far as new customers are concerned, express consent to the dissemination of such information is required.

Credit reference agencies[73]

Another area of concern relates to the disclosure by banks to credit reference agencies. It is not clear under which of the *Tournier* exceptions this practice would fall – in 'the interests of the bank' or 'duty to the public to disclose' or, whether disclosure in these circumstances can be justified at all. As credit default is on the increase and customers will, as result, have to pay higher charges, it may well fall under a 'duty to the public to disclose'.

In so far as the giving of this information is associated with disclosure within a banking group, it may be better housed under the qualification 'in the bank's interest'.

Section 4.2 of the Banking Code deals with credit reference agencies. It provides that information about a customer's debts owed to the bank may be disclosed to credit reference agencies under the following circumstances:

1   where the customer has fallen behind with his payments and has not made proposals satisfactory to the bank for repayment following formal demand and the customer has been given at least 28 days' notice of the banks intention to disclose;
2   where the customer has given the bank written consent;
3   where the customer has a cheque referred to drawer, the information is placed on a cheque verification service; or
4   where the amount owed or arrears amount is in dispute, the fact (but not the amount) of this dispute will also be disclosed.

---

73   A credit reference agency is defined in s 6.4 of the Code as 'an organisation which holds information which is of relevance to lenders'.

The bank will not give any other information about the customer to credit reference agencies without the customer's prior written consent.

Disclosure with express or implied consent

Express consent occasions no difficulty – the customer will have expressly consented to disclosure. Where a customer refers a creditor to his bank for a credit report, for example, no difficulty will arise.[74] A more complex issue is where a bank seeks to rely on disclosure with the customer's implied consent. As a matter of practice, a customer's consent is implied where disclosure is made to a guarantor or prospective guarantor regarding a guaranteed account.

Status opinions/bankers references

As a service to customers, a bank often obtains status opinions on the creditworthiness of third parties by addressing a request to the bank of the third party. While the perennial question in this regard is whether the express consent of the customer is required (and a court has yet to decide this issue), the better view seems to be that it is not necessary provided certain general requirements are met. These requirements are, among others, that the information given be in general terms, is correct and given to another bank or made known to a customer of the supplying bank.[75] Generally, the practices in South Africa are regulated by the 'Agency Agreement' adhered to by all clearing banks and may fall within the scope of banking business with the practice being regarded as impliedly authorised by the customer, a view alluded to by Atkin LJ in *Tournier*.

A further issue concerns the potential delictual liability (tort) of the bank giving the reference to third parties. In *Standard Chartered Bank of Canada v Nedperm Bank Ltd*,[76] the court had to decide whether and under what circumstances a bank incurred liability for a banker's reference or status opinion concerning a customer. The plaintiff sued the defendant for damages allegedly suffered as a result of a negligent misstatement made by the defendant. That liability for negligent misstatement or negligent misrepresentation is part of our law is accepted.[77] On appeal, the court found that the report provided was inaccurate and misleading as the company concerned was not trading normally and was heavily depending on borrowings from the defendant bank. On the question of negligence, the court had no difficulty in holding that, given the comprehensive and intimate knowledge of defendant's officials of the affairs of the company, a skilled banker, acting reasonably, would not have given the report in question. As Corbett CJ said: 'It seems to me, therefore that the bank had either to give a true report [that is, a report which truly reflected its knowledge of the position] or decline to give a report.' The court held, further, that the case was not of the kind that 'raises the spectre of limitless liability or places an

---

74 Smith, n 4 above.
75 Malan, note 2 above, p 382.
76 WLD 12673/89, 19 March 1992, overruled on appeal in 1994(4) SA 747 (A).
77 *Administrateur, Natal v Trust Bank van Africa Bpk* 1979 3 SA 824 (A); *Bayer SA (Pty) Ltd v Frost* 1991 4 SA 559 (A) 568. See Malan, note 2 above, p 382ff.

undue or unfair burden upon the bank'; the defendant could have refused to give the report or it could have disclaimed liability for negligence.

Fiduciary relationship between a bank and its customer

A fiduciary relationship exists between a bank and its customer where the bank takes on a role of investment and user or otherwise provides a service where the customer relies on the banks advice.

Durr v Absa Bank Ltd[78] concerns investment advice given by a broker employed in the broking division of a bank. The facts were these: the second respondent (S) was the regional manager of the broking division of the United Building Society, which later became the United Bank and ultimately the first respondent (ABSA). The broking division offered financial services and advice. In performing this function, the second respondent advised the appellant to invest in the Supreme Group of companies (Supreme). However, Supreme was unable to pay its debts, and was eventually liquidated.

From the evidence, it appeared that S had relied on marketing material which he had received and on a conversation with one of the directors of the group. In S's view, the director had satisfactorily accounted for various unusual features of the investment, including Supreme's ability to offer very high interest rates and broker commissions. S had also met the director personally. This meeting gave him no reason to doubt the integrity of the director or the soundness of Supreme. Furthermore, there had been no adverse criticism of the group in the media or elsewhere. S was thus satisfied that the information that he had obtained was sufficient to justify a recommendation to invest in Supreme. For that reason he did not think it necessary to call for a prospectus or audited financial statements.

In the court below,[79] Van Zyl J found that S had not been negligent: 'he had far exceeded that standard of care, skill and diligence which might reasonably be expected of the ordinary broker.'[80] There was also no evidence to suggest that the first defendant itself had been negligent.

In an appeal against that decision, two questions arose for decision. First, what levels of skill and knowledge were required of S (the relevant standard of care), and, secondly, was the standard against which that skill and knowledge should be measured that of the ordinary or average broker, or that of a regional manager of the broking division of a bank professing investment skill and offering expert investment advice?

In respect of the first, he relied on *Van Wyk v Lewis*,[81] that 'in deciding what is reasonable the court will have regard to the general level of skill and diligence possessed and exercised at that time by the members of the branch of the profession to which the practitioner belongs', but 'the decision of what is reasonable under the

78   1997(3) SA 448 (SCA).
79   *Durr v Absa Bank Ltd* 1996 CLD 472 (C).
80   1996 CLD 472 (C) at 485.
81   1924 AD 438.

circumstances is for the court; it will pay high regard to the views of the profession, but is not bound to adopt them'.[82]

As regards the second question, Schutz J concluded that the 'appropriate standard is that of the regional manager of the broking division of a bank professing investment skills and offering expert investment advice'.[83] On the basis of that characterisation, S's expert advice as the average or typical broker was irrelevant.[84]

The question that followed was whether S had satisfied the standard of care expected of an expert financial and investment adviser holding himself out to be such. Schutz JA stated that the basic rule [85] is that:

'lack of skill or knowledge is not *per se* negligence. It is however, negligent to engage voluntarily in any potentially dangerous activity unless one has the skill and knowledge usually associated with the proper discharge of the duties connected with such an activity.'

The court held that S had not performed his duty and was consequently negligent. The first respondent's negligence followed, as it was accepted that it was vicariously liable for S's actions.

CONCLUSION

In South Africa, as elsewhere, banks will continuously have to balance the duty of confidentiality they owe to their clients with their heightened obligations to disclose confidential information. As increased disclosure is called for by statute and in the wake of terrorism, it is doubtful whether the duty of secrecy as upheld in *Tournier*[86] will endure, and secrecy may be defined more by the exceptions to it than the duly itself.

82   1997(3) SA 448 (SCA) at 460–461.
83   1997(3) SA 448 (SCA) at 464A.
84   1997(3) SA 448 (SCA) at 463G.I.
85   Stated by W A Joubert (founding ed) (1995) LAWSA, vol 8, para 94.
86   *Tournier v National Provincial and Union Bank of England* [1924] 1 KB 461.

26 Spain

Juan Miguel Goenechea

INTRODUCTION

The principle of bank secrecy and the corresponding duty of credit institutions to maintain confidential information obtained in respect of clients was traditionally rendered as a commercial usage of widespread compliance and part of the Spanish banking system. It was widely accepted that the principle was inspired by, and based upon, the special nature of the relationship between the banker and his client that involves a special degree of confidence placed by the client on his financial adviser and credit provider.

Since the enactment of the Spanish Constitution of 1978, the principle of bank secrecy has been closely linked to the right of citizens to their privacy and to the obligation of professionals to keep confidential matters concerning their clients. At the same time, and whilst the principle was gaining explicit constitutional support, Spanish legislation eroded its scope by introducing limits in areas such as tax, supervision of credit entities by regulators and avoidance of money laundering activities. The principle of bank secrecy has only very recently been explicitly acknowledged and regulated by positive legislation: the recently enacted Law 44/2002 of 22 November, on the reform of the financial system, has recognised the existence of the banking secrecy by adding a new additional provision to Law 26/1988 of 29 July, on discipline and supervision of credit entities.

In this chapter we will analyse the current legal status of the principle of bank secrecy in Spain. For this purpose, the presentation is divided into five different sections:

1 legal basis of the principle of bank secrecy;
2 scope of the principle;
3 remedies available under Spanish law in case of breach of the duty of bank secrecy;
4 limits to the general principle set out by Spanish legislation; and
5 a special reference to related obligations of confidentiality as regards the Spanish securities market.

LEGAL BASIS OF THE PRINCIPLE OF BANK SECRECY

Before the enactment of the Spanish Constitution dated 27 December 1978, there was an important controversy in academic circles as to the legal basis of the principle of bank secrecy. For a number of scholars, the principle was an implied term of contracts entered into between clients and banking institutions.[1] The general principle contained in art 57 of the Spanish Commercial Code and art 1.258 of the Civil Code, by virtue of which contracting parties are obliged to comply not only with the terms of what has been expressly agreed in the contract, but also with those conditions deriving from good faith, usage and the law, supported this conclusion.

Others took into consideration existing legal provisions creating a duty of confidentiality in specific circumstances and in respect of particular entities, so as to extend its scope to cover the relationship between banking institutions and their clients.[2] These legal provisions were as follows:

1 Article 23 of the Statutes of the Bank of Spain approved by Decree of 24 July 1947, which under the heading 'Bank Secrecy' prohibited the Spanish Central Bank from facilitating to third parties any information in relation to funds deposited in current accounts opened by an identified person or entity, with the exception of information released to the interested party, its representative or the Spanish courts. A judgment of the Supreme Court of 28 November 1928 had ruled the application of the Statutes of the Bank of Spain to private banks in the absence of any other applicable regulation.

2 Article 16 of Decree Law of Nationalisation of the Bank of Spain dated 7 June 1962, which created a central credit risk information-gathering service available to all private banks and that obliged these to send periodical information to the Bank of Spain in respect of the concession of credits to third-party clients. Banks were allowed to request information from the Bank of Spain, but were obliged to a special duty of secrecy as to the information obtained.

Another important sector of Spanish scholars understood that the legal basis of the principle of bank secrecy laid in a commercial usage borne from banking practice due to the special relationship of confidence between a banker and the clients.[3] (The existence of a commercial usage in respect of bank secrecy could still be sustained today, provided that no specific legislation had been enacted, since the principle meets the two main requirements to be considered a commercial usage and therefore part of Spanish law: it has been a widespread practice for a long time in the Spanish banking sector, and there is a conviction that the duty of secrecy binds all credit institutions. In fact, all credit entities have accepted this special duty as part of the provision of banking-related services to clients).

The enactment of the Spanish Constitution in 1978 provided a further element to reinforce and substantiate the legal basis of the principle binding banking

1   See eg J M Otero Novas *El Secreto Bancario. Vigencia y Alcance.* Revista de Derecho Bancario y Bursátil 1985, pp 736 and 737.
2   See eg L M Cazorla *El secreto bancario* Madrid 1978, p 78, and R Jiménez de Parga *El secreto bancario en el Derecho español.* Revista de Derecho Mercantil 1969, p 399.
3   See eg Garrigues *Contratos Bancarios.* Madrid 1958, p 52, and M J Guillén Ferrer *El secreto bancario. Sus límites legales.* Valencia 1997, p 79.

institutions, as eventually confirmed by the judgment of the Spanish Constitutional Court of 26 November 1984. In essence, the court understood that the principle of bank secrecy was one of the rights, and a corresponding obligation, created under the Constitution deserving protection and of mandatory compliance, as follows:

1   From the point of view of clients, the Spanish Constitutional Court understood that bank secrecy was part of, and an expression of, the right of Spanish citizens to have their privacy guaranteed as provided by art 18 of the Constitution. In this respect, movements of current accounts and the information that in general may be gathered by a credit institution regarding its clients would form part of clients' privacy and, therefore, would merit the protection of the Spanish Constitution and its enforcement in case of breach.

2   From the point of view of financial entities, the Spanish Constitutional Court established a constitutional support for their obligation of confidentiality in art 20 of the Spanish Constitution that regulates professional secrecy. The general principle of professional secrecy could be invoked by credit entities so as to protect, with certain limits as described below, information gathered from clients in the course of their relationship.

The Constitutional Court, however, did not grant an unlimited protection to the principle of bank confidentiality. In the case at hand, the court limited it by the application of a further principle contained in the Spanish Constitution obliging Spanish citizens to collaborate in sustaining public expenditure through a tax system. This principle should allow the Spanish tax authorities to investigate and seek information from credit institutions as regards their clients, subject to procedures and requisites established by law that should, to the extent these were followed, preserve the privacy of the client subject to investigation. As the Constitutional Court established, the right to privacy should prohibit an illegal and arbitrary investigation into the private affairs of individuals and entities (including current account movements) if this was not carried out following the requisites and conditions set out by law.

A subsequent Constitutional Court ruling in the form of a summons dated 23 July 1986 reaffirmed the doctrine contained in the 1984 judgment by stating that the principle of bank secrecy formed part of the economic privacy of entities and individuals which was only limited when other constitutional rights deserved protection and the law established the procedure and necessary requisites to balance both principles.

During the following years, additional legislation explicitly acknowledged the principle of bank confidentiality and its enforceability under Spanish law in the field of the Spanish securities markets and with respect to the Bank of Spain.

As regard the Spanish securities market, Law 24/1988 of 28 July has provided in its art 81 the overall obligation of entities and individuals; that in carrying out their profession or functions or due to any other reasons, should they obtain information in relation to the securities markets, they must keep it confidential and safeguard it from any unlawful or improper use, without prejudice to reporting and co-operation duties to judicial and administrative bodies. Any such individual or entity shall adopt appropriate measures to avoid any abusive or unfair use of said information, and, if it cannot be avoided, to remedy the consequences arising from such abusive or unfair use.

In more detail, Royal Decree 629/1993 of 3 May has established a general code of conduct applicable to all entities and individuals performing activities within the Spanish securities market. According to the code, which is mandatory even on entities merely providing advisory services, all the information that entities active in the securities markets may obtain from clients in order to identify them and gather their financial situation, investment expertise and purpose of the investment will be confidential and will not be used for the market member's own benefit or that of a different party. Royal Decree 629/1993, also provides that these entities and individuals must have an internal code of conduct to regulate the activities of their officers, employees and representatives.

Law 3/1994 of 14 April, implementing the Second Banking Co-ordination Directive[4] in Spain and amending Royal Legislative Decree 1298/1986 of 28 June, has imposed on the Bank of Spain a special duty of confidentiality and secrecy in respect of any information and documentary materials obtained in the course of its prudential supervisory role on credit institutions. The same obligation applies to all officials that perform or have carried out activities in the Bank of Spain. These individuals are precluded from making any declaration, testifying, publishing or exhibiting any data or reserved document even after leaving their position with the Bank of Spain. As exceptions to the overall obligation to maintain confidential the above information, Royal Legislative Decree 1298/1986 sets out the following:

1   when the affected party has expressly agreed to such disclosure;
2   the data has been aggregated to other information for mere statistical purposes;
3   the information has been requested from a criminal court, or in connection with a bankruptcy/insolvency proceeding (provided the information does not relate to third parties involved in the relaunching of the relevant entity), or in respect of disciplinary proceedings initiated against credit entities;
4   information released to other regulatory and supervisory bodies in Spain so that these may perform their duties, including auditors;
5   information submitted by the Bank of Spain to the European Central Bank or central banks members of the system of European Central Banks or any other authority supervising payment and clearance systems;
6   information released by the Bank of Spain to supervisory entities of foreign countries, provided that reciprocity exists and rules of secrecy are similar to those applicable in Spain;
7   information provided by the Bank of Spain to Spanish settlement and clearing systems, provided it is aimed at allowing the correct operation of any such systems;
8   information that may be needed to prevent money laundering activities;
9   information released with the prior authorisation of the Ministry of Economy to the Tax Authorities in accordance with, and subject to, the conditions set out in arts 111 and 112 of the General Tax Law (Law 230/1963 of 28 December);

---

4   Council Directive 89/646/EEC.

10   information provided by the Bank of Spain to the Ministry of Economy or to the Spanish regional governments; and

11   information requested by a parliamentary investigation committee.

This special duty of secrecy of employees and officials of the Bank of Spain has been further recognised by Law 13/1994 of 1 June, on the Autonomy of the Bank of Spain and in the Internal Regulation of the Central Bank of 14 November 1996. We will refer to this legislation in the course of this chapter.

Notwithstanding the above, it was not until the enactment of Law 44/2002 of 22 November, on the reform of the financial system, that the banking secrecy was specifically recognised by positive legislation in connection with pure commercial banking activities. The Seventeenth Additional Provision of Law 44/2002 has added a new additional provision to Law 26/1988 of 29 July, on discipline and supervision of credit entities, establishing the duty of credit entities operating in Spain to keep bank secrecy.

This recently enacted legislation sets forth that entities and any other persons subject to the supervision of credit entities (ie managers and directors of credit entities and significant shareholders and their managers and directors) are obliged to safeguard and keep strictly confidential (without communication to third parties) all information relating to balances, operations and any other client's transactions. As general exceptions to this duty of confidentiality, Law 44/2002 mentions all information (i) which the client or applicable law has allowed communication to third parties or (ii) in respect of which an obligation to communicate to supervisory authorities exists or a request in connection therewith has been made by the supervisory authorities. In these exceptional cases, the delivery of confidential data must comply with the instructions of the client or with those provided by applicable law.

An additional exception to the duty to keep confidential clients' information is that delivery of confidential information among credit entities pertaining to the same consolidated group is not subject to the restrictions imposed by Law 44/2002.

Law 44/2002 finally states that any breach of the aforementioned regulations will be deemed a serious offence, which will be punished according to the ordinary sanctions procedure provided under Law 26/1988 (see below for a description of the sanctions regime).

SCOPE OF THE PRINCIPLE OF BANK SECRECY

Before the enactment of Law 44/2002, since Spain lacked a specific legal regime applicable to the principle of bank secrecy (especially for commercial banking activities), its scope needed to be determined in conjunction with the rules, referred to above, that had for many years been the legal basis of its binding nature under Spanish law.

Today, the new regulations have confirmed that the obligation to keep confidentiality refers to all information relating to balances, operations and any other client transactions. Although these new regulations have not explained in more detail what the scope of the principle is, it can be argued, based on the new rules enacted and on the fact that the bank secrecy had previously been considered by a majority of scholars as a commercial usage binding upon a credit institution in its dealings with clients, that the principle of bank secrecy must be construed as having a broad scope that covers all the information obtained by credit entities from clients, since it derives from the special relationship created based on confidence and trust. Confidentiality will therefore cover the following information:

1   all that gathered by the bank whilst entering into particular and usual banking transactions (ie deposit taking, credit accounts, lending), thus including balance sheet details, turnover, volume of sales, identity of clients and the specific terms and conditions and purpose of the relevant banking operation; and

2   all that factual information and opinions surpassing the economic terms of the particular transaction entered into or service provided to the client, and that may be of a personal or economic nature and that must be deemed to have been released by the client to their banker in the context of their professional relationship.

This broad conclusion has been supported since 1978 by the constitutional basis of the principle of bank secrecy. To the extent that the duty of bank confidentiality is connected with the right of privacy of clients as protected by the Spanish Constitution, such right (and the corresponding obligation on the provider of banking services) must be interpreted broadly and may only be limited to the extent that it enters into conflict, or needs to be interpreted in conjunction, with another right protected by the Spanish Constitution and such limits are set out in law. Below we will analyse in light of the Constitutional Court's judgment of 26 November 1984 the scope of the principle of bank secrecy and, in relation to the particular facts subject to revision, namely the level of information that credit entities are obliged to provide to the tax authorities as regards movements of bank accounts held by clients.

Another specific area of concern is the reports prepared by credit institutions regarding the economic situation of their clients. Although a number of scholars have understood in the past that the principle of secrecy should cover only details regarding particular and usual banking transactions, it seems, taking into consideration the nature of the principle of bank secrecy as a long-standing commercial usage before the enactment of the new legislation and the recognition granted to the principle by the Spanish Constitutional Court as part of the right of Spanish citizens to their privacy, that the release of any report that may serve to identify the client or/and a particular transaction entered into with a credit institution and/or the economic or financial position of the client requires the prior approval of that client. This conclusion is further supported by the fact that the Law 44/2002 regulations that recognise the existence of a duty to keep confidential information regarding clients of a credit entity refer to 'the information relating to balances, operations and any other clients' transactions'.

As regards additional legislation, it is worth mentioning that Royal Legislative Decree 1298/1986 and the Internal Regulations of the Bank of Spain consider privileged information subject to the duty of secrecy to be all the data, documents and information gathered by the Bank of Spain in the performance of the functions vested upon it by existing legislation. Thus, all such information gathered as agent bank to the Spanish Treasury, currency exchange provider and supervisor of the banking system, including, in particular, credit entities, will be subject to the duty of confidentiality.

In the securities market, all information obtained by market participants, including credit entities, in respect of investors, issues and transactions in the market must be kept confidential and safeguarded from improper use as provided for in art 81 of Law 24/1988. In this context, it is important to determine the level of activities and services that credit entities established in Spain (including branches of foreign institutions and EU-based entities under the Second Banking Co-ordination Directive,[5] as implemented in Spain by Law 3/1994) may provide to clients, since information obtained in the provision of those services will be affected by the duty of confidentiality and proper use. In essence, credit entities may perform in Spain all the activities restricted to duly authorised professionals in the securities market (ie investment services companies: namely, securities companies and agencies and portfolio management companies). These include, inter alia:

1   the receipt of orders from clients and their execution or providing for their execution;
2   the intermediation in the placement of securities on the account of issuers and their underwriting;
3   the negotiation of securities on their own account;
4   the provision of credit to the market; and
5   the provision of deposit and discretionary portfolio management services to clients.

In addition, it is provided in the code of conduct contained in Royal Decree 629/1993 that the information obtained from clients by market participants, including credit entities, in compliance with their obligation to 'Know Your Customer' (financial position, market knowledge, purpose of the investment) in order to provide a proper and professional service, will be covered by the principle of secrecy.

Below, we will analyse the limits applicable to the principle of bank secrecy affecting its scope. These limits refer, essentially, to the powers of administrative and judicial authorities to obtain information from credit entities. It is also natural to understand that the scope of the principle of bank secrecy must be limited and constrained by the will of the person or entity protected by it. Thus, if the bank has obtained permission to release any information from the person to whom the information relates, such disclosure must not be deemed in breach of the principle of bank secrecy. This conclusion is contained in Law 44/2002, which, as explained above, exempts from the duty of confidentiality not only the information which must be disclosed by mandate of law or regulatory authority as provided by law, but also the information dissemination of which has been consented by the client.

The approval by the affected client as a limit to the principle of bank secrecy was already considered in Royal Legislative Decree 1298/1986. This Decree exempts from the obligation of confidentiality vested on officials of the Bank of Spain that information released with the consent of the affected party. Although partially

5   Council Directive 89/646/EEC.

superseded by Law 44/2002, Circular 3/1995 of 25 September of the Bank of Spain that regulates the central credit risk information gathering system of the Central Bank, has allowed for information in respect of an individual to be made available to a credit institution with which such client has no contractual relationship only if the client's prior written consent has been obtained. Similarly, the regulations aimed at protecting personal data (specially Organic Law 15/1999 of 13 December, on the protection of personal data) provide, when referring to the activity of companies devoted to inform about the financial position of third parties, that any personal data used in that regard must be obtained from public sources or with the consent of the affected party. In the field of personal data, Organic Law 15/1999 sets forth the general rules applicable to the management of data, including communication and storage regulations and rights vested on the holders of said data. In particular, these regulations limit the rendering of outsourcing services to companies which administer personal data, by requiring certain minimum contents in the relevant outsourcing agreement, aimed at protecting the confidentiality of the data. Additionally, Organic Law 15/1999 limits transfers of personal data to persons or companies located in countries not providing an equivalent protection level to that achieved in Spain, subject to certain exceptions.

The issue of bank confidentiality is also linked to the provision of Internet services by credit entities. The duty to keep confidential all personal data regarding the client is also applicable to these transactions. In connection therewith, Law 34/2002 of 11 July, on information services and electronic commerce, which develops Council Directive 2000/31/EC, sets forth the general rules applicable to providers of Internet services located in Spain (information to be displayed at the web page, prohibition of unsolicited commercial emails, validity of electronic agreements and resolution of disputes, inter alia). This Law will also be generally applicable to providers of Internet services located within the EEA or within the EU, provided that the services relate to specific subjects (such as intellectual property, direct insurance, contracts with natural persons qualifying as consumers etc).

Finally, it is worth mentioning whether the bank may limit claims for breach of confidentiality. This issue has to be considered from the standpoint of general liability rules. In that regard, exoneration of liability can only be admitted, if agreed to, in the case of negligence, but not in the case of wilful misconduct; likewise, limitation of liability is generally accepted if agreed to between the parties. However, these general rules are restricted in the event that one of the parties (ie the client of the bank) is a consumer; should this be the case, a clause exonerating or limiting the bank's liability for breach of confidentiality included in a set of general terms and conditions not discussed by the parties could be deemed abusive and, thus, null and void.

REMEDIES

Due to the existence of a variety of rights and principles serving as the legal basis to the principle of bank secrecy under Spanish law, there are also an important number of remedies available or that, arguably, could be used in the case of a breach by a credit entity of its obligation of keeping confidential information gathered from its clients. For the purpose of this section, we have analysed the following possible actions or claims that may be brought by a client against the credit entity which has infringed its obligation of bank secrecy:

A claim based on the protection granted by the Spanish Constitution over the right to privacy

As we have already mentioned above, the Spanish Constitutional Court has established that the principle of bank secrecy is an expression of the right to privacy contained in art 18 of the Spanish Constitution.[6] In this respect, Organic Law 1/1982 of 5 May has developed art 18 of the Constitution, allowing for a claim to be brought before the courts for an alleged breach of privacy and empowering the courts to take the necessary measures and steps to put an end to the violation and to reinstate the injured party in the peaceful exercise of his right. Organic Law 1/1982 also envisages the possible adoption of measures by the courts to prevent any further unlawful breach of the right of privacy and the right of the affected party to be compensated for damages suffered. Such damages will be measured taking into consideration the use that may have been made of the information obtained and the benefit obtained by the entity or person in breach. The statute of limitation for any legal action taken pursuant to a breach of art 18 of the Spanish Constitution is four years from the time such action could have been taken by the damaged party. Law 62/1978 of 26 December further develops the judicial protection of constitutional rights (including those deriving from art 18 of the Constitution) and allows for an especially quick summary procedure to be used before the courts in a claim based on a breach of the right of privacy contained in art 18 of the Spanish Constitution.

A criminal claim due to the breach of the duty of professional secrecy binding credit entities

The judgment of the Spanish Constitutional Court of 26 November 1984 declared the close connection between the principle of bank secrecy and the duty of professional confidentiality owed by professionals to third parties contained in art 20 of the Constitution. This has served as the basis for a number of Spanish scholars to defend the possible initiation of a criminal claim in the case of a breach of the obligation of secrecy owed by a banker to his client[7] (the Spanish Supreme Court also seemed to sustain this position in its judgment of 24 September 1968 in which it ruled that a criminal offence had been committed by employees of a non-banking business entity that had divulged details and information from clients to third parties). Article 199.2 of the Spanish Criminal Code approved by Organic Law 10/1995 of 23 November imposes on a professional that has breached a duty of confidentiality by divulging information obtained in the course of the profession, a penalty of imprisonment for between one and four years, a fine of up to €216,367.20 and a prohibition to perform his past professional activities for a period ranging between

---

6   Constitutional Court judgment of 26 November 1984.
7   See eg A Jorge Barreiro *El delito de revelación de secretos (profesionales y laborales).* Revista La Ley, 1996-3, p 1.298; F Morales Prats *Comentarios al Nuevo Código Penal (Dir: G Quintero Olivares)* 1997, p 996.

two and six years. Under Spanish law, a criminal action may only be initiated against individuals and not legal entities. In accordance with art 31 of the Spanish Criminal Code, however, the administrator or person acting on behalf of a legal entity meeting the requisites and conditions of a criminal action will be deemed criminally responsible for such conduct. The statute of limitation for this type of offence is established by the Criminal Code as five years from the last date in which the offence was committed.

A claim based on the breach of a duty vested on the credit entity with respect to its banking relationships

As already mentioned, before the enactment of Law 44/2002, a majority of Spanish scholars have understood the legal basis of bank secrecy to lay, in addition to the 1978 Constitution, on a commercial usage created through the widespread perception in the banking sector of the existence of that principle and its mandatory nature. This commercial usage would allow a third-party client that has entered into a particular contractual arrangement with a credit institution (ie loan, credit, opening of account) to claim a breach of an implied term of its contract if the banker discloses information delivered to it without the client's consent. This conclusion has been supported (and continues to be supported following the enactment of Law 44/2002) by the terms of art 1258 of the Spanish Civil Code that oblige contracting parties to comply not only with the conditions expressly contained in the relevant contract, but also with all other terms that may derive not only from good faith and usage and also from applicable law. The remedies available to the client will therefore include those provided by the Spanish Commercial and Civil Codes for a breach of contract: the right to be indemnified for damages suffered. The statute of limitation, in this case, will be 15 years from the date any such claim for breach of contract could have been exercised.

On the other hand, if the disclosure of the confidential information by a credit institution was made outside a specific contractual relationship, including in respect of information gathered from preliminary contacts not deriving in a contract or in respect of advisory services not provided in the context of a contractual relationship, the client would need to rely on the general principles of the Spanish law on tort. Under art 1902 of the Spanish Civil Code, any individual or entity causing damages to a third party due to actions taken or conduct performed knowingly or with negligence is liable to indemnify such third party for those damages. Accordingly, the client would be allowed to be indemnified for the damages suffered due to the disclosure by the credit institution, in breach of its duty of professional diligence, of the information gathered. The statute of limitation in this case will be one year from the date when the injured party became aware.

An administrative action by the Bank of Spain based on the disciplinary regime of Law 26/1988, as amended by Law 44/2002

Protection of bank confidentiality through disciplinary measures has been developed by Law 44/2002. As mentioned above, Law 44/2002 has specified that the breach of the obligation of safeguarding confidential information will be deemed a serious offence under Law 26/1988. Pursuant to Law 26/1988, a serious offence may lead to the imposition of the following sanctions:

1   To the credit entity:
    (a) a public admonition, to be published in the Spanish Official Gazette; and/or
    (b) a fine up to 0.5% of its equity or up to €150,000, whichever is higher.
2   To the responsible managers or members of the board:
    (a) a private admonition;
    (b) a public admonition;
    (c) a fine up to €90,000 to each of the responsible managers or directors; or
    (d) a prohibition to act as managers or directors of a credit or financial entity, including, as the case may be, a temporary suspension in their respective offices not exceeding one year (this sanction can be imposed together with the aforementioned fine).

Law 26/1988 sets forth several criteria to determine the actual sanction to be imposed among those capable of being chosen. Additionally, this law states that members of the board of a credit entity will be liable due to serious offences except in the event that they (i) have not attended the relevant meeting with a justified cause or have voted against the relevant resolution which is in the origin of the offence or (ii) the relevant offence is exclusively attributed to delegated bodies, general managers or other persons with powers in the credit entity.

A claim before the recently created Commissioner for the Defence of Banking Services' Clients and the Commissioner for the Defence of the Investor

Law 44/2002 has also created the Commissioner for the Defence of Banking Service' Clients and the Commissioner for the Defence of the Investor, dependent, respectively, upon the Bank of Spain and the National Securities Market Commission. (An additional Commissioner has been appointed for the insurance industry.) These Commissioners will be devoted to protect the rights of consumers of financial services. They will (i) consider any complaints made by consumers and users of financial services and they will forward them to the relevant supervisory bodies within the Bank of Spain or the National Securities Market Commission where a possible breach of transparency or client protection duties may exist, and (ii) advise consumers and users of banking services on their rights in connection with transparency and client protection regulations. As a requisite for having access to the Commissioners, the client must first file a claim before the clients' complaints desk that all credit entities and investment services companies are obliged to have or, as the case may be, before the clients' ombudsman that any entity or group of entities may appoint. Where a credit entity or an investment services entity decides to appoint a clients' ombudsman, the resolutions issued by the ombudsman against the relevant entity will be binding. Law 44/2002 authorises the Ministry of Economy to develop the regulation on complaints desks, ombudsman and Commissioners.

Law 44/2002 also states that while the relevant Commissioner is not formally appointed, the currently existing Bank of Spain's Complaint Service, entrusted with the consideration of complaints by clients against credit institutions that have allegedly breached disciplinary rules or 'good banking practices', will continue its operations. Under the regime of this Complaint Service, a claim can be brought before the Complaint Service in connection with any alleged breach by a credit institution of its obligation of secrecy with respect to information gathered from clients. The effectiveness, however, of this course of action is limited: under the terms of the regulations that currently govern the Complaint Service, if it ruled against the credit institution, it would merely create a file with the documentation and investigation available and shall keep it available to the affected client and the courts. The resolutions to be issued by the Ministry of Economy developing Law 44/2002 will determine whether the powers of the Commissioner for the Defence of Banking Services' Clients remain those described for the Complaint Service or are otherwise extended.

An administrative action by the securities market regulator or the Bank of Spain for breach of a provision protecting clients' interests

Finally, as stated above, securities market regulations in Spain impose on market participants – including credit institutions providing services in respect thereof – an overall duty of confidentiality and the obligation to safeguard the information obtained in the course of providing those services. Regulations further impose on credit entities active in the securities market the obligation to abide by a code of conduct that includes the duty to maintain confidential details obtained from clients as to their financial situation, knowledge or expertise in investments and the purpose of the investment so as to comply with the obligation imposed on market participants to 'Know Your Customer'. Failure by a credit institution to meet these obligations may qualify as a 'serious offence' or a 'less serious offence', punishable from a private caution up to a fine equal to 2% of the aggregate amount of share capital plus reserves of the entity, including suspension or limitation of activities in the market for a period of up to one year. Members of the board of the entity convicted of a 'serious offence' may receive a punishment themselves, varying from a public caution to a suspension from their post for a period of up to one year.

LIMITS

The principle of bank secrecy has been acknowledged and recognised by Spanish courts, with unquestionable legal and constitutional basis, a long time before its express recognition regarding pure banking activities pursuant to Law 44/2002.

Notwithstanding this, and as provided by the Spanish Constitutional Court and now recognised by Law 44/2002, it is not a right or principle without legal boundaries. In this section we will analyse the main limits to the principle of bank secrecy introduced by Spanish legislation. Law 44/2002 does not specify the limits of the principle of bank secrecy; on the contrary, it merely provides that these limits are those set forth in law or by the consent of the affected client. Apart from the consent of the affected party, we may distinguish the following limits.

Limits deriving from the Spanish Constitution

The Spanish Constitutional Court ruling of 26 November 1984, whilst confirming the right of clients to bank secrecy as part of their right to privacy, concluded that this was not an unlimited right, especially if it entered into conflict with another right deserving protection under the Spanish Constitution. In the case at hand, the Constitutional Court ruled that the right of privacy was limited by the obligation of Spanish entities and individuals to support the general expenditure of the state by contributing to the tax system (art 31 of the Spanish Constitution). The disclosure of bank account movements and transactions in respect thereof could be thus justified in the need to secure compliance with the obligation contained in art 31 of the Constitution, provided that the appropriate legal measures were complied with so as to avoid any arbitrary and discretionary interference in the privacy of the individual. The summary decision of the Constitutional Court of 23 July 1986 confirmed the status of the principle of bank secrecy as part of the right of individuals and entities to their privacy with special constraints as regards the Spanish tax system.

Organic Law 1/1982 of 5 May also contemplated the existence of limits to the rights and principles contained in the Spanish Constitution. In a general sense, it established that the rights protected by the Constitution could be limited by the laws and social custom. Thus, no illegal breach of the principle of privacy could be deemed to exist when an exception was contained in a law safeguarding the basic elements of the right and avoiding any possible discretionary or abusive use of the exception. In addition, the Organic Law included, as a further exception, the possibility that the beneficiary of the right consented to the interference in his privacy; if granted, this consent could be revoked at any time.

Tax-related limits

The scope of the principle of bank secrecy has been especially eroded when it has entered into conflict with the Spanish tax legislation. In the ruling of 26 November 1984, the Constitutional Court admitted the right of the Spanish tax authorities to investigate bank accounts and their movements (with certain restrictions as explained below), provided the relevant conditions set out in the law were complied with and such investigation was approved by the appropriate authorities.

Subsequent to the ruling of the Constitutional Court, the General Tax Law 230/1963 of 28 December was modified by Law 10/1985 of 26 April. The amended art 111 of the General Tax Law introduced the following new regulation:

1   a general principle under which credit entities could not rely on the principle of bank secrecy to deny compliance with a request for information duly submitted by the tax authorities; and
2   the following conditions having to be met by the tax authorities' request for information regarding account movements, deposit and credit accounts operations and, in general, banking transactions –
    (a) the request would need to be authorised by the General Directorate of Tax or the territorial Delegate of the Treasury;
    (b) the solicitation would need to determine the transaction subject to investigation;

(c) it would also need to identify the affected taxpayer; and

(d) set out the period of time to which the duty of disclosure applied.

Article 111 of the General Tax Law was further amended by Law 31/1991 of 30 December to clarify and eventually extend the level of detail that the Spanish tax authorities could seek to obtain from Spanish credit institutions. In essence, the amendment included the possibility that the authorities could request the disclosure of payment orders and issue of cheques and, more important, information regarding the origin and destiny of account movements, payment orders and cheques issued.

The new terms of art 111 of the General Tax Law soon received criticisms from scholars[8] due to the ability granted to the tax authorities to request information regarding the origin and destiny of movements. As a consequence, the Spanish Supreme Court, in a summons dated 30 September 1992, requested from the Constitutional Court a ruling in respect of the latest amendment to art 111 of the General Tax Law. The Supreme Court argued a possible breach of the doctrine established by the Constitutional Court's judgment of 26 November 1984 by the new text of art 111 of the General Tax Law in defining the level of information that could be gathered from clients when reviewing bank statements and accounts movements. According to the Constitutional Court's ruling of 26 November 1984, and without prejudice to the conditions and requirements that would need to be introduced by law to ensure non-discretionary interferences with individuals' privacy by the tax authorities, the disclosure by credit entities of bank statements could not violate the right or privacy under the Constitution since those statements could only provide generic information of the underlying transactions, but not the relevant and particular details of such transactions, including their motives or considerations. Based on this ruling, the Supreme Court hinted at the possibility that the obligation contained in the revised art 111 of the General Tax Law to disclose the origin and destiny of account movements and payment orders could be considered an obligation to release not only generic information about transactions, but their particular details and underlying motives as well, information that could be protected by the Spanish constitutional right of privacy.

Unfortunately, the Constitutional Court's judgment of 28 June 1994 did not clarify this important issue. It did, however, declare unconstitutional the last amendment introduced in art 111 of the General Tax Law, based on a formal rather than substantive defect: the inappropriateness of an annual budget law (such as Law 31/1991 for the annual budget of 1992) permanently to regulate issues with effect beyond the state incomes and expenses of the fiscal year in question.

Notwithstanding the above, the Spanish legislator has taken into consideration the concerns of the Spanish Supreme Court and those of scholars who had argued against the revised text of art 111 of the General Tax Law. The last amendment to the General Tax Law introduced by Law 25/1995 of 20 July has clarified that the requests for information regarding the 'origin' and 'destiny' of account movements and payment

---

8   See eg P M Herrera Molina and A de Prada García *Los preceptos de la LGT modificados por leyes de presupuestos: ¿una bomba de relojería jurídica? (Comentario a la cuestión de inconstitucionalidad sobre los arts. 111.3 y 128.5 de la LGT)*. Revista de Derecho Financiero y Hacienda Pública, no 227, p 823 ff.

orders should only cover the identity of the persons or accounts being the origin and destiny of such movements or payments. Arguably, this last amendment might prove insufficient to meet the concerns vaguely supported by the Spanish courts. Only a new Constitutional Court ruling could help dissipate the controversy surrounding the current text of art 111 of the General Tax Law.

Within the tax field, the obligation to keep confidential the information obtained by authorities and public officials and servants in connection with the management of taxes (subject to the limits stated by law), has been also recognised by Law 1/1998 of 26 February, which regulates the rights of taxpayers. Furthermore, Law 1/1998 establishes a general duty vested on officials or civil servants to keep the absolute secrecy as to confidential data concerning taxpayers, subject only to exceptions provided by law.

The duty to provide information to the Spanish courts

The principle of bank secrecy has been further restricted by the obligation imposed in art 18 of Organic Law 6/1985 of 1 July on the judicial power, upon public and private entities or persons to provide assistance, in the manner provided by law, to the judiciary in the development of judicial functions.

Banking entities, therefore, will be subject to the general requirements contained in the Spanish courts' procedural rules to assist civil and criminal courts in their activities. As regards the Bank of Spain specifically, notwithstanding the fact that Royal Legislative Decree 1298/1986 of 28 June, as amended by Law 3/1994 of 14 April, only obliges the Bank of Spain to comply with requests for information from civil courts in connection with insolvency and bankruptcy proceedings (see above), it seems clear that the Central Bank will be equally obliged to assist civil courts in all other types of proceedings.

Similarly, as regards the securities markets and the services provided by credit entities in connection therewith, art 81 of Law 24/1988 has expressly provided that entities active in the market shall be exempt from their duty of confidentiality in respect of the information requested by administrative authorities or the judiciary in accordance with the law.

In respect of the assistance due to civil courts, art 330 of the Civil Procedural Law establishes the obligation on third-party entities (including credit entities) that are not party to a civil litigation to disclose private documents when, at the request of one of the litigants, the court understands the disclosure of such documentation to be relevant in order to render its judgment. The court shall hear the affected credit entity holding the relevant information and issue a summary ruling in that connection. The party requested by the court can claim that the documents are not removed, so that they may be disclosed to, and inspected by, the secretary of the court in the place where they are deposited. If, on the other hand, the credit institution is a party to the litigation, the documents will need to be disclosed and the proceeding referred to above will not apply.

As regards criminal proceedings, Spanish Law establishes the obligation without limitation of third parties to disclose any information requested from a criminal court. The court will, however, be obliged to take the necessary measures to protect the secrecy and privacy of the requested third party if the data held by such party was eventually not of interest for the relevant criminal investigation. Organic Law 6/1985 sets out the general principles for international judicial co-operation in Spain when no international treaty is applicable. According to art 276, Spanish courts will obtain judicial assistance from foreign courts through a formal request addressed to the Justice Ministry that will forward it, via the Foreign Affairs Ministry and the relevant Spanish Embassy, to the competent authorities. Articles 277 and 278 oblige the Spanish courts to assist foreign judicial authorities, provided the following conditions are met:

1   Spanish courts benefit from the same assistance in the jurisdiction making the request;
2   the proceedings or the subject matter of the request do not fall within the exclusive jurisdiction of the Spanish courts;
3   the contents of the activity to be carried out fall within the powers of the relevant Spanish court;
4   the request meets all the necessary requisites of authenticity; and
5   the request is not contrary to Spanish public policy.

As regards international treaties and in respect of civil matters, Spain is a party to the 1970 Hague Convention on the Taking of Evidence Abroad in Civil or Commercial Matters and the 1975 Convention of the Interamerican Conference on Rogatory Letters. On matters of criminal proceedings, Spain is a party to the 1954 European Convention on Judicial Assistance on Criminal Matters.

In connection with injunctions issued by courts, arts 590 and 591 of the Civil Procedural Law allow courts to request from financial institutions information about the assets of a litigating party so that these may be subject to a freezing order before the final outcome of court proceedings. Certain case law has determined the obligation of the courts, prior to issuing any injunction, to determine the identity, exact nature and details of the accounts opened by the affected litigant and the amounts that must be subject to the relevant freezing order.[9] Nevertheless, Spanish courts have in the past issued all-embracing injunction orders affecting all accounts (and sums therein) opened by the relevant litigant in all and every branch of the credit entity affected (there have been cases in which courts have delivered injunction orders to the Banker's Association for them to have affect on all associated credit entities).

The supervision of the Bank of Spain and the securities market regulator (National Securities Market Commission)

The principle of bank secrecy has been further restricted by the prudential supervision exercised over credit institutions by the Bank of Spain and, as regards services

---

9   See eg Resolution of the First Instance Jugde no. 7 of Palma de Mallorca dated 16 June 1998. This Resolution was subsequently overturned by the Provincial Court of the Balearic Islands on 3 February 1999, which ruled that all-embracing injunction orders affecting all accounts in a relevant credit entity could be issued without identifying the details of the accounts.

provided in connection with the securities markets, by the National Securities Market Commission (CNMV). Law 26/1988 of 29 July has granted the Bank of Spain overall responsibility for the supervision and inspection of credit entities established in Spain and branches of foreign credit entities opened in Spanish territory (with limits as regards branches of EU credit entities).

Law 26/1988 and its developing secondary legislation have set out the disclosure and information requirements regarding accountancy that credit entities must provide to the Bank of Spain on a periodical basis so that it may carry out its supervisory functions. Circular 4/1991 of 14 June of the Bank of Spain has detailed the procedures, principles and level of information that credit entities will need to comply with as regards the keeping of their accounts. Article 6 of the Circular establishes the obligation of credit entities to have those procedures and information available to the Bank of Spain for its supervision and inspection. Article 39 of the Circular further empowers the Bank of Spain to request from credit entities any additional information to the periodical data submitted by credit entities that is deemed necessary to clarify or detail the information received or for any other purpose connected to the prudential supervision of credit entities.

In addition to the terms of Law 26/1988, and as part of the supervisory role of the Bank of Spain, Law 13/1992 of 1 June and its developing secondary legislation have detailed the solvency and capital requirements that credit entities in Spain, on a consolidated basis, will need to comply with in line with the requirements of Council Directives 89/299/EEC, 89/646/EEC, 89/647/EEC and 92/30/EEC. This legislation also determines the level of information to be provided periodically to the Bank of Spain so that it can supervise compliance with capital adequacy ratios and investment limits as regards large risks that can be taken by a consolidated group of credit entities.

Failure by credit entities to comply with the above disclosure obligations towards the Bank of Spain may be considered, depending on the importance of the information not delivered and the particular circumstances of each case, a very serious offence or a serious offence sanctioned from a public caution to the imposition of a fine up to 1% of the equity of the entity, or even the loss of the licence to operate as a credit entity. Members of the board of the affected entity will also be deemed responsible if they acted with knowledge or negligence and could be sanctioned with a wide variety of punishments ranging from a fine up to €150,000 to a prohibition to act as a director or manager of a credit entity during a period of up to ten years.

It has been debated by scholars whether the seemingly all-embracing obligation of disclosure contained in Law 26/1988 and Law 13/1992 should include particularities of transactions entered into by credit entities with third-party clients.[10] In this context, scholars have argued against the duty of full disclosure based on the terms of the old, but still in force, art 49 of the Banking Law of 31 December 1946, which obliged banks to collaborate with the Central Bank in its supervisory functions without having to disclose details of particular transactions and operations. It seems, in the present writer's opinion, that art 49 of the Banking Law should not serve

---

10   See eg M J Guillén Ferrer *El secreto bancario. Sus límites legales.* Valencia 1997, p 237.

today as a limit to the extensive powers of investigation and supervision vested in the Bank of Spain by Laws 26/1988 and 13/1992. The prudential supervision of the Bank of Spain, especially as regards the solvency of credit entities, is a key element to safeguard the interests of end consumers in the banking sector, and constitutes the basis of the principle of recognition of other EU member state resident entities.

As regards protection of personal data, the recently enacted Law 44/2002 has amended the legal regime applicable to the central credit risk information gathering service of the Bank of Spain (CIR), adapting its regime to the general rules contained in Organic Law 15/1999 of 13 December, on protection of personal data. Based on the new regulation, the declaring entities (mainly credit entities and the Bank of Spain) are obliged to communicate to the CIR all data necessary to identify the persons with whom credit risks exist and the characteristics of these persons and risks. In turn, all declaring entities have the right to request and obtain from the CIR reports on any given person, provided that this person (i) keeps with the requesting entity some kind of risk, (ii) has requested a loan or a similar transaction or (iii) is a guarantor or main obligor in any payment document or obligation which the relevant entity is considering to acquire. The declaring entities are obliged to keep confidential all information obtained from the CIR, which must be solely used for the purposes of evaluating risks or granting credits. In addition, the communication of risk information by the declaring entities to third parties (other than the CIR) is prohibited, except if (i) made with the express consent of the affected party or (ii) if the relevant data refer to legal entities and are communicated to a financial entity pertaining to the same consolidated group as the declaring entity or (iii) if the data referred to an individual or natural physical persons are necessary to be communicated to any other financial entity pertaining to the same consolidated group for purposes of compliance with risk concentration and equity ratios regulations. The CIR also has the duty to ensure the confidentiality of the data recorded with the CIR; however, communication of this data by the CIR to other foreign supervisory bodies is permitted, provided that similar protections to those granted by Spanish regulations exist in the receiving countries.

In the securities markets, credit entities are allowed by virtue of Law 24/1988 of 28 July to perform all activities that securities companies and agencies are capable of performing as duly licensed entities to operate in the Spanish securities markets (see above). In this respect, and as provided by art 84 of Law 24/1988, credit entities will be subject to the supervision of the CNMV in the course of carrying out activities and providing services in the securities markets. Thus, banks, savings banks, branches of foreign entities and credit entities providing services in Spain without a permanent establishment will need to abide by the rules of conduct contained in Law 24/1988 as developed by secondary legislation and will be subject to the supervision of the CNMV. Article 85 of Law 24/1988 empowers the CNMV to request all information deemed necessary from market participants, obliging them to make available to the CNMV and even giving publicity, if so requested, to registers, documents and books. The CNMV is further empowered to carry out the inspections considered necessary over entities active in the securities market subject to its supervision. In turn, art 90 of Law 24/1988 sets forth that all information collected by the CNMV as regards their supervision and inspection functions will be subject to professional secrecy and safeguarded. However, there are certain exceptions to this general obligation of secrecy, as follows:

1   when the affected party has expressly agreed to such disclosure;
2   when the data has been aggregated to other information for mere statistical purposes;
3   when the information has been requested from a criminal court, or from a civil court (although in this latter case, supervisory requirements of the relevant investment services company must be kept secret);
4   information requested by judicial authorities in connection with a bankruptcy/ insolvency proceeding of an investment services company (provided the information does not relate to third parties involved in the relaunching of the bankrupt or insolvent company);
5   information requested by a court or an administrative authority in respect of disciplinary proceedings;
6   information released to the Spanish regional governments, the Bank of Spain and other regulatory and supervisory bodies in Spain for them to perform their duties, including auditors;
7   information that may be needed so as to prevent money laundering activities;
8   information requested by a parliamentary investigation committee;
9   information released by the CNMV to supervisory bodies of foreign countries, provided that reciprocity exists and rules of secrecy are similar to those applicable in Spain;
10 information provided by the CNMV to Spanish settlement and clearing systems, provided it is aimed at allowing the correct operation of any such systems;
11 information released with the prior authorisation of the Ministry of Economy to the Tax Authorities in accordance with, and subject to, the conditions set out in arts 111 and 112 of the General Tax Law (Law 230/1963 of 28 December); and
12 information provided by the CNMV to the Ministry of Economy or to the Spanish regional governments.

Restrictions contained in provisions aimed at avoiding money laundering

Law 19/1993 of 28 December implemented in Spain Council Directive 91/308/ EEC on the prevention of money laundering. According to the referred Law and related regulations, credit entities are obliged to disclose to the Executive Service of the Commission for the Prevention of Money Laundering dependent from the Bank of Spain information in respect of:

1   any transaction where there are indications or certainty that it is connected with money laundering activities deriving from drug trafficking, terrorism or organised crime;
2   any transaction involving physical cash movements or cheques exceeding €30,050;

3 all operations exceeding the above amount with counterparties resident in a tax haven as defined under Spanish law; and

4 any information requested from the Executive Service.

In principle, the information delivered to the Service will need to include: the identity of the parties to the transaction (including the beneficial participants); the nature, amounts, dates and place of performance of the operation; and any indicative circumstance of its illegal origin. The obligation to inform the Executive Service exists when the relevant funds are effectively the proceeds of crime, but also whether the origin of the funds is legitimate but there are indications or certainty that they are going to be used in terrorist activities. Law 19/1993 specifically exempts credit entities from any liability towards clients for any breach of their duty of confidentiality deriving from a contract or otherwise at the time of making, in good faith, the relevant disclosures provided in the Law. Regarding terrorism, Spain is also a party to the International Convention for the Suppression of the Financing of Terrorism, enacted in New York in 1999, which refers to rules similar to those set forth in Law 19/1993 already in force.

Royal Decree 338/1990 of 9 March, which regulates the tax identity number, sets forth certain limits to the confidentiality of banking transactions, establishing that credit entities must request the tax identity number to persons requesting cash payment of bank drafts issued by a credit entity or issued by any third party (provided in this last case that the amount cashed exceeds€3,005). Credit entities are also obliged to communicate to the tax authorities all drafts issued against cash, goods or securities, except those issued against a bank account.

Limits deriving from auditing regulations

As regards limits deriving from auditing regulations, Law 19/1988 of 12 July, on auditing, states that companies subject to audits are obliged to provide any and all information required by the auditor to perform the audit of their financial statements. Having taken into account that, pursuant to law, credit entities must audit their financial statements, in certain circumstances the obligation vested on audited credit entities to comply with the requests made by the external auditor may be considered an exception to the duty of secrecy.

Restrictions set forth in connection with parliamentary investigation committees

The regulation governing parliamentary investigation committees also imposes certain limits to the principle of bank secrecy, stating that financial entities, as well as tax authorities, must submit any data or information requested by a parliamentary investigation committee, provided that:

1 those data are referred to persons holding or having held an office as senior officials in the government, public administration, public entities or companies controlled by the public administration;

2 the investigation is related to the duties performed by the relevant person; and

3   the committee understands that lacking such data and information it would not be possible to complete the investigation.

Restrictions contained in the Spanish regulations for the defence of competition

Finally, it is worth mentioning the wide scope of the powers of inspection vested by Law 16/1989 of 17 July, on the Service for the Defence of Competition, the administrative body entrusted with the investigation of concentrations of a significant size and conducts that may limit or restrict competition in the Spanish market or constitute an abuse of dominant position. In the course of the investigations, officers of the Service may also request oral explanation in situ. According to art 33 of Law 16/1989, officers of the Service are empowered to investigate, obtain copies and even retain for a maximum period of ten days, documents, books and records that are deemed necessary for the due application of the Law. Legal entities and individuals are obliged to collaborate with the Service, making the requested documents and data available to that administrative body. The obstruction to the investigation may lead to the imposition of fines up to €901.50 per day.

SPECIAL REFERENCE TO SPANISH SECURITIES MARKET REGULATIONS

We have already mentioned the obligation contained in art 81 of Law 24/1988 upon participants in the Spanish securities market to maintain the confidentiality of and safeguard information gathered whilst providing services in respect thereof so that it cannot be improperly used by third parties, without prejudice to reporting to and fulfilling their co-operation duties with judicial and administrative bodies. Any such individual or entity shall adopt appropriate measures to avoid any abusive or unfair use of said information, and, if it cannot be avoided, to remedy the consequences arising form such abusive or unfair use.

In addition to the above, art 81 of Law 24/1988 has implemented in Spain Council Directive 89/592/EEC and prohibited on a general basis the abusive use of so-called inside information.

Subject to certain exceptions, art 81 generally precludes any party or person having inside information (and who acknowledges or who, at least, should have acknowledged the special nature of such information) from carrying out the following activities, directly or indirectly, on their own behalf or on behalf of a third party:

1   to prepare or enter into a transaction in the market regarding the securities to which the information refers or financial instruments or contracts related to these securities (subject to certain exceptions, such as the design of the transaction which constitutes the inside information, or any other transactions made pursuant to applicable regulations);
2   to communicate such information to third parties except in the ordinary course of their employment, profession, post or duties;
3   to recommend to a third party to purchase or to dispose of such securities or financial instruments or contracts, or to encourage that any other third party

purchases or disposes of such securities, instruments or contracts based on such information.

Article 81 of Law 24/1988 defines 'inside information' as any information that, being specific and referring to one or various issuers of securities or financial instruments or contracts or to one or various securities or financial instruments or contracts, is not public and, had it been made public, could have influenced an investor's decision and hence the price in the market (or organised trading system) of the relevant security or securities, financial instruments or contracts in any significant manner. This definition applies also to negotiable securities or other financial instruments for which the listing in an organised market or trading system has been requested.

Article 99 of Law 24/1988 considers any breach of the prohibition contained in art 81 as a 'very serious offence'. In addition to this, Organic Law 10/1995 introduced for the first time in Spain a criminal offence regarding the use of inside information. According to art 285, any individual with confidential information that may be relevant for the quoted price of a listed security to which he may have had access in the course of a professional or business activity is precluded from using it or disclosing it to a third party with the intention of obtaining a benefit or causing a loss of €450,759 or more. The offence is punishable with imprisonment of one to six years and a fine up to three times the benefit obtained or ranging between €432 and 216,367.20.

Finally, Law 24/1988 considers the problem of information gathered by professionals providing a variety of services in the securities market and the possibility that such information be released or be available through different departments where conflicts of interest could arise. Art 83 of Law 24/1988 obliges market participants, including those merely providing investment advisory services, to ensure that the information gathered through the performance of an activity is not accessible directly or indirectly by the staff of the same entity employed in another activity, thus eliminating possible conflicts of interest. As a development of this, the recently enacted Law 44/2002, has introduced several amendments in Law 24/1988 aimed at avoiding the flow of inside information within investment services companies and entities acting in the securities market or giving investment advice.

Furthermore, in order to prevent any leaking of inside information and to safeguard all confidential information before it is disclosed to the public, Law 44/2002 imposes certain duties on the issuers of securities during the phase of study and decision on the structure of any transaction, including, inter alia, (i) limiting the number of persons dealing with the inside information, (ii) setting up measures to preserve the security of the information flow, (iii) maintaining updated records of the persons having had access to the inside information or (iv) informing these persons of their confidentiality duties.

These new provisions supplement those previously established by Royal Decree 629/1993 defining a general code of conduct, mandatory upon entities acting in the securities markets, including credit entities, by virtue of which the appropriate 'Chinese Walls' in respect of different departments providing different services in the securities markets need to be introduced to ensure that no flow of information between departments is possible and, thus, ensuring that final investment decisions are taken by each department separately. Law 44/2002 expressly provides for the obligation of investment services companies and entities acting in the securities market to adapt their internal codes of conduct to the new provisions in force.

27 Sweden

André Andersson
Jesper Johansson

INTRODUCTION

Bank confidentiality has a long tradition in Sweden, dating back to the seventeenth century. Its main purpose is to protect customers who have a need for confidentiality, primarily regarding trade secrets, but also regarding personal circumstances.

However, not only customers gain from bank confidentiality. Trust and mutual confidence between banks and their customers are essential to banking business, and confidentiality is a necessary condition for this. Bank confidentiality thus serves an important purpose in banking business and thereby supports not only the interests of the customers, but also the interests of the banks, the business community and the public at large.

Bank confidentiality may, however, be misused in order to conceal illegal and even criminal behaviour. The public thus also has an interest in limiting bank confidentiality, and therefore Swedish rules have been provided with several exceptions. The current rules on bank confidentiality attempt to balance the duty of loyalty to the customers to keep information about them confidential, on the one hand, and the interest of the public to disclose illegal behaviour, on the other.

THE NATURE AND EXTENT OF BANK CONFIDENTIALITY

The general rule on bank confidentiality

Swedish bank confidentiality is partly founded on a contractual basis and partly stipulated by law. The general statutory rule is found in the Banking Business Act (Bankrörelselag (1987: 617), the BBA), Ch 1, s 10:

> 'The relations of individuals to a bank may not be disclosed without legal cause.'

There is no further legislation regarding bank confidentiality and there are very few precedents. The legal literature contains only a few works in this area.

The rule is applicable only to the private sector. Confidentiality in the public sector is governed by the Secrecy Act (Sekretesslagen (1980: 100)), which, however, will not be further discussed in this chapter.

Many issues regarding confidentiality are solved internally in the banks and it should be noted that Swedish banks in general have a good reputation for following the rules on confidentiality. The banks are supervised by the Swedish Financial Supervisory Authority (Finansinspektionen, the FSA).

A customer of the bank

The expression 'the relations of individuals to a bank' refers to the relations of individual persons and entities to a bank in the bank's capacity as a bank. The individuals and entities referred to shall be customers in the bank's banking business. Thus, information relating to, for example, the bank's employees, landlords and lawyers does not fall under the scope of bank confidentiality.

The bank is prevented from disclosing the relations between the bank and its customers. The bank is also prevented from disclosing the fact that an individual is a customer of the bank. If an individual ceases to be a customer of the bank, the bank still has an obligation to keep the information confidential. A person who negotiates or has been negotiating with the bank about becoming a customer shall, as regards bank confidentiality, be treated as a person who is or has been a customer of the bank.

Information covered by the confidentiality

Information is covered by bank confidentiality if the individual typically may have a reason to consider it as confidential and may wish to keep it confidential. The rule is vague and it is often hard to establish whether certain information should be treated as confidential. If there is uncertainty, the bank should consider the information as confidential.

The confidentiality covers the relations between the individual and the bank. However, the concept 'between' should not be interpreted narrowly; the confidentiality covers all information related to the relationship. The information covered by bank confidentiality is normally of an economic or financial character. However, information of a more personal character is also covered.

Information which an officer of the bank receives from the customer in his capacity as an employee of the bank is naturally covered by the confidentiality. In addition, the confidentiality covers information which the officer has learned about in a way other than in his capacity as an employee of the bank. The confidentiality also covers information not expressly given by the customer to the bank, but which the bank has been able to obtain through observations or conclusions. The rules on confidentiality thus apply regardless of how the bank has obtained the information.

Information known to the general public

Bank confidentiality does not cover information already known to the general public or known to a substantial number of persons. Nor does the confidentiality cover information which everybody is able to obtain without a major effort.

Disclosure or use of the information

According to the wording of the statutory rule on bank confidentiality, the bank may not disclose relations between the bank and an individual. However, it is also clear that the bank may not use the information in any other way if such use may be in conflict with the customer's interests. If the bank unlawfully uses the information, the bank is liable for any damage the customer suffers, regardless of whether the information is also disclosed to a third party.

Bank confidentiality prohibits all possible kinds of disclosures, the handing out of documents as well as giving oral information.

THE REMEDIES AVAILABLE

Generally on available remedies

The obligation to keep certain information confidential is civil. Thus, a breach of the obligation is not a criminal offence. The main remedy is a liability for damages imposed on the bank and the bank officers. It should also be noted that the bank may take disciplinary action according to Swedish labour law against an employee if the employee violates the rules on bank confidentiality.

The bank's liability for damages

The wording of the rule in the BBA does not state who has the obligation to keep certain information confidential. However, it is absolutely clear that the bank has this obligation. This means that the bank is primarily liable for economic damage resulting from a breach of confidentiality committed by any of the bank's bodies (for example, the board of directors or top management). The bank is also vicariously liable for damage resulting from breaches committed by another person if the bank is responsible for such person's actions. This includes employees assisting the customers (such as employees in the securities brokerage business) and employees who in their employment in any other way learn about the customers' relations with the bank. Normally, the bank is also liable if a person commits a breach of the confidentiality after he has left his position with the bank. However, the bank is not liable for damage if the shareholders or the auditors disclose confidential information.

In most cases, liability for damage presupposes wilfulness or negligence. However, it has been discussed in legal writing and debate whether the bank should be liable for damage even if the bank has not caused the damage wilfully or through negligence, ie that the liability should be strict. There are no precedents and the extent of the banks' liability is therefore unclear.

Other parties' liability for damages

In addition to the bank, a number of other persons have an obligation to keep certain information confidential. Among these are founders, trustees, members of the board of directors, delegates, liquidators and auditors. All members of the board of directors have this liability (including the employee representatives and board members appointed by the government). The chief executive officer is liable either as a member of the board or as a delegate. In addition, the shareholders have an obligation to keep information confidential.

All of the aforementioned persons have a legal obligation to keep certain information confidential. However, only some of them also have a liability for damages to a third party if they violate the obligation. The rules on liability for damages to customers of a bank are found in the BBA and are only applicable in relation to savings banks and membership banks. As regards banks which are incorporated as limited liability companies, which is the case for the majority of the banks in Sweden, there are no rules on damages to customers payable by the different directors and representatives of a bank for breaches of the rules on bank confidentiality. It is hence not possible for a customer who has suffered damage resulting from a breach of bank confidentiality by a bank incorporated as a limited liability company to claim for damages from anyone else but the bank.

Towards a customer, the liability of a founder, a member of the board of directors, a chief executive officer or a delegate of a savings bank or a membership bank arises if they wilfully or as a result of negligence contravene the BBA (including the rule on bank confidentiality) and thereby cause damage to a customer.

> 'A founder, a trustee, a member of the board of directors or a delegate who wilfully or as a result of negligence causes the bank to suffer damage when performing his duties shall be liable for the damage. The same applies where a shareholder, a member or any other person suffers damage through contravention of this Act.'[1]

The auditors of a membership bank or a savings bank are liable for damage caused by them through a wilful or negligent contravention of the BBA (including the rule on bank confidentiality). Where an accounting firm is auditor, both the firm and the auditor principally responsible for the audit shall be liable for such damage.

> 'An auditor is liable for damage on the grounds mentioned in section 1. He is also liable for any damage caused wilfully or by negligence by his assistants.'[2]

As is the case for the directors and other representatives of banks which are incorporated as limited liability companies, it is not possible for a customer of such bank to receive damages from an auditor of such bank should the auditor disclose information covered by the bank confidentiality.

A member of a membership bank or a person that is entitled to vote without being a member of the bank has a liability for damage caused by him through a wilful or grossly negligent contravention of, among other statutes, the BBA (including the rule on bank confidentiality). However, members rarely obtain information covered by confidentiality. It should be noted that if information becomes widely spread among a large number of members (for example, at a general meeting), the information will lose its confidential character.

---

1   BBA, Ch 5, s 1.
2   BBA, Ch 5, s 2.

'A member of a membership bank or a person entitled to vote without being a member is liable for the damage which he, wilfully or by gross negligence, causes the membership bank, another member or any other person by being an accessory to a contravention of this Act, the Act on Annual Accounts for Finance Institutes and Securities Companies [Lag (1995: 1559) om årsredovisning i kreditinstitut och värdepappersbolag], or the Act on Membership Banks [Lag (1995: 1570) om medlemsbanker].'[3]

Shareholders of banks, which are incorporated as limited liability companies, do not have any liability to pay damages to customers should the shareholder disclose information covered by the bank confidentiality.

Naturally, other employees and officers of the bank also have an obligation to keep information confidential. Normally, however, they do not have a liability for damage towards the customers, if they violate the obligation.

Third parties do not have any obligation to keep information confidential.

Reduction of awarded damages

The liability to pay damages described above may under certain circumstances be reduced having regard to the nature of the action, the extent of the damage caused and other circumstances.

'Where a person is liable for damages under sections 1–3, the amount of damages may be reasonably reduced having regard to the nature of his action, the extent of the damage caused and other circumstances.'[4]

Joint and several liability for damages

The liability to pay damages is joint and several if more than one person is liable for the damage according to the rules described above. If somebody, due to a joint and several liability for the damage, pays more than his share of the damages, he is entitled to reimbursement from the other liable persons to a reasonable extent.

'Two or more persons liable for the same damage are jointly and severally liable insofar as the liability for any one of them has not been reduced pursuant to paragraph one. A person liable having paid damages is entitled to reimbursement from the others to a reasonable extent having regard to the circumstances.'[5]

EXCEPTIONS

General

The main purpose of bank confidentiality is to protect the interests of the individual customers and the banks. However, these interests are to an increasing extent being

---

3   BBA, Ch 5, s 3.
4   BBA, Ch 5, s 4, para 1.
5   BBA, Ch 5, s 4, para 2.

balanced by the risk that the confidentiality may be used to conceal illegal or criminal behaviour. The public interest to prevent this has therefore resulted in a large number of exceptions to the obligation to keep confidentiality.

According to the general rule on bank confidentiality, the information 'may not be disclosed without legal cause'. There are a large number of situations when 'legal cause' must be considered to exist. These exceptions cover, first, where there is an obligation for the bank to disclose certain information and, secondly, where the bank has a right to disclose information, even though there is no obligation to do so.

Consent from the customer

Bank confidentiality mainly exists in order to protect the customers, and the bank may disclose information if the customer gives his consent. A consent may be withdrawn at any time.

If the bank's obligation to keep confidentiality had been based merely on a contractual relationship, the banks could have been able to disregard the confidentiality obligation totally through agreements with the customers. However, bank confidentiality exists also on a statutory basis and not all kinds of 'consents' or agreements may set the obligation of confidentiality aside. For instance, a bank may not in advance, through clauses in standard forms or in general terms, generally remove itself from the obligation of confidentiality. Such 'consents' would probably not be considered valid. However, a customer may in a specific case give his consent for the bank to disclose certain information, for example, Internet banking.

Information handled internally within the bank

A bank has to handle information (including confidential information) internally in order to carry out its ordinary business. This is not in conflict with the obligation of confidentiality, as long as it is done in the bank's duty of loyalty. This could involve disclosure of information by officers to the management, within the management or by the bank to its auditor.

However, if the information were to be distributed generally within the bank, the information would lose its confidential character. Such distribution is in conflict with the obligation of confidentiality and it is therefore necessary to keep confidential information within a limited group of persons in the bank.

Information exchanged between a parent bank and a subsidiary may be handled in the same way as information distributed within the bank.

Information provided by a bank to an outsourced part of its business is subject to the main rule and may not be disclosed without legal cause, which is assessed on a case-by-case basis.

The Financial Supervisory Authority

The Financial Supervisory Authority (Finansinspektionen, the FSA) promotes stability and efficiency in the Swedish financial market. The FSA supervises banks and other financial institutions and monitors, for example, the banks' compliance with applicable legislation. The FSA may, when carrying out its supervisory functions, request the banks to provide the FSA with necessary information. The banks shall, if requested to do so, disclose the information regardless of bank confidentiality.

> 'A bank is subject to supervision by the Financial Supervisory Authority. The bank shall provide the Supervisory Authority with information on its business and other circumstances connected therewith as required by the Authority.
> The Supervisory Authority may conduct an investigation in a bank whenever the Supervisory Authority considers it necessary.'[6]

A bank authorised in another jurisdiction is primarily supervised by the competent authority in the bank's home jurisdiction. However, the FSA also supervises Swedish branches of foreign banks and banks who conduct cross-border activities in Sweden, in co-operation with the competent authorities in such banks' home jurisdictions. Swedish banks may in a similar way be supervised also by the competent authorities in other jurisdictions, even if the primary responsibility rests with the FSA. Swedish bank confidentiality does not prevent banks from providing the FSA and/or other competent authorities with requested information.

The information obtained shall, as a general rule, be kept confidential by the FSA. The FSA may, however, provide the competent authorities in other states in the EEA with information, regardless of this confidentiality.

Information to the tax authorities

The tax authorities have been given extensive powers to obtain information from banks in order to make it possible for the tax authorities to perform their work and to make tax control more efficient.

The Swedish system for simplified tax returns is based on the fact that the banks, among others, provide the tax authorities with information. This has resulted in extensive obligations for the banks to provide the tax authorities with information regarding interest, capital balance and nominee shares. In addition, the tax authorities can request a bank to provide them with information regarding the legal relations between the bank and an individual. The tax authorities do not have to suspect any illegal behaviour, nor is it a prerequisite for the request that the interest of the tax authorities to obtain information in any objective way is considered to outweigh the customer's interest of confidentiality. These obligations also apply to foreign banks and other foreign companies conducting financing and insurance activities in Sweden through a branch or another permanent establishment.

---

6   BBA, Ch 7, s 1.

'The tax authority may order anybody, who is or may be required to maintain accounting records ..., to give a statement of a transaction between him and somebody else or disclose a document or submit a copy of a document which concerns the transaction.'[7]

The obligation to give the above-described information is also applicable to foreign banks, and other foreign companies conducting financing and insurance business cross-border into Sweden. Such companies are obligated to submit a written document to the FSA, stating that they undertake to report to the tax authorities the information required pursuant to the Act on Simplified Tax Return and Statement of Earnings and Tax Deduction before they start doing business into Sweden.

'Foreign companies that conduct banking activities, ..., in Sweden without establishing a branch or a corresponding establishment here, must before the business activities are initiated submit a written undertaking to the Financial Supervisory Authority that they will submit statement of earnings and tax deductions in accordance with this statute.'[8]

Testimonies and production of documents to a court

Swedish law contains a civil duty to testify in court. This duty is in certain cases limited by reason of secrecy. However, bank confidentiality does not restrict or limit the obligation to testify, and bank officers have to disclose information when testifying, regardless of the fact that the information is normally covered by bank confidentiality. Among those who may be obliged to testify are the bank management, other employees of a bank and a bank's auditors. A witness may not disclose information which has no relevance to the case in which he is heard.

However, a witness may refuse to testify regarding circumstances which are considered as trade secrets, unless there are extraordinary reasons. This covers not only the witness' own trade secrets, but also other trade secrets which are to be kept confidential by the witness.

Trade secrets include such information regarding a business enterprise or its operations which is kept secret and which, if disclosed, typically would result in damage to the entity's ability to compete. The definition implies that it has to be information used in the operation of a business; personal knowledge of an employee in itself is not protected. The information also has to be secret, meaning, first, on a subjective level, that the entity has an ambition to keep the information secret; and, secondly, on an objective level, that the entity has taken measures in order to protect the information and prohibit the access to it by unauthorised parties. From how the business is conducted it should be clear to the employees that the information shall be kept secret. The group of persons with access to the information must in some sense be limited, but the information can be protected even if known by several people. The disclosure shall also typically result in damage to the entity's ability to compete.

---

7   Act on Simplified Tax Return and Statement of Earnings and Tax Deduction (Lag (2001: 1227) om självdeklarationer och kontrolluppgifter), Ch 17, s 4, para 1.
8   Act on Simplified Tax Return and Statement of Earnings and Tax Deduction, Ch 13, s 1.

Bank officers may have information constituting trade secrets of the bank as well as information which is a customer's trade secrets. As stated above, a witness may refuse to testify. However, because of the rules on bank confidentiality, a bank officer must use this possibility to refuse to give testimonies regarding the customers' trade secrets.

A Swedish bank which is a party to, or an officer of a Swedish bank who testifies in, legal proceedings in a foreign country shall follow the Swedish rules on bank confidentiality.

Swedish law contains an obligation to produce documents to a court which may be of importance as evidence in proceedings. A bank may be ordered by a court to produce documents which are normally covered by bank confidentiality, even if the bank is not a party to the proceedings. However, the limitation regarding trade secrets when testifying also applies to the obligation to produce documents.

Foreign courts can ask for evidence to be obtained before a Swedish court. Basically, the rules regarding testimonies and production of documents described above shall apply also in these cases.

Information to prosecutors and the police

An individual's dealings with a bank may be of interest to prosecutors or the police when they investigate crimes. There are two formal ways for the prosecutors or the police to obtain information from banks: (i) through a search of premises; or (ii) through seizure.

A search of premises may be conducted concerning a person suspected of a crime in order to find material which has been seized or in order to gather information of importance for the investigation of the crime. A search of premises may also be conducted at a bank in order to achieve the above-mentioned purposes, if the crime has been committed in the bank, if the suspect has been arrested in the bank or if there is a particular reason to believe that material which has been seized or other information of importance will be found. A bank has no obligation to disclose information to the prosecutor or the police in other cases.

In addition, a bank may disclose information normally covered by bank confidentiality in order to provide the prosecutor or the police with information of importance for an investigation without a seizure or search of premises. Provided the bank is very cautious, it can be reasonably helpful towards the prosecutors or the police. A seizure or a search of premises is normally not needed for the bank to be able to do this.

It should be noted that the above-mentioned concerns the situation when the bank itself has no reason to suspect the customer of a crime. If the bank knows or has reasons to suspect that a customer has committed a crime, the bank should not use bank confidentiality in order to protect the suspect/criminal. If the bank learns or suspects that a crime has been committed, the bank has a right to disclose the information in question, regardless of requests from the prosecutor/police.

Foreign courts may also request coercive measures. Property may be seized at the request of a foreign court if it could reasonably have importance for an investigation of a crime or if the object of the seizure has been the subject of a crime. A search of premises may be used to locate such property.

Information to the enforcement service authorities

According to the Enforcement Code (Utsökningsbalk (1981: 774)), banks (and other third parties) are obliged to provide the enforcement service authorities with information that may be of importance when the authorities shall judge whether a seizure or a restraint may be obtained. The information that may be disclosed regardless of the confidentiality shall concern the customer's claims on the bank or other 'dealings' with the bank. The bank shall disclose the information to the extent the information may be of importance in order to determine whether the debtor has any possessions that may be restrained. The bank is allowed (but has no obligation) to inform the customer of the measures taken by the enforcement service authorities.

Disclosure in the interest of the bank

Another important exception to the obligation of confidentiality is the bank's right to protect itself and its interests towards its customers and others. In doing this, for example, in legal proceedings or when taking coercive measures, the bank may disclose information normally covered by bank confidentiality. However, a bank may not disclose information in a litigation against a customer if the customer's damage from the disclosure is substantially larger than the gain for the bank.

Information to the Bank of Sweden

Swedish banks have an obligation to provide the Bank of Sweden (Riksbanken) with certain information. This obligation shall be fulfilled regardless of bank confidentiality.

Information to other public authorities

In principle, bank confidentiality shall also be kept in relation to public authorities. The bank is obliged to disclose information only when it is a statutory requirement. The most important and extensive exceptions have been discussed above. There are many additional exceptions, such as the obligation to disclose information to the Data Inspection Board, to chief guardians and to the supervisory authorities for bankruptcies.

In addition to the obligations to disclose information, the banks are entitled to disclose information in other situations. If there is a significant public interest for disclosure of information and there is no duty of loyalty to the customers preventing the disclosure, information may be disclosed. In doubtful cases the information should be kept confidential.

Information to foreign courts and authorities

Foreign authorities may be involved in legal proceedings in Sweden in which case the rules described above will be applicable. As a general rule, Swedish courts are not available for public law claims by foreign authorities, for example, regarding tax or crime. However, in some situations there may be a legal requirement for Swedish authorities to assist foreign authorities, for example, pursuant to Swedish international treaties.

Information to other third parties

As stated above, an individual may be given access to information covered by bank confidentiality in legal proceedings (through a testimony or a directive to produce documents) or in connection with enforcement by the enforcement service authorities. As a general rule, bank confidentiality shall be maintained in other cases. However, there are also statutory exceptions to this rule and, for example, the following persons have a right to information in certain situations: the shareholders in the bank, liquidators, guardians, the estate of a deceased person, auditors and spouses.

A bank may sometimes also be allowed to give information to other banks, for instance, when a credit is being moved, when a credit has been granted by a syndicate or in relation to a second ranking security (see below regarding credit information). However, the general rule is that banks shall not be treated differently from other third parties and that bank confidentiality shall be kept between banks.

There are also situations where a guarantor of a person is entitled to receive information from the bank in respect of the customer of the bank whose obligations the guarantor is guaranteeing.

OTHER REGULATIONS RELATING TO BANK CONFIDENTIALITY

In addition to the general rules on bank confidentiality, there exist other rules regarding how and when banks may disclose or use information, including the following statutory regulations.

The Personal Data Act

The EC Directive of 1995 on the protection of individuals with regard to the processing of personal data and on the free movement of such data[9] was implemented in Sweden by the Personal Data Act (Personuppgiftslagen (1998: 204)), which contains regulations for registers and data regarding private individuals stored using electronic data processing (EDP). The Personal Data Act provides rules regarding how data concerning private individuals shall be kept, handled and made available in order to prevent improper encroachment on the integrity of registered individuals.

---

9   Council Directive 95/46/EC.

The Personal Data Act prohibits the disclosure of information that may be used in conflict with the Personal Data Act. These restrictions apply together with the rules on bank confidentiality. It is difficult to establish which rules are the most far-reaching. The conclusion must be that that a bank should be extra cautious when disclosing information relating to private individuals if the information is stored on EDP.

The Credit Information Act

The Credit Information Act (Kreditupplysningslag (1973: 1173)) regulates the providing of credit information professionally. The Act includes rules on which information may be stored and provided. It prohibits the storage and providing of information regarding political or religious belief, race, crime and diseases and information regarding inability to pay, unless the inability has been declared by a court or similar authority.

Although information may be provided according to the Credit Information Act, bank confidentiality will still prevail if applicable.

Under certain circumstances, a bank may disclose credit information without being in conflict with the rules on bank confidentiality. Information may be disclosed when the information includes a positive judgment of the customer's creditworthiness, since the customer in these cases must be supposed not to have any objections against a disclosure. It is harder to decide whether a bank may disclose unfavourable credit information without the customer's consent. As stated above, a bank may disclose information regarding customers if the reasons for the disclosure are significant enough. Since correct and fairly extensive credit information is of great importance to the business community as a whole, a bank may in principle give credit information. However, great precaution should be taken in order not to violate the rule on bank confidentiality. The credit information should be very general in nature and not include specific information regarding the customer's relationship with the bank.

Through changes in the Credit Information Act the rules apply also to information given between banks from 1 July 1997.

The sanctions against breaches of the act are penal in nature and an offender may be sentenced to prison for up to a year if the offence is considered gross.

The Insider Act

Insider trading is prohibited under the Insider Act (Insiderstrafflag (2000: 1086)). A person who has received non-public information which is likely to influence the price of financial instruments materially is prohibited from trading, on his own behalf or on behalf of another person/entity, with such instruments on the market. Nor may he cause or induce any other person/entity to trade in such financial instruments.

The prohibition applies primarily to persons who have employments, assignments or other positions which normally involve access to information that is significant for the price of financial instruments and to persons who have received information which concerns a company in which they own shares. However, the prohibition also applies to other persons who possess insider information, provided the direct or indirect source is a person referred to above, but these latter persons are not prohibited by the Insider Act from causing another person to trade. Banks and bank officers are not excluded from these regulations and bank officers are among those who typically may have insider information.

The sanctions against insider trading are penal in nature and an offender may be sentenced to up to four years' imprisonment if the offence is considered gross. Any gains from insider trading may be declared forfeited if this is not deemed unreasonable.

The Money Laundering Act

The EC Money Laundering Directive of 1991[10] was implemented in Sweden 1993 by the Money Laundering Act (Lag (1993: 768) om åtgärder mot penningtvätt, the MLA), last revised in April 2002, together with the Money Laundering Regulation (Förordning (1993: 1526) om åtgärder mot penningtvätt) and was later augmented by the Money Laundering Records Act (Lag (1999: 163) om penningtvättsregister). The purpose of the MLA is to make it more difficult to get hold of funds which have been obtained through a crime (money laundering). To accomplish this, the MLA contains a provision obligating a bank to investigate all transactions which the bank suspects concern funds obtained through a crime. The bank shall inform the National Police Board about all circumstances indicating money laundering. Bank confidentiality does not prevent the disclosure of such information.

The offences of money laundering, and aiding and abetting certain specified money laundering activities, are each punishable by up to six years' imprisonment, or a fine, or both. Wilful or grossly negligent failure to examine potential, or to report specified, money laundering activities is punishable by a fine. The same applies to disclosing to the customer or any third party that an examination has been performed that a report has been filed or that the police are investigating.

SUMMARY

Swedish bank confidentiality is civil and the basic rule is that 'the relations of individuals to a bank may not be disclosed without legal cause'. The confidentiality is sanctioned through liability in damages for the bank and, in respect of savings banks and membership banks, for certain persons, for example, the members of the board of directors and the members.

There are extensive exceptions to the rule on confidentiality, mainly in the interest of the public. The most important exception may be the right for the tax authorities to obtain information from the banks. Other important exceptions deal with the disclosure after consent from the customer, information handled internally within the bank and information to prosecutors and the police. In addition, other legislation may be of importance for a bank when handling information, for example, the Personal Data Act and the Insider Act.

10   Council Directive 91/308/EEC.

28 Switzerland

Dr Stefan Breitenstein

INTRODUCTION

Swiss banking secrecy, or bank confidentiality, is by no means as absolute as some people outside Switzerland tend to believe. It is, however, also not going to be abolished as many foreign commentators predict. Rather, it will continue to adapt over time to the changing legal, commercial and political environment. Conceptually, Swiss banking secrecy has remained unchanged since its introduction in 1934. However, its application and the scope have evolved substantially over the last 20 years. The definition of the scope of the banking secrecy by the Swiss legislators has always required a balance between the protection of the privacy of bank customers and law enforcement by the states inside and outside their boundaries. The increased globalisation of the previously national economies and the substantial harmonisation of financial laws have lead to an increased co-operation in international law enforcement. As a result, the balance of interest has gradually shifted from the protection of bank customers' privacy to international co-operation in law enforcement. The changes to Swiss banking secrecy clearly reflect this development. As described in more detail below, Swiss banking secrecy gradually eroded over time in matters of criminal legal assistance, enforcement of financial market regulations (insider trading), consolidated supervision of internationally active banking groups, money laundering and, most recently, terrorist financing. The only major area where the protection of privacy of bank customers still prevails over law enforcement is international tax enforcement. In this area, banking secrecy continues to be upheld, except where tax fraud is involved. In this connection, it should be noted that Switzerland applies a very narrow definition of tax fraud and normally requires an intentional deceit by means of false documents or documents containing untrue information.

NATURE AND EXTENT OF THE BANKER'S DUTY OF CONFIDENCE

Nature

Non-contractual

The Swiss Civil Code (CC)[1] protects the privacy rights of any legal or physical person in general by its art 28. Long before Switzerland had a banking law, the Swiss Federal Supreme Court recognised that the privacy rights of a person included information relating to his financial affairs.[2] It is therefore generally recognised in Swiss law that confidential information obtained by a bank concerning its customers and their financial affairs is protected by the privacy rights of the Civil Code.[3]

An intrusion of the privacy rights in breach of art 28 of the CC is also qualified as a tort in the meaning of art 41 of the Swiss Code of Obligations (CO).[4] Accordingly, a breach of banking secrecy could, depending on the circumstances, lead to civil law sanctions even if the bank's confidential information is not covered by a contractual relationship but concerns third parties. Possible sanctions include court injunctions and the award of damages. Tort claims for violation of bank confidentiality are, however, rare, since in most cases there exists a contractual basis for a claim which is normally the preferred basis for such claims.

An ordinary action under art 28a of the CC may take some time, which normally frustrates the claimant who is seeking quick relief. A claimant who can make a prima facie case evidencing that (i) his privacy rights have been illegally injured or the injury is imminent, and (ii) the injury will render harm to him which cannot be easily recovered is entitled to provisional measures under art 28a of the CC, such as temporary injunctions or restraint orders. Swiss law does not, however, grant a court the power to award punitive damages. In this connection, it is important to note that the payment of taxes which the claimant is obliged to pay under the applicable law is not considered a damage in the meaning of Swiss law. Penalties payable by the claimant for avoidance of taxes are attributed to the claimant's own fault and compensation is therefore generally not awarded.

Contractual

The relationship between a bank and its customers is generally contractual in nature and governed by a number of provisions of the CO. The qualification of the relationship between the bank and its customers largely depends on the services

---

1   CC 10 December 1907, RS 210.
2   Decision of the Federal Tribunal (hereinafter BGE) 64 (1938) II 162 (169).
3   B Kleiner and R Schwob in Bodmer, Kleiner and Lutz *Kommentar zum Schweizerischen Bankengesetz* (13th edn, 2002) BkL, art 47, n 106; D Guggenheim *Die Verträge der Schweizerischen Bankpraxis* (3rd edn, 1986) p 24; P Honegger and Th Frick 'Das Bankengeheimnis im Konzern und bei Übernahmen' in *Swiss Review of Business Law* (1996) pp 1–10; P Bernasconi 'Le secret bancaire suisse entre deux feux: procédures pénales et fiscales' in Bernasconi *Les nouveaux défis au secret bancaire suisse* (1996) pp 9–22.
4   CO 30 March 1911, RS 220; Kleiner and Schwob, n 3 above, BkL art 47, n 106; Guggenheim, n 3 above, p 24.

requested by the individual customer. It is, however, clear that most customer relationships contain some elements of a mandate.[5] The key provision for mandate contracts provides that the agent has to execute a mandate faithfully and diligently: art 398 of the CO. The bank has to treat as confidential all information the customer requests the bank to keep secret. The customer is considered the master of the 'secret'. Bank confidentiality is therefore a right of the customer and a duty of the bank. It is not a right of the bank.

Certain contractual relationships between the bank and the customer may not be qualified as mandates, but rather as a loan agreement or other non-mandate types of agreement, in which case the question arises whether the bank is under a duty of confidentiality. Most Swiss legal scholars take the view that the confidentiality covenant is customary and is at least implied in all banking agreements, unless disclosure is clearly required by the nature of the business transaction in question.[6] This is supported by the fact that the Swiss Federal Banking Law (BkL)[7] in its art 47 clearly establishes a duty of confidentiality to the bank, even though not in a civil law context. Unauthorised disclosure of confidential facts by the bank, therefore, constitutes a breach of contract. Consequently, the contractual duty of confidentiality and the protection of a customer's privacy rights guaranteed in art 28 of the CC form the basis for the banking secret protected by art 47 of the BkL.

The Swiss Federal Act on Exchanges and Securities Trading (SESTA)[8] provides among others for legal standards of professional conduct for securities dealers. Such standards include the duty to act faithfully and diligently.[9] As a result, securities dealers have to safeguard their customer's interest and keep customer information confidential if so asked implicitly or explicitly by the customer, even if the contractual relationship between the customer and the securities dealer does not in all respects qualify as a mandatory contract.[10] Cross-border transactions of foreign securities dealers providing their services into Switzerland are only subject to the Swiss confidentiality standards if the foreign securities dealers have an office with permanent employees in the form of a branch or representative office in Switzerland or if they are member of the Swiss Exchange (SWX). Without such presence in Switzerland, foreign securities dealers are not subject to the Swiss confidentiality standards.[11]

The remedies for breach of contract under Swiss law are either specific performance, which may mean an injunction prohibiting the disclosure of confidential information, or damages. Again, losses attributable to the customer's own fault cannot be claimed as damages or will at least result in a reduction of the compensation awarded. This

---

5   M Aubert, P A Béguin, P Bernasconi, J G Burg, R Schwob and R Treuilland *Le secret bancaire suisse* (3rd edn, 1995) pp 480–502.
6   Kleiner and Schwob, n 3 above, BkL, art 47, n 2; Aubert et al, n 5 above, pp 50–51.
7   BkL 8 November 1934, as amended, RS 952.0.
8   SESTA 24 March 1995, RS 954.1.
9   SESTA, art 11.
10   SESTA, art 11 sets a (contractually motivated) professional standard for faithful and diligent execution of client orders; compare G Hertig and U Schuppisser *Kommentar zum Schweizerischen Kapitalmarktrecht* (1999) SESTA, art 11, n 7ss.
11   Hertig and Schuppisser, n 10 above, SESTA, art 11, n 19s.

applies in particular to taxes and penalties which become payable as a result of an unauthorised disclosure of confidential information.

Criminal

It is a particularity of Swiss law that bank confidentiality is not only protected by civil and contract law but also by criminal law. Article 47 of the BkL makes breach of bank confidentiality a crime. This provision was included in 1934 in the BkL at a time when countries in the vicinity of Switzerland introduced legislation that attempted to gain control over the foreign assets of its nationals or discriminated against people for the mere reason of their race, religion or political belief. As these objectives were pursued by all kinds of intelligence and espionage, it was deemed necessary to enact a criminal provision protecting bank customers and defence against intrusion of Swiss sovereignty.

The present wording of art 47 of the BkL reads as follows:

'1.	Whoever divulges a secret entrusted to him or of which he has become aware in his capacity as officer, employee, mandatory, liquidator or commissioner of a bank, as representative of the Banking Commission, officer or employee of a recognised auditing company and whoever tries to induce others to violate professional secrecy, shall be punished by imprisonment for not more than six months or by a fine of not more than SFr. 50,000.
2.	If the act has been committed by negligence, the penalty shall be a fine not exceeding SFr. 30,000.
3.	The violation of professional secrecy remains punishable even after termination of the official or employment relationship or the exercise of the profession.
4.	Federal and Cantonal regulations concerning the obligation to testify and to furnish information to a government authority shall apply.'

It must be noted that two types of information are subject to the provision: (i) confidential information entrusted to the bank by its customers, and (ii) confidential information which came to the attention of the bank in the course of executing the customer agreement. Secrets related to the bank's own business are not covered by art 47 of the BkL, but may constitute business secrets protected by art 162 of the Swiss Penal Code (PC).[12]

Article 47 of the BkL is clearly criminal in nature and its enforcement is not dependent upon complaint of the damaged party, but must be prosecuted ex officio. Even negligent breach of banking secrecy can be punished. This indicates the historic importance the Swiss legislator attributed to banking secrecy as compared, for instance, with the attorney-client privilege, a breach of which will be prosecuted only upon complaint of the client and only if the breach was wilful.

In line with this provision of the BkL, the SESTA provides in art 43 for an equivalent provision incriminating the violation of professional secrecy of securities dealers or

---

12   PC 21 December 1937, RS 311.0.

of members of an exchange. The wording of art 43 of the SESTA is materially the same as art 47 of the BkL. Article 43 has, however, a somewhat wider scope of application since it not only protects the relationship between customer and securities dealer but also information a stock exchange receives when executing orders. Accordingly, the SESTA adds an additional layer of protection of customers who execute exchange transactions through banks or securities dealers.

Data protection

As of 1992, Switzerland has enacted a Federal Law on Data Protection (LDP)[13] which is designed to protect the individual's right to control the use of private data related to his person. Since the scope of application comprises private data, and includes information relating to the financial situation of a customer, the LDP is not strengthening the level of protection already provided by art 47 of the BkL and art 43 of the SESTA. These provisions constitute a lex specialis relative to the LDP. The rules set forth in the LDP on the processing, storing and transferring of data have no direct impact on the bank confidentiality and do not extend the duties of a bank or a securities dealer to safeguard its customer's confidentiality.[14]

In a case where a multinational banking group intends to transfer data abroad in order to centralise the data processing, special requirements of the LDP must, however, be observed. Under the LDP a data transfer is, in principle, only permissible to countries with data protection laws that are substantially equivalent to Swiss laws. If this is not the case, special agreements must be entered into in order to provide for the required data protection level. Further, the data transfer abroad must be notified to the Federal Officer for Data Protection if customer consent is not obtained. The data processing abroad of banks is governed by a special Circular of the Federal Banking Commission which is discussed in Recent developments below.

Administrative

Article 23ter of the BkL and art 35, para 3 of the SESTA stipulate that the Federal Banking Commission may take such measures as it deems appropriate to remedy irregularities in the conduct of a bank or securities dealer. Breach of banking secrecy as provided in art 47 of the BkL or breach of professional secrecy as provided in art 43 of the SESTA may constitute such an irregularity and entail administrative sanctions. These sanctions may range from a warning addressed to the bank or securities dealer to the effect that the persons who breached banking or professional secrecy be dismissed to the withdrawal of the banking or securities dealer licence.

Extent

In time

Bank's confidentiality obligation continues for as long as the customer whose secrets are involved has a reasonable interest to keep them confidential, even if the

13   LDP 19 June 1992, RS 235.1.
14   Kleiner and Schwob, n 3 above, BkL, art 47, n 112.

contractual relationship between the customer and the bank or the securities dealer has been terminated.

Territorial reach

All banks or securities dealers licensed to do business in Switzerland, either as Swiss legal entities or branches or representative offices of foreign banks or securities dealers or as members of the SWX, are subject to the banking or professional secrecy obligation with respect to the business activities in Switzerland.

Customer relationships of foreign branches of Swiss banks or securities dealers are, however, not protected by the criminal law provision of art 47 of the BkL and art 43 of the SESTA.[15]

Swiss legal scholars do not have a uniform opinion on whether a breach of Swiss banking secrecy by an act that occurs outside Switzerland is punishable under art 47 of the BkL.[16] As the provision on criminal protection of banking or professional secrecy would make little sense if anyone could cross the Swiss border and divulge protected information with impunity, the divulging of confidential information outside of Switzerland should also be subject to criminal sanction. The enforcement of such criminal sanction may, however, not be possible.

Persons bound by banking and professional secrecy

Persons bound by the secrecy obligation are those who in the course of discharging their duties and legal obligations obtain access to confidential customer information.

Public servants such as the members and officers of the Federal Banking Commission, officers of the Swiss National Bank, tax inspectors etc are bound by special confidentiality rules governing their respective offices which involve criminal sanctions as well.[17]

EXCEPTIONS

Customer consent

General

Bank confidentiality[18] is not only to the benefit of bank customers in the strict sense, but also to the benefit of third persons who had contacts with the customers or about

---

15 Kleiner and Schwob, n 3 above, BkL, art 47, n 100.
16 Affirmative Kleiner and Schwob, n 3 above, BkL, art 47, n 103; Aubert et al, n 5 above, pp 100–102 outlines the different positions and its repercussions.
17 Cf PC, art 320.
18 In the following sections, the terms 'bank confidentiality' or 'secrecy' and 'bank' shall also include 'professional secrecy' and 'securities dealer'.

whom the bank obtained confidential information in the ordinary course of its banking business. In order to facilitate reading, all those persons shall in the following be referred to as 'customers'.

Customer consent

As the customer is the master of the privileged information, his express or implied consent releases the bank from its confidentiality duty. Since such release must be legally valid, the bank may be in a difficult situation if it has reasons to believe that the consent of the customer may not have been given voluntarily but under material duress originating from a third party, including foreign public authorities. Under the CO consents given under material duress may be voided by the customer subsequently. Under these circumstances banks will usually try to obtain clear evidence that the consent expresses the customer's actual intent, for example, by means of prior written consent. Like any communication between the parties to a contract, such a consent will have to be construed in accordance with the 'principle of good faith' established by Swiss jurisprudence. This means communication with the client has to be understood as a reasonable person would have understood it under the given circumstances in good faith.[19] Given the fact that bank confidentiality not only protects a contractual right of the customer, but also his privacy, the test becomes particularly delicate in respect to court-ordered waivers.

Persons acting in lieu of the customer

The consent needs not to be given by the customer himself but may be given by any person authorised under the applicable law to act on behalf of the customer. Thus, consent may also be given by agents or proxies appointed by the customer, legal representatives such as parents, spouses (if applicable), tutors, officers and directors of a legal entity or successors, heirs and assignees or executors of the customer's will.[20] However, such consent may not be effective if information concerning the customer is of a strictly personal nature. The situation becomes particularly difficult for the bank when the customer is no longer available to clarify inconsistent or partial consent.

Litigation involving the customer

If the customer sues the bank

Article 47 of the BkL does not contain an express exception referring to an action of the customer against the bank. However, a customer who sues the bank, but insists that the bank abstains from disclosing facts covered by bank confidentiality when defending its position, acts against the general principle of good faith. Accordingly, banks are entitled to disclose confidential information to courts to the extent necessary or useful for their defence without breaching their duty of confidentiality.

---

19   Cf BGE 111 (1985) II 276 (279).
20   Aubert et al, n 5 above, pp 299–351.

If the bank sues the customer

Bank confidentiality does not prevent customers from being sued by Swiss banks. The customer may not invoke bank confidentiality as a defence in an action by the bank for breach of contract.

The bank as third party claimant/defendant

Frequently, Swiss banks are involved in litigation between a customer and a third party, because they hold assets which form the object of the dispute and which may be subject to civil or criminal attachment orders. In these cases, the banks are entitled to protect their own interests by claiming preferential rights such as liens, rights to set-off or other security rights which they may have.[21] According to Swiss jurisprudence, banks must disclose their interests in time otherwise their rights are forfeited.[22] The exercising of such preferential rights does not constitute a breach of bank confidentiality.[23]

Compulsion by law

Civil proceedings

Article 47, para 4 of the BkL expressly reserves federal and cantonal provisions on the duty to testify or to disclose information to public authorities. With respect to civil proceedings, three different systems have been adopted by the federal and the cantonal legislatures.[24]

The first system expressly waives testimony by all persons bound by a professional secret, which is generally deemed to include bank confidentiality.[25]

The second system mentions all professions entitled to refuse testimony without, however, mentioning banks, which means bank officers are obliged to testify.[26]

The third system requires the judge to balance the interests involved in each single case and to thereafter decide whether a bank officer has to testify.[27]

Usually, the obligation of banks to submit documents is subject to the same rules.[28] Where bank confidentiality is protected, courts may take various measures in order to prevent protected information from being disclosed, such as limiting the access of

---

21   Kleiner and Schwob, n 3 above, BkL, art 47, n 91.
22   BGE 109 (1983) III 22; 111 (1985) III 21; 112 (1986) III 59; 113 (1987) III 104; 117 (1991) III 74.
23   BGE 109 (1983) III 22.
24   Cf also Guggenheim, n 3 above, pp 26–28; Aubert et al, n 5 above, pp 133–210.
25   This applies to Berne, Geneva, Glarus, Neuchâtel, Jura and Vaud.
26   This applies to Appenzell (AI), Basle (City and Country), Obwalden, Solothurn, Schaffhausen, Schwyz and Thurgau.
27   This applies to Aargau, Appenzell (AR), Fribourg, Grisons, Lucerne, Nidwalden, St Gallen, Ticino, Uri, Valais, Zug and Zurich and also to procedures governed by the Federal Code of Civil Procedure (4 December 1947, RS 273).
28   Kleiner and Schwob, n 3 above, BkL, art 47, n 41; Aubert et al, n 5 above, p 139.

the parties to the file, excluding the public from hearings, covering certain parts of documents, sealing of documents and examination thereof by the judge in the absence of the parties in order to determine whether or not they should be excluded. In addition, courts may appoint an expert who himself is bound by banking secrecy.[29]

Such protective measures raise difficult questions of due process and require a careful balancing of the interests involved in each single case. Irrespective of the applicable cantonal system, a bank must provide a court with otherwise protected information in marital disputes if one spouse requests information on the financial situation of the other.[30]

Arbitration

Arbitration courts do not have the power to compel testimony or to subpoena documents.[31] Moreover, an arbitration court cannot release a bank from its secrecy obligation without the consent of the customer as master of the secret, since art 47, para 4 of the BkL only reserves federal and cantonal procedural law but not arbitral rules.[32] However, by taking recourse to the ordinary court arbitrators may gain access to privileged information and indirectly force banks to give evidence under the applicable local procedural rules.[33]

International judicial assistance in civil matters

Switzerland grants judicial assistance in civil proceedings to the members of the Treaty on the Law of Civil Procedure signed in The Hague on 1 March 1954 (the 1954 Convention).[34] According to art 11 of the 1954 Convention, the same coercive measures apply in judicial assistance procedures as in domestic civil procedures. This means that the applicable cantonal rules of civil procedure decide about the scope of the protection of bank confidentiality.[35] With respect to countries that are not members of the 1954 Convention, Switzerland will act upon letters rogatory as a matter of comity only and leave it to the cantons whether or not they want to apply coercive measures with regard to depositions of witnesses and submission of documents.

---

29   Cf arts 38, 51, 52, 55 and 56 of the Federal Code on Civil Procedure.
30   Cf CC, art 170, para 2.
31   Kleiner and Schwob, n 3 above, BkL, art 47, n 40.
32   Aubert et al, n 5 above, pp 141–142.
33   Compare art 184 of the Swiss Statute on Private International Law (PIL Statute) (18 December 1987, RS 291) and art 27 of the Concordat on Arbitration (27 March 1969, RS 279); art 27, para 2 of the Concordat expressly reserves the right of the arbitration court, if necessary, to refer to the cantonal court where the arbitration court is seated and request the respective evidence proceedings to overcome the limits set by the bank confidentiality. The same applies for international arbitration courts seated in Switzerland (art 184, para 2 of the PIL Statute); cf Aubert et al, n 5 above, pp 141–143.
34   RS 0.274.12.
35   J Schwarz 'Das Bankgeheimnis bei Rechtshilfe gemäss dem Haager Übereinkommen vom 18. März 1970 über die Beweisaufnahme im Ausland in Zivil- oder Handelssachen' in *Swiss Journal of Jurisprudence* (1995) pp 284–286.

The canton of Zurich and most other cantons exclude judicial assistance in fiscal, military and political matters or if judicial assistance is contrary to Swiss public policy and reserve the power to refuse judicial assistance completely if the foreign country does not grant reciprocity. Upon request by the foreign authority and if the parties agree thereto, evidence can be taken in accordance with foreign procedural rules; however, coercive measures will always remain subject to the applicable cantonal rules.[36]

This autonomy of cantonal rules of civil procedures with regard to the protection of bank confidentiality was not modified by the adoption of the Hague Convention on the Taking of Evidence Abroad in Civil or Commercial Matters dated 18 March 1970[37] (hereinafter the 1970 Convention) in force since 1 January 1995. Pursuant to art 11 of the 1970 Convention, a person has the right to withhold testimony, provided the laws of the requested state allow for such a right. Accordingly, an evidence request pursuant to the 1970 Convention will be executed pursuant to the procedural rules of the cantonal lex loci.[38] Whether bank confidentiality remains protected is, therefore, still subject to the federal and cantonal rules of civil procedures as described above. The 1970 Convention does not have a substantive impact on these procedural rules.

Collection of debt and bankruptcy

Proceedings concerning forced execution of debt and bankruptcy are governed by the revised Federal Law on Debt Enforcement and Bankruptcy (SchKG), effective as of 1 January 1997.[39] Once the execution officer has seized a bank account, the bank cannot refuse information by invoking bank confidentiality.[40] Banks are therefore obliged to provide customer information at a relatively early stage of the enforcement proceedings, otherwise they risk criminal prosecution.[41] This also applies to civil attachments which are granted as provisional measures upon summary proceedings without strict proof of a claim, provided the attachment is based on an enforceable title.[42]

In bankruptcy proceedings the trustee of a bankrupt customer is entitled to full disclosure of account information.[43] In the bank's own bankruptcy the trustee or the officially appointed liquidator has full access to all information concerning the banking relation. Foreign bankruptcy trustees may, however, have to resort to a Swiss ancillary bankruptcy proceeding pursuant to art 166ss of the Swiss Private International Law Statute (PIL Statute) of 18 December 1987 under which the Swiss trustee is given full access to the account information.[44]

---

36 Cf PIL Statute, art 11 and Zurich Statute on Organisation of the Judiciary, arts 116 and 117.
37 RS 0.274.132.
38 Cf Aubert et al, n 5 above, pp 602–608; Schwarz, n 35 above, p 285; Bernasconi, n 3 above, pp 12–14.
39 SchKG, RS 281.1.
40 BGE 112 (1986) III 98; 102 (1974) III 6; leading case BGE 75 (1949) III 106 (109).
41 PC, art 324, para 5.
42 Cf Kleiner and Schwob, n 3 above, BkL, art 47, n 38; BGE 109 (1983) III 22 (24).
43 Kleiner and Schwob, n 3 above, BkL, art 47, n 35.
44 Kleiner and Schwob, n 3 above, BkL, art 47, n 90.

Consolidated supervision of international banking groups

In the past, bank confidentiality could substantially interfere with the information internal supervision needs in internationally active banking groups. It has been correctly argued that the obvious need for consolidated risk assessment and supervision to maintain the safety and soundness of the banking institution outweighs the single customer's interest in unrestricted bank confidentiality.[45] As of 1 February 1995, the BkL expressly provides for a provision regulating the upstream information flow in internationally active banking groups. Article 4quinquies of the BkL authorised Swiss subsidiaries to forward to their foreign parent companies, which are themselves supervised by a banking or financial market supervisory authority, customer information or documents not publicly available which are necessary for the purpose of consolidated supervision, provided, however:

1   such information is used exclusively for internal control or direct supervision of banks or other financial intermediaries subject to a respective licence;
2   the parent company and its supervisory authority responsible for consolidated supervision are bound by official or professional secrecy standards; and
3   such information may not be transmitted to third parties without prior consent of the subsidiary bank or without a general authorisation in a treaty.[46]

It is now generally recognised that a Swiss banking subsidiary of an internationally active banking group may under the above conditions transfer customer-related information to the parent company without breaching of bank confidentiality.[47] Such information flow primarily affects bank customers that are borrowing money from the Swiss banking subsidiary or have credit lines outstanding.

It is noteworthy that the SESTA does not provide an analogous provision to art 4quinquies of the BkL. Although the supervisory regimes in the BkL and SESTA are virtually identical, and there are good reasons to permit the upstream information flow,[48] a limitation of the securities dealer confidentiality would require a statutory basis. The lack of such statutory basis has, in practice, not caused problems, since internationally active securities dealers normally also hold a banking licence in Switzerland, thus allowing the application of art 4quinquies of the BkL.

On-site inspections in Switzerland

Since 1 October 1999, Switzerland has permitted limited on-site inspections with Swiss banking subsidiaries and branch offices by foreign bank supervisors as part of the consolidated supervision of internationally active banking groups. Such on-site inspections require, however, the prior approval of the Federal Banking Commission, which is granted if the following requirements are met:

---

45   Cf Kleiner and Schwob, n 3 above, BkL, art 47, n 96; Aubert et al, n 5 above, pp 410–411; Honegger and Frick, n 3 above, pp 4–7; W de Capitani 'Das Bankgeheimnis im Konzern' in *Swiss Review of Business Law* (1997) pp 76–81.
46   Cf language of art 4quinquies of the BkL.
47   Cf Honegger and Frick, n 3 above, p 5; Kleiner and Schwob, n 3 above, BkL, art 47, n 96ss; Aubert et al, n 5 above, pp 426–427.
48   Cf R Watter and R Malacrida 'Das Börsengesetz im internationalen Kontext' in Meier-Schatz *Das neue Börsengesetz der Schweiz* (1996) p 162.

1 the requesting foreign authority is responsible for the consolidated supervision in accordance with the home country rule;
2 the information received is exclusively used for the banking supervision;
3 the foreign authority is bound by official or professional secrecy; and
4 the foreign authority is not transmitting the information received, without prior approval of the Federal Banking Commission, to other authorities that are entrusted with supervisory duties in the public interest. The transmission of information to penal authorities is not permitted whenever legal assistance in criminal matters would be excluded.

The scope of the permissible on-site inspections includes the adequate organisation, the risk monitoring and assessment, the compliance with equity and risk diversification requirements and the reporting obligations of Swiss subsidiaries. In case the foreign authorities wish to review assets and deposits of individual customers, such review is effected by the staff of the Federal Banking Commission and transmission of subsequent reports of the Federal Banking Commission to the foreign authorities is subject to judicial review. This procedure protects the bank confidentiality of private clients adequately. The bank confidentiality of commercial clients is, however, waived due to prevailing interests in a consolidated supervision of internationally active banking groups.

Criminal proceedings

With regard to Swiss criminal proceedings, the situation is relatively straightforward.[49] During the stage of mere preliminary investigations by the police, bank confidentiality remains protected. However, based on art 47, para 4 of the BkL, the Federal Code of Criminal Procedure[50] as well as all cantonal rules on criminal procedure can require banks to testify before official prosecutors and in criminal courts.[51] When testifying bank officers have to draw the attention of the judge to the fact that answers to questions may involve disclosure of banking secrets. It is then up to the judge or the prosecuting officer to determine whether the information is relevant and necessary for the purpose of the prosecution.

If a judge freezes an account by a blocking order in connection with a criminal investigation against a customer, the bank may inform its customer about such freeze unless the judge orders the bank to desist from notifying the customer. Since such a freeze and desist order may put the bank in a difficult position; in case the customer requests the execution of certain transactions from the blocked account or when the customer tries to withdraw money from his account, the Swiss Bankers' Association

---

49 Cf Kleiner and Schwob, n 3 above, BkL, art 47, n 39; Aubert et al, n 5 above, pp 144–155; Bernasconi, n 3 above, pp 14–17; Ch Baer 'Revision des Rechtshilfegesetzes und des Bundesgesetzes zum Rechtshilfevertrag mit den Vereinigten Staaten von Amerika' in *Swiss Review of Business Law* (1995) pp 80–84.
50 Federal Code of Criminal Procedure 15 June 1934, RS 312.0.
51 BGE 95 (1969) I 439 (444); 96 (1970) I 737 (749); 104 (1978) IV 125 (129).

has in co-operation with the chief magistrates of the cantonal justice and police authorities issued recommendations on how to deal with such blocking order.[52]

Delicate problems arise for banks if disclosure of documents and information is requested with regard to third parties not involved in the alleged offence. Generally, Swiss rules on criminal procedures are governed by the principle of appropriateness. Accordingly, the means used by the government in enforcing the laws must be appropriate to the objectives pursued. This requires a balancing of interests between the public interest in the enforcement of the laws and the interests of protecting privacy of the parties involved.[53] The federal and cantonal rules on criminal procedure provide for several protective measures, among which are the sealing of documents seized until a judge decides in a formal procedure whether the information is relevant for the criminal investigation and should serve as evidence. Documents may also be admitted only partially by blanking out sections containing protected information.[54] As it is not admissible to have 'secret files' in Swiss criminal procedure, the possibility of making certain documents accessible only to the judge but not to the other parties does not exist and would be contrary to the principles of due process.

International legal assistance in criminal matters

International legal assistance in criminal matters by Swiss authorities has become more important in recent years due to the international integration of the financial markets.[55] Pursuant to the Federal Statute on International Judicial Assistance in Criminal Matters dated 20 March 1981 (the Criminal Assistance Statute),[56] the Treaty with the United States dated 25 May 1973 (the US Treaty),[57] the respective federal statute dated 3 October 1973[58] and the European Convention on Judicial Assistance in Criminal Matters dated 20 April 1959 (the European Convention),[59] banks can be compelled to testify and to submit documents before the courts of the requesting countries. This legislation was subject to a substantial revision which has been implemented effective 1 February 1997.[60]

---

52 Cf Recommendation of the Swiss Bankers' Association addressed to the Cantonal Prosecuting Authorities on Blocking and Cease and Desist Orders dated 17 March 1997 (Empfehlung an die kantonalen Strafverfolgungsbehörden betreffend Kontosperren und Schweigepflicht der Bank vom 17. März 1997, Zirkular Nr 1286D).
53 See BGE 98 (1972) Ia 418.
54 Cf art 69, para 3 of the Federal Code of Criminal Procedure.
55 Reportedly, approximately 400 judgments were rendered between 1990 and 1994 by the Swiss Federal Supreme Court relative to requests for mutual assistance in criminal matters: cf Bernasconi, n 3 above, p 14.
56 RS 351.1.
57 RS 0.351.933.6.
58 RS 351.93.
59 RS 0.351.1.
60 Cf 'Botschaft betreffend die Änderung des Rechtshilfegesetzes und des Bundesgesetzes zum Staatsvertrag mit den USA über gegenseitige Rechtshilfe in Strafsachen sowie den Bundesbeschluss über einen Vorbehalt zum Europäischen Übereinkommen über die Rechtshilfe in Strafsachen' dated 29 March 1995, BBI 1995 III pp 1-59; R Wyss 'Die Revision der Gesetzgebung über die internationale Rechtshilfe in Strafsachen' in *Swiss Journal of Jurisprudence* (1997) pp 33–43.

The following will summarise the most important features of Swiss legal assistance in criminal matters.

Whether legal assistance is granted by Switzerland is determined primarily by the applicable treaty provisions. If no treaty applies or if a request goes beyond Switzerland's treaty obligations assistance may be granted under the Criminal Assistance Statute. The Criminal Assistance Statute, however, does not impose a legally enforceable obligation on Switzerland to grant assistance to the requesting country.[61] However, Swiss authorities are bound by the provisions of the Criminal Assistance Statute and therefore a refusal of assistance is only possible on grounds set forth in the applicable treaty or the Criminal Assistance Statute.[62]

First, it has to be reviewed whether the request concerns a proceeding in criminal matters. As such, a term is defined broadly, the Federal Supreme Court has, for example, held that legal assistance would be justified in a matter being investigated by the Commission des Operations de Bourse (COB), the French securities industry supervisory authority, although the COB is not a judicial authority. The court held that the preliminary investigations of the COB were susceptible to develop into a criminal procedure, and therefore approved the legal assistance request.[63]

In the absence of a treaty, Switzerland may refuse legal assistance if the requesting country does not grant reciprocity, except where a particularly serious offence, national interests, the interest of the incriminated person or of a Swiss victim demands otherwise.[64] Assistance may also be refused when it is contrary to essential Swiss national interests.[65]

No legal assistance will be granted if the foreign procedure does not adequately provide for protection of human and civil rights or otherwise suffers from grave defects.[66] Furthermore, assistance is excluded generally for military offences and offences of a predominantly political character,[67] ie if they were committed in a fight for or against political powers or have a close connection with such fight,[68] except in some particularly serious cases such as genocide or if very detestable means were used (for example, hijacking, taking of hostages).[69] The term political crime is narrowly construed.[70]

In addition, no assistance will be granted if the offence was aimed at reducing fiscal charges or taxes (except with respect to gambling and traffic in drugs, weapons and explosives[71] or evading regulations concerning currency, or economic policy).[72]

---

61 Criminal Assistance Statute, art 1, para 4.
62 Kleiner and Schwob, n 3 above, BkL, art 47, n 59.
63 See BGE 118 (1992) Ib 457; cf also BGE 109 (1983) Ib 47.
64 Criminal Assistance Statute, art 8; BGE 110 (1984) Ib 173 (176).
65 Criminal Assistance Statute, art 1a, para 2; US Treaty, art 3, para 1(a).
66 Criminal Assistance Statute, art 2.
67 Criminal Assistance Statute, art 3, para 1; US Treaty, art 2, para 1(c).
68 BGE 113 (1987) Ib 175; 109 (1983) Ib 71; 106 (1980) Ib 309.
69 Criminal Assistance Statute, art 3, para 2.
70 BGE 113 Ib 175 (180).
71 US Treaty, art 2, para 1(c).
72 Criminal Assistance Statute, art 3, para 3; US Treaty, art 2, para 1(c).

Legal assistance is only lifting bank confidentiality if coercive measures can be applied by the Swiss authorities. Under the Criminal Assistance Statute, as well as under the European Convention and the US Treaty, coercive measures are generally only admissible if the offence being prosecuted contains the elements (other than intent or negligence) of an offence punishable under Swiss law (requirement of dual criminality).[73]

The US Treaty also requires that the incriminated offence be one listed in its Annex.[74] If the request concerns other crimes, Switzerland may grant assistance and apply coercive measures only under the Criminal Assistance Statute. However, neither the requirement of dual criminality nor the Annex are applicable with respect to certain cases of organised crime, in which Switzerland will grant legal assistance even in tax matters if exponents of organised crime are involved and such assistance is necessary for effective law enforcement.[75] This means that, in cases of organised crime, it is possible to grant legal assistance to the US also with respect to offences against tax, antitrust and securities laws.

As Switzerland endeavours to prevent misuse of information furnished by way of legal assistance, it will request the foreign authority not to use such information for the prosecution of any offence for which Switzerland would not grant judicial assistance if it were made the object of a separate request (requirement of speciality).[76] In practice, the Swiss authorities require an express confirmation of the requesting country in the absence of a treaty.[77] Consequently, any further use of information requires the approval of the Swiss authorities unless the offence for which legal assistance was sought is being re-qualified by the requesting country in light of the information provided and the re-qualified offence would continue to be eligible for mutual assistance, or the information is used against perpetrators otherwise involved in the prosecuted offence.[78]

Switzerland refuses coercive measures for forcing a witness to appear in proceedings held abroad. Therefore, a Swiss bank officer summoned to appear in foreign proceedings must not do so if this would jeopardise the bank confidentiality.[79]

The Criminal Assistance Statute as well as the US Treaty provide for a certain degree of participation by foreign authorities and application of certain procedural rules in the execution of the request for judicial assistance. Thus, foreign judges or prosecutors and similar officers may be present when depositions are taken and when documents are seized. However, even under the US Treaty and the Criminal Assistance Statute, performance of the legal assistance requested is primarily the task of the cantonal authorities who, as far as coercive measures are concerned, apply their own cantonal

---

73 Criminal Assistance Statute, art 64, para 1; reservation by Switzerland made under European Convention, art 5, para 1(a); of the US Treaty, art 4, para 2(a).
74 US Treaty, art 4, para 2(a).
75 US Treaty, arts 6 and 7.
76 Criminal Assistance Statute, art 67; US Treaty, art 5.
77 BGE 110 (1984) Ib 173 (177); 107 (1981) Ib 264 (271).
78 Criminal Assistance Statute, art 67, para 2.
79 Criminal Assistance Statute, art 69; US Treaty, art 23ss and European Convention, art 8ss.

procedural rules[80] and foreign officers must take a passive role, except where federal law determines otherwise.[81]

In practice, the Swiss magistrate is often unable to determine which documents or information are relevant to a complex case. He will be tempted to consult with his foreign colleague when screening documents and questioning witnesses. Therefore, the danger exists that the foreign officer may obtain access to confidential information before the right to such access has been determined in judicial proceedings.[82] The Swiss Federal Supreme Court held that when in doubt the Swiss magistrate must exclude the presence of foreign representatives.[83] This rule has not changed, even though the new art 65a of the Criminal Assistance Statute now provides that the presence of foreign officials during the execution of the request may be requested.[84]

Measures to protect confidential information, where admissible, are the same as provided by the laws on federal and cantonal criminal procedure unless a treaty contains specific rules.[85] For example, the US Treaty provides for an exclusion of US representatives until it has been determined whether or not the relevant information can be disclosed.

The determination whether Switzerland grants legal assistance is made in a special procedure in which the persons concerned, including banks, who are asked to provide information, may challenge the legal assistance and appeal to cantonal courts and the Federal Supreme Court.[86]

Administrative assistance

Swiss banks and securities dealers and Swiss branches of foreign banks and securities dealers are subject to supervision by the Federal Banking Commission, to which they must fully disclose all information required for effective supervision.[87] Officers and staff of the Federal Banking Commission are strictly bound by their own secrecy obligation.[88]

Since customer relationships of a Swiss bank's foreign branch are not covered by art 47 of the BkL, disclosure of the relevant information to the competent foreign authorities is not subject to criminal sanctions by Switzerland. The disclosure of confidential customer information by the staff of the foreign branch will normally be governed by the relevant foreign law.[89]

Parallel to the ever increasing globalisation of the players in the financial markets, the cross-border co-operation among banking and securities supervisory agencies

---

80   Criminal Assistance Statute, arts 16ss and 64 and US Treaty, art 37, para 2.
81   BGE 113 (1987) Ib 157 (169); 106 (1980) Ib 260 (261); 103 (1977) Ia 206 (214); cf also European Convention, art 3, para 1.
82   Cf also Bernasconi, n 3 above, pp 16–17.
83   BGE 113 (1987) Ib 157 (169).
84   Cf Criminal Assistance Statute, art 65a, para 1.
85   US Treaty, art 12, para 3(d) and (e).
86   Cf Wyss, n 60 above, pp 35–37.
87   BkL, art 23bis, para 2; SESTA, art 35, para 2.
88   PC, art 320; cf Kleiner and Schwob, n 3 above, BkL, art 23, n 13.
89   Kleiner and Schwob, n 3 above, BkL, art 47, n 100.

has been continuously expanded in the past years. Accordingly, the BkL provides for administrative assistance in favour of foreign supervisory authorities to implement international co-operation among supervisory agencies. The relevant provision became effective on 1 February 1997.[90] Pursuant to art 23sexies of the BkL and art 38 of the SESTA, the Federal Banking Commission may, on the one hand, request information or documents from foreign bank and financial market supervisory authorities in order to assure its consolidated supervision of internationally active banking groups under the home country rule.[91] On the other hand, the Federal Banking Commission may assist foreign supervisory agencies. It may forward confidential information and documents related to the matter for which assistance is requested to a foreign supervisory authority provided the following requirements are met:

1   The transmitted information will be used exclusively for the direct supervision of banks, exchanges, broker dealers and other financial intermediaries subject to a licensing requirement.
2   The foreign supervisory agency is bound by official or professional secrecy.
3   It will not transmit the information received to a competent regulatory body which is entrusted with supervisory tasks being in the public interest in the foreign state without the prior approval by the Federal Banking Commission. Transmission of information to any criminal authorities is not allowed if criminal assistance would be excluded.[92]

These provisions are designed to provide bank-related data and customer-related data to foreign supervisory authorities. The transfer of customer related data is, however, subject to judicial review allowing a review of whether the interests of a foreign supervisory authority prevail over the protection of bank confidentiality.[93] In connection with the third requirement, the Federal Banking Commission requests a specific confirmation of the foreign supervisory authorities confirming that they are in a position to meet Swiss requirements for administrative assistance. By 2001, supervisory authorities of most countries with internationally active banks had issued such confirmations.[94]

---

90   BkL, art 23sexies and SESTA, art 38; cf Kleiner and Schwob, n 3 above, BkL, art 23sexies, nn 1–21; U Zulauf 'Rechtshilfe-Amtshilfe, Zur Zusammenarbeit der Eidgenössischen Bankenkommission mit ausländischen Aufsichtsbehörden im Rahmen der neuen Banken-, Börsen- und Anlagefondsgesetzgebung des Bundes' in *Swiss Review of Business Law* (1995) pp 50–62.
91   BkL, art 23sexies, para 1; SESTA, art 38, para 1.
92   BkL, art 23sexies, para 2; SESTA, art 38, para 2.
93   BkL, art 23sexies, para 3; SESTA, art 38, para 3.
94   Australia: Australian Securities & Investments Commission (ASIC); Belgium: NASDAQ Europe, EUROTEXT Brussels; Denmark: Danish Supervisory Authority (Finanstilsynet); Germany: Bundesaufsichtsamt für den Wertpapierhandel (BAWe); France: Commission des Opérations de Bourse (COB); Great Britain: Department of Trade and Industry (DTI, FSA (virt-x)); Hong Kong: Securities and Futures Commission (SFC); Italy: Commissione Nazionale per le Società e la Borsa (CONSOB); The Netherlands: Stichting Toezicht Effectenverkeer (STE); Portugal: Commissão do Mercado de Valores Mobiliários (CMVM); Sweden: Swedish Financial Supervisory Authority (Finansinspektionen); Spain: Comisión Nacional del Mercado de Valores (CNMV); US: US Commodity Futures and Trading Commission (CFTC) and Securities and Exchange Commission (SEC).

Administrative assistance is currently mainly used for cross-border insider investigations. Until 2001, the Federal Banking Commission has issued 115 assistance orders, half of which were challenged before the Swiss Federal Supreme Court.[95] A substantial body of case law has developed in the meantime. Following the Swiss Federal Supreme Court decisions, administrative assistance with the US SEC and the Italian CONSOB is currently on hold. With respect to the SEC, the Federal Supreme Court held that the requirements for administrative assistance are not met since the litigation releases of the SEC are not consistent with the obligation not to pass the received information to other authorities without prior approval by the Federal Banking Commission. The conceptual difference of the Swiss and the US supervisory system has lead to this unsatisfactory situation which can only be solved by legislators.

Tax authorities

Swiss banks, including branches of foreign institutions, have to account for stamp duties on purchase and sale of securities, including transactions made for the account of customers, and for withholding taxes on dividends paid to shareholders and interest paid to their customers. The Swiss Federal Tax Authority is entitled to inspect the relevant files and has, therefore, access to the customer data contained therein. The federal laws on stamp duties and withholding taxes prohibit, however, the use of customer data for any purpose other than enforcement of the respective taxes.[96] The information may not even be used for assessing other federal taxes, such as federal income tax. In line with this disclosure duty, banks have to testify in criminal proceedings regarding evasion of Swiss stamp duties and Swiss withholding taxes by their customers.[97]

With respect to the bank's own income taxes, the bank has to disclose the same information to the tax authorities as any other taxpayer. However, the tax authorities have no power to compel disclosure of any information protected by bank confidentiality.[98] If such information is directly relevant to the assessment of the bank's taxes, for example, reserves for bad debts, compensation for damages paid to customers etc, the bank has to exhaust other means, such as submission of certificates by independent auditors or an independent expert, before disclosing the information to the authorities.

A similar situation exists under the Swiss Federal Law on Value Added Tax (hereinafter VAT Law).[99] Whereas ordinary banking transactions are not subject to VAT, certain services of a bank such as asset management and fiduciary transactions are nevertheless taxable if the services are provided to persons domiciled in Switzerland.

---

95 Federal Banking Commission *Annual Report* (2001) p 39.
96 Art 37, para 5 of the Federal Law on Stamp Tax, 27 June 1973, RS 641.10; art 40, para 5 of the Federal Law on Withholding Tax, 13 October 1965, RS 642.21.
97 BGE 104 (1978) IV 125.
98 Cf Aubert et al, n 5 above, pp 242–243; X Oberson 'Questions actuelles concernant le secret bancaire dans la procedure fiscale' in Bernasconi *Les nouveaux défis au secret bancaire suisse* (1996) pp 61–62.
99 VAT Law 2 September 1999, RS 641.20.

Services provided to persons domiciled outside of Switzerland are exempt from VAT. In order to receive such an exemption, the Swiss federal tax authorities request proof that the recipient of the services is domiciled abroad. According to the tax authorities, a bank may submit all relevant documents containing the identity and the foreign domicile of the customer. The bank cannot invoke bank confidentiality. However, the tax authorities are allowed to use the customer information only for purposes of assessing VAT and are bound to preserve bank confidentiality.[100]

With regard to income and wealth taxes of the bank's customers, both cantonal and federal tax law require the bank to certify the relevant information to the customer only. Thus, the bank cannot be compelled to submit documents or information directly to the tax authorities for the purpose of tax assessment or tax audit of its customers.[101] Nevertheless, in criminal proceedings for tax fraud the bank has to testify as in any other criminal procedure.[102] Tax fraud is defined as: 'an intentional deceit of the tax authorities by means of documents containing untrue information for the purpose of obtaining an illegal tax advantage ...' (compare BGE 96 (1970) I 337ss). However, subsequently the definition has been broadened and been brought in line with the notion of fraud as defined in art 146 of the PC to include other types of malicious deceit, such as a 'shady conspiracy of the tax subject with third persons', or 'special machinations, tricks or a whole construction of lies', or even mere silence if it can be foreseen that the victim will not double-check given a particular relationship of trust.[103] The latter will hardly ever exist vis-à-vis the tax authorities, whereas the other terms of malicious deceit may extend the term 'tax fraud'. The traditional definition still applies with respect to direct federal taxes.[104]

The consequence of this development in domestic Swiss law may be less interesting than the effect in the area of international legal assistance. Though, in the same case in which the Federal Supreme Court seemed to announce a broader definition of 'tax fraud', it tightened the conditions for granting legal assistance (to Germany under the European Convention) by requesting that in tax fraud cases the request must present a prima facie case and sufficient facts to support a reasonable suspicion. This is contrary to the principle adhered to in other cases of legal assistance, according to which the facts as presented in the request will be generally accepted by the Swiss authorities without examination on the merits.[105]

Normal tax evasion by means of failing to declare certain income items or assets is not considered a crime in Switzerland but only a misdemeanour and, therefore, the bank cannot be compelled to testify in the relevant enforcement proceedings or to disclose customer data. However, this rule does not apply to withholding tax and stamp duties.[106]

---

100 VAT Law, art 62, para 3 and Broschüre Nr 14 Finanzbereich der ESTV, art 2.1.3.2.
101 Kleiner and Schwob, n 3 above, BkL, art 47, n 45a.
102 BGE 108 (1982) Ib 231 (236).
103 BGE 111 (1985) Ib 242 (248).
104 Art 186 of the Federal Law on Direct Tax, 14 December 1990, RS 642.11.
105 BGE 111 (1985) Ib 242; 114 (1988) Ib 56; 115 Ib 68; 116 Ib 96; cf also Criminal Assistance Statute, art 3, para 3.
106 Kleiner and Schwob, n 3 above, BkL, art 47, n 50.

Based on the treaties ratified by Switzerland concerning avoidance of double taxation, bank confidentiality remains protected.[107] This continues to be true even after the agreement in principle between the EU and Switzerland regarding a new withholding tax on interest for bonds held by EU residents, the details of which are not yet known.

Other administrative authorities

Unless expressly provided by law, banks have no duty to disclose privileged information in administrative proceedings. A notable exception concerns acquisition of interests in Swiss real estate by foreigners, which is strictly regulated.[108]

Insider dealing

Since 1 July 1988, insider dealing constitutes a crime. Under art 161 of the PC, any director, manager, auditor, attorney or agent of a company or a co-operative, or an entity controlling it or controlled by it, and any member of the governmental body or agency or a public servant or any auxiliary person thereof may be considered an insider. Persons directly or indirectly informed by an insider are considered 'tippees' if they know or should have known that the information is illegally disclosed by the insider.

Disclosure and use of inside information is punished if it relates to shares, participation certificates, bonds, debentures, other negotiable instruments or rights issued by Swiss or foreign companies listed on an official exchange or an official secondary market in Switzerland, or if it concerns options for the purchase or sale of such securities. Securities traded merely 'over-the-counter' are not included. Information is considered as inside information if it is confidential and concerns a planned rights issue, a merger or a similar occurrence of comparable importance, if it can be foreseen that its disclosure to the public will substantially affect the price of the securities. Under the case law of the Swiss Federal Supreme Court, a change in the profit forecasts does not constitute an inside information in the meaning of the PC. Apart from disclosure to third persons for the purpose of obtaining a profit, the insider also violates the law if he uses the information to obtain a profit for himself or for a third person. The penalties range from a fine to imprisonment of up to three years.

As a consequence of art 161 of the PC, bank confidentiality can be lifted in domestic insider trading cases (pursuant to the respective cantonal and federal statutes on criminal procedure, banks are required to testify before prosecutors and criminal courts) as well as in international legal and administrative assistance proceedings with respect to foreign insider cases. The same holds for the recently introduced criminal provision on market manipulation: art 161bis of the PC.

Under the US Treaty, the two governments signed a Memorandum of Understanding dated 10 November 1987, by which Switzerland also agreed to grant assistance in

---

107 Kleiner and Schwob, n 3 above, BkL, art 47, n 88.
108 Cf the respective Federal Law dated 16 December 1983, RS 211.412.41; arts 22, para 3 and 31.

so-called 'civil proceedings' relative to insider dealings conducted by the Securities and Exchange Commission.

The administrative assistance procedure has developed to an efficient tool to prosecute cross-border insider cases. Under the case law of the Swiss Federal Supreme Court and the practice of the Federal Banking Commission, the interest of an efficient cross-border insider prosecution outweighs the interests of the bank's customer in protecting his privacy. Administrative assistance is routinely granted by the Federal Banking Commission which is among others the result of the case law that put a very low threshold on the suspicion that insider dealing occurred. It is sufficient for foreign authorities to state that immediately prior to the public disclosure of the insider information trading volume increased and prices changed. The Federal Banking Commission does not have to review such statements made by the foreign authorities.[109]

Money laundering

The Swiss legislation against money laundering rests on four mutually re-enforcing pillars and constitutes a combination of administrative law, industry self-regulation and criminal provisions. The first and main pillar consists of the Federal Law Against Money Laundering in the Financial Sector of 10 October 1997 (Money Laundering Act).[110] The second pillar consists of the new Federal Banking Commission Ordinance on Money Laundering dated 17 January 2003 (FBC Money Laundering Ordinance) specifying bank's duties under the Money Laundering Act as well as with regard to terrorist financing.[111] The third pillar consists of the self-regulatory system put in place by the Swiss Banking Association in the form of the Swiss Banks' Code of Conduct with regard to the Exercise of Due Diligence, as amended (CDB 03), which embodies the 'Know your Customer' rules of the Swiss banks. Finally, the fourth pillar consists of the criminal provision regarding money laundering contained in arts 305bis and 305ter of the PC. All four pillars directly affect bank confidentiality.

The Money Laundering Act

The Money Laundering Act entered into force on 1 April 1998 and aims to prevent money laundering within the meaning of art 305bis of the PC. The Money Laundering Act applies to all financial intermediaries, which not only includes banks and securities dealers but also financial intermediaries such as investment advisors, so far not under supervision by any regulatory agency. The Money Laundering Act sets forth a number of due diligence obligations as well as obligations to act in the event of suspicion of money laundering and puts in place a system of supervision through self-regulating bodies of the financial industry. The due diligence obligations include first of all the verification of the identity of the bank customer upon entering into a

---

109 BGE 125 (1999) II 65 and 126 (2000) II 406; see also Federal Banking Commission *Annual Report* (2001) p 39.
110 RS 955.0
111 See the website of the Federal Banking Commission at www.cfb.admin.ch.

business relationship. Such verification includes, in particular, the identification of the beneficial owner of the funds. In this regard, banks have to require the customer to provide a written declaration disclosing the identity of the beneficial owner if (i) the customer is not the beneficial owner or the beneficial ownership is in doubt, (ii) the customer is a domiciliary company, and (iii) a cash transaction is effected for a large sum, ie 25,000 Swiss Francs or more. A further verification of the identity of the customer and the beneficial owner is required in the course of the business relationship if doubts arise as to the identity of the customer or the beneficial owner of the funds. In cases where a transaction or the business relationship appears to be unusual (except where it is manifestly legal), or there is reason to believe that the assets are the proceeds of a crime or that a criminal organisation has the power to dispose over them, the bank is under the duty to investigate the economic background and the purpose of the transaction and the business relationship. Such special investigation must be documented in writing. The Money Laundering Act requires a bank to draw up its documentation regarding the transactions effected and its due diligence investigations in such a manner that the qualified third parties can accurately understand the transactions and the business relationship and verify the compliance with the Money Laundering Act. The documentation must be retained in a form that enables the bank, within a reasonable time period, to comply with information requests or freezing orders of authorities. After the termination of the business relationship or the completion of the transaction, documents and records must be kept for at least ten years. Finally, banks must ensure that their staff is adequately trained to ensure full compliance with the Money Laundering Act.

If a bank knows or presumes, on the basis of founded suspicion, that assets involved in the business relationship are related to money laundering or that they are the proceeds of a crime or that a criminal organisation has a disposal right over the assets, it shall without delay notify the reporting office for money laundering. Further, the bank has immediately to freeze the assets it holds for the customer to the extent they are related to the reporting. The freezing of the assets shall continue to be effective until the receipt of a decision by the competent prosecuting authorities about a freezing order, but for a maximum of five working days after the notification. As long as the assets are frozen, the bank shall not notify the customer or any third party concerned about the reporting.

The duty to report and to freeze assets in cases of suspicion of money laundering conflicts with bank confidentiality. For this reason, art 11 of the Money Laundering Act explicitly confirms that a bank which reports a suspicion under the Money Laundering Act and freezes funds concerned cannot be prosecuted for violation of bank confidentiality and can also not be held liable for breach of contract, provided it can show that it applied the due diligence required by the circumstances. The Money Laundering Act does not specify the meaning of 'due diligence required by the circumstances'. In any case, there exists, so far, no published court decision as to violation of bank confidentiality or possible related breach of contract under this provision.

For the purpose of the Money Laundering Act, banks are supervised by the Federal Banking Commission.

The FBC Money Laundering Ordinance

The FBC Money Laundering Ordinance will become effective on 1 July 2003 and contains detailed rules regarding the fight against money laundering. It establishes a number of principles, sets out organisational measures to be implemented by banks and establishes principles of due diligence that have to be observed by banks to prevent money laundering. The principles set out in the FBC Money Laundering Ordinance include the prohibition to accept assets of which the bank knows or should have known that they originate from a crime committed in Switzerland or abroad. Crime, in particular, also includes the bribing of foreign officials. Further, a bank is not allowed to maintain a business relationship with companies or persons of which the bank knows or should have known that they are part of a terrorist or criminal organisation or support or finance such organisations. The banks are also not allowed to maintain business relationships with other banks that do not maintain a physical presence (offshore banks) in the country of the incorporation unless they are part of an adequately supervised banking group.

The FBC Money Laundering Ordinance requires banks to put in place a electronic transaction supervising scheme that allows to identify transactions with an increased risk profile. Transactions with an increased risk profile have to be defined by the banks on the basis of criteria such as money inflow and outflow, material deviation with regard to transaction type, volume and sequence as compared with the ordinary course of the business relationship, and material deviation with regard to transaction type, volume and sequence as compared with similar business relationships. In any case, transactions with an increased risk profile include cash deposits of more than 100,000 Swiss Francs at the beginning of the business relationship and any founded suspicion of money laundering. In order to enable banks to establish founded suspicions of money laundering, the Ordinance contains an extensive annex that lists specific types of transactions.

For the 'Know your Customer' rules, the Ordinance explicitly refers to the CDB 03. With respect to payments made abroad, Swiss banks are now obliged to indicate the name, account number and domicile of the payee in order to allow the tracking of money trails. In connection with customers or transactions with an increased risk profile, Swiss banks have to undertake reasonable inquiries regarding the background of the customer and the transaction. These inquiries have to be documented. Business relationships with politically exposed persons[112] can only be entered into with the approval of the management of the bank, who have to review annually the continuation of the business relationship.

---

112 Section a of art 1 of the FBC Money Laundering Ordinance defines politically exposed persons (PEPs) as (i) the following persons with prominent public functions abroad: Head of State or Head of Government, high politicians on the national level, high functionaries in administration, justice, military and political parties on the national level, high officers of companies of national importance controlled by the state, and (ii) any company or person that evidently has a close family, personal or business relationship with any of the persons named above.

The Swiss Banks' Code of Conduct

In an attempt to preserve the international reputation of the Swiss banking community and to establish rules ensuring the 'Know your Customer rules' and a business conduct that is beyond reproach when accepting funds from new customers, the Swiss Bankers' Association promulgated a code of conduct on a self-regulatory basis as early as 1977. This code of conduct has regularly been amended and is currently defined as the 2003 Agreement on the Swiss Banks' Code of Conduct with regard to the Exercise of Due Diligence, effective as of 1 July 2003 (CDB 03). All Swiss banks which are party to the CDB 03 undertake:

1 to identify the client when establishing a business relationship and, if in doubt, request a confirmation from the client as to who beneficially owns the deposited values,
2 not to support capital flight actively, and
3 not to aid and abet tax evasion actively by providing misleading representations.[113]

The CDB 03 contains specific guidance as to the identification of individuals and legal entities residing or domiciled in Switzerland or abroad.

A bank is further obliged to ascertain that the customer is the beneficial owner of the assets to be deposited by means of a written statement to be signed by the customer if it has any doubt that the customer who identified himself does not beneficially own the assets. Normally, the bank may assume that its client also is the beneficial owner. The CDB 03, however, provides for guidance when a bank should have doubts, in particular, when a power of attorney is conferred on someone who clearly would not have sufficiently close links to the customer, or the financial standing of someone requesting to carry out a transaction is known to the bank and the assets deposited or about to be deposited are disproportionate to that individual's financial capabilities. In these cases, the bank must require a written confirmation by the customer that he beneficially owns the assets, on the so-called Form A.

Interestingly, if the beneficial owner of the assets is not identical to the customer, ie if the beneficial owner has no contractual relationship with the bank, the bank may neither accept instructions from him nor forward information to him, otherwise it would risk being in breach of bank confidentiality. Moreover, the Federal Supreme Court has recently held that the beneficial owner of assets has no standing to challenge an order against the contractual counterparty of the bank in legal assistance procedures.[114]

Failure to comply with the CDB 03 may lead to an investigation by the independent supervisory board for the CDB, and eventually to sanctions against the bank such as a fine of up to 10 million Swiss Francs. Further, violations of the CDB 03 may jeopardise the banking licence since the proper business conduct of the bank is no longer assured.

---

113 CDB 03, art 1.
114 BGE 121 (1995) II 459 (462).

Criminal provisions

The criminal provisions with respect to money laundering include arts 305bis and 305ter of the PC.

Article 305bis, para 1 of the PC holds, in essence, that whoever commits an act which is likely to jeopardise the investigation of the source or the location of assets or their confiscation which as he knows or must assume originate from a crime shall be punished with imprisonment or with a fine. The offence must be designed to prevent the investigation of the origin, the discovery or the confiscation of assets. Since straightforward financial transactions, such as the acceptance of deposits could, basically, qualify as money laundering activities, the Federal Banking Commission takes the view that banks should refrain from certain transactions, such as labelling accounts with pseudonyms not identifiable as fictitious names.

Pursuant to art 305ter, para 1 of the PC, a person who accepts and holds deposits, or manages investments must establish with all due diligence the identity of the beneficial owner. The standards for establishing such identity are set out in the CDB 03. Accordingly, if a bank complies in form and substance with these standards, it will exclude the risk of committing a criminal act within the meaning of art 305ter, para 1 of the PC.

Article 305ter, para 2 of the PC establishes the right of banks to inform the Swiss criminal authorities if they recognise circumstances indicating money laundering activities. While this notification right of banks still exists, it has, in practice, been superseded by the notification duty contained in the Money Laundering Act.

Recent developments

Dormant accounts

The core issue of the now settled dispute on Holocaust-related claims was the treatment of dormant accounts by Swiss banks. The Swiss Civil Code and art 47 of the BkL regarding bank confidentiality put very high standards of proof upon heirs of deceased bank customers for locating bank accounts and being recognised as the legitimate new owner of such accounts. Due to lack of available proper inheritance documentation, most Holocaust victims and their heirs were not in a position to meet these strict standards of proof and be recognised by Swiss banks as legitimate owners of bank accounts. As part of the settlement of the dispute on Holocaust-related claims, Swiss banks were required to publish dormant accounts, which seems at the outset incompatible with bank confidentiality. The solution adopted was a pragmatic one. The Federal Banking Commission took the view that where there is no master of the secret anymore, there can also not be a banking secrecy. Therefore, the banks have to act in the best interest of the heirs of former bank customers, which is to learn about their entitlements.

Currently, a new federal law on dormant assets is in preparation which will provide for a statutory duty of banks to avoid the breaking up of customer relationships by organisational means. After a dormancy period of ten years, assets have to be reported to a newly created Contact Office. Such Contact Office will maintain a list of dormant assets. Persons who are establishing prima facie evidence of a claim are granted access to such list. After a dormancy period of 50 years, unclaimed assets accrue to the Swiss Confederation, provided, however, that five years prior to accrual the list of dormant assets is published.

US backup withholding tax

In 2001, the US introduced a new backup withholding tax on dividend and interest paid on US securities. In connection with this new tax scheme, Swiss banks have entered into qualified intermediary agreements with the Internal Revenue Service (IRS). In order to protect bank confidentiality, these agreements provide that compliance with the qualified intermediary agreement is reviewed by external auditors which, in most cases, are the same audit firms auditing the Swiss bank for Swiss statutory and banking purposes. Such audit firms are instructed by the IRS and report directly to the IRS. Such reports shall, however, not contain the name of customers and the identity of beneficial owners. This scheme allows the maintenance of bank confidentiality and assures compliance with US tax laws. Some authors have, however, raised concern about certain reporting requirements with regard to non-US persons. As a result of the uncertainties, a number of non-US private clients have decided no longer to invest in US securities.

Outsourcing

In recent years, many Swiss banks have resorted to the outsourcing of certain functions, in particular, data processing. In response to this development the Federal Banking Commission has issued on 26 August 1999 a circular setting out the principles of governing outsourcing. The circular was amended on 22 August 2002. It aims to assure the proper organisation of banks and the protection of bank confidentiality. The principles include the duty of the bank to secure with adequate technical and organisational measures bank confidentiality. Bank customers have to be informed about the outsourcing. Such information may be contained in the General Business Conditions if the outsourcing is made within Switzerland. In case of outsourcing involving the transfer of customer data abroad, the bank customer must be informed in detail in a separate document beforehand. The bank customer must be given the opportunity to terminate the banking relationship without financial consequences. These rules assure that the bank customer has been given a choice before limitations on the protection of bank confidentiality are put in place.

Securitisation and bank confidentiality

A valid assignment of claims requires under Swiss law that the assignor discloses at least the name of the debtor and the amount of the assigned debt to the assignee. Accordingly, securitisation conflicts with bank confidentiality since the name of the bank customer and the amount of his debt owed to the bank are protected by bank confidentiality. Securitisation of customer receivables by Swiss banks therefore requires a waiver of the bank confidentiality by the bank customer concerned. Without such waiver securitisation would constitute a breach of bank confidentiality, which not only could lead to civil damage claims but also to criminal sanction and a withdrawal of the banking licence. Some authors have even argued that an assignment in breach of the bank confidentiality is void. The Swiss legislator does not consider it necessary to change bank confidentiality in order to facilitate asset securitisation.

Internet banking and bank confidentiality

Internet banks and Internet banking are not governed by special banking laws but rather have to comply with the normal banking law including, in particular, bank confidentiality. Since information transmitted on the Internet is not protected, banks that use Internet communication with their customers risk violating bank confidentiality. Therefore, all banks engaging in Internet banking require Internet banking customers to sign an appropriate waiver of bank confidentiality.

Terrorist financing

Article 5 of the new FBC Ordinance on Money Laundering prohibits Swiss banks from maintaining any business relationships with organisations or persons of which the bank knows or should know that it is a criminal or terrorist organisation, or a person which is part of such an organisation or supports or finances such an organisation. Further, banks are not allowed to finance such persons or support them otherwise.

Even before the entry into force of the FBC Ordinance, the fight against terrorism and terrorist financing has been seamlessly included in the anti-money laundering legislation. The 'Bush' lists published by the US government were communicated to all Swiss banks, with either the request to immediately notify any assets of the listed persons or organisations to the Notification Office and freeze the assets or, depending on the requirements of the 'Bush' lists, conduct a special clarification inquiry in accordance with art 6 of the Money Laundering Act to clarify the economic background of the account holder. These measures lead to the freezing of a number of accounts. In accordance with the Money Laundering Act such freeze is, however, temporary and will last only until criminal proceedings or criminal assistance proceedings have been completed.

29 United States

Danforth Newcomb
Michael Gruson

INTRODUCTION

US law requiring financial institutions to treat customer information confidentially reflects the general nature of jurisprudence in the US. Financial privacy law can be found both in federal law and the law of individual states. It is found in court decisions, statutes, administrative regulations and even in informal guidance published by bank regulatory agencies. To understand the US law of financial privacy, one must examine both the sources for that law and the historical context in which it arose.

Until recent years, US financial privacy law dealt mostly with the proper reach of domestic government access to bank records. There were some cases that considered the issue of private party ability to obtain such information. Interestingly, until recently, there has been little concern about access to financial information by either private parties or governments from outside the US, a theme that is important in many other nations, such as Switzerland, Luxembourg and Uruguay.

Financial privacy law in the US started with a few decisions in various state courts, so we will first consider the leading decisions from those courts. In more recent years, federal statutes have dominated the scene and largely supplanted the state case law. We will next examine the tension in the US between privacy concerns and anti-money laundering provisions. Finally, with the advent of computers and the marketing of electronic data, the US, like Europe and elsewhere, has seen a rise in concerns about financial data used for commercial purposes and a corresponding legislative response.

The picture that will emerge shows a dynamic and multi-layered legal structure that only partially addresses financial privacy in the US.

THE DEVELOPMENT OF US CASE LAW OF FINANCIAL PRIVACY

Somewhat surprisingly, a bank customer's right to privacy of account information is not frequently litigated in the US. While US laws and regulations governing banks are found both at the state and federal level, the rights of bank customers historically

615

were found in the laws of the individual states. Prior to the 1960s, there was no substantial case law that articulated a duty of financial privacy owed by a bank to its customers. An article in the Harvard Law Review published in 1890 by Louis Brandeis (who was not yet a US Supreme Court Justice) and Professor Samuel Warren was an early argument for the right of privacy.[1] A leading scholar of the law of torts, Professor William L Prosser, some 70 years later, published an article entitled 'Privacy' in the California Law Review.[2] However, neither article seems to have engendered significant judicial adherence as applied to the rights of bank customers. Cases that have attempted to determine the scope of financial privacy usually arose from what was perceived to have been an excess of investigative zeal by police authorities.

An early but isolated case in New Jersey

An early example is *Brex v Smith*.[3] In this action, the members of the Newark city police force sought to enjoin the state prosecutor from reviewing the bank accounts of each of the city's police officers. The only stated reason for the review was to 'assist him in some investigation he is making'.[4] It is notable that this action was brought in a court of equity in the days before unification of equity courts and law courts. Generally, the equity courts were far more willing to develop creative solutions for situations which appear to be novel or not otherwise previously decided by the law courts. The decision in this case is not a model of clarity, weaving together both concepts of implied contract and an apparent tort theory of a right of personal privacy. The court seems to have been most concerned by the fact that the prosecutor failed to follow the usual procedures for an investigation by empanelling a grand jury and issuing subpoenas. Accordingly, the judge issued an injunction barring the prosecutor from his sweeping inquiry of the banks concerning the accounts of all of the policemen. This decision seems to have had little effect on the US jurisprudence of financial privacy for more than 30 years.

The first thoughtful analysis from Idaho

The first case carefully to consider the relationship between a bank and its depositors was decided by the Supreme Court of Idaho in December of 1961, *Peterson v Idaho First National Bank*.[5] Mr Peterson's employer requested from the bank information regarding his account which the bank voluntarily disclosed. Peterson then filed a complaint against the bank to recover damages for alleged violations of his right to privacy. The trial court dismissed the claim on the grounds that it failed to state a claim upon which relief could be granted. The Idaho Supreme Court, speaking through its Chief Justice, reversed that dismissal. In doing so, the court first considered the scholarly treatises on the right to privacy by Professors Prosser and Warren and

1   Louis D Brandeis and Samuel D Warren 'The Right to Privacy' (1890) 4 Harv LR 193.
2   William L Prosser 'Privacy' (1960) 48 Calif LR 383.
3   146 A 34 (NJ Ch, 1929).
4   146 A 34 at 35 (NJ Ch, 1929).
5   367 P 2d 284 (Idaho SC, 1961).

Justice Brandeis. The court also considered the Restatement of Torts, § 867 which defined the right of privacy as unreasonably and seriously interfering with another's interest in not having his affairs known to others.[6] The court also noted that the state of California has a constitutional provision which guarantees the right to privacy and concluded that a majority of the states recognised such a right.[7] The court concluded, however, that Peterson's right to privacy had not been damaged as there had been no communication to the public of the information beyond his employer, which was an essential element of the tort of invasion of privacy.

Rather than stopping at that point, the court then considered whether the plaintiff was entitled to relief on some other ground. The court began this analysis by positing that the relationship between a bank and its depositor, at least in certain circumstances, is one of an implied contract of agency. Accordingly, an agent is subject to a duty to its principal not to use or communicate confidential information. The court found no cases directly on point, including *Brex v Smith*, the New Jersey Chancery Court case. The court concluded by negative inference from other cases relating to a bank's obligations to comply with lawful subpoenas and other investigative process that 'inviolate secrecy is one of the inherent and fundamental precepts of the relationship of the bank and its customers or depositors'.[8] On the basis that it is implicit in the contract of the bank with its customer that no information may be disclosed by the bank unless authorised by law or by the customer, the court concluded that the bank must be liable for breach of such an implied contract. This decision was the first US decision carefully to analyse the basis for a claim of financial privacy by a bank customer and has been subsequently cited as the seminal case in this area.

Florida considers contract and tort theories

Eight years later, the intermediate appellate court of Florida clearly faced the choice between a contract theory of financial privacy and a tort theory. In *Milohnich v First National Bank of Miami Springs*, a depositor alleged damage arising from disclosure by the bank to private third parties of confidential information.[9] The majority opinion concluded that a bank had an implied contractual duty to maintain the confidentiality of its customers' information. In doing so, the court relied on *Peterson v Idaho First National Bank* and the English precedent of *Tournier v National Provincial and Union Bank of England*.[10] In a concurring opinion, one judge argued that the complaint did not adequately allege a contractual relationship but did allege that the bank committed a business tort and that accordingly the proper measure of damages was based upon a tort theory of damages rather than a contractual one.

The exception for suspicious activity in a Maryland case

In *Suburban Trust v Waller*, the Maryland intermediate appellate court considered what obligations and duties a bank had when it was suspicious of a customer's

---

6   Restatement (Third) of Torts § 867 (1998).
7   Cal Constitution, art I § 1 (1972).
8   367 P 2d 284 at 291 (Idaho SC, 1961).
9   224 So 2d 759 (Fla Dist Ct App, 1969).
10 [1924] 1 KB 461.

transactions and reported those suspicions to the police.[11] The court started its analysis by recognising that the relationship between a bank and its customers is one of a debtor and creditor or a contractual relationship. In following the implied contractual theory, the court examined the *Tournier* precedent carefully and then considered the discussion in *Peterson v Idaho First National Bank*, as well as the decision in *Brex v Smith*. The court then considered the circumstances under which a bank's obligations of confidentiality are released or the circumstances under which a bank has a public duty of disclosure. Again carefully referencing the *Tournier, Brex* and *Peterson* cases, the court concluded that a customer in Maryland has a right to expect confidentiality of all information regarding his account absent compulsion by law. In reaching that conclusion, the court's decision was buttressed by the adoption by the Maryland general assembly three years earlier of a statute that explicitly created a duty of confidentiality between fiduciary institutions and their customers.[12] Accordingly, the Maryland court held that, absent legal compulsion or expressed or implied authorisation from the depositor, the bank was under a duty to keep confidential information about its depositors' transactions and accordingly upheld the verdict against the bank for voluntarily disclosing its suspicions concerning the nature of the depositor's transactions. As will be discussed in the next section, this decision came just a few years before a federal requirement for reporting of suspicious activity was imposed.

An Indiana case finds broader exceptions to privacy

In 1985, the Indiana intermediate appellate court considered what limitations or exceptions existed in the law of implied contract between a bank and its depositor as to confidentiality.[13] At trial, a jury had returned a verdict in favour of a bank customer who claimed to have been injured by the disclosure by the bank of information to a police officer conducting an arson investigation. After the customer's acquittal on the arson charges, he sued the bank on a number of theories. The Indiana court found that, while there was a right of privacy, a bank customer had no legitimate expectation that bank records were within the zone of protection for such privacy. The court also found that the verdict as to slander was erroneous as the bank had a qualified privilege based on its duty to provide information in connection with a proper police investigation. Finally, as to the verdicts with respect to a breach of an implied contract between the depositor and the bank, the court concluded that, while there is an implied duty on a bank of confidentiality, the exceptions noted in the *Tournier* case and in the Indiana Law of Slander and Privacy permit a bank to give information to law enforcement officers without a subpoena or search warrant. The presiding judge in a dissenting opinion concluded that a bank's disclosure of information without legal compulsion constitutes a breach of a contractual duty between the bank and its customer. The dissent found the reasoning in the Maryland case, *Suburban Trust Co v Waller*, to be persuasive and accordingly concluded that the court should recognise that a bank's duty of confidentiality to its customers does not end upon a policeman's informal oral request for information.

---

11   408 A 2d 758 (Md Ct Spec App, 1979).

12   Md Fin Inst Code Ann § 1-302.

13   *Indiana Nat'l Bank v Chapman* 482 NE 2d 474 (Ind Ct App, 1985).

New York case law has not found a duty of financial privacy

It is somewhat surprising that the courts of New York have not had more jurisprudence concerning a bank's obligations of confidentiality given the prominent position New York holds in the banking community in the US. It was not until 1978 that a New York intermediate appellate court considered the question indirectly. In *Graney Development Corpn v Taksen*, the court considered the nature of the confidential relationship between a bank and its borrowers.[14] In doing so, it assumed that there was a duty of confidentiality between a bank and its depositors based on a common law right of privacy. The court refused, however, to extend that duty to a borrowing relationship. Accordingly, the court's assumption about the duty of confidentiality is mere dicta and not binding precedent.

It was more than ten years after the *Graney* decision before the issue was once again considered. This time, the federal appellate court sitting in New York was faced with the question of whether New York law had recognised a duty of confidentiality for depositors.[15] The case arose when a New York bank became suspicious of deposits made by a Bermudian couple and reported those suspicions to the Attorney-General in Bermuda who conducted an investigation, and as a result the couple plead guilty to violations of Bermuda's currency restrictions. The two Bermudians then came to New York and brought an action in the federal courts of New York under the diversity jurisdiction against the New York bank. The court dismissed various federal claims, which we will consider later in this chapter.

The plaintiffs also sought recovery on a common law theory under the law of the state of New York. The Court of Appeals examined the state law claims at great length reviewing the development of state law theories in various jurisdictions outside of New York and considered carefully both the case law in New York and the state legislation relating to privacy generally. The federal appellate court in the end concluded that the state of New York had not yet adopted a financial privacy for bank depositors and went on to conclude that the issue was sufficiently significant that it would be a mistake for a federal court to attempt to predict the outcome of that issue in the courts of the state of New York. Accordingly, the court abstained from ruling on the matter and dismissed the state law claim with an express reservation that the plaintiffs could refile their claim in the New York state courts.

The plaintiffs accepted the court's invitation to refile their claim in the state court and did so in a matter entitled *Young v Chemical Bank*.[16] Justice Baer sitting in the trial courts of New York county analysed the precedents and concluded that no prior New York court had found a duty of confidentiality imposed upon a bank with respect to customer information. The court went on to conclude that such a duty existed based upon the quasi-fiduciary relationship between a bank and its depositors which the court believed was akin to the attorney-client relationship or the doctor-patient relationship. The court also looked at the exceptions to that duty, concluding that there was an exception where the bank acting in good faith had a reasonable

---

14 400 NYS 2d 717 (Sup Ct Monroe County), *affd*, 411 NYS 2d 756 (1st Dept 1978).
15 *Young v Chemical Bank* 882 F 2d 633 (2nd Cir, 1989), *cert denied*, 493 US 1072 (1990).
16 *Young v Chemical Bank* 208 NY LJ 21 (1992).

basis for a belief that a crime was being committed. Under the circumstances, the bank was privileged to initiate contact with law enforcement authorities concerning its suspicions. Since this decision was at a motion to dismiss stage before factual evidence had been gathered, the court suggested that additional fact finding would be needed to resolve whether there had been a breach of the duty of confidentiality.

Shortly after issuing this decision, Justice Baer retired from the state courts (to take up a position as a judge in the federal courts of New York) and the case was reassigned to Justice Myriam J Altman. Justice Altman granted a motion for re-argument of the case and dismissed the case finding that all of the damages the plaintiffs sought were barred under New York precedent.[17] This decision may have been influenced by recently enacted federal anti-money laundering legislation, which will be discussed later in the chapter.[18] Justice Altman's decision rested on a proposition that the plaintiffs may not profit from their own criminal conduct. While Justice Baer had been sufficiently concerned about this doctrine to limit the extent of the recovery in his decision, Justice Altman concluded that the plaintiffs' admission of criminal conduct in Bermuda as a result of their guilty plea barred any recovery by them for the conduct of Chemical Bank in reporting its suspicions about the depositors' activities. Justice Altman's decision vacated the prior ruling that for the first time had found a duty of confidentiality in New York law. Effectively, Justice Altman's decision put a stake in the heart of any common law duty in the state of New York for banks to keep information of its depositors confidential.

California cases balance privacy and investigation

In the mid-1970s, a trilogy of cases arose in California that addressed the extent of exceptions to the duties of confidentiality and for the first time clearly showed the shift from judge-made case precedent as the basis for a duty of confidentiality to new emerging federal legislation that has become the predominant source of obligations and exceptions today. In *Burrows v Superior Court*, the California Supreme Court addressed California's constitutional provision against unreasonable searches and seizures which is similar to the provision of the US federal constitution.[19] In *Burrows*, a police detective having obtained information about various bank accounts contacted several banks and requested that they provide copies of bank statements and other materials relating to a depositor's transactions. At least one bank voluntarily provided bank statements to the officer without the benefit of any legal process being served on the bank. The court, in analysing the duties of the bank, harkened back to the original *Brex* concern about unfettered access by the police authorities to financial records. In *Burrows*, the court concluded that voluntary unregulated disclosure to police authorities without the benefit of the procedures inherent in issuing a subpoena exceeded the expectations of privacy that citizens legitimately had on the basis of both the California constitution and the Fourth Amendment to the Federal Constitution and accordingly ruled that the evidence

17   *Young v Chemical Bank* no 2211/89 (Sup Ct NY County, 15 April 1993).
18   31 USC § 5318(g)(3) (1992).
19   529 P 2d 590 (Cal SC, 1974).

obtained from the bank without the benefit of the subpoena was not useable in the trial of this depositor.

In weighing the balance between legitimate inquiry by investigative authority and an expectation of privacy as to financial records, the court analysed two other decisions that rose in the previous year and began the discussion of these issues as formulated by the federal legislature. The touchstone of a citizen's legitimate expectations as to privacy which the *Burrows* court considered determinative was the subject of two US Supreme Court decisions arising out of California.[20]

FEDERAL STATUTES BECOME THE PRIMARY SOURCE OF LAW

Before considering those cases, we should turn to the enactment of federal legislation which becomes, after 1970, the dominant source of jurisprudence with respect to a bank's obligations of confidentiality to its customers.

The Bank Secrecy Act was the first federal law

In 1970, the federal government enacted anti-money laundering legislation under the title of Bank Secrecy Act.[21] That title was something of a misnomer since the primary provision of the Act required banks to retain for a period of five years copies of records relating to most significant banking transactions. This legislation arose from a concern by regulators that, as modern records storage methods and the volume of transactions proliferated, there would not be sufficient records available to trace financial transactions without a uniform requirement for a retention.[22] In addition to the retention requirements, the statute provides that banks are required to report on two broad categories of transactions that do not generate records, namely the receipt from outside the US of currency and other monetary instruments and domestic cash transactions in excess of $10,000. Neither of these types of transactions inherently creates an audit trail. The regulations promulgated pursuant to this legislation require that two reports be filed by banks with government: a so-called Currency Transaction Report (Form 4789) and a Currency and Monetary Instrument Report (Form 4790).[23] The cash reporting requirements imposed on banks by the Bank Secrecy Act are subject to certain exemptions for transactions from other domestic financial institutions and, under certain fairly carefully controlled circumstances, commercial enterprises. Parenthetically, it is worth noting that a similar requirement has been imposed on commercial enterprises pursuant to Internal Revenue Code.[24] The Code requires taxpayers to file a Form 8300 for cash payments in excess of $10,000 received in a trade or business.

---

20 *California Bankers Ass'n v Shultz* 416 US 21 (1974); *United States v Miller* 425 US 435 (1976).
21 12 USC § 1951 (2002).
22 12 USC § 1951 (2002).
23 31 CFR §§ 103.22 & 103.23 (2002).
24 26 USC § 6501 (2002).

It is important to note that the Bank Secrecy Act by itself imposes no penalty for violations, but rather delegates to the Secretary of the Treasury authority to issue regulations, the violations of which are subject to both civil and criminal penalties. While much of the statute's requirements and the subsequent regulations simply codify practices that banks have had for years in retaining records and in some cases reporting certain kinds of transactions, the statute and its implementing regulations were a significant development in the law of customer confidentiality. For the first time there was a uniform national standard for record retention. The Act also finished the basis for a developing requirement for reporting suspicious transactions to the federal government.

The initial regulations and the statute adopted a presumption that transactions in cash in excess of $10,000 were sufficiently likely to be suspicious as to be worthy of reporting to the government. The evolution of that presumption is one of the most interesting aspects of US anti-money laundering policy because, almost as soon as the regulation established the rigid $10,000 threshold, a practice known as 'smurfing' developed. Street-level money launderers would deposit or withdraw funds just below the threshold amount to avoid the report and do so with such frequency as to permit substantial volumes of funds to be transferred without any report being required. This 'cat and mouse' game evolved over the years until the development of a requirement that 'suspicious activity' be reported with only the broadest attempt at a regulatory definition of what exactly amounts to suspicion. Under the regulations, as promulgated since 1996, banks are required to report any transaction which has no business or apparent lawful purpose and is not the sort in which the particular customer would normally be expected to engage.[25] The institution is permitted to inquire as to whether there is a reasonable explanation for the transactions after examining all of the facts, including the background and possible purposes for the transactions. Nevertheless, this very subjective standard is a dramatic departure from the initial presumption of suspicion inherent in the first regulations promulgated under the Bank Secrecy Act.

Reaction to *United States v Miller* strengthens financial privacy

Shortly after the Secretary of the Treasury issued the initial implementing regulations in April of 1972, a constitutional challenge to the Bank Secrecy Act and its regulations was mounted by the California Bankers Association in the federal courts of California.[26] The principal basis for the challenge was that the Act and its regulations violated the Fourth Amendment to the Federal Constitution's guarantee against unreasonable searches and seizures. Under an expedited procedure for challenging the constitutionality of statutes, the matter was argued in January 1974 before the US Supreme Court and decided four months later. The court concluded that depositors had no reasonable expectation of privacy with respect to their financial records maintained at banks and as required by the BSA Regulations to be available for government investigators. Similarly, the cash reporting requirements, both domestic and foreign, did not contravene the provision of the Fourth Amendment restrictions

25   31 CFR § 103.18 (2002).
26   *California Bankers Ass'n v Shultz* 416 US 21 (1974).

on searches and seizures. The decision reserved the question of whether the record retention requirements, when coupled with a subpoena, would violate the Fourth Amendment as there was no factual basis for such a matter to be considered in that decision.

In a decision two years later, *United States v Miller*, the question of the power to subpoena bank records in aid of a criminal prosecution was resolved by the court again concluding that the Fourth Amendment did not restrict the ability of Congress and the Secretary of the Treasury to require the retention of bank records.[27] The court made a careful distinction between private records maintained in an individual's home and records of his transactions held outside his home at financial institutions.

Third-Party Record Keepers Act creates a narrow and limited protection in tax investigations

Within months of the court's decision in *United States v Miller*, Congress adopted an amendment to the Internal Revenue Code, as part of the Tax Reform Act of 1976, known as the Third-Party Record Keepers Act.[28] Congress reacted to the court's holding that there was no expectation of privacy with respect to financial records kept at banks.[29] The Third-Party Record Keepers Act requires that, whenever the Internal Revenue Service issues a summons for a production of records of any person other than the person who receives the summons, the target of the summons shall be notified and provided an opportunity to intervene in any proceedings for the enforcement of the summons, as well as an opportunity to stay compliance with the summons pursuant to the Internal Revenue Code. The definition of a third-party record keeper picks up a broad range of financial institutions, consumer reporting agencies, brokers, attorneys, accountants and, in an amendment in 1982, barter exchanges. While the Third-Party Record Keepers Act was limited to summonses issued under the administrative authority of the Internal Revenue Code, Congress soon moved to apply broader restrictions on the federal information gathering again in reaction to the Supreme Court holding in *United States v Miller*.

Right to Financial Privacy Act creates some limitation on federal investigations

The broader reaction by Congress to the Supreme Court's decision in *United States v Miller* came in 1978 with the enactment of the Right to Financial Privacy Act.[30] This statute limits federal (but not state or local) governmental access to information, but contains significant exceptions and limitations. The Act covers information of individuals and small partnerships of up to five individuals but does not protect corporate customers' or other legal entities' information. Broadly, the statute prohibits financial institutions in the US from disclosing customer information to the federal

---

27 425 US 435 (1976).
28 Those provisions are codified in 26 USC § 7609(a) (2002).
29 Pub L no 94-455, 1976 USCCAN (94 Stat) 3797 n 8. The same legislation limited use of 'John Doe' summons to 'fish' for information.
30 12 USC §§ 3401-2 (2002).

government unless there has been a consent by the customer to such disclosure, or the government agency has issued an appropriate administrative summons or subpoena, a search warrant or a judicial subpoena. In certain circumstances, a so-called formal written request may also meet the requirements of the statute. In addition to a requirement of the appropriate 'means of access' to obtain the information, the customer must first be notified by the government, and the government must certify to the financial institutions that such notice has been provided to the customer and that an appropriate waiting period has elapsed. This affords the customer rights similar to those under the Third-Party Records Keepers Act to challenge the issuance of the means of access. Rarely are customers able to prevent the financial institution from providing the information required by the summons or subpoena. The principal practical effect, however, is that the previous practices of either enormously broad subpoenas or informal requests for information and unsupervised scanning of the files of a financial institution by a federal agent have been stopped.

There are important exceptions in the Right to Financial Privacy Act, including an exception with respect to the issuance of grand jury subpoenas in criminal proceedings, that do not require notice to the customer. It is also important to note that access by one agency in compliance with the Right to Financial Privacy Act may result in that agency transferring its information to other authorities in the government which it believes are seized with jurisdiction to address matters found in the documents received from the financial institutions. However, there is a requirement that the transmittal be accompanied by a certification after the fact describing the nature of the inquiry.

Anti-money laundering and anti-terrorist financing legislation

From the somewhat modest privacy heights that federal legislation reached with the enactments of the Third-Party Record Keepers Act and the Right to Financial Privacy Act, the pendulum of federal legislation again swung back in succeeding years, particularly since 11 September 2001, towards greater disclosure on the part of financial institutions. The original anti-money laundering provisions that emanated from the 1970s Bank Secrecy Act received significant expansions and enhancements in two pieces of legislation, the Anunzio Wiley Anti-Money Laundering Act and the so-called USA Patriot Act of 2001.[31] Anunzio Wiley broadly enhanced the obligations of banks to affirmatively participate in anti-money laundering efforts by adoption of specific policies, including a requirement that suspicious activities be reported. The Patriot Act, enacted after the terrorist attacks of 11 September 2001, expanded that regime to cover many other financial institutions beyond banks, including securities firms, insurance companies, money transmitters and mutual funds.

---

31 31 USC §§ 5311-5331 (2002).

Patriot Act combines anti-money laundering and anti-terrorist financing provisions

The Patriot Act, somewhat like the original Bank Secrecy Act, simply laid out broad goals for these institutions and left to the implementing regulators the detailed requirement applicable to financial institutions. The regulations promulgated pursuant to the Patriot Act have been slow to be issued. These regulations reflect the difficulties of applying banking industry procedures to other financial institutions. The Patriot Act requirement that all US financial institutions have anti-money laundering programmes has engendered a great deal of institutional uncertainty among most segments of the financial industry. This has been particularly difficult in those parts of the market which have segmented operations, such as the mutual fund business, where the ultimate account holder may have little to do with the investment advisor or custodian institution that holds his account. Accordingly, in the mutual fund industry, the regulations currently permit the delegation or sub-contracting of certain anti-money laundering requirements to those institutions that deal directly with the beneficial owners.[32] Nevertheless, the overall effect of the two statutes has been to broaden the anti-money laundering requirements and, accordingly, the obligation of financial institutions to both identify customers and retain information concerning transaction histories. The Patriot Act also reinforces prior requirements to check customers against government lists of terrorist and prohibited persons.

Suspicious Activity Reports are now widely required

One of the most significant developments is the expansion of the number of institutions required to file Suspicious Activity Reports. The Patriot Act required not only banks, but also broker-dealers and money service businesses to file such reports.[33] There currently are indications that this requirement will be further expanded to include institutions such as mutual funds.[34]

A Suspicious Activity Report is required for any transaction of $5,000 or more where the institution knows, suspects, or has reasons to suspect that the transaction:

1 involves funds derived from illegal activity;
2 is designed to evade the requirements of the reporting regulations; or
3 has no business or apparent lawful purpose and is not of the sort in which the particular customer would normally be expected to engage, and the institution knows of no reasonable explanation for the transaction after examining the available facts, including the background and possible purposes of the transaction.

Under these conditions, the institution must file a Suspicious Activity Report. These triggering events were not changed by the Patriot Act. However, the application to

---

3 2 FinCEN, 67 Fed Reg 21117 (29 April 2002) (codified at 31 CFR § 103).
3 3 31 CFR §§ 103.18, 103.19, 103.20 & 103.21 (2002).
3 4 Secretary of the Treasury, Board of Governors of the Federal Reserve System and the Securities and Exchange Commission 'A Report to Congress in Accordance with § 356(c) of the USA Patriot Act' (31 December 2002) p 37.

non-banking financial institutions of this definition, which had up until the adoption of the Patriot Act been used primarily for banking institutions, has proved to be difficult for many financial institutions that do not record the customers' transaction in the same way that banks do. In many cases, such institutions do not deal directly with the customer, but provide bulk services to other segments of their industry.

Accounts for shell banks are prohibited

A second aspect of the Patriot Act which has had a significant influence on financial privacy in the US is its prohibition on US financial institutions maintaining correspondent accounts with foreign institutions that do not have a physical presence in any jurisdiction and that are not affiliated with another bank, so-called 'shell banks'.[35] The definition of correspondent account is far broader than the traditional use of that term, so many additional relationships have been caught up in this regulation.[36] The shell bank provisions have a 'safe harbor' that permits correspondent accounts at covered financial institutions that have obtained an appropriate certificate from the foreign financial institution. This provision and the provisions with respect to delegation by mutual funds of certain obligations have led to an initial flurry of contractual certifications and assurances being exchanged among financial institutions, particularly those in the US, and those that have accounts with institutions in the US as to the foreign institution's compliance with various anti-money laundering regimes. Until the regulations under the Patriot Act have weathered the test of time, and the industry has adapted to those regulations, it can be expected that there will be a fair amount of uncertainty in this area.

Private banking due diligence is mandated

The Patriot Act also requires enhanced due diligence with respect to private banking accounts, which are defined as having a minimum aggregate deposit or assets of not less than $1 million and as having been established on behalf of one or more individuals.[37] Such an enhanced due diligence programme must include steps to ascertain the identity of all of the nominal holders and all of the beneficial holders of the account and to obtain information about the lines of business and sources of wealth of such persons, as well as the sources of funds deposited in the account. In addition, banks are required to determine whether any of the individuals are so-called 'senior political figures'.[38] In which case, the institution must have procedures that are designed to detect and report transactions that may involve the proceeds of foreign corruption, and the due diligence programme should assess the risk factors that would require specific transaction monitoring in such cases.

---

35 Patriot Act § 313; 31 CFR § 103.135 (2002).
36 31 USC § 5318A(e)(1)(B) (2002).
37 Patriot Act § 312; 31 USC § 5318(i)(4)(B)(i) (2002).
38 Patriot Act § 312(a)(i)(3)(B); 31 USC § 5318(i)(3)(B) (2002); 31 CFR § 103 (2002).

Know Your Customer

These provisions for transaction monitoring and enhanced due diligence of certain customers are a substantially diluted version of an earlier 'Know Your Customer' practice (KYC) and transaction profiling originally promulgated by bank regulators in 1998. Those proposals were subsequently withdrawn after a storm of protest, largely from non-banking centre legislators and rural constituents who found such profiling of all customer accounts to be intrusive and offensive to their sense of privacy.[39]

Information sharing finds statutory protection

Another outgrowth of the Patriot Act has been the adoption of provisions for anti-terrorist and anti-money laundering information sharing among financial institutions.[40] The regulations provide that the information sharing can be used for no purpose other than to identify and report activities relating to terrorism or money laundering and that the information can only be used in connection with the decision to close or maintain an account or engage in a transaction.

The broad provisions of the Patriot Act which permit regulatory adjustments to suit the goals articulated in the legislation are likely to result in a relatively stable environment for financial institutions on the legislature front, accompanied by adjustments in the regulatory structure that were similar to the initial history of the Bank Secrecy Act after its adoption in 1970. The likely course will be a series of revisions in the initial regulations after sufficient experience has developed in the financial community so as to persuade the regulators, particularly the Department of Treasury, that there are either less burdensome or more effective procedures. This trend can best be illustrated in the shift from the Bank Secrecy Act's initial reliance on the presumed suspicious activity of $10,000 in currency being used for a banking transaction or being transmitted across boundaries to the much greater reliance now on the use of Suspicious Activity Reports as a far more targeted method for identifying transactions in the financial flows of the US economy which warrant investigative attention.

Federal statutory law with respect to financial privacy then can be seen to follow somewhat the same pattern as the case law development. The Federal Legislature, like the judges deciding the cases, has sought to set a balance between unfettered freedom for government investigators and restrictions on such investigations which would impede what the Congress believed to be legitimate law enforcement objectives. The initial Bank Secrecy Act legislation of the 1970s was a modest requirement compared with the provisions adopted in the most recent Patriot Act. When the judicial interpretations supporting the Bank Secrecy Act, particularly *United States v Miller*, concluded that there were no protections in the federal constitution with respect to financial records, the Congress reacted by adopting both the Third-Party Record Keepers Act and the Right to Financial Privacy Act. While both statutes have broad exceptions for legitimate law enforcement procedures, their prohibitions on unfettered investigative discretion and private co-operation

39 Daily Report for Executive no 43, 63 Fed Regs 67516, 67524, 67529 and 67536 (5 March 1999).
40 Patriot Act § 314(b); 31 USC § 5318(h) (2002); 31 CFR § 103.110 (2002).

between the financial institutions and the investigative agencies have continued since the enactment of the statutes in the late 1970s.

The second important trend in this statutory development has been the increased requirement since the Bank Secrecy Act in 1970 for financial institutions to keep records and, in certain circumstances, call the government's attention to transaction and other information about customers where there appears to be reasonable basis for suspecting criminal conduct. Once again, even in this area, a balance has been struck. On the one hand, the Patriot Act requires identity information be obtained. But on the other, the 1999 regulatory efforts to require transaction profiles for every customer were withdrawn after substantial public outcry against the keeping of such information for all customers across the board. The more limited efforts in the Patriot Act to collect additional information about so-called private bank customers with accounts in excess of $1 million and foreign political figures reflect a practical political compromise at which the legislature could reasonably argue there was a basis for heightened due diligence.

The Patriot Act is the latest statute in US federal anti-money laundering laws that started in 1970 with the Bank Secrecy Act. Whether there will be a reaction to perceived excesses of the Patriot Act in the next few years, as there was in the late 1970s with the Third-Party Record Keepers Act and the Right to Financial Privacy Act, is yet to be seen. What is clear today is that the current federal law requires financial institutions to collect and retain customer identity and transaction information and report suspicious activity. Privacy restrictions on government access to this information are minimal. Federal statute provides customers only the most fundamental protections and grant access for governmental investigations with only limited procedural restrictions.

Statutes provide limited protection in a few states

Nineteen of 50 states of the US have adopted legislation that protects to some degree a customer's financial information. Generally, there is an express exception to that protection for various forms of authorised access by investigators. Several of these statutes also require notice to the customer of process to gain access to his information. These statutes are generally more comprehensive than the Right to Financial Privacy Act, creating a general protection for the financial information and then authorising procedures for permitted access. However, most states do not have such statutes and some that do have them limit the protection to electronic fund transfer information or other narrow classes of information.[41]

---

41 Ala Code § 5-5A-43 (2002); Alk Code § 06.05.175 (2002); Cal Govt Code § 7460 (2002); Conn Gen Stat Ann § 36-9j (West, 2002); Conn Gen Stat Ann § 36a-41 (West, 2002); Conn Gen Stat Ann § 36a-42 (West, 2002); Conn Gen Stat Ann § 36a-43 (West, 2002); Conn Gen Stat Ann § 36a-45 (West, 2002); Fla Stat Ann § 655.059 (West, 2002); Fla Stat Ann § 659.062 (West, 2002); 205 Ill Comp Stat Ann 5/48.1 (West, 2002); Iowa Code Ann § 527.10 (West, 2002); La Rev Stat Ann § 9:3571 (West, 2002); Mass Gen Laws Ann ch 167B § 7 (West, 2002); Mass Gen Laws Ann ch 167B § 16 (West, 2002); Me Rev Stat Ann ti 9-B § 161 (West, 2001); Md Code Ann, Fin Inst § 1-302 (2002); Minn Stat Ann § 13B.06 (2002); NH Rev Stat Ann § 359-C (2002); NC Gen Stat § 53B-1 (2002); ND Cent Code § 6-08.103 (2001); Okla Stat Ann ti 6 §§ 2201–2206 (2002); Or Rev Stat § 192.550 (2001); Utah Code Ann 1953 § 7-14-1 (2002); 8 Vt Stat Ann 10203 (2002).

So, while statutes and case law in the few states where they exist provide more comprehensive protection for financial information than does the Right to Financial Privacy Act and the Third-Party Record Keepers Act, there are only a minority of states with such protection. Even in states where such protection exists, it does not pose much of an obstacle to access such information by either government investigators or private litigants.

CROSS-BORDER DISCOVERY

Given the relative paucity of financial privacy jurisprudence in the US and the broad exceptions to any such restrictions available for legitimate domestic investigation by government and private litigants, it comes as little surprise that much of the US jurisprudence on financial privacy relates to the intersection between the efforts of US civil and criminal investigations, to obtain information and the restrictions found in the laws of other nations to disclosing such information. Once again, as in the domestic arena, this law started with the development of individual cases, but has in recent years largely shifted to government-to-government arrangements that obviate the need for individual judicial determinations of conflicts of jurisdiction.

The *Interhandel* case is the leading case

The starting point for consideration of US procedures to obtain information protected by foreign financial privacy laws is the so-called *Interhandel* case.[42] In that case, the Supreme Court concluded that 'fear of criminal prosecution constitutes a weighty excuse for non-production'.[43] A Swiss holding company sought the return of certain assets held during the Second World War by the US government's economic sanctions programme. The claim was dismissed when the Swiss company was unable fully to comply with the civil discovery requirements in the New York case because of Swiss financial privacy provisions. The Supreme Court reversed the dismissal of the claim and sent the case back to the trial court for further proceedings.[44]

It is ironic that in the *Interhandel* case, a private foreign plaintiff was suing the US government over foreign policy matters. This case falls somewhere in the middle of a continuum between a civil action between two private parties and a criminal investigation by the US government. That continuum is important to understand when reviewing the subsequent cases that address whether foreign privacy laws present an effective obstacle to US investigations and civil discovery.

The Restatement summarises the case law

The American Law Institute's Restatement of the Law of the Foreign Relations of the United States has attempted to codify the myriad of cases that have addressed this

---

42 *Societe Internationale Pour Participations Industrielles Et Commerciales, SA v Rogers* 357 US 197 (1958).
43 357 US 197 at 211 (1958).
44 357 US 197 (1958).

continuum. The Restatement attempts to set out where courts should come down on the question of foreign discovery. The Restatement's formulation of the rule is that in deciding whether to order production of information located abroad, a US court should take into account:

1   the importance to the investigation or litigation of the documents or information requested;
2   the degree or specificity of the request;
3   whether the information originated in the US;
4   the availability of alternative means of securing the information; and
5   the extent to which non-compliance with the request would undermine important interests of the US, or compliance with a request would undermine important interests of the state where the information is located.[45]

A practical view of discovery case law

While many courts have applied the Restatement's test to the facts of a particular case, the practical distillation of those cases would appear to be that criminal investigations generally are successful in compelling production of foreign information.[46] Conversely, where the parties are private parties engaged in a civil dispute, the courts are often reluctant to enforce cross-border subpoenas.[47] Even with respect to civil discovery between private parties, there is a significant difference in the outcome depending upon whether the holder of the information is a party to the action. Generally, if the holder of the information is a party in the case, the courts will impose sanctions for non-production which penalised that party's continued involvement in the case similarly to the procedures followed in the *Interhandel* case. So, if a financial institution is a non-party custodian of records and receives a subpoena in a civil action between two other private parties for records protected by non-US financial privacy laws and located outside the US, there is some prospect that the institution will be successful in defending on the basis of the non-US financial privacy law. Conversely, in criminal cases, even where the financial institution is an uninvolved custodian of records, the *Bank of Nova Scotia* case is authority for the use of cross-border subpoenas for the production of information despite the existence of foreign financial privacy laws.

Hague Convention as an alternative method

In addition to the use of subpoenas, there are a variety of alternative means which are available for the gathering of information from outside the US. Most common are letters rogatory, either on the basis of international comity or pursuant to the Hague Convention on Taking Evidence.[48] It is important to note, however, the US Supreme

---

45 Restatement (Third) of Foreign Relations § 442 (1998).
46 See *Re Grand Jury Proceedings (Bank of Nova Scotia)* 740 F 2d 817 (11th Cir, 1984), *cert denied*, 469 US 1106 (1985); but see *Re Sealed Case* 832 F 2d 1268 (DC Cir, 1987).
47 See *Ings v Ferguson* 282 F 2d 149 (2nd Cir, 1960); *Laker Airways Ltd v Pan Am World Airways* 607 F Supp 324 (SDNY, 1985).
48 23 UST 2555, TIAS no 7444.

Court decision in the *Aerospatiale* case, which made it clear that the Hague Convention, as a treaty, is the supreme law of the land, but it is not the only means for gathering foreign evidence in civil cases.[49] Accordingly, financial institutions may find themselves subject to attempts to reach financial information outside the US through subpoenas despite the availability of the Hague Convention.[50] There is authority at least in New York state that post-judgment subpoenas to financial institutions for information about accounts of customers outside of the state of New York are not enforceable when such subpoenas are in aid of execution of a judgment which would not be enforceable outside that state.[51]

Compelled consents raise conflict of jurisdiction

There are also cases in the US in which the bank customer is a party to the action where the courts have required the customer to sign a waiver or authorisation under the foreign financial privacy law authorising disclosure of his account information.[52] The court enforces its order either through the coercion of sanctions within the litigation or, in criminal matters, through the sanctions of court's contempt authority. In reaction to this practice, courts where the information is located have ruled that such waivers are not effective under their law.[53]

Multilateral co-operation is the most frequently used method

In gathering information in criminal investigations, the federal government's experience in litigating cases, such as the *Bank of Nova Scotia* case and the compelled consent cases, had the practical effect of forcing a careful review of the expenditure of resources necessary to gather foreign information through the use of unilateral means. As a consequence of that evaluation, today it is relatively rare that such techniques are used when there are viable alternatives available.[54] The emphasis in recent years by the federal government has been on expanding the alternative co-operative means of information gathering so as not to be forced to resort to cross-border subpoenas.

Financial Intelligence Units institutionalise co-operation

The most frequently used tool is informal co-operation among enforcement authorities. In recent years this has led to the development of so-called Financial

---

49 *Societe Nationale Industrielle Aerospatiale v United States Dist Court* 482 US 522 (1987).
50 See eg *Dietrich v Bauer* no 95 Civ 7051, 2000 WL 1171132 (SDNY, 16 August 2000); but see *Intercontinental Credit Corpn v Roth* 595 NYS 2d (Sup Ct NY County, 1991) which held that, at least in New York, a judgment creditor seeking information about foreign bank accounts is required to pursue the Hague Convention where such procedures are available.
51 *Walsh v Bustos* 46 NYS 2d 240 (NYC City Ct, NY County, 1943).
52 The leading case that popularised this procedure is *United States v Ghidoni* 732 F 2d 814 (11th Cir, 1984). The procedure was subsequently validated by the Supreme Court in *Doe v United States* 487 US 201 (1988).
53 *Re ABC Ltd* 1984 CILR 130 (Grand Court of Cayman Islands, 1984).
54 US Dept of Justice *US Attorney Manual* (1997) §§ 9–13.525.

Intelligence Units under the auspices of the OECD's Financial Action Task Force.[55] The Egmont Group is a network dedicated to the enhancement and development of the informal co-operation through Financial Intelligence Units. As of June 2002, more than 40 countries had joined the Egmont Group and established Financial Intelligence Units.

Mutual legal assistance treaties create legal obligations

The US also has a network of more than 40 bilateral mutual legal assistance treaties with an ever increasing number of countries.[56] These treaties are supplemented by a network of executive agreements in which an agency of the US government enters into specific co-operation agreements with its counterpart in another nation.[57] These executive agreements are particularly prevalent among the securities regulating agencies and the anti-trust regulators. There is no centralised repository in which the executive agreements can be found or are publicly available. However, the US Department of State website indicates which countries are currently party to mutual legal assistance treaties with the US.[58] Another form of treaty that has particular relevance with respect to taxation matters is the so-called Tax Information Exchange Agreement.[59] The US has recently negotiated a number of treaties to facilitate the exchange of tax information between the US and other nations. Finally, both as a matter of bank regulation and pursuant to the Patriot Act, bank regulatory agencies have recently placed significant requirements on US banks with foreign branches and foreign banks with US branches for access to information relevant to customer accounts that have connections to the US.[60] These provisions are contained in regulations which usually require mechanisms by which information can be made promptly available in the US concerning the identity and transactions of any accounts having connections to the US banking system.[61]

The practical upshot of these alternative means of accessing non-US financial information is that in most cases the outcome of the case turns on the specific facts and the range of available alternatives in that case. Cross-border subpoena, while available and often threatened, can frequently be dealt with by early intervention and negotiation accompanied by use of alternative methods. The key is usually representation by a US counsel with extensive experience in these matters.

55 The Hague *Statement of Purpose of the Egmont Group*, 13 June 2001, available at www1.oecd.org/fatf/Ctry-orgpages/org-egmont_en.htm.
56 As at 12 January 2003: see travel.state.gov/mlat.html.
57 See travel.state.gov/mlat.html.
58 See travel.state.gov/mlat.html.
59 26 USC § 927 (2002).
60 Patriot Act § 319(b); 31 USC § 5318(k)(2)–(3) (2002).
61 Patriot Act § 319(b); 31 USC § 5318(k)(2)–(3) (2002).

A FEDERAL STATUTE CREATES RESTRICTIONS ON DISCLOSURE TO THIRD PARTIES

Until 1999, federal statutes did not restrict access of private litigants or state or local officials to the information the financial institutions obtain and retain, with the limited exception that suspicious activity reports are not discoverable in private litigation.

In other words, federal statutes provide no restrictions on private litigants or non-federal government, and only limited restrictions on federal government, to access most of the information required to be retained under federal anti-money laundering laws. This gap in US privacy law was remedied in 1999 as a by-product of new federal legislation that addressed primarily the commercial use of consumer financial information. The Gramm-Leach-Bliley Act[62] is the first US statute that deals with the disclosure of non-public personal information of private individual consumers. In summary, the GLBA prohibits a financial institution from disclosing non-public personal information about a consumer to non-affiliated third parties unless the institution satisfies various notice and opt-out requirements and the consumer has not elected to opt out of the disclosure.[63] The opt-out requirement operates in effect as a consent by the consumer to disclosure.[64]

---

62 The Gramm-Leach-Bliley Act of 1999 (herein GLBA), Pub L no 106–102, 106th Cong, 1st Sess (12 November 1999), 113 Stat 1338–1481 (1999), amended the Bank Holding Company Act of 1956, 12 USC § 1841–1850 (2000) and other statutes. The relevant sections of the GLBA are codified in 15 USC §§ 6801–6809 and 6821–6827 (2000). In May 2000, the OCC, the Board, the FDIC and the Office of Thrift Supervision (herein OTS) published substantially identical regulations relating to privacy of consumer financial information. 12 CFR Pt 40 (OCC); 12 CFR Pt 216 (reg P) (Board); 12 CFR Pt 332 (FDIC); 12 CFR Pt 573 (OTS). See the joint release accompanying the regulations, 65 Fed Reg 35, 162–236 (1 June 2000). See also the proposed regulation, 65 Fed Reg 8,788–8,816 (22 February 2000) and the accompanying joint release, 65 Fed Reg 8770–8,816 (22 February 2000). Since the regulations are identical, this chapter only refers to reg P of the Board. See also 16 CFR Pt 313 (2002) Regulation of the Federal Trade Commission (FTC) carrying out the financial privacy rules of the GLBA for financial institutions subject to the FTC's enforcement authority pursuant to 15 USC § 6805(a)(7) (2000); 17 CFR Pt 248 (2002) regs S–P of the Securities and Exchange Commission carrying out the financial privacy rules of the GLBA for brokers, dealers and investment companies pursuant to 15 USC § 6805(a)(3), (4) and (5) (2000). See Charles M Horn 'Financial Services Privacy at the Start of the 21st Century: Conceptual Perspective' (2001) 5 NC Banking Inst 89; Neal R Pandozzi 'Beware of Banks Bearing Gifts: Gramm-Leach-Bliley and the Constitutionality of Federal Financial Privacy Legislation' (2001) 55 U Miami LR 163; Michael A Benoit and Nicole F Munro 'Recent Federal Privacy Initiatives Affecting the Electronic Delivery of Financial Services' (2001) 56 Bus Law 1143.

15 USC §§ 6821–6827 (2000) prohibit pretext calling or 'customer identity theft' to obtain personal financial information through false or fraudulent means. See Department of the Treasury, the OCC, the OTS, the Board and the FDIC *Interagency Guidelines Establishing Standards for Safeguarding Customer Information Rule*, 66 Fed Reg 8616–8641 (1 February 2001). For the proposed rule, see 65 Fed Reg 39, 471–489 (26 June 2000). The enactment of the bank secrecy provisions of the GLBA was spurred by the alleged misuse of account information by US Bancorp to telemarketers and the debiting of customer accounts for transactions with third-party vendors without customer authorisation. See *Hatch v US Bank National Association* DN Civil Action no 99-872 (D Minn, 4 October 1999) (action by the Attorney-General of Minnesota). See Stephen F Ambrose Jr and Joseph W Gelb 'Consumer Privacy Regulation and Litigation' (2001) 56 Bus Law 1157 at 1158–1159 for a discussion of the case.

63 See 12 CFR § 216.10(a)(1) (2002); 15 USC § 6802(a) & (b)(1) (2000).

64 The financial institution must have given the consumer a reasonable opportunity to opt out of the disclosure and the consumer does not opt out of disclosure: 12 CFR § 216.10(a)(1)(iii) & (iv) (2002).

The GLBA only protects the non-public personal information regarding consumers, a *consumer* being 'an individual who obtains or has obtained a financial product or service from a [financial institution] that is to be used primarily for personal, family, or household purposes'.

The GLBA applies to financial institutions. The GLBA defines *financial institution* as 'any institution the business of which is engaging in financial activities as described in section 4(k)[, BHCA]'.[65] Financial activities are the activities set forth in 12 CFR § 225.86.[66] It follows that the definition of financial institution goes far beyond those institutions that are customarily considered to be financial institutions.[67]

Non-public personal information means (i) personally identifiable financial information, and (ii) any list, description or other grouping of consumers (and publicly available information pertaining to them) that is derived using any personally identifiable information that is not publicly available.[68] *Personally identifiable financial information* means any information (i) a consumer provides to a financial institution to obtain a financial product or service from the institution; (ii) about a consumer resulting from any transaction involving a financial product or service between a financial institution and a consumer; or (iii) the financial institution otherwise obtains about a consumer in connection with providing a financial product or service to that consumer.[69] The term does not include publicly available information.[70]

The GLBA requires a financial institution to establish a policy regarding its practices for the protection and the disclosure of non-public personal information.[71] The financial institution must notify[72] each consumer who has a customer relationship with the bank (a *customer*)[73] about this policy at the beginning of the customer relationship and afterwards once a year.[74] The information has to include the financial institution's

65   15 USC § 6809(3)(A) (2000). See 12 CFR § 216.3(k); 12 USC § 1843(k) (2000).
66   12 CFR § 225.86 (2002) (reg Y).
67   In so far as the OCC, the FDIC, the Board and the OTS have jurisdiction, *financial institution* means state member banks, BHCs and certain of their non-bank subsidiaries or affiliates, state uninsured branches and agencies of foreign banks, commercial lending companies owned or controlled by foreign banks, Edge Act or Agreement corporations (12 CFR § 216.1(b)(1) (2002)); banks insured with the FCIC (other than state member banks), insured state branches of foreign banks and certain subsidiaries of such entities (12 CFR § 332.1(b)(1) (2002)); FDIC insured savings associations and certain of their subsidiaries (12 CFR § 573.1(b)(1) (2002)).
68   12 CFR § 216.3(n) (2002). See 15 USC § 6809(4) (2000).
69   12 CFR § 216.3(o) (2002).
70   12 CFR § 216.3(n)(2) and (p) (2002) (publicly available information means any information that a financial institution has a reasonable basis to believe is lawfully made available to the general public from government records, widely distributed media, or disclosures to the general public that are required to be made by federal, state or local law).
71   See 15 USC § 6803(a) (2000); 12 CFR § 216.6(a)(8) (2002). The disclosure must also address disclosure to affiliates.
72   The financial institution must provide 'a clear and conspicuous notice that accurately reflects [its] privacy policies and practices': 12 CFR § 216.4(a) (2002). *Clear and conspicuous* is defined in 12 CFR § 216.3(b) (2002). See 15 USC § 6803(a) (2000).
73   The notice must be given to (i) an individual who becomes the financial institution's *customer* (ie a consumer who has a customer relationship with the financial institution: 12 CFR § 216.3(h) & (i) (2002)) not later than when the financial institution establishes a customer relationship and (ii) a *consumer* before the financial institution discloses any non-public information about the consumer to any non-affiliated third party: 12 CFR § 216.4(a)(1) and (2) (2002).
74   12 CFR § 216.5 (2002); 15 USC § 6803(a) (2000).

policies and practices regarding the disclosure of non-public personal information relating to customers and former customers to non-affiliated third parties as well as to the financial institution's affiliates, and, in general, regarding the protection of non-public personal information about consumers.[75] The notice must inform customers as to what non-public personal information is collected from them, how this information is maintained and used, and with what persons this information is shared.[76]

The progress in financial institution secrecy made by the GLBA lies in the fact that after having received this information, the customer/consumer has a so-called right to 'opt out', ie he may direct the financial institution not to disclose his non-public personal information to non-affiliated third parties. By exercising this right, the consumer prevents the external use of his data.

Even if a consumer has not made use of his choice to opt out, the financial institution may not disclose to a non-affiliated third party, except to a consumer reporting agency, any information that gives access to a customer's account for the purpose of telemarketing, direct mail marketing, or other marketing through electronic mail to the customer.

If the consumer has not opted out of the disclosure of his non-public personal information to non-affiliated third parties, a non-affiliated third party that receives from a financial institution non-public personal information is under an obligation itself not to disclose such information to any other person that is a non-affiliated third party (limit on reuse of information).[77]

There are numerous exceptions to the privacy protection of the GLBA, the most important being:

1   *Business customers.* The GLBA does not cover the privacy of bank customers that are companies[78] or individuals who obtain financial products or services for business, commercial or agricultural purposes.[79] These non-protected customers have only recourse to the protection provided by common law.
2   *Affiliates.* The consumer cannot elect that non-public personal information not be disclosed to the financial institution's affiliates – an *affiliate* being any company that controls, is controlled by, or is under common control with, the financial institution. This exception is especially noteworthy when considering

---

75 The notice must include, among other things, (i) the categories of non-public personal information that the financial institution collects, (ii) the categories of non-public personal information that the financial institution discloses, (iii) the categories of affiliates and non-affiliated third parties to whom the financial institution discloses non-public personal information, (iv) the same information about the financial institution's former customers and (v) an explanation of the consumer's rights to opt out of the disclosure: 12 CFR § 216.6(a) (2002). See 15 USC § 6803(b) (2000). If a financial institution does not disclose, and does not wish to reserve the right to disclose, non-public personal information about customers or former customers to affiliates or non-affiliated third parties, the financial institution may simply state that fact, in addition to certain required information (simplified notice): 12 CFR § 216.6(c)(5) (2002).
76 See 15 USC § 6803 (2000).
77 15 USC § 6802(c) (2000). See 12 CFR § 216.11 (2002). This prohibition on reuse of information does not apply if the disclosure to another third party would be lawful if made directly to such other third party by the financial institution: 15 USC § 6802(c) (2000).
78 *Company* is defined in 12 CFR § 216.3(d) (2002).
79 See the definition of *consumer*, 12 CFR § 216.3(e) (2002).

the combination of banks, insurance companies and securities companies in one FHC group permitted by the GLBA. Thus, for instance, an insurance company may provide to its bank affiliate customer information.[80]

3   *Outsourcing and third-party providers; joint marketing.* A financial institution is always allowed to forward data even to a non-affiliated third party to perform services for or functions on behalf of the financial institution, for instance, to carry out marketing tasks or in the case where the financial institution wants to outsource some activity. However, in this case the financial institution is required to enter into a confidentiality agreement with the third party that prohibits the third party from disclosing or using the information other than to carry out the purposes for which the financial institution disclosed the information. The services that a non-affiliated party performs for the financial institution may include marketing of the financial institution's own products or services or marketing of financial products or services offered jointly by several financial institutions.

4   *Processing and servicing of transactions.* A financial institution is always allowed to disclose non-public personal information when this is *necessary to effect, administer or enforce a transaction*[81] that a consumer requests or authorises, or in connection with:
   (a) servicing or processing a financial product or service that a consumer requests or authorises;
   (b) maintaining or servicing the consumer's account with the financial institution, or with another entity as part of a private label credit card programme or other extension of credit on behalf of such entity; or
   (c) a proposed or actual securitisation, secondary market sale (including sales of servicing rights), or similar transactions related to a transaction of the consumer.

5   *Governmental authorities.* The GLBA only addresses the disclosure of information to private third parties. The GLBA does not apply to disclosures to governmental authorities in accordance with the Right to Financial Privacy Act and other federal reporting statutes[82] or to state insurance authorities,[83] disclosures made to comply with federal, state or local laws or rules, disclosures made to comply with an investigation or a subpoena or summons by federal, state or local authorities, or disclosures made to respond to judicial process or

---

80 Note, however, that the privacy notice must contain information on the categories of affiliates to whom the financial institution discloses non-public personal information (12 CFR § 216.6(a)(3) (2002)) and that the simplified notice is only available if the financial institution does not disclose, and does not wish to reserve the right to disclose, non-public personal information about customers and former customers to *affiliates* or non-affiliated third parties: 12 CFR § 216.6(c)(5) (2002). Since third-party providers and servicers of a financial institution are non-affiliated parties, a financial institution's disclosure policy must address disclosure to such providers and servicers: 12 CFR §§ 116.6(a)(5) & 116.13 (2002).

81 *Necessary to effect, administer or enforce a transaction* is defined in 12 CFR § 216.14(b) (2002).

82 15 USC § 6802(e)(5) (2000); 12 CFR § 216.15(a)(4) (2002). See eg 12 USC § 3401ff (2000) (Right to Financial Privacy Act of 1978); 31 USC ch 53, sub-ch II (2000) (Records and Reports on Monetary Instruments and Transactions) and 12 USC ch 21 (2000) (Financial Record Keeping).

83 15 USC § 6802(e)(5) (2000); 12 CFR § 216.15(a)(4) (2002).

government regulatory authorities having jurisdiction over the financial institution.[84]

6 *Consumer reporting agency.* The GLBA does not prohibit disclosure to a consumer reporting agency in connection with the Fair Credit Reporting Act.[85]

7 *Sale or merger.* The GLBA does not prohibit disclosure in connection with a proposed or actual sale, merger, transfer or exchange of all or a portion of a business or operating unit of the financial institution if the disclosure of non-public personal information concerns solely consumers of such business or unit.[86]

8 *Rating agencies.* The GLBA does not prohibit disclosure of information to rating agencies of the financial institution and the financial institution's attorneys, accountants and auditors.[87]

9 *Miscellaneous.* The GLBA does not prohibit disclosure of information:
   (a) to protect the confidentiality or security of the financial institution's records pertaining to the consumer, the service, product or transaction;
   (b) to protect against or prevent actual or potential fraud, unauthorised transactions, claims or other liability;
   (c) for required institutional risk control or for resolving consumer disputes or inquiries;
   (d) to persons holding a legal or beneficial interest relating to the consumer; or
   (e) to persons acting in a fiduciary or representative capacity on behalf of the consumer.[88]

A consumer can, of course, always authorise an individual disclosure of non-public personal information even if such consumer has generally opted out of disclosure.[89]

The financial privacy provisions of the GLBA do not supersede state law, except to the extent that state law is inconsistent, and then only to the extent of such inconsistency.[90] State law is not inconsistent if it affords greater protection than the privacy provisions of the GLBA.[91] This provision will cause much uncertainty.

CONCLUSION

The US law of financial privacy is a patchwork of cases and, most importantly, federal statutes that do not provide a comprehensive or coherent regime to protect financial information. Rather, in almost all cases, the law was a reaction to perceived excesses that invaded an undefined zone of privacy. Far more comprehensive and coherent are the duties placed on financial institutions by anti money-laundering laws and regulations to collect and retain information about customers and their transactions.

---

84 15 USC § 6802(e)(8) (2000); 12 CFR § 216.15(a)(7) (2002).
85 15 USC § 6802(e)(6) (2000); 12 CFR § 216.15(a)(5) (2002). See 15 USC § 1681ff (2000) (Fair Credit Reporting Act).
86 15 USC § 6802(e)(7) (2000); 12 CFR § 216.15(a)(6) (2002).
87 15 USC § 6802(e)(4) (2000); 12 CFR § 216.15(a)(3) (2002).
88 15 USC § 6802(e)(3) (2000); 12 CFR § 216.15(a)(2) (2002).
89 15 USC § 6802(e)(2) (2000); 12 CFR § 216.15(a)(1) (2002).
90 15 USC § 6807(a) (2000).
91 15 USC § 6807(b) (2000).

Index